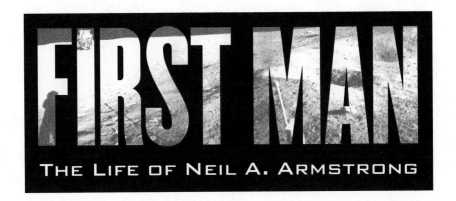

FIRST MAN

THE LIFE OF NEIL A. ARMSTRONG

James R. Hansen

Simon & Schuster

NEW YORK • LONDON • TORONTO • SYDNEY

SIMON & SCHUSTER
Rockefeller Center
1230 Avenue of the Americas
New York, NY 10020

For information about special discounts for bulk purchases,
please contact Simon & Schuster Special Sales at
1-800-456-6798 or business@simonandschuster.com

Designed by Paul Dippolito

Photo credits and jacket captions appear on page 769.

Manufactured in the United States of America

1   3   5   7   9   10   8   6   4   2

Library of Congress Cataloging-in-Publication Data

Hansen, James R.
First man : the life of Neil A. Armstrong / James R. Hansen.
p.   cm.
Includes bibliographical references and index.
ISBN 0-7432-5631-X
1. Armstrong, Neil, 1930–   2. Astronauts—United States—Biography.
3. Project Apollo (U.S.)   4. Space flight to the moon.   I. Title.

TL789.85.A75H36   2005
629.45'0092—dc22

[B]   2005049992

ISBN-13: 978-0-7432-5631-5
ISBN-10:   0-7432-5631-X

For Jennifer and Nathan

The privilege of a lifetime is being who you are.

—JOSEPH CAMPBELL, *REFLECTIONS
ON THE ART OF LIVING*

Contents

PART EIGHT: DARK SIDE OF THE MOON

FIRST MAN

Prologue

After the Moon mission was over and the Apollo 11 astronauts were back on Earth, Buzz Aldrin remarked to Neil Armstrong, "Neil, we missed the whole thing."

Somewhere between 750,000 and 1 million people, the largest crowd ever for a space launch, gathered at Florida's Cape Kennedy in the days leading to Wednesday, July 16, 1969. Nearly a thousand policemen, state troopers, and waterborne state conservation patrolmen struggled through the previous night to keep an estimated 350,000 cars and boats flowing on the roads and waterways. One enterprising state auto inspector leased two miles of roadside from orange growers, charging two bucks a head for viewing privileges. For $1.50 apiece, another entrepreneur sold pseudo-parchment attendance certificates with simulated Old English lettering; an additional $2.95 bought a pseudo space pen.

No tailgate party at any Southeastern Conference football game could match the summer festival preceding the first launch for a Moon landing. Sunglassed spectators dressed in Bermuda shorts or undressed in bikinis, even at this early hour firing up barbecue grills, opening coolers of beer and soda pop, peering through binoculars and telescopes, testing camera angles and lenses—people filled every strand of sand, every oil-streaked pier, every fish-smelling jetty.

Sweltering in 90-degree heat by midmorning, bitten up by mosquitoes, still aggravated by traffic jams or premium tourist prices, the great mass of humanity waited patiently for the mammoth Saturn V to shoot Apollo 11 toward the Moon.

In the Banana River, five miles south of the launch complex, all manner of boats choked the watercourse. Companies such as Grumman Aircraft had hired the larger charters for the day to give their employees a chance to witness the product of their years of effort. Aboard a large cabin cruiser, the *Grapefruit II,* wealthy citrus grower George Lier of Orchid Island, Florida, playfully tossed grapefruit at passersby. Just offshore, two small African-American boys sat in a ramshackle rowboat casually watching the mayhem that was making it so hard to catch any fish.

On a big motor cruiser owned by North American Aviation, builder of the Apollo command module, Janet Armstrong, the wife of Apollo 11's commander, and her two boys, twelve-year-old Rick and six-year-old Mark, stood nervously awaiting the launch. Fellow astronaut Dave Scott, Neil's mate on the Gemini VIII flight in 1966, had arranged what Janet called a "*numero uno* spot." Besides Scott, two of Janet's friends—Pat Spann, a neighbor from El Lago, Texas, whose husband worked in the Manned Spacecraft Center's Mission Support Office, and Jeanette Chase, who helped Janet coach the synchronized swimming team at the El Lago Keys Club and whose husband served in the Recovery Division at MSC—were also on board, as were a few NASA public affairs officers and Dora Jane (Dodie) Hamblin, a journalist with exclusive coverage of the personal side of the Apollo 11 story for *Life* magazine.

Above them all, helicopters ferried successive groups of VIPs to re-served bleacher seating in the closest viewing stands a little more than three miles away from the launchpad. Of the nearly 20,000 on NASA's special guest list, about one-third actually attended, including a few hundred foreign ministers, ministers of science, military attachés, and aviation officials, as well as nineteen U.S. state governors, forty mayors, and a few hundred leaders of American business and industry. Half the members of Congress were in attendance, as were a couple of Supreme Court justices. The guest list ranged from General William Westmoreland, the U.S. army chief of staff in charge of the war in Vietnam, and Johnny Carson, the star of NBC's *Tonight Show,* to Leon Schachter, head of the Amalgamated Meat Cutters and Butcher Workers, and Prince Napoleon of Paris, a direct descendant of the emperor Napoleon.

Vice President Spiro T. Agnew sat in the bleachers while President Richard M. Nixon watched on TV from the Oval Office. Originally, the White House had planned for Nixon to dine with the Apollo 11 astronauts the night before liftoff, but the plan changed after Dr. Charles Berry, the astronauts' chief physician, was quoted in the press warning that there was always a chance that the president might unknowingly be harboring an incipient cold. Armstrong, Aldrin, and the third member of their crew, Mike Collins, thought the medical concern was absurd; if the truth be known, twenty or thirty people—secretaries, space suit technicians, simulator technicians—were coming into daily contact. Apollo 8's Frank

Borman, whom NASA had designated as Nixon's special space consultant, assailed Berry's warning as "totally ridiculous" and "damned stupid" but stopped short of arguing for another reversal of plans, "because if anyone sneezes on the Moon, they'd put the blame on the president."

Two thousand credentialed reporters watched the launch from the Kennedy Space Center press site. Eight hundred and twelve came from foreign countries, 111 from Japan alone. A dozen journalists came from the Soviet bloc: seven from Czechoslovakia, three from Yugoslavia, and two from Romania.

Landing on the Moon was a shared global event which nearly all humankind felt transcended politics. British papers used two- and three-inch high type to herald news of the launch. In Spain, the *Evening Daily Pueblo*, though critical of American foreign policy, sent twenty-five contest winners on an all-expense-paid trip to Cape Kennedy. A Dutch editorialist called his country "lunar-crazy." A Czech commentator remarked, "This is the America we love, one so totally different from the America that fights in Vietnam." The popular German paper *Bild Zeitung* noted that seven of the fifty-seven Apollo supervisors were of German origin; the paper chauvinistically concluded, "12 percent of the entire Moon output is 'made in Germany.' " Even the French considered Apollo 11 "the greatest adventure in the history of humanity." *France-Soir*'s twenty-two-page supplement sold 1.5 million copies. A French journalist marveled that interest in the Moon landing was running so high "in a country whose people are so tired of politics and world affairs that they are accused of caring only about vacations and sex."

Moscow Radio led its broadcast with news of the launch. *Pravda* rated the scene at Cape Kennedy front-page news, captioning a picture of the Apollo 11 crew "these three courageous men."

Not all the press was favorable. Out of Hong Kong, three Communist newspapers attacked the mission as a cover-up for the American failure to win the Vietnam War and charged that the Moon landing was an effort to "extend imperialism into space."

Others charged that the materialism of the American space program would forever ruin the wonder and beautiful ethereal qualities of the mysterious Moon, enveloped from time immemorial in legend. After human explorers violated the Moon with footprints and digging tools, who again could ever find romance in poet John Keats's question, "What is there in thee, moon, that thou shouldst move my heart so potently?"

Partaking of the technological miracle of the first telecommunications satellites launched earlier in the decade, at the U.S. embassy in Seoul, 50,000 South Koreans gathered before a wall-sized television screen. A crowd of Poles filled the auditorium at the American embassy in Warsaw. Trouble with AT&T's Intelsat III satellite over the Atlantic prevented a live telecast in Brazil (as it did in many parts of South America, Central America, and the Caribbean region), but Brazilians listened to accounts on radio and bought out special newspaper editions. Because of the Intelsat problem, a makeshift, round-the-world, west-to-east transmission caused a two-second lag in live coverage worldwide.

Shortly before liftoff, CBS News commentator Eric Sevareid, who at age sixty-six was seeing his first manned shot, described the scene to Walter Cronkite's television audience: "Walter . . . as we sit here today . . . I think the [English] language is being altered. . . . How do you say 'high as the sky' anymore, or 'the sky is the limit'—what does that mean?"

Nowhere on the globe was the excitement as palpable as it was throughout the United States. In east Tennessee, tobacco farmers picking small pink flowers from tobacco plants crowded around a pocket-size transistor in order to share the big moment. In the harbor at Biloxi, Mississippi, shrimpers waited on the wharf for word that Apollo 11 had lifted off. At the Air Force Academy in Colorado Springs, where 7:30 A.M. classes were postponed, fifty cadets hovered around one small TV set. "Everybody held his breath," a twenty-year-old senior cadet from Missouri said. "Then, as the spaceship lifted off the ground, we began to cheer and clap and yell and scream." In the twenty-four-hour casino at Caesars Palace in Las Vegas, the blackjack and roulette tables sat empty while gamblers stood spellbound in front of six television sets.

The multitude of eyewitnesses assembled on and around the Cape, Merritt Island, Titusville, Indian River, Cocoa Beach, Satellite Beach, Melbourne, throughout Brevard and Osceola counties, as far away as Daytona Beach and Orlando, prepared to behold one of the most awesome sights known to man, second only perhaps to the detonation of an atomic bomb.

William Nelson, an engineering planner from Durham, Connecticut, sat with his family of seven and, gazing at the Apollo rocket looming eleven miles away, said excitedly, "They tell me I'll be able to feel the earth shake when it goes off. Once I see it, I'll know that it was worth all the heat and mosquitoes. All I know is that my kids will be able to say they were here." The voice of Jacksonville, Florida's Mrs. John Yow, wife of a stockbroker, quivered as she uttered, "I'm shaky, I'm tearful. It's the beginning of a new era in the life of man." Charles Walker, a student from Armstrong's own Purdue University, told a newsman from his campsite on a small inlet in Titusville, "It's like mankind has developed fire all over again. Perhaps this will be the kindling light to put men together now." In the VIP stands nearest the launch complex, R. Sargent Shriver, the U.S. ambassador to France who was married to Eunice Kennedy, a sister of the deceased president John Kennedy, who had committed the country to landing on the Moon, declared, "How beautiful it is! The red of the flames, the blue of the sky, the white fumes—those colors! Think of the guys in there getting that incredible ride. *Incroyable!*"

CBS's sixty-one-year-old commentator Heywood Hale Broun, best known for his irreverent sports journalism, experienced the liftoff with several thousand people along Cocoa Beach, some fifteen miles south of the launchpad. He told Cronkite's audience of tens of millions, "At a tennis match you look back and forth. On a rocket launch you just keep going up and up, your eyes going up, your hopes going up, and finally the whole crowd like some vast many-eyed crab was staring out and up and up and all very silent. There was a small 'Aah' when the rocket first went up, but after that it was just staring and reaching. It was the poetry of hope, if you will, unspoken but seen in the kind of concentrated gestures that people had as they reached up and up with the rocket."

Even those who came to the launch to protest could not help but be deeply moved. Reverend Ralph Abernathy, successor to the late Dr. Martin Luther King Jr. as head of the Southern Christian Leadership Conference and de facto leader of the American civil rights movement, marched with four mules and about 150 members of the Poor People's Campaign for Hunger as close as they were allowed to get to the sprawling spaceport. "We are protesting America's inability to choose the proper priorities," said Hosea Williams, the SCLC's director of political education, who claimed money spent to get to the Moon could have wiped out hunger for 31 million poor people. Nonetheless, Williams stood "in admiration of the astronauts," just as Reverend Abernathy himself "succumbed to the awe-inspiring launch," declaring, "I was one of the proudest Americans as I stood on this soil. I think it's really holy ground."

"There's so much that we have yet to do—the hunger in the world, the sickness in the world, the poverty in the world," former president Lyndon B. Johnson told Walter Cronkite shortly after watching the launch from his bleacher seat, wife Lady Bird at his side. "We must apply some of the great talents that we've applied to space to all these problems, and get them done, and get them done in the spirit of what's the greatest good for the greatest number."

With ten minutes left on the clock, the thoughtful Eric Sevareid said on-air to Cronkite, "There's not a carnival atmosphere here, really. You've got the snack shops and all the rest, all the trailers, but there is a quiet atmosphere, and when the van carrying the astronauts themselves went by on this roadway just now, there was a kind of hush among the people. Those things move very slowly as though they're carrying nitroglycerine or something. You get a feeling that people think of these men as not just superior men but different creatures. They are like people who have gone into the other world and have returned, and you sense they bear secrets that we will never entirely know, and that they will never entirely be able to explain."

In central Ohio, a thousand miles from the viewing stands in Florida, the little burg of Wapakoneta, Armstrong's hometown, counted down. Streets were virtually empty, with nearly 6,700 residents glued to their television sets. Downtown stores, displaying framed pictures of Neil and red, white, and blue pennants proclaiming the town's piece in "the biggest event of the century," delayed their opening until after liftoff.

The quiet, even quasi-religious anticipation followed weeks of commercial and patriotic uproar in the town. At the center of the chaos was 912 Neil Armstrong Drive, the one-story, ranch-style home of Viola and Steve Armstrong, into which the couple had moved just a year earlier. Neil's parents had attended the Gemini VIII launch in 1966. Their son had also arranged for them to witness Apollo 10's liftoff in April. But for this flight, he advised them to stay at home, saying "the pressure might be too great" for them at the Cape. The night before the launch, however, a reporter counted a total of 233 cars circling their suburban block.

Six months earlier, Viola Armstrong had been sitting at her kitchen table placing pictures—most of them of Neil—in photo albums when she heard the news on TV that Neil was to be the commander for Apollo 11: "A flood of tears gushed from my eyes. There was tumult within me. I sobbed in anguish. Soon I was on my knees in prayer." Over the years since she had given her life to Jesus Christ as a young teenager, she had uttered many fervent prayers, "but never was there a prayer like this one. I had actually heard the announcement with my own ears that our son had been chosen to be on the coming Moon landing team!"

In the months leading up to the launch, Neil's mother and father were "besieged by newsmen of every category," from England, Norway, France, Germany, and Japan. Viola recalled, "Their prying questions ('What was Neil like when he was a little boy?' 'What kind of a home life did he have?' 'Where will you be and what will you be doing during the launch?' etc. etc.) were a constant drain on my strength and nervous system. I survived this only by the grace of God. He must have been at my side constantly."

NASA sent a special protocol officer to Wapakoneta from Huntsville, Alabama. "Tom Andrews was blessed with the most beautiful head of red wavy hair that anyone ever saw," Viola remembered. "Plus he was common like us, so we felt very much at ease with each other. He said, 'Now, Mrs. Armstrong, I'll answer your doorbell, answer your phone, and help you folks in any way that I can.' My! He was welcomed with open arms."

To facilitate their coverage of Apollo 11 from Wapakoneta, the three major TV networks erected a shared eighty-five-foot-high transmission tower in the driveway of the Armstrong house. The Armstrong garage was turned into a pressroom with messy rows of telephones temporarily installed atop folding picnic tables.

Because Neil's parents still had only a black-and-white television, the TV networks gave them a large color set on which to watch the mission. On a daily basis, a local restaurant sent down a half dozen pies. A fruit company from nearby Lima delivered a large stock of bananas. A dairy from Delphos sent ice cream. Frito-Lay sent large cartons of corn chips. A local dairy, the Fisher Cheese Co., Wapakoneta's largest employer, proffered its special "Moon Cheeze." Consolidated Bottling Company delivered crates of "Capped Moon Sauce," a "secret-formula" vanilla cream soda pop. Neighbors and friends contributed delicious foods of the midwest summertime.

The proud mayor of Wapakoneta requested that every home and business display an American flag (and preferably also the Ohio state flag) from the morning of the launch until the moment "the boys" were safely back. Among a few locals, the media spotlight inspired a different kind of civic embellishment. Some told exaggerated stories, even outright lies, about their special connection to the astronaut. Even kids took to spinning yarns: "Listen, my dad is Neil Armstrong's barber!" or "My mom was the first girl ever to kiss Neil!" or "Hey, I chopped down Neil Armstrong's cherry tree!"

Since the Armstrongs' Auglaize County phone number was public knowledge, Tom Andrews arranged to have two private phone lines run into the family's utility room, off the kitchen. Around noontime the day before the launch, Neil called his mother and father from the Cape. "We enjoyed a very pleasant conversation," recalled Viola. "His voice was cheerful, and he said he thought they were all ready for the takeoff the next morning. Daddy said, 'Will you call us again before you leave?' and he said, 'No, I'm afraid I won't be able to call again.' These words were spoken very softly. We asked God to watch over him, and then we had to say 'good-bye.' "

Neil's sister and brother attended the launch. June, her husband, Dr. Jack Hoffman, and their four daughters flew to Florida from their home in Menomonee Falls, Wisconsin. Dean Armstrong, his wife, Marilyn, and their two daughters drove down to Florida from their home in Anderson, Indiana. Both children called their mother and father the day prior to the launch. June said, "Momma, if you feel someone squeezing your hand these days, you'll know it is me." Viola replied, "Oh, thank you, darling. You know I already have one hand in the Lord's hand, and now I have yours in the other. Now I'm sure I can go ahead."

Late that night Neil's wife Janet telephoned Viola to report that she and the boys had not been able to see Neil, but they had talked with him briefly by telephone and had wished him a successful flight. A government car had driven them to see the gigantic rocket spectacularly alit with the spacecraft atop it. Janet told Viola that at dawn they would be heading out onto the Banana River in the corporate yacht. "Janet, too, was full of cheerfulness," Viola remembered. "She felt the crew was ready."

Viola's recall of that extraordinary morning remained sharp until her dying day: "Streets about our house were blocked off. Old Glory was flying everywhere. The weather was quite hot, and the skies were clear and beautiful. Stinebaugh Construction had installed two window air conditioners for our comfort. Tom Andrews guarded our doors and our very selves. Lawmen were at watch outside. Our local WERM radio station had its truck out in front, too. TV and radio personnel were busy setting up their equipment.

"Visitors, neighbors, and strangers gathered around to watch and listen, including my mother, Caroline; my cousin, Rose; and my pastor, Reverend Weber. Stephen and I sat side by side, wearing for good luck the Gemini VIII pins that Neil had given us. For so long I had been talking with my Lord, and for so long He had been giving me strength. It seemed as though there was something around me holding me up. These were tense moments, yet the watchful eye of the *Life* people was constantly upon us, snapping pictures, especially, I thought, when we were looking our worst. Reverend Weber with his prayers at intervals was most comforting. We all had explicit faith in NASA and our boys, and I had a feeling that our Heavenly Father was the Supreme Commander over all. . . . When the final countdown began, I felt someone gentle and firm supporting me right through the liftoff. There was our Neil with Buzz and Mike off on a journey to the Moon!

"It seemed as if from the very moment he was born—farther back still, from the time my husband's family and my own ancestry originated back in Europe long centuries ago—that our son was somehow destined for this mission."

PART ONE

AN AMERICAN GENESIS

*Even the greatest American is an immigrant or has
descended from immigrants.*

—VIOLA ENGEL ARMSTRONG

*America means opportunity. It started that way. The
early settlers came to the new world for the opportunity to
worship in keeping with their conscience, and to build a
future on the strength of their own initiative and hard
work. . . . They discovered a new life with freedom to
achieve their individual goals.*

—NEIL A. ARMSTRONG, "WHAT AMERICA MEANS TO
ME," *THE READER'S DIGEST,* APRIL 1975

CHAPTER 1

The Strong of Arm

Two obscure European towns took special meaning from the first human steps on another world. The first was Ladbergen, in the German province of Westphalia, about thirty-five miles from the Dutch border. Here in the northern Rhine region stood an eighteenth-century farmhouse-and-barn belonging to a peasant family named Kötter, the same common folk from which Neil Armstrong's mother, Viola Engel Armstrong, descended. Five hundred miles to the northwest, on the Scotch-English border, lay Langholm, Scotland, home of the Armstrong ancestry. One branch of its lineage led to Neil's father, Stephen Koenig Armstrong.

In March 1972, not quite three years after the Apollo 11 landing, Neil was named Langholm's first-ever honorary freeman. To the cheers of eight thousand Scots and visiting Englishmen, Armstrong rode into town in a horse-drawn carriage, escorted by regimental bagpipers dressed in Armstrong tartan kilts. The glorious reception marked a reversal of fortune for the Armstrong name. Chief magistrate James Grieve, arrayed in an ermine-trimmed robe, gravely cited a four-hundred-year-old law, never formally repealed, that ordered him to hang any Armstrong found in the town. "I am sorry to tell you that the Armstrongs of four hundred years ago were not the most favored of families," Grieve instructed. "But they were always men of spirit, fearless, currying favor in no quarter, doughty and determined." Neil responded wryly: "I have read a good deal of the history of this region and it is my feeling that the Armstrongs have been dreadfully misrepresented." Neil then "smiled so broadly," said the local newspaper account, "that you could tell he loved every last one of the ancestral scoundrels."

The Armstrong name began illustriously enough. Anglo-Danish in derivation, the name meant what it said, "strong of arm." By the late thirteenth century, documents of the English nation—including the royal real estate records *Calendarium Genealogicum*—listed the archaic "Armestrange" and "Armstrang."

Legend traced the name to a heroic progenitor by the name of Fairbairn. Viola Engel Armstrong, who immersed herself in genealogy in the years after her son's immortal trip to the Moon, recorded one version of the fable. "A man named Fairbairn remounted the king of Scotland after his horse had been shot from under him during battle. In reward for his service the king gave Fairbairn many acres of land on the border between Scotland and England, and from then on referred to Fairbairn as Armstrong." Offshoots of the legend say that Fairbairn was followed by Siward Beorn, or "sword warrior," also known as Siward Digry, "sword strong arm."

By the 1400s, the Armstrong clan emerged as a powerful force in "the Borders." The great Scottish writer and onetime Borderlands resident Sir Walter Scott wrote four centuries later in his poem "Lay of the Minstrel" of the flaming arrows emblematic of endemic clan feuds: "Ye need no go to Liddisdale, for when they see the blazing bale, Elliots and Armstrongs never fail." Or as another Scottish writer put it, "On the Border were the Armstrongs, able men, somewhat unruly, and very ill to tame."

By the sixteenth century, Armstrongs were unquestionably the Borders' most robust family of reivers—a fanciful name for bandits and robbers. Decades' worth of flagrant expansion by the Armstrongs into what had come to be known as "the Debatable Land" eventually forced the royal hand, as did their purported crimes of burning down fifty-two Scottish churches. By 1529, King James V of Scotland marshaled a force of eight thousand soldiers to tame the troublesome Armstrongs, who numbered somewhere between twelve thousand and fifteen thousand, or roughly 3 percent of Scotland's population. Under the pretext of a hunting expedition, James V marched his forces southward in search of Johnnie Armstrong of Gilnockie, known locally as "Black Jock." Their fatal standoff in July 1530 was immortalized in the "Ballad of Johnnie Armstrong of Gilnockie," which is still sung in the Borders of Scotland, and by a stone monument inscribed: "Here this spot was buried Johnnie of Gilnockie . . . John was murdered at Carlinrigg and all his gallant companie, but Scotland's heart was ne'er sae [so] wae [woe], to see sae many brave men die."

In his nineteenth-century collection of ballads *The Border Minstrelsy,* Sir Walter Scott identified William Armstrong, nicknamed "Christie's Will," as a lineal descendant of the famous Johnnie Armstrong of Gilnockie. Scott may have been right. Historians have inferred that Will was the oldest son of Christopher Armstrong (1523–1606), who was himself the oldest son of Johnnie Armstrong.

Walter Scott's nineteenth-century stories do not coordinate very precisely with seventeenth-century genealogy. All information about Christie's Will gives his birth year as 1565. His infamous kidnapping of Lord Durie, made legendary by Scott, could only have happened around 1630, when Will would have been sixty-five years old. Reportedly, the same Christie's Will fought for the crown early in the English Civil War and died in battle in 1642; he would have been seventy-seven.

In the 1980s a private genealogical research firm in Northern Ireland suggested to Viola Armstrong that Christie's Will was the likely founder of her husband's family in Ulster in northern Ireland. Conveniently, he was one of the few Armstrongs with a known biography.

As early as 1604, records show a William Armstrong settling in Fermanagh, where by 1620 no fewer than twenty-five different Armstrongs (five headed by a William) lived as tenant farmers. Militia muster rolls for Ulster from the year 1630 indicate that thirty-eight Armstrong men (six named William) reported to duty.

Contrary to Viola's conjecture, no Neil Armstrong progenitors ever settled in Ireland. They stayed in the Borderlands until they immigrated directly to America sometime between 1736 and 1743. Fittingly, for the family history of the First Man, the ancestry goes back literally to Adam.

Adam Armstrong, born in the Borderlands in the year 1638 and died there in 1696, represents Generation No. 1. Coming ten generations before the astronaut, Adam Armstrong is the great-great-great-great-great-great-great-great paternal grandfather of the first man on the Moon. Cemetery records indicate that he died in Cumberland Township, Green County, Pennsylvania, in 1749, most likely making him the first of Neil's bloodline to immigrate to America.

Adam Armstrong had two sons, Francis (year of birth unknown), who died in 1735, and Adam, born in Cumbria, England, in 1685. At age twenty, Adam Armstrong II married Mary Forster, born in Cumbria the same year as he. Together the couple had four children—Margaret (b. 1706), William (b. 1708), Adam Abraham (b. 1714 or 1715), and John (b. 1720)—all baptized in Kirkandrews Parish, Cumberland, England. Adam Abraham Armstrong also came to America, probably with his father, likely in the mid- to late 1730s.

These Armstrongs were thus among the earliest settlers of Pennsylvania's Conococheague ("Caneygoge") region, named "clear water" by the

Delaware tribe. Adam Abraham Armstrong worked his land in the Conococheague, in what became Cumberland County, until his death in Franklin,
Pennsylvania, on May 20, 1779, when he was sixty-three or sixty-four. But already by 1760, his oldest son John (b. 1736), at age twenty-four, had surveyed
the mouth of Muddy Creek, 160 miles west of the Conococheague and some
60 miles south of Fort Pitt. There John and his wife, Mary Kennedy (b. 1738,
in Chambersburg, Franklin County, Pennsylvania), raised nine children, their
second son, John (b. 1773), producing offspring leading to Neil. According to
regional genealogy expert Howard L. Leckey, John and Mary's sixth child,
Abraham Armstrong (b. 1770), was "the first white child born on this (western) side of the Monongahela River." While not close to being historically accurate, Leckey's point underscores the early Anglo movement west beyond
the ridge of the Alleghenies. Therein lay the major provocation for the out-
break of the French and Indian War in 1756.*

Following the Revolutionary War, thousands of settlers poured into
the Ohio Country, a land that one of its first surveyors called "fine, rich,
level . . . it wants nothing but cultivation to make it a most delightful
country."

In March 1799, twenty-five-year-old John Armstrong and his wife Rebekah Miller (b. 1776), as well as John's younger brother Thomas Armstrong (b. 1777), his wife, Alice Crawford, and their infant, William,
traveled by flatboat down Muddy Creek to Pittsburgh, then steered into the
Ohio River some 250 miles down to Hockingport, just west of modern-day
Parkersburg, West Virginia. The two families coursed their way up the
Hocking River for 35 miles to Alexander Township, Ohio. Homesteading
outside what became the town of Athens, Thomas and Alice raised six children. John and Rebekah eventually settled near Fort Greenville, in far
western Ohio.

To "defend" the frontier in the early 1790s, General "Mad" Anthony
Wayne built a series of forts from southwestern Ohio into southeastern
Michigan. In August 1794, Wayne's "Legion" defeated a Native American
confederation led by Shawnee chief Blue Jacket at the Battle of Fallen Tim-

---

* Armstrong family involvement in the French and Indian War, and in the American Revolution, remains incompletely documented, but there is no doubt that some offshoots of the
family (and definitely some in-laws) served in military capacities. The husband of John
Armstrong's younger sister Hannah (1742 or 1743–1816), Irish-born John Moore (1741–
1818), entered the War for Independence as a private and may have served as a combat surgeon. John Armstrong, with the help of his sons, built along the Monongahela a "strong
house" refuge for patriots.

bers on the Maumee River near Toledo. At Fort Greenville the next year, chiefs of the Shawnee, Wyandot, Delaware, Ottawa, Miami, Eel River, Wea, Chippewa, Potawatomi, Kickapoo, Piankashaw, and Kaskaskia relinquished claims to the entire bottom two-thirds of Ohio.

Following the War of 1812, in which many tribes had allied themselves with the defeated British, came the Treaty of Maumee Rapids in 1817, which placed all of Ohio's remaining Native Americans on reservations, followed in 1818 by a supplemental treaty struck at Fort Barbee, near Girtystown, 42 miles north of Fort Greenville, on the St. Marys River.

Neil's ancestor John Armstrong (Generation No. 5) and his family witnessed negotiations for what became the Treaty of St. Marys, the last great assemblage of Indian nations in Ohio. David, Samuel, John Civil, Sally, Rebecca, Mary, Jane, and Nancy settled with their parents in 1818 on the western bank of the St. Marys. From the first harvests, the Armstrongs seem to have earned enough to secure the deed to their 150-acre property, paying the two dollars per acre stipulated by the federal Land Act of 1800. St. Marys township collected taxes in 1824 from twenty-nine residents totaling $26.64, a dear ninety cents of which was paid by John Armstrong for "2 horses" and "3 cattle," for what became the "Armstrong Farm," the oldest farm in Auglaize County.

David Armstrong, the eldest of John's children (b. 1798) and Margaret Van Nuys (1802–1831) were Neil's paternal great-grandparents. It seems they did not marry. Margaret soon married Caleb Major, and David married Eleanor Scott (1802–1852), the daughter of Thomas Scott, another early St. Marys settler. Baby Stephen stayed with his mother until her premature death in March 1831, when Margaret's parents, Rachel Howell and Jacobus J. Van Nuys, took in their seven-year-old grandson. Stephen's father David died in 1833, followed by his grandfather in 1836.

Stephen Armstrong (Generation No. 7) received his grandfather Van Nuys's legacy of roughly two hundred dollars in cash and goods when he turned twenty-one in 1846. The census of 1850, a year in which farmers made up 83 percent of Ohio's 2.3 million population, listed Stephen as a "laborer." After years working for a family named Clark, whose farm was in the low-lying "Black Swamp" of Noble Township, Stephen managed to buy 197 acres (Ohio farms then averaged only about 75). Later he secured the deed to 138 additional acres held since 1821 by the Vanarsdol family (related to the Armstrongs by marriage) as well as the rights to 80 acres held since 1835 by Peter Morrison Van Nuys, Stephen's maternal uncle.

How the Civil War affected Stephen Armstrong is unknown. When the conflict broke out in 1861, Stephen was only thirty-four. Union service records do not indicate that he fought in the war, though by war's end, nearly 350,000 Ohioans had joined the Union army. Of these, some 35,000, fully 10 percent, lost their lives.

Stephen married Martha Watkins Badgley (1832–1907), the widow of George Badgley and mother of two sons, George and Charles Aaron, and two daughters, Mary Jane and Hester ("Hettie"). Stephen must have met and wed "Widow Badgley," six years his junior, by 1863 or 1864, because on January 16, 1867, Martha gave birth to Stephen's son, Willis Armstrong, named after his guardian James Willis Major. Previously, the couple had lost two consecutive babies in childbirth.

When Stephen Armstrong died in August 1884 at age fifty-eight, he owned well over four hundred acres whose value had nearly quintupled from the 1850s purchase price of roughly fifteen dollars per acre to over $30,000—the equivalent today of over half a million dollars.

Stephen's only natural son, Willis, inherited most of the estate. Three years later, Willis married a local girl, Lillian Brewer (1867–1901). The couple, both twenty years old, lived in the River Road farmhouse with Willis's mother Martha. Five children were born in two-year intervals between 1888 and 1897. But in 1900 Muriel, the eldest, fell from her horse and died from head injuries, and then in 1901 Lillie died trying to give birth to yet another child.

Bereaved, Willis began a part-time mail route. One regular mail stop was at the highly respected law firm of John and Jacob Koenig. Their unmarried sister Laura Mary Louise worked as their stenographer and secretary, and, sometime in late 1903—about the time two brothers from nearby Dayton were test flying an airplane over coastal North Carolina's Kitty Hawk—Willis began courting her. When they married in June 1905, Laura was thirty-one years old.

Willis gifted Laura not only an expensive wedding ring and precious gold lavalieres, but a honeymoon by train to Chicago, where Willis bought his new wife a dining room suite and a table service for twelve of pure white Haviland china. Returning to St. Marys, he purchased a house on North Spruce Street. Later, he moved the family into an impressive Victorian on a corner of West Spring Street.

It was here that Stephen Koenig Armstrong, Neil's father, grew up. The first of two children born to Willis and Laura (Mary Barbara was born in 1910), the boy was welcomed on August 26, 1907, by half sisters Bernice, seventeen, and Grace, ten, and half brothers Guy, fifteen, and Ray, twelve.

Laura was thirty-three when her first child was baptized, an occasion commemorated by the Koenig family with a vial of water from the River Jordan.

What most defined Stephen's boyhood, however, were economic misfortune and a streak of family bad luck. Willis sank most of his money into an investment scheme whereby his brother-in-law John Koenig envisioned Fort Wayne as a regional interurban rail hub. Seeing a clear path to fortune, Willis mortgaged his farms.

Unfortunately for the investment, the Fort Wayne and Decatur Interurban Electric Railway was built in perfect concert with the rise of the automobile. Fatalities from a pair of highly publicized 1910 railway accidents included the man who headed the Bluffton, Geneva, & Celina Traction Company, which subsequently aborted a plan to build a new westward line out of Fort Wayne. The resulting financial disaster soured family relations, including Willis's marriage.

In the spring of 1910, Stephen's eighteen-year-old half brother Guy was lured to Maricopa, California, north of Los Angeles, by reports of a bountiful gusher, only to perish in an April 1912 oil rig accident. Back in St. Marys, the Armstrong house caught fire in 1914. Six-year-old Stephen escaped with just his corduroy suit on his back.

In 1916, Willis, forty-nine years old and deeply in debt, quit his mail route and headed for Kansas with "oil on the brain." Willis traveled to the Mid-Continent Range with his twenty-one-year-old son Ray.

In early 1919, after the end of World War I had significantly weakened demand for oil, Willis returned to Ohio with an unknown—likely modest—sum. Within weeks, Willis moved the family back to the River Road farm, still heavily mortgaged. Soon crippled by chronic arthritis, Willis relied on Stephen to work the fields; finishing his education was a task on which Stephen's mother insisted.

Even before Stephen graduated from high school in 1925, he had decided not to pursue the farming life. He wrote as much to his older half brother Ray in Los Angeles. Back in St. Marys, Stephen Armstrong dreamed of opportunities out West.

Yet right there in his midst was a pretty, highly intelligent, sensitive, and soft-spoken young woman with whom he fell in love. Her name was Viola Louise Engel.

CHAPTER 2

The Strong of Spirit

Ralph Waldo Emerson came close to expressing a universal truth when he claimed, in 1860, "Men are what their mothers made them."

Stephen Armstrong's family had been living in America for well over a century when Viola's grandfather, Frederick Wilhelm Kötter, sailed into Baltimore harbor aboard *Johannes* in October 1864. In a family effort to circumvent enforced conscription into Prussian prime minister Otto von Bismarck's military, eighteen-year-old Fritz Kötter's father sold part of his farm to pay their son's passage to America.

From Baltimore, Frederick made his way to Cincinnati and then north via the Miami and Erie Canal to the little burg of New Knoxville, Ohio. A state whose German immigrant population exceeded 200,000 (predominating in thirty-seven of eighty-eight counties) held obvious appeal to the native of Ladbergen, Germany. Kötter soon found a wife, but she died, perhaps in unsuccessful childbirth. In the early 1870s, after purchasing eighty acres of land near the village of Moulton, six miles to the north of New Knoxville, Fritz married a first-generation German-American, Maria Martha Katterheinrich. They Americanized their name to Katter. Two newborn daughters died, but the couple later enjoyed the healthy birth of six sons and one daughter, Caroline Matilda, born on February 6, 1888. Nineteen years later, on May 7, 1907, Caroline gave birth to her first and only child, Viola.

Some of Viola's most vivid childhood memories involved watching her German-speaking grandmother, Maria Martha Katter, prepare traditional recipes. An apple pancake topped with a chunk of butter and sorghum molasses was Viola's best-loved treat, and a half century later, she would tell her son Neil to "hurry home from the Moon" because she would have his favorite apple dessert ready and waiting for him.

Whereas the Armstrongs for three centuries had been Presbyterian,

Viola's family worshiped at the St. Paul Reformed Church, whose doctrine derived from Martin Luther's Catechism, the Heidelberg Catechism, and the Augsburg Confession, drawing on a fundamentalist tenet: "The Holy Scriptures of the Old and New Testaments are recognized as the Word of God and the ultimate rule of Christian faith and practice."

After the Moon landing, Viola summarized her beliefs: "My faith is deep and simple. I believe our body houses the soul within us—our body is a living temple of God, therefore it is sacred."

Young Viola sat for long stretches singing hymns. She prayed—sometimes in German—before meals and at bedtime. According to her daughter June, Neil's younger sister: "Mother never preached. She'd take us to church and [hear] us say our prayers good night. But she never preached."

The Bible was her rock. She respected the King James Version for "the way it is written." In 1929, her mother's wedding gift was *The Red Letter New Testament,* "With the Words of Jesus Christ Printed in Red." Viola's underlining and margin notations reveal treasured passages, among them Psalm 37—"Trust in the Lord, and do good" and "the meek shall inherit the earth."

"I do believe my mother was deeply in love with the father she never knew," her daughter June has expressed. On May 4, 1909, Martin Engel (1879–1909), a butcher by trade and not yet thirty years old, died of tuberculosis, with his wife and baby daughter at his side. On May 7, Viola's second birthday, her father was buried in Elmgrove Cemetery, near the Armstrong farm, which John and Rebekah Armstrong had settled in 1818.

Viola frequently asked about her father. He "loved his home and his family very much," related twenty-one-year-old widow Caroline Katter Engel of the man who played the violin beautifully "by ear," owned a typewriter and an Edison phonograph, and wore stickpins and cuff links. Viola was left to romanticize him.

Caroline's parents cared for Viola while she cooked for the wealthy McClain family. In 1911, Dr. Vernon Noble (the son of Dr. Harry Noble, who had delivered Viola) diagnosed liver cancer in Caroline's mother, Maria. Viola remembers being banished so that an "awful surgery" could be staged on the family dining room table.

To Viola, the undertaker's funeral wreath was a symbol "that God had taken one of His flock home." Viola took to pretending that the Katter barnyard, like Elmgrove, "was a cemetery. I would bring flowers (weeds) and lay them on the stones, feeling so sad, actually crying tears."

The veil of tragedy lifted until 1916, when Grandfather Katter became fatally infected with erysipelas, "St. Anthony's fire." "Suddenly a most beautiful white angel appeared at the foot of his bed," Viola believed. "The angel had really called him Home."

For Caroline Katter, loss yielded to happiness when a romance blossomed between herself and a local farmer, two years her junior, by the name of William Ernst Korspeter, whom she had met at the Reformed Church in St. Marys. The church was the site of their marriage on October 7, 1916.

Cleardale School in Washington Township was about a mile's walk from Viola's new home. Only sixteen children (many of them siblings) enrolled during her seventh- and eighth-grade years (1918–20). Viola recorded, "I am sort of lonesome as I am the only one in my [eighth] grade. . . . I haven't missed a day so far, which I hope I never will."

The previous school year, Viola had kept a "commonplace book" filled with "Memory Gems," such as D. L. Moody's adage, "If I take care of my character, my reputation will take care of itself."

Even as a young girl, Viola established the touchstones of her parenting philosophy: "Oh, you who have a mother dear; / Let not a word or act give pain; / But cherish, love her, with your life; / You ne'er can have her like again" [unattributed]. Certainly, son Neil learned these lessons well.

In a decision she would come to regret, Viola forewent the pursuit of her teaching qualifications at Normal School and instead matriculated at Blume High School in Wapakoneta, where she graduated in a class of ninety-three students.

Viola's favorite teacher, a Miss Pera Campbell, taught American classics from history to satire. Religious and moral themes of Nathaniel Ward, Cotton Mather, and Jonathan Edwards naturally interested her. "We learn, if we never have before," she wrote of Edwards's *Sinners in the Hands of an Angry God,* "that we must be born again, or converted, sometime in our life." From Philip Freneau's romantic elegy "The House of the Night," she learned "what death really is and should be." Life beckoned as well, as evidenced by a keepsake sketch of Venetian gondolas annotated in Viola's hand, "The picture looks at me with eyes that penetrate."

Her high school years appear to have been very happy. A slender girl with unassuming ways, Viola seems to have been "one of the sweetest, brightest, and most charming of friends," while maintaining high academic marks in what today would be considered demanding college-level coursework. A student of the piano since the age of eight, she was known for her love of music. This quality, along with inventiveness, concentration, organization, and perseverance, she passed along to her son Neil.

Yet, Viola's dearest aspiration was to devote her life to Christ: "I had longed to be a missionary, going to distant lands, but being an only child, my parents discouraged me." She instead earned twenty cents an hour clerking at St. Marys' Glass Block Company, touted as the "Largest Department Store in Western Ohio."

It was then that Viola started seeing Stephen Armstrong, who himself had just graduated from St. Marys Memorial High School, Wapakoneta's archrival. The two first spoke during a youth group meeting at St. Paul Reformed Church. Their "courting" unfolded within fairly strict bounds: "We went places close around, but only on Sunday afternoons or evenings. We had a wonderful time together," Viola reminisced. "I guess when you love one another you really don't need much money." The ardor of their young love disguised their many differences.

For Christmas 1928, Viola and Stephen exchanged engagement rings and announced their plans to marry. Like most young couples, they were not unaware of the challenges ahead but knew "somehow we would manage." Their wedding was set for October 8, 1929, at 2:30 P.M.

Viola prayed, "asking God to help us always to do right, that we might be pleasing in His sight. I told Him that I wanted us to be right for each other. I asked Him to help us have a beautiful marriage and be useful and helpful people while we lived here on earth. These talks with God made me strong to face the future, whatever it might bring."

The ceremony took place in the small living room of the Korspeter farmhouse at an altar made of red and yellow cockscomb, marigolds, and pink and lavender asters. Viola, her hair curled that morning, wore a streetlength dress of blue transparent velvet and black satin pumps with silver buckles. She carried a bouquet of four pink rosebuds. Stephen dressed in a hand-tailored, finely striped navy blue suit, a white carnation in his lapel. His best man, Guy Briggs, was dating Viola's best friend and bridesmaid, Marvel Hoeper. Stephen's beautiful younger sister, Mary Barbara, served as maid of honor; the day before the wedding, she had turned nineteen. Reverend H. R. Burkett of St. Paul Reformed Church officiated. His wife played the piano—Lohengrin's processional and Mendelssohn's "Wedding March" for the recessional. Viola's friend LaRue Stroh sang "O Promise Me" and "I Love You Truly" before immediate family and friends. Viola had made her own wedding cake, an iced angel food in three graduated layers ornamented with rosebuds and garlands, and hand-churned the ice cream served out of bell-shaped molds.

For a honeymoon, the couple drove "Papa" Korspeter's automobile sixty miles for their first-ever trip to Dayton, where they nervously signed in for their overnight stay at the Biltmore. Stephen spent $275 on a 1927 Chevy two-door, leaving precious little to spare. Two weeks later, on October 29, 1929, Wall Street's stock market crashed and the Great Depression began.

Stephen moved Viola into the River Road farmhouse, where she helped his mother with the cooking and housework. Opportunity arose when the county auditor and a friend of the family offered him part-time work as an appraiser. Stephen went to Columbus, the state capital, to sit for the civil service exam, and in February 1930, he received his passing marks as well as an appointment to assist Robert Horn, Columbiana County's senior auditor. Arrangements were made to auction off the farm and to move his parents into a small house in St. Marys. Stephen and Viola saw a godsend in a promising new job and a life together—and a baby on the way.

Viola claimed, "Immediately I became aware that I had conceived. Oh, the thoughts kept racing through my mind, oh, really and truly, Stephen and I were going to have a child." When she was alone, she "fell on her knees and thanked God with all my heart." She promised to teach the child "the very best I knew how" and "to give him back to God, to use as He saw fit." She prayed her baby would "grow up to be a good and useful person."

In mid-May 1930 Stephen and Viola, six months pregnant, drove the 230 miles to Lisbon, near the Pennsylvania border. They were "thrilled beyond words" to have electric lights and hot and cold running water in their furnished two-room apartment.

Two weeks before her due date, set for August 4, Viola prepared to give birth at her parents' farmhouse, in the same front room in which Stephen had courted and married her. On a bedside table, she carefully laid out the layette she had made herself, every stitch "one of love and expectation."

The evening of August 4, 1930, found Viola sitting at the kitchen table writing a letter to Stephen, who remained in Lisbon: "The baby and I will be all right—you know, honey, if it's God's will. Today is the fourth and we haven't any little Teddy yet—but the day isn't up yet." As she closed the letter, a severe pain overcame her and a gush of amniotic fluid ran down her leg. Dr. Vernon Noble, who had had to be called in, said, "Well, I cannot save the child, but we will try to save the mother." Finally, at 12:31:30 on August 5, 1930, he managed to deliver the baby—a boy—with the assistance of Stephen's sister Mary Barbara. The child's jaw structure resembled his father's. But his nose and eyes were all Viola.

When Grandmother Caroline placed the boy dressed in his new clothes into his mother's arms, all Viola could do was look at "that beautiful little dear" and thank God over and over again. Exhausted from her ordeal, she fell fast asleep. Caroline picked up Viola's letter and added a postscript:

Viola's Mother: Papa Stephen. Baby weighs 8³/₄ lb. Viola was very sick from 9:30 P.M. to 12:31 A.M. Dr. had to take it with instruments. But Viola seems to be getting along fine, but she is weak and sore. Baby is very pretty. Don't worry about Viola. If she takes worse we will let you know. Will write more tomorrow. Viola sent her love to you.

Viola and Stephen called their son Neil Alden. Viola liked the alliteration, "Alden Armstrong," and the allusion to Alden from Henry Wadsworth Longfellow's classic poem "The Courtship of Myles Standish." No one in either family had ever been christened "Neil." Perhaps they knew that "Neil" was the Scottish form of the Gaelic name Néall, which translated as "cloud," or that, in its modern form, it meant "Champion."

PART TWO

TRANQUILITY BASE

Neil read a lot as a child and that was his escape. It wasn't an escape from *anything; it was an escape* to *something, into a world of imagination. As a boy he felt secure enough to risk escaping, because he knew, upon returning, he would be in a nice place.*

—JUNE ARMSTRONG HOFFMAN

CHAPTER 3

First Child

With first love, teenage Viola thought she had experienced the pinnacle of human emotion. But, at age twenty-three, the birth of her baby forever changed that belief. "Oh, how good it was to hold him in my arms—truly the flesh and blood of Stephen and me, completely fashioned by God, truly a precious blessing given to us to have, to hold, to cherish, to love, and to teach the beauty of life."

Ten days after delivering Neil, Viola rose from bed, "caring for the baby instead of mamma doing it all." Contrary to 1930s societal norms, Viola "was able to breast-feed him as well as our two later babies. This I prayed so hard for, and my prayers were answered."

The doctor did not permit her to attend her father-in-law Willis's funeral, but with Stephen at home she arranged for Neil to be baptized by Reverend Burkett, the minister who had married them, in a "hallowed place, truly sacred," the same living room where the couple's marriage and Neil's birth had taken place. "Our hearts were all running over with thanksgiving for our beautiful son. . . . In my heart I dedicated him to God, and promised I would do my best to rear him according to God's Holy Word."

Stephen's job with the Bureau of Inspection and Supervision of Public Offices (a branch of the auditor's office in the Ohio Department of State) demanded an immediate transfer from Lisbon to Warren, Ohio, forty miles to the north, where he would assist a Mahoning County senior examiner. The Armstrong family would make *sixteen* moves over the next fourteen years, in an Ohio odyssey including stops in Lisbon (1930), Warren (1930), Ravenna (1931), Shaker Heights (1932), Cleveland Heights (1932), Warren (1933), Jefferson (1934), Warren (1936), Moulton (1937), St. Marys (1938), Upper Sandusky (1941), and Wapakoneta (1944).

Viola found Neil to be a serene and untroubled baby. Yet family photographs captured the boy's tendency toward shyness. A visit to Santa Claus when he was about three left Neil "A little bit scared. See, you can see that funny little look." Staging a photo with his birthday-present puppy dog, Tippy, Viola had to exhort a reluctant Neil, "Stand up there like a man!"

She read to Neil constantly, instilling in her son the love of books shared with Neil's grandmothers Caroline and Laura. The boy learned to read extraordinarily early and could read street signs by age three. His father Stephen, in a 1969 interview before the Apollo 11 mission, explained: "He's a deep thinker. He likes books. He's made the statement many times that he wished he could have books all around him."

During his first year in elementary school, in Warren, Neil read over one hundred books. Though the boy started his second-grade year in the rural consolidated school in Moulton but finished at St. Marys, Neil's teacher, Mrs. Dorothy Hutton Adams, found him reading books meant for fourth- and fifth-grade pupils. Together with school superintendent C. C. McBroom, they decided to move him up to Mrs. Grace Wierwille Schrolucke's third-grade class, which made him eight years old when he started St. Marys' fourth grade the following autumn. Nonetheless, he received top grades and his teacher, Miss Laura Oelrich, said she "couldn't keep him busy all the time."

Wherever the family went, Neil acclimated well and made friends easily. According to Neil, "as far back as I can remember, I was always moving. I didn't think so much about it."

No children were Neil's more constant companions than his younger sister and brother. On July 6, 1933, when Neil was almost three, June Louise Armstrong was born in Warren, Ohio; a year and a half later, on February 22, 1935, Dean Alan Armstrong arrived in Jefferson.

Though they always felt loved and cherished by their parents, young June and Dean sensed that their older brother was "mother's favorite." "When it was time to plant potatoes out at our grandparents' farm, Neil was nowhere to be found. He'd be in the house, in the corner, reading a book. Also, I don't think all of us were allowed to get [model airplane] glue all over everything! But he was." June recalls, "He never *did* anything wrong. He was Mr. Goody Two-shoes, if there ever was one. It was just his nature."

As older brothers go, June says, Neil "was definitely a caretaker." The first time she ventured onto the high board at Upper Sandusky, Neil cheered her on from the water below: "Jump! Jump! It's okay." He always waited for her before heading home, usually carrying her towel so it would not get caught in the spokes of her bike.

With brother Dean, who was five years younger, relations were more difficult: "I never violated Neil's space. It would have had to have been an invitation." Though the brothers were in the same Boy Scout troops, Neil outpaced Dean in badges earned and socialized with his older friends from school. They both loved music, but Dean enjoyed competitive sports and played on the varsity basketball team. Neil was "consumed by learning," like his mother, while Dean was more like his dad, "a fun-loving person" who did not care much for books. Dean boasts that Neil "only had two dates in high school and I had to get both of them for him," a remarkable claim considering that Dean was only twelve when Neil, age sixteen, graduated.

"I've never competed with Neil in any way," Dean asserts, but sister June isn't convinced: "Dean *wasn't* left out, but that's still the way he perceives it." Friends of the family also wonder about Dean's feelings. But Neil's senior prom date, Alma Lou Shaw, who also knew Dean well, says, "I never experienced anything to make me feel he was envious of Neil."

"Neil was just not made to hurt anyone," Dean acknowledges, "very much like mother." Stephen had a bad temper, Stephen's father Willis had a bad temper, and Dean realized that he did, too. Childhood Monopoly games found Neil always serving as banker—and almost always winning. At the height of Dean's inevitable frustration, he "would kick the middle of the card table and send all the money and cards flying. All Neil ever said, as calmly as he could, was, 'Okay, this game is over.'" In Dean's view, his brother never displayed any "outer fire."

Neil's unusual combination of coolness, restraint, and honesty could be read as inscrutable. But he was rarely that in the eyes of his mother. "He has a truthfulness about him," Viola said in a summer 1969 interview with *Life* magazine writer Dodie Hamblin. "He either had to be truthful and right, or he didn't think he'd engage in it. I really never heard him say a word against anybody, never. That hurt him. If he heard somebody say something against somebody, that too would hurt him." June compares that essential quality in Neil to her mother: "Mother thrived on goodness." She never said a curse word stronger than "Lordy." As the family disciplinarian, her style was not physical but moral: "She wanted us to be good."

But a person's being "good" did not preclude resolution to the point of stubbornness. Neil "thinks things through," Apollo 11 crewmate Michael Collins answered when asked about this facet of Armstrong's personality, but "Yes, I would have to say stubborn rather than whatever the opposite of stubborn is." Dean suggests the synonym "self-willed": "Neil always does things on his terms. Our parents never tried to change him in any way. They were happy with him the way he was." June regards the quality from a different angle: "The way Mother treated him fostered a high level of self-confidence." To which Dean adds: "I don't think he 'scared' that much."

If anyone ever did scare Neil Armstrong, it was his father, who himself was a product of the "old school" of stern parenting. According to June, "One of his favorite phrases was, 'Straighten up!' " Judicious in any personal statement, Neil has always been especially reserved when discussing his father: "My father's job kept him away from our home most of the time, so I didn't think of him as being close to any of the children and did not notice if he seemed to be closer to one than another." When asked whether Neil and his father were close, June replied: "No, they weren't close. I may have been the closest to my father, but even that was not close." Mother hugged the children but Father did not. In June's recollection, "Neil probably was never hugged by him and Neil didn't hug, either."

When Neil wrote home from college, he addressed the envelopes to "Mrs. S. K. Armstrong." His letters greeted "Dear Mom and Family." Dudley Schuler, one of Neil's closest high school friends, found the Armstrongs "very close and very loving—a really nice family." Area residents found Stephen Armstrong "amiable," but it was Viola who stood out. "Neil's mother was one of the nicest persons I've ever known," proclaims Alma Lou Shaw-Kuffner. Dudley Schuler concurs: "She couldn't find fault in anybody." Though he called Steve "a great father," high school friend Arthur Frame regarded Viola as "really the spine of the family."

"I don't remember any discord in the family," recollects sister June. "I don't remember my parents arguing."

A certain element of tension did intrude in 1943, when Stephen's mother, Laura, after living alone in St. Marys for thirteen years following Willis's death, broke her ankle. Stephen and Viola took the sixty-nine-year-old woman into their home in nearby Upper Sandusky, an arrangement that became permanent when they moved in 1944 to Wapakoneta.

For Viola, Laura's thirteen-year stay, until her 1956 death at age eighty-two, was a daily cross to be borne. "Always, always there," remembers June, who from age ten on had to share her bedroom with Grandmother Laura. She "wasn't an interfering person," but her preference to be treated as "more of a guest" was particularly hard on Viola. Yet Viola was "the flexible one," June notes. She actually "stood it better than my father," who "would become more irritated with it." As for Neil, who was thirteen years old when

Grandmother Laura arrived in the household and who would leave home for college soon after his seventeenth birthday, the impact was minimal.

The same could not be said for the effect on Neil and his siblings of the evolution of Stephen and Viola's marriage. On the surface, the relationship appeared solid. But underneath, the conjugal union seems to have run an all-too-typical course, from loving passion to emotional distance.

One divisive issue was religion and the accompanying moral trappings of temperance, in drink and language. Stephen never talked openly about his religious ideas. Nor has Neil ever done so. Viola wrote shortly after the Moon landing that "Stephen's love of the Master never seemed to be as deep as mine." The same was true for Neil, Viola knew, though she always found that harder to admit to herself.

That is not to say that Neil did not believe in God, as a few uninformed writers and proponents of atheism—notably the famous American atheist Madalyn Murray O'Hair—suggested during the rush of Apollo 11 publicity in 1969. It is clear that by the time Armstrong returned from Korea in 1952 he had become a type of deist, a person whose belief in God was founded on reason rather than on revelation, and on an understanding of God's natural laws rather than on the authority of any particular creed or church doctrine.

While working as a test pilot in Southern California in the late 1950s, Armstrong applied at a local Methodist church to lead a Boy Scout troop. Where the form asked for his religious affiliation, Neil wrote the word "Deist." The confession so perplexed the Methodist minister that he consulted Stanley Butchart, one of Neil's fellow test pilots as well as a member of the congregation. Though uncertain of the principles of deism, Butchart praised Neil as a man of impeccable character whom he would and, during their flying together, did trust with his life. Unlike many Christians he had met, he had never heard Neil once utter a profanity, nor to his knowledge had anyone else. Taking Butchart at his word that Neil would positively influence young Scouts the minister gave Neil the position.

By Neil's own admission, he did not become aware of deism through any history or philosophy class. By the time he was in high school, his favorite subject was science, under the direction of department head and Dean of Boys John Grover Crites, a master of science education from Ohio State University. Crites came to Blume High School in Wapakoneta in 1944, the same year the Armstrongs moved to town. A man in his early fifties, Crites taught chemistry, physics, and advanced mathematics; he was the type who, according to one of Neil's classmates, "gave the kids [who shared

his interests] all the experience and all the knowledge they could absorb."
With Crites's help, Neil won the Freshman General Science Award given by
Bowling Green State University. During his senior year, Crites selected him
for Buckeye Boys State, an American Legion–sponsored weeklong government program held at Miami University in Oxford, Ohio. Dudley Schuler
identifies Crites as "an idol," "a tremendous man," and "a great influence
on Neil."

Living into the 1970s, Crites was available for interviews on the eve of
the Apollo 11 mission. "Science was [young Neil's] field and his love,"
Crites reported to journalists. Neil not only kept "a goal in mind," but "he
was the type of fellow who always tested out a hunch. He was always seeking
an answer to some future question," always on course to find the "right answer." This critical spirit made him "a natural for research."

It would also have set him on collision course with his mother over religion, if he had ever allowed that to happen. According to Dean, whenever
his mother spoke about religion, Neil would listen politely and in silence,
offering some terse comment only if pressed. Perhaps young Neil developed this conflict-avoidance strategy in a more general context, but surely
his relationship with his mother was the primary reason for it.

John Crites observed: "Neil was the type of boy who never let anyone
know that he knew anything. You had to ask to get an answer, but he expressed himself well in written form." Fellow engineers, test pilots, astronauts, space program officials, and other colleagues concur. "I did not see
Neil argue," remembers NASA mission flight director Eugene Kranz. "He
had the commander mentality . . . and didn't have to get angry." According
to Charles Friedlander, who directed the astronaut support office at Kennedy Space Center, "I saw that in the crew quarters. If something difficult
came up, he would listen politely. He'd think about it and talk to me about
it later if he had something to say."

Like many journalists covering the space program, CBS's Walter
Cronkite also experienced Neil's nonconfrontational—some have even said
evasive—style. On CBS's *Face the Nation* on Sunday, August 17, 1969, three
weeks after the Apollo 11 splashdown, the issue of Madalyn Murray O'Hair
publicly declaring Neil an atheist resurfaced. Cronkite asked: "I don't really
know what that has to do with your ability as a test pilot and an astronaut,
but since the matter is up, would you like to answer that statement?" To
which Neil replied, "I don't know where Mrs. O'Hair gets her information,
but she certainly didn't bother to inquire from me nor apparently the
agency, but I am certainly not an atheist." Cronkite followed up: "Appar-

ently your [NASA astronaut] application just simply says 'no religious preference.'" As always, Neil registered another answer as honest as it was vague and nondescript. "That's agency nomenclature which means that you don't have an acknowledged identification or association with a particular church group at the time. I did not at that time." At which point, Cronkite dismissed the matter. According to Neil's brother Dean, Cronkite on another occasion asked Neil if he felt closer to God when he stood on the Moon's surface, to which Neil gave a totally ridiculous non sequitur: "You know, Walter, sometimes a man just wants a good cigar." No available transcript confirms that Neil ever said this—or that Cronkite ever asked this exact question. But even if the brief byplay never actually occurred, it only underscores Dean's keen recognition of his brother's conflict-avoidance strategy.

Janet Shearon, Neil's first wife of thirty-five years, also faced frustration in this regard. But his mother, unlike everyone else, did not have to guess what was on his mind or in his heart. "Neil was a pleasure for us to raise in every way," Viola wrote on October 27, 1969, to a Methodist minister in Iowa—a man whom she had never met but who sought to correspond with her about the religious significance of her son's recent Moon landing—"but when he was a senior in high school, and even more in college, he began wondering about the truth of Jesus Christ. I felt sure he was praying less. . . . [Today] he is not teaching his own two fine sons about Jesus Christ. This fact causes a million swords to be pierced through my heart constantly."

Nonetheless, Viola found a way in 1969 to interpret her son's life journey in a positive, Christian way: "As I look back, I can see how the pattern of his life has all dovetailed together. I believe God gave him a mind to use and maybe destined him to the work he has been doing. As a child and as a young man he loved and was completely fascinated by the heavens and God's great creation. It seemed as if the heavens were calling him—so great was his undying interest. He has been fine and good, a scholar, a thinker, and a diligent worker." Since the Moon landing, "I've listened to every speech of his very carefully. Though not an eloquent speaker, I feel every word is fine and thoughtful and every one from the heart. His thinking is big and his thoughts are far reaching. He seems to be inspired by God, and speaking his Will. For this I am over and over thankful."

It was a mother's loving rationalization against which Neil Armstrong, her precious first child, would never argue.

CHAPTER 4

The Virtues of Smallville

For Neil Armstrong, rural Ohio represented comfort, security, privacy, and sane human values. Leaving NASA in 1971, Armstrong would seek a return to the ordinary on a small farm back in his native state. "I have chosen to bring my family up in as normal an environment as possible," he would explain. Upon hearing that fellow Apollo 11 astronaut Michael Collins had told a reporter that Neil, by moving back to Ohio, was retreating to a castle and pulling up the drawbridge, Armstrong countered: "You know, those of us who live out in the hinterlands think that people that live *inside* the Beltway [as Collins did] are the ones that have the problems."

Armstrong's down-to-earth view dates back to his boyhood. During these same years, another product of an Ohio boyhood, cartoonist Jerry Siegel, envisioned a hero named Superman who hailed from Smallville. This biographical detail was a vital component of his fictional character, whose powers could only be fostered by an environment that promoted the triad of revered abstractions: "Truth, Justice, and the American Way."

It was not Smallville but Warren, Jefferson, St. Marys, Upper Sandusky, and Wapakoneta that harbored Neil Armstrong. None of these burgs registered a population in the 1930s and 1940s much above five thousand. In these genuine Smallvilles, young people—with the right kind of family and community support—grew up embracing ambition.

In addition to Neil Armstrong, that mind-set marked all seven of the original Mercury astronauts: Alan B. Shepard Jr., of East Derry, New Hampshire; Virgil I. "Gus" Grissom of Mitchell, Indiana; John H. Glenn Jr., of New Concord, Ohio; Walter M. Schirra Jr., of Oradell, New Jersey; L. Gordon Cooper Jr., of Shawnee, Oklahoma; and Donald K. "Deke" Slayton of Sparta, Wisconsin. Only the hometown address of M. Scott Carpenter—Boulder, Colorado—might register on a larger scale, but, during Carpenter's youth in the 1930s and 1940s, Boulder counted just over ten thousand citizens.

In the view of the Original Seven, if the famous ephemeral quality that came to be known as "The Right Stuff" existed at all, it derived socially from their common upbringing. "Small-town values are a mark of distinction of the Project Mercury pilots," Walter Schirra wrote in his autobiography *Schirra's Space* (1988). John Glenn, the first American astronaut to orbit, concurred: "Growing up in a small town gives kids something special." Children "make their own decisions" and "maybe it's no accident that people in the space program, a lot of them tended to come from small towns."

For most of the history of the U.S. space program, a greater number of astronauts have come from Ohio than from any other state. Still today, of the four states producing the most astronauts (the others are California, New York, and Texas, the country's most populous states), Ohio ranks first in terms of astronauts per capita, with one native-born astronaut for every 662,000 people.

Though the amiable atmosphere of small-town life in Ohio, real or imagined, faced a serious crisis in the 1930s, young Neil noticed hardly any financial hardship: "The small towns, the ones that I grew up in, were slow to come out of the Depression. We were not deprived [Stephen Armstrong's annual salary was just above the 1930 national average of $2,000], but there was never a great deal of money around. On that score we had it no worse and no better than thousands of other families." To some of his boyhood friends, the fact that Neil's father had a job meant that the Armstrongs were rich, and they told Neil so.

Neil's first employment came in 1940 when he was ten—and weighing barely seventy pounds. For ten cents an hour, he cut grass at Upper Sandusky's historic Old Mission Cemetery. Later, at Neumeister's Bakery, he stacked loaves of bread and helped make 110 dozen doughnuts. He also scraped the giant dough mixer clean: "I probably got the job because of my small size; I could crawl inside the mixing vats at night and clean them out. The favorite of the senior bakers was the hot-buttered bread, but the greatest fringe benefit for me was getting to eat the ice cream and homemade chocolates."

When the family moved to Wapakoneta in 1944, Neil clerked at Wahrer's West End Grocery and then at Heller and Bowsher Hardware. Later he did morning and evening chores at Rhine and Brading's drugstore for forty cents an hour. His parents let him keep all his wages, but expected him to save a substantial part of it for college.

An incident from Neil's Boy Scout days in Upper Sandusky seems to confirm his superior work ethic. Early one morning Neil and two of his fellow Scouts, John "Bud" Blackford and Konstantine "Kotcho" Solacoff, set off for Carey, Ohio, ten miles to the north, on their twenty-mile qualifying hike toward a badge required to make Eagle Scout. After eating lunch at a windmill-shaped restaurant the boys started back. According to Kotcho Solacoff though "fatigue was setting in . . . Neil kept pushing us to go faster and faster so he could get to work. We told him to go ahead." Neil started "the Boy Scout pace," alternately walking and then running intervals between roadside telephone poles. "By the time we got home," Kotcho recalls, "we were not only exhausted but we had painful cramps in our legs." The next day Kotcho and Bud found that Neil had made it to the bakery on time.

Of the 294 individuals selected as astronauts between 1959 and 2003, over two hundred (more than four in every five) had been active in scouting. This included twenty-one women who served as Girl Scouts. Forty of the Boy Scouts who became astronauts had made it to Eagle status. Of the twelve men to walk on the Moon, eleven participated in scouting. On this list stand both Neil Armstrong and his Apollo 11 crewmate Buzz Aldrin, though Aldrin stayed in Scouts only briefly.

In the opinion of Bud Blackford, "The Scouts can take a lot of credit for Neil Armstrong." When the family moved to Upper Sandusky in 1941, the town of roughly three thousand people still had no Scout troop. The Japanese attack on Pearl Harbor on December 7, 1941—breaking news of which Neil heard on the radio when his father called him inside from playing in the front yard—soon changed that. On the following day, when the U.S. Congress declared war, the Boy Scouts of America placed its entire resources at the service of the government. As Neil remembers, news of the war "was around us all the time, in the newspaper, on the radio. And of course there were a lot of stars in the windows of the families who had children that had gone off to war." As Bud Blackford recalls, "A new troop was formed right from scratch," to be led by Protestant minister J. R. Koenig, "a real taskmaster sort of fellow."

The new troop, designated by the national organization as Ohio's Troop 25, met monthly in a room above the Commercial Bank building in downtown "Upper." Thirty-two boys joined, whom Reverend Koenig lined up by height and had them count off into four "patrols." Neil's group called itself the Wolf Patrol and elected Blackford as patrol leader, Solacoff as assistant patrol leader, and Neil as the scribe who penciled the minutes into "a beat-up three-ring binder."

Troop 25 and its Wolf Patrol became, in Neil's words, "immersed in the wartime environment." Airplane recognition was a Scout forte that suited Neil perfectly. He and his friends made models that their Scout leader sent on to military and civil defense authorities so their experts could better distinguish friendly from enemy aircraft. Troop 25 skit night had the Wolf Patrol skewering Axis leadership. Blackford played Hitler, Solacoff imitated Mussolini, and Neil was a German general. "The show received great acclaim under the circumstances," Blackford recalls.

When the terse Reverend Koenig was assigned to an out-of-town ministry, Ed Naus, "less of a disciplinarian," stepped in, assisted by Neil's father. "He was not a Scoutmaster," Neil explains, "but he was very helpful and very involved." In Bud Blackford's eyes, Stephen Armstrong and Ed Naus were a "wonderful combination."

Blackford remembers that Steve Armstrong encouraged the troop to start a monthly newspaper. At his office in the courthouse, he typed the editorial staff's stories, news items, and a few dumb jokes ("You serve crabs here?" "We serve anyone, sit down.") onto unforgiving mimeograph paper that yielded such masthead misspellings as features editor "Niel." *The Pup Tent News* was first released on Flag Day, June 14, 1943.

In their Wolf Patrol, Neil, Bud, and Kotcho entered into one of those indelible adolescent friendships that thrived on good-natured rivalry. Kotcho Solacoff remembers a chem-lab prank: "I said, 'Here Neil, try some $C_{12}H_{22}O_{11}$.' To my surprise and horror, Neil grabbed a pinch full and put it in his mouth. I yelled, 'Spit it out, it's poison!' Neil said, '$C_{12}H_{22}O_{11}$ is sugar.' I said, 'I know, but I didn't think you did.' That was the last time I took for granted that I knew something that he didn't."

The antics escalated at the Bowling Green State University Science Fair. "Neil had made a steam turbine out of scraps of wood and a little alcohol lamp that heated the little boiler. Every time he lit that lamp, his turbine would turn with such speed and eloquence. Bud and I had to save some face. So we built a little pinhole camera. The pictures were quite fuzzy but visible. The day came for the science fair. Neil's little turbine was spinning without missing a beat. He was teasing us that the judges would fall down laughing when they saw our science project. Several hours went by before the judges got to Neil's turbine; it wouldn't work. . . . the axles on the turbine warped and locked in place from overuse. A week or so later, the certificates from the science fair arrived. Bud and I got a superior, the highest award. Neil got a fair rating. Neil was furious. While telling the story recently at a class reunion, Neil wanted me to know that he had finally forgiven us. That little turbine can now be seen in the Neil Armstrong Museum in Wapakoneta, Ohio."

Wapakoneta has been consistently identified as Neil Armstrong's hometown, but it was his three years in "Upper" that Neil cherished most of all. Yet, as much as the entire family enjoyed their residence from 1941 to 1944 (Neil's age eleven to fourteen) at 446 North Sandusky Avenue, circumstances forced the family to make one last move, the one to "Wapak."

This time, Neil recalls, his father "thought he might get drafted" even though he was thirty-six years old, "on the upper edge" of "draft material." Wapakoneta, some fifty miles southwest of Upper, was farther from Stephen's work, but, explains Neil, "Mother had her parents nearby."

Stephen bought a large two-story corner home at 601 West Benton Street. As always, Neil had no particular trouble adjusting to his new environs, and he immediately became active in Boy Scout Troop 14. Blume High School was located just six blocks from his home. His high school transcript shows that his best grades were always in math, science, and English. Contrary to some historical accounts that have misunderstood Blume High School's grading system, he never received any poor, unsatisfactory, or failing grades. His lowest grades were in drawing (freshman year), Latin (sophomore year), American history (junior year), typing (junior year), and metalworking (senior year), but even in those classes he never earned less than a "fair."

Always musically inclined, Neil joined the school orchestra, boys' glee club, and band. Despite his small size, he played one of the largest instruments, the baritone horn, because he liked its distinctive tone. He joined Hi-Y, a student organization, served on the yearbook staff, and acted in the junior class play. Elected to the student council in grades eleven and twelve, in his senior year Neil served as vice president.

Neil even lent his baritone to a neighborhood ragtime combo, with Jerre Maxson and Bob Gustafson on trombones, and Jim Mougey on clarinet. The Mississippi Moonshiners' one paying job was a two-night gig playing Spike Jones tunes at grange halls in nearby Uniopolis and St. John—for five dollars to be split four ways. According to a laughing Gustafson, "Neil knew only one song by heart." That was "The Flight of the Bumblebee." "Oh, God, I can still hear that one today!" Jerre Maxson, now deceased, gave Neil's musical abilities a higher grade: "Neil was a very good musician. He had a strong after-beat, and really kept us going." Maxson took note of

Neil's cerebral approach, recalling his saying that "music contributed to 'thought control.'"

Of the Moonshiners' rendition of "The Star-Spangled Banner," Jerre Maxson admitted, "We were so bad that only half the people stood up. Before we got done, everyone had sat down." "We would probably never have been successful commercially," Neil adds wryly.

High school friends remember Neil not as shy or introverted, but as "a person of very few words" who "thought before he spoke." Remembers Bob Gustafson, "I think he wanted to be sure everything was right." According to Ned Keiber, "He just had things to do and he did them and he didn't talk about it." "I wouldn't call Neil shy," explains Arthur Frame, who for years subsequently served as Neil's stockbroker. "If you are someone who has something to say or has done something that he thinks is worthwhile, he'll participate in it wholeheartedly. But it's all on his terms."

Neil went on very few dates in high school, but "most of us really didn't have steadies," remembers Dudley Schuler. Maybe a boy would meet a girl and walk her home; "that was about it." According to Schuler, Neil "was as interested in girls as the rest of us, but he never really had a steady date, not a steady girl."

Neil's most memorable date, as it was for many high school students, was his senior prom.

"I think I was his first date, as a date kind of thing," recalls Alma Lou Shaw-Kuffner. "It was no romance between us. I think his mother said to him, 'You've got to go with somebody,' and he figured, 'What the heck.'"

"That was a big thing—to get the car," remembers Dudley Schuler, who double-dated with Neil, Alma Lou, and Dudley's girlfriend Patty Cole in the Armstrongs' brand-new Oldsmobile. "The last thing [Stephen Armstrong] told Neil was, 'You don't go to Dayton.'"

By the time the car had traveled halfway to Dayton, Neil got cold feet. "If we got in an accident," Schuler remembers the rationale, "we'd be in trouble because everybody would know we had gone to Dayton." Instead, Neil drove them over to the amusement park at Russell's Point at Indian Lake. But the park was closed. "We were going to stay out all night," Alma Lou reminisces, "so we just drove." At about three o'clock in the morning, the two young couples in their formal wear found an all-night diner in Lakeview, where they ate breakfast, then started home.

Somewhere between the little towns of New Hampshire and St. Johns, about twenty miles west of Wapakoneta on U.S. Highway 33—with Dudley and Patty sound asleep in the backseat—Neil nodded off. "It was like four o'clock in the morning," Schuler recalls, "and all of a sudden we hit this ditch on the wrong side of the road." Neil could not free the car, and the girls' prom gowns got grass-stained from trying to push. Just as day started to break, a man on his way to work in Lima pulled the automobile out.

The car would not start. The rescuer's car had to pull the big Oldsmobile until the engine triggered. Neil, now wide awake, drove his father's car westward into Wapakoneta. "Stop the car here," Dudley told Neil, "and if doesn't start again, we'll push it across and get it started when we coast down Fire Alley." As feared, the car would only start by rolling it downhill. Neil managed to pull it into an all-night garage where they found a truck driver who discovered a loose wire.

"We thought we were out of the woods," Schuler explains, "until the next morning when Neil's dad found that the whole side of the car was scratched." The girls were left to explain the grass stains on their dresses. Alma Lou's mother observed, "You *must* have had an interesting evening."

The month following the prom, sixteen-year-old Neil Armstrong graduated from Blume High School. Among his seventy-eight classmates, his grades placed him in the upper 10 percent, eleventh in his class. Accompanying Armstrong's senior class picture in the Blume High School yearbook for 1946–47 was the telling epigram, "He thinks, he acts, tis done."

In the quietly congenial world of the series of midwestern towns that amounted to the truest Tranquility Base that he would ever know, Armstrong prepared to meet the world. He would dare risking his peace and comfort on something he discovered there.

That "something" was flying.

CHAPTER 5

Truth in the Air

Jacob Zint relished his role as Wapakoneta's Mr. Wizard. A lifelong bachelor who lived with two bachelor brothers in a sinister-looking three-story home at the corner of Pearl and Auglaize streets, just a few blocks from the Armstrong home, Zint worked as an engineering draftsman for the Westinghouse Company in Lima. On top of his garage, the scientifically minded Zint built an observatory, a domed rotunda ten feet in diameter that revolved 360 degrees on roller-skate wheels. An eight-inch reflecting telescope pointed outward at the stars and planets. Through Zint's best eyepiece, the Moon appeared to be less than a thousand miles away, rather than the actual quarter million miles' distance. It was a setup that would have pleased the eccentric sixteenth-century astronomer Tycho Brahe, one of Zint's heroes.

Jake Zint would have forever remained an obscure local oddball if not for his self-proclaimed connection to young Neil Armstrong. One evening in 1946, when the future astronaut was sixteen, Neil, his friend Bob Gustafson, and a few other members of Boy Scout Troop 14 paid a visit to Zint's home. Their purpose was to qualify for an astronomy merit badge. Because Zint, age thirty-five, did not like people coming to his place unasked, the Scoutmaster, Mr. McClintock, had painstakingly prearranged the appointment.

In Zint's estimation, the moments that followed represented a turning point in the life of young Neil Armstrong. The Moon, so Zint said, "seemed to be Neil's main interest. He would dote on it," as well as expressing "a particular interest" in "the possibility of life on other planets. . . . We hashed it over and concluded there was no life on the Moon, but there probably was on Mars." So taken was Neil with Zint and his observatory that his visits "continued even after he went away to Purdue University." On the eve of the Moon launch, Zint even claimed, Neil sent, via a visiting newsman, his old astronomical mentor a special message: "The first thing he's going to do when he steps out on the Moon is find out if it's made of green cheese."

Headline after headline during June and July 1969 featured the Zint connection to Armstrong: "Neil Dreamed of Landing on Moon Someday," "Astronomer Jacob Zint Provided Neil A. Armstrong's First Close-Up Look at Moon," "Neil Armstrong: From the Start He Aimed for the Moon," "Astronaut Realizing Teen-Age Dream," "Moon Was Dream to Shy Armstrong," and "Jacob Zint, Wapakoneta Astronomer, Says, 'Neil's Dream Has Come True.' " Many of the stories included a picture of a smiling Zint, his arms resolutely folded, standing in front of the telescope that supposedly provided Armstrong's first close-up look at the Moon.

Neil's great moment of landing on the Sea of Tranquility became Zint's own high point back in Wapakoneta: "At 2:17 A.M. on July 21, Jacob Zint hopes to have his eight-inch telescope trained on the southwest corner of the moon's Sea of Tranquility. Weather permitting, the sighting will complete an odyssey in time and space that began here 23 years ago when a small blond boy named Neil Alden Armstrong took his first peek at the Moon through Mr. Zint's lenses." Everyone wanted to know what Zint was thinking at the moment of the historic landing: "It's unbelievable, when I think of all those times Neil and I talked of what it would be like up there," he told many interested reporters. "And now he's up there."

Perversely, nothing that Jacob Zint, now deceased, ever had to say about his relationship with Armstrong was true—not a bit of it, though Zint's telescope, along with his dismantled astronomical rotunda, sits in a favored location inside Wapakoneta's Auglaize County Museum.

"To the best of my recollection," Armstrong admits today with reluctance and typical reserve, so as not to overly impugn the reputation of Wapakoneta's highly publicized amateur astronomer, "I was only at Jake Zint's observatory the one time. As for looking through Zint's telescope and having private conversations with Zint about the Moon and the universe, they never happened. . . . Mr. Zint's story grew after I became well known," Neil says. "All of his stories appear to be false," though Neil never bothered to correct them or insist that Zint refrain from telling them.

Most people in 1969 had no reason to disbelieve what was being reported so widely in the newspapers. Moreover, Zint's prophetic version of Neil's "destiny" just seemed, as one journalist put it in July 1969, "Almost Too Logical to Be True."

"When all that came out, I thought it was fishy," remarks Alma Lou Shaw-Kuffner. "It didn't sound right to me, either," echoes Ned Keiber.

Zint's voice was one among many, including Neil's favorite science teacher, John Crites. Under a harvest Moon that was "just gorgeous," Crites recalled, he inquired about Neil's future plans. "Someday," Neil replied, pointing to the full Moon, "I'd like to meet that man up there." "That was in 1946," Crites told reporters in 1969, "when no one had a thought of going up there."

"That's fiction," Neil comments tersely. "All my aspirations in those days were related to aircraft. Space flight would have been an unrealistic ambition."

In their bicycle shop less than sixty miles south of the Korspeter farm where Neil was born, Dayton's Wilbur and Orville Wright had experimented with different types of wings and propellers, built a wind tunnel for aerodynamic analysis, and prepared successive models of their aircraft concept for flight testing at Kitty Hawk, North Carolina. After achieving their goal of inventing the first powered and controlled airplane in December 1903, the Wrights returned to their Ohio home. In a large meadow on the outskirts of Dayton known as Huffman Prairie, they steadily improved their Flyer. By late 1905 the brothers had achieved the first truly practical airplane.

Many accounts of Armstrong's boyhood relate that Neil read about the Wrights as a first grader. That seems to be just another edifying myth. Neil explains. "I don't remember reading about the Wrights or anything about *any* of the books I read in the first grade."

"When Neil was approximately two or three years old," Stephen Armstrong recalled in 1969, "he coaxed his mother into buying a little airplane at the ten cents store, and there was an argument between a ten- and twenty-cent plane. Of course, his mother bought him the twenty-cent plane. From that time on, he liked airplanes because he was always zooming around in the house and out of the house."

Neil took his first airplane ride at about six years old when the family was living in Warren.* Over the years he has heard and read so many different versions of the story that he says, "I don't know what's true. It's my belief that [the plane] was offering rides for a small fare [twenty-five cents], to tour around the city." His father remembered it this way: "One time we

* According to a volunteer group in Warren, Ohio, that has worked through the early 2000s to turn the Warren airport site into a historical exhibit, the date of Neil's inaugural flight was July 26, 1936. If that date is correct, Neil was still only five when he experienced his first airplane ride, his sixth birthday not coming for ten more days.

were headed—at least his mother thought we were headed—for Sunday school, but they had an airplane ride [at the Warren airport] that was cheaper in the morning and then a price that escalated during the day. So we skipped Sunday school and took our first airplane ride."

The machine that took them up was a high-wing monoplane, the Ford Trimotor, nicknamed the "Tin Goose" for its skin of corrugated aluminum. First flown in 1928, the airplane employed fixed landing gear, accommodated up to twelve passengers in wicker chairs, and cruised at a speed of about 120 miles per hour. The pilot was a man named Johnny Finta. Neil's father volunteered during a pre–Apollo 11 interview, "Those old Ford Trimotors; they really rattled. I was scared to death and Neil enjoyed it."

Sometime during his adolescence Neil began to have a recurring dream: "I could, by holding my breath, hover over the ground. Nothing much happened. I neither flew nor fell in those dreams; I just hovered. But the indecisiveness was a little frustrating. There was never any end to the dream." According to Carl Jung, flight dreams express one's desire to break free of restrictions, limitations, and difficulties. Alfred Adler thought that flying in a dream tapped into an impulse toward superiority and domination. Sigmund Freud connected dreams of flight to the libido and expression of sexual desire. (A simpler interpretation is that flying is fun.)

In 1873, the Russian space flight visionary Konstantin E. Tsiolkovskii (1857–1935), aged sixteen, imagined a spaceship driven by centrifugal force: "I was so worked up that I couldn't sleep all night." Through the streets of Moscow, young Tsiolkovskii wandered through a blinding snowstorm. "By morning I saw that my invention had a basic flaw. My disappointment was as strong as my exhilaration had been. . . . Thirty years later, I still have dreams in which I fly up to the stars in my machine, and I feel as excited as on that memorable night." The creative imagining stayed with the Russian for the rest of his life, which lasted well into the Stalinist period. Along the way, "the father of cosmonautics" conceived of such advanced ideas as rocket staging, high-energy liquid propellants (such as liquid oxygen and liquid hydrogen), Earth-orbiting space stations, space suits for what would become known as "space walks," and even self-sustaining ecological starships capable of intergalactic travel. In Tsiolkovskii's view, a human future in space was inevitable. "The Earth is the cradle of civilization," he wrote, "but one cannot live in the cradle forever."

Even more haunting was the dream of Robert Goddard (1882–1945), the American rocket pioneer. At age seventeen, Goddard climbed to the top of his backyard cherry tree. "It was one of the quiet, colorful afternoons of sheer beauty which we have in October in New England," recalled God-dard in notes for his autobiography, "and as I looked toward the fields to the east, I imagined how wonderful it would be to make some device which had even the *possibility* of ascending to Mars, and how it would look on a small scale, if sent up from the meadow at my feet. . . . I was a different boy when I descended the tree from when I ascended, for existence at last seemed very purposive." For the rest of his life, Goddard celebrated October 19 as his "Anniversary Day." After his marriage in 1924, he lived with his wife in a house near where the cherry tree stood. When he subsequently moved his rocket-testing experiments from Massachusetts to New Mexico, he visited the tree whenever he could: "Got rocket weighed and ready, in afternoon. Stopped at cherry tree at 6 P.M." (Oct. 19, 1927). "Took out trailer to farm, with Sachs. Went out to cherry tree" (Oct. 19, 1928). "Worked on flow pat-terns in afternoon. Went to cherry tree—Anniversary Day" (Oct. 19, 1932). In the fall of 1938, Goddard received a letter from a Massachusetts friend informing him that his cherry tree had been uprooted in a nor'easter. In his journal that night (Nov. 10, 1938), the father of American rocketry wrote, "Cherry tree down—have to carry on alone."

In the case of Neil's boyhood nighttime reveries, "I can't say they were related to flying in any way. As I look back on it, it doesn't seem like there was much relationship, except for being suspended above the ground." Neil dismisses his dream: "I tried it later, when I was awake; it didn't work." Yet, he still recalls the dream some sixty years later.

Curiously Armstrong, like Goddard, did have a memorable boyhood tree-climbing experience. At age eight, Neil set out to scale the biggest tree in his St. Marys backyard. In a way, navigating the height of the stately silver maple may have been Neil's first attempt to think like an engineer, and to explore the sensations of flight.

His sister June still characterizes Neil's fifteen-foot fall as "awful." "He hit smack on his back. He was white as a ghost and not moving at all. All of a sudden, he opened his eyes and looked up. I said, 'Should I get Mama?' All he could do was barely shake his head no. Then he said weakly, 'Yeah.' So I ran yelling into the house for Mom to come."

"Never to trust a dead limb" was young Neil's takeaway. "I climbed trees, like all boys. I never thought of it as being related to my character." Nonetheless, the incident serves as an allegory for his life—as an engineer, test pilot, and astronaut—presaging his strong preference for solitary chal-lenges that task the mind more than the body; his desire to experience the unique perspective of unusual heights; his ambition for temporary escapes from an earthbound existence; the greater drama and criticality of his descents and landings over his takeoffs and ascents; and his extreme good fortune in coming away from serious accidents virtually unharmed.

Neil himself rejects the notion that "there is any psychological backdrop to this." Yet, some of the most illuminating studies of the character of engineering reveal that "the ideas of engineering are in fact in our bones and part of our human nature and experience" and that for engineering design the "first and foremost objective" is "the obviation of failure." The engineering mind develops from earliest childhood, when falling down, literally, is a part of growing up.

"I began to focus on aviation probably at age eight or nine," Neil recalls, "inspired by what I'd read and seen about aviation and building model aircraft." An older cousin, Kenneth Benzing, the nephew of Viola's father Martin Engel, lived down the block in St. Marys and once Neil "saw what he was able to do" with balsa wood and tissue paper, he became hooked.

The first model Neil remembers building was a high-wing light aircraft cabin, most likely a Taylor Cub, papered in yellow and black. "It never occurred to me to buy models *with* engines," because motors cost extra money and required gasoline—both of which were in short supply during World War II. If powered, his models were driven by twisted rubber bands, like those tried in the 1870s by the French aeronautical experimenter Alphonse Pénaud (1850–1880).

Neil's models filled up his bedroom plus an entire corner of the basement. According to Dean, Neil built so many planes that he would fly ones that he was tired of or did not like—sometimes aflame—out the upstairs window. June remembers Neil gathering "five or six at least, then he runs down the stairs and out the front door to the end of the driveway," one of those old-style driveways where two parallel strips of cement ran through a grass center. "So we're leaning out an open window upstairs, flying these airplanes. Oh, I know Mother would have just died." Neil would mark the landings with sticks, then "bring them back so we could do it again."

Armstrong did not fly models out of upstairs windows often, though: "I usually hung my models with string from the ceiling of my bedroom. I had put a lot of work in them and didn't want to crash them, so when I flew one of those airplanes it was a rare occasion.

"My focus was more on the building than the flying," Armstrong recalls. In flying competitions, "you couldn't have success with the model that wasn't built well," Neil emphasizes. "While I was still in elementary school my intention was to be—or hope was to be—an aircraft designer. I later went into piloting because I thought a good designer ought to know the operational aspects of an airplane.

"I read a lot of the aviation magazines of the time, *Flight* and *Air Trails* and *Model Airplane News,* anything I could get my hands on." His employer, Richard Brading, confirmed that "Neil never bothered reading comic books."

While Armstrong's friends drew biplanes with fixed landing gear, Neil drew low-wing monoplanes with retractable tricycle landing gear. "At the time, we thought his airplanes would never get off the ground," laughs Kotcho Solacoff. Arthur Frame remembers that Neil during World War II "was most interested in the fighter-type model as opposed to a bomber."

As part of the Aeromodelers Club at Purdue University, "I would win a number of events or get second place." Neil recollects racing his "gasoline-powered 'control-line' models, flown on wires and operated at the center of a circle," to speeds well in excess of 100 miles per hour. "I absorbed a lot of new knowledge and found people, some of them World War II veterans, who had vastly more experience and intuition on how to be successful flying."

"He tried awfully hard to get out there and get ahold of the real thing," his mother remarked. Foregoing model airplane kits, fifteen-year-old Armstrong saved toward the cost of flying lessons, nine dollars an hour (roughly ninety 2005 dollars). Making forty cents an hour at Brading's Drugs, Neil worked twenty-two and a half hours to pay for a single lesson.

Early Saturday mornings Neil hitchhiked or "rode a bike with no fenders" out to the Wapakoneta airfield known as Port Koneta.

"They did what they called 'top cylinder overhauls,' " Neil recalls, "or just 'top overhauls,' for short." Once Neil turned sixteen and had his student pilot's license, he could fly the airplane. "That's the way I built up flight time, by doing slow time [to coat the valves with high-octane gasoline] after top cylinder overhauls." "He was a little grease monkey out there," Neil's mother once explained. "And for everything he did, why they gave him flying lessons. He learned to fly."

For many years now the small grass airfield outside Wapakoneta has been abandoned. As Neil's father scornfully predicted, "The place is just gonna turn back into a cornfield," and regrettably it has done just that.

When Port Koneta opened up, "There were a lot of people around town talking, telling [aviation] stories all the time, and as a young guy I was absorbing all that."

The aircraft flying at Wapakoneta were mostly old army planes and trainers. There was a BT-13 made by Vultee and a low-wing Fairchild PT-19. One of the newest airplanes was the Aeronca Chief, a light high-wing monoplane—made in nearby Middleton, Ohio—featuring side-by-side instead of in-line seating for two and a control wheel instead of a control stick. A more basic version known as the Champ was Aeronca's best-selling model. It was in one of the three Champs at Wapakoneta that Neil Armstrong learned to fly.

Three veteran army pilots gave Neil flying lessons: Frank Lucie, Aubrey Knudegaard, and Charles Finkenbine, the youngest of the trio, then in his early twenties. Armstrong flew first with Lucie, and most often with Lucie and Knudegaard. "I thought they were excellent pilots, but what did I know! They were certainly much better than I was" at handling the controls.

Of the seventy students in Neil's high school class, about half of whom were boys, three—Neil, Ned Keiber, and Ned Binkley—learned to fly that summer of '46. Each soloed about the same time. Neil has always refused, therefore, to say that his learning to fly was all that unusual. Ned Keiber's older brother, who was ex–air corps, also flew at the field. (Ned remembers, "We'd stop and pick Neil up.") A couple of women from the Wapakoneta area were even learning there.

It was a little unusual, though, that Neil earned his pilot's license before he got an automobile driver's license. "He never had a girl. He didn't need a car," explained his father. "All he had to do was get out to that airport." Unfortunately, the logbook the boy kept for his first flights was lost in Neil's Houston house fire in 1964.

"I believe you could solo in a glider at age fourteen," Neil said, "but in a powered airplane you had to wait till you reached your sixteenth birthday," which he celebrated on August 5, 1946. That day Neil earned his "student pilot's certificate," then made his first solo within a week or two.

The spontaneity of the event meant that the student pilot was in no position to alert family or friends. "You just heard the instructor unbuckle his belt, saw him look at you knowingly, felt his hand placed confidently on your shoulder, and thought to yourself, 'Oh, oh, here I go.' " Not that Neil would have told anyone about it if he had known. "Flying was pretty much something he did on his own," Dudley Schuler remembers. "Neil was a lone wolf in this respect."

Dean, who helped mow grass and weeds at the airfield, was on scene to observe his brother's progress, though he personally never had any desire to fly. Viola was too nervous to watch her son fly, but she never tried to stop him from doing it. Part of the reason, according to June, was that the confident Neil "never expressed any fear when he talked about it."

Armstrong has only vague recollections of his first solo, for which he got the nod from Frank Lucie. "The first time you solo any airplane is a special day," Neil states. "The first time ever you solo is an exceptionally special day. I'm sure there was a great deal of excitement in my mind when I got to do that first flight."

Fellow student pilot Ned Keiber witnessed it: "I was getting ready to leave and Knudegaard said to me, 'Hang around, you might get a free Coke out of this.' So I hung around and I watched him solo." Neil recalls the mechanics: "I managed to make a couple takeoffs and landings successfully and bring it back to the hangar without incident." Keiber's assessment: "He didn't bounce it like I did on the landings."

One of the positive results of making his first solo, Neil realized, was financial. Without the need for an instructor, he only had to pay seven dollars an hour instead of nine. But the advantage was theoretical, as only ever more hours in the air would satiate his zest.

Developing his own piloting technique on the grass fields, Neil "got in the habit of putting the airplane into a substantial slip on final approach where I would come down pretty steep so I could land on an early part of the grass runway and then have plenty of time to roll out and come to a stop." But "the navy instructors did not like that technique at all," Neil explains, chuckling.

It was at the Wapakoneta airport that young Neil first witnessed the darker side of flying. On the afternoon of July 26, 1947, twenty-year-old flying student and World War II navy veteran Frederick Carl Lange struck a power line and crashed his Aeronca Champ in a hayfield. Lange, who had forty-five hours in the air under a GI training program, died at the site from a skull fracture. His passenger, instructor Charlie Finkenbine, survived shock and minor lacerations.

As luck had it, Neil was on the road back from the Shawnee Council Boy Scout camp near Defiance, Ohio. Dean remembers, "We saw the plane go down [Neil questions whether any of them actually did see it go down]. My dad was driving, pulled off, and we all ran over there and tried to administer first aid." According to the *Lima News,* Neil, "jumping a fence, rushed to the aid of the plane occupants. 'I'm all right, take care of Carl,' Finkenbine said as Armstrong opened the door to the ship." The newspaper reported that Lange died in Neil's arms. But in such a traumatic situation Neil says that he never really knew when Lange died.

During his career, Neil would become an expert accident investigator due to his ability to pinpoint the cause of a crash. "It was a field at an intersection of roads and they were doing a practice emergency landing. The instructor is always cutting the power and saying, 'Okay, you've lost your engine, let's see you make an emergency landing someplace.' What they apparently didn't see until it was too late was a wire [part of the St. Marys Rural Electrification Cooperative] that crossed the field diagonally with no posts on it. A pilot usually monitors the poles, which are much easier to see, rather than the wires. They came in and hit that wire with their landing gear, and they nosed in. Took a pretty severe impact."

Newspapers reported Neil flying with Lange several times, but Neil says he never did, as he is unsure whether he ever knew the Lima native. Some biographical accounts adhere too closely to the Christian magazine *Guideposts'* post–Apollo 11 "as-told-to" article from Viola. Entitled "Neil Armstrong's Boyhood Crisis," the melodrama had a confused Neil spending a solitary two days in his room reading about Jesus and pondering whether he should keep flying: Neil does not remember doing anything like that. According to June, "I never felt he was affected by it in any way." Certainly it did not dampen his enthusiasm for flying.

By the time of Carl Lange's death, Armstrong had flown two cross-country solos—first to Cincinnati's Lunken Airport in a rented Port Koneta Aeronca. Round-trip, the flight spanned some 215 miles, each log bookending his sitting for the navy scholarship qualifying exam. To preregister for classes at Purdue University, Neil flew to West Lafayette, Indiana, a flight of about 300 miles.

Contrast Ned Keiber's perspective: "The longest cross-country that I ever did was about twelve miles. I could still look over my shoulder and see the airport." One can only imagine the astonishment of the West Lafayette airport personnel when a sixteen-year-old boy got down out of his airplane, asked for refueling, and started walking toward campus.

CHAPTER 6

Aeronautical Engineering 101

On October 14, 1947, one month after Armstrong started at Purdue University, an air force test pilot—one with whom Armstrong would later fly—broke through the mythical "sound barrier." The name of the hotshot flier was Captain Charles E. "Chuck" Yeager, and the revolutionary airplane he piloted beyond Mach 1 was the rocket-powered Bell X-1.

Armstrong does not remember exactly when he heard the news of the first transonic flight over the Mojave Desert of Southern California. Before the military shrouded its transonic research program in secrecy, stories about the X-1's performance appeared in the *Los Angeles Times* and *Aviation Week*. Aeronautics faculty and students nationwide were discussing the meaning of "shattering the sonic wall."

For Neil, however, this new era in flight dawned bittersweet. "By the time I was old enough and became a pilot, things had changed. The great airplanes I had so revered as a boy were disappearing. I had grown up admiring what I perceived to be the chivalry of the World War I pilots—Frank Luke, Eddie Rickenbacker, Manfred von Richthofen, and Billy Bishop. But by World War II, aerial chivalry seemed to have evaporated. . . . Air warfare was becoming very impersonal. The record-setting flights—[John] Alcock and [A. W.] Brown, [Harold] Gatty, [Charles] Lindbergh, [Amelia] Earhart, and [Jimmy] Mattern—across the oceans, over the poles, and to the corners of Earth, had all been accomplished. And I resented that. All in all, for someone who was immersed in, fascinated by, and dedicated to flight, I was disappointed by the wrinkle in history that had brought me along one generation late. I had missed all the great times and adventures in flight."

As Armstrong entered college, the National Advisory Committee for Aeronautics (NACA), NASA's predecessor, along with the newly established U.S. Air Force, moved ahead ambitiously to construct new research facilities devoted to transonics, supersonics, and hypersonics (the speed

regime, at around Mach 5, where the effects of aerodynamic heating became pronounced).

Armstrong's time in the aeronautical engineering program at Purdue
University spanned—including a three-year stint in the military—from
September 1947 to January 1955. That seven-and-a-half-year stretch saw an
astonishing new era of global aeronautical development. Three months
after the historic X-1 flight, the NACA activated the country's first hypersonic (capable of Mach 7) wind tunnel. A few months later, early in Armstrong's second semester, an army rocket team under Dr. Wernher von
Braun launched a V-2 missile at White Sands, New Mexico, to an altitude of
seventy miles. Armstrong's first full calendar year at Purdue witnessed the
first flight of Convair's XF-92 airplane, with its innovative delta wing; the
flight of the first civilian test pilot, Herbert H. Hoover (not related to
the U.S. president), past Mach 1; the tailless X-4 aircraft's first test flights;
and the publishing of an aerodynamic theory that proved critical to solving
the high-speed problem of "roll coupling."

Armstrong left Purdue and reported for military duty during what
would have been his spring semester of 1949. During those months, the
U.S. Army established its first formal requirements for a surface-to-air
antiballistic missile system; President Truman signed a bill providing a
5,000-mile guided-missile test range, which was subsequently established at
Cape Canaveral, Florida; and a single-stage Russian rocket with an instrument payload of some 270 pounds flew to an altitude of sixty-eight miles.
During that summer, as Armstrong took flight training at Pensacola, a
V-2 rocket carried a live monkey to an altitude of eighty-three miles (the
monkey survived but died on impact); the American military made its first
operational use of a partial pressure suit during a piloted flight to 70,000
feet; and the first U.S. pilot ever to use an ejection seat escaped his jet-
powered F2H-1 Banshee while speeding over coastal South Carolina at
500 knots.

By the time he returned to his AE program in September 1952, Armstrong realized that the world of aeronautics was becoming the world of
"aerospace." In 1950, the first missile launch at Cape Canaveral occurred,
lifting a man-made object to the highest speed yet achieved, Mach 9. In
1951, the air force started its first ICBM program, forerunner to the Atlas
program, which took the first astronauts into orbit. The following year, a
centrifuge opened at the navy's medical aviation laboratory in Johnsville,
Pennsylvania, that could accelerate human subjects up to speeds producing

40 g's. It was an instrument of torture that Armstrong himself would later endure. In that same year, NACA researcher H. Julian Allen predicted that reentry-heating problems for missiles and spacecraft could be avoided by changing their nose shapes from sharp to blunt. Not just the Mercury, but also Neil's Gemini VIII and Apollo 11 spacecraft would be built around the "blunt-body" principle. During Neil's first year back in the classroom, in November 1953, NACA test pilot A. Scott Crossfield in Douglas's D-558-2 became the first person to fly at Mach 2. When Armstrong left Purdue with his degree a year later, he went to work for the NACA. In fact, Neil became a test pilot at the NACA's High-Speed Flight Station in California, where he would come to fly the experimental X-15 hypersonic aircraft seven times.

It was into this new world, one that gave birth to the Space Age faster than most anyone at the time could imagine, that Neil Armstrong found himself immersed by the time he left college in January 1955. It is extraordinary that an individual who lived through such a revolutionary age of flight would have ever thought to trade his present for the past.

In the early 1940s, fewer than one in four Americans completed high school, and fewer than one in twenty went to college. An eighth-grade education was the average in many rural communities. With the passage of the GI Bill in 1944, the proportion of college-goers began to rise but, by the early 1950s, only to about 25 percent of those who were college-age.

Neil was only the second person in the history of his family to attend a university, the first being his great-uncle John Koenig, who had earned a law degree. College education as a family first was a precedent shared by many of the astronauts and engineers who were to become associated with the young space program. Both of Neil's parents, particularly Viola, had encouraged their son to think beyond the education they themselves had achieved. No goal, no sacrifice, was more important.

It took special efforts for Neil to go to college, particularly to engineering school. Wapakoneta's Blume High School did not offer all the prerequisites—in particular, trigonometry. So Armstrong and two other engineering-minded students went to Franklin H. Laman, Blume's principal, who in turn called on Doris Barr, a 1945 graduate of Oberlin College. "I handled trigonometry as independent study," Mrs. Barr remembered from her Cincinnati retirement home in 2002, since she had taught geometry to all three of the students during their junior years ("Neil was so quiet I hardly knew he was there"). "Neil had very good math skills." Barr recounts. "He didn't really need a teacher. I just handed him assignments and talked to him about his answers when he turned them in."

Armstrong was acquainted, through his father, with just one engineer—a graduate of the Massachusetts Institute of Technology, a school to which Neil applied and was accepted. The MIT alum (a Dayton resident whose name Neil cannot recall) told Neil "that it wasn't necessary to go all the way to MIT [830 miles] to get a good engineering education." Neil instead set his sights on Purdue University in West Lafayette, Indiana, only 220 miles from Wapakoneta.

Armstrong had heard about the U.S. Naval Aviation College Program's four-year scholarships. The program required a commitment of seven years: two years of study at any school accredited by the navy, followed by three years of service, after which the student finished his last two years of college. The Holloway Plan—created by Admiral James E. Holloway Jr. (who, incidentally, became the father-in-law of NASA astronaut Walter M. Schirra)—intended, in Neil's words, "to build up the naval air reserve strength, which [the navy] felt was going downhill because [young men] after the war really didn't want to do [reserve work] anymore."

Armstrong's medical examination recorded a weight of 144 pounds and a height of five feet nine and one-half inches; doctors categorized his general build and appearance as "athletic," his posture "good," and his body frame "medium." His chest measured a narrow thirty-three inches and his waist a slim twenty-nine inches. His blood pressure was 118 (systolic) over 84 (diastolic). A heart rate of 88 beats per minute standing and 116 beats after exercise first registered Armstrong's tendency, frequently noted in his years as a test pilot and astronaut, to run a little high.

The medical form also recorded twenty hours of solo flying time in the past twelve months. At seven dollars per hour in the air, Armstrong had spent $140 (about $1,350 today) on flying since his first solo flight. That the taxi ride from Cincinnati's Lunken Airport to the downtown test site cost him seven dollars seemed "an astronomical amount of money because I could fly the airplane for seven dollars an hour."

Viola Armstrong had raised her son to pursue sound financial goals: "You know, money was scarce, college was expensive, and he knew *somehow* he had to get to college. . . . He wasn't really that interested in a military career. But it was a means to an end, and so . . . he was going to *try* it. And, of course, he was one of the ones [a mere fraction of all applicants] selected. . . . I'll never forget," Viola happily related, "I was in the basement getting some fruit to bake some pies, and he called so loud. 'Mom, Mom!' It scared me to death and I dropped the blackberries on my foot. I believe I broke my toe—it was black and blue and sore for weeks. And he said, 'Oh, Mom, they accepted me.' " Neil recalls "great jubilation that I had been accepted and that I had a way to go to college, paid. That was a wonderful deal."

According to Neil's navy appointment letter, dated May 14, 1947, his score of 38 points equated to 592 on Princeton's Scholarship Aptitude Test (SAT), which would likely have ranked in the top quartile among all college-bound seniors.

One month before receiving the good news from the navy, Purdue University had admitted Neil. "I just couldn't have been happier with what I was doing, going into engineering."

If Armstrong had chosen MIT over Purdue, his overall education would likely have been more theoretical though not necessarily superior. As David S. Stephenson, one of Neil's freshmen classmates testifies, Purdue's AE program was "more nearly a 'shop-culture' school than a 'school-culture' school." "Purdue was very hands-on at that time," remembers Tommy Thompson, another of Neil's classmates. In their first semester, students in the new School of Aeronautics learned to weld, machine and heat-treat metals, and do sand casting.

Affirms Donald A. Gardner, yet another student (and Holloway scholar) who began the AE program with Neil in the fall of 1947, "I certainly needed the background provided by the [required] shop courses."

"We took all pretty much the standard stuff," Neil recalls, nineteen credit hours involving eight different classes. Six days a week he had three hours of classes each morning and three hours of lab each afternoon. As Donald Gardner explains, "Students didn't protest. . . . The character of the engineering programs in the late forties and early fifties was hard work and plenty of it."

Armstrong tested out of freshman English, "which surprised me a lot," but he still had to take a three-hour English composition course resulting in his lowest grade of the semester, a 4 on a 6-point scale. A 6 was Purdue's "Highest Passing Grade" and a 3 the "Lowest Passing Grade." A 2 indicated a "Conditional Failure" and a 1 a "Failure." (When the university began giving letter grades in the summer term of 1953, a 4 equated to a C grade.) Freshman engineering students at Purdue did not take calculus but instead faced five hours of algebra and trigonometry in the fall followed by five hours of analytical geometry in the spring. Neil earned a 5 in the first and a 4 in the second. Additional courses included General Chemistry, a well known Purdue freshman "flunk-out" course (four credits, grade of 5), Engineering Drawing (two credits, grade of 6), and Welding and the Heat Treatment of Metal (two credits, grade of 5), plus two more requirements: an uncredited weekly series of engineering lectures and physical education (one credit, grade of 5).

Unlike the other four young men who entered Purdue in the fall of 1947 as part of the Holloway Plan, Neil did not take courses in naval science. Nor did he belong to Naval ROTC (NROTC), instead fulfilling the requirements by playing in the university band (two credits, grade of 5), which at the time functioned as a military band.

Overall, his first-semester grades were moderately good, averaging 4.94 on Purdue's 6.00 scale. With another nineteen-hour load, his second semester average dipped to 4.36, setting his cumulative GPA to 4.65, equivalent to a low B average. In an age predating grade inflation, Armstrong's first-year academic performance was solid though not spectacular. As with beginning students everywhere, his freshman year was "kind of a whirl."

Tommy Thompson, who came from Rochester, New York, recalls: "Purdue, with an enrollment of something over twelve thousand students, was still dominated by returning GIs. The university [then] had about five hundred students sleeping in the field house. I spent my freshman year in a rooming house across the river in Lafayette. I think there were about six of us that shared a room. Most of the year I biked to classes." Neil did not room with Thompson, but he, too, resided that first semester in a Lafayette boardinghouse. After that, he rented a room in a house closer to campus, at 400 North Salisbury Street.

A rare surviving letter written by Armstrong near the end of his second semester details his college routine:

Sunday P.M.

Dear Mom & Family,
   Thanks for the laundry, letters, & girl Scout Cookies. The other fellows saw them & when I got home last night, they were nearly all gone.
      You don't have to worry about my getting a job this summer. I am

going to summer school. It's an order. I have my schedule for classes
all-ready. It is:

    Differential Calculus.

    8–10 A.M.—Mon.,   Tue,   Wed.   Thu.   Fri.

    Physics

    10–12 A.M.— "   "   "   "   "

    Physics Lab

    1–3 P.M.—   Tue.   Thu.

That's all, but it's a load. The two labs are the only afternoon classes
and there are no Saturday classes. I should be able to get home on week-
ends some times pretty easily. There will be a lot of homework in the sum-
mer even though there aren't many classes.

Today, we went to Indianapolis to the first model airplane contest. My
control lines broke on the first official flight so I didn't have a chance to
win anything.

I think I am doing better in my studies lately. I enjoy analytics [though
he received a final grade of 4] *and I understand a little of the chemistry we*
are studying [also a 4 grade].

I'll send the laundry again & hope you'll send Les's blanket back. There
are six weeks of school left yet. (6) I won't be out until the middle of June. I
saw a show tonight that was the best I had seen in a long time. It is called
"Sitting Pretty" with Clifton Webb, Maureen O'Hara, and Robert Young. I
especially recommend it to you & Dad. It is a comedy. I'm running out of
paper, so I'll stop.

                                                Love, Neil

In the fall of 1948, "The navy wrote me a letter," Neil explains today,
outlining "some new options" in the Holloway program: take the four semesters as planned or begin military service early, after three regular semesters plus a term of summer school. Given that the engineering
curriculum was built around two-part courses—Thermodynamics I followed by Thermodynamics II, integral calculus coming right after differential calculus, and so on—"I thought it wasn't good to cut that in the middle."
When he told the navy "I'd go to the end," the navy answered. "Well, you
made the wrong choice. You're going to come out early."

Armstrong took seventeen credit hours that fall, including Descriptive
Geometry, a second semester of physics and another one of calculus, a
speech class, plus more physical education and band. Perhaps his anticipa-

tion of leaving for the navy affected his academic performance, because his grades were the lowest of any Purdue semester—a 4.17 GPA, caused by three 3s, including one in calculus. While his 3 in physical education might be explained by the fact that Neil was never overly interested in sports or exercise, the bigger mystery is why he also received a 3 in band, an activity that he had enjoyed since junior high. When asked about it, Neil answers, "I have no idea."

When Neil left for navy flight training in February 1949 after four semesters at Purdue, he was only eighteen and a half years old. When he returned to the university in September 1952, he had just turned twenty-two. For the first time since second grade, Armstrong was not younger than the majority of his classmates. "I was really getting old," he relates, laughing. "When I went back to [the] university, kids looked so young!" According to his Purdue friend and fellow navy pilot Pete Karnoski, Neil was "still the quiet, pleasant type, easygoing and friendly, still a young kid, even though he had seen some fighting in Korea."

Coming to Purdue for the second time, "I really knew what I wanted to do." After significant exposure to operational flying and handling high-performance jets, he thought "maybe there was a way to find a combination where I can do both airplane design and piloting." An internship in the summer of 1954 at the Naval Flight Test Center at Patuxent River in Maryland cemented his career goal.

Sharper focus and greater maturity resulted in improved grades, as did the fact that Armstrong was now taking specialized courses in his major. In his first semester back, he earned three grades of 6 and two of 5. One of his 6s was in Calculus II, in which before leaving for the navy he had managed no better than a 3. In no engineering course did Neil receive a grade lower than 5. Those courses included Statics and Kinetics, Aircraft Layout and Detail Drafting, and Mechanics of Materials, in which he earned 6s, and Elementary Heat Power, Fluid Mechanics, and Thermodynamics, in which he earned 5s. He even made it through Differential Equations with a 5.

In the fall of 1950, a young and energetic Caltech graduate, Dr. Milton Clauser, had taken over Purdue's aeronautics department. Believing that the AE program was "not rigorous enough" and that it was "slanted toward a terminal degree program for those going directly into industry," Clauser proposed more theoretical courses and fewer laboratories—a curious move by a man who was most recently head of mechanical design for Douglas Aircraft.

Yet Clauser's new curriculum was geared toward the emerging field of "engineering science." Armstrong did not choose to pursue the new Theoretical Aeronautics option that premiered at Purdue in the fall of 1954, but he did, in his final semester of coursework, take its very challenging course on vector analysis.

Doctoral candidate Les Hromas served as the instructor for the Wind Tunnel Laboratory that Armstrong took in the fall of 1953. "Two navy flight veterans were in that Wind Tunnel class," recalls Hromas. "Neil and his friend Tom Thompson." Hromas recalls as "rather humorous" his classroom objective of demonstrating to two navy flight veterans—one of whom (Neil) had flown seventy-eight combat missions in Korea—what makes an airplane fly.

In the same fall 1953 term, Armstrong taught a section of GE (General Engineering) 224, Aircraft Layout and Detail Design, a course he had aced just the year before. According to Richard H. Petersen, a 1956 Purdue graduate who later became the director of NASA's Langley Research Center, "We would draw at drafting tables. Neil would roam around and offer comments or suggestions."

Just as Neil's academic life improved during his second stay at Purdue, so did his social life. He pledged a fraternity, Phi Delta Theta, and lived in the frat house (at 503 State Street). "We [pledges cleaned] it imperfectly," Neil remembers, "but *far* better than contemporary standards." Those were also the days of "The Paddle," which, according to Armstrong, was "used effectively" for fraternity initiations and misconduct.

Marvin Karasek, "an amazing pianist and composer," was Phi Delta Theta's musical director who wrote all the songs for a musical in the 1952 Purdue *Varsity Varieties* all-student revue. Armstrong, whom Karasek recruited as a Phi Delt, sang in Karasek's show and still remembers most of his lyrics. When Karasek moved on to graduate school the following spring, Neil succeeded him as the fraternity's musical director.

For the next two *Varsity Varieties,* Armstrong wrote and codirected his own short musicals. The first of his shows, in fall 1953, was *Snow White and the Seven Dwarves.* Codirected by Chi Omega's Joanne Alford, whom Neil took out on a couple of dates, it featured music from the famous Walt Disney film, including "Someday My Prince Will Come." However, Neil's humorous prince "wore a black suit, shirt, tie, and fedora and drove in a black MG convertible." The second production, which Neil entitled *The Land of Egelloc* ("college" spelled backwards)—alternatively titled *La Fing Stock*—was synopsized in the program: "New words have been given to the familiar music of Gilbert and Sullivan [transposed into minor keys] for this satire on college honoraries."

Armstrong's showmanship might have affected his grades. In the semester of *Snow White,* he received C grades in two courses, Psychology for Engineers and Dr. Hsu Lo's Aircraft Vibrations, and a D in Electrical Engineering (Direct Current). While busy in *The Land of Egelloc,* he received C grades in Aircraft Power Plant Laboratory and in Vector Analysis and withdrew from a course in Introductory Nuclear Physics.

No doubt the thought of eighteen-year-old Janet Shearon, the first love of his life, further distracted Neil from his academic work. He met Janet, who was studying home economics, casually at a "trade party" cohosted by Janet's sorority, Alpha Chi Omega, and Neil's fraternity. The second time they spoke was early one morning when she was on her way to a home economics lab and he was delivering the school newspaper, the *Purdue Exponent.* Neil also drove a tomato truck for a local cannery and in the summertime sold kitchen knives door to door.

He also had intermittent weekend responsibilities as an officer in the U.S. Naval Reserve, carpooling with his Purdue navy buddies to the Naval Air Station in Glenview, Illinois, north of Chicago, to fly F9F-6 jets. In civilian garb, he flew among fellow veteran military pilots as part of the Purdue Aero Flying Club, which he chaired during the 1953–54 academic year. Lafayette's Aretz Airport housed the club's few small planes: an Aeronca and a couple two- and four-place Pipers.

One weekend in 1954, Armstrong suffered a minor accident following an air meet in Ohio. Neil thought he would fly a club Aeronca to Wapakoneta, but a rough landing in a local farmer's field caused, according to Neil, "damage sufficient to prevent flying it back, so I took off the wings and returned it to West Lafayette on a trailer." Dean, chuckling, tells the story a little differently: "They had to disassemble it and haul it back to Lafayette on our grandfather's hay wagon."

Armstrong finished his last coursework in early January 1955. He did not attend commencement exercises, instead returning to Wapakoneta to prepare for his job in Cleveland at NACA Lewis. Purdue sent by mail the diploma awarding his bachelor's of science degree in aeronautical engineering. His final grade point average of 4.8 on a 6.0 scale did not win him any academic awards or honors, but it represented a highly respectable performance in a very demanding field stretched out over nearly seven years. After returning from the navy, his GPA averaged a 5.0. This included the equivalent of A or B grades in twenty-six out of a total of thirty-four courses.

For the rest of his life, engineering would be Armstrong's primary professional identity. Even during his years as a test pilot and as an astronaut, Neil considered himself first and foremost an aeronautical engineer, one whose ambition to write an engineering textbook set him apart from virtually all of his fellow fliers. It is only in this context that one can truly understand a statement that a frustrated Armstrong would make to a Cincinnati newspaper reporter in 1976: "How long must it take before I cease to be known as a spaceman?"

Two of the most important—and rarely acknowledged—points about the Apollo lunar landing program are that it was engineering—much more than science—that accomplished the Moon landing, and that an engineer, not a scientist, was the first to set foot on another world.

PART THREE

WINGS OF GOLD

I'll always remember him for the way he could talk about flying, no bragging, no great statements, just a man who was cool, calm, intelligent, and one of the best fliers I ever knew.

—PETER J. KARNOSKI, ARMSTRONG'S ROOMMATE
FOR BASIC TRAINING, CLASS 5-49, NAVAL AIR
TRAINING COMMAND, NAS PENSACOLA

Where do we get such men? They leave this ship and they do their job. Then they must find this speck lost somewhere in the sea. When they find it, they have to land on its pitching deck. Where do we get such men?

—"ADMIRAL GEORGE TARRANT," FICTIONAL
CHARACTER IN JAMES A. MICHENER'S
THE BRIDGES AT TOKO-RI

CHAPTER 7

Class 5-49

If Neil Armstrong had not become a naval aviator, he would not have been the first man to walk on the Moon.

The first American to fly into space, Alan B. Shepard Jr., was a U.S. Navy aviator. So was the commander of the very first Apollo flight, Walter M. Schirra. Of the one dozen human beings privileged to walk on the Moon, seven of them wore, or had worn, the navy's wings of gold. Most remarkably, six of the seven mission commanders who piloted Apollo spacecraft down to lunar landings were naval aviators. This included not only the first man to walk on the Moon but also the last man to leave its surface to date, Eugene A. Cernan, in Apollo 17. In between Armstrong and Cernan, fellow navy pilots Charles "Pete" Conrad Jr. (Apollo 12), Alan Shepard (Apollo 14), and John W. Young (Apollo 16) flew Apollo spacecraft down to the lunar surface. Navy captain James A. Lovell Jr. would also have done so if not for the near-tragic mishap occurring on Apollo 13's outbound flight. Only David R. Scott (commander of Apollo 15) did his military flying with the U.S. Air Force. Interestingly, the head of NASA's Astronaut Office who handpicked all of the Apollo commanders, Donald "Deke" Slayton, was himself an air force officer.

Since the days of John Paul Jones, navy men have been practicing celestial navigation. It was a natural evolution for what became the world's greatest navy to take military advantage of the new ocean of space. As early as 1946, the navy commenced feasibility studies of global command and control of the U.S. fleet via Earth satellite vehicles. The Naval Research Laboratory and Office of Naval Research's Viking rockets set a number of altitude records, including a flight in May 1949 that reached an altitude of 51.5 miles.

In 1955, the Eisenhower administration selected navy's Vanguard to become the first U.S. satellite. A joint effort with the National Academy of

Sciences, Vanguard lagged behind the Soviet Sputniks, first launched in the fall of 1957. That December, the Vanguard program suffered the nationally televised humiliation of a launchpad explosion at Cape Canaveral. No one was killed, but the disaster—dubbed by the press as "Flopnik" and "Kaputnik"—forced President Dwight D. Eisenhower to green-light the alternative U.S. army satellite program headed by Dr. Wernher von Braun. On the last day of January 1958, von Braun's team launched the nation's first satellite, Explorer I, on the first try. Vanguard remained grounded until March 1958.

Still, much about the emerging U.S. space program would be defined by "the Navy Way." The service's TRANSIT satellites, first launched in April 1960, established satellites' effectiveness as navigational aids. Three of the seven original Mercury astronauts were naval aviators (Shepard, Carpenter, and Schirra) and one (Glenn) flew as a marine. Five of the "New Nine," the second group of astronauts, of which Armstrong was a member, were navy pilots (Armstrong, Conrad, Lovell, Stafford, and Young). Apollo 12, the second lunar landing mission, had an all-navy crew (Conrad, Bean, and Gordon). Four navy flyers (Conrad, Kerwin, Weitz, and Bean) and two Marine Corps officers (Lousma and Carr) participated in Skylab missions. An all-navy crew occupied the very first Skylab, in 1973. At the helm of the first Space Shuttle flight—the mission of the orbiter *Columbia* in April 1981— sat yet another all-navy crew (Young and Crippen). Navy captain, Shuttle pilot, and International Space Station astronaut Jeff Ashby has observed: "It is as if ISS is our first ship and we are learning to sail."

The training of a naval aviator harnesses men (and since the 1970s, women) to machines, culminating in landing an airplane on the deck of an aircraft carrier. Between February 1949, when he reported to the commander of the 4,000-acre naval air training base in Pensacola, Florida, and August 1950, when, just two weeks after his twentieth birthday, he ceremoniously received his navy wings of gold, Neil Armstrong passed the test.

Recalling his days as a Holloway scholar in the fall of 1948, Armstrong surmises, "I suppose the navy saw the Korean War coming" and "needed to ratchet the volume up a little bit, so they called us up early." Orders arrived on January 26, 1949, for Neil, as well as Purdue classmates Donald A. Gardner, Thomas R. "Tommy" Thompson, Peter J. "Pete" Karnoski, and Bruce E. Clingan, to start flight training.

Neil went by train from Wapakoneta to Cincinnati, where the group convened, joined by two Holloway students from Miami of Ohio University, David S. Stephenson and Merle L. Anderson, for the 720-mile rail journey to Pensacola. On February 24, 1949, eight days after passing medical exams at the naval air station, they pledged their oath as midshipmen, the lowest grade of officer in the U.S. Navy.

The navy designated the Pre-Flight training group to which Armstrong (serial number C505129) and his six friends were assigned as Class 5-49, the fifth class to begin training at NAS Pensacola in 1949. New classes formed about every two weeks that year, for a total of nearly two thousand trainees. Yet during World War II, as many as 1,100 cadets *per month* were beginning Pre-Flight. In 1945 alone, 8,880 men completed flight training with the U.S. Navy.

Forty midshipmen belonged to Class 5-49, which included roughly the same number of naval cadets, "NavCads," enlisted men selected for navy flight training. "Pre-Flight" ground school lasted four months.

For sixteen weeks in the classroom, Armstrong and his mates took intensive courses in Aerial Navigation (128 hours), Communications (fifty-five hours), Engineering (forty hours), Aerology (i.e., meteorology, thirty hours), and Principles of Flight (eighteen hours). They studied aerodynamics and the principles of aircraft engines. They learned how to send Morse code and understand the basic tenets of weather forecasting. As Neil remembers, there was "very little time away from the grind."

Much of that grind involved learning how the navy wanted things done: eighty-seven hours of Physical Training, sixty hours of the Essentials of Naval Service, thirty hours of Military Administration Courtesy and Bearing, and thirteen hours of Gunnery. In the first weeks of Pre-Flight, recalls classmate Tommy Thompson, "we learned such important things as how to polish our shoes, how to wear the uniform, how to march, how to take orders, how to handle weapons, the difference between a lieutenant and an admiral, et cetera."

Armstrong and the others were drilled by marines, taught flight basics by marines, and disciplined by marines. Lieutenant Mano, dubbed "Mighty Mouse" after his five-foot-four stature, was a disciplinarian who, Armstrong recalled, "probably gave everyone low grades" in Physical Training. Lieutenant Colonel R. D. Moore, who was in charge of the Military Department, graded Neil for his final assessment on Military Courtesy (Neil's mark: 3.0, "Very Good), Military Behavior (3.3, "Outstanding"), Military Drill (3.0, "Very Good"), Initiative (3.0, "Very Good"), Social Adeptness (2.9, "Very Good"), Stability (2.8, "Very Good"), Character (3.4, "Outstanding"), and Leadership (2.7, "Fair").* Any violation of conduct was punished. According to Pete Karnoski, "Everybody, even Neil, walked [disciplinary] 'tours.' " Records indicate only one "Delinquent Report" for Armstrong, dated March 31, 1949, resulting in ten demerits and a four-hour Saturday tour.

At liberty, midshipmen might converse with a pretty young lady at Pensacola's San Carlos Hotel or take her for a dinner at the Harbor View Restaurant, where red snapper was accompanied by the young aviator's new favorite drink, Ballantine India Ale. At the white-columned Officer's Club at Mustin Beach, where American divorcée Wallis Simpson met King Edward VII years before, girls from Mobile came over to Pensacola every Friday and Saturday night to meet the young naval-aviators-to-be. As Midshipman Pete Karnoski recalls, "the attraction was reciprocated." And Neil? According to Karnoski, "Yes, Neil was one of us in those sorts of endeavors."

Training continued with a mile-long swim in the base's Olympic-size pool. Midshipman Thompson remembers, "I was not much of a swimmer beyond a basic dog paddle, but Neil was a strong swimmer. About ten laps or so into it, Neil literally swam right over me, and I sank. We all completed the mile, but some of us just barely."

Another torture drill was the Multi-Phase Ditching Trainer, called the Dilbert Dunker after a World War II–era cartoon characterization of "the screwup navy pilot." As seen in the 1982 film *An Officer and a Gentleman,* the fully clothed aviator candidate was fitted with a parachute then strapped into a simulated cockpit sent on rails into a swimming pool. The aviator candidate's task was to unharness, knock out the flipped canopy, exit the sinking plane, and swim up to the surface before running out of breath. Many members of Class 5-49 required the help of frogmen to survive the Dilbert Dunker. Classmates remember that Armstrong was among those who handled the trial with ease.

Class 5-49 finished its sixteen weeks of Pre-Flight on June 18, 1949. Armstrong's specific marks—Principles of Flight, 3.62; Communications,

---

* Without knowing the scores of the other students in Class 5-49, it is impossible to assess Armstrong's performance relative to his peers'. With two "Outstandings," five "Very Goods," and one "Fair," it seems that Neil's scores were above average but not at the very top of the class. It is known that James J. Ashford, a member of Training Class 2-49 who later was killed in action while serving with Armstrong in VF-51, received "Outstandings" in all categories, with a 4.0 in "Character."

3.59; Aerial Navigation, 3.51; Engineering, 3.31; Essentials of Naval Service, 3.09; Aerology, 3.07; Military, 3.01; Gunnery, 2.94; and Physical Training, 2.90—averaged 3.27 on the navy's 4.0 scale, which, according to classmates, would have ranked him near the top 10 percent of the class.

On June 24, 1949, six days after completing Pre-Flight training, Class 5-49 moved to Whiting Field for Stage A of flight training. The largest of NAS Pensacola's auxiliary airfields, Whiting (named in 1943 for Commander Kenneth Whiting, a pioneer in carrier aviation) consisted of North and South airfields located about a mile apart, each equipped with four 6,000-foot-long paved runways.

Armstrong's instructor at North Whiting was a man by the name of Lee R. P. "Chipper" Rivers. "He was a very good instructor," Neil recalls, talkative in the navy tradition of a "chipper," whose cockpit coaching was "quite authoritarian, but fun loving."

Stage A consisted of twenty "hops," the first eighteen of which were dual instruction flights. "In basic training," Tommy Thompson remembers, "we sat in the rear seat and the instructor in the front. Consequently, our visibility was somewhat limited. I expect that for Neil this was less of a problem, as he already knew how to fly, albeit in a much smaller aircraft." A-19 became the "safe for solo" check flight and A-20 the first solo in the North American SNJ, the most famous of all World War II trainers, with retractable landing gear and a radial engine of 600 horsepower. "The SNJ was a big step up from both the Aeroncas and Luscombes for me," Armstrong explains. Its greater "finesse and control force" flew "very much like the F6F Hellcat that was the predominant navy fighter in World War II." All in all, the SNJ was an "ideal training plane."

Neil's first hop in the SNJ occurred on Wednesday, July 6, 1949, and first solo (A-20) nine weeks later on September 7, 1949. Throughout Stage G, Chipper Rivers recorded Armstrong's progress:

July 8 (A-2): Average to above. Student looks around very good & appears to be at ease. Applies instructions above average.

July 11 (A-5): Good hop. Satisfactory progress.

July 13 (A-5): Good on procedures for stalls; however, he has difficulty maintaining constant attitudes. Coordination is weak.

July 18 (A-7): Rough on coordination. Is slow to use tabs when attitude is changed.

July 19 (A-8): Rough coordination, especially in turns. Tries to level off at 90-degree position on approaches instead of making a continuous turn. Has a little trouble maintaining heading on touch and go takeoffs.

August 5 (A-9): Doesn't use tabs enough—coordination in general is rough. Poor speed and attitude control in landing pattern.

Armstrong's flight A-10, on Tuesday, August 9, was graded by instructor S. W. McKenzie as "Satisfactory," with three areas rating "Below Average": Taxiing ("too fast, too much throttle"), Landing Pattern ("weak speed control"), and Approaches ("cuts throttle and turns immediately into field").

Back with Rivers for the next four flights, Armstrong worked to improve on his deficiencies—most notably, landing:

August 11 (A-11): Entire period with exception of spin and H.A. [High Altitude] emergency was spent on landings, handled with all the different flap settings. Good hop.

August 13 (A-12): Aileron and erratic rudder pressures on recoveries. Slow reacting, improper procedures on low altitude emergencies.

August 15 (A-13): Shows very good progress on landing pattern & landings. Mixed up on wind directions on first two high altitude emergencies. Poor pattern.

August 16 (A-14): Unsure of himself on high altitude emergency.

Armstrong made his fifteenth hop on August 23 with yet another instructor, J. W. McNeill, who rated the attempt an overall "Unsatisfactory," specifically "Unsatisfactory" for his approaches ("overshot wind-line every time"), and five "Below Averages," on taxiing ("too much power, rides brakes"), stalls ("recovers nose too low, over controls"), landing ("levels off too high"), emergencies ("no flaps on low emerg[ency], too short on high altitude emerg[ency]"), and headwork ("was not thinking enough"). D. J. Badger, the officer in charge, reviewed with Neil his entire flight training performance. Badger could have required additional instruction, ordered an A-15 reexam, or referred his case to the Student Pilot Disposition Board, but chose to return Neil to training "with no action."

Although Armstrong's problems with altitude and speed control and judging his approaches to landings continued on hops sixteen and seventeen, Chipper Rivers gave Neil many more average than below-average marks. The eighteenth hop, on August 30, was again a check flight. Even though Rivers graded the flight below average in three areas (Transitions, Landing Pattern, and Approaches), he judged Neil "safe for solo." The following day, Armstrong took off with Instructor Praete for the solo check flight, soon grounded because of bad weather. Still, Praete saw clear to award Neil an "up" for the flight. On Wednesday, September 7, 1949, Armstrong made his first navy solo without an instructor. Afterward, a couple of Neil's mates observed navy tradition by cutting off the lower half of his tie, and Neil gave Chipper Rivers a bottle of his favorite whiskey. Armstrong's Stage A evaluations totaled 1 "Unsatisfactory," 27 "Below Average," 192 "Average," and 59 "Above Average."

Although his flying was not without its defects, it showed great promise, widely recognized by fellow members of Class 5-49. Classmate Pete Karnoski: "I remember walking out to my plane, the SNJ trainer, one morning as Neil taxied by. He looked very comfortable and sure of himself in that plane. He waved to me as he passed by." Classmate David Stephenson concurs: "[He was] confident, but not cocky." Bruce Clingan adds: "Neil had a head start on most of us by virtue of his experience as a private pilot. Beyond that, I think he had a tremendous natural talent. If it involved flying, he was very good at it."

Stage B of Basic Training—maneuvers—began the very next day after Armstrong's first solo flight. Neil made seventeen flights in nineteen days and received eighty-six "Average" marks, twenty-eight "Above Average," and only eight "Below Average" (five of them for wingovers). On none of the flights did Neil receive a "down." Neil's check flight instructor for Stage B, O. T. Menefee, on September 27, 1949, made the final evaluation: "Student obviously knew all work and was able to fly most of it average to above. Towards last of period he got so nervous it began to show up in his work. *Should be able to continue on in program and make an average pilot* [author's emphasis]."

Stage C—aerobatics—began the following week at Corry Field, a few miles northwest of Pensacola. Armstrong proved "above average" from the start at "inverted stall, wingover rolls, & loops" (Oct. 5, C-1); "All acrobatics excellent" (Oct. 15, C-8); "Acrobatics well above average" (Oct. 18, C-11); "Precision maneuvers very smooth" (Oct. 24, C-18). Three different C-stage instructors gave Armstrong a total of thirty-two "Average" marks, thirty-eight "Above Average," and only two "Below Average." All seventeen of his flights were "ups."

Stage D had Armstrong and his fellows "flying" in the Link Trainer. Dating to the late 1920s, the machine (which would stall and spin if maneuvered incorrectly) was equipped with the stick, throttle, and rudder pedals of a single-engine fighter, as well as a layout of standard navigation instruments.

But the real test came "under the hood," in the rear seat of the SNJ. In Partial Panel flying, the instructor (in the front seat) could turn off the gyro horizon and directional gyro. Armstrong intuited by logic to trust only the instruments, an ability he would later apply to piloting a spacecraft through the vacuum of space.

Armstrong's D stage was marred by "weak transitions" (Oct. 26, D-2) in trim and heading. His worst flight (Nov. 14, D-9) produced four "Below Average" marks, and his Partial Panel instructor, E. C. Reddick, commented, "Altitude control is poor. Climbs during turns. Airspeed is erratic during glides. Does not coordinate rudders properly during rollout to a level attitude." For his ten Stage D instrument flights, however, Neil received nothing but "ups."

Armstrong's next five flights (completed from November 15 to 18) involved the Radio Range Phase of D stage, where he received 43 "Above Average," 28 "Below Average," and 138 "Average" marks. His instructors continued to focus on Neil's poor altitude control.

Armstrong made his two mandatory night flights (Stage E) on Friday, November 4, both of them resulting in "ups" (eleven "Average" marks and seven "Above Average"). Instructor Martin commented, "Student has a very good mental attitude" and "knows procedures."

By Thanksgiving 1949, Armstrong had completed the first five stages of Basic Training. He had made forty hops with 39.6 hours in dual instruction and 19.4 hours solo.

Saufley Field, an outlying landing field (OLF) northwest of Pensacola off Perdido Bay, was the site for formation flying (Stage F, eighteen hops, November 28, 1949, through January 30, 1950), conducted simultaneously with Primary Combat (Stage H, January 18 and 21, 1950) and Cross-Country Navigation (Stage I, January 23 and 25, 1950), for which he received very favorable evaluations.

Armstrong received two Stage F "downs": on December 5, 1949 (F-5), when "Student was sucked far behind on most of rendezvous. Wing position was very erratic. Failed to pass signal on break up," and on January 7, 1950 (F-12), when "Rend[ezvous] and join-ups badly sucked, continually fouling up people behind. Lags behind in position. Doesn't know sequence very well." Following the F-5 review, Armstrong was given "one increment" of extra instruction; following F-12, he was "returned to training with no action," no doubt because LCDR R. S. Belcher believed Neil possessed too much potential to delay his progress. Neil repaid the trust by experiencing no significant problems in his last six F hops. For the last four he received seven "Above Average" marks and only one "Below Average."

For Stage G's sixteen gunnery flights (January 30, 1950, through February 15, 1950, at Saufley), Armstrong turned in thirty-five "Above Average" scores, only thirteen "Below Average," and not a single "Unsatisfactory." Though ground strafing and dive-bombing proved challenging, his marksmanship was superior—with eight of his "Above Average" grades coming in the Firing category. "One great afternoon after a gunnery mission," Pete Karnoski recalls, "Neil and I came back to Saufley together. He was on my right wing and we flew along like a couple of aces, almost wingtip to wingtip. Dangerous you think, but, hey, at that age, you're indestructible!"

"I enjoyed the training immensely," Armstrong reminisces, "but they had a way of adding a degree of intensity to it. There was always a lot of pressure to try to do things with perfection." Not that Neil disliked competition. "It was every man for himself," according to David Stephenson. "One person might advance along his track faster than someone else in the same class," Armstrong explains.

Those students who made it to Carrier Qualifications entered the crucible in which naval aviators were made. In late February 1950, Armstrong began final Basic Training at Corry Field. Field Carrier Landing Practice (FCLP) occurred on a 500- to 600-foot runway painted onto an OLF twenty-three miles west of Pensacola, known as "Bloody Barin" for the large number of accidents that occurred there during World War II.

Neil's class of ten spent the next three weeks learning to follow "a landing signal officer completely," Armstrong explains. "The LSO had a paddle in each hand and he would, just by the arrangements of the paddles, tell you that you're a little high or a little low, a little fast, or you need to turn a little more.

"If the LSO deems you cannot complete a successful landing or a safe landing," Armstrong relates, "he will wave his paddles at you—a so-called wave-off—and you're immediately commanded to add full power and 'go around' and try again." At Barin Field, Neil learned "to keep both eyes open."

Neil's principal instructor for K Stage, R. M. Sullivan, rated Armstrong's performance at Barin: "Ruff [rough] altitude control" (K-3, February 24); "Drops nose in turn . . . Overshoots . . . Very ruff landing. *Ruff*" (K-4, February 24); "Showing great deal of improvement" (K-6, February 25); "Long. Not lined up." (K-7, February 27); "Ruff rudder control" (K-8, February 27); "Average work" (K-11, March 1). Still, Sullivan awarded Neil 97 of 110 marks "Average" or above; of the 13 below-average marks, 6 were problems that Neil experienced with "Final Approach." Following the K-12 check flight, Neil was "field qualified" and ready to make his first landing at sea.

Thursday, March 2, 1950, was one of those indelible days for a naval aviator. Armstrong headed out over the Gulf of Mexico to make Stage L's required six landings on the USS *Cabot,* a light carrier (CVL designation) steaming a short distance off Pensacola. "The SNJ was a relatively low-speed airplane," and, he remembers, "even if you had thirty knots across the deck, you could take off easily, without a catapult." Landing, of course, was the major challenge. Naval wisdom holds that "a good carrier landing is one from which you can walk away. A great carrier landing is one after which you can use the aircraft again."

Armstrong likens his first carrier landing to his first solo back in Wapakoneta, another "very emotional achievement" in his flying life. Grounded as he is in technical details, Armstrong is more comfortable speaking about "we" or "you" rather than "I": "It is certainly a highly precise kind of flying. It works because you, in a very precise manner, get the airplane through that very small window that will allow it to land successfully on a very short flight deck."

He relates that he received no wave-offs on his first carrier landings, a showing worth nine "Average" marks and two "Below Average" grades—one for Final Approach ("poor line up—flat") and one for Speed ("fast starts"), solid enough that he "Qualified this date in carrier landings aboard the USS *Cabot.*"

Carrier qualifications ended Basic Training and punched tickets to Advanced Training.

"I requested fighters and fortunately was assigned to fighters" at NAS Corpus Christi. "The fighter pilots always said that only the very best men got to be fighter pilots," Neil admits, laughing. "My own guess is that a large part of it had to do with what needs the navy had at the time you graduated, because in my particular class, most of my classmates happened to get what they asked for, while I can recall people from a different generation saying nobody got what they asked for."

According to his mother, Neil "chose the single-motor fighter plane," because, in his words, " 'I didn't want to be responsible for anybody else. I'd better just watch my own self.' He thought if he had more motors, why then he'd be hauling more people, taking more people, and he said, 'I'd better just be responsible for my own self.' "

Viola's maternal projections may have caused her to misunderstand Neil's motives for wanting fighters: "I was assigned the F8F-1 Bearcat as my advanced training aircraft, which I was delighted with because it was a very high performance airplane." First flown in 1944, the Bearcat, with its full "bubble" canopy, was the last propeller-driven fighter aircraft built by Grumman for the navy. Many consider it the finest piston-engine fighter in service with the U.S. Navy at the end of World War II. A small plane with an outstanding power-to-weight ratio (provided by a 2,100-horsepower Pratt & Whitney eighteen-cylinder radial engine), the F8F-1 offered both great agility and great speed, up to 434 miles per hour (377 knots). Compared to anything that Armstrong had ever flown (the SNJ possessed only 600 horse-power and flew to a top speed of 178 knots), the Bearcat was a hot rod, with fantastic acceleration and climbing ability.

At Cabaniss Field, one of Corpus Christi's six outlying auxiliary bases, he began his indoctrination with VF ATU (Advanced Training Unit) No. 2 on March 28, 1950. In the three months ending June 21, 1950, Neil made thirty-nine flights and logged over seventy hours in the air, all but one hour of it solo. Only once did he receive an unsatisfactory mark, on June 6, 1950, during Gunnery & Tactics, when instructor H. W. Davis was unhappy with Neil's Air Discipline for taxiing to the parking area before going out to the weapons dearming area. His other two weak flights, both during gunnery runs, came a week earlier, on May 31, when Neil "recovered too sharply & blacked out. Lost sight of flight & unable to find them until after many radio transmissions," and a week later when he "reversed toward tow too late & sucked back often times never getting into firing range" and "recovered slightly to side instead of ahead, lost banner so no gun results." His last five flights at Cabaniss showed considerable improvement—with ten "Above Average" marks and only one "Below Average" (on June 20) for not flying sufficiently straight and level on instruments.

By mid-July 1950, Neil was back at NAS Pensacola preparing to make his next six required qualification landings, this time in the cockpit of an F8F Bearcat. As in Basic Training, Field Carrier Landing Practice came as the K Stage. On his fifteenth FCLP hop on August 10, Armstrong was deemed "Field Qualified."

His next day's destination was the Gulf of Mexico and the USS *Wright* (CVL-49). Armstrong again experienced a good day at sea—not a single "Below Average" mark. According to Neil, holding back a smile, "The Bearcat was able to take off in a very short distance. They wanted you still steering down the runway when you passed all the senior officers who were standing on the bridge." This was not just a matter of military decorum. "As soon as your wheels lift[ed] off, then you're going to be susceptible to wind tending to drift you one way or the other," possibly right into the bridge.

Class 5-49 and Korean War mate Herbert Graham remembers how a small training group flew out in formation. Approaching the carrier, all the planes went into a racetrack pattern and took six turns shooting landings then taking off. According to Graham, "Neil and I wanted to finish first for bragging rights." Graham got in his first five landings with Neil right behind him. Then, due to his position in the pattern, Graham had the chance to get his sixth before Neil or anyone else. When he was ready to land, however, the LSO waved him off. The plane ahead of him had not yet cleared the deck, leaving it "fouled." Graham had to go around again.

Fortuitously, the deck cleared just as Neil's plane approached and he became the first in his group to make his sixth landing. In Neil's case, as Graham describes it, "luck, opportunity, preparation, and skill converged," a phenomenon he recalled years later when he heard that "something similar happened on Neil's being selected for the first Moon landing."

CHAPTER 8

Fighter Squadron 51

On August 16, 1950, five days after Armstrong aced his carrier qualifications in the F8F, Naval Air Training Command Headquarters at NAS Pensacola informed the midshipman by letter that he had "successfully completed the full course of the prescribed syllabus of training for Naval Aviators" and was "hereby designated a Naval Aviator (Heavier-than-Air)."

Graduation took place a week later, on August 23; Neil's mother and sister drove 825 miles to attend. Stephen, June explains, "was to testify in an [audit] case and [tried but] could not be excused. I remember both Mother and Father being very disappointed."

After a short leave, Midshipman Neil Armstrong reported to ComAir-Pac, i.e., air command of the Pacific Fleet—"for duty involving flying." Armstrong explained: "Typically you're going to ask for an assignment that is similar to your recent training. In my case, it was fighters, so I was going to ask for a fighter squadron, and the choice would be East Coast or West Coast. There was a lot of talk about a war either in Indochina or Korea, but I don't think that was related to my choice of the West Coast. I'd never been to the West Coast and thought it would be nice to see that part of the country, so I asked for West Coast and I was given the West Coast."

Reaching California in early September 1950, Armstrong served ten weeks with Fleet Aircraft Service Squadron (FASRON) 7—based at NAS San Diego (NAS North Island as of 1955). Commander Luke H. Miller reported "Midshipman Armstrong has been attached to this command in a pool status awaiting assignment to an air group."

From October 27 to November 4, 1950, Armstrong trained at the close-air support school run by the Marine Corps at its amphibious base on the south strand of Coronado Island down from NAS San Diego. "That was good fun while I was waiting for my fighter assignment," Armstrong remembers. "A lovely flying experience." Fifty miles north at marine Camp Pendleton, mock aerial combat drills set "offense" pilots (Neil continued to fly an F8F-2) to find and attack "enemy" ground targets and disrupt the "defense."

On November 27, 1950, ComAirPac ordered Armstrong, along with Pre-Flight buddy and FASRON 7 mate Herb Graham, to "proceed immediately and report to the Commanding Officer of Fighter Squadron FIFTY ONE, for duty involving flying." Fighter Squadron 51 was a veteran squadron just then returning stateside aboard the USS *Valley Forge* (CVA-45). It was the first of three cruises to the Far East that VF-51 would make during the Korean War.

Armstrong wanted to fly jets in VF-51 (until August 16, 1948, VF-5A), the first all-jet squadron in the United States Navy. William W. "Bill" Bowers of VF-51 recalls that "in the early jet days, most single-engine pilots wanted to fly jets. So those who got into it early, around 1949–50, considered themselves fortunate." Some of them were also "a little more prideful than they should have been." VF-51 member Ken "K. C." Kramer concurs: "There was a great mystique about flying high-performance jets and we all played into that."

As Herb Graham tells it: "When VF-51 was being formed in 1950, jets and jet-trained pilots were scarce and VF-51 was to be an all-jet squadron flying F9F-2s. Neil was in that assignment pool . . . and he was an excellent young pilot. It was a dream spot. Everyone wanted to fly jets and be a fighter pilot."

VF-51's commanding officer was Lieutenant Commander Ernest M. "Ernie" Beauchamp. A flight instructor at NAS Pensacola before the attack on Pearl Harbor, Beauchamp (pronounced "Bee-chum") flew Grumman F-6F Hellcats in World War II with VF-8, a key player in the victory in the Philippines. Aboard USS *Bunker Hill* in mid-1944, Beauchamp's squadron, under Commander William Collins, in six months' time took down 156 Japanese aircraft, producing thirteen different aces, pilots who had destroyed five or more enemy aircraft in air-to-air engagement. Commander Collins himself had nine kills; Beauchamp had eight (four confirmed and four probable). But Ernie was more than an outstanding fighter pilot. He had a brilliant mind for fighter tactics. In the spring of 1945, Beauchamp took command of Fighter Squadron VF-1 (later VF-74), aboard the USS *Midway,* but the war in the Pacific ended before the squadron could deploy.

Beauchamp stayed in the navy after the war, retaining his squadron command before taking a staff post with the Deputy Chief of Naval Operations for Air (DCNO-AIR) in the Navy Department in Washington. On

June 25, 1950, the very day the Korean War started, Lieutenant Commander Beauchamp left his desk job to assume command of VF-51, which became as close to a handpicked squadron as the navy ever got.

Serving temporarily at NAS North Island as officer-in-charge of a brand-new jet transition unit (JTU) for flyers from reserve F4U squadrons that had been recalled to active duty, Lt. Commander Beauchamp not only saw the records but also observed the performance of a large number of pilots. "Only two or three pilots in the [then] currently deployed VF-51 would be available for a second tour," Beauchamp explained in 2002 from his retirement home in Corona Del Mar, California. Beauchamp managed to secure the assignments of four of his veteran aviators. Lieutenant Richard M. Wenzell had finished first in his test pilot training class and at the Naval Air Test Center at Patuxent River in Maryland and had performed most of the control and stability testing on the navy's new Panther fighter jet. This was the very plane that VF-51 would be flying. The "dean of instruction" in Beauchamp's JTU, Wenzell became VF-51's operations officer. Pensacola flight instructor Lieutenant William A. Mackey had flown under Beauchamp in VF-1 and had recently completed the JTU at Whiting Field, along with Lieutenant Daniel V. Marshall and LCDR Bernard Sevilla, two other VF-1 veterans who Beauchamp in 1950 signed onto VF-51.

Still, Beauchamp was short on pilots. On the word of "Wam" Mackey, Beauchamp recruited four additional aviators from Whiting Field: JTU instructors LTJG Robert E. Rostine (who "made every plane he ever flew look good") and LTJG John Moore; along with JTU graduates and class 5-49 members LTJG Thomas B. Hayward (future Chief of Naval Operations) and LTJG Ross K. Bramwell.

One day after arrangements had been finalized, none other than World War II double ace (fourteen kills) Marshall Beebe—the new commander (CAG) for Air Group 5—came storming into Beauchamp's office. "What the hell are you doing? You can't have all four of those guys! Some of those guys are going to VF-52."

All four stayed in the 51st. "Skipper" (as the pilots called Beauchamp) told his chosen nine officers to wield "a fine mesh screen" for eleven additional "nuggets," or new aviators who had not yet received an assignment.

Beauchamp, Mackey, and Wenzell, in Beauchamp's words, "took every opportunity to fly with each of the nuggets on the recommended list." Armstrong insists, though, that he never flew with Wenzell, Mackey, or Beauchamp prior to his assignment to the squadron; so "whatever Ernie found out about me, he must have learned from other sources." Possibly the recommendation for both Armstrong and Herb Graham came from their commanding officer in FASRON 7, Luke H. Miller.

No one has ever claimed credit for identifying Armstrong as a person to bring into VF-51. Nor has Armstrong ever speculated about it.

Filling out the group with Armstrong and Graham were, in alphabetical order, ENS James J. Ashford, LTJG William W. Bowers, LTJG Leonard R. Cheshire, ENS Hershel L. Gott, ENS Herbert A. Graham, ENS Robert J. Kaps, ENS Kenneth E. Kramer, ENS Donald C. McNaught, ENS Glen H. Rickelton, LTJG George E. Russell, and LTJG Harold C. Schwan. Carrying on with VF-51 from the *Valley Forge* cruise were LTJG Francis N. Jones and LTJG Wiley A. Scott. Harley Thompson was pulled out of VF-51 to become a naval liaison officer with the air force in Japan, and squadron veteran Red Gardner was killed in an F9F training accident at NAS San Diego. The squadron was fortunate to retain experienced chiefs and first-class petty officers in maintenance, ordnance, and supply. New to the squadron were nonflying intelligence officer LTJG Kenneth I. Danneberg and ground maintenance officer ENS Howard "Howie" Zehetner.

The VF-51 nuggets still faced a competitive selection process. One potential disadvantage for Armstrong was that, at the time of his assignment to the squadron in late November 1950, he had not yet flown a jet.

VF-51's Bill Bowers, a veteran of World War II, remembers that his first hop in a jet—at the one-month transition unit in Pensacola in a single-seat TO-1, the navy's version of the F-80—was "terrific." "Not just the higher speed," Bowers notes, "it was the smooth, vibration-free flow of power from the new engines." Some say the transition from props to jets was "like switching from a high-powered race car with a 'four on the floor' stick to a faster one with 'automatic' drive." Others say the changeover was a little more problematic. Wam Mackey remembers from JTU training in Pensacola that the TO-1 was "a pretty complicated jet fighter" with "very short legs" on the fuel supply.

On Friday, January 5, 1951, Armstrong first took off in a Grumman F9F-2B. The "spectacular" first flight in the Panther lasted a little over an hour, and was another "one of those magic moments" in Neil's career as a pilot. "That was very exciting to me, to be in the front lines of the new jet fighters."

Though Neil was only a few months past his twentieth birthday, his fellow aviators held him in high regard. Herb Graham called Neil "quiet without being shy. He was confident without bragging. He listened intently." Wam Mackey characterized Neil as "very serious and very dedicated. . . .

He was a fine young pilot—a very solid aviator, very reliable." But it was Beauchamp himself who most needed to be impressed, and he was. Until he read a book published in 1997 by VF-51 aviator John Moore, Beauchamp was not even aware that Neil reported into the squadron as a midshipman. "I must have known it at the time," Beauchamp recalls, "but I always thought of him as a fully qualified designated naval aviator." Neil's mental approach to flying was very similar to his commanding officer's. "Our skipper . . . was a great guy but very regulation," Hal Schwan recalls. "He didn't believe in any outward show—no flashy paint jobs on the airplane or anything like that. He told us we should get attention by how well we performed."

Because the squadron possessed so few jets (only six planes for twenty-four pilots), flying was, in Armstrong's words, "a bit scarce"—about three flights per week per aviator through the first two and half months of 1951. By mid-March, the winter fog had lifted and VF-51 had a full complement of aircraft allowing each pilot to fly between five and seven hops per week, periodically maintaining their instrument proficiency by flying "under the hood" in old twin-engine Beechcraft SNB trainers.

Armstrong always kept a pilot's logbook, but he never kept a diary. One of his mates in VF-51, Ensign Glen H. "Rick" Rickelton, did. As the squadron trained, the specter of the enemy loomed. "I am anxious to go west and try some of this stuff for real," Rickelton wrote on May 21, 1951.

"We felt that we would possibly be fighting swept-wing MiG-15s," recounts Herb Graham. "They cruised above our top speed and could climb at a higher speed than we could dive. It was similar to the start of World War II when the navy F4F Wildcat fighters were faced with the much higher-performance Japanese Zero." Having read the combat action report covering the Panther's encounters with the "superior performance" MiG back in late 1950, Beauchamp felt "grave concern" that if MiGs were "manned by pilots as aggressive and well trained as ours that our own pilot and plane losses would have been great."

According to Armstrong, "We didn't know to what extent we would be offensive, in the sense that we would be dropping bombs or shooting guns, to what extent we might be defending the fleet against Chinese or Russian incoming aircraft, or to what extent it might be air-to-air or air-to-ground. I was very young, very green."

Would Armstrong have enjoyed mixing it up with a MiG? "I probably would have enjoyed it," he admits, "but I don't know that I would have won against a MiG in an old Panther." In retrospect, the Panther was an immature design that did not fly particularly well compared to the next wave of jets. "But we didn't know that at the time," Armstrong explains. "It didn't have particularly good handling qualities. Pretty good lateral directional controls, but very stiff in pitch. Its performance both in absolute altitude, max speed, and climb rate were inferior to the MiG by a substantial amount."

Contemplating the threat of facing the Russian MiG, and struggling to keep their focus through a grueling training schedule, unmarried pilots lived in the bachelor officers' quarters at North Island. Rick Rickelton observed in his diary that Neil behaved as one of the guys. "Neil had a lot of fun," Wam Mackey recollects of the squadron "beer musters" and officers' dinners, "but he was serious about his work."

If Armstrong's age and youthful looks did not single him out, his hobbies did. Besides being an avid reader, he remained passionate about building models. Herb Graham, who shared a room with Neil in the BOQ, remembers seeing Neil carving a block of wood, "starting on the body of a pulse jet. He had made a model of the engine and needed a plane to use it. Neil was already flying the best of the navy fighters, but he wanted more." Later, aboard the *Essex,* Armstrong built a small wooden boat and then out of a hat drew the name of one of the married guys who had children. Mackey won it and took it home for his boys. To his great regret—and to the greater regret of his boys by the time of Apollo 11—Mackey later gave it away to his local Fraternal Order of Police during a Christmas toy collection drive. Neil also built a model of the MiG-15, which he hung in VF-51's ready room.

Training once again built toward the finality of carrier "quals" in the Panther, this time on the 27,100-ton carrier USS *Essex* (CV-9), recently modernized at a cost of $40 million. Neil had previously made a grand total of twelve carrier landings—six in the SNJ and six in the F8F. The older pilots, especially the ones who had fought in World War II, had many more carrier landings in prop planes, but they had no more experience in jet landings than Neil did. "The speeds tended to be higher on the jet," Neil notes. "We were flying at slightly over a hundred knots typically in a pattern, which was maybe twenty knots faster than we'd been flying with the Bearcat." The squadron flew night FCLP at Brown Field near the Mexican border.

"I happened to be a day fighter pilot," Armstrong is glad to say. "We had night fighters on the ship I was on, and I thought they were crazy." He qualified in the bright light of day on June 7, 1951, roughly two months before his twenty-first birthday and just two days after his preset "date of rank" for promotion to ensign. (In order to bring Neil "in proper lineal position with his contemporaries," the navy subsequently revised the date from June 5 to June 1, 1951.)

On final approach, with his powers of concentration intent on the paddles of the landing signal officer, Armstrong reduced his speed to just above a stall, about 105 knots. In an instant, the ramp of the *Essex* flashed below him, the jet dropped abruptly, and its all-important tailhook blessedly snagged one of the arresting wires. With only 150 feet left before the airplane smacked rudely into the protective barriers, Armstrong's F9F Panther jerked fiercely to a stop, having gone in a heartbeat from about 105 knots to teeth-rattling zero.

"Neil was a great precision pilot and did very well in this area," recalls "K. C." Kramer. "He had the skill and the nerve," adds Herb Graham. Armstrong faced the LSO and his little green record book seven more times that day. "We got graded on every landing," Kramer explains, "so there was some sense of competitiveness among the pilots."

Following the exhilaration of his first carrier landing in a jet, Armstrong experienced the thrill of a "cat shot," cannonading airborne by one of the navy's powerful H8 hydraulic catapults. "The first few catapult launches took faith," remembers Herb Graham. Armstrong concurs: "There was a degree of uncertainty. If, for one reason or another, you got a little bit of a weak shot, you could come perilously close to the water." It was at this point, following a total of eight successful carrier landings by Neil that day, that Lieutenant Commander Beauchamp must have finalized his choice of Armstrong as one of VF-51's officers beginning the cruise on the *Essex*. A month earlier, Beauchamp, in recognition of Neil's abilities, had assigned him to serve as both the squadron's assistant education officer and its assistant air intelligence officer. Based on Beauchamp's input, Captain Austin W. Wheelock, commanding officer of the *Essex*, noted in Armstrong officer's fitness report dated June 30, 1951: "Ensign ARMSTRONG is an intelligent, courteous, and military appearing officer. As a naval aviator, he is average to above average and is improving steadily. He is recommended for promotion when due." Armstrong's combined 215 hours in the SNJ, 102 hours in the F8F, 33 hours in the SNB, and 155 hours in the F9F made for a total of 505 hours in the air since Neil joined the navy.

On Monday, June 25, 1951, Fighter Squadron 51 received its orders. Three days later, at 1430 on June 28, the *Essex* upped anchor. As she approached the Hawaiian Islands on July 3, most of the carrier's aircraft flew ahead to Oahu's southwestern tip.

At NAS Barbers Point, the squadron's aircraft were first equipped with heavy (four 250-pound general-purpose or four 260-pound fragmentation) bomb racks. Ken Kramer remembers: "We had expected that we would be fighting MiGs, and we had practiced our dogfighting tactics probably more than any other squadron before us." If the navy's Pentagon aircraft procurement unit "had only gone with the North American Fury [the progenitor of the Sabre jet] instead of the Panther," Kramer has speculated, "we would have been the pilots fighting the MiGs" in the Sabre jet being built by North American Aviation for the air force. "Instead, we became a ground attack squadron," "a big letdown for us" as naval aviators.

Yet, the navy's decision to add the bomb racks was sound. The FJ-1 lacked carrier suitability; among other reasons, the plane kept losing its tailhook in its landing gear. VF-51 became a fighter-bomber unit because, as CO Ernie Beauchamp put it, "it was the only game in town." In the eastern half of Korea into which VF-51 would be flying, there were simply no MiGs to engage.

During the training in Hawaii (from July 4 through 31), it was unclear whether all of VF-51's officers would make the cruise. On July 11, 1951, Rickelton wrote in his diary: "We are still wondering if they are going to have to kick us ensigns off the ship due to lack of room for planes." Neil Armstrong, a brand-new ensign and the squadron's youngest officer, felt equally vulnerable.

There was still a chance no one at all would be going. On June 23, 1951, the Soviet delegate to the United Nations had proposed a truce between North and South Korea. Treaty negotiations, started on July 10, at Kaesong near the 38th parallel, were still taking place on July 25, the day that Rickelton optimistically recorded in his diary: "I think the war is as good as over." Starting on August 1, United Nations forces, in order to consolidate their front lines, resumed limited attacks, which the Communists called an act of aggression. By August 18, heavy fighting resumed. Five days later, the Communists broke off peace talks, charging the United States with violations of neutrality and with restarting the war. September 1951 would see some of the bloodiest fighting of the war. At the Battle of Bloody Ridge, the U.S. Army's 15th Field Artillery Battalion set a record by firing 14,425 rounds in a twenty-four-hour period. On its heels came the monthlong Battle of Heartbreak Ridge, costing the United States 3,700 casualties to North Korea's nearly 25,000-man loss.

By the time belligerency resumed on August 23, 1951, the *Essex* was fifteen days out of Pearl Harbor (having left on August 8, four days away from what had been a quick stop at the U.S. Naval base at Yokosuka [pronounced *Yah-koos̈-kah*], Japan, and already on station some seventy miles off the northeast coast of Korea near the harbor at Wonsan). Joining Fighter Squadron 51 aboard the *Essex* were one squadron of F4U Corsairs (VF-53), one squadron of AD Skyraiders (VA-54), and one squadron of F2H-2 Banshee jets (VF-172). Also embarked were four VC detachments: VC-61 with F9F-2P photo planes; VC-3; VC-11; and VC-35 ("VC" designating a "composite squadron" trained in night attack and defense, air early warning, and antisubmarine warfare). The replacement at Pearl Harbor of the Banshee squadron for VF-52 (and its F9F-2s) was an unhappy surprise for the Panther pilots, who took no delight in the notion they might play second fiddle to the Banshees.

They need not have worried.

CHAPTER 9
Fate Is the Hunter

Skipper Beauchamp foresaw the perils of his squadron's upcoming cruise. In its four months of combat in Korea in late 1950, Carrier Air Group 5, while aboard USS *Valley Forge,* had lost fourteen aviators, more than 10 percent of CVG-5's entire complement of pilots. True, VF-51 itself had suffered only one casualty. Beauchamp knew that his own squadron might not be so lucky.

The men of VF-51 were more excited than scared about the prospects of combat. They were, in Ernie Russell's words, "in the company of fellow travelers at the peak of their potential, overflowing with energy and good spirits, and embarking on the adventure of their life."

A bad omen for what was to come, typhoon Marge battered the *Essex* for two straight days, rolling the ship just ten degrees shy of its thirty-five-degree capsize point. In his journal for August 20, VF-51's Bob Kaps wrote, "Same rolling, pitching motion. Becoming very disagreeable, says my stomach." Several of the men got sick and hardly anyone got good rest. "I didn't get much sleep," Rick Rickelton noted in his diary, "Every time I would doze off I would get banged against the side of my bunk. I woke up so mad I almost broke my fist on the . . . bulkhead."

On August 22, the *Essex* joined Task Force 77 about seventy miles off Wonsan. Looking out the large bay door of the hangar deck, Armstrong saw his first American carrier battle group. The carrier *Bon Homme Richard;* the battleship *New Jersey;* two cruisers, the *Helena* and *Toledo;* and some fifteen to twenty destroyers numbered among some two dozen warships that would swell in the following months to marshal as many as four carriers and three cruisers in simultaneous action.

The previous day, the pilots of Fighter Squadron 51 had gotten airborne, though bad weather on August 22 and 23 grounded them again.

Air Group 5's first stretch of combat operations commenced on

August 24, when CVG-5 launched seventy-six sorties against "targets of opportunity." It was not Armstrong's turn to fly that first day. Nor did he participate on the twenty-fifth in a massive air raid on the railyards at Rashin near the Soviet border—the first time navy fighters (both Panthers and Banshees) ever escorted air force bombers over hostile territory.

According to Armstrong, "The four-plane division was the mainstay of the operation." A division consisted of two sections of two airplanes each. In flight, the sections stayed separated (as opposed to the World War II–era partner maneuver "Thach Weave") by a quarter mile to a half mile.

Beauchamp divided his twenty-four pilots into six divisions scheduled to receive approximately the same number of hops. The Skipper led the first division with Bob Rostine as his section leader. Benny Sevilla led the second with Wiley Scott as section leader. Dick Wenzell and Tom Hayward led the third, Wam Mackey and Chet Cheshire the fourth, and Danny Marshall and Bill Bowers the fifth. The head of the sixth division was John Carpenter. An air force major, Carpenter came to VF-51 on an air force–navy exchange program. Carpenter's section leader was John Moore. The junior officers flew as wingmen. At the start of the cruise, Armstrong usually flew as Carpenter's wingman, in the division with John Moore. Later, Neil flew mostly with Wam Mackey. Like the other pilots, Armstrong also flew a number of photo escorts, which were not done in divisions.

Though Armstrong "was one of the boys," as Hersh Gott declares, a special interest in education did set him apart somewhat. According to Beauchamp, "It was not unusual to find Neil in the ready room after dinner at the blackboard with a piece of chalk in his hand illustrating a math problem, an aerodynamic principle, or so forth." Early in the cruise, Armstrong taught an algebra class to some thirty interested enlisted men. So wrapped up in one lesson, Armstrong missed muster for a scheduled squadron briefing. It took a call over the ship's PA system to get his attention. Neil burst through the rear door of the ready room and apologized for being late. As VF-51's John Moore has told the story, Beauchamp accepted no excuses:

Beauchamp: "Neil, where were you?"

"Down below, sir."

"What were you doing down below?"

"Sir," said Armstrong, "I am teaching an algebra class to some of our crew and tonight I had a scheduled class meeting. Sorry, sir."

The skipper demanded an explanation from his youngest ensign. Armstrong answered, "It's no big deal, sir. Some of our guys asked me if I would do it and I said, sure. No big deal."

The fact that CAG Marshall Beebe always asked for the squadron's youngest aviator as his wingman did not go unnoticed. Ken Kramer relates, "I never discussed Neil with Beebe, but it is a fact that CAG chose to fly with Neil whenever he flew the F9F-2 Panthers. I think they had a very good relationship." Armstrong concurs: "I flew with Commander Beebe some and thought he was quite a good air group commander, the first I'd known and certainly the first in any operational circumstances or any combat circumstances. . . . I was delighted when I had the chance to fly with him."

Flying as Beebe's wingman did not afford Armstrong any protection from danger; in fact, CAG's aggressive approach to combat flying may have put Neil even more into harm's way. Beebe "seemed to be completely fearless," Hal Schwan says. "I was on missions with him where there would be a lot of antiaircraft fire—we would go in and make our run and he would call everybody to go up and orbit while he would go down to see if another strike was needed. I can remember looking down and thinking, 'My God, that guy just doesn't care!' "

Beebe had a well-deserved reputation for staying "feet dry"—overland—for too long, maximizing air time over enemy targets but leaving the planes with barely enough fuel to make it back to their carrier. Wam Mackey remembers: "We'd always have a hell of a time when we got to the 'bingo' point [the minimum fuel needed to return to the carrier safely]. We'd say, 'CAG, help me out,' and he'd say, 'Okay, I'm just going to take one more look around.' " More than once, Beauchamp expressed his displeasure with Beebe for pressing everyone's luck. Some of the pilots in Air Group 5 called Beebe "the greatest of the 'follow me, boys!' "

On a couple of occasions Beebe managed to get authorization for his jets to fly up into MiG Alley in the uppermost regions of North Korea, though the requisite defensive maneuvering against MiGs would have used up too much fuel to afford safe return to their carrier. Balancing the risk against the unknown military gain, some of Beebe's aviators wondered privately, What the hell was the man thinking?

Armstrong has never criticized Marshall Beebe for his aggressive flying, though he has said, "I do remember when I would have appreciated a couple of hundred more pounds of fuel in the landing pattern."

Armstrong's first action over North Korea came on Wednesday, August 29, when he escorted a photoreconnaissance plane above the 40th parallel over the port of Songjin, then flew a routine combat air patrol over the fleet. Three of the next four days (except for September 1, when the task force replenished its fuel and supplies), he flew armed reconnaissance over Wonsan, Pu-Chong, and again up to Songjin. A few VF-51 aircraft encountered small-arms ground fire on the twenty-ninth, but the squadron's first taste of potent AA fire did not come until September 2. Beauchamp's divisions' main objective was disruption of the transport system that fed the North Korean and Chinese armies. "We did that by blowing up trains and bridges and tanks," explains Armstrong, "and just being as contrary as we could."

In its first ten days of action, Air Group 5 experienced a nasty rash of casualties. On August 23, LTJG Leo Franz in a Corsair from VF-53 disappeared in heavy overcast. In a "shocking incident" early on Sunday morning, an AD-3 (Attack Douglas) Skyraider piloted by LTJG Loren D. Smith of VC-35 was "seen to burn in midair and then crash into the water," killing both Smith and his radioman, Philip K. Balch. Bob Kaps (nicknamed "Bottle") reported: "Night heckler [typically a Corsair attack plane] exploded after catapult. Bomb & napalm load gave them no chance." Covering the week ending Sunday, September 2, the ship's combat action report noted, "Not a day had gone by but at least one plane had been hit by AA," the casualties provoking "a more pronounced outlook on the point of survival." Bottle Kaps wrote in his journal, "Have already decided I'm not the hero type."

The next week almost ended Neil Armstrong's life.

On Monday morning, September 3, 1951, following a briefing in the ready room, Armstrong suited up for what was to be his seventh combat mission since arriving in the Korean theater. Although years later Armstrong would take even greater care with the complicated suit so vital to an astronaut's survival in the vacuum of space, donning a naval aviator's two-part "poopy suit" drew comparisons to putting on a straitjacket. The inner lining, similar to a child's snowsuit, was relatively comfortable compared to the tight rubber outer garment that resembled a frogman's suit. According to one naval aviator, "If your face turns blue and you gasp for breath, you know the suit fits properly." All of this trouble for an outfit that might keep a downed pilot alive in the cold ocean water for twenty minutes, yet that was considerably better than the ninety seconds without it. Carrier lore held that one successful ditching was all any pilot had the right to expect. This made the experience of Paul Gray, the thirty-five-year-old commander of VF-54, all the more remarkable. During the *Essex* cruise, Gray ditched an AD Skyraider into the sea five times and was rescued each time.

Having struggled into the rubber exposure suit, next came an outer shirt, a survival jacket, a holstered .38-caliber Smith & Wesson pistol, extra ammo, a life jacket, and gloves. As with his fellow aviators, Armstrong finished his raiment by tying a silk scarf around his neck. The scarf was not simply stylish; it was necessary to help stop water from getting into the immersion suit from around the neck if a ditching did occur.

The call to "Flight Quarters!" commenced a noisy, frenetic choreography on deck. The "plane captain" started the jet engines even before the pilots arrived to make their assisted climb into the cockpit, where the plane captain connected the shoulder and lap straps and arranged the parachute harness. Following a check of his oxygen mask and the status of his life raft and radio, the aviator was primed for the ship's powerful H8 catapults. His cat shot that day would be Armstrong's twenty-eighth in three months.

Armstrong's mission was to fly an armed reconnaissance mission into a hot zone that U.S. naval intelligence called "Green Six." Located west of Wonsan, Green Six was the code name for a narrow valley road that ran south from the village of Majon-ni, southwest of Wonsan to the interior border of South Korea.

The principal targets for September 3, 1951, were freight yards and a bridge. According to Rick Rickelton, who was flying wing for Mackey, "We really ran into a terrific concentration of AA; fairly heavy stuff. I think I could have walked on it." Flak hit Lieutenant Frank Sistrunk's AD Skyraider from VF-54 while Sistrunk was bombing the bridge. His plane smoking badly, Sistrunk headed toward the safety of the east coast thirty air miles away. Halfway to the beach and at an altitude of about 2,000 feet, the Skyraider nosed into a steep dive and crashed. Sistrunk became Air Group 5's fourth casualty during the *Essex* cruise, following Franz, Smith, and Balch.

Armstrong, flying with John Carpenter, made a number of attacking runs that day. So many different versions of what happened next to Neil have been told over the years that it is difficult to sort out what really occurred.

The complete official version of Neil's incident was reported, doubtlessly with input from Armstrong and other division pilots, by Marshall Beebe to the commanding officer of the *Essex* just days after the incident.

Ensign Neil ARMSTRONG of VF-51 saved his own life with a piece of exceptionally fast headwork. He'd been attacking a target in very hilly country. While he was in his run he was hit by AA. He lost elevator control but in a fraction of a second he rolled in all the back tab he could get. His aircraft, well loaded with ordnance, came so close to the ground that he sheared off two feet of starboard wing on a power pole. By babying the stick and the trim tabs he was able to fly to friendly territory and to safety. The stall characteris-

tics of the plane were such that a landing speed of over 170 knots would be necessary without positive elevator control, which dictated the bailout. This was the first ejection seat bailout by an Air Group Five pilot. ARMSTRONG ejected himself, cleared the seat, opened his chute and landed near K-3 without further incident.

According to Beebe's report, Neil's emergency occurred "at approximately the same time" that Sistrunk was hit and killed.

Naval Aviation News, during wartime a "restricted" publication, capsuled Armstrong's close call in its December 1951 issue under the title "One Stub Wing":

The Panther jet Ens. Neil Armstrong was using to strafe trucks near Wonsan spun out of control and nosed downward, badly hit by AA. Armstrong struggled frantically with the controls. The plane leveled finally at about 20', struck a pole and tore off three feet of its right wing. The pilot nursed the crippled fighter back to 14,000 feet and headed for friendly territory. Radio out, landing gear jammed and rockets hung, Armstrong bailed out.

Safely back aboard the *Essex* two days later, Armstrong reportedly commented, "Twenty feet from Mother Earth at that speed is awful doggone low!"

In the 1960s, NASA publicists and news media reporting Armstrong's military background relied on "facts" presented in these two accounts. The superlative historian of military aviation Richard P. Hallion also cited them in his 1988 book *The Naval Air War in Korea:*

As an Essex *Panther strafed a column of trucks near Wonsan, flak knocked the jet into a spinning dive. In its cockpit, the young fighter pilot instinctively regained control over the hurtling plane, recovering into level flight a mere twenty feet off the ground. The Panther immediately collided with a telephone pole, clipping three feet from its right wing. Again the pilot managed to regain control, and he staggered back up to 14,000 feet, reaching friendly territory before ejecting safely. Two days later, Ensign Neil Armstrong returned to VF-51.*

According to Hallion, Armstrong displayed in this combat experience "the qualities of courage and skill that would lead to his selection as the commander of the first lunar landing mission in 1969."

Regrettably, some of the salient facts about Armstrong's flight of September 3, 1951, have been wrong from the start. Flying as Carpenter's wingman, he was not strafing a column of trucks; he was making a bomb run. Also, antiaircraft fire did not hit him, even though AA saturated the valley that day. Nor did Neil get blasted into some sort of pole. Rather, at approximately 350 miles per hour, Armstrong sliced through a cable, presumably a North Korean–devised booby trap for low-flying attack aircraft. And it was not two feet (according to Beebe) or three feet (according to *Naval Aviation News*) of Neil's right wing that got clipped off; closer to six feet was shorn. There was never any spinning out of control—that seems to have been an invention of *Naval Aviation News*, since Beebe had not mentioned it. Nor did Armstrong lose his radio or badly damage his landing gear. Other than those critical essentials, everything else written about Neil's combat incident was basically true. Certainly, the part about Armstrong's quick thinking was right on the mark.

Fortunately, Armstrong's Panther jet cut into the cable at about 500 feet, flying at an angle where it could aerodynamically compensate the loss of half a dozen feet of wing. Instantaneously, he thought about the loss of the small fuel tank at the tip of his right wing (the "tip tank"), plus the serious damage to his starboard aileron, the moveable control surface attached to the trailing edge of the wing.

Armstrong radioed his division head, John Carpenter. As Neil recollects, "I was having to carry a lot of aileron already, to keep the airplane in balance, and if I got a little too slow where I didn't have enough aileron, it was going to snap. I was going to lose control of the airplane." Major Carpenter concurred. The only real option for Neil was to eject.

A bad choice for jumping out was . . . anywhere over North Korea. Only a few American pilots had made it back from overland ejections. Neil explains, "Navy guys like to come down in the water; it was a soft landing" over the sea, patrolled by intrepid navy rescue helicopters.

Carpenter stayed with Armstrong until he ejected as planned in the vicinity of an airfield near Pohang, designated K-3, located far down the coast of South Korea and operated by the U.S. Marines. The term "punching out" does not do justice to the "kick in the butt" of the Panther's British-made Stanley Model 22G ejection seat, which was survivable at anything over 500 feet when not compromised by any sort of "sink rate." Armstrong's was Fighter Squadron 51's first-ever ejection-seat bailout.

The jump was also Armstrong's first. This fact contradicts VF-51's John Moore's *The Wrong Stuff,* which had Ernie Beauchamp assigning Neil the collateral squadron's duty of "survival officer." As such, Armstrong attended a briefing at the NAS El Centro's parachute school, then strapped on a chute, found a pilot who would take him up, and bailed out. Beauchamp, in Moore's words, "came out of the few hairs he had left and told Armstrong, 'I can't believe that you went ahead and jumped! You might get hurt, and we can't afford to have anyone injured.' " Allegedly, Neil replied, "But, sir, you told me to go find out about it, so I did!"

Moore told a great story. Unfortunately, his tale was one of mistaken identity. It was not Armstrong but Herb Graham who took his parachute instruction a step beyond that required.

Rather than the parachute itself, it was the winds aloft along the Korean coast that saved Armstrong's life. Neil "intended to come down in the water," but misjudging the wind, he floated inland and landed in a rice paddy. Aside from a cracked tailbone, Neil was virtually unhurt.

No sooner had Armstrong picked himself off the ground when a jeep drove up from K-3. Inside the jeep—Neil could barely believe his eyes—was one of his roommates from flight school, Goodell Warren. "Goodie" was now a marine lieutenant operating out of Pohang airfield.

Warren told Armstrong that the explosions he was hearing out beyond the coastline came from North Koreans laying mines in the bay. If Neil's parachute had stayed on course, he might very well have splashed down in the deadly minefield.

Late in the afternoon of September 4, Armstrong returned to the *Essex* aboard a "codfish"—for "carrier onboard delivery"—mail and personal transfer craft.

Ken Danneberg, VF-51's intelligence officer, remembers, "Naturally we had to rough him up a bit." As per ejection procedure, Armstrong had removed and dropped his helmet, which broke when it hit the ground. According to Danneberg, Neil "had that broken helmet in his hand and a smile on his face. We didn't say 'good to see you back, glad you're alive.' John Moore and I jumped right on him, 'You know, Neil, you're going to have to pay the government for that helmet.' " Kidding aside, everything that Armstrong had done "received a lot of favorable notice for his cool handling of the situation," Herb Graham remembers.

In letters home, Armstrong virtually never mentioned combat, and certainly not what happened to him that day. All he did was make a note in his logbook for September 3, 1951: "Bailed out over Pohang." Next to it he drew a little picture of an open parachute with a tiny figure of a man hanging from it. As for the airplane itself, Neil's F9F-2 (Bureau of Aeronautics

No. 125122) was the first Panther lost to Fighter Squadron 51. What happened to the crash remnants is unknown.

There was no celebration the night Armstrong returned to the *Essex*. Earlier that day, two of his squadron mates, James Ashford and Ross Bramwell, had been killed in action. Twenty-four-year-old Bramwell lost control of his aircraft after getting hit by enemy flak. Armstrong flew in the same division as the twenty-five-year-old Ashford and might have been in ops with him if not for his ejection the day before. During a reconnaissance mission in the region between Simp'yong and Yangdok, northwest of Wonsan, Ashford's jet, heavily loaded with ordnance, failed to pull out while making a rocket run on a truck, then flew into the ground and exploded. As one of his VF-51 mates thought at the time, "What a price to pay for a goddamn truck!"

"It was just the dumbest goddamn thing," fumed intelligence officer Ken Danneberg, "to take a ten-million-dollar airplane, and pilots in whom the government had invested a few million more, and send them down after incidental targets [to] get the living bejesus shot at them."

According to Beebe's combat action report, through September 4, 1951, "The Air Group had destroyed seven bridges, ninety railroad cars, twenty-five trucks, twenty-five oxcarts, two hundred and fifty troops, and damaged about twice as many of each, the price being the lives of five pilots, one aircrewman and ten aircraft." In his journal that night, Bob Kaps wrote: "Another bad day. This war is really hitting home. . . . Two damn fine guys lost and for what?" Rick Rickelton noted in his diary: "The worst part of it is the heartsick people who are left behind." On September 5, the entire task force took a day off from combat to replenish, giving them a chance to reflect.

"There was great concern among our senior officers and even some speculation whether the casualties might be sabotage," Armstrong remembers, "because some of the accidents were unexplained. Leaders were doing what leaders do: trying to figure out how to make the situation better. And my sense is, it did get better. We certainly didn't have the number of losses later that we had early. I don't know if inexperience or circumstance or what might account for all the early losses.

"They never missed an opportunity to shoot at you," Armstrong relates. "We saw all kinds of guns, all kinds of sizes, and some were radar-controlled and some were not. They had those long-barreled 85s that could reach up a long way. There was always a lot of concern about getting hit. I had a lot of bullet holes in the airplanes I flew, but usually got them back.

"If the target was particularly valuable," Armstrong recalls, "then they really put a lot of guns around it. They didn't have missiles in those days, fortunately. That would really have made life more complicated for us."

Armstrong's next flying came on September 10, a day when the *Essex* air group flew 101 sorties. Over the next nine days, Neil flew four combat air patrols, one photo escort (again to Songjin), and four armed reconnaissance missions. The recco on the tenth took him as far north as the Changjin (Chosin) Reservoir, where a British-owned power plant was a prime target, though the group would later learn of an agreement between London and Washington to keep the plant intact. Herb Graham has asserted, " 'Intelligence' seemed to spend more time telling us about targets that were off limits than they did giving us good targets to hit. It did seem, at times, that we were risking our lives fighting a war with our hands tied." When it came to target selection, Armstrong admits, "those were frustrations we lived with."

The biggest disaster of the entire *Essex* cruise happened not in the air but on the carrier's deck. At the end of a beautiful clear day on September 16, 1951, a F2H Banshee from VF-172 came in for an emergency landing. LTJG John K. Keller fought to bring his Banshee—left with limited aileron control and no flaps following a midair collision—home. At the head of his Panther division, Ernie Beauchamp had just entered the *Essex* landing pattern. The Skipper was turning crosswind for final approach when he heard Keller, "with a great deal of stress, maybe even panic in his voice," calling for a "straight in." Beauchamp put on power, picked up his wheels and flaps, and cleared the landing approach, as did the other three planes in his division, flown by Rostine, Kaps, and Gott.

A series of mistakes escalated into catastrophe. Still shaken by his plane's jolting collision over the enemy target, Keller, the son of a University of Michigan professor, forgot to lower his tailhook for landing. Somehow in the urgency of the moment—perhaps due to the plane's westward approach into the bright orange ball of the setting sun—the hook spotter and the LSO (William Chairs, a Naval Academy graduate) mistakenly thought Keller's hook was down. The oversight brought the eight-ton Banshee slamming into the deck at nearly 130 knots. Bouncing high into the air, the plane jumped all of the heavy crash barriers, then tumbled headlong into an array of aircraft just moved from the aft flight deck to the starboard catapult area to make room for the returning aircraft. Some of those pilots and plane captains had yet to exit their planes.

The mushrooming explosion of parked planes—some fully fueled with almost a thousand gallons of high-octane gas—was tremendous. Hersh

Gott, still aloft with Beauchamp's division, was checking off in preparation for landing when somebody radioed, "Jesus Christ, look at it burn!" The *Essex*'s forward flight deck was a ball of fire. The only choice for Beauchamp's division was to fly over and land on the *Boxer*, where they stayed overnight.

The consequences of the crash were obscene. Four men burned to death. Engulfed in the gaseous envelope of the flames, five others leaped into the ocean some seventy feet below, only to be gravely imperiled by burning aviation gasoline on the surface. A tractor shoved the offending Banshee overboard, with its dead young pilot still inside, and did the same to a few other burning airplanes. By the time the conflagration was extinguished several hours later, seven men had died. Sixteen were seriously injured. Eight jets in all had been turned to cinders. Fortunately, the Skyraiders, loaded as they were with fuel plus a 5,000-pound bomb load, were parked safely over to the other side.

As luck had it, Neil Armstrong was serving as the squadron duty officer that day. Rules prescribed that on the day he "had the duty," the SDO would not fly—as Armstrong did not on September 16—and that he would stay at his position in the ready room. Consequently, when the Banshee crash occurred, Armstrong did not see any of the fire and took no part in the firefighting activities.

Under Armstrong's direction, "I had just taxied a plane forward and was walking back down the flight deck," Rick Rickelton recorded in his diary that night. "This F2H jumped the barriers. I ducked under it as it went by and it crashed into the planes parked behind me. It immediately exploded. I started making tracks but got burned on the hands and neck although not bad." The Panther that Rickelton had taxied was one of those pushed over the side in an effort to slow down the fire.

Rickelton got off easy compared to senior VF-51 pilot John Moore, who volunteered to taxi one last Panther to spell the younger officers who had just sat down to dinner in the wardroom. The signalman waved frantically at Moore to park his jet on the very edge of the flight deck, starboard side, away from Keller's incoming Banshee. The shriek of the ship's crash whistle crescendoed as the Banshee bounced airborne and blasted into Moore, igniting his plane and knocking it onto the ship's catwalk. "The heat was horrible," Moore recalled. "I dived with all my might out of the cockpit and felt myself falling, still in this ball of fire."

No more than ten feet away, the huge gray hull of the ship sped by him at twenty knots. Hardly believing he was still alive, Moore instinctively pulled the toggle of his life jacket, noticing that his hands were badly burned. As soon as his Mae West vest inflated, Moore realized his miscalculation. He needed to swim underwater, not stay on top of it. Wave after wave of burning fuel swept over him, frying his skin, especially around the neck and face. Finally, a rescue helicopter from the *Essex* lifted him back on deck. Another whirlybird dispatched from the nearby *Boxer* retrieved other men overboard. To get Moore to the sick bay located far aft, they had to navigate his wire stretcher through a maze of parked airplanes and tie-down cables, shoving Moore's body underneath one plane at a time.

To treat Moore's wicked burns, a doctor applied Vaseline-coated gauze bandages over his entire body, leaving only narrow slits across his eyes and lips. The next day he was flown to a hospital in Japan, where he stayed for several weeks. Amazingly, following a rehabilitation in San Diego until early 1953, he rejoined the Screaming Eagles aboard the *Valley Forge,* as a division leader during its third and final Korean cruise.

Moore's burns were the most severe injuries suffered by a VF-51 aviator in the Banshee crash. According to CAG Beebe, "The flight deck personnel and squadron personnel nearest the crash made courageous efforts to aid the people injured by the initial explosion. Taking no heed of personal safety they disarmed and removed ordnance loads and moved aircraft out of the danger zone." Wade A. Barfield, the VF-51 plane captain for the aircraft taxied by Rick Rickelton, died, as did another VF-51 plane captain, Charles L. Harrell. The squadron also lost Earl K. Niefer, a well-liked and experienced crew chief. Three other members of the VF-51 crew were badly burned but survived. In his journal for that day, a woeful Bob Kaps wrote: "Essex hard luck reached a climax."

For the next three days, the men of the *Essex* mourned. With the loss of Armstrong's plane, the deaths of Ashford and Bramwell, the serious injuries to Moore, and the fiery destruction of four additional Panthers in the Banshee disaster, a demoralized Fighter Squadron 51 counted only nine serviceable aircraft, down from sixteen, and twenty-one pilots, down from twenty-four.

It was a somber *Essex* crew that gathered at 1400 for a memorial service while en route to Yokosuka on Thursday, September 20, 1951. The service honored the memory of the thirteen men in CVG-5 killed since the cruise began. Armstrong considered himself lucky. He survived his September 3 flight by the skin of his teeth. Furthermore, had he not served as squadron duty officer the day the Banshee crashed, Armstrong, the most junior pilot in Fighter Squadron 51, would by rank likely have been on the deck taxiing one of the Panthers.

For Armstrong, it turned out that ill Fate was not the hunter. Rather, it was almost as if the young flier was being safeguarded so as to become the grand prize of some extraordinary Destiny.

CHAPTER 10

The Ordeal of Eagles

Arriving at Yokosuka in the early evening of September 21, 1951, Neil Armstrong experienced his first overseas "rest and relaxation." For some of the men, R&R meant alcohol and women in the bars of Tokyo and Yokohama, but not for Armstrong or many of his fellow aviators in VF-51. The U.S. Navy had taken over a number of resort hotels on the east side of Japan, the most beautiful and luxurious of these "R&R camps" being the Fujiya Hotel, in the cool shadow of magnificent Mount Fuji (Fujiyama or Fujisan to the Japanese). Armstrong more than once enjoyed the wonderful food, drink, and service, all for very little charge. The resort even had a golf course caddied by elderly Japanese ladies who found "your ball" anywhere you hit it. A neophyte golfer, Neil discovered incentive enough to try the game, which he later came to love.

Sightseeing in and around Tokyo, Armstrong took many pictures that he later developed into slides. He especially admired the famous Daihatsu, or Great Buddha, in the ancient capital city of Kamakura.

Neil purchased two landscape paintings that hang to this day in his home. He designed the furnishings and garden in his Houston house to express the Japanese influence he found "unique and interesting." Equally inspiring as Eastern aesthetic were the Japanese people, so thoroughly villainized by World War II propaganda. According to his mother, Neil remarked upon his return home from the navy in 1952, "Never sell them short, because they are highly alert and have brilliant minds."

The *Essex* stayed in port for ten days. Sailors alternated shore leave with three or four days of shipboard preparations, with most of the men of VF-51 making time to visit John Moore in the hospital in Yokohama.

On October 1, 1951, the *Essex* headed to the northeast coast of Korea to rejoin Task Force 77. Armstrong flew ten times during this second combat period. October 5, 9, and 11 were routine air patrols, and three days

101

were photo escort missions, the flight on October 24 locating concealed targets in the Wonsan region that were then eradicated in a devastating strike.

To be fast, light, and versatile enough to protect the photo plane, the fighter escort was armed with only its 20-millimeter cannon. The photo plane itself flew straight, level, and unarmed (its Panther jet nose guns replaced with camera equipment) over the hottest spots in North Korea. "You'd get photos one day," Hersh Gott says, "and they'd show a lot of damage and the next day they would be fixed" by large labor gangs working under the cover of night. At the completion of one mission, a photo pilot vented his frustration to VF-51's Ernie Russell by jumping on the wing of Russell's plane and saying, "Let's go shoot something. Anything!"

On October 22, 1951, Armstrong's division found two trains for the ADs and Corsairs to destroy, and then itself went on to hit several supply points. On the twenty-sixth, his division hit bridges and busted rails in the region of Pukch'ong, over which he had flown photo escort twelve days earlier. On the thirtieth, Neil was part of an attack that flew quite far north, well above the 40th parallel, to the area between Tonch'on and Kapsan. It was during this flight that Armstrong may have gotten his first look at the Yalu River, beyond which lay China: "That wasn't our normal territory. We were better off busting bridges down in the middle of the country rather than being exposed to the dangers of being up close along the border." The day before, on the twenty-ninth, he flew about as far west as he ever got, during a fighter sweep in the area of Sinanju. North of Pyongyang at the mouth of the Ch'ongch'on River on the northwestern coast, here was MiG Alley. Bob Kaps reported "many anxious moments but no engagements" with MiGs.

Fighter Squadron 51 suffered nary a casualty during this second tour. Overall, the entire air group lost only three pilots and the aircraft that carried them, a great improvement over the initial weeks of the first operational period. During the month of October, the squadron expended 49,299 20-millimeter rounds and dropped 631 general-purpose 100-pound bombs. This represents a slight slowdown of combat—partly through lost days of flying due to bad weather—compared to the twenty-one squadron pilots' very first weeks in action when VF-51 fired 96,417 rounds, dropped 396 bombs, and shot off 626 rockets. Neil personally fired an estimated 7,000 rounds, dropped 48 bombs, and fired 30 rockets during the initial two-and-a-half-month combat period. During his twenty-six flights, of which nine were combat air patrols, he accumulated over forty-one and a half hours of air time.

Following another refurbishing of the ship in Yokosuka lasting from October 31 to November 12, 1951, the *Essex* and its air group returned to action, again off Wonsan Bay. With the onset of winter, carrier activities in the Sea of Japan turned miserable. With temperatures topping out in the low forties Fahrenheit and lots of rain, there were several days in November when no flying could be done. On November 26, Bob Kaps noted in his journal, "Seas have reached the roll-em-out-of-their-sacks stage. Don't know what keeps the planes from toppling over the side."

Armstrong flew only six times in November, two of them CAPs (November 19 and 29). His first combat flight during this third tour, which took place on the eighteenth, was a recco from Wonsan to Pukch'ong. During the mission, developing bad weather forced many aircraft to shift their targets from bridges to rail-cutting operations, which Neil pursued at Kilchu on the twenty-first and at Tonch'on on the twenty-seventh and again on the twenty-eighth. Both strikes involved busting up the coastal rail line that ran down from the Soviet border to Wonsan.

For bombing such precision targets as narrow-gauge North Korean railways the Panthers' symmetrical airframes provided a superior bombing platform to the props. Attacking in twenty-degree glides with dive brakes extended, the Panthers would release their bombs at 800 to 1,000 feet while flying at a speed of between 300 and 320 knots.

During November and December 1951, Fighter Squadron 51 dropped 672 general-purpose bombs, most of them 250-pounders. It also dropped 16 fragmentation bombs. In all during this two-month period, the Screaming Eagles unloaded onto North Korean targets a total of 135,560 pounds of bombs, well over twice as much weight as the squadron had dropped in the previous two and a half months since first arriving in Korea. During the last two months of the year, strafing remained the most effective weapon for VF-51, with 43,087 rounds fired, an average of 2,051 rounds per pilot.

"We would jettison armaments prior to returning," Armstrong explains, "and we tried to jettison on targets of opportunity." Wam Mackey declares, "I can't remember ever having come back with any ordnance."

In December 1951, prior to leaving again for refurbishing in Yokosuka on the thirteenth, Armstrong took to the air eight times. Three of the flights were photo escorts—to the Kowan-Yonghung region, just north of Wonsan (on the third), over Wonsan harbor (on the tenth), and to Tonch'on via Songjin (on the eleventh). One was an armed recco (on the first) to Yang-dok. The other four (December 2, 5, 6, and 9) were CAPs, but only three of them were uneventful.

On December 2, at high altitude and over water, the engine in Arm-strong's Panther jet quit on him. Flameouts were a serious problem plagu-ing gas-turbine engines. Neil's flameout was caused by a fuel control mechanism being stuck at a low-altitude setting due to salt corrosion. Ad-vancing the throttle at the higher altitudes required by CAP missions had injected too much fuel into the mix, extinguishing the jet's flame. Fortu-nately, the jet relit and Armstrong finished his flight without further trou-ble.

During its third tour in the Sea of Japan, VF-51 had some close calls but suffered no fatalities. On December 14 the *Essex* arrived in Yokosuka, where it would spend Christmas 1951. In a shipboard Christmas Eve pro-gram, Armstrong, Gott, Kaps, Sevilla, Jones, Hayward, and a few of VF-51's enlisted men, "had some makeshift choir robes and each singer had an electric candle or a flashlight made to look like a candle," Neil remem-bers. "We sang Christmas carols, primarily," then treated a number of Jap-anese orphans in the audience to candy and holiday fare.

Most men waited until Christmas Day to open presents from loved ones. On the day after Christmas, the ship bound for yet another combat tour in Korea, Rick Rickelton wrote in his diary: "I had a very merry Christmas considering I couldn't be home." The *Essex* then ran into "some of the heav-iest weather we have seen yet." In the face of winds of nearly 85 knots for a full day, the carrier made almost no progress. Considering the dangers and near-arctic conditions to be faced back on station off the North Korean coast, Bob Kaps asked in his journal, "Who's in a hurry?"

Essex's fourth tour proved to be by far the nastiest, most strenuous, and longest lasting of the entire cruise. For thirty-eight days from December 26, 1951, to February 1, 1952, the pilots of Air Group 5 flew a total of 2,070 sor-ties, an average of 86 per day (not counting the days when no flying was done due to replenishment or bad weather). Armstrong himself flew 23 missions during the period, with a total time in the air of over 35 hours. On only four days when the air group got into the air did Neil not fly.

Twenty-three cat shots, twenty-three carrier landings, all in one month, all in combat conditions: this was the experience of the young aviator from Wapakoneta, tightly bound in the MK III Anti-Exposure Suit that had been newly issued to him while in Yokosuka over Christmas. Relying on half-frozen catapults and bone-cold aircraft carrying icy guns and frosty bomb loads, Armstrong and his mates performed an unenviable job, day after day, over a remote enemy land.

On Friday evening, January 4, 1952, which ended the first week of the *Essex*'s fourth tour, the men of CVG-5 got happy news from CAG Beebe. At the end of January they were to leave for Yokosuka, spend two weeks in port, and then head back to "dear old Uncle Sam." Kaps wrote in his journal: "HAPPY DAY! Hardly seems possible but I'll buy it." Rickelton noted: "The word sounds pretty official and needless to say joy reigned in the bunkroom. I guess I won't tell the folks till I'm positive. I figure 20 more flying days till home. . . . We should be home by the end of February. There's good news tonight!!"

That was the last diary entry the twenty-three-year-old ensign from New Mexico made. Less than thirty-six hours later on an early-morning rail cut north of Wonsan, Rick Rickleton's Panther was hit by flak. A real tiger of a fighter pilot, Rickelton always went in as low as he could, maybe a little too low if his aircraft was heavily loaded with ordnance, as the division's planes were on that frigid January morn. When hit, the F9F nosedived right into the ground.

Kap's forlorn journal entry spoke for all of VF-51: "Rick shot down—plane exploded—no chance. Damn fine pilot and guy. Padre said mass for him, as he has done for them all. Hope the Lord can see through this mess, don't think I can. There has to be a reason for prolonging this business but I just don't see it."

With Rickelton gone, Wam Mackey's division needed another wingman. The job fell to Armstrong. For the rest of the cruise Neil flew primarily in Rickelton's spot with Mackey, Chet Cheshire, and Ken Kramer. Later in life, during a reunion of the Screaming Eagles, Armstrong would cheer and honor the brother and the nephews of Rick Rickelton by saying of Rick: "He was our fighter pilot."

Two days after Rickelton's death, Wam Mackey remembers, "The admiral came down to the wardroom and said, 'I've got some bad news: such and such a ship has had problems and is going to be delayed in relieving us, and we are going to have to come back one more time."

Sinking VF-51's morale ever lower, according to Armstrong, was "our general feeling that most Americans were not aware, or at least as aware, of what was going on in Korea as they had been in World War II. There was a substantial difference in the level of information and in their interest."

Limits on information also frustrated the aviators, who "questioned everything," Armstrong relates.

"There's just a lot more intensity to combat," Armstrong explains, "and more consequence to making a bad move. These guys tend to be people who like challenges and like to meet them head-on." As for the chance of dying, "It's a reality that you live with, and I guess you think the odds are with you if you keep your head and don't do anything foolish. . . . The naval aviators that I knew were determined to do a first-class job. . . . They were doing a job they thought was important." Some of Neil's mates looked at the situation more fatalistically. "For me, the adjustment to being a target was the roughest," explains Herb Graham. "I reached a reasonable peace of mind when I considered myself dead and stopped worrying about it."

Historians have debated the ultimate value of the interdiction program, though the constant pressure applied by airpower played a role in forcing the Communists to the peace table. "It didn't cut off the supplies," Armstrong relates, "but I'm sure the harassment had an enormous effect."

From the beginning of the war, bridges were principal targets in the interdiction campaign. According to official Pentagon wartime statistics, navy planes destroyed 2,005 North Korean bridges out of a total of 2,832 that U.S. military forces destroyed in all.

Over time the navy learned—at great cost—that the key to effective bridge strikes was coordinating the props and the jets into a single unified and well-timed assault. Marshall Beebe and the squadron commanders of Air Group 5 hatched the basic plan on the *Essex* in the latter months of 1951. Jets, with their higher and steeper "drop-down approach" to a target and their faster escape speed, had a significantly better chance of penetrating a bridge's defenses. Yet the jets were not the best instruments for actually taking out a bridge. That took 2,000-pound bombs, which jets could not carry. The job of the jets was to quell the antiaircraft fire. Then came the Corsairs, which also bombed and strafed the AA positions, followed finally by the Skyraiders deploying the heavy ordnance. Typically, at least twenty-four aircraft would be involved in a major bridge strike: eight jets, eight Corsairs, and eight Skyraiders.

"We [in the Panthers] wanted to hit them right before the ADs were ready to drop their bombs," Hersh Gott explains, "so that it would keep their gunners down. When they saw us start our dives, they cleared out of those gun emplacements. I sure would have if I'd been a gunner down there."

The successful new tactic, adapted by Beauchamp from air strikes in World War II, was quickly adopted throughout Task Force 77, with one alteration. To prevent the dust created by the jets' airbursts from concealing the props' bomb targets, the air groups directed the jets to move their suppression points of aim farther from the bridges.

Though Armstrong flew flak suppression on his fair share of bridge strikes, the only specific notation in his logbook came on January 8, 1952, two days after Rickelton's death, when CVG-5 destroyed two bridges. Whether Neil flew as part of the attack on "The Bridges at Toko-Ri" cannot truly be answered, because the events depicted in James A. Michener's 1953 novel by that title (made the following year into a Hollywood movie starring William Holden, Mickey Rooney, and Grace Kelly) were highly fictionalized.

Armstrong recalls that Michener, just off a Pulitzer Prize for his first book, *Tales of the South Pacific,* was a guest on the *Essex* during the last months of 1951. Himself a navy veteran of World War II, Michener was writing a series of articles on the naval air war for *The Saturday Evening Post.* "I think he went on two or three tours, at four or five weeks at a crack," Neil recalls. "He would just sit around the wardroom in the evening or in the ready room in the daytime and listen to guys tell the actual stories. He didn't ask questions much or anything; he just kind of absorbed it all." It was here, while on Neil's ship, that Michener began to think about writing a book that became *The Bridges at Toko-Ri.*

"So most of the things that happened in the book . . . were actual events," Armstrong recounts. "I thought *The Bridges at Toko-Ri* was an excellent representation of the kinds of flying that we were doing there. It was identical, same kind of aircraft and the same class carrier."

While living aboard the *Essex,* Michener interviewed Ernie Beauchamp two or three times. Marshall Beebe, to whom Michener dedicated his book, cameoed in the film's opening scene as a pilot calling in a downed pilot report. The rescue helicopter pilot (played in the movie by Mickey Rooney) was at least partly based on one or more incidents involving VF-51's colorful landing signal officer, "Dog" Fannon.

Over the years, a number of people have compared Michener's novel to the historical record. What most have found are recognizable elements of at least four actual missions in the Toko-Ri story.* Armstrong does not speculate on whether he flew on any of the four. All he has ever said is that "I flew into equally difficult places."

Perhaps for reasons of better storytelling, Michener did not accurately present the role of the jets in the coordinated strikes. In the book, Michener disregarded the jets' technical lack of bomb capacity and had the jets bombing the bridges.

Although the new tactics lessened air group casualties, there was no way to go after so many well-defended targets without losing some men and machines. On January 6, 1951, Rick Rickleton died. That same day Lieutenant Harold J. Zenner of VF-54 lost an eye when fragments of metal from an AA shell and small pieces of Plexiglas from his own canopy hit him in the face. On the ninth, Ensign Raymond G. "Gene" Kelly, also of VF-54, was fatally hit by AA fire following a bombing run on a bridge. On the eleventh, yet another pilot from VF-54, Joseph H. Gollner, crashed into the sea after what seemed to be a normal takeoff. On the nineteenth, a VF-172 Banshee flown by air force major Francis N. McCollon was hit by antiaircraft fire during a strafing run, then crashed and burned.

But the death that hit Armstrong and the rest of the men of VF-51 by far

---

* On January 3, 1951, divisions of VF-51 flew flak suppression in a concerted attack against heavy gun emplacements protecting a trestle-type railway bridge near Yangdok, west of Wonsan in Green Six. Armstrong was flying CAP that day, but Wam Mackey's division (Cheshire, Rickelton, and Kramer) was involved, and Mackey remembers the flak being so heavy over the target that "it looked like someone had pulled a circus tent open and all these balloons [of antiaircraft fire] were coming up out of it." Mackey thought to himself, "Good God! Please say they [the ADs following behind] got it [the bridge] on the first pass!" (WAM to author, Sept. 21, 2002, pp. 22–23). Unfortunately, they did not, "so we had to rendezvous and come back and do it a second time." Yet not a single plane was lost.

On January 5, Armstrong was again assigned to CAP. The targets were near the town of Potan, northeast of Pyongyang. A January 8 strike destroyed two bridges, and Neil participated in it as part of Carpenter's division. So did Bob Kaps as part of Beauchamp's. In his journal that night, Kaps noted: "Flew FLAK suppression for drop strike. They [the AD pilots] did a good job. Don't envy any of them" (Kaps journal, Jan. 8, 1952). This particular strike occurred the same day that the squadron heard it would be staying in the Korean theater until March.

Yet another coordinated bridge attack took out four more bridges in the region around Potan on January 18. It was another day that Neil did not fly. The last big coordinated effort of the fourth tour occurred on January 23. It involved two VF-51 divisions, Mackey's and Wenzell's. On that day Armstrong flew a photo escort mission over Tonchon. Locating a number of railway locomotives sitting in a marshaling yard, his mission resulted in two of the locomotives being destroyed.

the hardest, after Rick Rickleton's, was that of another one of their own, LTJG Leonard R. Cheshire, on January 26, 1951.

Like Rickelton, Cheshire was from New Mexico—Albuquerque, to be exact. So impressed was division leader Wam Mackey with the two young men that he thought at the time, "If everybody from New Mexico was like those two boys, I'm going to move to New Mexico." A tall, thin, angular man with dark brown hair, Cheshire had been married to Dorothy just before he left for Korea. After the war was over, Chet planned to return to the Land of Enchantment and become a teacher.

In a cubicle in the junior officers' bunkroom (an area the senior officers referred to as "Boys' Town"), Armstrong and Cheshire slept right across the aisle from each other, on lower bunks. The two men—the squadron's youngest member and the other the squadron's oldest junior officer—became close friends. "In the combat environment," Neil explains, "you welcome lighthearted conversation that takes your mind away from the realities of the war around you. But we also talked a great deal about the serious side of life: philosophy, theology, history, et cetera. Chet was a very thoughtful person, and I learned a great deal from listening to his perspectives on those issues." Both Neil and Cheshire also spent time reading books. In the evenings, Cheshire often read out loud while the others, in the words of Hal Schwan, "would sit around and listen almost like a bunch of little kids." In the first weeks of January 1952, Chet was well into a reading of *The Caine Mutiny,* a recent bestseller by novelist Herman Wouk.

On Saturday, January 26, 1951, Mackey's division was making its second run on a camouflaged train sitting in the Kowan area, just adjacent to Wonsan Bay, when Cheshire's plane was hit by AA. According to Ken Kramer, Cheshire's wingman, "We were in a racetrack pattern, which allowed us to keep each other in sight while we made individual dives on the target. Chet had just completed his dive and I was rolling into my dive behind him when he got hit." At that instant, Cheshire radioed urgently to Mackey, "Wam, I'm hit, and I'm hit bad!"

Mackey called Kramer to "get up there fast" because Kramer was closest. Already heading that way at 100 percent power, Kramer could see Cheshire's plane in flames originating right behind the cockpit, where the plane's 1,000-gallon tank of high-octane fuel was located. Gaining a little altitude, Cheshire blew off his canopy in what appeared to be preparations for ejection. But he did not eject. Instead, he turned toward Wonsan harbor and brought his plane down as though he was going in for a water landing. Kramer, who was nearest the flaming airplane, called Cheshire several times to eject, but Chet never answered. "By this time," Kramer remembers, "I was flying right off his starboard side with a clear view of his cockpit and he never moved. I believe he was already dead at this point."

As Armstrong tells it, "It was clear he was going to ditch, but for some unknown reason, just before ditching, at a very low altitude he ejected—too low for his parachute to open. He hit the water, but I could not see that clearly from my position. When we got in a good viewing position, I thought he was on the surface. By the time the rescue helicopter arrived, however, he was nowhere to be seen."

It is Kramer's view that Cheshire's ejection seat went off, not because Chet was still alive to trigger it, but because the intense fire engulfing his cockpit set it off. Perhaps Cheshire had tried to eject back when he blew the canopy. Powered by a 75-millimeter shell, the cartridge fired the same type of ejection seat that had launched Armstrong to safety from his damaged Panther back in September 1951. This time it must have misfired, then ignited later when Chet's plane was gliding in just above the water.

In his journal, Bob Kaps recorded the tragic news in words that mirrored what Armstrong and everyone else in VF-51 so deeply felt: "It happened again today. Chet this time. Hit and burning—bailed out too low in Wonsan Bay. Just don't see the justice of it all. Chet, of all people. Poor Dorothy— what words could possibly explain. He had so much to live for. Heaven help this world of ours on judgment day."

That evening over the ship's PA system, Chaplain J. J. Buzek said a prayer, as he always did, for the men who lost their lives or had been reported as missing in action: "O God, we humbly beseech thee for the soul of the pilot, our shipmate, Leonard Cheshire, who died this day. Deliver him not into the hands of the enemy, but command that he may be received by the holy angels and conducted into paradise. God bless you all, men." Since the ship had left Hawaii for Korea back in August 1951, Chaplain Buzek had said this prayer for Marshall Beebe's men twenty-eight times.

James A. Michener wrote poignantly (but also incorrectly) about Cheshire's death in an article entitled "The Forgotten Heroes of Korea," which appeared on May 10, 1952, in *The Saturday Evening Post*. It is Armstrong's belief that Michener used several stories derived from the life of Chet Cheshire in *The Bridges at Toko-Ri* as the basis for the novel's doomed hero, Lieutenant Harry Brubaker, who was also a married, thoughtful, older man from a western state. It is little wonder that Michener's book remains one of Neil's favorites. And little wonder that Neil also eventually finished reading Wouk's *The Caine Mutiny,* to himself, though it took him many months before he had the heart to pick up reading where his good friend Leonard R. Cheshire had left off.

At 1330 hours on February 1, 1952, the *Essex* left Task Force 77 for Yokosuka, ending tour number four after thirty-seven grueling days out of port. Bob Kaps's journal entry spoke for everyone: "Happy day. . . . Sure glad to have that one over." Flying well over 2,000 sorties during that stretch (441 of them done by VF-51), Air Group 5 had fired nearly 400,000 rounds of ammunition, dropped almost 10,000 bombs, shot off approximately 750 rockets (the majority by the Banshees), and hit the enemy with just under 3,000 pounds of napalm. This resulted in 1,374 railroad track cuts, the destruction of 34 bridges and damage to 47 more, along with a multitude of damaged or destroyed war matériel and infrastructure. In accomplishing these attacks, CVG-5 lost five men, two of them from VF-51, and the services of more than a dozen aircraft.

Armstrong's fifth and final tour of combat started on February 18, 1952. Mercifully, it lasted only two weeks. Neil was in the air every one of the days that flying was done, for a total of thirteen flights. The first, on February 20, involved gunnery training, and six were CAPs. The others were armed reccos. On the morning of the twenty-fifth, Neil finished the work of the night hecklers in a morning attack that destroyed both locomotives and forty cars on a long train.

The weather stayed cold, overcast, with rough seas. On the twenty-first, the day Armstrong flew a recco to Yonghung, a Corsair pilot from VF-53, LTJG Francis G. Gergen, crashed while escorting a battle-damaged AD through a heavy snowstorm to a friendly field. It was the only death experienced by the entire air group during this final tour.

Armstrong says of the VF-51 aviators: "If they had that choice, on most days they'd say, 'I ought to go fly, go face those guns again. I'd rather do that than stay here and read.' Because they were that kind of people. They enjoyed the flying" and kept close track of how many missions they had flown, how many cat shots they had made, how many carrier landings achieved, and so forth, not wanting the other guys to get ahead of them. To the very last days of the cruise, as Hal Schwan explains, "It wasn't a question of how difficult it was to fly so many missions; rather, it was more a question of trying to get out on more missions than you were scheduled." The engineer in Armstrong regarded wartime survival primarily in terms of odds and probabilities.

Armstrong's last flight in the Korean War came on March 5, 1952. On that day, the pilots of VF-51 transferred their flyable planes to the *Valley Forge*. The Panther jet that Neil flew was U.S. Navy Bureau of Aeronautics No. 125123, a plane he had flown only twice before (photo escort to Songjin on September 17 and recco escort to Wonsan and Pu-Chong on November 18). He flew BuAer Nos. 125132 and 125100 ten times and nine times, respectively. Overall, he flew every one of VF-51's F9Fs at least once, except the few that were lost early.

Armstrong flew a total of seventy-eight missions. Thirty of them were CAP, fifteen were photo escort, and one was for gunnery training. In the other thirty-two, he flew recco, fighter sweeps, rail cuts, and flak suppression. In all, Neil was in the air for over 121 hours. Over a third of that time came in the extraordinarily tough month of January 1952.

On March 11, 1952, after a few days in Japan, the *Essex* departed for Hawaii and from there stateside—or, as Bob Kaps called it, to "the land of dreams." Finally on March 25 came the glorious sight of the California shoreline. "Seems years since we left this very dock," Kaps wrote in his journal. "May the Lord will that none will have to go through it again."

As did his fellow aviators, Armstrong arrived home with a chest full of war medals. Neil typically downplayed his own achievements, saying, "They handed out medals there like gold stars at Sunday school." His first award, the Air Medal, came in recognition of his first twenty combat flights; his second, a Gold Star, in recognition of his next twenty. With his mates, Neil also received the Korean Service Medal and Engagement Star. As with most military honors and recognitions, Neil may have most appreciated his first, the Air Medal, which covered the series of flights that included his ejection over Pohang. This citation read:

> *For distinguishing himself by meritorious achievement in aerial flight as a pilot of a jet fighter in Fighter Squadron FIFTY ONE, attached to the U.S.S. ESSEX, in attacks on hostile North Korean and Chinese Communist forces. During the period from 21 August 1951 to 9 October 1951, in the face of grave hazards, Ensign Armstrong participated in twenty flights including strikes on transportation and lines of communication at HAMHUNG, MAJON-NI, PUKCHONG, and SONGJIN. He performed his assigned*

missions with skill and courage. His devotion to duty was at all times in keeping with the highest traditions of the United States Naval Service.

The person who most influenced Armstrong on the *Essex* cruise was, undoubtedly, Ernie Beauchamp. Neil developed "enormous respect" for the Skipper. "I thought he was a superior leader," Armstrong states. "I learned from our skipper that it's not how you look; it's how you perform." If Beauchamp's eyes had not gone bad, he most likely would have become an admiral. But after losing his wings in the late 1950s for failing to pass an annual eye exam, Beauchamp left the navy for McDonnell Aircraft Corporation.

In naval aviation, "Almost everything we did, we did as teams," Neil emphasizes. "Eight eyes [per four-pilot team] are better than two in looking for trouble and looking for targets." "We just seemed to click together very well," explains Hal Schwan. "We had the closest and best operating organization imaginable. All of the people were top-notch people. That was really all you thought about." And still do. Most of its members have kept in touch for the past fifty-plus years.

The Screaming Eagles was an amazing group of professionals. The early American astronauts are hardly more impressive. Eight members of VF-51 flew more than one hundred combat missions. One became a Blue Angel, the navy's stellar flight-exhibition team. Two became captains. Another became the navy's top admiral and chief of naval operations (CNO). Five became test pilots. Three were inducted into the Test Pilot Hall of Fame. The Golden Eagles, an elite association of naval aviation pioneers limited to 200 active members, at one time counted five men from VF-51 (Armstrong, Beauchamp, Hayward, Mackey, and Moore), perhaps the most ever from any one squadron. One can only imagine what sort of achievements might have been made by their other mates, forever young, who died over half a century ago in battle: Ashford, Bramwell, Rickelton, and Cheshire. From all of them, Armstrong learned a quiet, dignified pride.

Just under 34,000 Americans were killed in the Korean War, with over 23,500 of them dying in action. An additional 10,000 were wounded, and 7,000 became prisoners of war. The great majority of the casualties were U.S. Marines or soldiers in the U.S. Army. Compared to what the infantry went through in the ground war, the experiences of the men in the air—navy, marines, and air force—may seem comparatively inconsequential. Fewer than 500 navy personnel died in the war—492 to be exact. Twenty-seven of them fell during the *Essex* cruise.

At one point in Michener's novel *The Bridges at Toko-Ri,* the admiral in command of Task Force 77 tells the doomed jet aviator, the fictional Harry Brubaker, "All through history free men have had to fight the wrong war in the wrong place. But that's the one they're stuck with." Even more poignantly, Michener's book concludes with the admiral looking out over the deck of his aircraft carrier, sadly pondering the young aviator's death in combat and asking, "Where do we get such men?"

PART FOUR

THE REAL RIGHT STUFF

Aeroplane testing . . . demands for satisfactory results the highest training. It occupies no special place by virtue of this—it merely comes into line with the rest of engineering. Now, one can learn to fly in a month . . . but an engineer's training requires years. It is evidently necessary, therefore, that engineers—men with scientific training and trained to observe accurately, to criticize fairly, to think logically—should become pilots, in order that the development of aeroplanes may proceed at the rate at which it must proceed if we are to hold that place in the air to which we lay claim—the highest.

—CAPTAIN WILLIAM S. FARREN, BRITISH
ROYAL AIRCRAFT FACTORY, 1917

In the end the accuracy of the results really depends upon the flyer, who must be prepared to exercise a care and patience unnecessary in ordinary flying. Get careful flyers whose judgment and reliability you can trust and your task is comparatively easy; get careless flyers and it is impossible.

—CAPTAIN HENRY T. TIZARD, TESTING SQUADRON
OF THE BRITISH ROYAL FLYING CORPS, 1917

CHAPTER 11

The Research Pilot

One evening in a bull session aboard the *Essex* in 1951, Neil Armstrong told his bunkmates about the research of Dr. Robert Goddard, America's leading rocket pioneer and founder of the American Rocket Society. During his freshman year at Purdue, Armstrong had joined both the American Rocket Society (ARS) and the Institute of Aeronautical Sciences (IAS), two organizations that would later merge to become the predominant aerospace engineering society, the American Institute of Aeronautics and Astronautics (AIAA). Though neither Goddard nor the American Rocket Society registered with Neil's fellow junior officers, what resonated was Neil's "amazingly prophetic statement" that "he would like to be the first man on the Moon."

Unlike the apocryphal stories told by Wapakonetans Jacob Zint and John Crites—the truthfulness of which Armstrong categorically denies—Neil qualifies his alleged statement to his VF-51 mates. "I think Wernher von Braun's book *Conquest of the Moon* did not come out until [1953]. I was interested in spaceflight but did not believe it would occur in my lifetime. Von Braun's book proposed that if all the countries of Earth combined their resources, humans could go to the Moon by the year 1978. So I very much doubt that I made the statement."

Armstrong's contract with the navy expired three years from the time he started his flight training. That meant he should have been free to return to college in February 1952. However, Fighter Squadron 51 was still in combat: "My options were either to extend my time in the service or swim home, so I extended." On February 1, 1952, while he was still serving aboard the *Essex,* the navy terminated his regular commission and reappointed him as an ensign in the U.S. Naval Reserve.

Arriving back in the States with his shipmates on March 25, 1952, Neil spent the next five months based ashore in Southern California ferrying aircraft in and out of Naval Air Station San Diego for Air Transport Squadron 32. His final fitness report, signed by VR-32's commanding officer C. B. Cottingham, read: "ENS Armstrong. . . . is willing to learn and has repeatedly demonstrated his willingness, initiative, and industry. With broader experience in administrative responsibilities he should develop his talents as an officer and become of great value to the naval service. He presents a fine military bearing, and is recommended for promotion when due."

Armstrong left the navy on August 23, 1952, in the month of his twenty-second birthday. He received $442.70 in separation pay and $157.20 in travel allowance. Promoted to lieutenant junior grade in May 1953, he remained in the U.S. Naval Reserve until he resigned his commission on October 21, 1960, all the while remaining "physically qualified for all duty with waiver," the waiver being a "trick knee" sustained in a college boxing bout.

Back in school at Purdue, Neil flew regularly with Naval Reserve Aviation Squadron 724 at NAS Glenview, outside Chicago, under the jurisdiction of the Ninth Naval District based at Great Lakes, Illinois. LCDR Leonard R. Kozlowski, the commanding officer of VF-724, filed Armstrong's fitness report dated June 5, 1954: "LTJG Armstrong has . . . already displayed a high degree of interest and initiative." Six months later (and one month after Neil graduated from Purdue), Kozlowski reported: Neil "has frequently demonstrated outstanding performance in providing useful suggestions regarding Squadron tactics." Later reports called Neil "an extremely efficient pilot" and "an outstandingly proficient Naval Aviator." As a test pilot for the National Advisory Committee for Aeronautics at Edwards Air Force Base at Muroc Dry Lake, northeast of Los Angeles, Neil did his reserve flying with VF-773 at NAS Las Alamitos, near Long Beach. But his boss at Edwards, Joseph Vensel, put a stop to Neil's committing his time to additional flying, prompting LCDR A. A. Johnson to note in Neil's final fitness report: "This officer has been a good squadron officer and pilot. He has the ability to accept greater responsibility in the Naval Reserve Program, and it is regrettable that his civilian employment forced him to terminate his activities with this unit."

Graduating from Purdue in January 1955, Armstrong entertained several tempting options for employment. He could have stayed in the navy. Interviews with Trans-World Airlines (TWA) and Douglas Aircraft Company led to job opportunities. Neil also briefly considered graduate work in aeronautical engineering.

Seeking a position in the small fraternity of engineering test pilots in early 1955, Armstrong could have gone one of two ways. If he had taken a job offered by Douglas or a competing firm, he could have become a *production test pilot.* As such Neil would have test-flown each new aircraft of a given type as it rolled off the production line to demonstrate manufacture according to contract specifications.

His second option, and the one he took, was to become an *experimental test pilot,* as epitomized by the fledgling Society of Experimental Test Pilots, committing in 1955 "to assist in the development of superior aircraft." Elite test pilots most often trained at either the U.S. Air Force school at Edwards Air Force Base in the Mojave Desert of California, or the U.S. Navy school at the Patuxent River Naval Air Station in Maryland, where Armstrong spent the summer between the semesters of his senior year in college helping to supervise carrier landing qualification tests and to analyze the performance of the navy's new steam catapults. The SETP would welcome Neil as a charter member and later elect him one of its distinguished Fellows.

The position that most interested Armstrong was that of *research pilot.* A special class of experimental test pilot, the research pilot strove to advance the science and technology of flight across a broad front. Employment opportunities existed primarily at private research organizations or the federal government, most prominently the National Advisory Committee for Aeronautics. From boyhood, Armstrong had regularly followed the results of ongoing NACA research in *Aviation Week* and other aviation magazines, and NACA reports were part of the curriculum in his aeronautical engineering classes at Purdue.

In the summer before his last semester, Armstrong presented his credentials to the NACA. Specifically, he applied to be a test pilot at the NACA's High-Speed Flight Station at Edwards AFB, the facility where the X-planes were being flown. As Edwards had no openings, the NACA, unbeknownst to Armstrong, circulated his application to all of its research centers. Neil's recollection is that an engineer from the NACA's Lewis Flight Propulsion Laboratory in Cleveland, Ohio, by the name of Isadore Irving Pinkel "asked if he could come down and talk with me." I. I. Pinkel headed the physics division at Lewis; Pinkel's brother, Benjamin, was in charge of the thermodynamics research division. Sometime during the fall of 1954, brother Irving interviewed Neil at Purdue's Phi Delta Theta house. Pinkel could not offer Armstrong much money, but rather promised him the excitement and personal satisfaction inherent in the world of aeronautical research.

Armstrong accepted the post at Lewis laboratory. It did not hurt that the job kept him in Ohio, because by this time Neil was seriously considering marrying his college sweetheart, Janet Shearon, who herself was a midwestern girl, from suburban Chicago.

Assigned originally to the lab's Free-Flight Propulsion Section, Armstrong's official job title was Aeronautical Research Pilot, responsible, as he noted on a naval reserve questionnaire, for "Piloting of aircraft for research projects and for transportation, and engineering in free flight rocket missile section." His first test flight at Lewis came on March 1, 1955. For civil service purposes, the NACA labeled Armstrong a "research scientist." Yet, as with most NACA employees, his work served the organization's legislated mission, "the scientific study of the problems of flight, with a view to their practical solutions."

The chief test pilot at Lewis was William V. "Eb" Gough Jr. Like Armstrong, Eb Gough had earned an engineering degree (Kansas State University, 1937) and became a naval aviator facing Japanese Zeroes in World War II. Reaching the rank of lieutenant commander, Gough was the fourth navy pilot ever to qualify in helicopters, the thirty-fifth to qualify in jets. When the war ended, Gough became a test pilot for the NACA.

Gough's older brother by ten years, Melvin N. Gough (born 1906), epitomized the NACA research pilot. In 1926, the twenty-year-old Johns Hopkins–trained engineer struggled to convince one of NACA Langley's senior test pilots of some results he had obtained in the lab's new Propeller Research Tunnel, then the world's largest. The pilot stared down the young engineer, "Son, have you ever flown an airplane?" According to Gough, "I started taking ground school instruction the next year."

Mel Gough trained at the navy's flight school in Pensacola. He returned in the spring of 1929 to NACA Langley as a fully qualified naval aviator, proving the adage that it was much easier to make a pilot out of an engineer than it was to make an engineer out of a pilot. As chief, since 1943, of Langley's Flight Research Division, Mel Gough directed a team of a half dozen talented engineer-pilot hybrids, including John P. "Jack" Reeder, Robert A. Champine, John M. Elliot, John A. Harper, and James V. Whitten. Still today, Neil regards Reeder as "the best test pilot I ever knew."

When Armstrong joined the NACA in February 1955, most of its research pilots were trained engineers. Yet as most of the NACA's flight research took place at Langley, at the High-Speed Flight Station colocated at Edwards Air Force Base, or at the Ames Aeronautical Laboratory in Northern California, outside of San Francisco, at Lewis Armstrong numbered one of just four test pilots, with Eb Gough, William Swann, and Joseph S.

Algranti, future chief of the Aircraft Operations Division at the Manned Spacecraft Center in Houston.

Armstrong stayed at Lewis for less than five months, investigating new anti-icing systems for aircraft, for many years a special focus of Lewis laboratory. More significant to Armstrong's future proved his work at Lewis in his very first space-related flight program, studying high Mach number heat transfer.

In early tests, various air-launched models descended at speeds reaching Mach 1.8. On March 17, 1953, a T40 rocket air-launched by a Lewis test pilot achieved the hypersonic speed of Mach 5.18, the first time that the "NACA flew successfully an instrumented vehicle to greater than Mach 5."

On May 6, 1955, Algranti and Armstrong flew the forty-fifth test in this series. The pilots steered their P-82, North American's Twin Mustang, over the Atlantic Ocean beyond the NACA's Pilotless Aircraft Research Station at Wallops Island, off Virginia's Eastern Shore. Attached to the belly of the P-82 was a solid-rocket model designated ERM-5. A conventional ballistic shape with a sharp nose, slender body, and tail fins, the ERM-5 was equipped with a T-40RKT rocket motor that had been developed by the Jet Propulsion Laboratory in Pasadena. Reaching the optimum altitude, Algranti released the model, designed to test heat transfer characteristics and boundary-layer transition at high Reynolds numbers.* The ERM-5 reached a hypersonic speed of Mach 5.02 and an acceleration rate of 34 g.†

Armstrong "did a lot of analyzing data; designing components for advanced versions of the rockets, and doing calculations, and drawings for them." The proactive identity of the engineering test pilot that was fostered by the NACA—and by its successor, NASA—fit Armstrong perfectly. Neil has always felt that even though the NACA position was the lowest-paying job he was offered coming out of college, "it was the right one."

"The only product of the NACA was research reports and papers," Neil has explained. "So when you prepared something for publication, you had to face the technical and grammatical 'Inquisition.'. . . The system was so precise, so demanding. It assured that anything that was graphical would

---

* A key parameter in aerodynamics, Reynolds numbers—named after the nineteenth-century English scientist Osborne Reynolds—are a nondimensional parameter representing the ratio of the momentum forces to the viscous forces about a body in a fluid flow. Generally speaking, the higher the Reynolds number, the more realistic are the results of any model tests to actual full-scale performance.

† "G" (g) is the unit of measurement for bodies undergoing acceleration that is equal to the acceleration of gravity—approximately 32.2 feet per second at sea level.

be readable and understandable, and if it were to be projected on to a screen, there wouldn't be any letters that were too small to read by the audience. They [female editorial authorities trained as English teachers or librarians] just went into that kind of detail. . . . That is what NASA needs today."

Neil's last test flight in Cleveland occurred on June 30, 1955. A week or so earlier, Abe Silverstein, Lewis's deputy director, had called. "I walked over to his office," Armstrong recalls, "and he said he had gotten a letter from Edwards and would I still like to transfer out there. I would have been very pleased to continue at Lewis if that was the only thing available to me." But Edwards was a test pilot's Shangri-La, the place where the sound barrier had been broken, and where the newest and most revolutionary experimental aircraft—the X-1A, X-1E, X-3, X-5, Douglas D-558-2, YRF-84F, F-100A, and YF-102—were being piloted to speeds of Mach 2 and beyond.

In early July 1955, after a brief visit with his family in Wapakoneta, Armstrong took off in his car for Southern California. Cross-country automobile trips were not new to Neil. When he returned from Korea, he still did not own a car. To get back home to Ohio, he rode with VF-51 mate and Wisconsin native Hal Schwan. According to Schwan, "One of us would drive and the other one sleep, and we would just keep pounding along—San Diego to Chicago in less than forty-eight hours."

On that earlier military leave in Wapak, Neil had purchased his first car, a brand-new 1952 Oldsmobile, the same make his father then owned. That two-door Olds 88 cost him just over $2,000 cash. Ken Kramer remembers Neil's effort, long before the popularity of vanity license plates, to secure his initials "NAA." The closest Neil got was Ohio plate "N4A." "We all expected him to use a black marker and extend the slanted line in the '4,' " Kramer jokes, "but he never did." Dean Armstrong had come out to California in the summer of 1952 following Neil's return from Korea. The brothers took the new Olds sightseeing from Mexico to Canada before heading home. They visited ten national parks, mostly camping out, and hiked to the bottom of the Grand Canyon.

So it was really Neil's fourth cross-country automobile trip that took him to his new job at Edwards in July 1955. On the way Armstrong planned to make one important stop. That was in Wisconsin, to visit his wife-to-be, Janet Shearon.

CHAPTER 12

Above the High Desert

Gazing northward on a clear day from her little cabin's 5,000-foot-high perch upon the side of the San Gabriel Mountains that separates the Antelope Valley from Los Angeles, Janet Armstrong could see for 150 miles. Far to the northwest, she perused the Tehachapi Mountains, tracing a spectacular pass from the Mojave Desert floor to the fertile green fields of California's central San Joaquin Valley. To the northeast lay granite buttes amid huge sandscapes, such distinguishable western landmarks as Saddleback and Piute. Though the harsh summer sun baked the land an ugly brown, in the springtime, after a wet winter, the entire valley bloomed into a vast garden rainbow.

Between 1905 and 1913, the City of Los Angeles, at a cost of $23 million (the equivalent of some $430 million today), built a 223-mile aqueduct (later a landmark along Armstrong's daily commute to Edwards). In the early 1920s, the state paved the valley's first road, the Sierra Highway. In 1925, an enormous deposit of anhydrous sodium borate, useful in the manufacture of glass and ceramics, was discovered in the tiny town of Boron, on the edge of one of the valley's largest dry lakes, the flattest of all the world's geological features. Eventually, the mining of "Borax," which came to be used widely as a cleaning compound, produced the world's largest open-pit mine.

Into this process of industrializing the western desert came a number of government facilities. The U.S. Army set up a bombing range in 1933 on Muroc Dry Lake, adjacent to Boron. "From my point of view," Armstrong has said, "it was clearly a superb flying place. The skies were blue most days, and you didn't have to worry about clouds or instrument flying."

With the phenomenal growth of American airpower during World War II, Muroc Field mushroomed in size and purpose, the site's succession of aviation firsts culminating in 1947, when the Bell X-1 broke the mythical sound barrier. The newly established U.S. Air Force that year took over the army operation, later renaming it Edwards Air Force Base in honor of Glen W. Edwards, a young air force captain who lost his life at Muroc in a June 1948 crash of Northrop's experimental YB-49 Flying Wing. It was at Edwards that the first supersonic fighter to enter U.S. military service, North American's YF-100A, debuted in May 1953. Later that year, the NACA's A. Scott Crossfield, the Edwards test pilot whom Armstrong came in 1955 to replace, became the first person to fly at Mach 2. Although Edwards Air Force Base and the NACA's High-Speed Flight Station (HSFS) were officially independent entities, most people referred colloquially to both facilities simply as "Edwards."

From the lofty vantage of the San Gabriels, the huge Edwards complex appeared much closer than its actual fifty miles' distance, and Janet Armstrong could see the airplanes flying overhead. "I used to get up there," Janet remembers, "and watch the early X-15 flights. You could see the X-15 when it dropped because it left a separate contrail [from the B-52 launch aircraft]. . . . Well, you couldn't quite see it [drop] if you happened to be blinking your eyes. Then you could watch it all through its powered flight and then you would lose it. But then, if you looked real hard at the lake bed, you could see the dust that it kicked up when it would land." A pair of binoculars brought the action all that much closer to her. Occasionally when he was flying more routine aircraft than the X-15, Neil flew over their Juniper Hills cabin and waggled his wings at his young bride.

Neil and Janet had met as students at Purdue University the year Neil returned from Korea. He was a twenty-two-year-old junior and she was eighteen and a freshman. What attracted Neil was Janet's poise and bearing, her smarts, her good looks, and her lively personality. Born in Cook County's St. Luke's Hospital on March 23, 1934, Janet Elizabeth Shearon was the daughter of Dr. Clarence Shearon and his wife, Louise. A native of South Dakota, Dr. Shearon was chief of surgery at St. Luke's who taught at his alma mater Northwestern University's medical school in Evanston, on the shore of Lake Michigan. A specialist in reattaching tendons to make damaged fingers and hands work again, he coauthored a textbook published in 1932 by the American Medical Association Press, *The Process of Tendon Repair: An Experimental Study of Tendon Suture and Tendon Graft.*

The Shearon family lived a very comfortable upper-middle-class life in the town of Wilmette, Illinois, an affluent suburb of Chicago located just north of Evanston. Life in Wilmette rated well above average: household income, house size and value, the percentage of the population who completed high school and went on to college. Well below average were the unemployment rate, the percentage of the population that was black, the percentage of people renting houses, and the crime rate. Even today, the average household income and house value in Wilmette are high: over $110,000 and $450,000, respectively.

Interestingly, Dr. Shearon owned and flew his own airplane, a Piper Cub. He regularly logged weekend round trips to the family's lake cottage in Eagle River, in far northern Wisconsin, where his wife and three girls usually spent their entire summer. "I've never learned to fly a plane," Janet once said, "though I've always wanted to. . . . My mother and oldest sister actually flew, but I never did because I was always too young." Later, during married life, Neil would occasionally let Janet take the controls of their Beech Bonanza, "but I never made a landing or a takeoff in the Bonanza." As late as 1969, Janet expressed a determination to become a licensed pilot, yet that dream never materialized.

In November 1945, when Janet was twelve, her father died suddenly of a heart attack. Although her father's career as a physician had kept him away from home a lot, Janet dearly loved him. On the verge of her teenage years, the loss of her father was devastating, "gravely affecting the way I grew up, and my thinking." As the third and last daughter, Janet did not always get along well with her mother, who, like Janet, was quite strong-willed. So her father always had—and always would—loom large in Janet's mind as her hero, the one person who most truly recognized and appreciated her worth, including her skills as a swimmer.

Graduating in 1952 from Winnetka's New Trier High School, one of the Chicago area's largest and highest-achieving township high schools, Janet chose to attend a college in her home region. Purdue University offered a nationally prominent program, established in 1926 as the School of Home Economics, then defined as "the science and art of home management."

Purdue was an excellent choice for Janet's ambition to become a modern homemaker, wife, and mother. As part of her busy college life, Janet stayed active by swimming intramurally and joining the women's synchronized swim team. She pledged to Alpha Chi Omega, a sorority whose motto, coincidentally enough, was "Together let us seek the heights." Among its many traditions was Alpha Chi's "sweetheart song":

Down deep in the heart of each Alpha Chi girl
Is the dream of a love that is true.

He's loving and he'll always be faithful
And somewhere he's waiting for you.

One of Janet's good friends in college turned out to be the man who would become the last Apollo astronaut to leave the surface of the Moon, Eugene Cernan. A 1952 graduate from Proviso High School in the Chicago suburb of Maywood, which was New Trier's main sports rival, Cernan matriculated at Purdue the same fall semester as did Janet. He pledged the Phi Gamma Delta fraternity and moved his sophomore year into the frat house. His roommate was William Smith, who had gone to New Trier High School with Janet and had dated her occasionally. Cernan met Janet through Smith: "She was a young, attractive coed, very effervescent, very pleasant, very nice. . . . She was a sorority girl. She was all the right things."

"Neil knew me for three years before he ever asked me for a date," Janet recalled during the Apollo era. "That wouldn't be so bad except that, after we were married, his roommate told me that the first time Neil saw me he came home and told the roommate that I was the girl he was going to marry. Neil isn't one to rush into anything."

Neil returned to Purdue from Korea in 1952, and Dean started at the school a year later. Dean believes he met her before Neil did. "Janet is as strong as horseradish," Dean explains, "a dynamic and self-confident person. . . . She looks you in the eye. Her body language is dramatic—the way she crosses her arms to say 'What do you mean by that?' " One day during her junior year in 1955 after Neil had graduated and was working in Cleveland, Dean arrived at her off-campus apartment to drive her to school. Janet told him that Neil and she had gotten engaged. "It shocked the heck out of me that they were engaged," Dean remembers, "because I had no idea that he was serious with her." Neil had never been serious with anyone before.

"Maybe opposites attract," Dean has remarked about the pairing of Janet and his brother. "They are really sort of opposites," Gene Cernan seconds. Janet was outgoing and talkative, "very much so." According to Cernan, "Neil and Jan must have just found something in common. . . . Maybe they mutually filled in voids. . . . Jan was a classy gal and I could see her being attracted to class—being attracted to someone who was not trying to impress her. You know, 'Sure, baby, I fly jets,' 'I just got back from Korea' thing. She probably had to drag that out of him. Neil was the same Neil. He's never changed since I've known him."

The courtship was unusual in that there really wasn't any. The betrothed were virtual strangers to each other. "We never really dated," Janet explains today. "My philosophy was, 'Well, I'll have years to get to know him.' I thought he was a very steadfast person. He was good-looking. He had a good sense of humor. He was fun to be with. He was older. He had a better sense of maturity than a lot of the boys I dated, and I had dated a lot of boys on campus."

Curiously, neither Neil nor Janet remember the exact timing or circumstance of their engagement, other than that it occurred while Neil was working in Cleveland. On his way to Edwards that July, Neil detoured to northern Wisconsin where Janet was working as a summer camp counselor. According to Janet, Neil joked that "if I would marry him [on the spot] and come along in the car, he'd get six cents a mile for the trip. If I didn't he'd only get four." Recalling Neil's father's sole piece of advice upon the couple's engagement was for her not to ride with Neil in a car, Janet decided, equally in jest, to join him in California later. Their wedding took place at the Congregational Church in Wilmette on January 28, 1956. Dean served as his brother's best man and June as one of Janet's attendants. "It was very lovely," Viola Armstrong remembered. The newlyweds honeymooned in Acapulco.

The couple took an apartment in Westwood, so Janet could take classes toward her college degree at UCLA. Neil returned to his bachelor's quarters on North Base at Edwards and commuted to Westwood on the weekends, a round-trip of over 180 miles. According to Neil, "That was for one semester. Then we moved up to the Antelope Valley and rented a house in an alfalfa field. That was down on the desert floor [at 5026 East Avenue L, within the city limits of Lancaster]. Then we moved into another rental house up in Juniper Hills. When we went up there, we found and bought the property with the cabin on it."

The move, in late 1957, meant that Janet never earned her degree, something she always regretted.

Compared to the creature comforts of the Shearon home in agreeable Wilmette or even her family's summer place in Wisconsin, life in the rustic 600-square-foot cabin overlooking Antelope Valley qualified Janet for membership in the Daughters of the Pioneers. The cabin was intended for weekend use. Its floor was bare wood. There were no bedrooms per se, just a room with four bunks. The cabin had a tiny bath and a small kitchen, but only primitive plumbing and no electricity. Even after Neil finished installing the wiring, Janet did all of the cooking on a hot plate. They enjoyed neither hot water nor a bathtub. As Neil recalls, "a shower was a hose hung out over the tree limb." To bathe their first baby, Eric (whom they came to call Ricky), Janet got a plastic tub, filled it with hose water, and waited ten minutes for the sun to warm it. Only slowly, after a lot of remodeling, did the cabin really become livable. Yet both Neil and Janet "loved it." The remote physical setting up in the San Gabriel Mountains was gorgeous and, with very few neighbors, provided "total relaxation away from everything."

Eric Alan Armstrong was born at the Antelope Valley Hospital in Lancaster on June 30, 1957. A daughter, Karen Anne Armstrong, was delivered at the same hospital on April 13, 1959. The Armstrong's third and last child, Mark Stephen, was born on April 8, 1963, after the family moved to Houston in the fall of 1962. (In mid-1956, the couple lost a child when Janet spontaneously miscarried.)

Armstrong's job at Edwards, as Janet once said, "was some fifty miles . . . but only one stop sign away." Neil carpooled with fellow High-Speed Flight Station employees who lived in the tiny towns of Littlerock and Pearblossom right below Juniper Hills. Charles Garvey made models in the HSFS woodshop. Betty Scott worked as a human "computer," one of the NACA employees—virtually all women—who, in an age before electronic computers, did the tedious mathematical work of converting all the flight data into meaningful engineering units. Her first husband, Herb Scott (Betty later married Jim Love), also rode in the carpool, as did Bill LePage.

Being a test pilot made Armstrong the worst of the carpoolers. "He wasn't very reliable," Betty Love admits. "It might happen that he had to stay and work on a simulator. But the guys out in the parking lot would sit and wait and finally he'd send word out or come out himself and say . . . he'd take a company car home. We used to roust him. The guys did; I didn't. He took it and handed it right back! He was no pussycat."

At Edwards, some of the stories of Armstrong's driving have become legendary. Milton O. Thompson, a fellow test pilot and later chief engineer at what became the NASA Dryden Flight Research Center, chronicled Neil's "automobility" in his 1992 book on the X-15 program, *At the Edge of Space:*

Neil lived in a small house on a couple of acres in Juniper Hills on the southern edge of the Antelope Valley. Neil had several cars, none of which were in good mechanical condition. Neil worked out a pretty good procedure to compensate for the questionable condition of his automobiles. His home was up in the hills above the Pearblossom Highway. He would simply start rolling down the hill in one of his cars on the way to his job at Edwards. If the

car started running and sounded good, he would continue on across Pear-
blossom Highway and head for Edwards. If it did not start, or it sounded
bad, he would simply make a left turn at the highway and coast on down to
an automotive repair shop. He would then walk back up and try another
car. Later that day after work, he would stop at the shop to pick up the other
car. He really had a car repair production line going. The mechanic at the
repair shop knew him well.

Typical of many stories told about Neil after he became famous, this one, too, has been embellished over the years.

Armstrong did have an interesting little collection of motorcars. Soon after he moved to California, he traded his 1952 Oldsmobile toward a new Hillman convertible, a snappy European import. "Then a fellow at the High-Speed Flight Station had a '47 Dodge," Neil explains. "He threw a rod on the way to work, so he sold me the car for fifty dollars 'as is.' I hauled the car up to the cabin and rebuilt the engine. A friend, Keith Anderson, reground the shaft and the cylinders and put in oversize rings and rebuilt the carburetor. It ran very well after that. It is probably true that from time to time I would go down to Vern's Garage—mostly for the Dodge." Neil particularly wanted the Dodge in good running order because the '47 model had a backseat "where you could put your legs straight out without hitting the front seat." The legroom was great, "and in a carpool situation that was pretty nice."

"I don't know if you could say that Neil drove like he flew or flew like he drove," Betty Love said, posing a riddle. "Neil always sat back in the [driver's] seat like he was in an easy chair and crossed his left leg over his right knee. . . . And he would drive that way!" Love once started a carpool conversation about the snow level in the San Gabriels, inquiring of Armstrong "if he ever put his [airplane] wingtip so he could fly along the snow level [and if the snow] would all be the same altitude or did it just look like that from the road." Intrigued by the question, Neil kept looking off at the snow line as he drove. A moment later "there was a car coming towards us—a pickup truck, actually—and I was ready to tell Neil that he'd better be careful, but it was already too late. He was already over the line," recalls Betty Love, "and he ran the truck into a ditch, and it happened to be an air police." Neil showed the MP his identification and "instead of bawling him out, they saluted him and told him to go on his way but to be more careful of where he was on the road." Clearly, some privileges came with being a test pilot.

Another time the Armstrongs and a group of friends left on a Saturday morning for a picnic and canoeing on nearby Jackson Lake. "All the kids wanted to ride with Neil," Betty Love remembers. "They wanted to ride in a convertible," but after what must have been an exciting ascent up the narrow, winding hilltop roads leading to lake country, "nobody wanted to come home with Neil. . . . Even Jan stayed in the car that she had gone up in—she and her little ones—and Neil came home by himself."

Contrary to Betty Love's riddle, it is not a question of whether Neil drove like he flew or flew like he drove, for he did neither. Driving a car in the earthbound two dimensions simply did not engage his mind in the powerfully stimulating way that flying an airplane did.

Armstrong reported to work at the High-Speed Flight Station on July 11, 1955. His formal job title was Aeronautical Research Scientist (Pilot).

Originally, the NACA employed only twenty-seven individuals in its Muroc Flight Test Unit. Its entire operation was hemmed in on a few dozen acres at "South Base." In 1951 Congress appropriated an additional 120 acres and $4 million. Via a new concrete parking apron and taxiway, this dual-hangared facility, which opened in June 1954, gave the NACA High-Speed Flight Station (formally named on July 1, 1954) ready access to the enormous runway that stretched southwest to northeast on the west side of the dry lake bed. At 15,000 feet long and 300 feet wide, it was, in Armstrong's words, "a wonderful runway for those big machines."

High-Speed Flight Station chief thirty-six-year-old Walter C. Williams epitomized the NACA tradition of "engineer in charge," having led the first detachment of NACA personnel from Langley to Pinecastle, Florida, and from there on to Muroc in 1946 for the purpose of flying the X-1. He ran the NACA's desert flight research operation until joining the Space Task Group in September 1959 to develop launch operations and oversee the building of a worldwide tracking network. As one of the top men in Project Mercury, Williams served as the director of flight operations for the first three Mercury flights, those made by Shepard, Grissom, and Glenn in 1961 and 1962.

Williams "was a gung-ho individual," remembers one of his engineers, Clyde Bailey. "Yet he was particularly concerned about safety." So lean was Williams's HSFS administratively that his "Office of the Chief" consisted solely of himself and one secretary. His Research Division's main office was staffed by just four people: Williams's number-two man, De Elroy E. Beeler; his assistant Hubert M. Drake; and two secretaries. Eleven people ran the offices of Williams's four divisions—research, operations, instrumentation, and administrative. "Real research work" and its supporting activities got done in divisional subsidiaries known as branches and sections.

Armstrong's Flight Branch was part of the Flight Operations Division, grouped with the Operations Engineering Section, Aircraft Maintenance Branch, Fabrication and Repair Section, Inspection Section, and Operational Aircraft Maintenance Section. The latter, Aircraft Ops, employed fifty-five workers, more by far than any other single organization at the station. Total HSFS staff numbered 275, a fraction of the nearly nine thousand at Edwards AFB.

Flight Operations Division reported to forty-four-year-old Joseph R. Vensel. A former research pilot at Lewis, Vensel had gone off flight status after losing a good bit of his hearing and transferred to Edwards in the early 1950s. Vensel's authority extended to all aircraft maintenance, inspection, and operations engineering. Ops Engineering required Vensel be knowledgeable about aircraft design, because research aircraft often needed new wings, tails, appendages, or other alterations built on-site in NACA shops. Assisted by secretary Della Mae Bowling, Vensel worked out of room 237 of the NACA building. In the adjacent office were the desks of all his test pilots.

Under Vensel was Neil's immediate boss, the head of Flight Branch, thirty-five-year-old chief test pilot Joseph A. Walker. Born in 1921 in Washington, Pennsylvania, Walker earned a bachelor's degree in physics from Washington and Jefferson College in 1942. Entering the Army Air Corps, he flew P-38 fighters in North Africa during World War II, earning the Distinguished Flying Cross and the Air Medal with seven oak clusters. In March 1945, Walker became a test pilot for the NACA in Cleveland, contributing the next six years to the laboratory's aircraft-icing research by "droning around in the crappiest winter weather that they could find in the Great Lakes region." As part of what was becoming a virtual pipeline between Lewis and the HSFS, Walker came to Edwards in 1951. His promotion to chief test pilot came just months before Neil arrived. A close friendship would grow not just between the two men, but between their wives as well.

The twenty-four-year-old Armstrong once again ranked the most junior pilot. Joe Walker's ten years of research pilot experience included an estimated 250 flights at Edwards, well over one hundred in experimental aircraft including the Bell X-1, Douglas D-558-1 and D-558-2, Douglas X-3, and Northrop X-4. Between January 1952 and April 1954, Walker had made seventy-eight test flights in the Bell X-5 alone. The X-5 was America's first high-performance variable-geometry ("swing wing") aircraft, though its spinning tendencies had killed air force pilot Raymond Popson in October 1953.

Even more experienced than Walker was HSFS test pilot A. Scott Crossfield. It was Crossfield whom Armstrong came to replace, yet, recalls Armstrong, "We were side by side in the office for nearly a year. . . . [He] had announced that he was going to be the pilot on the X-15 program, whoever won it. He had [employment] agreements with all the different bidders." (North American Aviation was the eventual winner over Douglas, Bell, and Republic.)

At thirty-four years old in 1955, Crossfield was already a legend. A naval aviator who trained but saw no combat during World War II, Crossfield had earned a degree in aeronautical engineering from the University of Washington in 1946. Joining the NACA as a research pilot at Muroc in June 1950, he flew hundreds of research flights, including eighty-seven in the rocket-powered X-1 and sixty-five in the jet-powered D-558-1 and D-558-2 aircraft. In November 1953, Crossfield became the first person ever to fly at Mach 2—or faster than 1,320 miles per hour—when he took to the sky over Edwards in the D-558-2 Skyrocket.

Fellow HSFS test pilots in July 1955 were Stanley P. Butchart and John B. McKay. Both men were thirty-three years old (born in 1922) and both were naval aviators during World War II. Butchart had served in the same torpedo-plane squadron with future U.S. president George H. Bush, VT-51. In 1950, both Butchart and McKay received degrees in aeronautical engineering—Butchart at the University of Washington, Crossfield's alma mater, and McKay, at the Virginia Polytechnic Institute. After a brief stint at Boeing as a design engineer on the body of the B-47 bomber, Butchart came to the HSFS as a research pilot in May 1951. McKay began with the NACA slightly earlier, but as an intern, and did not assume pilot status until July 1952. Both men flew a variety of research aircraft, including the D-558 and X-5. Butchart became the station's principal multiengine pilot. Hundreds of times he flew a B-29 Superfortress up over 30,000 feet in order to air-launch a research aircraft.

Stan Butchart first met Armstrong in March 1955 at NACA Langley, soon after Neil had started his job at Lewis. "Hey, I want you to meet the newest pilot," Eb Gough had said to Butchart in the chow line at the Langley cafeteria. "Neil still had on his old navy flight jacket and I thought, 'Boy, this kid is not even out of high school yet!' He looked so young." Gough told

Butchart that Edwards was really where Armstrong wanted to be. Looking at Armstrong's résumé, Butchart figured that "somebody had to pick him up quick." Walker and Vensel agreed and tabbed him for Crossfield's slot.

Armstrong started flying the first day he arrived at Edwards, in a P-51 Mustang, one of America's most significant and most beloved military airplanes. "It was quite elegant," Armstrong says. "Just didn't have the performance of the F-8F.

"I was in a learning mode for the first few weeks," Armstrong recalls, flying almost every day, either in the P-51 (with an F-51 designation) or in the NACA's R4D, a military version of the celebrated Douglas DC-3 transport. "They were telling me the various activities that I should be looking for [leading up to an air launch]. They would be venting the oxygen tanks and starting the turbopumps for the exhaust. I had been introduced to the aircraft on the ground, but this would be my first time actually to observe it in flight. . . . As they became more confident in my abilities, and as I became more experienced, they gave me more and more jobs."

Though in position to chase D-558-2 Skyrocket and X-1A launches that ultimately aborted, on August 3, Armstrong saw his first actual drop while flying chase in the F-51 on Crossfield's D-558-2 flight investigation of stability and structural loads at supersonic speeds. Later that month, Armstrong also checked out in the YRF-84F, the prototype of Republic Aviation's swept-wing jet fighter (maximum speed 670 mph), and first crewed on the B-29. Armstrong's first launch assist on a research aircraft came on August 24, 1955, again with Crossfield piloting the Skyrocket.

"Generally, the person in the left seat was in command of the drop," Neil explains. "The person in the right seat did most of the flying. Over the years I flew in both positions probably an equal number of times." Without question, this was challenging flying. "We were usually taxing the performance limit of the aircraft because there was a lot of excess drag due to having the [research] aircraft slung beneath the B-29's belly. We also wanted to get as high as we could for the launches," typically up in the 30,000- to 35,000-foot region, which would take an hour and a half or more. After that, "it was a matter of getting into the proper position."

In air launching lurked unanticipated dangers. On August 8, 1955, just an instant before Joe Walker was to be dropped in the X-1A, an explosion within its rocket engine rocked the B-29. "I thought we'd hit another airplane," remembers pilot Stan Butchart, "and in those days there wasn't anybody else up there above twenty thousand feet!" Alarmed by the big bang, Walker immediately scrambled up and out of the X-1A and into the bomb bay of his mother ship. The X-1A was too damaged to fly, and the B-29 could not risk landing with it still hooked to its underside. Butchart had no choice but to jettison the research aircraft into the desert. The machine exploded on impact, ending the X-1A program.

Armstrong saw the whole thing. "Neil Armstrong was real new," Butchart remembers, "and he was flying off our wing in the F-51. So we gave him a good introduction to how the game went." It was learned later that a gasket blew when Walker threw the switch to pressurize the liquid oxygen and water alcohol in the X-1A's fuel tanks.

The cause of the accident proved to be a simple leather gasket made by the Ulmer Company to seal propellant plumbing joints. When saturated with liquid oxygen, Ulmer leather was so unstable that a shock of any magnitude caused the gasket to blow. Unfortunately, a number of accidents occurred—involving the X-1-3, X-1A, X-1D, and X-2—before engineers identified the malfunctioning gasket and a fix was made.

Eight months after arriving at Edwards, Armstrong experienced one of his own closest shaves ever, during what should have been just another routine air launch. It happened on Thursday, March 22, 1956. In the NACA's launch B-29 modified and designated P2B-1S, Armstrong was flying in the right seat with Stan Butchart in command to his left, along with five crew members. Their job that day was to take the number two D-558-2 research airplane up to an altitude of a little over 30,000 feet and then drop it so HSFS research pilot Jack McKay could take it through a flight investigation of its vertical tail loads.

Approaching 30,000 feet, one of the B-29 engines quit. Passing the controls over to Neil, Butchart turned around to consult with flight engineer Joseph L. Tipton. "Butch, number four quit," Tipton told the pilot, pinpointing the far right starboard engine. With no power, the propeller blade on number-four engine windmilled in the air stream.

"I wasn't too concerned about it, really," recalls Butchart. "B-29 engines are not all that dependable." On his control panel, Butchart had four "feathering" buttons designed to shut down, or "feather," the rotation of a propeller up to three times. Feathering his far starboard engine, he expected the propeller to come to a standstill. Instead, just as the prop came close to stopping, it started spinning again. With Neil flying the plane and Butchart "kind of scratching my head thinking about what was going on," the maverick propeller came back up to full speed, matching and then even *exceeding* the rpm's of the other props.

The B-29 pilots were learning firsthand that "a windmilling propeller that has lost its governor will rotate proportionally . . . to the true airspeed of the aircraft. So if you speed up," Neil explains, "the propeller's going to go faster. If you slow down, the propeller should slow down." Armstrong and Butchart faced a critical choice: "try to slow down and hope we can keep the rpm of the propeller under control" or "speed up and get rid of the rocket plane underneath."

Butchart hit the same feather button a second time. The propeller kept spinning wildly. Down to his last chance, Butchart hit the button again, with the same result. In the meantime McKay down in the cockpit of the Skyrocket called up, "Hey, Butch, you can't drop me! My Grover loader valve just broke." (The valve regulated the buildup and release of fuel pressure in the D-558.) Given that the rebel propeller could fly loose at any moment, Butchart announced: "Jack, I've got to drop you!"

Already, Butchart had motioned over to Armstrong to nose down the B-29. If the speed at launch was anything less than 210 mph, the Skyrocket would come out in a stall—falling but not *flying*. But in gaining speed by nosing over, the runaway prop spun just that much faster, increasing its likelihood of busting loose according to an altogether predictable law of physics known as centripetal disintegration.

Butchart put his hand on the emergency release lever and pulled. Nothing happened. He pulled two or three times. Nothing. Then he reached up and hit the two toggles that armed the "pickle switch" (conventionally used to drop bombs) which the NACA had adapted to drop its research airplanes. The D-558-2 fell away sharply from the B-29—and not a second too soon. Butchart has always wondered whether the very act of dropping the D-558-2 might have been jarring enough to the B-29's flight stability to push the runaway propeller beyond the limit. Whatever the trigger, the prop almost instantaneously let go.

The blades flew off in every direction, one of them slicing through the air intake scoop on the B-29's number-three engine, through its bomb bay where test pilot Jack McKay had been sitting in the Skyrocket a few seconds earlier, and hit its number-two engine on the other side.

Getting the B-29 down for landing was not going to be easy. The starboard number-three engine was still running, but its instrument readings—throttle control, oil pressure, and fuel pressure—had shut down. The pilots shut the engine down. Number one had not been damaged, but it had to be shut down because of the wicked torque it caused out on the far port side with neither of the starboard engines running. Butchart and Armstrong had to fly the B-29 down from 30,000 feet with only one engine.

Butchart tried to take over the flying from Armstrong, but his wheel was loose and floppy. He looked over and said, "Neil, you got control?" and Neil answered, "Yeah, a little bit." Both pilots had rudder and longitudinal control, but Butchart did not have pitch control, nor did he have any control of roll because his cables to the ailerons were shot. What controls Armstrong had were all dicey.

"So we just made a slow, circling descent, tried never to get to a very large bank angle, and were successfully able to make a straight-in landing on to the lake bed," Armstrong remembers. According to Butchart, during the descent "Neil kept saying, 'Get your gear down! Get your gear down!' and I said, 'Wait a minute. I have to make sure I can make that lake!' because there was no way of going around and I couldn't use too much power even on [number] two because we couldn't hold the rudder down. We were both standing on rudder. . . . So it was pretty tense coming down."

With typical understatement, Armstrong has summed up the experience: "We were very fortunate. It could have turned ugly."

McKay in the Skyrocket landed safely. The matter of his malfunctioning Grover loader valve caused him no trouble on the way down.

Over the course of his seven-year career at Edwards, Armstrong piloted or copiloted a launch plane more than one hundred times. He dropped or flew chase for every type of NACA/NASA research airplane then flown at Edwards. Virtually every day that conditions were suitable for flying, the young test pilot took to the air. From the time he came to Edwards in July 1955 to the time he left to join the astronaut corps at the end of September 1962, Armstrong made well over nine hundred total flights, an average of over ten flights per month. Averaging something less than twenty workdays per month (given holidays and vacation time), Neil was flying more than half the days he worked.

His busiest time was his first three and a half years (July 1955–December 1958) and his last year (January to September 1962); his least busy was 1959. It wasn't that Neil worked less hard in 1959; he was simply assigned to projects requiring fewer flights. Flight Operations Division logbooks indicate approximately 2,600 hours total flight time, roughly fifteen and one half weeks of twenty-four-hour days in the cockpit of some of the country's most advanced, high-performance, and risk-laden experimental aircraft. Most of his flights came in jets. More than 350 of his flights took place in one of the famous "Century" series fighters: the North American F-100 Super

Sabre, the world's first fighter capable of sustained supersonic speeds in level flight; McDonnell F-101 Voodoo; Convair F-102 Delta Dagger; Lockheed F-104 Starfighter; Republic F-105 Thunderchief; and Convair F-106 Delta Dart.

The first time Armstrong broke the sound barrier came in October 1955, an F-100A flight investigation of longitudinal stability and control characteristics involving various wing slots and slats in different leading-edge configurations.

In June 1956, Armstrong started flying the F-102, newly supersonic thanks to NACA aerodynamicist Richard T. Whitcomb's recent development of the so-called area rule, by which the drag of a wing and the drag of the body of an aircraft must be considered as a mutually interactive aerodynamic system. "I flew the YF-102, which was the pre-area-rule F-102," Armstrong remembers. "Kind of a dog of an airplane," it was "not a lot of fun to fly," and "I don't think I could ever get it supersonic." Applying the area rule by pinching the waist of its fuselage measurably improved the F-102's speed and overall performance even with approximately the same engine thrust. Because it was a delta-wing airplane, the F-102 did suffer, however, from very high induced drag, that is, drag due to lift. "It was a very nice flying airplane, [with] very nice handling qualities," Neil explains, "but if you turned, it would really slow down. It was the only plane I've ever been in where you could do a 'split S' in afterburner and slow down in the process!"

In the NACA's F-102s, Armstrong "did a lot of landing work, because we more than anyone else at that point in time were flying the rocket airplanes and having to make unpowered landings." Armstrong also flew dead-stick landings in the F-102 as well as the F-104: "These would vary the geometry of the pattern and the [flight] speeds and the energy management aspects of the trajectory to come up with a conclusion, what is the probable best technique?"

About a third of the 900-plus flights piloted by Armstrong at Edwards were true "research" flights. The other two-thirds involved familiarization flights, chase, piloting air launches, or flying transport. Considering the two-year period from 1957 to 1958 as a representative sample shows that Armstrong flew the greatest number of flights in the R4D/DC-3 followed by the F-100A, F-104, B-29, F-100C, and B-47. Besides the F-51 Mustang and the aforementioned Century series fighters, Armstrong logged time in the venerable T-33 "T-Bird," a two-seater derivative of the F-80 Shooting Star fighter; North American's F-86E Sabre; McDonnell's

F4H Phantom; Douglas F5D-1 Skylancer; and Boeing's KC-135 Stra-totanker. Armstrong pushed past Mach 2 in Bell's X-1B and X-5, and went hypersonic in the North American X-15. He also piloted a unique experimental vehicle called the Parasev.

The flights Armstrong made lasted on average less than one hour apiece, particularly the research flights. Typically, less than ten flights in any year lasted more than two hours and only four or five lasted more than three hours. Many of these longer flights took place in the R4D/DC-3 on transport missions to other NACA laboratories, to aircraft manufacturers, or to military bases, or involved taking the B-29 up to high altitude for air-launch operations.

"Our principal responsibility was engineering work," Armstrong explains. "We did not do a lot of flying. It was program development, looking at the problems of flight. It was a wonderful time period, and it was very satisfying work, particularly when you found a solution."

Almost everyone who has ever rated Armstrong as a pilot, including his commanders back in the navy, has made a connection between his piloting skills and his engineering background and talents. Flight Research Center colleague Milt Thompson has written that Neil was "the most technically capable of the early X-15 pilots" and "the most intelligent of all the X-15 pilots, in a technical sense." Bruce A. Peterson, the NASA test pilot whose spectacular (and, amazingly, nonfatal) accident in the M2-F2 lifting body at Edwards in 1967 served as the opening footage for the popular '70s television show *The Six Million Dollar Man,* says that Neil "made a point of wanting to understand everything." William H. Dana, who as a NASA research pilot flew in some of the most significant aeronautical programs ever carried out at what became NASA Dryden Flight Research Center, emphasizes how "bright" Armstrong was about the aircraft he flew: "He understood what contributed to a flight condition. . . . He had a mind that absorbed things like a sponge and a memory that remembered them like a photograph. That set him apart from mere mortals." On one occasion, Armstrong was talking in the company of fellow NACA pilots about lift-drag ratio, one of the most significant parameters in aerodynamics. Neil said that "L over D was a function of airspeed, angle of attack, and the wing area, and I thought [otherwise]," Dana relates. "So I looked it up and it turned out Neil was right."

As impressive as Armstrong's abilities were to pilot-engineers, aeronautical engineers who did not fly appreciated Armstrong as a pilot even more. At Edwards in the late 1950s and early 1960s, Neil often worked with

Eugene J. Matranga, a 1954 graduate in mechanical engineering from Louisiana State University. "Neil ran circles around many test pilots, engineering-wise," Matranga has declared. "The other guys who flew seat of the pants knew instinctively what to do, but they didn't always know why. Neil knew why." In Matranga's view, Armstrong was "the best engineering test pilot that I ever dealt with.

"As long as he could convince himself that something was going to be successful," Armstrong's "openness to doing things," in Matranga's opinion, compared favorably to a "pretty hard and fast reluctance on the part of many pilots" to surrender any of their authority to nonfliers. "Neil did not have that bias."

Some pilots who weren't engineers were not nearly as impressed with Armstrong's flying. Chuck Yeager was the most prominent detractor, joined by William J. "Pete" Knight, Armstrong's colleague on the X-15. That Yeager and Knight were air force pilots, whereas Armstrong was a naval aviator flying for NACA/NASA as a civilian, may partially explain the criticisms. Yet a greater reason was that neither Yeager nor Knight were engineers. Yeager did not go to college; Knight never earned a college degree. Asked how an engineering pilot like Armstrong flew, Knight responded, "It's more mechanical than it is flying, basically. I think that's why Neil got into trouble on numerous occasions [in his flying], because some things didn't come natural to him. . . . [He was] flying the airplane all right and doing everything necessary, but not being aware of some of the other important things that were going on."

While "trouble" would, in fact, pop up from time to time in Armstrong's flying at Edwards, ultimately, there can be no doubt that Armstrong's experience and talents as a professional engineer served the cause of his flying career extremely well. Those who handpicked him in 1962 for the second class of astronauts, without question, favored Neil's engineering qualifications.

A telling admission came from Christopher C. Kraft Jr., a NACA flight researcher and one of the founding fathers of the American space program: "I was prejudiced for the fact that this guy's been a NACA test pilot. So he's probably head and shoulders above. . . . I shouldn't say it that strongly. But he was above the capability of the other test pilots we had in the loop because he'd been through the daily contact with flight engineers, of which I was one."

According to Kraft, key people on the astronaut selection board, notably NACA veterans Robert R. Gilruth, Walter Williams, and Dick Day, felt even more partisan in Armstrong's favor, especially Williams and Day. Both men were themselves engineers rooted in the NACA's engineering research culture. Both came to NASA's Manned Spacecraft Center after spending years in flight research with NACA/NASA at Edwards, where they had come to know and admire young Armstrong. "Neil was about as good as you could come by in evaluating a man from a test-pilot-performance capability," Kraft states. The only real uncertainty about Armstrong's choice as an astronaut in 1962 came down to whether *he,* Neil A. Armstrong, personally *wanted* to become an astronaut.

For why choose to become an astronaut when Armstrong was already so deeply and so creatively involved in what were the biggest, most technically challenging flight programs ever attempted? Two of these programs—the X-15 and Dyna-Soar—had as their goal not just flying *piloted winged* vehicles at *hypersonic* speeds, but flying them *transatmospherically,* into and back from space.

CHAPTER 13

At the Edge of Space

The rarefied conditions into which Armstrong "zoomed" in his sleek fighter jet were far closer to those on the Martian surface than anything down on Earth. Streaking upward past 45,000 feet he passed the biological threshold at which a person could survive without the protection of a spacesuit. When his near-vertical climb reached 90,000 feet, atmospheric pressure fell to a scant 6 millibars, about 1 percent of the pressure at sea level. Outside his cockpit, the temperature dipped to 60 degrees below zero F.

This *was* space. The only way to control his plane at the top of its ballistic arc was to invoke Newton's Third Law and expel some steam via jets of hydrogen peroxide. A pilot in a near vacuum could maneuver his airplane in pitch, yaw, and roll just as manned spacecraft would later do. With all the energy from the zoom dissipating, Armstrong's jet came close to a virtual standstill, sitting on its tail. For over half a minute at the top of his climb, he experienced a feeling of weightlessness. At about 70,000 feet, Neil had shut down the engine to prevent it from exceeding its temperature limit. The cockpit's ingenious auxiliary pressurization system released a squirt of compressed gas.

The engine's *not* running at the top of the arc was critically important to the goal of the flight test. If not shut down, the engine would have introduced yaw motions challenging Neil's capacity to control the aircraft.

Streaking down nose-first into the atmosphere, enough air molecules eventually passed through the jet's intake ducts to allow Armstrong to restart his engine, and, at a speed of about Mach 1.8, begin his recovery from the unpowered dive. From that point on, with luck, the rest of the flight was routine all the way down to the runway. If Neil did not get an engine restart, he could make a dead-stick landing. If necessary, in the moments after touchdown, he could pull a lanyard to deploy a drag chute housed just below the plane's vertical stabilizer to decrease his landing roll-out distance.

In this fashion, Neil Armstrong and his fellow NASA test pilots at Edwards—at the controls of a long pointy jet plane nicknamed "The Missile with a Man"—made the country's first dramatic excursions to the edge of space.* They did so for research purposes more than half a year before Commander Alan B. Shepard became the first American astronaut to fly in space.

These facts fly in the face of popular lore. Thanks to author Tom Wolfe's 1979 bestseller *The Right Stuff,* and the 1983 Hollywood film adaptation, most people believe that the man who first flew *in an airplane* to the edge of space was U.S. Air Force test pilot Captain Chuck Yeager. Yeager made his December 10, 1963, flight in a rocket-equipped version of the Lockheed F-104A (designated NF-104A), the episode providing the stirring conclusion to Wolfe's provocative account of the early days of the Space Age. Wolfe's final sequence begins when four of the seven celebrated astronauts *still had not flown* into space, with the solitary Yeager taking the NF-104A up over Edwards, firing its auxiliary rocket motor, and zooming up so high that in the movie version Yeager glimpsed stars. Never mind that such a sight was optically impossible due to light reflecting off the Earth. Shooting for the stars—in an airplane named Starfighter—was the stuff of legend.

Reaching the dizzying height of 108,700 feet (Yeager wanted to set a new altitude record), his plane pitched up and went out of control. In his 1985 autobiography, Yeager claimed that a rocket thruster on the nose malfunctioned and stuck open, but some pilots at Edwards knowledgeable about the NF-104A and Yeager's piloting of the aircraft that day have

---

* The zooms flown by Armstrong and other NACA pilots in the F-104 were designed primarily to investigate reaction controls. According to Armstrong, "We would accelerate to Mach 2 at about 35,000 feet, pull up to the programmed climb angle, shut down the engine at about 60,000 feet (to prevent engine overheating), then, at 75,000 to 80,000 feet, began a planned control sequence with the reaction control system [a three-axis reaction control system utilizing hydrogen peroxide rockets on the wingtips and in the nose]. The top of the zoom was usually about 90,000" (NAA to author, Nov. 26, 2002, p. 15). "We were the first to do this kind of maneuver," Armstrong states (NAA: e-mail to author, Jan. 22, 2004). "I am confident that we had the only aircraft so configured and were the first to use reaction controls in this mode."

suggested that Yeager "plain screwed up," letting his pitch attitude and angle of attack get away from him.*

Whatever caused its pitch-up, Yeager's plane fell over on its back and went into a flat spin. Spiraling down and down from over twenty miles high, Yeager struggled to right himself. At 21,000 feet, he popped open the parachute rig stored in the tail of the NF-104A, a desperate move that failed to get him out of the spin. At 14,000 feet, he had no option but to eject. Blasted out of his plane, Yeager became entangled in his ejection seat and, awash in leftover rocket fuel, suffered horrible burns to his face and hands. As shown in the movie, he hit the ground hard and in excruciating pain. Nonetheless, Yeager resolutely got to his feet, loosely gathered up his chute, and, with flight helmet under his arm, walked almost staidly away from the burning wreckage toward an oncoming ambulance. That is, at least, the glorified Hollywood image. More accurately, a motorist from a nearby highway immediately rushed to assist Yeager, only to vomit at the sight of Yeager using

---

* The most authoritative sources for the suggestion that Yeager "plain screwed up" have been Major Robert W. Smith, a 1956 graduate of the air force's Test Pilot School (TPS) at Edwards and the primary pilot in the NF-104A program; Colonel William Haynes, one of Smith's TPS classmates and an officer involved at the time in the air force's X-20 Dyna-Soar program; and Robert G. Hoey, then the air force's deputy flight test engineer at Edwards. According to these sources, the stability derivatives from Bob Smith's previous NF-104A flight of November 1963 had not yet been reduced when Yeager, then the commander of the TPS, decided to take the airplane up for his own assault on the world altitude record (for a ground-launched airplane), a record that Smith had just set at 118,600 feet. Both Smith and Hoey tried to get Yeager to wait until the data was completed. They also strongly encouraged him to spend at least a little time in the NF-104A simulator. But Yeager refused both pieces of advice, insisting that "If Smith can fly it, I can." If he had trained on the fixed-base simulator, according to Hoey, Yeager would have learned, among other things, the right way to recover the aircraft from a flat spin via deployment of an emergency chute. A pilot's natural inclination was to do what Yeager did: to push forward *gently* with the stick, an instinctive move that only accelerated the plane's nosing up. The best thing to do, as could be learned in only the simulator, was to come *full forward* on the stick, even though normal pilot experience indicated that action would turn the plane upside down. Yet it was only that counterintuitive use of the stick that could have gotten the NF-104A out of a flat spin using the chute. Yet another Edwards pilot has suggested that Yeager failed to reset the trim tab during the recovery and, because of this, was unable to control the nose pitch-up when the drag chute was jettisoned.

The real tragedy of Yeager's rush to fly the NF-104A, in the opinion of these air force insiders, was that, when Yeager failed to recover from the spin and nearly lost his life, the consensus at the TPS was that the NF-104A was too dangerous an aircraft to be flying zooms. So the air force canceled the NF-104A project, Smith said, "thereby depriving the school and its students of a tool that would have allowed real cutting-edge training and development of some crackerjack test pilots." For a critique of Yeager's version of what occurred during his December 1963 flight in the NF-104A, see "Yeager's View, in Review," at NF104.com. On this Web site, the views of Smith, Haynes, and Hoey are all expressed.

the man's penknife to cut off one of his lined gloves, as well as parts of two badly burned fingers stuck to the rubber lining.

Unfortunately, so much else about Yeager and his December 1963 flight as romantically inflated in *The Right Stuff* and elsewhere is factually inaccurate.* Most important, Yeager and the U.S. Air Force Test Pilot School at Edwards were not responsible for "develop[ing] the first techniques for maneuvering in outer space," as some air force publications and Web sites have claimed; NACA/NASA was, with the F-104 and previously with the X-1B. (The X-1B flights occurred between November 1957 and January 1958, but they were not effective in terms of reaction-control research.) And Yeager was not even close to being the first pilot to zoom into the high stratosphere. As we have seen, some NASA test pilots began to make zooms to 90,000 feet as early as the fall of 1960, a full *three* years prior to Yeager's December 1963 flight. And in the rocket-assisted NF-104A, air force pilots performed zooms into the upper stratosphere before Yeager, as did Lockheed test pilot Jack Woolams.

Also, well before December 1963, a far more remarkable and historically significant flying machine had pushed the envelope considerably further than any zooming F-104. This machine was the X-15, the fastest and highest-flying manned winged vehicle ever built—and one that Chuck Yeager never flew. Conceived by the NACA in the early 1950s and built by North American Aviation (later North American Rockwell) under the sponsorship of the air force, the navy, and the NACA, the X-15 was constructed not just to explore the hypersonic flight regime existing above Mach 5 but also to study the possibilities of flying a winged vehicle outside the sensible atmosphere (the region where aerodynamic control surfaces will function). First flown in June 1959, the rocket-powered X-15 was a veritable "aerospace plane." By the end of 1961, the year President Kennedy committed the nation to the Moon landing, the X-15 attained its primary design goals of flying to a speed in excess of Mach 6 (over 4,000 mph) and to an altitude of over 200,000 feet (or nearly thirty-eight miles high). In 1962, a year that saw the Mercury flights of astronauts Glenn, Carpenter, and Schirra, air force pilot Robert White, in a pressure suit similar to the Mer-

---

* In response to Tom Wolfe's *The Right Stuff,* Armstrong has said: "I haven't read the book critically. I did see the movie. I thought it was very good filmmaking but terrible history: the wrong people working on the wrong projects at the wrong times. It bears no resemblance whatever to what actually was going on."

cury space suit, flew the X-15 more than fifty miles high (264,000 feet), the altitude that technically qualified him as an "astronaut" according to a policy invented by the U.S. Air Force (and never endorsed by NASA). The total number of X-15 pilots who earned "astronaut wings" according to the air force definition was eight. That was one more than the original group of Mercury astronauts, only six of whom made it into space (and only four into orbit) as part of the Mercury program.

Following over thirty zooms in the F-104, Neil Armstrong would fly the X-15 seven times before joining the second class of American astronauts in September 1962. Neil never made it above the fifty-mile mark, but on April 20, 1962, in his sixth X-15 flight, he did reach 207,500 feet, just under forty miles high.

In retrospect, the movement of aeronautics from subsonic to transonic, then to supersonic and on to hypersonic (and beyond that to "hypervelocity") seems inevitable. As the emerging Cold War crystallized into an atomic face-off between the United States and the Soviet Union, the sharpest focus for hypersonic enthusiasm lay in the development of an intercontinental ballistic missile (ICBM) armed with nuclear warheads. Yet for those enthusiasts for whom aeronautics still meant piloted, winged *airplanes,* the ambition was to design a rocket-powered vehicle to take men and cargo on hyperfast flights across global distances, on trajectories that, at their apex, flew out into space.

Rocket-powered experimental research airplanes were air-dropped into flight. Armstrong piloted his first on August 15, 1957, the first check-out flight of the modified X-1B, zooming to about 60,000 feet. Although it was the highest altitude that Armstrong had yet flown, at only 11.4 miles the dynamic pressure simply was not low enough to test the reaction controls.

In landing the aircraft, his nose landing gear "failed." According to Neil's official report, he "inadvertently touched down at 170 KIAS [Knots Indicated Airspeed], nose wheel first." "It didn't really *fail,*" Neil admits, "I broke it. I was landing on the lake bed, and it was fairly normal. But at touchdown the airplane began to porpoise and, after several cycles of the porpoising, the nose wheel bracketry failed. I felt devastated, of course, but that was improved a little when I found out that was the thirteenth or fourteenth time [due to the coupling of the geometry] that had happened [with the X-1 series]."

In his second flight in the X-1B on January 16, 1958,* Armstrong re-members, "we dropped too close to Edwards Dry Lake [due to some sys-tems problems on the X-1B], so we aborted the zoom." The X-1B flew only one more time, on January 23, 1958, when Armstrong and Stan Butchart air-dropped pilot Jack McKay for a zoom to 55,000 feet, one that did not slow enough at the top to check out reaction controls. Immediately after McKay's flight, mechanics found irreparable cracks in the rocket motor's liquid oxygen tank (by then, the X-1B was about a ten-year-old plane), end-ing the entire X-1B program.

Supersonic jets differed from their slower predecessors in the design of their relatively shorter swept-back wings, denser shapes, and a much greater mass concentration around their fuselages. Unexpectedly, this al-tered geometry brought on some serious aerodynamic difficulties known as "roll coupling" (also called "inertial coupling" or "roll divergence").

As Armstrong reported to work at the HSFS in the summer of 1955, no problem was receiving more attention than roll coupling. Not only was the problem endangering the F-100, it had also threatened the D-558-2, X-2, and the NACA's newest research airplane, the Douglas X-3. A long, slen-der, dart-shaped aircraft that rates as one of the fastest-*looking* aircraft ever designed, the X-3 Stiletto experienced coupling instability during abrupt roll maneuvers that caused it to go wildly out of control. Built for Mach 2, the X-3 was barely able to reach Mach 1.2 because it never received the higher-rated-thrust turbojets intended for it. The NACA retired the plane, which was underfunded and lacked expected engine performance, in May 1956 after only twenty flights. So all the attention turned to the F-100. Quickly, a fix was found—the addition of a much larger tail. Then, flying its own modified F-100C, the NACA tested a new automatic control tech-nique—one that used pitch damping as a means of lessening the divergency yaw during high roll rates—to resolve the roll coupling problem more gen-erally. Armstrong checked out in the airplane on October 7, 1955, and pi-loted many of the flights for that program during the next two years.

This partially automatic flight-control system that Armstrong helped to develop for the F-100 was one of the first to incorporate "feedback com-

---

* Besides twice flying the X-1B as part of the reaction-control research, Armstrong sought a possible fix to a problem known as aileron "buzz." This was a dangerously rapid vibration of an aileron (considered a type of flutter) that occurred especially at transonic speeds. Neil's X-1B flights involved fitting peculiarly shaped wedges on the ailerons to see if they might solve the buzz problem.

pensation." In essence, the idea was for the control surfaces on the aircraft (ailerons, rudder, elevator, and such) to communicate as part of an integrated, self-regulating system. What was needed for the X-15 was a novel system that automatically monitored and changed the "gains," i.e., the ups and downs in voltage necessary to adjust the flight control system, without requiring too much work from the pilot.

The stability augmentation system used on the first two X-15s did not live up to expectations. Armstrong explains: "Because the X-15 covered such a wide speed range, it was impossible to set the gains in the flight control system to a single value that was optimum for all flight conditions. You had to continually be changing the gains because at one minute you're at Mach 1, the next minute you're at Mach 5." This was "a complex and bothersome nuisance, a high workload environment."

Starting in April 1960, Neil consulted with engineers at the Minneapolis-Honeywell Corporation on "a very unique, self-adjusting system." After Honeywell installed the prototype system—called MH-96—on an F-101 Voodoo in early 1961, Armstrong traveled to Minnesota in March 1961 to fly it. Based largely on Neil's favorable written reports, NASA decided to install the MH-96 on the final X-15 (X-15-3), which was scheduled to be test flown for the first time late in 1961. Given his role in the MH-96's development, NASA assigned Armstrong to pilot the first flight.

In Minneapolis as at Edwards, Neil explains, "We used airplanes like the mathematician might use a computer, as a tool to find answers in aerodynamics."

The NACA's High-Speed Flight Station virtually invented the flight simulator for research purposes. In 1952, the NACA convinced the air force to buy an analog computer known as GEDA (Goodyear Electronic Differential Analyzer). Set up on the military base and maintained by electronics technicians, the inspiration and talent for turning the machine into a real flight simulator fell to two young engineers from the NACA, Richard E. Day and Joseph Weil. They programmed the necessary equations of motions into GEDA, gave it a simple broom-handle control stick, and set it up to "fly" what amounted to the first "virtual" airplane with a variation on "degrees of freedom" (roll; move forward and backward; and go up, down, and sideways). Day and Weil chose to give their pioneering simulator one freedom less, massively simplifying the overall equations by holding the forward speed constant. Changes in any one of the five flight quantities fed back into the program's equations, changing the quantities of the other four.

By the time Armstrong arrived at Edwards, flight simulators had made important contributions to a number of research programs, notably the X-1B and the X-2, the latter of which the NACA was supposed to receive after the air force finished testing it. Unfortunately, a needless tragedy with the X-2 stopped that from happening.

Dick Day warned his air force associates not to push ahead so fast with the X-2, piloted by Iven Kinchloe, Frank "Pete" Everest, and Milburn G. Apt. Data from their work with the GEDA was confirming evidence from NACA wind tunnel tests that the X-2 would experience "rapidly deteriorating directional and lateral (roll) stability near Mach 3." On April 25, 1956, the X-2 broke the sound barrier for the first time. Less than a month later, it flew past Mach 2. By midsummer it was pushing Mach 3. When Mel Apt took the X-2 up on September 27, 1956, *for his very first flight in the aircraft,* his flight plan called for "the optimum maximum energy flight path," one that, without question, would rocket him past Mach 3—and into roll coupling.

The fatal crash happened just as Dick Day thought it might. At 65,000 feet and a speed of Mach 3.2, Apt lost control of the X-2 due to roll coupling and became unconscious. By the time he came to, it was too late. He died instantly when the plane screamed into the desert floor.

On the ground that day in the company of air force test pilot Iven Kinchloe, Armstrong observed the disaster from start to finish: "Mel's flight was to be the last air force flight of the X-2 prior to turning the aircraft over to the NACA. So there was a good deal of interest in each X-2 flight. NACA HSFS was wedded to the concept of step-by-step testing so we were appalled that the air force would be putting any pilot on such a difficult profile on his first flight. In the air force quest for yet another record, they were deviating substantially from the NACA approach. So we tended to blame the air force officials for the accident, the loss of Mel, and the loss of the one-of-a-kind aircraft."

The irony is that, in Mercury, Gemini, and Apollo, NASA did approximately the same thing as the air force did with the X-2. The difference was, in Armstrong's view, that "our simulators in the space program were so much more sophisticated and accurate, and our preparation was so much more intense, that we convinced ourselves that the pilots could handle whatever situation we might encounter in flight."

The Apt tragedy deepened the NACA's commitment to the development of its research simulators. From GEDA and Dick Day's other very early simulators came the Sim Lab, which Armstrong inhabited with increasing frequency: "I was often in the Simulation Lab at the request of one of our flight test engineers or simulation engineers to check out something about some simulator mechanization. We were trying to increase our understanding of aircraft handling qualities, damping limits, and what was causing instability."

In the Sim Lab, Neil learned "that there were many ways to induce errors into the programming. Often the outputs to the instruments were improperly mechanized so the instrument would not accurately represent the airplane motions. I found this to be true much later in Houston and always took the time with a new simulator to check the accuracy of its response."

"In those days, pilots didn't really trust simulators," remembers flight simulation programmer Gene L. Waltman, who came to work at the HSFS in July 1957, shortly before the transition from the NACA to NASA, "especially the older pilots." For most of them, "what went on in a simulator just didn't look or feel right." Dick Day remembers one older pilot who after being coaxed into the Sim Lab and making a single simulation, said to Day, " 'Well, that's enough. Let's go to the bar.' And that's the way his actual flights looked." On the other hand, according to Day, "Neil believed in the simulations. . . . because he could see the results." "Always picking up new things and researching new things," Armstrong may have spent more time in simulators than any other pilot then at Edwards.

Long before the Mercury astronauts "rode the wheel," Armstrong also became one of the first NASA test pilots to endure the torture of the navy's Johnsville centrifuge "to see whether the g field that you had to go through in a rocket-launch profile would adversely affect your ability to do the precision job of flying into orbit." Armstrong explains the purpose of the research: "We hypothesized that it would be possible to pilot an aircraft into orbit—that a vertically launched rocket could be manually flown into orbit without the need for an autopilot or any sort of remote control."

A team of seven pilots took part in the experiment: Armstrong, Stan Butchart, and Forrest "Pete" Petersen from the FRC; two other NASA pilots, one from Langley and one from Ames; and two air force pilots. Lying on their backs and strapped into molded seats contoured to fit the form of the individual pilot in his pressure suit, Armstrong and his mates were put through the wringer. Every possible force and stress and every possible flight condition was brought to bear on the pilots as they whirled dizzily at the end of the fifty-foot-long arm. At the highest speed and angle of the wheel, they experienced acceleration rates as high as fifteen g's. Only a couple of the pilots handled g forces that high, and Armstrong was one of them. Gene Waltman, one of the FRC technicians on the scene, remembers

Armstrong saying that at fifteen g's so much blood left his head that he could only really see one of the instruments in the simulated cockpit. "I'd watch them get sick!" recalls Roger Barnicki, another FRC technician specializing in pilots' flight suits. "Neil was not one that got sick. Neil was one that did his fifteen and got out of there!"

Neil recalls, "We persuaded ourselves at least—I don't think we persuaded others—that it was, indeed, a doable task, operating the controls of a launch vehicle or aircraft accelerating at those high rates." With FRC engineers Ed Holleman and Bill Andrews, Armstrong coauthored a NASA report announcing the surprising results. Many people in the aerospace community questioned the finding that g-forces up to about eight g's actually had very little effect on a pilot's ability to operate flight controls until it was proven to be true in the X-15 and Mercury programs.

Armstrong later went back to Johnsville to fly X-15 entry trajectories with various flight control system settings. "This was the most complicated centrifuge simulation ever created, as it attempted to provide a complete closed-loop simulation with the lateral and vertical components of the accelerations produced due to the pilot control actions reproduced in the centrifuge's gondola cockpit."

But the key component of X-15 flight preparation was the electronic simulator. Two main X-15 simulators were built. Both of them were analog machines, because digital computers were still far too slow to do anything in "real time." North American erected the simulator called the "XD" on company property on what is now the south side of Los Angeles International Airport. Armstrong visited several times to experience the simulation of all six degrees of freedom. Flying down in an R4D, Day remembers Neil regularly asking for an ILS (instruments) approach into Los Angeles airport. "We did several flights down, basically entries. We would go up to 2,500 or 3,000 feet and we would do entries at different angles of attack and then plot angle of attack versus maximum dynamic pressure. It turned out to be a straight line, which was a special equation. And Neil learned that in case he had trouble."

Under Dick Day's direction, NASA built at Edwards an X-15 simulator that replicated the X-15 cockpit. According to Armstrong, the machine was "probably the best simulator that had ever been built up to that time, in terms of its accuracy and dependability." In preparation for each one of his seven X-15 flights, he spent fifty to sixty hours in the simulator.

"The actual X-15 flights were only ten minutes long, and generally in the simulator you didn't have the ability to do the landing," Neil explains.

"You'd just do the in-flight, and they were only a couple minutes long. We would put together a little team—the pilot, one of the research engineers, and one of the guys from the computer group—and say, 'Here's what we want to do,' and they'd take what data we had and put it in and find out what we could learn from it. You could kind of begin to understand a problem."

It is amazing just how fast the X-15 program came together. The contract was awarded to North American at the end of September 1955, then, barely a year after building began on the aircraft in September 1957, the first one rolled out of the factory. Six months later, in March 1959, the X-15 made its first captive flight and, three months after that, its first glide flight. On September 17, 1959, less than four years since the project's inception, Scott Crossfield took the most complicated and radically new aircraft design ever conceived through the paces of its first powered flight.

Armstrong was very much a part of the intense preparation: "The systems were pretty complex, a lot of things were new. The pressure came from the fact that you had to recognize what you're going to do when the systems go wrong."

Wind tunnel tests indicated that the X-15 at low speed possessed a very low lift-drag ratio (L/D), that is, one producing very little aerodynamic lift. Once its rocket burned itself out, the X-15 would come down fast and steep. Normal power-off landing techniques were inadequate.

Under the direction of a talented HSFS engineer by the name of Wendell H. Stillwell, flight tests involving the X-4 raised "some fairly significant concerns" for the X-15. As the unpowered F-104 "came down like a streamlined brick," Stillwell suggested a low L/D landing program using the F-104A (and the F-102 though the plane did not have as low an L/D).

Beginning in the summer of 1958, Armstrong flew L/D approaches testing "various and sundry combinations of speed brakes and flaps" well into 1961.

Everybody involved in the X-15 program seemed to hold an opinion about the best landing approach. Scott Crossfield believed the X-15 should descend in a smooth curve as in carrier landings. Crossfield used speed brakes and a drogue chute to replicate this approach in an F-100, and to his way of thinking it worked well. Then there was the concept from Fred Drinkwater, a test pilot at NASA Ames. Based on his own low L/D studies made in a F-104, Drinkwater felt that a long, straight-in approach—one made at relatively high speed—was ideal.

Armstrong and the other NASA pilots at Edwards had issues with both approaches. Based on their own low L/D program, they proposed a third version, which they believed offered greater flexibility. According to project engineer Gene Matranga, "Our technique involved a 360-degree spiraling descent starting at about 40,000 feet" right above the desired touchdown point on the runway. From that "high key" position, the pilot moved into a 35-degree bank (usually made to the left) while maintaining an air speed of 285 to 345 miles per hour. At roughly 20,000 feet, after some 180 degrees of the spiral had been completed, the X-15 reached the "low key." At this point, the aircraft was headed in the opposite direction of the landing runway and was about four miles abeam of the touchdown point. From the low key, the turn continued through the other 180 degrees until the X-15 lined up with the runway at about a five-mile distance. The rate of descent through the spiral averaged over two miles per minute, which meant it took on average about three minutes to go from high key to that point where the X-15 was ready to head straight in for landing.

To determine where the flare should begin, Armstrong and Walker were forced to resort to the imprecise explanation of "I feel it." In this case Matranga understood: "We tried to work mathematical models for determining the starting point, and it just could not be done. It was just something that the pilots, with their own experience, knew intuitively, and it could, from flight to flight, vary pretty significantly."

Scott Crossfield still preferred his way, even though his low and slow technique involved a substantially higher sink rate. In June 1959, in the X-15's very first free flight, Crossfield's landing was a little touchy due to a pitch damper failure and pilot-induced oscillation. In its second powered flight three months later, also flown by Crossfield, the vehicle's nose gear door failed due to a rough landing on Rogers Dry Lake. In the following flight, in November 1959, Crossfield broke the back of the airplane when it hit hard coming down on Rosamond Dry Lake. According to the official report, the structural failure occurred on landing "due to design flaw and excessive propellant weight," but the NASA engineers at Edwards knew otherwise. Even North American questioned Crossfield's landing technique. According to Gene Matranga, "We had a big meeting at North American following that incident, and I can remember Larry Green, who was the company's chief engineer on the X-15, saying, 'Scottie, you've used your technique three times. You almost bought the farm on the first flight, and you almost bought the farm on the last flight. Let's try theirs for a change.' "

North American adopted the spiral technique that Armstrong and his mates worked out in their F-104 program. The Crossfield approach was scrapped, and the technique developed by NASA became standard. In fact, the basic technique developed at the Flight Research Center worked well later in the so-called lifting body program, and it also worked well for the Space Shuttle.

Along with Matranga, Armstrong coauthored two papers on the F-104 low L/D landing investigations. The first (also coauthored by HSFS engineer Tom Finch) Neil presented at a meeting of the Institute of Aeronautical Sciences (IAS) in Los Angeles in July 1958. Dick Day, who was present at the meeting, tells the story: "Tom Finch was going to make the presentation, but they wanted the pilot there who had been through these lower L/D landings. So, Walt Williams [the head of the High-Speed Flight Station] went out and found Neil and dragged him through the back door by his ear! Literally, by his ear! It wasn't really that Neil didn't want to do it. I think Walt was just showing him off to the audience, 'Here he is!' And Neil went along with it."

Another technical paper coauthored by Armstrong during this period involved the design of the sidearm controller for the X-15. The traditional center-stick control was difficult to position accurately under the high accelerations during rocket firing and the high decelerations of atmospheric entry. Armstrong and his mates at the Flight Research Center proposed that a small, secondary control stick be mounted on the right console, whereby the pilot could make all control movements by small wrist actions from a fully supported position. A third, left-hand control stick would operate the reaction controls. "We were not certain whether such a controller should command rotation or nose position," Armstrong explains. "It wasn't easy even to decide what that flight stick should look like," and indeed it did not end up looking like the others. "We decided that the stick would pivot at the panel and then a motion up would lift the nose and a motion right would push the nose right."

Armstrong's systematic engineering approach again shined through: "We had worked on sidesticks for a number of years ahead of time, and what we found was quite surprising. We tried to find where the hinge points were in the wrist—and the wrist is a complex mechanism. If you picked something that seemed right to one pilot, the next pilot wouldn't like that at all. So we took ergonomic measurements of the motions of the hand, and it turned out that the hinge points for one person won't be the same for another. So we developed a variety of kinds of sticks and tried them in various kinds of jet aircraft. We had the opportunity to put those ideas into the X-15 during its design process so that, in fact, the sidestick turned out pretty usable. We were able to find a design that would be okay for everybody."

Part of the sidearm controller test program took place in conjunction with Cornell Aero Lab at Cornell University in Ithaca, New York, a laboratory to which Armstrong made a few visits. Cornell had a variable-stability aircraft, a Lockheed NT-33A Shooting Star, which Armstrong flew and which the lab's test pilot eventually took out to Edwards. In one of the test flights he flew in the T-33, Armstrong inadvertently broke off the experimental sidestick installed in the airplane.

Other technical papers coauthored by Armstrong came out of his work on the creation of the X-15's so-called High Range. This was the supersonic flight-test instrumentation range stretching through Nevada and California through which the X-15 would be flown. Armstrong explains: "The X-15 needed several hundred miles of space to fly the hypersonic trajectories it would fly. I was involved in the development of this high-speed range, or 'High Range,' and the combination of radar, communications, and telemetry that would be required to get data quickly, accurately, and in a minimum amount of time. The airplanes were a big investment, and the cost per flight was high, so it was important to be able to maximize the efficiency of getting the data."

In one paper coauthored with NACA/NASA researcher Gerald M. Truszynski that was presented at the winter 1959 meeting of the Society of Experimental Test Pilots, Armstrong spoke about "Future Range and Flight Test Area Needs for Hypersonic and Orbital Vehicles." With the development of more and more high-speed aircraft such as the B-58 and B-70 that could fly at Mach 2 for extended periods of time, it was important to plan to pinpoint the vast geometric space necessary to test the data. Armstrong discussed the development of the High Range (through which the X-15 had not yet been flown), but went beyond it to consider future—so-called Round Three needs—for flight test areas. (The X-1 and what followed from it had come to be called Round One; the X-15 represented Round Two. These were not terms invented by Truszynski and Armstrong but had emerged in the aerospace industry in the late 1950s as the air force started talking about a successor to the X-15 capable of a speed of Mach 12.) Along with Truszynski, an expert on radar tracking and telemetry instrumentation, Armstrong wrote a number of papers on instrumentation ranges for aircraft, including classified ones that dealt with even more advanced test ranges "where we were proposing taking off from a Caribbean island and flying westbound against the Earth's rotation and landing at Edwards, which could allow you to get quite high Mach numbers in a relatively short space—into almost nearly orbital Mach numbers, while still being suborbital."

Crossfield flew the X-15 a total of thirteen times before North American turned it over to NASA–air force–navy partnership. Armstrong watched as many of those flights as he could. Two of Crossfield's flights were in the number-one airplane, the rest in number two. The highest speed he reached in any of them was Mach 2.9, the highest altitude 88,116 feet, and the farthest distance 114.4 miles. As Armstrong explains, "The contractor was expected to demonstrate certain basic, acceptable characteristics of the airplanes operationally, and that was a negotiation between buyer and seller. Beyond that, when it got into areas that had not ever been investigated, that was the responsibility of NACA/NASA."

Armstrong was the last of the first group of NASA pilots to fly the X-15. The first to do so was Joe Walker, followed by Jack McKay. Walker, NASA's senior pilot, flew after Crossfield's eighth flight, and Major Robert M. White, the senior air force pilot, flew for the first time after Crossfield's tenth. The air force wanted White to go before Walker, but negotiations between all the parties involved, which included the U.S. Navy, put NASA first. "I was not party to those discussions," Armstrong notes. "The air force did like to set records—and that's understandable. They could use that as a motivational tool and as a promotional, advertising tool to encourage people to join the air force, 'That's where the action is.' I've never had any problem with that. Walker and White were sort of taking stair steps, the two of them, alternating flights, and the rest of us filled in behind. I was the most junior guy there, so I was kind of at the tail end, and that was fine with me."

Armstrong did not fly the X-15 for the first time until November 30, 1960. Prior to that, he did fly chase on two occasions, for Bob White's flight past Mach 3 on September 10, 1960, and for the flight made five weeks later, on October 20, 1960, by Lieutenant Commander Forrest Petersen, the first successful program flight for the navy. In all, Neil flew chase for the X-15 on six occasions. Many more times than that, Neil was located in the Edwards control center, on the microphone with the pilot, and monitoring the radar and telemetry. The last time he flew chase as an Edwards employee was on June 29, 1962, when NASA colleague Jack McKay flew the number-two airplane nearly to Mach 5. After becoming an astronaut and transferring to Houston, he did fly chase one other time when he happened to be visiting Edwards on NASA-related business. This happened on August 15, 1964, during an X-15-1 flight piloted by Jack McKay, when Neil took NASA pilot John Manke with him for an "informal" chase: "We were interested in seeing how a T-38 would perform as a chase aircraft. . . . We were with the B-52 at launch and accelerated to about Mach 1.4, but we couldn't make it back to Edwards in time for the X-15 landing."

For the majority of X-15 flights, four chase planes were employed; in the longer-range flights, a fifth was added. Armstrong remembers his duties as chase: "We would have chase aircraft at the launch flying in formation with the B-52 with the X-15 under its wing and watching all the procedures. It helped to be knowledgeable about both airplanes [the X-15 and B-52], to know what you were watching for as they would go through the prelaunch checklist. If anything was going wrong, it was the chase pilot's responsibility to report on what he could see at the back end—the business end—of the aircraft. If the engine lit [on the first try], then the X-15 pulled away very rapidly and the chase pilot just went home. On some flights the launch chase might be able to get to Edwards at the same time as the X-15. But most flights, he couldn't beat him home. There were 'catchers' at the other end that would intercept, and sometimes there might be an 'intermediate' chase plane in case the X-15 landed at one of the intermediate landing fields. The job of the catcher was to look for the X-15—and it wasn't easy to see sometimes—catch up, join up, and rendezvous with the airplane, so you were available if there was anything inside the X-15 that wasn't working—airspeed, altitude, or so forth. We had windows break in the X-15; visibility in it was poor. For the X-15 pilot, it was nice to have somebody along, outside, looking at the airplane."

At 10:42 A.M. Pacific time, on Wednesday, November 30, 1960, Armstrong sat in the cockpit of the number one airplane high over Rosamond Dry Lake anxiously waiting to be launched in an X-15 for the first time. At the controls of the B-52 drop plane were Major Robert Cole and Major Fitzhugh L. "Fitz" Fulton. Flying the chase planes for Neil were Joe Walker and Lieutenant Commander Forrest S. Petersen in F-104s and Captain William R. Looney in an F-100. Overall, it was the twenty-ninth flight in the X-15 program, the seventeenth involving the X-15-1, and the seventh made by a NASA pilot.

With Neil at the controls for the first time, the purpose of flight number 1-18-31 was simply pilot familiarization, but there was nothing ever very simple about flying the X-15. "The first one was just a checkout for me,"

Armstrong relates. He had been in the X-15 simulators for hundreds of hours, but the real thing was very different. "When you're dressed up in that pressure suit, and you get the hatch closed down on you, you find that it is a very, very confined world in there. The windshield fits over you so snugly that it's very difficult to see inside the cockpit. You realize that this is a real different machine!" Looking out of the windshield, Neil saw nothing at all of the aircraft he was flying. "It's exciting. There's a lot of tension when you're in that situation even though you know it's been done before. Everybody else has been able to handle it, so you ought to be able to. Still, a high-tension time."

At 45,000 feet, Fitzhugh in the B-52 started the same sort of countdown that would be used later in space shots: "Ten seconds, launch light is on. Five, four, three, two, one, launch." Armstrong had been air-launched before, in the X-1B, but the X-15 came off much more dramatically, with more of a clank. Then came the challenge of getting the rocket motor started, *right away.*

The engine powering Neil's X-15 was the XLR-11, built by Reaction Motors. The XLR-11 was comprised of two rocket motors, an upper and a lower. Each motor had four chambers and each chamber gave 1,500 pounds of thrust, a total of 12,000 pounds of thrust. But chamber number three, on the upper (number-one) engine, would not light, reducing the total thrust to 10,500 pounds. Even if up to four chambers had not been operating, the vehicle still could have been flown, though it would have had to stay close to base and immediately enter into a constant turn that prepared it for landing. More than four chambers missing and the pilot had to shut down whatever chambers were firing, jettison fuel, and get down. Fellow test pilot Jack McKay, acting akin to what in the manned space program would come to be known as the "CapCom" (for capsule communications officer), told Neil to "go ahead and proceed with the original flight plan."

If Reaction Motors had not been behind schedule with its new XLR-99 engine, Armstrong could have been flying a much more powerful machine. The XLR-99 produced 60,000 pounds of thrust, five times more than the XLR-11. Crossfield flew the new engine on contractor flights in November and December 1960, but the engine was not ready for government flights until March 1961. With the XLR-99, the X-15 could fly much faster and higher. But the original XLR-11, Neil explains, "gave us the ability to be flying the airplane and learning about its subsonic, transonic, and low supersonic characteristics. The landing would be the same as it would be with the bigger engine, so we faced the same challenges, learning how to properly get that thing onto the ground." The first two flights Armstrong made in the X-15 were with the XLR-11, his last five with the more powerful XLR-99 engine.

Other than the number three chamber on the upper engine failing to light, Armstrong's first X-15 flight went without incident. After the aircraft came level at 37,300 feet, Neil put it into an eight-degree climb that took him to an altitude of 48,840 feet before "pushover," or nosing back downwards. His maximum speed was only 1,155 mph, or Mach 1.75, a fact that provoked him to say over the radio, "I bet those [chase] [F-]104s are outrunning me today." At one point, Walker even taunted, "We're overrunning you," to which Neil countered, "No, you're not." But Walker and the rest were pleased with what they saw from Armstrong that day. During Neil's approach to landing on Rogers Dry Lake, one that took place less than ten minutes after launch, Walker exclaimed, "Atta boy!" Armstrong answered teasingly, "Thanks, Dad," his humorous moniker for the thirty-nine-year-old Walker, nine years his senior.

Armstrong's second X-15 flight, and his first for research purposes, came ten days later, just before the noon hour on Friday, December 9, 1960, also in the number-one airplane. Flight number 1-19-32 first tested the X-15's newly installed "ball nose."

Until this flight, the X-15, typical of all research aircraft up to this time, had a front-mounted boom with vanes to sense airspeed, altitude, angle of attack, and angle of sideslip in a free aerodynamic flow field. At such high altitudes and high speeds, the X-15 would melt its nose boom, destroying measurement data.

The ingenious solution was to design a sphere that could be mounted on the front of the aircraft. The sphere would be subject to the highest temperatures on the airplane, but it could be cooled from the inside by liquid nitrogen. Equidistant from the circumference were sensor ports in the middle of the ball as well as on the top and bottom. The "eight ball" moved automatically in pitch and yaw to keep the pressure equal on both of the ports, pointing the center hole directly into the free flow. The angle of the ball movement amounted to the airplane's angle of attack. Similarly, the ball nose received precise indications of angle of sideslip and dynamic pressure, which then gave airspeed.

"It wasn't a particularly difficult thing to fly for the first time, if it worked," Armstrong explains. Dropped by the B-52 at the standard 45,000 feet over the Palmdale VOR station by Captain Jack Allavie and Major Robert Cole, the X-15 climbed to 50,095 feet at a speed of Mach 1.8.

Burnout of the rocket came immediately after Neil extended the aircraft's speed brakes. The ball nose worked extremely well, so well that it would be used throughout the remainder of the X-15 program. Neil's own performance was, again, solid. Flying chase were Lieutenant Commander Petersen and Major Bob White in F-104s and Major Daniel in an F-100F. Upon touchdown, Joe Walker, acting as "NASA 1," radioed up from the control center, "Real nice flight, boy!"

It would be over a year before Armstrong would make another X-15 flight. Throughout 1961, Armstrong continued to work on the new automatic flight-control system for X-15-3, the aircraft in which he would make his third through sixth X-15 flights starting in December 1961. Until then, there would not be nearly so much test flying for Neil as in previous years. But there would be more travel than ever, much of it done on commercial airliners, back and forth to Minneapolis-Honeywell and, even more so, to Seattle, where he consulted for NASA on the air force's new X-20 space plane program, known as Dyna-Soar.

It would be in Seattle in late spring 1961 where one of the worst tragedies that could ever befall a young family began.

CHAPTER 14

The Worst Loss

Seattle, the state of Washington's Emerald City, can in early June be down-right blissful: fresh air, golden sunshine, azure skies, verdant landscapes. On such a day, the loving parents of two young children might think that nothing could ever possibly go wrong.

The family was temporarily in the city because Neil was working at Boeing, the contractor on Project Dyna-Soar, a joint NASA–air force program that was developing a manned hypersonic boost-glider as a follow-on to the X-15. Some of its advocates had thought that the Dyna-Soar vehicle, designated X-20, might beat Project Mercury's ballistic capsule into space. But Alan Shepard's suborbital flight just a few weeks earlier, on May 5, 1961, put an end to that part of the dream. Yet Dyna-Soar lived on.

Visiting the public park on Lake Washington had become a regular weekend outing for the Armstrongs in Seattle. Along with swimming, Ricky enjoyed riding the swing, the merry-go-round, and the teeter-totter as would any boy about to turn four years old. Karen, two years old, ran through the park in her own great big adventure.

Neil and Jan called their little girl Muffie. As a teenager in Wapakoneta, Neil had a friend by the name of Fred Fisher whose sweet younger sister was named Karen. In the little girl's eyes, Neil could do nothing wrong. When he visited the Fisher home, Neil, unlike Fred's other friends, paid attention to little Karen "Cookie" Fisher. Shortly before heading off to Purdue, Neil told his sister June that if he ever had a daughter he wanted to name her Karen. When a daughter was born on April 13, 1959, the couple named her Karen Anne Armstrong. Instead of Cookie, Neil chose for Karen the nickname Muffie, an endearing form of Muffin.

A good father naturally loves all his children. Yet there is often something special between a father and a daughter, perhaps especially with Neil, whose formative relationships were with his mother and his sister rather

160

than his father and his brother. June discerned "how he loved Rick [his first-born], but when Karen was born, he was just a different man."

While leaving the public park on Sunday, June 4, 1961, Muffie had one of those typical childhood spills. "Karen was running from the grass down to the street," Janet remembered, "and it was such a big step, she tripped and fell. You could see the knot right there on her head. We went immediately home. She had a little nosebleed with it, and we thought maybe she'd had a little concussion. By that evening we noticed that her eyes weren't operating properly." The Seattle pediatrician Janet consulted the next day while Neil was at work told Janet to have Karen checked out thoroughly back in California, where the family was headed at the end of the week.

Karen's regular pediatrician in Lancaster, Dr. Phil Stumm, sent her on to an ophthalmologist, who immediately saw that there was a problem. The eye doctor told Janet to see how the child did at home and to bring her back in a week.

"I was teaching swimming during this time," Janet explained, "and putting on a water show involving synchronized swimming." A mother of one of Janet's students was a registered nurse. While Ricky swam and took lessons with the others, Karen stayed with the nurse, who was alarmed to observe that Karen seemed to be getting progressively worse. She kept tripping and her eyes were almost constantly crossed. The nurse told Janet to hospitalize Karen for a comprehensive series of tests.

Janet made the arrangements, because Neil, upon returning from Seattle, had left immediately to do some work at Minneapolis-Honeywell: "He didn't know anything about it, so I finally called him and told him I was hospitalizing her." That day the girl's eyes began to roll and she could not talk plainly anymore.

Daniel Freeman Memorial Hospital was a Catholic hospital on North Prairie Avenue in Inglewood, southwest of downtown Los Angeles. There, at a facility grounded in the tradition of the Sisters of St. Joseph of Carondelet, a team of physicians led by Dr. Eric Yuhl and Dr. Duke Hanna put the little girl through a battery of tests, culminating in a pneumoencephalogram. Prior to the invention of CT scanning, a pneumoencephalogram was the only diagnostic tool for the inner parts of the brain. The invasive procedure required a spinal tap and an injection of air into the patient's spinal canal. The injected air displaced spinal fluid as the air rose to the patient's head—specifically, into the cerebral ventricles—when the patient was turned upright. Radiographic visualization then allowed the doctors to evaluate the midline brain structures and the brain stem.

The X-rays showed that Karen had a glioma of the pons, a malignant tumor growing within the middle part of her brain stem. Brain-stem tumors were, and still are, the most dreaded cancers in pediatric oncology. Quite rare, such tumors account for about 10 percent of all childhood brain tumors, of which there are only about 1,500 newly diagnosed cases in the United States each year. Even today, with the availability of chemotherapy, the prognosis for brain-stem gliomas is remarkably poor: a majority of children still die within a year of diagnosis.

"They immediately started X-ray treatment on her to try and reduce the size of the tumor," Janet recalled. "In the process, she completely lost all her balance. She could not walk; she could not stand . . . She was the sweetest thing. She never, ever complained." Everyone at the hospital was "so good to her and so kind." They would let Janet stay with her: "I was with her around the clock, or Neil was there. He took a week off [the flight logs at Edwards indicate that Neil was off from June 26 through July 6 and again on July 13 and 14] and we stayed in a motel down there. One of us kept Ricky and one of us stayed at the hospital." The initial week of radiation was followed by six weeks of outpatient treatment.

"During this time, she learned to crawl again and eventually she learned to walk again," Janet noted. "Ricky was a big, big help there. He had just turned four. Eventually her eyes straightened out. Of course, she had a big bald spot from the X-rays. Then it got so I could bring her home on weekends and took her back to L.A. through the week." Over the seven-week period, the hospital gave Karen the maximum 2,300 roentgens of X-ray. "She took the radiation beautifully," according to her mother. "She never had any sickness."

For the next month and a half, Karen's condition improved. The radiation temporarily arrested the tumor. Neil frequently consulted with his sister June and her husband Dr. Jack Hoffman, a physician who had just set up a private practice in Wisconsin. "We had a lot of phone calls back and forth," says June. "I'm the eternal optimist, but my husband told me, 'No, she'll be dead within six months.' "

Before long, all of Karen's symptoms were back—the difficulty with coordination and walking, the crossed eyes and double vision, the inability to speak clearly, the sagging of one side of the face. The person who first noticed signs of Karen's regression was brother Ricky, her regular playmate. Returning to Daniel Freeman Memorial Hospital, Neil and Janet knew there was only one possible treatment remaining: cobalt. The invention of the cobalt machine in the 1950s had been a major breakthrough in cancer treatment. Instead of relying on X-rays, which could not penetrate deep-seated tumors, the gamma-ray beam generated from the breakdown of radioactive cobalt 60 irradiated much deeper. Unfortunately, cobalt killed not only cancer cells but also healthy tissue. Side effects could be more unpleasant and more damaging, especially for a two-year-old girl.

Neil and Janet decided to try the cobalt, but Karen's weakened little body could not take it. The doctors at Freeman Memorial were very straightforward with the Armstrongs. Rather than hospitalizing her again, everyone involved realized she would be happier at home. The family even traveled to Ohio for the holidays. "She made it through Christmas," Janet recounted. "She couldn't walk by this time—she could crawl—but she was still able to enjoy Christmas. It seems like the day Christmas was over, she just went downhill. . . . It just overcame her."

Through the ordeal, Neil and Janet received particularly thoughtful support from Joe Walker, Neil's boss, and from Joe's wife Grace, who were their best friends in California. The Walkers had recently experienced their own tragic loss. In June 1958, their two-year-old son, Robert Bruce Walker, had died suddenly, the result of a radically deficient immune system brought on by an extreme case of food allergy. "After Robbie died," Grace Walker-Wiesman tearfully remembered, "I was really searching for what it must mean that a child comes into this world and then is taken away. When I heard about Karen, I desperately wanted to do something to help."

"Jan brought Karen around a number of times," Grace recalled. "We put her in the high chair and tried again with some Jell-O or pudding. She was a gay little thing. She would try to eat it and then she would just throw it up. Janet said to me, 'I'm going to go over to the doctor and see if there is *something* we can do.' " But there was nothing that could help.*

---

* Grace Walker, for one, has always wondered whether there might have been an environmental factor involved in the death of Karen Armstrong: "There has been any number of brain tumors out in that valley. There was a family up in the hills near where Janet and Neil lived that had two children die of brain tumors. In 1951, when we came to Edwards, the government was still doing a lot of aboveground atomic testing in Nevada. When it did, a day or so after, we would have these terrible east winds, just blowing dust and dirt. You almost never get an east wind in the desert; it's usually northwest all the time. I've often thought that we probably had atomic fallout lying around on those hills and going into water systems all over. I think someone told me that Antelope Valley Hospital did a study on brain tumors in the area and could not find any connection. But I wouldn't be surprised." GWW to author, Reedley, CA, Dec. 14, 2002, transcript, p. 10.

From its establishment by President Truman in 1951 until its closing in 1992, the Nevada Test Site (NTS), a Rhode Island–sized testing ground northwest of Las Vegas, conducted the majority of America's nuclear weapons tests. More than nine hundred atomic explosions took place at the NTS, the great majority of them in the 1950s and early 1960s.

Somewhat earlier, Neil also paid Grace Walker a visit: "I remember Neil bringing Karen over without saying anything, just a visit on a Saturday. They wanted to see our new baby [a daughter born in September 1961]. So I got her out of the bassinet and put her on the bed, and Neil carried Karen over so she could touch her and kind of hold her. Karen was a valiant little girl. I wanted to do something overt, but I didn't feel Neil would consider it acceptable—putting hands on Karen or saying a prayer or something. But I felt that Neil came to me because he wanted somehow to encourage Karen and to hold on to a hope, just a wild hope, like parents do. You could see that he loved his little girl very deeply."

On Sunday morning, January 28, 1962, Karen Anne Armstrong died at home in the family's Juniper Hills cabin after an agonizing six-month battle with the inoperable brain tumor. The week leading up to her death must have been particularly difficult on Janet as Neil was away on job-related travel to Florida. The little girl succumbed to pneumonia, a complication caused by her weakened condition. The day she died was Neil and Janet's sixth wedding anniversary.

Final rites were held at the Mumaw Funeral Home at 2:00 P.M. on Wednesday, January 31, with burial in the children's sanctuary at Joshua Memorial Park, both in Lancaster. The Reverend Carroll N. Parker of the Community Methodist Church in Pearblossom officiated. A poem printed on the remembrance card read: "God's garden has need of a little flower, it had grown for a time here below. But in tender love He took it above, in more favorable clime to grow." The well-known passage from the Gospel of St. Luke offered a final prayer: "Suffer little Children to come unto Me— for of such is the kingdom of God." The small stone marking her grave read "Karen Anne Armstrong, 1959–1962." In between these two lines was carved the precious little nickname Neil had given her: Muffie.

In honor of Neil's daughter, the Flight Research Center grounded all test planes the day of her funeral. (The fact that Karen had died was recorded in the FRC flight log for January 28.) One man who paid his respects, FRC engineer John McTigue, recalled Neil being very "composed"

Many of the early detonations occurred aboveground and resulted in some devastating health effects on "downwinders." Due to weather patterns, most of the fallout landed, not to the southwest of the testing ground, in the direction of the Antelope Valley, but to the northeast, in northern Nevada and in western Utah. The NTS was bounded on three sides by Nellis AFB, an airfield into which Armstrong occasionally flew while he worked at Edwards. The influence of any nuclear fallout causing higher cancer rates in the Antelope Valley has never been specifically studied.

at the funeral, though everyone knew he was suffering deeply. Grace Walker also remembered Neil being very stoic and showing little emotion, in contrast to Janet, who was visibly shaken. Despite their close friendship, Grace also remembered not hugging Neil that day or ever: "I think he always felt like that wasn't the thing to do."

Very seldom was Neil Armstrong not in control of his emotions. Grace Walker observed Neil channeling his grief for Karen, just as her husband Joe had done in the aftermath of their son's death in 1958. "Joe was very supportive for me, but I would say it is a pilot thing. Most of them act pretty stoic. They would say they had an 'okay flight' and then they would go into the bathroom and vomit. I think Joe was a little more supportive for me than Neil was for Janet. Now I say that not as a criticism, but just the way that Neil was—he was very tight emotionally. But the whole attraction to those men—outside of their being good-looking and daring—was their laid-back nature and sense of humor."

People who knew Armstrong well indicated that Neil never once over the years brought up the subject of his daughter's illness and death. In fact, several of his closest working associates stated that they *did not know* that Neil *ever had a daughter.*

Quickly after his son's funeral, Joe Walker went right back to work; so did Neil after Karen's. Neil was back in the office on Monday, February 5, and back in the air the day after that. Armstrong took no other time off from the job until a family trip to Ohio in mid-May, though there was another monthlong stay in Seattle from February 26 to March 20, when Neil was again consulting on the Dyna-Soar program.

"That hurt Jan a lot," Grace claims, that Neil went right back to work. "She is a very directed and self-sufficient person, but she really needed support after that. She desperately needed her husband to help her. Neil kind of used work as an excuse. He got as far away from the emotional thing as he could. I know he hurt terribly over Karen. That was just his way of dealing with it.

"Jan was angry for a very long time," said Grace. "Angry at God, and I think at Neil, too. The dynamics between a married couple are already so complicated. . . . I don't think they were communicating too well." Unwilling to get into combative verbal exchanges, "Neil would leave Janet in limbo."

To help Rick through the loss, Neil and Janet got their son a new pet. (Their previous dog, a Belgian shepherd, had run off with a pack of wild dogs.) Rick named him Super, perhaps because Superman was indestructible. "They came by that day and Ricky was so happy," Grace remembered. In response to a question from *Life* reporter Dodie Hamblin in 1969, Janet stated that Ricky, twelve years old at that time, definitely still remembered his sister. But "he doesn't speak of her much anymore. . . . He was a different child after all this." *

Grace Walker and a handful of other close friends did what they could to support Janet and Ricky emotionally: "We did things with the kids." Slowly but surely she saw Janet making a stronger effort to keep life going. During the summer of 1962, Janet became pregnant with her third and last child, Mark. By the fall, the family was making its move to Houston.

Still, one wonders about the lasting effects of Karen's death upon Neil and Janet Armstrong, both individually and upon their marriage, even though that marriage lasted another thirty-two years, until a divorce (initiated by Janet on the grounds of "irreconcilable differences") sent them on their separate ways in the early 1990s.

In a remarkable chapter of his 2003 book *All the Presidents' Children: Triumph and Tragedy in the Lives of America's First Families,* author Doug Wead describes how an unusually high number of U.S. presidents and their wives—Adams, Jefferson, Harrison, Pierce, Lincoln, Garfield, McKinley, Cleveland, Theodore Roosevelt, Eisenhower, Kennedy, George H. Bush— suffered the loss of a child. For a few, the death became the catalytic event in their ascendancy to the presidency.

It is tempting to apply to Neil Armstrong Wead's assertion that propelling the man outside the family and into public life enabled him "to be alone and escape the tenderness of the loss," for there is no question that, despite surface appearances, Karen's death shattered him to the core. "It was a terrible time," June reminisced, still teary-eyed forty years after her little niece's death. "I thought his heart would break. Somehow he felt responsible for her death, not in a physical way, but in terms of 'Is there some gene in my body that made the difference?' When he can't control something, that's when you see the real person. I thought his heart would break."

June recalled a telling incident from the spring after Karen's death, when Neil took his family to Wapakoneta for a short vacation and a small,

---

* Forty-six-year-old Rick Armstrong stated in September 2003 that he recalls "very little" about his sister Karen, whose death was "a closed subject." Asked specifically if Karen's death was a taboo subject in the family, Rick responded: "It wasn't stated that way. It just wasn't addressed." Was it just too painful to remember? "I think it must be." Rick Armstrong to author, Cincinnati, OH, Sept. 22, 2003, pp. 4–5.

informal family reunion. "A baby sheep had died" at the Korspeter farm, June recounted. "The men went out to the barn to attend to the dead lamb. My husband later told me that Neil could not go into the barn. Neil waited outside while the other men took care of the animal."

Such intense feelings of sadness and loss did not keep Armstrong from regularly visiting his daughter's grave. On several occasions after leaving California to become an astronaut, Armstrong returned to Edwards on NASA business, and when he did, he usually visited the children's sanctuary in Joshua Memorial Park. According to fellow NASA test pilot Bruce Peterson, "I would give him a ride, and he would want to stop by the cemetery. I would stay in the car. He'd go over and spend a little time by his daughter's grave site."

Later in life, during Armstrong's most celebrated days as an astronaut, there would be some curious personal moments that hearkened back to the loss of Karen. A number of newspaper stories following Gemini VIII and Apollo 11 show Neil holding a little girl in his arms. The most extraordinary of these appeared in a wire service article covering the Apollo 11 crew's post-flight visit to London, England, in October 1969. Under the headline "2-year-old Girl Bussed by Neil," the story began by explaining that Armstrong, Buzz Aldrin, and Mike Collins were about to set out for Buckingham Palace and an audience with Queen Elizabeth and Prince Philip. "But it was a tiny girl who came to see the spacemen only to be nearly crushed against a barrier who won the heart of the slender, blue-eyed Armstrong, the first man to set foot on the Moon. A policeman had picked up Wendy Jane Smith, two, when she was shoved against a barricade in front of the U.S. Embassy. Armstrong caught her eye and quickly stepped forward and kissed her while a crowd of more than three hundred cheered."

Was there an intensely personal—most likely, subconscious—relationship between Karen's death at the end of January 1962 and Neil's decision to submit his name for astronaut selection just a few months later? "I never asked him," June confesses. "I couldn't." Yet it is clear to June that, through his becoming an astronaut, Neil turned it all around: "The death of his little girl caused him to invest those energies into something very positive, and that's when he started into the space program."

CHAPTER 15

Higher Resolve

Armstrong has never related his decision to become an astronaut to his daughter's death: "It was a hard decision for me to make, to leave what I was doing, which I liked very much, to go to Houston. You don't have to be in any particular program or wear a particular color of shirt to find research questions that need answering.... But by 1962 Mercury was on its way, the future programs were well designed, and the lunar mission was going to become a reality. I decided that if I wanted to get out of the atmospheric fringes and into deep space work, that was the way to go."

Looked at in this way, Armstrong's views about his future began to evolve on October 4, 1957. On that day, the Soviet Union launched into orbit the world's first artificial satellite, Sputnik I, a stunning technological achievement that put a new sense of value and urgency on everything that the American aerospace community had been doing to prepare for flight outside the atmosphere. Previous to Sputnik, "space" had been a dirty word in the American political arena. When NACA official Ira H. Abbott in the mid-1950s mentioned the possibilities of spaceflight to a U.S. House subcommittee, one congressman accused Abbott of talking "science fiction." Armstrong acknowledges, "Spaceflight was not generally regarded as a realistic objective. It was a bit of pie in the sky. So although we were working toward that end, it was not something we acknowledged much publicly. Not necessarily for fear of ridicule, but probably somewhat."

The day Sputnik launched, Armstrong was in Los Angeles at a meeting of the Society of Experimental Test Pilots: "What was happening in the test-flight world was a very hard sell to the press, and it became completely impossible once Sputnik came across the sky.

"Sputnik did change our world. It absolutely changed our country's view

of what was happening, the potential of space. I'm not sure how many people realized at that point just where this would lead. President Eisenhower
was saying something like, 'What's the worry? It's just one small ball.' But
I'm sure that was a façade behind which he had substantial concerns, because if they could put something into orbit, they could put a nuclear
weapon on a target in the United States."

The Sputnik crisis quickly led to, among other things, the formal aboli-
tion of the NACA and its amelioration by NASA, from the start a much
higher-profile organization. NASA's first priority was to place a man in
space through a program known as Mercury. "We were certainly aware of
Mercury," Armstrong notes, "from our colleagues in the military, friends
and people we flew with daily, some of whom had been invited to consider
applying for the astronaut program." Of all the pilots who became the first
astronauts—Gordon Cooper, Gus Grissom, and Deke Slayton from the air
force; Scott Carpenter, Wally Schirra, and Alan Shepard from the navy; and
John Glenn from the marines—Neil knew only Schirra well, from working
with him at Patuxent River on the navy's preliminary evaluation of the
McDonnell XF-4H, which later became the F-4, a principal fighter for both
the navy and the air force. With a few of the others, he had sat in occasional
technical meetings and had seen them in the air or at the Edwards's officers'
club.

Unlike Chuck Yeager and other like-minded test pilots, Armstrong
did not denigrate the Mercury astronauts as "Spam in a can": "I didn't have
that feeling at all—the Yeager criticism of the whole idea of the way they
were approaching space. At the time the Mercury program was started, it
might have well gone that way. In a sense it did, in that they had a lot of
chimpanzee flights. But the Mercury crewmen insisted on making their
spacecraft an airplane-like device, with the same conventions as normal
airplanes, so that their normal instincts would be proper. So I think that
was a great contribution on the part of the Mercury guys. . . . I always
felt that 'form follows function,' that engineering would decide the best
way to go. I thought the attractions of being an astronaut were actually, not
so much the Moon, but flying in a completely new medium."

This is not to say that Armstrong did not continue to prefer a winged
pathway into space, via transatmospheric vehicles like the X-15 and X-20
Dyna-Soar. Even after the first suborbital Mercury flights in 1961, Armstrong thought "we were far more involved in spaceflight research than the
Mercury people.

"I always felt that the risks we had in the space side of the program were probably less than we had back in flying at Edwards or the general flight-test community. The reason is that we were exploring the frontiers, we were out at the edges of the flight envelope all the time, testing limits. That isn't to say that we didn't expect risks in the space program. But we felt pretty comfortable because we had so much technical backup and we didn't go nearly as close to the limits as much as we did back in the old flight-test days."

A significantly higher rate of fatalities in the world of flight test supports Armstrong's contention. Apollo 1 astronauts Gus Grissom, Roger Chaffee, and Ed White died in January 1967 when a fire broke out in their Block I spacecraft during a routine test while sitting on the launchpad at Cape Kennedy, and astronauts Theodore C. Freeman (in 1964), Charles A. Bassett and Elliot M. See Jr. (in 1966), and Clifton C. "C. C." Williams (in 1967), died in crashes of airplanes they were piloting; but not a single American astronaut was lost in an actual space flight until the loss of the seven members of the Space Shuttle *Challenger* crew in 1986. In contrast, the flight-test community buried many of its members. In 1948 alone, at Edwards alone, thirteen test pilots were killed. One of them was the air base's namesake, young Captain Glen Edwards; another was Howard C. Lilly, the first NACA test pilot to be killed during a research flight. In the next ten years, many test pilots lost their lives at Edwards. In the year 1952 alone, sixty-two pilots died there in the span of thirty-six weeks, an astonishing rate of nearly two pilots per week, many of them involving flight test. The navy's test-flight mortality rate was just as disturbing. At Patuxent River, Lieutenant Pete Conrad, in the words of author Tom Wolfe, wore "his great dark sepulchral bridge coat" to more funerals than most members of his Princeton graduating class of 1953 wore their tuxedos.

Armstrong might very well have chosen to remain in the challenging world of test flying. The X-15 program had hardly seen its last days. Neil's final X-15 flight occurred on July 26, 1962. Though it was the sixty-fourth flight in the program, there were still 135 more X-15 flights to follow in the next six years, before the program ended in October 1968. Between the time of Neil's first X-15 flight in November 1960 and his last in July 1962, the X-15 made thirty-five test flights; Neil flew seven, or one-fifth, of them. It has always been Neil's understanding that, if he had stayed on at Edwards, he would likely have become the X-15 program's chief test pilot. In that capacity, he would have flown the X-15 even more frequently, likely at a rate of one every four flights. "I liked the people I worked with at Edwards," Armstrong recollects. "There was no reason to try to change things to get into a new field. Staying with the X-15, that was very attractive. It was a real project. It was good. I enjoyed it." In the end, he just did not decide to do it.

In November 1960, NASA named Armstrong a member of the air force/NASA Dyna-Soar "pilot consultant group." Although the air force eventually complicated—some say, ruined—Dyna-Soar by trying to make it operational, the original intent of the Round Three vehicle was research. Its objective was demonstrating controlled *lifting* reentry, a technique (not unrelated to the *lifting-body* concept) that created enough aerodynamic lift to give a transatmospheric vehicle the cross-range necessary to maneuver down to established runways, as the Space Shuttle would later do. Lifting reentry provided a flexibility that the nonlifting, blunt-body ballistic capsules sorely lacked. Because it pushed technology so fast and so hard in so many areas (notably high-speed aerodynamics, high-temperature structural materials, and reentry protection concepts), Dyna-Soar, even more than the other X-series programs before it, served as a critical focal point for a wide range of future-oriented aerospace R&D.

Although NASA engineers at Dryden had considered the possibility of air-launching the X-20 from a B-52 or B-70 mother ship, the plan that NASA and the air force adopted was to loft the Sänger-like boost-glider into orbit on top of a Titan III. This raised the problem of how to rescue the X-20 and its crew if some emergency, like a fire or booster failure, occurred on the launchpad. Such a nightmare scenario almost happened in the Gemini program, when, in December 1965, Wally Schirra in Gemini VI-A came awfully close to yanking the seat ejection ring between his legs and blowing himself and fellow astronaut Tom Stafford up and off their Titan. Because Dyna-Soar was a winged vehicle capable (unlike Schirra's Gemini capsule) of real flying, a pilot inside the X-20, once blasted clear of his Titan booster, could perhaps fly the vehicle down safely to a runway landing.

Armstrong (who had published a technical report on his low L/D testing in delta-wing aircraft using an F-102) conceived of a way to test the rescue concept. "That was our thing at Edwards," Armstrong explains, "doing power-off landings." The small escape rocket being planned for Dyna-Soar shot the X-20 up several thousand feet and it occurred to Armstrong that "maybe we could duplicate that. So I set about finding out if we could and see if we could get an airplane for it." *

The F-104 might have been used again if not for the fact that two F5D-1 Skylancers had just become available to NASA. The F5D was an experimental fighter built by Douglas that the navy had decided not to produce. Only four of the aircraft were ever built, with two of the prototypes given to NASA in late 1960 essentially as castaways. Armstrong flew one of the F5Ds on September 26, 1960, during a visit to NASA Ames. Neil realized immediately that the F5D could serve particularly well in a study of Dyna-Soar abort procedures because its wing planform was a good match for the X-20's slender delta-shaped wing. Armstrong knew it took a plane like the F5D whose gear could extend out fully and safely at high speed, over 300 knots (345 mph): "So I went out and fiddled with the airplane to see what initial conditions I could get, what airspeed I could match, and how soon could I get the gear down to produce the drag for the L/D that I needed."

Armstrong began flight tests in the F5D in July 1961, just shortly after Karen Anne's illness was diagnosed. While he and Janet were initiating what became the little girl's first round of X-ray treatment, Neil occupied his mind with the problem of figuring out what kind of separation flight path and landing approach would best bring the X-20 down safely: "I fiddled with that. I think other guys also did it later, but I confirmed that it could be doable."

Between July 7 and November 1, 1961, Armstrong made no fewer than ten test flights in the F5D. By early October, he had developed an effective maneuver for the abort. Neil simulated the act of being shot away by the escape rocket by making a steep vertical climb in the F5D to 7,000 feet. At that point, he pulled on his control column until the "X-20" lay on its back. Rolling the craft upright, he initiated the low L/D approach. Landing

---

* In a letter published in *Air & Space Smithsonian* in 2003, William G. Cowdin, former program manager for the Dyna-Soar booster rocket maker Aerojet-General in Sacramento, Calif., reported an alleged conversation he had with Armstrong about Dyna-Soar abort procedure: "At that time there was debate as to whether a pilot could react fast enough to prevent a catastrophic event, or whether automatic sensors should be included in the design. Neil's response to me was 'Give me a stick and throttle and I will fly the SOB.' " William G. Cowdin, Burbank, Calif., "Hidden Figures of High Society," *Air & Space Smithsonian* 17 (Feb./Mar. 2003): 12. When shown this letter to the editor, Armstrong responded: "I am EXTREMELY skeptical about this quote. Dyna-Soar did not have a throttle and I am not prone to make that sort of statement in any circumstance. Perhaps someone else made such a statement." NAA: e-mail to author, Feb. 18, 2003.

came on a specially marked area on Rogers Dry Lake, a parcel that simulated the 10,000-foot landing strip at Cape Canaveral.

Late in the summer of 1961, NASA installed a Cinerama camera into the nose of the F5D to film the abort procedure. On Tuesday, October 3, 1961, Armstrong demonstrated the Dyna-Soar rescue during a special visit of Vice President Lyndon B. Johnson to Edwards. Two days later, Neil repeated the show for an audience that included Marvin Miles, the aerospace editor for the *Los Angeles Times,* who detailed the technique in a long feature.

Armstrong handled the F5D research flawlessly. Much of the flying that he performed for Dyna-Soar came during the troubled times following the diagnosis of Karen's tumor.

It was six weeks after Karen's death, on March 15, 1962, that the air force and NASA jointly named Armstrong as one of the six "pilot-engineers" for Dyna-Soar. The only other NASA pilot named was Milt Thompson, so the selection was quite an honor for Armstrong. The air force designees, all age thirty-two, were Captain Pete Knight, Captain Russell L. Rogers, Captain Henry C. Gordon, and Major James W. Wood. At thirty-one, Armstrong was the youngest of the group. "We were the pilots that were to do the development work, the simulator work, consulting on the aircraft, sitting in them, arguing through all the points," Armstrong recalls. If a small fleet of X-20s actually got built, the sextet would be the prime contenders for first flying the X-20 when it came on line, then scheduled for 1964.

As Armstrong looked into his professional future following his daughter's death, he saw three choices: "I could have kept flying the X-15. The X-15 was real. You *knew* it was real. . . . I was also working on the Dyna-Soar. That was still an on-paper airplane, but it was a possibility. Then there was this other project down at Houston, the Apollo program. Project Gemini had not been really much identified yet at that point. Recognize, that in this world of aerospace R&D, we constantly see projects come and go. For example, I never flew the D-558 Skyrocket, although I was assigned to that project for a long time. I never got to that goal. I can't tell you now just why in the end I made the decision I did, but I consider it fortuitous that I happened to pick one that was a winning horse. . . . I don't think there was a Eureka moment. . . . Apollo was just so overpoweringly exciting that I decided to give up these other opportunities to pursue it, even though I knew it may never happen."

Armstrong admits that the growing excitement surrounding Project Mercury may have had something to do with his decision. On February 20,

1962, three weeks after Karen's funeral, Mercury astronaut and fellow Ohioan John H. Glenn orbited the Earth three times in *Friendship 7*. No celebration since that for Armstrong's hero Charles A. Lindbergh in 1927 matched the national outpouring in honor of America's newest hero. If ever there was a time to entice a pilot out of his airplane and into a spacecraft, this was it. "Astronaut Glenn" appeared on the cover of countless newspapers and magazines in the winter and spring of 1962. *Life* put Glenn in his space helmet on its cover a full two weeks before he even made his Mercury flight; a ten-page, highly illustrated feature story entitled "Making of a Brave Man" called Glenn "a man marked to do great things."

Armstrong deliberated between four and five months over his decision to apply for astronaut selection. All the while, he continued to grieve for his daughter—and he continued to fly.

Armstrong himself claims there were no noticeable ill effects on his work at Edwards, but the picture appears more complicated. In the months immediately following Karen's death, Armstrong was involved in a series of flying mishaps at Edwards, an uncharacteristic stretch of "problem flights." His peers and superiors at Edwards came to worry that Neil had become, in their words, "accident prone."

Even the very best pilot commits the occasional error and experiences the random mishap in the course of routine flying. In his first years at Edwards, Armstrong likewise had a few minor incidents. In his first and only flight in the Bell X-5 in October 1955, shortly after beginning his job at the HSFS, the landing gear door fell off during takeoff. In part it was Neil's fault, because, in his attempt to get his landing gear fully retracted, he oversped the plane's gear limit.* Then, in August 1957, in an incident previously mentioned, he cracked the nose-gear wheel of the X-1B when the airplane began porpoising after touchdown on Rogers Dry Lake. In yet another mishap, he hurt his thumb badly when he accidentally shut the canopy of the

---

* Armstrong recalls his X-5 incident: "My checkout pilot was Jack McKay, and he explained that they often had trouble getting the nose gear to lock up. So, after takeoff, when retracting the gear, you were advised to nose over and go to about half a g. That would help get the nose gear up in place, due to less download on the gear. So I attempted to do it, but it didn't seem to be locking up. In the meantime, I was nosing over, getting in a nose-down position and, of course, the aircraft was speeding up, and I suspect that I actually 'oversped' the gear-limit speed, knocking the fairing door off. I never got the indication that the gear was completely retracted, so I put back down and wasn't able to conduct my flight plan. . . . I never got a chance to fly the airplane again. They decided it was at the end of its research lifetime." NAA to author, Cincinnati, OH, Nov. 26, 2002, transcript, p. 7.

YRF-84F on his hand as he was doing his final pre-takeoff checklist. Other than those few incidents, the record of Armstrong's flying at Edwards was remarkably unblemished. Even after Karen's hospitalization, Neil's flying showed no indication that his performance was suffering.

The same can be said about Armstrong's continued involvement in the X-15 program. Twice during Karen's illness—on December 20, 1961, and January 17, 1962—Armstrong piloted the rocket plane, his third and fourth of seven X-15 flights overall. Both flights came off without any hitch, at least not in Armstrong's performance.

Preparing for an X-15 flight took high intensity from everyone involved, but no one felt the pressure like the pilot. Furthermore, the X-15 flight scheduled for December 1961 with Armstrong at the helm was to be the first run of the number-three aircraft. Already the X-15-3—or more precisely, the plane's powerful new XLR-99 rocket engine—had a checkered history. On June 8, 1960, during what was supposed to be a final ground test by the contractor, the XLR-99 exploded on its test stand. "It was the biggest bang I'd ever heard," said North American pilot Scott Crossfield. "Fortunately for me and the airplane, the explosion blew the forward section—the tanks and the cockpit—out of the major part of the blaze. The firemen were right on their toes and they moved in to blanket the tanks and the fire area with foam." At first everyone thought the rocket engine had blown. As is often the case, the first impression was wrong. As soon as all the scattered parts could be found and cooled down enough to touch, a disenchanted group of engineers mostly from North American began a thorough investigation into what caused the explosion. Eventually the investigators determined that a frozen regulator, a faulty relief valve, and a rapid buildup of back pressure caused the center structure of the X-15's ammonia tank to ram and smash open the control system's hydrogen peroxide sphere. Not until the entire pressurizing and pressure release systems were thoroughly analyzed, redesigned, tested, and retested could another pilot step into the X-15 cockpit. By the time Armstrong got into the plane in mid-December 1962, the first flight of X-15-3 had been delayed by sixteen months, at a cost of $4 million.

The long delay and extra cost heightened anxiety over Armstrong's flight. "There's always concern about whether there had been damage that you didn't recognize," Armstrong admits, "but the engine went back to the plant and got torn apart and reassembled." Following a new round of engine ground testing, Neil had every reason to think that the X-15-3's problems, at least those causing the June 1960 explosion, had been solved.

Rebuilding the aircraft gave North American the opportunity to update the newest X-15 airplane's research equipment and outfit it with the MH-96 "black box" that Armstrong had been helping Minneapolis-Honeywell to develop for the program. Flight testing the innovative adaptive control system became the primary purpose of Neil's December 1961 flight.

The flight was scheduled to launch on December 19 but was aborted when instrumentation involving the X-15's ball nose did not read correctly, so it got pushed back to the next day. The flight (number 3-1-2 and the forty-sixth in the program) was not without problems. Immediately upon being dropped by Major Jack Allavie from his B-52 over Silver Lake east of Death Valley, all three axes of the new stability augmentation system on the MH-96 disengaged and "a severe right roll occurred with accompanying yaw and pitch excursions."

Armstrong recalls that the failure did not cause him much trouble: "One of the aspects of the MH-96 was its reliability. It was a system designed to run for 76,000 hours between failures." As it turned out, the system experienced a blip a lot sooner—at the very start of Neil's flight. Armstrong managed to reset the system on the first try, "so it wasn't really a problem" once he recovered from the strong right roll. "That was a medium-speed flight," Neil explains. "I think it was faster than I had ever flown before, though," up to a speed of Mach 3.76, or 3,670 mph. "The flight followed a carefully programmed order, principally to check out the operation of the MH-96, and I'm sure no one wanted to go to extreme flight conditions, extreme loadings, on the system on the first flight."

Armstrong observed that the MH-96 system produced at least one unconventional flight characteristic: "Most airplanes have what is called 'speed stability,' that is, you set it at 250 knots, it tends to stay at 250 knots. But with the MH-96 flight control system, which was a rate-command, attitude-hold system, it had no affinity for staying at a particular speed. It tended to stay at its particular angle, but if the thrust did not match the drag, the plane would either speed up or slow down, whichever was appropriate, without any apparent signal to the operator."

Air-launched at 14:45:50 Pacific time, Armstrong landed the X-15 a little less than ten and a half minutes later, after flying a distance of 150.9 miles. The highest altitude reached was 81,000 feet, which was not as high as Armstrong had gotten in several of his F-104 zooms. With Major Daniels, LCDR Petersen, and Major Rushworth flying chase, Armstrong brought the X-15-3 down gingerly onto Rogers Dry Lake just southwest of Boron.

"Although skid contact seemed quite gentle," Armstrong wrote in his pilot's report, "nose wheel touchdown and impact seemed to be somewhat harder than that of previous flights in #1 airplane. [Neil never flew X-15-2.] It was attempted to keep the runout along the painted right hand stripe of the runway. With a light to moderate left cross wind, the airplane finally veered to the right of the painted stripe and could not be returned."

Armstrong's next X-15 flight came on Wednesday, January 17, 1962, a week and a half before Karen Anne's death. The flight was again to evaluate the MH-96 system and was the first time for Armstrong past Mach 5. It was also the first time he ever flew above 100,000 feet. In fact, he surpassed both marks, with a speed of Mach 5.51 and an altitude of 133,500 feet.

"I think it went pretty much on plan," Neil relates. Launched by a B-52, this time over Mud Lake to the north of Edwards, the X-15-3 traveled a distance of 223.5 miles in a little less than eleven minutes before touching down safely on Rogers Dry Lake at 12:11:01 in the afternoon. Throughout the flight, Armstrong gave the X-15's sidestick quite a workout. Flying chase with Petersen and Rushworth were Captain Henry C. "Hank" Gordon, one of the air force pilots later to be named along with Neil for the Dyna-Soar program, and Captain James McDivitt, future commander of the Gemini IV and Apollo 9 space missions.

His X-15 flight on January 17, 1962, was Armstrong's last flight of any kind until a week after Karen's funeral, when on February 6 he took an F5D up over Edwards for a low L/D approach. In the entire month of February, Neil flew only three other days, on the twelfth, thirteenth, and sixteenth. The first two of these days involved flights in an F-104, one for "pilot proficiency," and the last another low L/D approach in an F5D. Armstrong worked on Dyna-Soar in Seattle from February 26 to March 20.

Upon returning to work at Edwards on Monday, March 23, Armstrong immediately began to prepare for his next X-15 flight (flight 3-3-4), scheduled for five days later. Most of his flying leading up to the twenty-eighth involved "touch-and-go" landings in an F-104. These flights amounted to practice landings of the X-15. When the day for the actual X-15 flight arrived, clouds and hazy overcast limited visibility, pushing the schedule back one day. On March 29, the X-15's stable platform heat exchanger iced up, and a faulty fire detector caused the plane's fire warning light to pulse intermittently. The following day, the launch panel in the B-52 showed a potential problem involving the rocket engine's cooling gas, leading to a stressful abort at zero seconds in the countdown. The day after that, the MH-96 analyzer failed during a preflight check.

Not until the morning of Wednesday, April 5, did Armstrong manage to make the flight (flight 3-3-7). Then, just as he was being dropped at altitude above Hidden Hills north of Death Valley (across the Nevada line), his rocket engine did not ignite. "Before lighting the engine, or attempting to light the engine, I'm sure that some malfunction lights lit up," Armstrong recalled in his postflight debriefing later that day, "but I did not see any light. All I saw was the igniter pressure go to zero and silence."

In an X-15, there was only time enough for one relight. The remaining time until touchdown was required to complete the jettison of the propellants. If a second relight was attempted, the X-15 would still have some propellants in the tanks at landing, which, in Armstrong's words, "was not desirable." He recalls what "sure seems like a long time the second time for that engine to light up."

Accelerating to a top speed of Mach 4.12, Neil thundered up to 180,000 feet. It was the first time he had reached a high enough altitude to fully integrate the MH-96 reaction controls. The test flight spanned 181.7 miles in a little over eleven minutes before landing at Rogers Dry Lake.

The airplane still had not been flown to the point of testing the MH-96 system limit, or "g limiter," in part designed by Armstrong, to prevent the pilot from exceeding 5 g's, and he "felt the obligation to demonstrate every component and aspect of the MH-96."

It was this commitment that led to Armstrong's making what some came to feel was his biggest pilot error in the X-15 program.

Flight 3-4-8 occurred on Friday, April 20, 1962. Armstrong remembers, "It was the highest I'd ever gone"—to 207,500 feet, an altitude that remained his highest until Gemini VIII. "The views were spectacular. The system ran pretty well up there. The reaction control systems were operating satisfactorily 'across the top.' It kept a good attitude reference. Everything worked well. It was well outside the atmosphere so that we were flying completely on reaction controls. Aerodynamic controls were completely ineffective, like flying in a vacuum."

Coming down from peak altitude, part of the flight plan was to check out the g limiter. Armstrong explains, "I thought I got the g's high enough, but it was not kicking in. That was my job, to check out that system."

Armstrong let the X-15 nose up just a little, causing it to balloon to a high enough altitude—roughly 140,000 feet—where "the airplane returned to the wings-level attitude with essentially no sideslip. At about fifteen or sixteen degrees angle of attack and four g, I elected to leave the angle of attack in that mode and I was hoping that I would see the g limiting in action. We had seen g limiting on the simulator operation at levels approximately four g to four and a half g and it wasn't obvious that we were not having any g limiting, so I left it at this four-g level for quite a long time hoping that this g limiting might show up. It did not, and apparently this is where we got into the ballooning situation."

Over the radio, "NASA 1" back at the main flight control center told Neil rather emphatically, "We show you ballooning, not turning. Hard left turn, Neil! Hard left turn!" "Of course I'm trying to turn," Neil explains forty years after the flight, "but nothing's happening. I'm just on a ballistic path and I get over on to a very steep bank angle trying to pull down into the atmosphere. But the aerodynamics are not doing anything. The plane's going to go where it's going to go. It's on a ballistic path. They're telling me on the ground to 'Turn!' but that's not any help to me. They could see on the instruments that my servos are at full stabilizer turning position. I rolled over and tried to drop back into the atmosphere, but the aircraft wasn't going down because there was no air to bite into.

"I had no reason to suspect that ballooning would cause any trouble, because I had fiddled around with this lots of times in the simulator and never, never had any kind of problem with bouncing out like that."

Eventually the X-15 fell back down into the atmosphere where Armstrong was able to start making the turn. But by that time, Neil recalls, the airplane had gone "sailing merrily by the field"—at a speed of Mach 3! By the time he rolled into a bank, pulled up the angle of attack, and started to turn back in a northeasterly direction toward Edwards, Armstrong found himself approaching Pasadena. Neil was forty-five miles south of Edwards and still above 100,000 feet. (Subsequent Edwards lore suggesting that Neil flew the X-15 as far south as the Rose Bowl seems an exaggeration, since forty miles south of Edwards is substantially north of the Rose Bowl. Downward visibility was very limited for the X-15 pilot, so Neil did not know how far south he got.)

"It wasn't clear at the time I made the turn whether I would be able to get back to Edwards. That wasn't a great concern to me because there were other dry lakes available. I did not want to go into another one, but I certainly would if I had needed to. My easiest choice was to land at a lake called El Mirage, and I could easily get there. The only other alternative at that point would have been Palmdale municipal airport, and I didn't want to get into their traffic pattern." So Armstrong committed himself to trying for

Edwards: "After I got on the track—the northbound track for Edwards—it was clear that I was going to be able to try to go in. I'd have to make a 'straight in.' "

Neil: *I have the home base in sight, Joe* [Walker].

NASA 1: *What is your visual estimate of the location?*

Neil: *Looks like I'm pretty, in pretty bad shape for the south lake bed.*

NASA 1: *You're at eight degrees alpha* [angle of attack].

Neil: *Affirmative. And I'm going to jettison* [auxiliary fuel] *now.*

Chase: *What altitude, Neil?*

Neil: *Got 47,000.*

NASA 1: *Yes, we check that. Have you decided what your landing runway is yet?*

Neil: *Let me get up here a little closer. I can definitely . . . see the base now.*

NASA 1: *Yep.*

Neil: *Check head bumper* [at the top of the ejection seat]. *I'm 41,000 feet.*

NASA 1: *We're 26 miles to the south lake and have you at 40,000.*

Neil: *Okay.*

NASA 1: *Stop jettison on the peroxide.*

Neil: *Rog. Okay, the landing will be on runway 35, south lake and will be* [a] *straight-in approach. I'm at 32,000, going to use some brakes to make it. Okay, I'm about, approaching, pretty hard to tell from here.* [At this point Armstrong is using speed brakes to reduce energy, which in retrospect confirms that his return to South Base could not have been as close a call as some people at Edwards later suggested.]

Chase: *Okay, I've got you now. I'm one o'clock to you.*

Neil: *Okay.*

Chase: *Don't know if I will be with you, though.* [The chase was not sure he could rendezvous before Neil landed, since he had been in position to join up for a landing on the north, rather than south, lake bed.]

Neil: *Okay, going to use some brakes to get in. Okay, the ventral is armed and the brakes are in.* [At the rear end of the X-15 were vertical stabilizers placed above and below the fuselage; these were the ventral and dorsal fins. Prior to landing, the ventral fin needed to be jettisoned by triggering explosive bolts. Had Armstrong jettisoned the ventral even earlier, he would have reduced the drag and extended his glide time.] *I'm landing on 35 and I'm about fifteen miles out from the end now. Peroxide-low light is out, on again, source is 1,600 pounds. I'm 290 knots.*

Chase: *Coming up on your left.*

Neil: *Okay, I haven't got hold of you yet. And a little brakes here. I'm going back to pressurize. Going to land in sort of the middle of the south lake bed. Brakes are in again, 280* [knots].

Chase: *Henry* [Gordon], *I'll take the left side if you want me to.*

Chase: *Rog.*

Neil: *You want to call the ventral jettison, Henry?*

Chase: *Okay.*

Neil: *Little shorter than I thought.*

Chase: *You can punch it* [the ventral] *off any time you want to, Neil, for drag.*

Neil: *Oh, I should have done that before, shouldn't I?*

Chase: *Yep. Start your flaps down now. Off. Okay, you're well in, go ahead and put her down. Very nice, Neil.*

NASA 1: *The posse will get there shortly.*

Chase: *In about thirty minutes!* [A sarcastic reference to the fact that all the recovery vehicles were up at the original landing site on the north lake bed.]

H-21 [helicopter]: *We'll be there, Neil.*

Armstrong's X-15 flight of April 20, 1962, established X-15 program records for the longest endurance (12:28:07) and for longest distance (350 miles, ground track). Local Edwards lore still relates that Armstrong was trekking right down amid the Joshua trees as he made his landing on the southern tip of Rogers Dry Lake; in fact, the jest was that the Joshua trees were passing by *above* Neil. But that was a gross exaggeration devised by the boys in the chase planes, the only ones close enough to Neil's set-down point to know exactly where it occured.

Fellow NASA test pilot Bruce Peterson was situated on the north lake bed waiting to send up locator flares. "Neil was supposed to land on runway 18 ["18" was short for 180-degrees heading] on the north lake bed," Peterson relates. "Then I heard on the radio that he was going to go to the south lake, so I got in my vehicle and I must have been doing a hundred miles per hour, racing down that lake bed to see if I could get to the south lake bed and throw some flares. I watched him come in and looking across the lake, you can't see relative distances. But I knew he was close to the edge of the lake."

One of the engineers who monitored the flight, John McTigue, remembers "later kicking myself in the backside because I didn't tell Neil to get rid of the lower ventral, because that would have reduced the drag some. But it was the only airplane that the little old lady in Pasadena had ever seen come roaring above her, the X-15!" Though he did not see Neil's landing, McTigue heard that Armstrong barely made it back to South Base. Gathering for the postflight debriefing, McTigue heard Joe Vensel, the head of FRC flight operations, ask pilot Forrest Petersen, "How far was Neil from the Joshua trees?" Petersen thought for a moment and said, "Oh, probably a 150 feet or so." A wry smile coming to his face, Vensel asked, "Were the trees to his right or left?!"

People who were not even at Edwards on April 20 came to believe that Armstrong made it back by the skin of his teeth. NASA pilot Bill Dana, who was to fly the X-15 sixteen times, had taken an F-104 to Albuquerque, New Mexico, that day, "but I sure heard about it when I got back! Neil just barely made it back to the dry lake bed. And that isn't exaggerated; it was close." Air force test pilot Pete Knight did not see any of the flight, either, but "oh, yes, I heard about it" when fellow pilots started teasing Neil for his "record cross-country flight." "We thought it was rather funny at the time," Knight recalls, "to bounce back up and get into the thin air where you can't turn. It's not too bright." Major Bob White, who was flying chase for Armstrong in an F-100, admits that he "kind of giggled over it a little bit" and "never did discuss the overshoot with Neil because it might have been a little bit embarrassing."

A number of people felt that Armstrong made some sort of mistake or such a long overshoot could not have occurred. Before his death in 2004

Pete Knight extrapolated: "I think it was a lax condition, not doing something wrong, but not paying attention to what was going on. Because certainly after you reenter the atmosphere, you can, if you don't get the nose down and keep the airplane from climbing again, you can climb pretty fast and get back out into where you can't turn too well. You can pull all you want, but you've got nothing to pull against. So, yes, it was a mistake. I think it was just a laxity, not in Neil's ability or dedication, but just in his focus."

Knight was not the only person who came to this conclusion. More important, it was an opinion held by D. Brainerd Holmes, the director of the Office of Manned Space Flight at NASA headquarters in Washington, DC. According to Armstrong, "when the report went to Washington, Brainerd Holmes was fairly . . . I'm not going to say 'critical,' but it sounded like a screwup to him . . . But I just assumed that was because he didn't really understand. He didn't have any technical knowledge of the problem involved."

Today, Armstrong admits, "in this case, it might have been well advised for me to think, 'Well, if the g-limiting isn't kicking in, I'm not going to push it. I'll leave that to the next flight and try it again.' "

The inherent problem was lack of accuracy in the simulator. According to early NASA simulation expert Gene Waltman, "maybe after the pilots had flown a while they would begin to recognize some differences between the way the plane behaved and the way the simulator acted. But it was not a case where the pilots went out and flew the X-15 every day to get really well familiar with it. There were definite limitations, on the order of one hundred volts for every 4,000 to 5,000 feet." Fellow NASA test pilot Bruce Peterson relates, "I made the first flight of the HL-10 lifting body in 1966 and it was almost unflyable. None of that did we pick up on in the simulator."

Whether Armstrong could have pulled the necessary g's to get the g limiter to kick in without getting off his flight profile, no one can be sure. "There were ways to do the test he did without going to Pasadena," suggests NASA test pilot Bill Dana. "But that's kind of second-guessing. He just didn't realize how far up the nose had gone."

Typically, Armstrong regards his infamous "overshoot to Pasadena" as "a learning thing." Bill Dana concurs: "Neil was doing what he thought was the right thing. And if it won him a trip to Pasadena, why, he would not be doing that again! Probably nobody ever zoomed out of the atmosphere again on the X-15, because the pilots were all trained on the danger of that action based on what happened to Neil."

"He wasn't a screwup and he wasn't accident prone," declares Roger Barnicki, a technician in the FRC's Research Pilots Branch who was responsible for Armstrong's and other test pilots' personal flight equipment. "This guy was by the numbers, not fanatical, but by the numbers."

Just four days after his X-15 overshoot, Armstrong was involved in a second incident testing the notion that Karen Anne's death may have been temporarily affecting his job performance. On Tuesday, April 24, 1962, Armstrong and Chuck Yeager made their only-ever flight together.

The X-15 flight plan necessitated emergency landing sites all along the trajectory. One of the farthest flung was Smith Ranch Dry Lake, located some 380 miles due north of Edwards, and east of Reno, Nevada.

Conditions on a dry lake bed needed to be carefully checked out, especially during the wet winter season. Employing a crude but effective method, teams of inspectors would walk the lake bed, dropping six-inch-diameter lead balls from a height of five feet. Measuring the diameter of the depressions made by the balls and comparing them to measurements that had been made on a firm, usable lake bed, the inspectors determined whether the lake bed would support the fifteen-ton weight of the X-15.

The winter of 1962 was a particularly wet one in the western desert. On the weekend prior to Karen Armstrong's death, Rogers Dry Lake became a real lake of measurable depth. Many roads leading to and from Edwards were closed and very little flying took place.

On Monday, April 23, NASA's Joe Walker took an F-104 up to Smith Ranch Dry Lake to check it out for possible emergency use, not by the X-15-2, which air force major Bob White was scheduled to fly the next day (because White's flight was to be the first-ever launched from Delamar Dry Lake, in eastern Nevada), but by X-15-1, which Walker himself was scheduled to fly down from Mud Lake on April 25 (poor weather delayed the launch until April 30). The NASA R4D Gooneybird, flown by Jack McKay and Bruce Peterson, reported that day that Smith Ranch might be sufficiently dry to support a landing by the time of Walker's launch on the twenty-seventh.

Paul Bikle, the head of the FRC, wanted to be absolutely sure of the condition of Smith Ranch Dry Lake for Walker's flight. On the twenty-fourth, after White's X-15-2 flight was canceled due to clouds, Bikle made a phone call to the air force side of the base. Bikle talked to Colonel Chuck Yeager, the new commander of the Aerospace Research Pilots School at Edwards—and who also, incidentally, had been copiloting the launch B-52 just that morning when White's flight was aborted due to clouds. Bikle and Yeager had served together postwar at Wright Field in Ohio, where Bikle, in Yeager's view, had been one of those conservative flight test engineers "who thought the X-1 was doomed." Still, Bikle agreed with Yeager's self-assessment that the colonel's firsthand knowledge of the dry lakes was "like the back of my hand." In Yeager's version, the conversation between the two men went like this:

Bikle: *What do you think about Smith's Ranch Lake?*

Yeager: *I was just up there yesterday in a B-57 looking at it, and it's wet.*

Bikle: *Well, my guys were over there today and they say it isn't wet.*

Yeager: *Well, then, be my guest!*

Bikle: *Would you go up there and land on it?*

Yeager: *No, I won't. It's wet.*

Bikle: *Would you fly Armstrong up there and attempt a landing?*

Yeager: *No way.*

Bikle: *Would you do it in a [NASA] airplane?*

Yeager: *Hell, no! I wouldn't do it in any airplane because it just won't work.*

Bikle: *Would you go up there if Neil flew?*

Yeager: *Yeah, as long as I'm not responsible for anything that happens. I'll ride in the backseat.*

Pairing a NASA pilot and an air force pilot for such a purpose was unusual, but not unheard of. Earlier that April, NASA's Joe Vensel had flown with Yeager in a helicopter survey of a number of wet lake beds.

The plane was a T-33. Armstrong sat in the front, Yeager in the back. On this sunny and warm afternoon, both men wore just flying suits and gloves. Even before taking off, according to Yeager's version:

I tried my damndest to talk Armstrong out of going at all. "Honestly, Neil, that lake bed is in no shape to take the weight of a T-33."... But Neil wouldn't be budged. He said, "Well, we won't land. I'll just test the surface by shooting a touch-and-go"—meaning he'd set down the wheels then immediately hit the throttle and climb back up in the sky. I told him he was crazy. "You're carrying a passenger and a lot of fuel, and that airplane isn't overpowered, anyway. The moment you touch down on that soggy lake bed, we'll be up to our asses in mud. The drag will build up so high, you won't be able to get off the ground again." He said, "No sweat, Chuck. I'll just touch and go."

According to Yeager, Armstrong managed the first half of that:

He touched, but we sure as hell didn't go. The wheels sank in the mud and we sat there, engine screaming, wide open, the airplane shaking like a moth stuck on flypaper. I said from the back, "Neil, why don't you turn off the sumbitch, it ain't doin' nuthin' for you." He turned off the engine and we sat there in silence. Not a word for a long time. I would've given a lot to see that guy's face.

Yeager's story portrays Armstrong in unflattering terms, its telling further marred by factual errors.*

"We went up there and looked it over," Armstrong recalls, "and it looked like it was damp on the west side but pretty dry on the east side. So I said to Chuck, 'Let's do a touch-and-go and see how it goes.' " At no time on the way up to the Nevada site, according to Armstrong, did Yeager ever try to talk him out of trying to land.

The touch-and-go took place with absolutely no trouble. Neil landed, ran the wheels over the surface, added power, and took off. The problem for Armstrong came next, when Yeager told him, "Let's go back and try it again, and slow down a little more."

---

* Even a casual reading of the different versions of the Armstrong story that General Yeager has told over the years shows a number of basic errors and inaccuracies. For example, in his 1985 autobiography, Yeager stated that the incident occurred during the NACA period, which ended in 1958; then in an interview with him conducted by the Academy of Achievement's Museum of Living History in 1991, Yeager said it took place "around 1965." Clearly, General Yeager's sense of time and chronology is not good, as many of the events discussed in his autobiography reveal. Just before the section of the book in which he tells the story of the flight to Smith Ranch Dry Lake, Yeager talks about a conversation with Paul Bikle and Bikle's reaction to Scott Crossfield's infamous F-100A collision with a hangar wall at Edwards, which took place in September 1954. The trouble with Yeager's story—in which he relates that while the sonic wall had been his, the hangar walls were Crossfield's—is that the incident occurred several years before Bikle came to the Flight Research Center. Bikle arrived at the FRC in September 1959, five years later.

"Okay, we'll do that," Neil agreed. "So we landed a second time and cut the power back and slowed down, and then I could feel it starting to soften a little bit under the wheels so I added some throttle, and then it settled some more, and I added some more throttle. Finally, we were at a full stop, full throttle, and we started to sink in." In Yeager's version, what followed was an uncomfortable scene that neither enjoyed. Armstrong relates otherwise: "Chuck started to chuckle. Slowly he got to laughing harder. When we came to a full stop, he was just doubled over with laughter."

As Armstrong and Yeager got out of the T-33, an air force pickup truck immediately drove up to them, a fact that Yeager never mentions. "The driver came out and he had a chain," Armstrong remembers. "So we put it around the nose gear and hooked it up to the truck and tried to pull the airplane out of the mud, unsuccessfully. We couldn't do it, so we just sat there on the wing." Neil actually took eight-millimeter film of the plane stuck in the mud with an inexpensive little movie camera that he had bought for his family: "I don't think anyone has ever seen the film. I don't remember ever showing it, because the image quality was not the best.

"What an air force pickup truck was doing there, I have no idea, in retrospect," Neil wonders. There was a perimeter road on the east shore of the 5,000-foot-high dry lake, but the nearest town, Austin, Nevada, was several miles away. Could Yeager have arranged for the pickup, possibly from Stead AFB near Reno, in anticipation of the T-33 getting stuck?

The mishap took place at about 3:30 in the afternoon. With the sun dropping behind the high mountains to the west, the temperature fell quickly. For men wearing only thin flying suits, it soon grew cold. "Any ideas?" Yeager claims he asked Armstrong, with Neil grimly shaking his head no. Sometime after 4:00 P.M., they heard the sound of NASA's Gooneybird approaching. According to Yeager, Bikle sent the plane up to Smith Ranch "because he suspected something might happen." But the logbooks at the Flight Research Center clearly show that the R4D flight left Edwards with pilots McKay and Dana at the controls before Neil and Yeager even took off for Smith Ranch. Its flight plan indicated a northeasterly route to Ely, Nevada, up and along the X-15's High Range. Because Edwards had not heard from the T-33, NASA radioed McKay and Dana to fly over to Smith Ranch and take a look.

In Yeager's story, he got back in the airplane, switched on the battery, and radioed McKay, "We only got one choice. If you land over next to the edge of the lake and keep the airplane rolling, you probably won't sink, and then we can get back off the ground. Give us some time to walk over to the edge of the lake. Don't slow the airplane down. Keep the door open and we'll jump aboard." If Yeager did actually radio this message to the NASA pilots, he failed to mention how he knew where the Gooneybird "probably wouldn't sink." It was because it was on that side of the lake that Armstrong had performed the touch-and-go safely in the first place.

Bill Dana does not remember any of the specific conversation on board the returning airplane, but he does recall the "ribbing" that Neil took from Yeager and that Neil "did not rise to the bait." It was clear to both Dana and McKay, as it certainly was to Armstrong, that "Yeager took delight in Neil's embarrassment." Back at Edwards long past sunset, Yeager remembers, Paul Bikle was still there. "I don't know what he said in private to Neil Armstrong," Yeager asserts, "but when Bikle saw me he burst out laughing." According to Bill Dana, "Bikle felt Yeager was the best test pilot he ever worked with, because Chuck had a total recall. When Yeager came back from a flight, he could say, 'Yeah, I pushed the left rudder a little bit, it rolled right, and then the nose went to the left. He could just about be a human script chart.'" Too bad Yeager's detailed memory did not extend to pilots he did not like.

In his autobiography and in subsequent published interviews, Yeager expressed several harsher sentiments toward Armstrong, culminating in this opinion: "Neil Armstrong may have been the first man on the Moon, but he was the last guy at Edwards to take any advice from a military pilot." To which Neil has only responded wryly, "On this occasion at Smith Ranch, I did take his advice!"

Armstrong and Yeager really did not know each other well. What Yeager was expressing in his dealings with Armstrong were long-standing animosities aimed at the entire civilian, NACA/NASA research pilot culture that had operated at Edwards alongside the military ever since the start of the X-1 program in the mid-1940s.

According to Yeager's autobiography, the NACA "wasn't thrilled" with the army's selection of him as the X-1 test pilot: "The NACA team thought I was a wild man." One of the stories that NACA old-timers still commonly tell about Yeager concerns why the army air forces selected him to fly the Bell X-1 for the assault on the sound barrier. It was not because Yeager was the most qualified to meet the unknown dangers of the first supersonic flight, they say; it was because AAF leadership considered him "the most expendable" of all their test pilots.

Yeager, who remembers being treated with this sort of condescension, called the NACA pilots "the most arrogant bunch" at Edwards: "There was nothing worthwhile that a military pilot could tell them. . . . I rated them about as high as my shoelaces. I lived balls-out, flew the same way. I had my own standards, and as far as I was concerned there was no room at Edwards for test pilots who couldn't measure up to the machines they flew. I was harsh in my judgments because a pilot either knew what he was doing or he didn't. The NACA pilots were probably good engineers who could fly precisely, but they were sorry fighter pilots." Of course, NACA pilots were not *supposed* to be *fighter* pilots; they were supposed to be *test* pilots. "Neil was a pretty good engineer" has always been Yeager's backhanded compliment, but "he wasn't too good an airplane driver." *

Armstrong assesses, "Yeager was a pilot, and a good one. He had limited understanding of aeronautical engineering and limited educational exposure. He really, I don't think, understood quite what we were trying to learn. He was very good at flying aircraft and doing aerobatics and loved getting into mock combat situations one-on-one. But he seemed to have less interest in precision and getting information and drawing conclusions from that. He seemed to be impatient—not so much bored—but impatient with the planning and the techniques [of] the NACA."

Back at the High-Speed Flight Station, Armstrong seemed to be suffering through a prolonged streak of bad luck. On Monday, May 21, Neil returned to work following his family vacation in Ohio.

Following a crew briefing for an X-15 flight scheduled for Major Bob Rushworth the next day, Joe Vensel told Armstrong to fly up and inspect Delamar Lake, about ninety miles north of Las Vegas. After a half-hour flight in an F-104, Neil set up an approach that would allow him to practice his dead-stick landings. "I did it just like we always did," he recalls. "We made our flare and came down steeply just like the X-15, simulating putting the gear down in the middle of the flare, touching down, and then adding power and taking off. On this occasion I was doing that, but I was looking into the sun and the glare was very difficult."

Very few of the intermediate lake beds benefited from painted stripes and other markings, as did the regular runways on the big dry lakes near Edwards. From one lake bed to another, the texture of a surface could

---

* Yeager also overlooked the fact that several of the NACA test pilots—Butchart, Walker, McKay, as well as Armstrong—had distinguished combat records.

vary dramatically as could the surface cracks in its clay crust. Every experienced desert pilot knew that landing on a dry lake was like trying to judge height above glassy water. It was a problem in photo optics not dissimilar to what Armstrong and others at NASA studied so carefully in preparation for the lunar landings.

Two factors contributed to the "accident" that happened. First, Armstrong failed to judge his height precisely enough. Second, he failed to realize that, when he extended his landing gear during the flare, the gear did not extend fully and lock in place, causing the fuselage to smack into the lake bed. "So I lost hydraulic pressure," Armstrong explains. "I wanted to leave the gear down; I couldn't pick it up, anyway. I couldn't make it back to Edwards on the fuel I had. It was quite a ways away. I decided to go to Nellis Air Force Base, near Las Vegas, which was a lot closer."

His radio antenna gone, Armstrong could not communicate: "So I had to make a no-radio approach where you go over the field and waggle your wings, and the people in the tower, they're supposed to see you and realize that you're making a no-radio approach."

What Armstrong did not know was the loss of hydraulic pressure had triggered the release of his emergency arresting hook. If Armstrong had known his arresting hook was down, his landing at Nellis AFB would have came off trouble-free; after all, he was a naval aviator with loads of experience making tailhook landings. The Nellis arresting gear consisted of a steel cable attached to a long length of ship's anchor chain, each link weighing over thirty pounds.

"There was a good jolt when I hit it," Armstrong relates, "and it was completely unexpected because I didn't even think about the hook being down, because I couldn't see exactly what my situation was." Down the runway for hundreds of feet, this way and that, links of heavy, broken anchor chain went careening like desert tumbleweeds. The F-104 stopped dead in its tracks.

It took the air force thirty minutes to clear the runway and considerably longer to rig a makeshift, interim arresting gear. Driven to the building where the base operations officer was on duty, Armstrong took off his gear, explained what happened to the perturbed base ops officer, and mustered his nerve to telephone back to NASA to report his accident.

By then everyone at NASA had been fearing the worst. When more than thirty minutes passed from Neil's last check-in, Della Mae Bowling, the flight ops secretary, tried contacting him but got no answer. Then another fifteen minutes passed, still with no word. For the next hour, Della Mae tried calling Neil every four or five minutes. The Edwards control tower had no information. A few minutes later the tower reported that Neil had encountered a problem but had landed safely at Nellis.

Soon, Armstrong was on the phone with Joe Walker, who told NASA test pilot Milt Thompson to go pick him up. The only two-seat aircraft available was an F-104B, which Thompson had not been checked out in. But Joe Vensel insisted, citing "no significant difference" between the B model (which had tip tanks) and the F-104A, which Thompson had flown many times. As soon he left the ground, Thompson knew Vensel "had stretched the truth a bit." "All over the sky" after takeoff, Thompson could not crank it around tight enough to line up with the runway at Nellis. On his second go-around, a strong crosswind caught Thompson's airplane, forcing him to plunk down hard enough to blow the left main tire. Chunks of rubber tumbled across the runway where thirty-pound links of steel chain had just been. A fire truck and base ops vehicle quickly joined Thompson's crippled airplane as he parked it off the center taxiway. The only person who felt worse than Thompson at this moment was Armstrong as he watched the base ops officer shut down the runway for the second time that afternoon thanks to the questionable performance of a NASA pilot.

The "Nellis Affair," as it came to be known in the unwritten annals of Mojave Desert aviation, did not end there. NASA now had two stranded pilots. It had no choice but to send a third plane to Nellis. Unfortunately, the Gooneybird was up at NASA Ames. The only available plane was a T-33, another two-seater. But, almost beyond belief, as Bill Dana headed in long and hot, it looked like he was going to overshoot the runway. "Oh no, not again!" lamented the base ops officer, while Neil hid his head in his arm and Thompson watched "transfixed." Fortunately, Dana got the airplane stopped in time. "Please don't send another NASA airplane!" the air force officer begged. "I'll personally find one of you transportation back to Edwards."

True to his word, when an air force C-47 happened to be passing through Nellis on its way to Los Angeles, the ops officer expedited the refueling to haul Thompson away. For years thereafter, the base ops officer related "the tale of the three hot-shot NASA test pilots" that ruined his runways. Whether the man realized later that one of them turned out to be the first man on the Moon is unknown.

"That was a bad day all around," Armstrong recalls. "We had a couple bruised airplanes, and we made the officials at Nellis irritated. The air force guys got sick and tired of these NASA guys coming and dumping old airplanes on them."

The following day, a group from NASA went out to Delamar to examine Armstrong's tire tracks. The day after that, an accident investigation board convened in Joe Vensel's office. According to Milt Thompson, the tracks on the lake bed told the whole story.* Armstrong was not present at the accident investigation board, as he left that day for Seattle and another round of consultation on Dyna-Soar. In his logbook for the day of the Delamar flight, Neil recorded the event as an "inadvertent touchdown." To him, that indicated that he "put the gear down to simulate the X-15 procedure and drag, but did not intend to touch down." So "the main cause was my misjudging in that glare situation resulting in an advertent touchdown prior to the gear fully extending."

A few of Armstrong's colleagues at Edwards believe that Paul Bikle, the FRC director, in his own mind did connect the short string of mishaps in Neil's flying to Neil's emotional state following his daughter's death, temporarily grounding Armstrong after the Nellis mishap. Bikle was known for handling his pilots sternly. "Bikle didn't diddle around," Stan Butchart remembers. "He always made a decision right then and there, yes or no. . . . You knew where you stood with him." Armstrong agrees: "Bikle was very pragmatic. He was good at correcting you when he thought you were off base, but he was never disagreeable in the process. He was a fun-loving guy and he tended to joke more than he talked when he was criticizing you. He'd rather make fun of you than make light of you."

---

* In his autobiographical *At the Edge of Space,* Milt Thompson detailed the findings of the "Nellis Affair" investigation board as they pertained to Armstrong's original accident and its aftermath: "On initial touchdown, the distance between the two main gear tires was less than it should have been with the gear fully down and locked. As the aircraft continued to settle, the tire tracks began to merge. The weight of the aircraft was forcing the gear down before landing gear green lights came on. [Armstrong] immediately applied power to abort the landing and get airborne. For what must have seemed like hours, the aircraft continued to settle before it began to rise. In this few seconds of actual time, the aircraft continued to settle far enough to allow the ventral fin and landing gear doors to contact the lake bed. The ventral, which contained the radio antenna, was damaged and the door actuator was broken on one door. This allowed the utility hydraulic fluid to escape, deactivating that system. One other result of the ground contact was the release of the emergency arresting gear hook. [Armstrong] managed to get the airplane started uphill before the fuselage struck the lake bed. As [he] struggled into the air, he realized he had damaged the aircraft and was losing hydraulic fluid, so he headed to the nearest airfield, which happened to be Nellis. He attempted to contact Nellis to request landing instructions, but received no response due to the damaged radio antenna. He then entered the traffic pattern and made a pass down the runway wagging his wings to indicate radio failure. He turned downwind and set up for his landing approach not realizing that his arresting hook was down and, as a result, he engaged the arresting gear in an abnormal manner shortly after the touchdown." *At the Edge of Space,* p. 115.

Armstrong declares that the only times he was ever grounded during his career at Edwards were for medical reasons and that Paul Bikle never grounded him or even talked to him about it. Perhaps Bikle did not have to. The day after the debacle in Nevada, Armstrong left on what turned out to be a two-week trip to Seattle. He flew round-trip on a commercial airliner, returning on June 4. The first two days back at Edwards, Neil stayed at home and did not fly. His first flight following the Nellis Affair came on June 7, when he piloted an F-104 in the company of Bill Dana.

Certainly, Armstrong by this time had decided to apply for astronaut selection. When exactly that happened is not clear. NASA formally announced that applications would be accepted for a new group of astronauts on April 18, 1962. This was two days before Armstrong's X-15 overshoot flight. Very possibly, Neil knew nothing about NASA's announcement until April 27. On that day, the FRC's in-house newsletter, the *X-Press,* ran a story entitled "NASA Will Select More Astronauts," specifying an additional five to ten slots. The new pilots would participate in support operations for Project Mercury and then join the Mercury astronauts in piloting the two-man Gemini spacecraft.

The requirements for selection could not have suited Armstrong better if had they been written for him specifically. The successful applicant had to be an experienced jet test pilot—preferably one presently engaged in flying high-performance aircraft. He must have attained experimental flight status through military service, the aircraft industry, or NASA. He had to hold a college degree in the physical or biological sciences or in engineering. He needed to be a U.S. citizen who was under thirty-five years of age (at the time of selection) and six feet or less in height. His parent organization, in this case NASA's Flight Research Center, had to recommend him for the job.

The director of the Manned Spacecraft Center in Houston, Robert R. Gilruth, would be accepting applications until Friday, June 1, 1962. Pilots meeting the qualifications were to be interviewed in July. Those who passed a battery of written examinations on their engineering and scientific knowledge were then to be thoroughly examined by a group of medical specialists. The training program for the new astronauts was to include work with design and development engineers, simulator flying, centrifuge training, additional scientific training, and flights in high-performance aircraft. Virtually the entire training syllabus involved activities that Armstrong had already done.

Curiously, the same day as the *X-Press* report, *Life* magazine published an issue headlined "Man's Journey to the Moon: Preview of the Greatest Adventure of All Time." The cover shot featured a man testing a "Moon-suit." Inside was a feature entitled "Our Next Goal, Man on the Moon." Sidebars and captions highlighted "Moonship and Rocket in the Works," "A Model Menagerie of Moon Vehicles," "Complex Mysteries to Solve Before Fixing a Flight Plan," and "The Hunt for Ways to Live There." Whether Armstrong saw this issue of *Life* is uncertain, but, even if he did not, its existence in April 1962 suggests just how deeply the idea of the Moon landing had penetrated the American psyche in the year since President Kennedy's lunar commitment. This deepening public interest in the possibility of a manned Moon landing "before the decade is out" surely played some small role in Armstrong's thinking about whether to become an astronaut.

So, too, may have his visit to the Seattle World's Fair. From May 9 to 11, 1962, Armstrong was in the city to attend the Second Annual Conference on the Peaceful Uses of Space, an event cosponsored by NASA, the American Astronautical Society, the American Rocket Society, the Institute of the Aerospace Sciences, and the Society of Experimental Test Pilots to explore the potential international applications of space science and technology. Armstrong with coauthors and fellow X-15 pilots Joe Walker, Forrest Petersen, and Bob White, all members of the test pilots' "100,000 Foot Club," gave a presentation on "The X-15 Flight Program." Other speakers at the conference included NASA Administrator James E. Webb ("The Role of Government in Scientific Exploration"), Vice President Lyndon B. Johnson ("The New World of Space"), director of NASA's Manned Spacecraft Center Bob Gilruth ("Projects Mercury and Gemini"), NASA's Director of Spacecraft and Flight Missions George M. Low ("Project Apollo"), and several other notables in space-related fields.

Attendance at this conference and at the conjoining Seattle World's Fair could not help but impress a person who was thinking seriously about a career in space exploration. The fair, whose theme was "the possibilities of life in the 21st Century," featured the 605-foot-tall Space Needle and the Monorail, both of which became Seattle landmarks. Festivities began on May 9 when former president Dwight D. Eisenhower started a clock in Seattle that was to count down to the end of the millennium. At the very same instant, President Kennedy, on Easter holiday in Florida, pressed a telegraph key that triggered a radio telescope in Maine that picked up an impulse from a star ten thousand light-years away and then lit up the fairgrounds.

The star attraction on the second day of the World's Fair was astronaut John Glenn, fresh off his orbital flight for Project Mercury two and half months earlier. "Throngs of awestruck admirers" lined Seattle's streets to catch a glimpse of the famous red-haired "spaceman."

• • •

Only one person besides Armstrong ever knew that Neil's application to Houston arrived late. This was Dick Day, the FRC flight simulation expert with whom Armstrong worked closely ever since Neil joined the NACA's High-Speed Flight Station. In February 1962, Day transferred from Edwards to Houston to become assistant director of the Flight Crew Operations Division at the Manned Spacecraft Center. In this capacity, Day oversaw all astronaut training programs and equipment. Two months after arriving in Houston, Day also found himself, thanks to his former boss at Edwards, Walter Williams, not just a member of the selection panel for the second group of astronauts but the panel's ad hoc secretary.

According to Day, Armstrong's application for astronaut selection missed the June 1 deadline. Day explained how and why Neil's application was processed anyway: "There were several people from Edwards who had gone on to Houston. Walt Williams, for one. Walt had gone on to be the operations director in Houston for the Space Task Group. He wanted Neil to apply, and I wanted Neil to apply. I really don't know why Neil delayed his application, but he did, and all the applications came to me, since I was the head of flight crew training. Neil's application came in late, definitely, by about a week. But he had done so many things so well at Edwards. He was so far and away the best qualified, more than any other, certainly as compared to the first group of astronauts. We wanted him in."

Technically, since Armstrong's application missed the deadline, NASA should not have accepted it. However, no one but Day and Williams knew the application arrived late. When it came in, Day slipped it into the pile with all the other applications prior to the selection panel's first meeting. Personally, Day had no concerns whatsoever about Neil's prospective performance as an astronaut—and Day knew the ups and down of Neil's flying record at Edwards as well as anyone, except for the details of what had happened since Day left Edwards in February 1962: "I never gave a thought to his personal affairs, and I don't think Walt Williams or anyone else did, either."

Armstrong does not remember sending his application in late. Yet he does credit Day, who died in 2004, for his powers of persuasion: "You were responsible for getting me to transfer over to Houston," Neil wrote Day in a 1997 e-mail.

Except for Monday, May 21—the day of the Nellis Affair—Armstrong did not spend a single day in his office at Edwards from Wednesday, May 9, to his return from Seattle on June 4. Undoubtedly, the application waited for him on his desk. If he completed it soon after returning to Edwards, the timing of its arrival in Houston would fit what Dick Day has indicated, about a week late.

To some at Edwards, Neil's decision came as a surprise. "He never mentioned anything to anybody," relates his good friend Stan Butchart. "We never knew that he had applied, unless maybe he had told Joe Walker. But Neil never said anything to me, and we were as close as we could be. The first thing we knew was when it was announced." Fellow NASA test pilot Bruce Peterson concurs: "I hadn't seen anything to indicate that Neil wanted to leave Edwards and go into the space program."

Virtually everyone at Edwards thought that Armstrong was a great choice to become an astronaut, especially when it was announced in early June 1962 that he was to receive the prestigious Octave Chanute Award. Presented by the Institute of the Aerospace Sciences, the Chanute Award went to the pilot that the IAS deemed had contributed the most to the aerospace sciences during the previous year. According to Dick Day, Paul Bikle, the director of NASA's Flight Research Center at Edwards and Day's own former boss, did not think so positively of Armstrong. Bikle chose not to recommend Armstrong for astronaut selection, because, in his mind, Neil's immediate past record in the air raised some serious concerns about his performance.

At the end of May 1962 Neil scheduled a two-week trip to Europe to coincide with the 21st Meeting of the Flight Mechanics Panel of the NATO Advisory Group for Aeronautical Research and Development, to be held in Paris from July 6 to 10. On his way to France, where Armstrong would present a paper (coauthored by Robert Rushworth), he was to stop in England in order to fly the new Handley Page HP-115, a very low aspect-ratio (70-degree leading-edge sweep) research airplane built to investigate the low-speed characteristics of the slender delta, the wing form being considered for the British supersonic transport that evolved into the Anglo-French Concorde.*

Paul Bikle pulled the plug on Neil's British sojourn. In a memorandum sent to NASA Headquarters on May 29, 1962, Bikle wrote, "Due to commitments of Mr. Neil A. Armstrong in relation to the X-15 program, it will

---

* What attracted Armstrong to the HP-115 was how its highly swept delta wing configuration, when flown in steep, unpowered, low L/D approaches and landings, could generate data useful in the design of the Dyna-Soar vehicle.

be impossible for Armstrong to participate in flights of United Kingdom aircraft" specified for the last week of June.

Whether the accelerating workload in the X-15 program was the only reason for Bikle canceling Armstrong's visit to England in the summer of 1962 is a question only Paul Bikle can answer, and he is no longer living. Given the series of mishaps in Neil's flying that spring—culminating in the Nellis Affair on May 21 and the accident investigation board that looked into it on May 23, just five days prior to Bikle sending the memo—and given Bickle's subsequent refusal to support Neil's astronaut application, one can only wonder whether Bikle privately did not want Armstrong over in England test-flying one of the RAF's newest experimental jets. Neil never understood Bikle's decision as such: "I am confident that Paul's memo was a form response. There could have been many reasons for his conclusion. We would have to know what the overall workload at the time was and how many FRC pilots were available to handle it." Forty-two years after Bikle canceled the British trip, Neil does not harbor any disappointment, "but I don't remember well enough to say I wasn't."

Armstrong did eventually have the chance to fly the HP-115, on June 22, 1970, eleven months after his Moon landing.

No one has ever understood the mentality of test pilots or astronauts better than Christopher Columbus Kraft Jr., the "Voice of Project Mercury" and the original director of NASA's manned spaceflight operations at Mission Control in Houston. Upon graduating with an aeronautical engineering degree from Virginia Tech in 1944, Kraft went to work in the Stability and Control Branch of NACA Langley's Flight Research Division where he rubbed elbows with such talented flight test engineers as Bob Gilruth, Charles Donlan, and Walt Williams, men who in the summer of 1958, following Sputnik, took Kraft with them into the Space Task Group, which planned and administered Project Mercury.

Kraft did not serve on the selection panel for the second group of astronauts, but he had a lot to do with defining the selection criteria. "Charles Donlan was in charge of that," Kraft recalls, "and he talked to me about it because he valued the association I was having with the first seven astronauts. I emphasized that we should go talk to the people who know the candidates, know their character, and know their capabilities. . . . People like Gilruth, Williams, and myself were looking for qualified test pilots.

"I hardly knew Armstrong out at Edwards," Kraft continues. "I didn't know about his daughter's death. I did know that he had had a few accidents—what pilot hasn't—but I never associated them with any psychological event. What I knew was that Walt Williams thought he was first rate. Certainly, based on what we knew about him, and what we saw when we met him, Gilruth and I and everybody else felt the same way."

Given the emphasis that Kraft, Donlan, and others placed on background and verbal checks, it is surprising that individuals in leadership positions in Houston did not know about Neil's personal situation—not that it would have changed their thinking about the strength of his credentials for astronaut selection one iota. Today Kraft believes there was "absolutely no way" Armstrong's piloting performance wasn't affected in the short term by the tragedy. "The human brain is no different than any other computer. It's a better computer, but it's got to have those kinds of faults in it. The pilot won't even be aware of it. The pilot is probably doing [the flying] to try to get away from it. He wants to go back and get in the fray. I think any good flight surgeon would not have let him fly for a while. But back at Edwards at that time, the only thing that a flight surgeon would have been doing is qualifying him physically every 'x' number of days. The chief test pilot up there [Joe Walker] should have been aware of the problem and kept him from flying. . . . Knowing Neil and knowing Janet, too, as I got to do, they might not have known how they were coping with it. They're both of the personality that would try to bury that."

Neil himself should be given the last word. *"Were you concerned at all about how your personal situation could have been affecting your job performance, especially your flying, in late 1961 and early 1962?"*

"I'd have to think that [my] performance was somewhat affected by the situation."

"Did Karen's death play any role in your decision to leave Edwards and become an astronaut?"

"I don't remember any factors from Karen's loss that influenced my work. Personally, it was a trying time. It might have affected my concentration on my work to some extent at the time, because we'd be going into the hospital and to the doctor. You know, a lot of families have these kinds of problems that they have to deal with. It's not that unusual, unfortunately, but you just have to deal with those kinds of things. We did."

Whether Neil and Janet Armstrong handled "those kinds of things" *together* as constructively as they might have is another question.

CHAPTER 16

I've Got a Secret

At 8:00 P.M. EST on Monday night, September 17, 1962, millions of Americans tuned in to the popular CBS television game show *I've Got a Secret.* By today's standards, *I've Got a Secret* was almost quaint, with its panel of urbane New York celebrities, an unadorned set, and a top prize of $80 to any guest who could stump the panel. This evening's panelists were the series regulars: actor and radio humorist Henry Morgan; the first Jewish Miss America and future public servant and philanthropist Bess Myerson; popular game show host Bill Cullen; and the actress Betsy Palmer. One of the show's attractions was the sophisticated but playful camaraderie among the contestants and host Garry Moore's genial and gracious demeanor. It was a formula that kept the show on the air from the early 1950s until 1976.

In response to Moore's usual greeting—"Will you come in, please?"—Neil's parents emerged through a doorway to take their seats at a desk to Moore's right. Facing the contestants, Viola, in a dark, knee-length cocktail dress and low-heeled pumps, and Stephen, in a gray business suit, introduced themselves. Then Viola and Stephen whispered their secret to Moore at the same time the words "Our son became an ASTRONAUT *today*" flashed on TV screens across the country. After the studio applause died down, the game began.

MOORE: Now, panel, to help you classify Mr. and Mrs. Armstrong's secret, the clue concerns a relative of theirs, and we'll start the game with Henry [Morgan].

MORGAN: Mr. Armstrong, is your relative's name Armstrong?

STEPHEN: That's right.

MORGAN: Has he ever made any public figure of himself?

STEPHEN: Yes.

199

MORGAN: Did he ever invent anything?

STEPHEN (pauses for a second): Not that I know of.

MORGAN: Whatever he did—I'm assuming he was in the newspapers and so forth—did he do it recently?

STEPHEN: Yes.

LOUD BUZZER

MOORE: Twenty dollars down, sixty dollars to go. We go to Bess Myerson.

Myerson asks several mundane questions before the buzzer sounds and Bill Cullen takes a shot.

CULLEN: I think I have it!

MOORE: Go ahead, buddy.

CULLEN: Mr. and Mrs. Armstrong are relatives of Jack Armstrong . . .

CULLEN AND FELLOW PANELISTS: the All-American Boy!

After a few moments of laughter, Moore gets the game back on track:

MOORE: Sixty dollars down and twenty dollars to go. And we go to Betsy Palmer.

PALMER (still laughing): Does it have anything to do with linoleum?

LOUD LAUGHTER

STEPHEN (smiling): No.

PALMER: Does it have anything to do with aeronautics?

STEPHEN: It does.

PALMER: Space?

STEPHEN: It does.

PALMER: Is your son going to fly out into space soon?

PALMER: Is he a new astronaut?

MOORE: That's it!

APPLAUSE

MOORE: Mr. and Mrs. Armstrong are a very happy and a very proud couple—they're still kind of in a state of shock—because this afternoon at three P.M., their son Neil was named one of America's new astronauts.

MOORE: So we want to congratulate you and all of the new astronauts and all of their families. We would have liked to have had many more of them here, but we felt so lucky to get them here from Ohio.

MOORE: Well, Mr. Armstrong, your son is one of the two civilians chosen. How long has he been flying, sir?

STEPHEN: Since before he was sixteen years of age.

MOORE: Before sixteen?

STEPHEN: Uh-huh.

MOORE: That would mean he had his wings before he had his driver's license, right?

VIOLA: That's right.

MOORE: I understand that he has been a test pilot since 1955, when he graduated from Purdue and was hired directly by NASA. Now, what did he do for NASA, sir?

STEPHEN: Well, he tested various jet planes of different speeds: Mach 1, 2, 3, and so on, until he came up to the X-15.

MOORE (reading from a prepared sheet): He flew the X-15 more than 3,900 miles per hour, over 207,000 feet. Now, how would you feel, Mrs. Armstrong, if it turned out—and, of course, nobody knows, but it turns out—that your son is the first man to land on the Moon? How would you feel?

VIOLA: Well, I guess I'd just say, God bless him and I wish him the best of all good luck.

Neil did not see his parents on TV that night; in fact, he did not even know his mother and father were appearing on the CBS program until after the fact, so cloistered did NASA keep its newest astronauts in the days leading up to their introduction to the country on Monday, September 17, 1962.

The space agency forced Armstrong to play its own version of *I've Got a Secret*. The episode started four days earlier when, while at work in his office at Edwards, Neil got *the* phone call from Deke Slayton, head of the astronaut office at the Manned Spacecraft Center, then still under construction on Clear Lake, southeast of Houston.

Deke came right to the point: "Hi, Neil, this is Deke. Are you still interested in the astronaut group?"

"Yes, sir," replied Armstrong.

"Well, you have the job, then. We're going to get started right away, so adjust your schedule and get down here by the sixteenth." Slayton told Armstrong that he could tell his wife but otherwise to keep the news quiet.

Even as a boy, it was never hard for Armstrong to keep a secret. His parents did not get the news about their son becoming an astronaut until sometime that weekend when they received a phone call at their Wapakoneta home from a NASA public relations officer who was helping CBS set up the Monday evening appearance on *I've Got a Secret*. Neil's sister June and brother Dean did not hear about Neil becoming an astronaut until even later. "He came through Wisconsin for a short visit around the Fourth of July," June recounts, "and he said to me, 'I'm on my way to Texas. I'm taking a couple tests.' He was kind of flippant about it, 'taking a couple tests.' Next thing, I hear the announcement he's been chosen as an astronaut!"

As for the call from Slayton to Neil, "I was happy to get that call," Armstrong relates. Slayton's call really could not have surprised Neil much. As early as midsummer 1962, newspapers had been reporting that Armstrong was going to be named the "first civilian astronaut." Based on information from "official sources," an article in the *Washington Evening Star* on July 18, 1962, opened: "An X-15 pilot, Neil Armstrong, will be the first civilian selected for training as an astronaut. Conceivably he could command America's first attempt to land men on the Moon."

NASA officials later denied the story, conceding that Armstrong was "definitely on the list" of 32 men out of an applicant pool of 253 who had survived the preliminary screening but indicating that no final selections had been made. Many close observers of NASA did not believe the denial. Nor did most of the astronaut finalists who came from the active military. One of the air force finalists, Michael Collins (who would not be chosen until the third class of astronauts, in October 1963), wrote home to his father: "I strongly suspect that at least one civilian will be included, for propaganda purposes, if nothing else, and Neil Armstrong will be on the list unless his physical discloses some major problem. I say this because he has by far the best background of the six civilians under consideration, and he is already employed by NASA." James A. Lovell, a navy finalist who NASA did choose for the second group, felt much the same way about Armstrong as Collins, later writing: "Given his Agency pedigree, the odds had been good he would make this cut."

Yet if one takes Slayton at his word, Armstrong's civilian status had nothing to do with his selection. "Nobody pressured us to hire civilians," Slayton wrote later in his autobiography. The truth was, as we have already seen, that no such pressure was needed, at least in Armstrong's case. All through the selection process, as Neil admits, his identification with the ways of NACA/NASA had been an advantage for him: "I was in Houston talking with people from my own organization, while for somebody coming off a fighter squadron or a carrier assignment, or coming over from a squadron, say, in Ramstein, Germany, this was a very different experience."

Armstrong was relatively confident that NASA would choose him as one of its next astronauts, but he could not be sure: "A number of us had combat experience. My education level was, I thought, competitive. My experience was rather broad, and having flown the rocket airplanes and things like that, and being involved in a variety of test-flight programs. Nevertheless, the areas that I didn't know how well I compared were physical, emotional, psychological, and perhaps how I was perceived by other people. I didn't know how I would grade in those categories. And any one of those could certainly evict you from the program."

During the four-month stretch from early June 1962, when he turned in his astronaut application late to Houston, to the day in mid-September when Slayton called him with the good news, Armstrong was too busy to worry much about whether he was going to become an astronaut. He spent the second week of June at the Lovelace Clinic in Albuquerque, New Mexico, ostensibly taking his annual NASA test pilot's physical but with the results of certain tests being relayed—unbeknownst to him—back to the Manned Spacecraft Center for evaluation as part of the astronaut selection process. Back at Edwards, Neil made a series of low L/D landings in the F-104; flew chase for Bob White's X-15-3 flight (on June 21) and Jack McKay's X-15-2 flight (on June 29); picked up his Chanute Award at an IAS event in Los Angeles (the evening of June 21); and flew a test program involving a radio altimeter for the Saturn rocket then under development.

On July 5, 1962, Armstrong left for his AGARD meeting in France, where he presented a paper, "A Review of In-Flight Simulation Pertinent to Piloted Space Vehicles." Coauthored by Euclid C. "Ed" Holleman of FRC's Dynamic Stability and Analysis Branch, the paper (AGARD Report 403) demonstrated "how the environment of actual flight may be used to simulate many phases of manned space exploration," culminating in "one of the most challenging and potentially most fruitful projects of the current space program"—an experimental flight vehicle then under development at the

Flight Research Center that could simulate the final several thousand feet of descent to a Moon landing. Over the next years, this simulator, in the form of the Lunar Landing Research Vehicle (LLRV), would make major contributions to the Apollo program. In the form of the Lunar Landing Training Vehicle (LLTV), which evolved from the LLRV, the machine in 1968 nearly cost Armstrong his life.

Returning from the Paris conference, Armstrong spent all of his time preparing for his final flight in the X-15. It was to be Neil's first time back in the number-one aircraft since his flight of December 9, 1960, when the cue-ball system replaced the nose boom for the first time. The objective of the flight was evaluation of the aircraft's aerodynamic stability and drag handling qualities at hypersonic speed and in the relatively low altitude range between 90,000 and 110,000 feet.

Although his X-15 flight on June 27, 1962 (number 1-32-53), resulted in the highest Mach number Armstrong ever attained in the X-15 program—Mach 5.74, or 3,989 mph—it did not come off, as most X-15 flights did not, without a hitch or two. The first sign of a problem came prior to launch when Neil saw that the hydraulic pressure in the aircraft's number-one auxiliary power unit (APU) was behaving erratically. Upon landing, the reading turned out to be the result of a rather serious oil leak, one traced by the engine mechanics to a pinhole crack in the cockpit source transmitter line, which left very little oil in the reservoir of the APU at shutdown.

Then smoke started to infiltrate the cockpit at just the time Neil was pushing the black rocket plane into the range of maximum speed. "The smoke was obvious," Armstrong remembers. "There really wasn't much to do about it. You couldn't open the cockpit and let it out. You're just stuck with it. But you're shielded from it because you're inside the pressure suit. You're okay unless it's some kind of fire hurting the aircraft systems. The best thing you can do is get the plane on the ground." Armstrong managed to land safely, the few control difficulties related to operating the new type of trim tab that had just been installed on his sidestick controller.

Following the X-15 flight, there was barely enough time for Neil to write up his pilot comments before he had to leave for Brooks Air Force Base in San Antonio. At Brooks he underwent an exhausting week of medical and psychological tests that went a long way toward finalizing the selection of the new astronauts. Not that the second group of candidates suffered what the original Mercury group had, yet, in Armstrong's opinion, "there were some painful experiences. My sense at the time was that some of these things must have been specially designed to be medical research rather than diagnostic techniques."

A few of the exams were especially diabolical. "There was one," Neil recalls, "where they syringed ice water into your ear for a long period of time until you sort of got uncaged, and another where you had your foot in ice water for quite a while. There were a lot of strange tests like that, which certainly were not standard 'annual physical' kinds of tests. . . . On another occasion, they sent us to Los Alamos, where the government had special facilities to weigh you underwater and compute your body mass density. A lot of strange things. There were also standard medical tests and some duplicating of what had been done earlier at Lovelace. But at Brooks there was a lot more focus on psychological testing."

One psychological trial that Armstrong distinctly remembers was an isolation test: "They put you in a black room where all sensory signals were removed. There was no sound, no light, and no smell. They told you to come out after two hours." Neil applied engineering principles: "I tried to compute a way to figure out how long two hours were. So I used the song, 'Fifteen Men in a Boardinghouse Bed' ":

> Fifteen men in a boardinghouse bed,
>   Roll over, roll over.
> One turned over and the other man said,
>   "Roll over, roll over."
> One man thought it would be a great joke,
> not to turn over when the other man spoke,
> but in the struggle his neck got broke,
>   Roll over, roll over.

"You go through the ditty at fifteen, then you go at fourteen, then you go at thirteen, so by the time you get to the end, it's pretty long. I could roughly compute how long that might take. I didn't have a watch or anything, but I sang that song until I thought about two hours were up. Then I knocked on the door and shouted, 'Let me out of this place!' "

Another one of the ordeals involved high temperature. Examiners put him in a small room where the temperature ranged from 140 to 145 degrees F. Following a counterintuitive strategy, Neil reduced his metabolic heat generation to an absolute minimum by doing absolutely nothing but sitting quietly in a corner, trying not to move, or even to think. "I don't know how well I did it, but I was able to stand it in there. Of course, those of us who came from Edwards were used to 115 degrees as a standard. We probably had an advantage over the guys who were stationed in Michigan."

One week working at Edwards following the exams in San Antonio, Armstrong traveled on August 13 to Houston's Ellington Air Force Base for a final round of medical and psychiatric tests: "It was a chance to chat about what this program might mean and have a chance to express my opinions on the values and the challenges of this kind of work." At Ellington Armstrong first came before NASA's astronaut selection panel, a group that included Deke Slayton, Warren North, Walt Williams, and Dick Day. Occasionally John Glenn or Wally Schirra drifted in and out of the room. "We talked about the general nature of the program," Armstrong relates. "I didn't find it at all difficult or pressuring or anything. I found it a natural conversation about the kinds of things I was interested in at the time."

All thirty-two of the finalists (thirteen navy, ten air force, three Marines, and six civilians) gathered one evening for cocktails and dinner with a small party of leading officials from the Manned Spacecraft Center. Armstrong remembers, "I didn't know too many of the people. I knew Schirra from the XF4H-1 evaluation. I knew some others a little," including Gus Grissom, who had flown at Edwards until he was transferred back to Wright-Patterson in 1957. Slayton and Cooper, too, had also been stationed at Edwards, but the fliers' duties had not overlapped. "We did not have military pilots in the Society of Experimental Test Pilots in the early days," Neil explains. "Most contact with the military pilots was on the job, so that contact was restricted to situations where NACA/NASA pilots were working on a project with air force pilots. And I don't recall being on any projects with Grissom, Slayton, or Cooper." Armstrong knew John Glenn and Al Shepard only from the occasional flight-test event, though he also recalls meeting both of them back in the summer of 1954 when he was working between semesters at Purdue on catapult design at Patuxent River. Scott Carpenter was the only Mercury astronaut that Neil had never met.

"I didn't have any difficulties with any of the Mercury astronauts," Neil recalls. "Some of them I knew to be quite able fellows with good experience. So, no problem in my mind." Only the three Mercury astronauts who had already made their spaceflights—Al Shepard, Gus Grissom, and John Glenn—had actually flown farther out of the atmosphere than Armstrong had in the X-15; and Neil was the only one in the entire group who had ever flown a rocket plane or won the Octave Chanute Award. Male ego and competitive spirit abounded at the Houston get-together, to be sure, but every pilot there respected the other men's flying credentials.

While Mike Collins and others have admitted to keeping "lookout for any abnormal behavior that might indicate someone had heard good news from NASA," Armstrong quietly concentrated on his regular duties back at Edwards. He flew nearly every workday during the three-week stretch prior to Deke Slayton's call, including chase for Bob Rushworth's X-15-2 flights on August 20 and 29.

Neil arrived at Houston's Hobby Airport late on Saturday, September 15, 1962. "There was nothing," Neil remembers. "It was completely quiet. Nobody was to know that we were coming in or that it was going to be announced. Leaks weren't as common in those days as they are now." To the extent that the dutiful men and women of the fourth estate knew anything about the upcoming NASA announcement, as Neil explains, "they protected the institution."

As instructed by NASA, Neil checked into downtown Houston's stately Rice Hotel under the code name "Max Peck." All eight of the other new astronauts did the same. "Everyone checked in as Max," Armstrong recalls, smiling ruefully. "I've been told that there really was a manager named Max Peck at that hotel." Armstrong was the last of the nine to arrive: "My recollection is that I got in pretty late that evening, but I did meet a couple of the other guys that night—some of them I recognized."

The next morning at Ellington, NASA's new class of astronauts first assembled under Slayton's direction. According to Armstrong, "It was a meeting where we officially got to know each other, got to know some of the other NASA people there." Walt Williams, the head of flight operations, ran the men through their job description. Bob Gilruth, the balding, reedy-voiced director of the Manned Spacecraft Center who had headed the Space Task Group from its inception, told them that with eleven manned Gemini flights on the schedule, at least four Block I Apollos (to be launched on the Saturn I), and a still undetermined number of Block II Apollos, including the one that would make the first lunar landing, "There'll be plenty of missions for all of you." Slayton warned them about some of the new pressures and temptations they would be facing. He told them to be careful about accepting gifts and freebies, especially from companies competing for NASA contracts. "With regard to gratuities," Deke added, according to some of the astronauts there, "if there is any question, just follow the old test pilot's creed: anything you can eat, drink, or screw within twenty-four hours is perfectly acceptable." Gilruth flushed noticeably and shook his head at this brazen pronouncement, while Walt Williams choked out, "Within reason, within reason!" Shorty Powers, NASA's public affairs officer, ended by briefing the astronauts on the upcoming press conference. He then organized the nine men for the first of what in the following days became an interminable sequence of photo shoots.

The University of Houston's 1,800-seat Cullen Auditorium was filled to capacity for the early afternoon announcement. Reporters and camera crews from all three of the major television networks, from the major radio broadcasting systems, from the wire services, from dozens of newspapers and magazines not just from all over America but overseas as well crammed into the theater's best vantage points, anxiously awaiting to learn the identities of America's new astronauts. Back on April 2, 1959, the newborn NASA had been taken by surprise by the public sensation surrounding the announcement of the original seven astronauts in a ballroom of Washington's Dolly Madison Hotel, near the White House. This time the more seasoned agency and its expanded public affairs operation were much better prepared for the media blitz. So, too, were the astronauts themselves.

The "New Nine"—Neil Armstrong, Air Force Major Frank Borman, Navy Lieutenant Charles Conrad Jr., Navy Lieutenant Commander James A. Lovell Jr., Air Force Captain James A. McDivitt, Elliot M. See Jr., Air Force Captain Thomas P. Stafford, Air Force Captain Edward H. White II, and Navy Lieutenant Commander John W. Young—were a truly remarkable group of men. In the opinion of key individuals responsible for the early U.S. manned space program, it was unquestionably the best all-around group of astronauts ever assembled. Certainly, Deke Slayton felt this way, as did Bob Gilruth, Chris Kraft, George Low, and many others both inside and outside the agency. Mike Collins has baldly declared that "this group of nine was the best NASA ever picked, better than the seven that preceded it, or the fourteen (Collins's own group), five, nineteen, eleven, and seven that followed."

The educational level of the second group was dramatically higher than that of the Mercury Seven, and with exactly the emphasis on rigorous engineering that NASA's astronaut selection panel had sought. A 1950 graduate of the military academy at West Point, Frank Borman had earned a master's degree in science in 1957 from the California Institute of Technology. Pete Conrad was the first astronaut from an Ivy League school—a

1953 graduate in engineering from Princeton University. Jim Lovell studied engineering for two years at the University of Wisconsin before moving on to the U.S. Naval Academy, where he graduated in 1953. Jim McDivitt finished first in his engineering class of 1959 at the University of Michigan. Elliot See, the only other civilian in the group besides Armstrong, was a 1949 graduate of the U.S. Merchant Marine Academy; just months before becoming an astronaut, he finished a master of science degree at the University of California at Los Angeles. Tom Stafford graduated in engineering from Annapolis in 1952 (then chose to be commissioned, not in the navy, but in the air force). Ed White completed a master's in aeronautical engineering from the University of Michigan in 1959, seven years after graduating with distinction from West Point. John Young earned his engineering degree in 1952 at the Georgia Institute of Technology. Armstrong had everything but his thesis completed toward a master's in aerospace engineering at the University of Southern California.

The group's experience as pilots and record in the world of flight testing was equally impressive. Borman had accumulated 3,600 hours flying time in jets (the most of any of the nine); at the time of his NASA appointment, Frank instructed in the air force's aerospace research pilot test school at Edwards AFB. Conrad had flown more than 2,800 hours, including 1,500 hours in jets; a graduate of the U.S. Navy test pilot school at Patuxent River in Maryland, Pete rose quickly through the ranks to become a flight instructor and performance engineer at the navy's Pax River establishment. Lovell had a total of 2,300 hours in the air, including 1,600 in jets; Jim was serving as a flight instructor and flight safety officer at the Oceana Naval Air Station in Virginia when his call came from Slayton. Jim McDivitt was an experimental flight test officer at Edwards who had logged 2,500 hours flying time, about 75 percent of it in jets. Elliot See flew as a civilian experimental test pilot for the General Electric Company; he had amassed more than 3,200 hours flying time, including 2,300 in jets. Stafford's last assignment was as chief of the performance branch of the air force's experimental test pilot division at Edwards. Tom was at the Harvard Business School when he was picked to be an astronaut. Some 2,500 of his 3,500 hours in the air had been in jet aircraft. Young finished training at the U.S. Navy Test Pilot School in 1959; for the next three years, John piloted a number of different experimental aircraft at the Naval Air Test Center at Pax River, including evaluations of the Crusader and Phantom fighter weapons systems. In 1962, prior to reporting to NASA, Young set world time-to-climb records to 3,000-

meter and 25,000-meter altitudes in a Phantom. Of his 2,300 flying hours, 1,600 had been in jets. Finally, there was Armstrong, with his seven years as a NACA/NASA test pilot at Lewis and Edwards. By the time he became an astronaut, Neil had amassed 2,400 hours of flying time, about 900 of it in jets. Plus he was the only one of the nine who had done any flying in rocket-powered aircraft.

The new astronauts were born in seven different states: two each from Ohio (Armstrong and Lovell) and Texas (See and White), and one from California (Young), Indiana (Borman), Pennsylvania (Conrad), Illinois (McDivitt), and Oklahoma (Stafford). The group's average age was thirty-two and a half, compared to thirty-four and a half for the seven Mercury astronauts when they were selected in 1959. The new astronauts weighed slightly more than did the first group—161.5 pounds per man as compared to 159 pounds—and their average height of five feet ten inches was two-tenths of an inch taller. At five feet eleven and 165 pounds, Armstrong was slightly above average size for his group, for one of the first times in his life.

All of the men were married, none of them had ever been divorced, and all of them had children. Frank and Susan Bugby Borman had two boys, and Pete and Jane DuBose Conrad had four boys. Elliot and Marilyn Jane Denahy See had two daughters, as did Tom and Faye Laverne Shoemaker Stafford. The homes of Jim and Marilyn Lillie Gerlach Lovell and of Jim and Patricia Ann Haas McDivitt both counted one boy and two girls. Ed and Patricia Eileen Finegan White and John and Barbara Vincent White Young both had one child of each gender. The Armstrongs, after the loss of Karen, had only Rick, but Mark would soon be on his way, born in April 1963. The oldest of all the children was Borman's son Frederick, who was eleven. The youngest were Christopher Conrad and Patricia McDivitt, both two. Of the twenty-one children in all, thirteen of them were six years of age or under when their fathers became astronauts. Over the coming years, none of these children would see nearly as much of their father as they would have liked.

Clean-cut and attired for the press conference in conservative dark business suits (except Conrad, who stood out in a white linen suit), the New Nine looked, to one observer, "more like junior executives on their way home to Scarsdale than spacemen who hope to set foot on the Moon." In response to questions from reporters, none of them gave answers worthy of quotation, but that did not matter. In 1962 America, astronauts were heroes in a league with Hollywood actor John Wayne. Anything they said was worth writing down.

"Gentlemen, what drew you to apply for the job?" came the first question from the press. Since he was first in line alphabetically, Armstrong was forced to give the initial response: "It was the general challenge of the unknowns of the program," Neil said haltingly, "and the general alignment of this part of it with our national goals."

The fact that none of the other answers were any better put than Neil's did not stop the audience in Cullen Auditorium from applauding after each man's comment. "I like to be on the first team," uttered Borman. "I want to be part of it," agreed Pete Conrad, an also-ran three years earlier when NASA selected the Original Seven, "I made up my mind years ago that if I ever had a chance, I'd volunteer for this." Jim Lovell felt the same way: "I'll have to agree with my compatriot. I've been interested in space work for a number of years." Elliot See commented, "I feel this is the most interesting and the most important thing I could possibly do." "It's a real honor to be a representative of one hundred eighty million American people," added Tom Stafford. "I felt I had something to give to this program," said Ed White, ironically, for what Ed ended up giving to the program was his life. Last to answer was John Young, who drew a loud laugh when he muttered, "I agree with those other eight guys," then adding seriously, "I couldn't turn down a challenge like that."

Armstrong's recollection "is that the questions at the press conference were typical, fairly unsophisticated questions—with answers to match." This two-pronged comment—the second part self-denigrating—illuminates much about what later became the misunderstood character of Armstrong's attitude toward the press.

NASA expected Armstrong to be at Cape Canaveral along with all the other new astronauts for Schirra's Mercury launch, but that was not scheduled until October 3. Leaving most of the preparations for the family's move to Texas in Janet's hands, Neil went right back to his job at Edwards. He flew every working day right through the end of the month: "I realized that in Houston I was not going to have the variety of aircraft available to fly whenever the opportunity presented itself, and so I was having a good time and enjoying the last weeks."

If his new bosses in Houston had known the risk factors of one particular experimental vehicle, they might have stopped Armstrong from flying it. That machine was the Paraglider Research Vehicle, known as the Parasev.

Back in the summer of 1960, Armstrong and fellow FRC test pilot Milt Thompson had heard a talk by a brilliant aeronautical engineer from NASA's Langley Research Center by the name of Francis M. Rogallo. A kite enthusiast, Rogallo explained the advantages of using a controllable paraglider rather than the customary parachute for the recovery of space vehicles. Armstrong and Thompson asked FRC director Paul Bikle for permission to build a simple research vehicle to test Rogallo's concept. When Bikle refused, citing the pilots' commitments to the X-15 and to other approved NASA programs, Armstrong and Thompson continued working on the design in their free time. "Our original idea was to make a 'rag wing' having a delta or triangular shape. We were going to hang it from a bicycle frame and control the center of gravity by how we pedaled. But wiser heads prevailed and we arrived at a Parasev design that had a little platform slung beneath it."

Flying a Cessna L-19 on June 28, 1962, Armstrong first took off with the Parasev in tow over Rogers Dry Lake and turned so sharply at the edge of the lake that the towline went slack, causing Thompson to crash-land on one of the really small dry lakes east of Rogers. Armstrong was not even aware there was a problem until Bruce Peterson came into the pilots' room and asked, "Where's Milt?" "So we got in the C-47," Peterson remembers, "flew out, and saw him sitting down there, shaking his fists at us." Milt Thompson admits: "We encountered numerous problems developing a good flightworthy vehicle."

By this time, Bikle had authorized their Parasev work—in part due to a 1961 NASA objective to develop parawing prototypes as a possible landing system for the Gemini and Apollo spacecraft, though safety concerns may well have been a factor. Construction of the Parasev moved to Dryden's shops, where simple light-aircraft fabrication techniques led to a functional prototype in a matter of weeks.

The first free flight was made by Thompson on March 12, 1962, a day Armstrong was in Seattle on Dyna-Soar business. Although Armstrong had been involved in the Parasev project from the start, he first flew the unusual vehicle on Monday, September 24, five days after he returned from the astronaut announcement in Houston.

"I would be leaving FRC for Houston in another week," Armstrong remembers, but he went on to fly the Parasev on the twenty-fourth, twenty-fifth, and twenty-sixth of September. "They were short flights, but twenty flights." Armstrong acknowledges that controlling the glider was extremely tricky: "The acceptable center of gravity box was pretty small, and the control forces could be surprisingly big. Its speed range was very narrow, and its L/D was substantially less than a pilot would like. Yet for a first effort, the paraglider was surprisingly successful."

Built and rebuilt several times, the Parasev eventually made more than one hundred flights at Edwards. Among the pilots who flew it was astronaut Gus Grissom, who, during a flight at Edwards on October 17, 1962, broke its nose gear on landing. The Rogallo parawing might have proved feasible for capsule reentry if there had been sufficient time to develop it fully. But the country's schedule for going to the Moon "before the decade is out" necessitated not an elegant reentry plan, just a workable one. In 1964, with both the Gemini and Apollo programs committed to water landings, NASA canceled all of its paraglider work.

Armstrong's last flight as an FRC employee occurred on Friday, September 28, 1962. It was yet another low L/D flight in an F5D. Following that weekend at home, Neil went by commercial air from Los Angeles, not to Houston, but to Orlando and thence on by car the short distance to Cape Canaveral, where he and the rest of the New Nine watched Schirra's *Sigma 7* Mercury flight go off without a hitch on Wednesday, October 3.

The very next day Neil was back at Edwards, as his civil service orders called for his permanent change of station from the Flight Research Center to the Manned Spacecraft Center to be made not until between the eleventh and the thirteenth of the month. In two days' time, he and L.A.-based Elliot See made the 1,600-mile (pre–Interstate highway) drive to Texas in See's car. Neil rented a furnished apartment very close to Hobby Airport, on Airport Road just off the Gulf Freeway, then set off with the other new astronauts to inspect the manned space program's contractor facilities nationwide.

Returning to Juniper Hills through Los Angeles on November 3, Armstrong traded in both of his used cars and bought a used station wagon spacious enough to haul all of the family's more precious belongings. The family's furniture and clothing had already been shipped to storage in Houston. Neil took Rick with him in the car, while Janet flew east by commercial airliner two days later, arriving in Houston the same day her men did. For the next few months, the Armstrongs lived in their furnished apartment until completion of their home in the new El Lago subdivision, a few minutes east of the Manned Spacecraft Center.

For the entire Armstrong family, it was the start of a brand-new phase, one that would take them not just to the Moon and back, but, in terms of how they lived their lives, also to some places they would have preferred not to go.

PART FIVE

NO MAN IS AN ISLAND

They say "no man is an island"; well, Neil is kind of an island. . . . Sometimes what he was thinking and his inner thoughts were more interesting to him than some-body else's thoughts were to him, so why should he leave his island, go wading out into the shallows to shake hands with somebody, when he's perfectly happy back in his little grass hut or wherever.

—MICHAEL COLLINS, GEMINI X
AND APOLLO 11 ASTRONAUT

The heavy, private burden borne by an astronaut's wife was not unlike the uncertainty felt by the wives of the sailors who took the Niña, Pinta, *and* Santa Maria *across the unknown seas to find a new world five hundred years ago.*

—EUGENE CERNAN, GEMINI IX, APOLLO 10,
AND APOLLO 17 ASTRONAUT

CHAPTER 17

Training Days

By the time NASA named Armstrong one of its nine new astronauts in September 1962, the idea of a manned lunar landing had passed with amazing rapidity from the realm of imagining the future into the world of engineering tomorrow's reality. Triggering that almost metaphysical transformation was a turbulent confluence of dramatic geopolitical events in the spring of 1961 that undermined respect for the fledgling presidency of John F. Kennedy and provoked Kennedy into making his astonishing commitment to a manned Moon landing.

On April 12, 1961, not yet fully three months into JFK's term, the Soviet Union stunned the world by achieving another space first. Just as it had back in 1957 with Sputnik, the world's leading Communist power beat the United States to the punch when cosmonaut Yuri Gagarin became the first human space traveler.

The pain did not end there, certainly not for the Kennedy administration. Three days after Gagarin's flight, a plot to invade Cuba and overthrow the Communist regime of Fidel Castro failed miserably on the island's southern coast at a place known as the Bahia de Cochinas (Bay of Pigs). Although the plot had been hatched by the Central Intelligence Agency during the Eisenhower presidency, President Kennedy hesitantly gave it his approval. When the confused CIA-backed invasion force got neither the expected air cover nor the insurgent support of native anticommunist forces, Castro's unexpectedly efficient army of twenty thousand quickly drove the invaders back to the beach. Facing intense criticism for what many around the world called an indefensible exercise in intervention, the Kennedy administration could do little but agonize over its complicity in the misguided attack. Pierre Salinger, Kennedy's articulate press secretary, later called the Bay of Pigs fiasco "the three grimmest days" of the Kennedy presidency—quite a statement given the apocalyptic gravity of the Cuban Missile Crisis that was yet to come.

JFK realized that only swift and dramatic action would restore American respect at home and abroad. To this purpose, Kennedy turned to the potential of the U.S. manned space program. Though Kennedy's reticent record on space dated back to his days in the U.S. Senate, the president saw in NASA and its astronauts a means to a political end.

The Mercury astronauts were America's newest heroes, even though only one of them had flown in space at the time Kennedy gave his speech (Alan Shepard's suborbital flight on May 5, 1961). As writer Tom Wolfe would later explain in *The Right Stuff,* the early astronauts were "the best of the best" on to which American society projected "the mantles of the single-combat warriors of a long-since-forgotten time."

Initially, President Kennedy was not convinced that even a manned Moon landing was bold enough to prove the point of American superiority over the Soviets, and even went so far as to suggest a manned landing on Mars. But NASA leadership assured him that the Moon was a worthy goal and that, with an unreserved national effort, the United States could beat the Russians to it.

"Now it is time to take longer strides—time for a great new American enterprise—time for this nation to take a clearly leading role in space achievement, which in many ways may hold the key to our future on earth." With these historic words, expressed before a joint session of Congress on Thursday morning, May 25, 1961, the dynamic forty-three-year-old president threw down the gauntlet: "I believe that this nation should commit itself to achieving the goal, before this decade is out, of landing a man on the Moon and returning him safely to Earth. No single space project in this period will be more impressive to mankind, or more important for the long-range exploration of space; and none will be so difficult or expensive to accomplish. . . . It will not be one man going to the Moon, it will be an entire nation. For all of us must work to put him there."

Armstrong was in Seattle working on the Dyna-Soar project the day Kennedy committed the country to shooting for the Moon. Neil does not remember his specific reaction to watching the nightly news or to reading about JFK's speech in the next day's newspapers other than excitement at the prospect of new technology and knowledge. In contrast to Project Mercury, wherein a small, one-person capsule traveled around the world for a few hours, a program to achieve a mission as complex as a manned Moon landing would have to be infinitely larger and more elaborate. Astronaut operations and spacecraft versatility would need to expand exponentially.

Neil does remember wondering what the Congress would do. "Because the president can proclaim, but it's the Congress that makes things happen. So that's really where the question was. As it turned out, Congress was motivated to support the president in this area, which I'm not sure I necessarily would have guessed at that point, based on my recollection of what up to then had been set as national priorities.

"The world was caught up in what the Soviets were doing," Armstrong recalls of 1961 and the Cold War. "It was a time of such incredibly high tension nationally and internationally. I think everyone felt we were right on the brink of World War III." For most Americans, that meant carrying on with their lives as best as they could. "The reality was, you've got your job to do and you just go ahead and do it, and keep doing it and hope for the best."

Very quickly after their selection, the New Nine got a close-up look at everything NASA was doing to push Apollo ahead. They attended the launch of the third manned orbital Mercury flight made by Wally Schirra on October 3, 1962. Most of the group had never seen a rocket launch before, from the Cape or anywhere else. An excited Pete Conrad watched with fingers crossed on both hands as the powerful Atlas lit up and roared upwards like a fiery sword. Nine hours and six orbits later, Schirra's *Sigma 7* spacecraft splashed down in the Pacific Ocean very close to its predetermined landing point near the carrier USS *Kearsarge.*

Three weeks later, the new group of astronauts headed out for the first in a series of contractor tours to the Pratt & Whitney Engine Facility at West Palm Beach, Florida, where the fuel cell for the Apollo spacecraft was being developed; to Baltimore, where the Martin Company was assembling Titan II rockets for the Gemini program, as well as to Martin's plant in Denver, where the ICBM version of the Titan II was being built. They then made their way to Aerojet-General Corporation in Sacramento, maker of the Apollo service module propulsion engine; to NASA's Ames Research Center south of San Francisco; and finally to the Lockheed Aircraft Corporation in Los Angeles. The builder of the Apollo launch escape system rocket, Lockheed was preparing to submit a bid for the Apollo lunar excursion module, a contract that eventually went to Grumman.

As Tom Stafford has noted, the trips were grueling: "We were all flying commercial, four of us on one flight, five on another . . . and everywhere we landed we faced a full schedule because we were not only new astronauts, but we were supposed to be the men who were going to the Moon. So they laid out lots of food and plenty of booze. The drinking never got out of hand. It was just a new challenge to be a celebrity, signing autographs, meeting the chief executives of major corporations."

Most of the buildings at the Manned Spacecraft Center were still under construction, so for several months all of the astronauts worked out of rented offices in the Farnsworth-Chambers Building in downtown Houston. "Every Monday morning all astronauts would get together at eight A.M. for the pilots' meeting chaired by Deke," Stafford explained. "There we would get our schedule for the week."

Much of the time Armstrong and the rest of the New Nine spent on the road. To become familiar with the Apollo launch vehicle—what in the end would become the Saturn V Moon rocket—they visited NASA's Marshall Space Flight Center in Huntsville, Alabama. They met the brilliant rocketeer Dr. Wernher von Braun for the first time. Just a few months earlier, von Braun had shocked his own people at NASA Marshall by shifting his support from earth-orbit rendezvous (EOR) to the more controversial lunar-orbit rendezvous (LOR) as the best way to land on the Moon. Then the astronauts spent a couple of days at McDonnell Aircraft Corporation in St. Louis. Besides meeting "Mr. Mac" himself, company founder James McDonnell, they saw how the Mercury spacecraft were built and how McDonnell planned to design and build the new Gemini spacecraft. Returning to the Los Angeles area just before Christmas, the New Nine received Apollo technical briefings from the Space and Information Systems Division of North American Aviation, Inc., at Downey, California, the prime contractor for the Apollo command and service modules. At Douglas Aircraft Company's facility in Huntington Beach, the visiting astronauts saw how the S-IVB upper stage was shaping up for the Saturn IB and the Saturn V.

The years 1963 and 1964 were all about astronaut basic training. George M. Low, a member of NASA's original Space Task Group and a leading official in the Office of Manned Space who later served as program manager of the Apollo Spacecraft Program Office, once explained the "fantastic amount of preparation" involved: "Although the astronauts along the way did enjoy some fun and games, by and large they were the hardest-working bunch of guys I ever knew. Nearly every one of them was motivated on the morning of the flight not to let 'the program' down."

As Armstrong remarks, "There wasn't anybody that had done this and could tell us how to do it, because nobody had the experience." Specialists in all the various areas pertaining to spaceflight "could tell us what they did know," and those who became systems experts could explain "the details of how the inertial guidance system or the computer or certain kind of engine valves and so on would operate, and how we might handle malfunctions.

"The early part of astronaut training was similar [to navy flight training]," Armstrong explains. "NASA felt that its new astronauts with little experience with the sophistications of orbital mechanics or the differences between aircraft and spacecraft needed a quick primer.

"With some of those subjects I felt fairly familiar," Armstrong states. "Orbital mechanics, for example, I had already studied at the University of Southern California. Some of them were new to me, but overall I didn't find the academic burden to be overly difficult. I doubt that anyone did. But it was something we had to plow through."

Along with the academic curriculum, Armstrong and his classmates went through a number of other formal training programs. In Operations Familiarization, they toured all pertinent launch facilities and studied the rigorous prelaunch procedures at Cape Canaveral and the new Mission Control Center in Houston. In Environmental Training, they were exposed to acceleration, weightlessness, vibration and noise, simulated lunar gravity, and the experience of wearing a pressure suit. Contingency Training involved not only desert and jungle survival schools but also learning how to use ejection seats and parachutes. Training in Spacecraft and Launch Vehicle Design and Development was accomplished by the astronauts' participating in different engineering briefings and mockup reviews held at NASA centers and at contractor facilities.

To keep their piloting abilities and judgment in the cockpit as sharp as possible, the astronauts also went through an Aircraft Flight Training program. This they did by making regular flights in T-33, F-102, and T-38 aircraft assigned to MSC, based at Ellington AFB. They also rode out parabolic trajectories in what at the time was simply called the "Zero-g Airplane" (later known as the "Vomit Comet"), a modified KC-135 aircraft that simulated zero-gravity conditions for roughly thirty seconds at a time. Neil had gone "over the top" in zooms in the F-104A Starfighter but those flights into weightless conditions provoked nothing like the queasiness brought on by the abrupt changes in gravity due to a parabolic drop. Four days in the Zero Gravity Indoctrination Program conducted at Wright-Patterson AFB during the last week of April 1963 (through the support of the 6570th Aerospace Medical Research Laboratories) introduced Armstrong to some of the more fascinating features of the nearly traction-less experience: floating free, tumbling and spinning, soaring across the cabin by pushing off the walls and bulkheads, eating and drinking in a near vacuum, and learning to use wrenches and other hand tools.

In late September 1963, the New Nine attended the Water Safety and Survival School at the U.S. Naval School of Pre-flight in Pensacola. For the four naval aviators in the group—Armstrong, Lovell, Conrad, and Young—much of this training, including another confrontation with the Dilbert Dunker, was old hat. What was new for all of the astronauts was learning how to stay afloat and then get hooked up out of the water into a sling for a helicopter rescue while wearing a bulky pressure suit. Gus Grissom's Mercury flight on July 21, 1961, had demonstrated just how dangerous such a water rescue situation could be. When the hatch to Grissom's capsule mysteriously fired open minutes after splashdown, the rescue helicopter could not manage to lift the flooded *Liberty Bell 7* spacecraft out of the ocean. In fact, the helicopter barely managed to save a flailing Grissom from drowning after his suit began to fill up with water.

None of the new astronauts had anything close to the experience riding a centrifuge that Armstrong did; many of them had never even seen one. John Glenn recalled from his torturous experience on "the wheel" that "at sixteen g's, it took just about every bit of strength and technique you could muster to retain consciousness." NASA aerodynamics expert and aerospace vehicle designer Maxime A. Faget, who visited Johnsville to watch the Mercury astronauts ride the wheel, challenged, "If you can get up to twenty g's, you will be my hero for life." As early as 1959, Armstrong had survived forces as high as fifteen g's.

The New Nine got its initiation to the miserable instrument on a four-day visit to Johnsville in late July 1963. During the stay, Neil made eight "dynamic runs" on the centrifuge, his time in the contraption totaling five hours. All the astronauts also rode a centrifuge built on site at the Manned Spacecraft Center.

The New Nine were issued Para-Commander parachutes (made by the Pioneer Parachute Company). "[Ground School at Ellington AFB] would tow you up into the air to about three hundred feet and cut you loose and then you maneuvered down to a landing," describes Armstrong. "We did that over land as well as over water, the latter near Galveston Island off the coast of Texas, in the Gulf of Mexico. That training went for quite a substantial period of time on an intermittent basis."

To all of the astronauts, not just the New Nine, applied the NASA directive to add helicopter flight to preparations for flight simulations of a lunar landing. This training was done two astronauts at a time beginning in November 1963 at Ellyson Field, a part of NAS Pensacola that had been used for navy helicopter training since 1950. Armstrong trained with Jim Lovell for two weeks in mid-November 1963. By the end of the period, Neil completed nineteen hours of dual flight time (with an instructor) in a Bell H-13 helicopter, one of the most popular light utility helicopters ever built. First introduced in 1951, the H-13, as Neil well knew, had been used in the Korean War for observation and reconnaissance and as a litter carrier for evacuation of wounded ground troops. Armstrong also finished three and a half hours of dual night flying in the larger Sikorsky H-34 helicopter, one of the most successful transport helicopters of all time. He finished off his training with three hours solo time in an H-13. Along with the flying, he took another seventeen hours of class work covering unique aspects of helicopter aerodynamics and various systems of the H-13 machine.

"I found that very fascinating," Armstrong recounts, "because I had not flown helicopters before. So I enjoyed that." But NASA's idea that learning to fly a helicopter would better enable its astronauts to make lunar landings, simulated or real, was problematic. As it turned out, "The helicopter was not a good simulation of the lunar module control at all. Had it been, we probably would have configured a helicopter such that it could duplicate the landing—and that could have been done with a great deal of less risk than flying the LLRV or LLTV. But we never could come up with anything that worked well. The natural requirements of helicopter aerodynamics precluded you from duplicating the lunar module's characteristics." Nevertheless, "the helicopter was valuable to understand the trajectories, visual fields, and rates of motion. You could pretty precisely duplicate the flight paths that you wanted to make; it was just that the controls you were using to do that were not at all the same."

As a footnote, Armstrong and Lovell were driving back to Houston from their helicopter training in Pensacola on Friday, November 22, 1963, the day that President Kennedy was assassinated. Neil remembers: "We were in our separate cars, but we were sort of caravanning back westward on I-10 when I heard the news bulletin on the radio." Neil had never met JFK, the man who was responsible more than any other single individual for what would become Armstrong's historic destiny. Ultimately, the events that sealed each of their places in history were of such immediate and imposing import on the lives of people all over the world that they became the subject of the two most asked "Where were you when . . ." questions of contemporary times: "Where were you when President Kennedy was killed?" And, "Where were you when Neil Armstrong first set foot on the Moon?" As for Kennedy's funeral in Washington and burial at Arlington National Cemetery, Armstrong did not attend. The official representative for the astronauts at those events was John Glenn.

Armstrong's experience exceeded all of the other astronauts' when it came to the critical area of flight simulators. "That is really understandable," Armstrong modestly explains, "because simulators were in their infancy in those times. Up until the time I got to Edwards, the only simulator experience I had—and perhaps the same with a lot of my contemporaries—was in the Link trainer where you learned to fly instruments. That was a very rudimentary, primitive state. But when I got to Edwards, they were developing simulators for research purposes—not for operational purposes—they didn't exist much for operational. So I got exposed to lots of formative experiences, and worked actively with the guys in the simulator lab constructing simulations to try to investigate problems. So, yes, it was just natural that I was at the place where the simulators were and most people weren't."

Still, in evaluating Armstrong's strengths as an astronaut, many historians have seriously underestimated the importance of Neil's background in flight simulation. It was a strength that Deke Slayton definitely did not miss when he handed out specialized technical assignments to the new astronauts in early 1963. Slayton gave Borman the Saturn boosters; Conrad, cockpit layout; Lovell, recovery and reentry; McDivitt, guidance and control; See, electrical systems and mission planning; Stafford, range safety, instrumentation, and communication; White, flight control; Young, environmental controls and pressure suits. "We didn't have a choice in the matter," Stafford remembered. "Deke just said, 'Here they are.' " Not for a second did Deke consider giving Armstrong anything other than the responsibility for trainers and simulators. "What is probably true," Armstrong states less boldly, "is that when I was assigned to a specialty, having simulators and training as my area of responsibility was pretty natural based on the fact that that was an experience where I had had quite a bit and the other fellows had literally none. So it was probably an easy pick for Deke."

In projects Gemini and Apollo, astronauts and spacecraft were to be committed to major, complex, and untried maneuvers that, of necessity, had to be carried through to completion, and usually on the first attempt.

Simulation was vital to their success. Very little simulation was necessary for Project Mercury, which had as its very specific objective the placement of a man in orbit and his return. Project Gemini, on the other hand, which came to life in 1962 as a bridge between Mercury and Apollo, entailed orbital rendezvous and docking. Rendezvous and docking were seriously more dangerous and complex maneuvers than simply sending a capsule into orbit. Being able to chase down another object in space and then linking up or docking with it to take on fuel or other vital components that were required for the continuation of the mission was an absolute requirement of Apollo's LOR mode. For that reason, learning how to rendezvous and dock, above all else, was Gemini's primary purpose. Without the proven ability to rendezvous and dock, the other major objectives of Gemini—notably, long-duration flights and EVA (Armstrong considers "space walking" a terrible term and "not a Gemini objective" until it "secretly emerged" after Alexei Leonov's EVA in March 1965)—were meaningless for Apollo.

No astronaut played a more vital role in the development of flight simulators for Gemini and Apollo than did Armstrong. Often Armstrong found that a simulator did not behave like the spacecraft actually would in flight: "One of the things that I particularly did with all the simulators was to find out if the designers of the simulator had mechanized the equations of motion properly. So I would always be flying the simulator into areas that most people would not ever go, to make sure that when you got to a discontinuity in an equation, there would not be a mathematical error that would cause the simulator to misbehave. I found a surprising number of times that they were not mechanized properly. That responsibility was natural for me because I had done the same work at Edwards; I was always making sure that the equations of motion were properly integrated into the computer."

As they had at Edwards, Armstrong's perspectives as a pilot added vital insights into simulator development. "The guys who were mechanizing the equations—sometimes contractors, sometimes NASA employees—oftentimes did not have the perspective of a pilot," Neil explains. "They couldn't visualize if you were pulling up to a vertical position and then rolling ninety degrees and then pitching forward back toward the ground, what that would mean to the pilot—what the pilot would actually see. Oftentimes they would mechanize the equations without any consideration of what was proper. They would just do the arithmetic without regard to the sense of being proper."

Armstrong made significant contributions to the Gemini launch-abort

trainer, a fixed-base simulator built in the astronauts' group training building at the Manned Spacecraft Center. According to Neil, "It was positioned
so that astronauts were oriented as they would be during launch, laying
on their back and facing up against an instrument panel ahead of you. We
duplicated the launch profile with various kinds of malfunctions—engines
going out and things—and depending on what went wrong, you had to
have a procedure for either continuing or aborting, or in some cases ejecting, whatever the case may be. That was a very good simulator. It did not
have the g-force on you, but we were able to tilt the seat back so that it
would give the impression of g changing, at least in the sense of getting a
feeling for the direction that the acceleration was taking. That was a very
useful simulator."

In setting up the system of specialization in early 1963, Slayton understood that far too much was happening too quickly in the program for the
astronauts individually to pick up on more than a small fraction of the technical whole. Deke's idea was for the astronauts to share knowledge and experience freely between their various assignments. Thus, in late 1963 and
early 1964, Jim Lovell, for example, whose specialty was recovery and reentry, wrote memos for the rest on "Parasail Primer" (July 26, 1963), "Gemini
Egress Development" (February 7, 1964), "Ballute Test Results" (February
11, 1964), and "Gemini Survival Kits" (April 27, 1964).

"There were a lot of memos flying around the office," Armstrong explains, but "once you got on a flight crew, a very large percentage of your
time was committed." Until the third group of fourteen additional astronauts came on board in early 1964, "we had a bit of a gap, in my perspective.
Some things weren't covered to the degree we would have liked."

Another responsibility the astronauts shared was NASA publicity and
making appearances before professional audiences, press, and the adoring
public. NASA public affairs officers early on accepted the astronauts' own
idea of a rotating publicity schedule. Usually lasting a week at a time, the
period of public appearances came to be known within the astronaut corps
as "the week in the barrel."

Armstrong's first week in the barrel started on July 6 when he flew to
Staunton, Virginia, on the edge of the Blue Ridge Mountains. From there
he was driven to the National Youth Science Camp being held at Camp Pocahontas in Pocahontas County, West Virginia. Neil next headed for Washington, where on July 8, he presented a technical briefing at NASA
Headquarters, visited the offices of several congressmen, and met with reporters. Following a night in a Washington hotel, he departed for New York

City's World's Fair, where he posed for cameramen in front of Space Park's X-15 exhibit and answered questions at a press conference. Early that evening he flew to Des Moines, Iowa, then on to Ames to address an aerospace workshop at Iowa State University and keynote a luncheon. A second aerospace workshop was at Drake University back in Des Moines, where Armstrong presented to an evening assembly of scientific societies. In that one day, Neil made five presentations. Exhausted by the incessant glad-handing and social conversation much more so than by giving his technical talks, he flew back to Houston from Des Moines early the next morning. The time in the barrel was the one aspect of being an astronaut that he could have lived without.

Armstrong found the transition from research test pilot to astronaut—except for the public celebrity—relatively easy and comfortable: "There were some similarities between the two in the sense that both were always planning and trying to solve problems and devise approaches, but since as astronauts we were trying to do an operational job, we were extremely focused. A research pilot tends to be more broad and generic, covering a range so that you have indications as to which might be the best path." In Gemini and Apollo, "we were looking for not a range of stuff, but for the best method that we could find that would give us the ability to go at the earliest possible time, with maximum speed, and with the highest level of confidence. Quite a different responsibility, yet the skills, the engineering approaches, and the equipment available to us were really quite similar."

As time passed in astronaut training, Armstrong's peers—not just in the New Nine but also in the Original Seven that came before and the Fourteen that followed—respected Neil's abilities as a pilot, engineer, and astronaut, admired his intelligence, and they wondered at his unique personality traits.

"My first impression of Neil was that he was quiet," stated Frank Borman. "Because he was so quiet and so thoughtful, when he said something, it was worth listening to. Most of us were, 'We're operational, let's-get-it-done people.' Of course, Neil was operationally oriented, too, but he would be more interested in trying to understand exactly what the inner mechanisms of the system were. . . . Most of us came out of the same mold. But Neil was different."

"Neil was a very reserved individual—that was a first impression," recalled Mike Collins. Personality-wise, in Collins's view, "Neil presented a certain façade, a certain persona. I didn't want to say, 'Hey, I think there's a chink in your armor here and I want to, you know, probe a little bit.' I never did that.

"I think he was more thoughtful than the average test pilot," Collins continued. "If the world can be divided into thinkers and doers—test pilots tend to be doers and not thinkers—Neil would be in the world of test pilots way over on the thinker side." Buzz Aldrin understood Neil's personality similarly: "Neil was certainly reserved, deep, and thoughtful. He would not utter things that would have much potential of being challenged later because of their spontaneity. I think you learned that in the test pilot business."

The Fourteen's Dick Gordon, who got to know Armstrong well for the first time when they trained together for the Gemini VIII flight of 1966 (Neil as commander and Gordon as backup pilot) described Neil's style of interacting with crew members as "very quiet." "He would take a long time coming to a solution, but when it was made, that was that."

"Neil was patient with processes," Collins differentiated. "Sometimes he could be impatient with people when they didn't meet his standards." Dick Gordon observed, "You could sense that he was upset about something, because he would tend to withdraw more than normal." "I don't remember seeing him lose his cool," Buzz Aldrin concurred. "He could be stubborn, with hidden reason."

In the opinion of William Anders, another member of the Fourteen, one who served in the backup crew for Apollo 11, "Neil was not going to get bamboozled. Neil was not a shrinking violet; he just wouldn't scream or yell. Generally, I don't ever remember him being wrong, but he caught me wrong a few times." "He didn't seem to meet anyone halfway," Collins has commented, with no criticism intended.

To call Armstrong shy can be misleading, Collins testified: "I think he was quite happy with his own persona. It was not so much that he was *unable;* it was more that he was *unwilling.* He was unwilling to share with other people and that, perhaps, can be interpreted as shyness."

"Neil wasn't an expansive guy," Bill Anders offered. "He was totally professional—not overly warm but not cold. I don't remember him and I sitting around having a casual conversation about 'What are your kids doing?' or 'Have you seen any good-looking blondes lately?' Not that Neil would not have a drink or two with you. But he was a straight arrow in all the ways that counted. . . . In my view, the character of the real person, Neil Armstrong, comes out generally higher than most of his colleagues."

"Neil is as friendly as you can get," says John Glenn. "He was laid-back, friendly, a nice guy, small-town just like where I came from. I don't think either of us put on any airs with one another."

Glenn and Armstrong got paired up in early June 1963 for jungle survival training, organized by the USAF Tropical Survival School, at Albrook AFB in the Panama Canal Zone. "We were just getting our jungle training like everybody else [in the Original Seven and New Nine]. One of the Choco Indian guys came around. After we had built our two-man lean-to of wood and jungle vines, Neil used a charred stick to write the name 'Choco Hilton' on it."

What Glenn and everyone else who ever spent any quality time with Armstrong enjoyed, and were surprised by, was Neil's sly sense of humor. John Glenn remembered, "I always got a kick out of Neil's theory on exercise." Armstrong joked with his friends that exercise wasted a person's precious allotment of heartbeats. Dave Scott, Neil's crewmate on Gemini VIII, recalls Armstrong coming into the astronauts' exercise room at MSC when Scott was sweating away pumping iron, getting onto a stationary bicycle, and setting its wheel at its lowest possible tension, and grinning at Dave, saying, "That a boy, Dave! Way to go!"

Yet even his conscientious approach to work was distinctly flavored with Armstrong's own salt. "He was a highly organized guy," expressed Mike Collins. "Neil tended to do things on his own schedule, and that sometimes may have appeared to be disorganized."

"The guy was really cool—cool, calm, and energized," described Dave Scott. "Neil was at his peak when he was operating at his peak. He was never in a frantic mode, but he was quick. . . . I was very comfortable with him, not that I could predict everything that he was going to say or decide. I think you had to work with him to understand him. He was very easy to work with. He was a very smart guy. He could make an analysis of a problem very quickly. The guy was really cool under pressure."

Every commander in the U.S. space program exercised a different leadership style, and every style was unique. None more so than Armstrong's. In Buzz Aldrin's words, "Neil was not the boisterous Pete Conrad; and he was not the authoritarian Frank Borman. You mostly had to wait for Neil to make a decision and often you wouldn't have a clue as to what was going on in his head in the meantime. You just couldn't see through him. But even that opaque quality helped make him a great commander."

CHAPTER 18

In Line for Command

The first members of the New Nine to be assigned to a flight crew were Tom Stafford and Frank Borman. In February 1964, Slayton paired Stafford up with Mercury veteran Al Shepard, the first American in space, as the prime crew for the first manned Gemini mission, designated Gemini III. Assigned as the backup crew for Gemini III were Gus Grissom and Frank Borman. Although as anxious as the next guy for a flight assignment, Armstrong experienced no disappointment. "I had no expectation of getting it. . . . I was so pleased to be associated with the program, because it was going. It was happening. It was exciting. The goals, I thought, were important to not just the United States, but to society in general. I would have been happy doing anything they told me to do."

Neil does seem to have been less concerned about just what job he had than were many of the astronauts. "I think they were all different people," Neil remarks. "I looked forward to an actual flight assignment as much as anyone, as opposed to being in the backup role, but the backup role, I thought, was an important job, and just might turn out that we had to be ready, and we were going to be ready. In some flights it did turn out that the backup crews, or members of them, had to step in."

The crew assignments for Gemini III, in fact, had to be changed before preparation for the flight even got going. Because Al Shepard suffered from a chronic inner-ear problem known as Ménière's syndrome that caused episodic vertigo (diagnosed back in August 1963), Slayton moved Grissom from backup to prime commander, and Gus picked John Young as his new mate. None too happy about the change, Tom Stafford became the backup for Gemini III, under the command of Mercury veteran Wally Schirra. Frank Borman was removed entirely from Gemini III and was held for a later, unspecified Gemini flight.

The mysterious matter of Slayton's method for assigning astronauts to flight crews has been discussed in many NASA history books and in virtually all of the biographies and autobiographies of the astronauts. "I have my own ideas of how Deke assigned the crews," Armstrong remarks, "and it's not easy to explain. I don't think it was a matter of simply switching crews back and forth and alternating. Deke's principle concern was getting a qualified capable commander on each flight.

"Deke had the secondary objective of putting people in the other slots so that they would be getting the proper training, preparation, or experience to slide them into a more important slot in their next assignment. . . ."

Within the flight crews, "we tried to divide the responsibilities such that each person was about equally loaded. We tried for each person to be able to know how to do everything if he had to, but we divided the responsibilities such that each would go into their area in substantially more depth. The job of the commander differed principally because he had the responsibility for the decisions, just as the commander of a ship or commander of an airliner. He was always responsible for his craft.

"I think the key thought above all else was having commanders coming up that would be right for that job and with the right experience to enable them to have a degree of confidence. Deke always said, and I think he was completely right, that he had to take the position that the guys had all come through the process, were all qualified to fly, should be able to fly, and should be able to accept any task they were given.

"Having said that, Deke did say, and wrote in his own autobiography, that all that being true, he still wanted to get the best people into the best slots that were best suited for them. As an additional, less important technical reason—but I think it [was] a reality that was just as strong—Deke felt an obligation to his Mercury colleagues. He always put Gus, Al, and Wally, particularly, as his first-line guys—and properly so. . . . They were the first class of astronauts; they had been under the highest scrutiny; they should get their first pick."

Not everybody was cut out to be a commander. "Some flights required more, or special, skills and experience than others," explains Armstrong. "There were special requirements where Deke wanted the second guy or the third guy on the list also to have about the right level of experience. If the mission didn't require that, he wanted to get guys in there so that they would get some experience, so he would have the ability to use them in more difficult challenges on subsequent flights."

Slayton's standard practice was to solicit the commander's input about potential crew members. "I know he did with me," Armstrong confirms. "I suspect he did with others." This limited Slayton's flexibility. "One rule we had," Armstrong notes, "was a guy could not be on two flights at the same time. The training preparation period was fairly extensive, so Deke would have a crew and backup crew completely committed for quite a long time period and they couldn't be touched for any other jobs. By the time you got three flights with crews assigned to them, you were using up twelve to about eighteen people, out of not so many. So he tried to think things through ahead of time. He thought that every flight was important, but particularly the early flights of a particular program—the early flights of Gemini, the early flights of Apollo. It was very important that we not stub our toe on those because of crew problems—because a failure early in a flight program jeopardized the entire program."

Neil was the only member of the New Nine that had a formal administrative responsibility within the Astronaut Office. In the office, Joseph S. Algranti ran aircraft operations, Warren North ran flight crew operations, and Slayton served as coordinator for astronaut activities. Helping out Deke was Al Shepard, who after his dizzy spells grounded him, became chief of the astronauts. Under Shepard in the organization was Gus Grissom, in charge of the Gemini group, and Gordon Cooper, in charge of the Apollo group. Deke gave Armstrong the responsibility for a third group called operations and training. Like Grissom and Cooper, Armstrong had a small number of fellow astronauts working under him in what Neil calls "a very loose operation."

"Deke gave me the assignment of coming up with something that would help him understand how many crews would be needed at any given point in time," Armstrong recalls. "So I took a very simple approach. I took the launch dates as we projected them for Gemini and Apollo. There were several different kinds of Apollo missions at that point in time—different categories of Apollo missions (e.g., C missions to test fly the command and service modules in Earth orbit, D missions to test combined CSM and lunar module operations in Earth orbit, G missions for the first lunar landing). So I used that kind of a schedule with just the launch dates and said, 'Okay, if that's right, then how many flight crews do we need?' I started at launch time and went back however many months that you would need the crew to be preparing. And none of these crew members were named—they were just individual A, B, C, D, and so on. I put in all these flights on a time line with block diagrams showing how many people had to be available. At the bottom I toted under each month how many astronauts were in flight status and how many available for flight. Along the bottom, the numbers might run twelve, twelve, twelve, twelve, ten, ten, ten, thirteen, fourteen, ten, eighteen, and twenty-one.

"As Apollo started to come in and overlapped with Gemini, that was the way it looked. I also toted other things. For example, we had to allow a certain amount of time for people to take vacation during the year. They had to take their annual physicals and do their collateral duties as well as be assigned to flight crews. We had to have people to handle some things that meant they could not be on flight status while they were doing them. We had to have people available to study the next spacecraft that was coming on line.

"It was quite a complex job. We actually had so few astronauts that almost everybody was assigned all the time. I would come off one crew assignment and within a few weeks be assigned to something else. That endured throughout the entire Gemini program."

Armstrong's schematic allowed Slayton to determine when additional astronauts needed to be brought into the program, culminating in Houston's announcement in June 1963 that NASA was looking for a new class of ten to fifteen additional astronauts. This third round of astronaut selection set a slightly more stringent age requirement (thirty-four years old rather than thirty-five). More significant, applicants no longer needed to be test pilots, in service of the broader scientific and engineering requirements of the Apollo lunar landing mission.

Although the New Nine had no formal role in selecting the new class of astronauts, some did recommend to Slayton and Shepard the names of particularly good candidates. Armstrong does not "recall specifically identifying anyone that I thought we needed to get to apply."

Eight of the fourteen new astronauts selected in October 1963 turned out to be test pilots, five from the air force—Donn F. Eisele, Charles A. Bassett, Michael Collins, Theodore C. Freeman, and David R. Scott—two from the navy—Alan L. Bean and Richard F. Gordon Jr.—and one from the marine corps—Clifton C. Williams. The other six were all pilots whose wide-ranging academic backgrounds and flying experiences added important new strengths to the astronaut corps. Edwin E. "Buzz" Aldrin Jr. had just finished a doctorate in astronautics at MIT. His dissertation on orbital rendezvous concerned an essential maneuver for the Moon landing. Air force fighter pilot William A. Anders held a master's in nuclear engineering. Navy aviators Eugene A. Cernan and Roger B. Chaffee both had engineering degrees from Purdue, plus Cernan had earned a master's in electrical engineering from the U.S. Navy Postgraduate School. Again there were two civilians in the group. Ex–marine corps pilot Walter Cunningham held a master's degree in physics from UCLA and was working for the RAND Corporation. Former air force pilot Russell L. Schweickart was just finishing a master's in aeronautics and astronautics at MIT.

It was in the company of these outstanding astronauts that Armstrong would actually experience spaceflight: with Dave Scott on Gemini VIII and with Buzz Aldrin and Mike Collins on Apollo 11.

On February 8, 1965, Armstrong received his own first assignment to a flight crew when Slayton named him as backup commander to Gordon Cooper on Gemini V. Although the mission's primary objective was demonstrating preparedness for a rendezvous in space, the astronauts intended to stay in space for the designated duration of eight full days. This was twice as long as the Gemini IV flight then being planned for Jim McDivitt and Ed White. As Mike Collins explains, " 'Eight days or bust' was their motto, and a covered wagon the motif of their crew patch."

Serving with Armstrong in the backup role was Elliot See. See supported Pete Conrad, who would sit in the right seat next to Cooper on the prime crew. Armstrong says, "Because everything was based on beating the Russians and getting there by the end of the decade, the schedule was overwhelmingly important."

Armstrong continues: "From a preparation point of view and competence-building point of view, it was very good because the secondary crew essentially learned everything about that flight so they could not only take that information forward but, during the prime flight, they could be useful at Mission Control Center—not necessarily at a CapCom job but being around and being available to talk to whomever wanted more information about how the astronauts in space did this particular thing or whether it would it be okay if Mission Control asked them to do this or that. So there was a very useful role for the backups."

As for his specific assignment as backup commander for Gemini V, Neil was "really pleased to be assigned to a flight, and quite satisfied to be in the position of backing up Gordon Cooper." On the spectrum of personality types within the astronaut corps, Cooper and Armstrong were opposites. "Gordo" did a lot of flamboyant kinds of things, while Armstrong never did any. Some key MSC managers responsible for the manned space program, notably Walt Williams, did not care for Cooper's foolishness and tolerated as little of it as necessary; virtually nothing Neil did ever bothered his bosses. Yet the differences between the two men never personally got in the way of their working together.

"We seemed to work well," Armstrong recollects. "Gordon was sometimes less dedicated than the rest of the guys about really learning how things should work. But Pete [Conrad, Cooper's crewmate] was very good about that. So I figured that if Gordo did miss something along the way, he was in good shape with Pete at his side. . . . I've subsequently read about Walt Williams and maybe some other people not being enthusiastic about having Gordon on Gemini V, but Deke stood up for him and Gordo did a good job."

After assignment to Gemini V, general training continued for Armstrong but now represented only about a third of his work time. A second third, as Armstrong recounts, "had to do with planning, figuring out techniques and methods that would allow us to achieve the best trajectories and the sequence of events." The final third of his time involved testing: "That was probably equal to thousands of hours in the labs and in the spacecraft and running systems tests, all kinds of stuff, seeing whether it would work and getting to know the systems well."

"We'd get home . . . sometimes," Neil states. "But the reality of the world in those days is that a lot of the testing took place at two o'clock in the morning or four-thirty in the morning, and we were spelling each other off. The four of us spent enormous amounts of time together, working out the details. I would not say that we never cracked a joke or talked about something off the project, but we were always ninety-eight percent focused on the job we had to do."

Getting ready for the backup role in Gemini V did not preclude Armstrong from serving in a supporting role in Gemini III, a flight made by Gus Grissom and John Young in the spacecraft *Molly Brown*, named by Gus Grissom after the heroine of the Broadway play *The Unsinkable Molly Brown*, in wry deference to Grissom's own Mercury capsule, *Liberty Bell 7*, which sank to the bottom of the Atlantic Ocean after splashdown in the second manned Mercury flight. For Gemini III, the first manned mission in the Gemini program, Neil reported for a week of work at the worldwide satellite network tracking station in Kauai, Hawaii. Designated as a "primary" station, Kauai, the farthest north of the major Hawaiian Islands, transmitted verbal commands to the orbiting Gemini spacecraft. "Secondary" stations, such as the Caribbean Sea tracking station on Grand Bahama Island (GBI), handled radar and telemetry information only.

In the view of some NASA folks, such assignments were partly a way for Slayton to give his astronauts a little rest and relaxation. According to Mission Control's Eugene Kranz, "Slayton would send astronauts out at the very last moment to all of the sites that were generally good locations to go to—Bermuda, Hawaii, California, Australia." If the astronauts were a little too aggressive about their responsibilities, as Kranz has charged Pete Conrad became when Pete showed up at the tracking station in Australia for Gemini III with word that Slayton wanted him to be in charge of the tracking site during the flight, it could lead to a tense situation.

Having served similarly in Hawaii during Gordon Cooper's Mercury 9 flight in May 1963, Armstrong was familiar with the place, its equipment, and its procedures. For Gemini III, he traveled to Hawaii roughly a week before the launch to help perform tracking and communications simulations: "We practiced the procedures and worked out the kinks. In the simulations, they would sometimes put in failures, so we would have to practice how to handle that."

Gemini III's objective was to demonstrate the ability of a spacecraft to change orbits by firing its maneuvering thrusters, a fundamental requirement in the rendezvous maneuver, which in turn was essential to the Moon landing. Specifically, Gemini III was to demonstrate the ability to move around effectively in space by making three carefully executed "burns," or timed firings of its rocket engines. As Armstrong remembers, *Molly Brown* performed flawlessly. The only real problems in the flight came at the end. The spacecraft landed about fifty miles short of its target, and the jerking deployment of the spacecraft's parachute threw the astronauts into their instrument panel, shattering Grissom's faceplate. "From the point of view of the responsibilities of the tracking station at Hawaii," Armstrong recalled, "I thought it went well." Happily, he played no part in the postflight hubbub provoked by astronaut John Young when he admitted in a news conference that he had smuggled a corned beef sandwich into the spacecraft, one that Wally Schirra had bought for him the night before the launch at Wolfie's, a local Cape deli.

During the twenty-one-week stretch between the launches of Gemini III and Gemini V, Neil spent no less than twenty-six days at the McDonnell plant in St. Louis where the Gemini V spacecraft was being tested and prepared for flight. "We all knew the spacecraft very well by the time it was shipped to the Cape," Armstrong notes. As the monthly calendars indicate, another twenty-plus days were spent in Florida at the Kennedy Space Center. Mixed in between were trips to California, North Carolina, Virginia, Massachusetts, Colorado, and elsewhere in Texas besides the Manned Spacecraft Center in Houston.

Armstrong and the other members of the GT-5 crew traveled, conservatively, during this roughly five-month period, well over 60,000 miles—or about a quarter of the way from the Earth to the Moon. Some of the flying was done commercially, but the astronauts did a significant amount of it themselves. This helped them keep up their proficiency as pilots. "I was getting a fair amount of flying," Neil confirms, "because we were just on the road a lot. It was mostly A-to-B flying. So maybe my instrument proficiency was up, but my ability to do test work was probably eroding a bit." Most of the flying he did in preparation for Gemini V was in the new T-38 aircraft. The Manned Spacecraft Center got a batch of the two-seater jet trainers for its astronauts to fly in August 1964. Their arrival pretty much put an end to any flying of the F-102s that the astronauts had been using previously, though they still occasionally made flights in the old T-33.

The Original Seven astronauts learned much of their celestial navigation at the domed Morehead Planetarium, built in 1949 on the campus of the University of North Carolina at Chapel Hill by alumnus John Motley Morehead III (the inventor of a new process for manufacturing calcium carbide and a founder of Union Carbide). For the Mercury program, a brilliant planetarium director by the name of Tony Jenzano designed and constructed versions of the Link flight trainer that mirrored the view from inside the space capsules. For Gemini, "Tony Jenzano was excellent at helping build up simulations," Armstrong recalls. From two barber's chairs within a "spacecraft" constructed from plywood, cloth, foam rubber, and paper, astronauts controlled the movement of a star-field projection that simulated spacecraft pitch and roll. Planetarium technicians even tilted the barber's chairs slightly from side to side to simulate the action of rocket thrusters that produced left and right yaw.

"Morehead was a superb facility with a good-sized projector and a large dome, highly realistic." The monthly calendars leading up to the Gemini V launch record that Armstrong paid three different visits to the Morehead Planetarium, totaling five days. Morehead's records show that Neil trained at the planetarium a total of eleven different times, lasting a total of twenty days. His last visit came on February 21, 1969, five months before the launch of Apollo 11. No Mercury, Gemini, or Apollo astronaut spent more time studying the stars at Morehead than Armstrong, followed by Pete Conrad, Gordon Cooper, Jim Lovell, and Wally Schirra, with totals of eighteen, seventeen, twelve, and eleven days, respectively.

"My interests were just from a rank amateur," Neil admits. "I did know some number of constellations just because I had a curiosity about the subject, but certainly the Morehead experience was excellent in bringing every-body up one order of magnitude in their ability to recognize the stars and constellations," paramount in the Gemini program for navigational compu-tations and astronomy-related experiments. Apollo flights, with their im-proved computer capabilities, required crew members to have "a good visual representation" to perform sextant sightings and navigational com-putations involving all thirty-six stars being used as the basis for NASA's ce-lestial navigational system.

Flying cross-country together in T-38s in preparation for their March 1966 Gemini VIII flight, Armstrong and Dave Scott regularly tested each other's knowledge of the stars. "We would be flying at a high altitude of 40,000 feet and we would turn the lights completely down in the cockpit," Neil remembers. "You got a wonderful view of the sky and it was a great op-portunity to practice." Asked whether he usually scored better than Scott in the quizzes, Neil answers slyly, "Well, I don't know."

On Apollo 9 in March 1969, Scott performed a lot of excellent star work that kept the onboard guidance and navigation computer properly aligned. Scott, who for his master's and for his Engineer in Aeronautics and Astro-nauts (EAA) degrees at MIT in 1962, had written on star-based interplane-tary navigation, credits his time practicing with Armstrong: "We didn't get much Southern Hemisphere practice" flying across America, but they "made up for that in the planetarium." According to Dave, "We used to pick out remote [fainter] stars and test each other on the constellations. If you can find a star quickly you can align your platform much more quickly than if you have to look at a star chart. You don't have time for that. You've got to know it."

The Gemini V team of Cooper, Conrad, Armstrong, and See, as well as the later Gemini VIII crew of Armstrong, Scott, and their backups (Pete Con-rad and Dick Gordon), grew into closely knit units. "All of the teams I was on were pretty close, but my sense is that the Gemini teams were more closely knit than the Apollo ones," Neil relates. Part of the reason was that the Gemini teams involved just four astronauts whereas the Apollo teams involved six. "That was part of it," Neil states. "Another part of it was that the splitting of duties in Apollo did not get you to spend nearly as much time together. With Gemini we'd all four of us be [at McDonnell] for three days or four days at a time. So we just spent an enormous amount of time to-gether—and we worked pretty well."

Gemini V launched on Saturday, August 21, 1965. The Titan II rocket shot the spacecraft aloft from Launchpad LC-19 just a few seconds before 9:00 A.M. EST, following a two-day hold due to weather conditions at the Cape and because of problems loading the cryogenic fuel. Gordon Cooper remembered: "Ours was the first spacecraft to go into space with a fuel cell: an on-site photochemical generator that produced its own energy. Previous spacecraft had relied on batteries, which would be too cumbersome and heavy given the amount of electronics the more advanced spacecraft were now carrying. In Gemini V, for example, we were taking into space the first onboard radar, and first computer, both of which drew substantial electric power. Proving we could fly with a fuel cell was paramount." For the engineers responsible for making sure that the "newfangled contraption" was reliable, notably MSC's Charles W. Matthews, head of the Gemini Project Office, the very idea of a problematic fuel cell literally produced nightmares.

Following backup crew member procedure, Armstrong and See were at the Cape for the launch, then returned to the Manned Spacecraft Center. "We actually talked to the spacecraft on VHF as it went overhead on our way back in our T-38," Armstrong recalls. "We landed back in Houston and immediately went to Mission Control and made ourselves available to help with the flight. Certainly in all the various problems that they bumped into on that flight, we were very much involved."

As Cooper later wrote, the fuel cell "nearly cost us our mission." On their third orbit, in the middle of one of their seventeen planned experiments, Conrad noticed that the oxygen pressure in the fuel cell had dropped for some unknown reason from 800 to 70 pounds per square inch, just when "we'd released a rendezvous pod, had it on radar, and were just getting ready to intercept it—an experiment designed to provide crucial information about never-before-attempted space rendezvous."

The pressure in the fuel cell eventually recovered, but by then the chance to demonstrate a rendezvous had passed. The flight of Gemini V ended one day short of "eight days or bust," splashing down a considerable distance (ninety miles away) from its rescue ship because someone on the ground had sent up incorrect navigation coordinates (involving the Earth's rotation rate) to the onboard computer. The mission amassed impressive data on the physiological effects of weightlessness (it took two days for the cardiovascular systems of Cooper and Conrad to recover), but the disappointing rendezvous outcome underscored that aspect for the next Gemini flights.

Three weeks after the splashdown of Gemini V, on September 20, 1965,

NASA formally named the crew for Gemini VIII. Armstrong would serve as the command pilot, as he had in the backup crew for Gemini V. Rather than Elliot See, who had been with Neil on the Gemini V backup crew, Slayton paired Neil with Dave Scott, the first member of the third class of astronauts to get a flight assignment. Assigned as backup to Neil and Dave were Pete Conrad, the pilot of the just completed Gemini V, and Dick Gordon, who like Scott was new to the Gemini program.

Only by misunderstanding Slayton's method of assigning crews does one conclude that Deke "replaced" Elliot See, who had seniority over Scott, on Neil's crew. Some astronauts, in fact, believed this was the case, as did many journalists covering the space program. Tom Stafford, for one, went to Al Shepard for an explanation.

"Deke's position was," states Armstrong, "small differences between crews should be just overwhelmed with other considerations. It should not be important."

Dave Scott's assignment was partially motivated by changes in the Gemini schedule. Furthermore, Slayton was concerned that See was not physically strong enough to do the ambitious EVA that was scheduled for Gemini VIII. The only EVA ever done by an American astronaut was Ed White's space walk in Gemini V, just three months earlier, in June 1965. Not even the athletic White could finish his twenty-two-minute space walk without his normally slow pulse shooting up to 180 beats per minute. With sweat in his eyes and a fogged-up visor, White struggled to rejoin commander Jim McDivitt, who in a worst-case scenario would have had to cut the umbilical cord, close the hatch, leave his mate to die floating in space, and head home.

Together, these circumstances moved See into a left-seat assignment on Gemini IX, where he would not have to make a difficult EVA. "Gemini VIII was a rendezvous and a long EVA flight—a big-time EVA flight," Neil explains. "Dave['s] flight experience was good. At MIT some of his [graduate] studies had been with rendezvous. He was big and strong—no question about his ability to physically handle the stuff. . . . I thought Dave was an excellent choice."

Not for a minute did Armstrong think that somehow he was abandoning See by accepting Scott as his crewmate: "No, I didn't think about that at all. That's partially because I worked with Deke. We also talked about strategies for moving people through the system. I had some concept of what was in Deke's mind." Others might not have understood it as well, but "There were so many other examples of people who changed out of crews, for all different reasons," cites Neil.

With his assignment in September 1965 to command Gemini VIII, the first phase of Armstrong's career as an astronaut came to an end. For the next six months, until the launch of Gemini VIII on March 16, 1966, Armstrong and Scott trained almost without interruption for their first spaceflight, the most complex ever tried to that point in the American space program—and one that almost cost them their lives.

CHAPTER 19

Gemini VIII

Cape Kennedy, Florida. 9:41 A.M. EST, Wednesday, March 16, 1966. This is Gemini Launch Control. We are T minus 114 minutes for Gemini VIII on Pad Nineteen and nineteen minutes away from the Atlas/Agena liftoff on Pad 14. Prime pilots for the mission, Astronauts Neil Armstrong and David Scott, were over the hatch and into the Gemini VIII spacecraft at thirty-eight minutes past the hour. They are now hooking up. . . . Both pilots will have an opportunity to observe the Atlas/Agena liftoff by looking through the windows of the Gemini VIII spacecraft at a television monitor mounted outside the spacecraft right above their hatches. . . .

Three and a half years into his career as an astronaut—1,277 days, to be exact—Neil Armstrong, thirty-five years old, finally entered a spacecraft, atop a fully fueled Titan II rocket, ready to make his first space shot.

9:58 A.M. This is Gemini Launch Control at T minus 2 minutes and counting on the Atlas/Agena liftoff. At Launch Complex Nineteen, they are just closing the hatches on the Gemini VIII spacecraft with Astronauts Neil Armstrong and David Scott on board . . .

Gemini VIII, the fourteenth flight overall in the U.S. manned space program, was definitely worth waiting for. A rendezvous in space had been made only once before, just four months earlier, and had never been managed by the Russians. It happened in December 1965 when astronauts Wally Schirra and Tom Stafford in Gemini VI coasted up from their orbit to stop only a few yards away from Gemini VII, with Frank Borman and Jim Lovell aboard. Now Gemini VIII was to perform not just a rendezvous but the first actual docking in space, by joining up with the specially designed, unmanned Gemini Agena Target Vehicle (GATV).

The Gemini VIII mission also called for thirty-three-year-old, Texas-born pilot Dave Scott to perform a far more complicated EVA than Ed White (Neil's residential neighbor) had accomplished in America's first space walk during Gemini IV in June 1965. Also promising to occupy the crew during their scheduled seventy-hour, fifty-five-orbit flight were on-board experiments involving zodiacal light photography, frog egg growth, synoptic terrain photography, nuclear emulsion, and atmospheric cloud spectrophotography. "We thought of it as being an absolutely super flight with great objectives," Armstrong recalls, "and we really loved the challenge.

"In ancient Greek mythology, Gemini meant the twins, Castor and Pollux," Armstrong explains. Armstrong and Scott designed the patch for Gemini VIII "having a ray of light emanating from Castor and Pollux going through a prism and reflecting the full spectrum of spaceflight."

As was true for the entire Gemini program, Gemini VIII's fundamental objective was preparing for the Moon landing. When NASA in the summer of 1963 decided, after a heated yearlong internal technical debate, that the lunar-orbit-rendezvous (LOR) method was the only way to get to the Moon by the end of the decade, it became absolutely essential to learn how to rendezvous and dock with another spacecraft.

It was up to Armstrong, as commander of Gemini VIII, to pull off, for the first time in the brief history of human spaceflight, those critical maneuvers. "The rendezvous and docking was certainly at the top of my priority list," Armstrong declares. "Wally Schirra and Tom Stafford had confirmed in Gemini VII–VI that the rendezvous strategy that we were using worked. So we knew it was doable. But Gemini VIII provided a substantial piloting challenge, and that certainly appealed to me.

"Second to the rendezvous and docking, I would place the entry to a target landing area as my main ambition about the flight. Of course, that didn't work out as we planned, because of the trouble we encountered after the docking" with the GATV.

As originally developed by Lockheed for the U.S. Air Force, the Agena was a second-stage rocket. As such, it proved so reliable that NASA mission planners as early as 1961 contemplated using it as a target vehicle in a rendezvous experiment, an idea that blossomed into Project Gemini. The re-purposed Agena needed a three-way data communications system, a radar transponder and other tracking aids, an attitude stabilization system, and a docking collar. Most complicated of all, the GATV needed a restartable engine capable of no less than five start-and-stop cycles in space (in contrast to the two-start engine that came standard in the original Agena rocket), enabling the docked pair of spacecraft to be maneuvered in any direction, even to a different orbit.

Several times during its troubled development from 1961 through 1965, NASA came close to pulling the plug on the entire GATV program. It had wanted to fly the machine as early as Gemini IV in June 1965. By the end of the year, a mere three months before the scheduled launch of Gemini VIII, NASA came up with a substitute: a poor man's target vehicle called simply the ATDA, or "augmented target docking adapter." So desperate was NASA for a rendezvous and docking target for Gemini that its engineers, as part of an emergency effort known as Project Surefire, bolted the ATDA (the front end of an Agena without its motor and tanks) to a piece of surplus Gemini hardware and fitted it to the end of an Atlas booster. Fortunately, the crude arrangement did not have to be used, at least not for Gemini VIII. In the nick of time, just eleven days before the scheduled launch of Armstrong's mission, a modified Agena was certified for launch.

10:00 A.M. We've got liftoff of the Atlas-Agena. Our network controller advises that liftoff was three seconds after the hour. . . . The flight dynamics plot looks very good. . . . Coming up on six minutes into the flight. . . . We are now 650 miles downrange and 120 miles in altitude. We are aiming for a 161-mile-high orbit. Agena confirms the shroud that encloses the target-docking adapter into which Neil Armstrong and David Scott will dock with this bird has separated.

A petty little prelaunch problem inside their own spacecraft almost cost Neil and Dave their chance to go after the Agena, now streaking into space: "Just after Dave and I slid through the hatches and into our couches, one of the guys in the flight preparation crew found some epoxy in the catcher mechanism on Dave's harness. It was very hard for us to do anything about it, so restricted we were in our seats, but Pete Conrad, our backup commander, and pad leader Guenter Wendt, after a little sweating, got the catch unglued. I didn't really pay much attention to it, because there were other things going on." Scott thought about it a little more than Neil. "Just a little thing like that," Dave surmised, "might have cost us the launch."

10:08 A.M. The astronauts have been busy in the spacecraft at Launch Complex Nineteen. . . . When Neil Armstrong heard that the Agena had ig-

nited and was performing well, he came back with a very strong and very happy "very good" remark. . . . During the last few minutes, we have checked the computers, and Flight Dynamics advises the Agena is in orbit. Its orbit is as follows: 162 nautical miles apogee and 156 miles perigee. This is as close as we could hope with an unmanned vehicle. It's cause for a lot of smiles here in the Control Center. One of the controllers is passing around cigars that are labeled, It's an Orbit. This is Gemini Mission Control Houston.

Janet stayed home with her two small boys in Houston and watched the liftoff nervously on television. Neil had gotten motel reservations for his parents, who were taken with other VIPs to the Cape Kennedy viewing stands by a NASA bus. A NASA protocol officer was constantly at senior Armstrongs' side, as was their daughter June and her husband, Dr. Jack Hoffman, and son Dean, and Dean's wife, Marilyn. The in-laws of both Neil's siblings (Florida residents) attended, as did Janet's mother, Louise Shearon, and Janet's sister Carolyn Trude and her husband. "My heart was in my throat the whole time," Viola Armstrong remembered years later. "I was speechless, but my thoughts were with God."

Neil himself experienced a "counterbalance" to the buildup of anxiety and anticipation in that "most times in airplanes when you're going to go fly, you go fly. But in spacecraft a lot of times you go to the launchpad and just sit for a couple of hours and then get out of the spacecraft and go back to your quarters. It happened so often that it was always a surprise when you really launched. You didn't really expect it" until you felt the rocket's anchoring bolts shear off for breakaway.

Inwardly, Armstrong definitely felt the excitement, his heart rate climbing during launch to a maximum of 146 beats per minute. During liftoff, Dave Scott's heart rate peaked at 128. Neil has always interpreted his higher heart rate as a positive and not as a sign of physical stress. Aeromedical investigations done in association with the X-15 program discovered that what at first appeared to be excessive heart rates in a pilot "should be considered as norms, forming a baseline for pilot response." Rather than indicating any inherent physiological problem, most of the increase in heart rate happened *in anticipation* of what a pilot knew would have to be an elevated performance on his part and thus reflected a "keying up" rather than a direct physical stress. If Armstrong's heart rate rose higher than that of fellow pilots and astronauts in such situations, perhaps it was because Neil was only more intent on preparing himself mentally for what he was about to do.

11:40 a.m. T-20 seconds and counting. Fifteen, ten, nine, eight, seven, six, five, four, three, two, one, zero, we have ignition, and we have liftoff [at 11:41:02 a.m.] . . . *Neil Armstrong reports the clock has started. Roll program is in, Armstrong says. Twenty seconds into the flight and Armstrong says the pitch program is in . . . Everything looks good. . . . Flight dynamics says we are "go" for staging. . . . The spacecraft is now about fifty-two miles downrange and Armstrong says we have staging and that the second stage has ignited. Armstrong said they noted the staging and saw a little fireball behind them. . . . Jim Lovell, the CapCom* [capsule communicator] *at Mission Control who is in communication with the spacecraft, has just advised Armstrong that he is "go" from the ground . . . Six minutes and five seconds into the flight and Armstrong advises they have completed their burn. They are free of the second stage.*

"When the Atlas/Agena went on time," Armstrong recalls, "that was a great sign. Then we went precisely on time with our Titan as well, which was a good sign, too, because it meant that our rendezvous schedule was going to be just like we'd practiced for.

"The Titan II was a pretty smooth ride," Neil remembers, "a lot smoother than the first phase of the Saturn V would be in Apollo. The launch was very definite; you knew you were on your way when the rocket lit off. You could hear the thrust from the engines, at least at low altitudes, but the noise did not interfere with communications. It was really quite acceptable. The g levels got to be pretty high in the first stage of the Titan—something like seven g."

At four minutes and eleven seconds elapsed time following liftoff, Scott said to his commander, "Hey, how 'bout that view!?" "That's fantastic!' Armstrong answered. "They were right, weren't they?!" Dave exclaimed. "Boy, oh boy!" Neil replied. "Here we go!"

From the nearly forty-mile height he had reached in his X-15 flight of April 1962, Armstrong had gotten a good look at the Earth's curvature, but that view was nowhere nearly as stunning as that which he and Scott experienced as the Titan II shot their spacecraft up to the 161 miles that became its orbital apogee. According to Neil: "First, all you see is blue sky and then as you get into the pitch-over program—you're upside down and you're pitching so that your feet are going up towards the sky and you see the horizon coming down through the top of the window. It's quite a spectacular sight because you're going over the Caribbean and you see all those blues and greens and occasionally an island here and there. . . . It would be nice to enjoy the view, but you're too worried about the engine keeping running."

Intermittent voice communications with Gemini VIII happened a few minutes at a time as the spacecraft circled the globe on its easterly path. Relaying between the cockpit and Houston was a worldwide tracking network with stations on Ascension, a British island in the South Atlantic; at Tananarive in the Malagasy Republic, on the island of Madagascar off the east coast of Africa; at Carnarvon, in western Australia; at Kauai, the northernmost Hawaiian Island; and at Guaymas, in Mexico on the Gulf of California.

Not until the astronauts were over Hawaii did they try to do much sightseeing. Armstrong, who was familiar with the Hawaiian Islands from his days in the navy and his sojourn at the Kauai tracking station during Cooper's Mercury flight and Gemini III, was able to make out Molokai, Maui, and the big island of Hawaii, but a bank of storm clouds obscured his view of Oahu and Kauai itself. Approaching the Baja, Neil set his eyes on his old navy base in San Diego and exclaimed, "Oh! Look at all those ships!" Both men then started looking for the shoreline of Texas, hoping to see Houston and to pinpoint the location of their homes just east of the Manned Spacecraft Center. But the demands of the mission quickly interrupted the scenic interlude. The job at hand was to chase down the Agena, presently some 1,230 miles away from Gemini VIII and moving in a separate, higher orbit.

The first task Armstrong needed to perform was aligning the spacecraft's inertial platform, a fixed base, or "stable table," that measured angles—and thus directions—in the void of space where all directions (up-down, right-left) are relative. In the Gemini spacecraft, the inertial platform consisted of three gyroscopes mounted at right angles to one other. As the spacecraft moved relative to the gyroscopes, the inertial measuring unit fed pitch, roll, and yaw angles to the onboard computer tracking the Agena via radar. Three accelerometers mounted in tandem with the gyroscopes measured the spacecraft's reaction to thruster firings.

A five-second burst of Gemini VIII's forward thrusters would slow the Gemini spacecraft into a position where its orbital inclination—that is, the angle between the plane of its orbit and that of the equator—matched up precisely with the Agena's. This critical moment came shortly before 1:15 P.M., at one hour and thirty-four minutes elapsed time into the mission, just as Armstrong and Scott crossed over the Texas coastline for the first time and headed out over the Gulf of Mexico.

"A fundamental requirement of rendezvous," Armstrong explains, "is to get your orbit into the same plane as the target's orbit, because if you're misaligned by even a few degrees, your spacecraft won't have enough fuel to get to its rendezvous target. So the plan is to start off within just a few tenths of a degree of your target's orbit. That is established by making your launch precisely on time, to put you in the same plane under the revolving Earth as is your target vehicle." But no matter how precisely the two launches are timed, the angles of inclination in the resulting orbits of the two spacecraft invariably prove to be slightly askew. In the case of Gemini VIII, a .05-degree difference between its inclination and that of the Agena's needed to be burned off.

Even under ideal circumstances, chasing down a target in space required unusually keen piloting. Armstrong's Apollo 11 crewmate Michael Collins was himself introduced to the dark mysteries of rendezvous while training for his own Gemini X flight of July 1966: "The pilot sees the Agena's blinking light out the window, points the nose of the Gemini at it, and fires a thruster to move toward the Agena. For a short time all seems well, and the Agena grows in size. Then a strange thing happens: the Agena begins to sink and disappear under the Gemini's nose. Then minutes later it reappears from below, but now it is going faster than the Gemini and vanishes out front somewhere. What has happened? When the Gemini fired its thruster to increase its velocity, it also increased its centrifugal force, causing its orbit to become larger. As it climbed toward its new apogee, it slowed down, so that it began to lose ground compared to the Agena. The Gemini pilot should have fired a thruster to move *away* from the Agena, causing him to drop down below it into a faster orbit, and begin to overtake it." Complicate those tricky maneuvers by throwing in orbits of different shapes, or orbits not in the same plane, or difficult rendezvous lighting conditions, or the need to bring the orbits of the two spacecraft together in a great hurry—in other words, any number of real-world complications of spaceflight—and the demands of rendezvous grew exceedingly stringent.

Without extensive simulator time, it is doubtful that any astronaut could ever have been truly ready to perform a space rendezvous. "Rendezvous simulation in Gemini was really quite good," Armstrong notes. "We achieved fifty to sixty rendezvous simulations on the ground, about two-thirds of which were with some sort of emergency. That means that some part of the equipment was either malfunctioning or inoperative during the rendezvous. We completed the rendezvous in all of them but two. But in the two that we missed there were unplanned malfunctions of the simulation experiment, so we never really missed . . . What the ground simulations could not do well was simulate the visual field we would be experiencing. It was okay at night: the star field was pretty good and the relative motion against the stars was pretty good. But when the target was in daylight, it couldn't do a very good job of reproducing that."

A guidance computer was needed to compute the location of the two spacecraft, to define the best transfer arc into the GATV's orbit, and, during the final phases of rendezvous, to solve precise mathematical problems based on radar lock-on with the Agena. Built for NASA by Federal Systems Division of IBM in Oswego, New York, the Gemini guidance computer was among the world's first computers to use digital, solid-state electronics for the purpose of assisting with the real-time guidance, navigation, and control of a flying machine. "This was a teeny-tiny computer," Armstrong relates. Measuring nineteen inches long and weighing fifty pounds, the computer fit inside the front wall of the spacecraft. Within this compact unit, tiny doughnut-shaped magnets comprising the computer's core memory stored 159,744 bits of binary information—less than 20,000 bytes—far less than even the very moderate storage capacity of the very first eight-inch floppy disks developed in the early 1970s, which was some 130,000 bytes. Adding only slightly to this capacity was a tape drive by which the astronauts could put alternate programs into the computer. Gemini VIII was the first space mission to benefit from the alternate-tape system. Even with what was then the most current computer technology, it was incumbent on the mission planners to reduce the complexities of rendezvous.

Mathematical models, simulations, and early Gemini flight experiences determined that the optimal altitude difference between the two spacecraft was fifteen miles, and that the ideal transfer angle—the angular distance the Gemini spacecraft needed to traverse during its rise to the higher orbit of the Agena—was 130 degrees rather than the 180 degrees (or halfway around the globe) called for by the so-called Hohmann transfer. This was the classical method of transferring from one circular orbit to another circular orbit with the greatest efficiency, as suggested by German engineer Walter Hohmann (1880–1945) in his 1925 book *Die Erreichbarkeit der Himmelskörper (The Attainability of Celestial Bodies)*. Employing the Hohmann transfer, as Armstrong explains, "you maneuver to perigee, your lowest point in an orbit, accelerate the vehicle, and then climb for half an orbit, arriving at the orbit of the target vehicle with essentially zero vertical velocity. That sounds good, but the disadvantage of the Hohmann transfer is that when you arrive at the target orbit, there is a lot of motion between your target and the stars in the background. You're looking at the target and everything is moving behind it, so it's difficult for you to know exactly how to control your own vehicle to make sure that you're on the proper approach. What our mission planners worked out was an approach path that allowed us to arrive at the Agena when it appeared to be a great big star fixed in the middle of the background and things weren't all going every which way. This technique used a little more fuel, but it gave us the advantage of having a much easier approach to our target vehicle, because we didn't have the background moving on us. With our target frozen against the star background, we could know we were on the right path. It automatically told us something important if the target started moving; it told us that we had a velocity component that we needed to take out." As for the best lighting conditions, it was found through analysis and simulation that the Sun should be behind the Gemini spacecraft during its braking phase to rendezvous. From these stipulations, the mission planners worked backwards to design launch times, ascent trajectories, and orbital parameters that set up the optimum conditions for Gemini's terminal phase of rendezvous leading to docking.

From the time of the spacecraft's first burn at one hour and thirty-four minutes into the mission (a period when the onboard computer operated in "catch-up mode") to the point in time that the spacecraft began terminal phase (when the astronauts manually switched the computer back to "rendezvous mode"), it took approximately two hours and fifteen minutes. Armstrong and Scott then decided to eat what turned out to be their only meal in space. Some six hours had passed since they had eaten their prelaunch breakfast (filet mignon, eggs, toast with butter and jelly, coffee, and milk) back in crew quarters at the Cape. Schirra and Stafford in Gemini VI had not taken the time to eat early enough in their mission, leaving them hungry and in need of energy by the time they rendezvoused with Borman and Lovell in Gemini VII.

Inside the meal packet labeled Day 1/Meal B was a freeze-dried chicken and gravy casserole. But a call from CapCom Jim Lovell in Houston, relayed through the tracking station at Antigua in the British West Indies, told the crew to get ready for their next burn—a phasing adjustment, or slight in-plane repositioning, requiring another platform alignment. Taking advantage of weightlessness, Armstrong and Scott used patches of Velcro to stick their packaged food on the ceiling of their spacecraft until the burn was complete. Retrieving their food half an hour later, the astronauts found the casseroles still dry in spots. Washing NASA's humble entrée down with fruit juice, Armstrong next tried a package of brownies, only to have crumbs float all over the cabin.

The next maneuver, a plane-change burn, came over the Pacific Ocean just before completing a second orbit, at 2:45:50 elapsed time. Punching the aft thrusters, Armstrong produced a horizontal velocity change of 26.24 feet per second, which brought Gemini VIII's nose down, perhaps imprecisely:

2:46:27   Armstrong: *I think we overdid it a bit.*

Not until the spacecraft was over Mexico was Neil's gut feeling confirmed. Lovell told him from the remote site line at Guaymas to add two feet per second to his speed by making another very short burn. As Scott later said, "It was . . . a pretty quick loose burn . . . without much preparation."

Armstrong explains how he and Scott brought Gemini VIII to the verge of the rendezvous: "We had gotten in plane and into an orbit where we were below the target vehicle so that we were traveling faster around the Earth than the target was, so we were catching him. Then we waited until we got to about one hundred thirty degrees behind the Agena. At that point we added some velocity and got into a transfer arc that was to take us up to the GATV orbit. When we got to this point we started making computations of our range and range rate to assure ourselves that we were on the right transfer arc. We did that both with the computer and manually with charts and also with the ground—all three ways. At intermediate points, we made small corrections based on the computations to improve our transfer arc, because it was impossible to get it exactly right. If we were off just a little bit, the errors got bigger. So we took the errors out and restarted the calculating. Knowing that it was inevitable that we would get a little bit out of plane (meaning that we would be going sideways when we got to the terminal phase of rendezvous), we made a number of fine adjustments on the way so we could hopefully arrive at the target with the target having zero relative motion against the stars and with us approaching at a reasonable rate that had us using a minimum amount of fuel in decelerating for final approach."

The terminal phase could not begin until Gemini VIII had a solid radar lock-on with the Agena. On the Agena was a transponder that answered the inquiring signal sent out by the Gemini spacecraft. The computer on board Gemini VIII measured the time it took for this signal to make a round-trip to the Agena and back. From this measurement, the Gemini computer twice calculated the range between the two vehicles, comparing the two transit times to deduce how quickly the spacecraft was closing on its target. Commander Armstrong kept range and range rates constantly in mind so as not to overshoot the target by closing in on it too fast.

At 3:08:48 elapsed time, while over the United States and in direct communication with Houston, Armstrong reported, "We're getting intermittent lock-on with the radar." Thirty-five minutes later, with the spacecraft over Africa, Neil reported a solid radar lock:

2:20 P.M. This is Gemini Houston Control. About two minutes ago, Neil Armstrong called in over Tananarive and he was able to confirm at that time that radar lock had been established.... He said the range was 158 nautical miles. This is an all-important element of a rendezvous mission— the establishment of that radar link. The pilots say that if they had to lose any of the several things involved in a rendezvous mission—that is, the platform, the computer, or the radar—the one they would rather not lose is the radar.

While still over Madagascar, Armstrong needed to perform another burn. The transfer arc in which Gemini VIII had been moving for the past couple of hours in order to catch up with the Agena had been elliptical, the pathway that was dictated, as Johannes Kepler explained, by the gravitational field of *one* body. At 3:40:10 after the launch, Armstrong nosed down his spacecraft and applied the aft thrusters. The burn resulted in a velocity change of 59 feet per second, which circularized Gemini VIII's orbit and put it more precisely in plane with the Agena.

It took a while before the crew could see its target. "It's hard to do at night," Armstrong explains. "We had the radar information giving us range, range rate, and position. At some point we knew we would see the target. But we had to be pretty close. According to the mission plan, what we wanted to do is be in the dark throughout 130 degrees of the transfer arc— or at least 125 degrees or so. Then at roughly ten miles out, the target would go into daylight. At that point it lit up like a Christmas tree. We could see it against that dark sky just like a gigantic beacon. When that happened, the star background became less important because we would be on a good trajectory, so we could make the final adjustments visually."

At 4:40 elapsed time, while over the Houston tracking station, Scott radioed the crew's sighting of an object seventy-six miles distant that was gleaming in the sunlight. They assumed it was the Agena. Busy preparing for maneuvers necessary for Terminal Phase Initiation (TPI), Armstrong did not comment on the sighting of the target for another three and a half minutes:

4:44:17 Armstrong: *Advise at seventy-six miles we've got what appears to be the Agena, and also we have a visual on another object, which, at this time is approximately twelve degrees above the Agena and appears to be in plane with it. It's possible that it could be a planet. . . . Oh, listen, Dave, I've got to align.*

With the Agena located ten degrees above Gemini VIII, Armstrong needed to align the inertial platform once again, in preparation for one of his last translation maneuvers. In it Neil would pitch up the spacecraft's nose some thirty degrees and cant the vehicle roughly seventeen degrees to the left. When that maneuver was completed successfully, he had time to take another look at the Agena:

4:47:33 Armstrong: *Okay, we have a good solid visual on the Agena at fifty-six miles. I'm taking a second look at it with the sextant.*

A few minutes later, the Agena vanished from view as it entered twilight, soon to reappear for the astronauts when the acquisition lights on the target vehicle, by command from Gemini VIII, blinked on:

5:02:18 Armstrong: *Going into darkness at—let's see, 05:02. We lost a visual on the Agena, and I had the ACQ light up right away. Range was forty-five miles. It's very hard to see, but it looks like a sixth-magnitude star, I'd say.*

"Once we completed our transfer arc," explains Armstrong, "we had to make final adjustments that would get us exactly into the same position and to the same speed as the Agena, so that we would be flying in formation. From that point, we did what was called 'station keeping.' This meant we stayed about one hundred fifty feet apart. We flew around the target but never got very far away from it. We had to stay in the same orbit as the Agena, because if we went astray by even just a little bit, the errors propagated. So we had to fly essentially in formation. Unlike with flying in formation with aircraft, where you fly in the same direction as the target and have the nose of your airplane pointed just like the nose of the airplane with which you are in formation, that was not required in space."

High over the tracking ship *Coastal Sentry Quebec* (CapCom James R. Fucci), which was positioned near the Caribbean island of Antigua, the crew of Gemini VIII prepared to apply the brakes to their spacecraft so that it would not close too quickly on the Agena and fly right by it. Delicately, Armstrong handled the braking by intermittently firing his aft thrusters in very short bursts, while Dave Scott called out Gemini VIII's range and rate:

5:42:52	Armstrong:	*Okay, I'm going to start braking down a little bit very shortly because we're at 15K [15,000 feet or 2.84 miles away]. We're inside 15K and I'd like to . . .*
5:43:04	Scott:	*Yes, we're inside 15K.*
5:43:08	Armstrong:	*How about if I brake off?*
5:43:09	Scott:	*Yes, I agree.*
5:43:25	Armstrong:	*Okay. Now give me a digital range for the remainder of twenty seconds.*
5:43:37	Scott:	*Okay. You're at 10,000 feet.*
5:43:40	Armstrong:	*Okay. And range rate?*
5:43:41	Scott:	*Forty-four feet per second, but let me get you another readout on that.*
5:43:44	Armstrong:	*Okay. I'm reading.*
5:43:47	Scott:	*Ready.*

Two minutes and twenty-one seconds later came the glare of the Agena's lights. Edging ahead at the glacial pace of five feet per second, a pace by which it would have taken a track athlete twenty-four seconds to run forty yards, Gemini VIII bore down on the Agena.

At this critical point in the rendezvous, Houston reported that, "all in all, the pilots are acting extremely 'ho-hum,' " and that the crew had to be "urged to say a bit more about their situation." The news from Mission Control was misleading, as Armstrong's excitement was clearly evident:

5:52:32	Scott:	*You're 900 feet.*
5:52:35	Scott:	*Five feet per second.*
5:53:01	Armstrong:	*That's just unbelievable! Unbelievable!*
5:53:08	Armstrong:	*I can't believe it!*

5:53:10	Scott:	*Yes, I can't either. Outstanding job, Coach!* [Starting in training, Dave often called Neil "Coach" or "Chief."]
5:53:13	Armstrong:	*Way to go, partner!*
5:53:16	Scott:	*You did it, boy! You did a good job!*
5:53:17	Armstrong:	*It takes two to tango.*
5:53:20	Scott:	*Say again?*
5:53:21	Armstrong:	*It takes two of us.*
5:53:25	Scott:	*Okay, we're at . . .*
5:53:27	Armstrong:	*Back off.*
5:53:32	Scott:	*Okay, We're 700 feet. Eleven feet per second. Let me redo that one. I like seven. You buy seven feet per second?*
5:53:52	Armstrong:	*Yes.*
5:53:56	Scott:	*Boy! Look at that sucker! That's beautiful!*

Two minutes later, CapCom Lovell, who had kept quiet so as not to bother Armstrong and Scott during the critical braking phase, broke in and asked the crew for an update on the rendezvous. Dave Scott knew that Armstrong deserved center stage:

| 5:56:19 | Scott: | *You tell them.* |
| 5:56:23 | Armstrong: | *Flight Houston. This is Gemini VIII. We're station keeping on the Agena at about 150 feet.* |

With relative velocity between the two vehicles canceled out, rendezvous—only the second ever made in the brief history of the Space Age—had been achieved.

Station keeping posed no particular problem for Armstrong: "The Gemini VII/VI combination flight had reported that it was quite easy to fly very close and maintain station keeping without worrying about bumping into the other spacecraft inadvertently. Schirra and Borman had indicated that it was very easy to do once they got in the proper position, and I found that to be true also. It was very easy to fly close. We flew around the vehicle and took pictures of the Agena from different perspectives, in different lighting."

Armstrong always used the term "we" when it came to flying any aircraft or spacecraft, but the requirements of the Gemini mission were too serious for him to share any of the piloting responsibilities with Scott, at least not yet:

6:03:52	Armstrong:	*Man, it flies easy! I'd love to let you do it, but . . .*
6:03:56	Scott:	*Oh, no!*
6:03:57	Armstrong:	*I think I better get my practice while I can.*
6:03:59	Scott:	*Man, I'll have my chance!*
6:04:00	Armstrong:	*Get yours later. Okay?*
6:04:04	Scott:	*Yes. I wouldn't even take it if you gave it to me. It's up to you to stick with it. The more you get now, the better you're going to be when . . .*
6:04:52	Armstrong:	*Man, this is easy!*
6:04:53	Scott:	*Is it really?*
6:04:54	Armstrong:	*This station keeping, there's nothing to it.*

Even after this exchange, Armstrong planned to let Scott fly the spacecraft sometime later in the mission: "I was going to have him fly it, but not then. I thought it would be much better to do it later. We were coming up on darkness, and we needed to get this job done. I had a lot of stuff I was supposed to practice in order to get the docking done, and I decided that he could fly the spacecraft after we undocked or after he did his EVA, one of the other times when we were still going to be around the Agena. I thought there would be another time for him to get his chance."

Armstrong and Scott kept their rendezvous station across most of that "day," knowing that the plan was to proceed with the docking before they moved into the next "night," when docking conditions would be far from optimal. In the orbit they were in, daylight lasted for about forty-five minutes.

The rendezvous began just west of Hawaii. The press noted the irony that Schirra and Borman, the command pilots for Gemini VI and VII, were at that very moment in an airplane also heading eastward for Honolulu, closing out a goodwill tour to the Far East. Earlier in the day, Schirra and Borman had tried to contact Gemini VIII via a radio transmission—call sign "Gemini 7/6"—sent by UHF to the Kauai station. Armstrong and Elliot See had made the same sort of friendly call to Gordon Cooper and Pete Conrad early in the latter's Gemini V flight.

Gemini VIII's location at daylight put it in the vicinity of USS *Rose Knot Victor* (CapCom Keith K. Kundel), tracking the spacecraft from off the northeastern coast of South America, at the very moment Armstrong was easing the spacecraft toward the docking at the barely perceptible closing rate of three inches per second:

6:32:21	Armstrong:	*Okay, we're sitting about two feet out . . .*
6:32:22	CapCom:	*Go ahead.*
6:32:23	Armstrong:	*. . . we'll go ahead and dock.*
6:32:25	CapCom:	*Roger. Stand by for a couple minutes here.*
6:32:42	CapCom:	*Okay, Gemini VIII . . . You're looking good on the ground. Go ahead and dock.*
6:32:50	Armstrong:	*Okay. We're going to go ahead and dock.*
6:33:40	CapCom:	*Okay, Gemini VIII. It looks good here from the ground. We're showing CONE RIGID. Everything looks fine for the docking.*
6:33:52	Armstrong:	*Flight, we are docked! Yes, it's really a smoothie.*

Celebration broke loose in Mission Control for a few mad seconds.

6:34:01	CapCom:	*Roger. Hey, congratulations! This is real good.*
6:34:07	Scott:	*You couldn't have the thrill down there that we have up here!*
6:34:10	CapCom:	*Ha! Ha! Ha!*
6:34:24	Armstrong:	*Okay. Just for your information, the Agena was very stable and at the present time we are having no noticeable oscillations at all.*
6:34:37	CapCom:	*Roger. Copy. Agena very stable and no noticeable oscillations.*

It came as a surprise to no one that both the crew and the flight controllers in Mission Control focused, during the first minutes of the docking, on the performance of the Agena, given how riddled with problems the GATV had been. Houston had difficulty verifying that the Agena was receiving and storing the commands uplinking for an upcoming yaw maneuver. Flight also wondered why the Agena's velocity meter did not seem to be operating. These two mysteries suggested to Flight Director John Hodge and his team of controllers a malfunction in the Agena's attitude control system:

6:55:38	CapCom:	*. . . If you run into trouble and the attitude control system in the Agena goes wild, just send in the Command 400 to turn it off and take control with the spacecraft. Did you copy that?*
6:55:58	Scott:	*Roger. We understand.*
6:56:01	CapCom:	*Roger. Okay. Stand by.*

Six minutes and seven seconds after this warning reminder, the Tananarive tracking station lost the spacecraft's signal as it moved into a dead zone in the worldwide tracking network, across the waters of the Indian Ocean. For the next twenty-one minutes, there would be absolutely no communications with Gemini VIII, now coupled in flight with the Agena as one integrated spacecraft.

Then came the next chilling words from Gemini VIII:

7:17:15	Scott:	*We have serious problems here. We're . . . we're tumbling end over end up here. We're disengaged from the Agena.*

Armstrong recalls the sequence of events leading to the in-flight emergency, the first potentially fatal one ever experienced in the U.S. space program: "We had gone into night just shortly after the docking was made. You didn't see a lot on the night side. You saw stars up above, and down below you might see lights from a city or lightning areas embedded in thunderstorms, but you didn't see much down below. I don't remember exactly what I was doing at the time, but Dave noticed from the ball indicator, and called to my attention, that we were not in level flight like we were supposed to be but rather in a thirty-degree bank angle."

As their spacecraft had moved into nighttime conditions, the astronauts had turned up the lights in their cockpit as far as they could go, making it almost impossible to detect any changes in their horizon line unless they were looking directly at instruments: "I made some efforts to reduce the bank angle, mainly by triggering short bursts from the Orbit Attitude and Maneuvering System [OAMS]. Then the banking started to go again, so I asked Dave to shut off the controls to the Agena. Dave had all the controls for the Agena on his side of the spacecraft."

To no avail, Scott commanded the target vehicle to turn off its attitude control system; he jiggled the target vehicle switches and cycled them on and off again; he energized and deenergized the entire Agena control panel. Armstrong relates, "I really believed that we wouldn't have any trouble with the docking, based on the simulations we did," but no one had conjured a simulation in which a *coupled* Gemini-Agena experienced such deviant motions. "If we had been able to practice in such a situation," Armstrong feels, "I'm sure we would have figured it out much more quickly.

"We had a couple of flights in the Gemini program under our belt by this point," Armstrong notes. "So it was natural to suspect that if there were a problem or mistake, it would come from the Agena, which had had quite a few problems in its development."

Reinforcing the bias against the Agena was the warning that Jim Lovell had issued, just moments prior to docking, that at any sign of trouble Armstrong and Scott were to get off the Agena and take control of their own spacecraft. "This was probably an unnecessary comment at this point in the flight, given all the prior concerns about the performance of the Agena," Armstrong notes, "but I'm sure somebody at Mission Control told Jim to remind us not to mess around if anything started acting up."

Neil simply said to his crewmate, "We're going to disengage and undock," and Dave Scott immediately agreed.

"Go," Armstrong said to Scott. "We disengaged successfully," Neil explains, "but I was a bit concerned because I didn't want to have a reimpact immediately afterwards with the Agena. So I pulled away sharply hoping I could increase the distance before one of us rotated back into the other one. That worked fine. We then immediately tried to get control of our own spacecraft, which we found we couldn't do. Immediately it was obvious that the problem was not the Agena's. It was ours."

The real villain was one of Gemini VIII's OAMS thrusters—specifically, thruster number eight, a small rocket with twenty-three pounds of thrust used to roll the aircraft. Apparently sometime while Armstrong had been using the OAMS to maneuver the Gemini-Agena combination, a short circuit stuck the thruster open.

"I didn't know at the time," relates Armstrong, that "you only hear the thruster when it fired; you didn't hear it when it was running steadily."

Gemini VIII was spinning dangerously out of control. According to Armstrong, "The rate of rotation kept increasing until it reached the point where the motions began to couple. In other words, the problem became not just a precariously high rate of roll but also the coupling of pitch and yaw," in engineering terms, the same sort of control dilemma as the inertial roll coupling that had so plagued the design of early supersonic aircraft.

"Our spacecraft turned into a tumbling gyro, the fastest motion of which was our roll rate. Our roll rate indicators only went up to twenty degrees per second, and all the roll rate indicators had shot up against the peg, so we were clearly beyond twenty degrees per second in all axes—although sometimes they mysteriously came swinging back all the way across." When the revolutions surpassed over 360 degrees per second, "I became very concerned that we might lose our ability to discriminate accurately," Armstrong recalls. "I could tell when I looked up above me to the controls for the rocket engine that things were getting blurry. I thought I could, by holding my head at a certain angle, keep the controls in focus, but I knew we were going to have to do something quickly to make sure that we could work on the problem without losing our vision or our consciousness."

Armstrong found his options narrowed to one, "to stabilize the spacecraft in order to regain control. The only way I could do that was to engage the spacecraft's other control system." This was the reentry control system (RCS), which was up in the nose of the spacecraft. As the RCS had two individual rings that were coupled, "its propellant tanks were not normally pressurized until shortly before their normal use. There was a single pushbutton switch that energized pyrotechnic valves that allowed high-pressure gas to pressurize the UMDH/N204 propellant tanks. Once the tanks were pressurized, each redundant ring (A and B) could be operated individually using electrical switches. Once we blew the squib valves, we used both rings to regain control. Then we shut off one of the rings to save its propellant for the entry phase. Mission rules dictated that once the squibs were blown, we were obliged to land at the next available landing site.

"We turned off the other control systems, the ones in the back end, and stabilized the spacecraft with only the front-end system," Neil relates. "It didn't take an awful lot of reentry control fuel to do that, but it took enough."

With the spacecraft now stabilized thanks to his firing of the RCS, Armstrong energized the thrusters, one by one. When he hit the switch for thruster number eight, Gemini VIII immediately started to roll again. "We found the culprit," Armstrong notes, "but we didn't have a lot of fuel in the back-end system left available to us at that point.

"Murphy's law says bad things always happen at the worst possible times," Armstrong says with a smile. "In this case, we were in orbits that didn't go over any tracking stations. We were out of radio contact almost all of the time, and for the short stretches when we were in contact, it was over the *Rose Knot Victor* or the *Coastal Sentry Quebec*. These ships at sea had limited ability to communicate back with Mission Control or to transmit data to Houston.

"By the time we went over a tracking station or two and were able to convey the nature of our problem so [Mission Control] knew what was going on, there wasn't any way they could help much at that point."

7:17:15	Scott:	*We have serious problems here. We're . . . we're tumbling end over end up here. We're disengaged from the Agena.*
7:17:22	CapCom:	*Okay. We got your SPACECRAFT FREE indication here.*
7:17:26	Scott:	*Say again.*
7:17:28	CapCom:	*We're showing your SPACECRAFT FREE. What seems to be the problem?*
7:17:35	Armstrong:	*We're rolling up and we can't turn anything off. Continuously increasing in a left roll.*
7:17:45	CapCom:	*Roger.*
7:18:22	CSQ (Fucci):	*Gemini VIII, CSQ.*
7:18:25	Armstrong:	*Stand by.*
7:18:33	Scott:	*We have a violent left roll here at the present time and we can't turn the RCSs off, and we can't fire it, and we certainly have a roll . . . stuck hand control.*
7:18:45	CapCom:	*Roger.*
7:20:05	Scott:	*Okay. We're regaining control of the spacecraft slowly, in RCS Direct.*
7:20:11	CapCom:	*Roger. Copy.*
7:21:12	Armstrong:	*We're pulsing the RCS pretty slowly here so we don't control roll right. We're trying to kill our roll rate.*

7:21:22	CapCom:	*Okay. Fine. Keep at it.*
7:22:35	CSQ:	*VIII, CSQ. How much RCS have you used and are you just on one ring?*
7:22:41	Armstrong:	*That's right. We are on one ring, trying to save the other ring. We started with two rings, but we are now on one ring.*
7:22:48	CapCom:	*Roger. What about RCS usage?*
7:22:51	Armstrong:	*Now okay. We're down to 1,700 pounds right now on RCSB.*
7:22:57	CapCom:	*Roger.*
7:22:58	Armstrong:	*We have about 2,350 on A.*
7:23:01	CapCom:	*Okay. Copy.*
7:23:35	CSQ:	*VIII, CSQ. How are you doing?*
7:23:39	Armstrong:	*We're working on it.*
7:23:40	CapCom:	*Okay. Relax. Everything's okay.*

Finally having put a stop to the maverick spinning, Armstrong took his first chance to explain what had happened, and Houston had its first chance to inquire into the fate of the Agena:

7:23:51	Armstrong:	*The spacecraft-Agena combination took off. Yaw and roll, and we had ACS off. . . .*
7:24:01	CapCom:	*Roger. Understand. Can you see the Agena now?*
7:24:04	Armstrong:	*We turned the spacecraft system on, tried to stabilize, and, in so doing, we may have burned out our lower left thrusters.*
7:24:13	CapCom:	*Okay. I copy. Can you . . . Do you have visual sighting of the Agena right now?*
7:24:17	Scott:	*No. We haven't seen the Agena since we undocked a little while ago.*

Armstrong recalls of his decision to start up the reentry control system: "I knew what the mission rules were . . . Once we energized the RCS and the integrity gets broken in both RCS rings, we had to land—and land at the next convenient opportunity.

"I had to go back to the foundation instincts, which were 'save your craft, save the crew, get back home, and be disappointed that you had to leave some of your goals behind.' "

6:44 P.M. This is Gemini Houston Control. We are eight hours and three minutes into the flight of Gemini VIII. And in view of the trouble encountered at seven hours into the flight as reported earlier, the Flight Director [John Hodge] has determined to terminate the flight in the 7-3 area. We plan to bring the flight down on the seventh orbit in what we call the third zone, which is approximately 500 miles east of Okinawa. It's in the far west Pacific. Our situation out there is as follows. A destroyer named the USS Leonard Mason is about 160 miles away at this time. It is proceeding towards the point, and it should take that destroyer probably five to six hours to reach it, which should come very close to the . . . Well, it may be a little delayed and get there after the landing itself . . .

Out of communication with the ground, Neil expressed his frustration about having to land, especially in such a remote area:

9:31:21	Armstrong:	*Do you have the coordinates for the landing point?*
9:32:38	Scott:	*It's right where they said it would be.*
9:32:43	Armstrong:	*Seven-three comes right there in the middle. That was minus three. That was the third choice, remote areas.*
9:32:58	Scott:	*Roger.*
9:36:20	Armstrong:	*Okinawa.*
9:36:24	Scott:	*Pardon?*
9:36:25	Armstrong:	*Okinawa. Well, I'd like to argue with them, about the going home, but I don't know how we can.*
9:37:55	Scott:	*Yes.*
9:38:02	Armstrong:	*I hate to land way out in the wilderness.*

Armstrong and Scott knew that rescues on open ocean did not always happen quickly. Even on land and with modern communications, it was hard to find something as small as a space capsule. Stories had circulated in NASA that it sometimes took the Russians forty-eight hours to find their astronauts after their parachuting down into places like Kazakhstan or Siberia.

As for arguing with Mission Control, "I was sure that, if there were a way, they would keep us up. I wanted to stay up. I was also sure, if it was reasonable to do so, there were people arguing that view on the ground. I didn't have to get into the fray."

The two astronauts had much to do to prepare for emergency reentry and splashdown: "Dave and I understood that we probably had several hours to get ready. From the ground we were given the retrofire location time, which was over Africa and on the night-side of Earth, so we prepared for retrofire activity. We were flying over the tracking station in Kano, Nigeria, when Houston started giving us the countdown for the retrofire time. We lost communication with the ground midway through that count so they didn't really know if the retro had come off or not. But the retrofire was stable and our readings of the retro change in velocity—that is, the amount of slowing down that we had done—was proper for the target that we wished to hit. Our guidance system seemed to be working properly, so we steered a course for Okinawa."

> *8:47 P.M. This is Gemini Houston Control. The pilots were counted down in the blind via the Kano station, and Neil Armstrong, while he said nothing leading up to the point of retrofire, came back with a very reassuring, "We have all four retros. All four have fired." A cheer went up here in the Control Center, and I'm sure everyone can understand why. . . . We want to emphasize again that there is practically no communication expected now for some time. We are going to try to reach them via the* Coastal Sentry Quebec *on high frequency after they emerge from blackout, but that signal will be marginal. Probably our first authoritative information will come via one of the C-54 aircraft maneuvering in the area east of Okinawa . . .*

As Gemini VIII came into daylight, "We appeared to be dropping at a prodigious rate," Neil recalls. "We could almost see those big mountains [Himalayas] coming up at us." The spacecraft's main chute deployed on time, orienting them with their view up rather than down, so "there was a mirror that we used, a small flight pocket mirror, and by looking into that I could look down over the side and see that we were, thankfully, over water."

10:39:54 Armstrong: *Do you have water out there?*

10:40:09 Scott: *All I see is haze. Oh yes, there's water! It's water.*

"Being an old navy guy, I much preferred coming down in the water to coming down in Red China," Armstrong remembers with a smile.

While they were coming down under the chute, Neil was the first to hear the sound of propeller airplanes in the vicinity. "We assumed it was friendly."

The splashdown itself turned out to be, in Neil's words, "not too bad." A C-54 rescue plane arrived quickly and dropped navy frogmen into the rough waters to attach a big flotation collar around the spacecraft. Nothing remained but to wait for the destroyer *Leonard Mason*. The wait turned into a nauseous ordeal.

"The Gemini was a terrible boat," Neil explains, "a good spacecraft, but not a good boat." Much to their regret, neither Armstrong nor Scott took their tablets of meclizine, used to avoid motion sickness. "So both of us really got seasick in due course," Neil admits. Fortunately, they were on a low-residue diet and did not have much in their systems to regurgitate.

After more than two hours, the frogmen, themselves queasy from inhaling the stench from Gemini VIII's burnt heat shield, opened the spacecraft's hatches, and the astronauts climbed out. For former sailor Armstrong, getting up and on board the destroyer happened much quicker and easier than it did for Scott. Dave, an air force pilot and untested on a Jacob's ladder, struggled up the rigid chain links and nearly fell back in the water. At the top, while tangled up in some rungs, the massive hand of an African-American seaman reached down and pulled him onto the ship. By that time, Neil was already well on board, reluctantly accepting handshakes from the crew.

Neil did not feel like shaking hands with anyone: "I was very depressed at this point. We had not completed all the things we wanted to do. We'd lost Dave's chance to do all those EVA marvelous jobs. We'd spent a lot of taxpayers' money, and they hadn't gotten their money's worth out of it. I was sad, and I knew Dave was, too. It was one of those bad days. The guys on the ship fixed a marvelous big dinner for us, but I could hardly eat a bite."

It took about fourteen hours for the ship to get them to Okinawa. In the party of VIPs at the dock stood Wally Schirra. Immediately after arriving in Hawaii with Frank Borman from their Far Eastern trip, NASA sent Wally back to Okinawa to help the assigned medical doctor and State Department protocol officer bring back his fellow astronauts without incident. "Our job was to protect Armstrong and Scott. We were to prevent people from washing out their minds and diluting information they had to report."

The ship's arrival at Buckner Bay in Okinawa caused more of a stir than anyone planned. Armstrong recollects the unfolding comedy: "The ship had been directed to proceed at flank speed and get us there with the recovered spacecraft as soon as possible. The captain of the destroyer was running his engines at full throttle, and he didn't have a chance to reballast the ship because he was burning off fuel at a great rate and was riding real high in the water. There was a big welcoming party on the dock. There was a band and people with signs and big banners. The ship approached the dock, the band was playing, and all the people were waving signs and yelling. An offshore wind caught the ship and just pushed it right away from the dock. So the captain turned away from the dock and made a new approach. The band stopped, the banners came down, and everybody milled around. When the ship came around and pulled towards the dock for the second time, the band started playing again and the banners went up and the people started yelling. But then out went the ship again! The wind took it right back out again!"

"If she doesn't make it this time," Schirra heard a crusty three-star admiral say, "I'll get a gun and sink her!" Finally, the humiliated captain of the *Leonard Mason* figured out his problem and made the necessary corrections to get his ship docked. By then, some of the banner carriers had left, and the oom-pah-pahs of the band had grown weak. Even in his depressed state, Armstrong found the incident "very humorous," but not as much as Schirra, a good-natured navy veteran, who was barely able to hold back his chuckles while standing at attention on the dock.

After a good night's sleep in Okinawa, the astronauts were flown in a C-141 jet transport to Hawaii. Not even that flight went without incident, as the plane lost oil pressure in its number two engine about 800 miles west of the islands. At Tripler Hospital, an army facility located on Oahu just west of Honolulu, they underwent a complete medical exam. They arrived back at Kennedy Space Center on March 19, three days after launching from the Cape. Reporters were kept away pending completion of a preliminary round of debriefings.

"Essentially every aspect of the operation was reviewed. We went through a number of discussions with different people [flight controllers, astronauts, launch operation, recovery systems, control systems], each of whom had a special interest, wanting to find out how his system worked or didn't work and what recommendations we had to improve it. We tried to tell them everything we knew."

Not until March 25 did Armstrong and Scott return to their homes in Houston. The next day NASA convened the crew's first post-flight press conference. Even several days of talking over technical matters with his associates did not alleviate Neil's depression: "It was a great disappointment to us, to have to cut that flight short. I'm sure I expressed the fact to the media that Dave and I were really disappointed that we didn't get to do everything we hoped to do and that we hoped to get another chance to do something equally good in a future flight."

International media paid a great deal of attention to the unprecedented spaceflight ordeal of Gemini VIII. All the networks in the United States broke into their regular evening programming with emergency news bulletins. (ABC's interruption of an episode of its immensely popular *Batman* series was rewarded with more than one thousand phone calls from complaining viewers.) At the Scott and Armstrong homes in Texas, additional camera crews joined the others already camped out in the front yards. The next morning's New York *Daily News* carried the banner headline "A Nightmare in Space!" Even staid *Life,* with its exclusive contract, elevated the events into melodrama.

Initially, the magazine positioned its coverage as "Our Wild Ride in Space—By Neil and Dave," but Armstrong put a stop to it. He called Hank Suydam, a *Life* writer assigned to Houston. Suydam wired his boss, Edward K. Thompson, *Life*'s editor-in-chief:

I JUST HAD A PHONE CALL FROM NEIL ARMSTRONG WHO WAS VERY UPSET AT THE ADVANCE BILLING IN THIS WEEK'S MAGAZINE WHICH READ "OUR WILD RIDE IN SPACE." HE ASKS THAT THE HEADLINES YOU USE WITH THEIR ACTUAL PIECE NOT CONCENTRATE SOLELY ON THE EMERGENCY AND NOT BE PHRASED IN WHAT HE CONSIDERS AN OVERLY JAZZY WAY. I TOLD HIM WE APPRECIATE HIS POINT. I EXPLAINED, HOWEVER, THAT WE DO HAVE TO USE HEADS TO CRYSTALLIZE THE ESSENCE OF VARIOUS PHASES OF THE STORY. I GAVE HIM A GENERAL ASSURANCE THAT WE WOULDN'T REPEAT THE ONE IN THE BILLING AND WOULD PROBABLY UTILIZE, FOR THE MOST PART, QUOTES FROM THEIR OWN PIECE.

The editor at *Life* obliged, but only partway. He toned down the piece, took the astronauts' byline off it, and changed its title to "High Tension Over the Astronauts."

Life went on to run articles on Gemini VIII in its next two weekly issues.

For the second article, a version of the title that Neil had resisted reappeared as "Wild Spin in a Sky Gone Berserk." The third article, entitled "A Case of 'Constructive Alarm,' " gave the astronauts their bylines, as the story was, in fact, based on first-person pieces written by Neil and Dave, through their words were so heavily edited that Armstrong again complained. In particular, Neil was upset at the cut of his final quote: "I think we'd put this almost identically, so I'll speak for both of us. We were disappointed that we couldn't complete the mission, but the part we did have, and what we did experience, we wouldn't trade for anything."

Editor-in-chief Ed Thompson addressed a personal letter to both Neil and Dave: "I know that you were not entirely satisfied with the result and I think we've thought up an approach for the future which will cause less bleeding on your part and on the part of *Life*. We shouldn't show you unedited copy; we should process it here, taking into account the space we have, etc., and then clear it with the Astronauts and NASA. That would eliminate a lot of misunderstandings. As in the past, we will pay the maximum attention to what you think of the edited result [and] will take the factual corrections you suggest. . . . As a friend I will personally be available on almost every closing to pour a little oil on troubled waters in case you want to call me. With the maximum of goodwill on everyone's part I think we can come to a meeting of minds somewhat easier and earlier."

While *Life*'s editors hyped the drama of the astronauts' personal stories, other media mined the ways that technology had failed Gemini VIII. "What Went Wrong?" headlined the *New York World-Telegram* on the morning after the flight. Some investigative journalists looked for scapegoats, but the great majority of the American press took its lead from President Lyndon Johnson's words on March 17: "From [the astronauts'] skill and strength, we all take heart, knowing that the personal qualities of all the astronauts and their colleagues will ultimately prevail in the conquest of space. We are very proud of them."

If the press had known that, in the hallways and men's rooms of the Manned Spacecraft Center, a few fellow astronauts were privately suggesting that the crew of Gemini VIII had handled their emergency improperly, thereby forcing NASA to terminate their mission early, the tone of the editorials might have grown negative.

According to astronaut Gene Cernan, "It didn't take long for some of the guys around the Astronaut Office to criticize Neil's performance. 'He's a civilian pilot, you know, and maybe he has lost some of the edge. Why didn't he do this, or why not do that? Wouldn't have gone in the spin if he would have stayed docked with the Agena!' " Astronauts who had been on the ground while Neil and Dave were fighting to survive in space were brutal. "Screwing up was not acceptable in our hypercompetitive fraternity," Cernan has admitted, "and if you did, it might cost you big-time. Who knew if the criticism might reach Deke's ears and change future crew selections in favor of the person doing the bitching? Nobody got a free ride when criticism was remotely possible. Nobody."

Armstrong never heard any of the second-guessing firsthand, and very few of the astronauts have ever gone on record with any negative thoughts about the Gemini VIII crew's performance. In his 2002 autobiography, *We Have Capture,* Gemini VI (and Apollo 10) astronaut Tom Stafford asserted simply, without explanation, that Neil's undocking from the Agena "turned out to be the wrong thing to do." The most candid critic, Walter Cunningham, had served at the Cape during the launch as capsule communicator for the flight crew—a position known (for some unknown reason) as the "Stoney." There it had been Cunningham's job to "call the liftoff" by counting backwards from ten and hollering "Liftoff!" Walt had not yet made a spaceflight of his own by March 1966. He never served on a Gemini crew; his first and only mission came on Apollo 7 in October 1968. Yet neither that relative inexperience nor the fact that he was in no position to observe any of the Gemini VIII flight (since he, Bill Anders, and their wives left on a nine-hour flight in a Cessna 172 back to Houston from the Cape immediately after liftoff) stopped Cunningham from opining. "After docking with the Agena," Cunningham reiterated in his 1977 autobiography, *The All-American Boys,* "a runaway thruster began rotating the vehicles. Malfunction procedures had been written and practiced by the flight crews for just such an eventuality, but at the onset of the problem improvisation seemed to be the rule of the day. When the excitement was over, the spacecraft was undocked and once more facing the Agena in space, but the crew had unnecessarily activated a backup control system."

The great majority of the astronauts never expressed or supported this harsh, inaccurate opinion. For one thing, malfunction procedures did *not* cover "just such an eventuality." It is true that, had the Gemini VIII crew been able to correctly diagnose the problem while docked and allowed the Agena to stabilize the combined spacecraft, they would not have had to energize the reentry control system. It is also true that the crew had practiced what to do when a spacecraft thruster stuck open. But they had *not* practiced such an emergency when the spacecraft was docked with the Agena. Contrary to what Cunningham (and some other critics) thought, it was also *not* possible to energize just one ring of the reentry control system, leaving the other one intact for reentry. When the astronauts energized the RCS, *both* rings were pressurized, which invoked the mission rule.

"I didn't hear any of the criticism," stated Frank Borman, who along with Schirra accompanied the Gemini VIII crew back to Hawaii after greeting them in Okinawa following their rescue. "I wouldn't have participated in that crap if there was. I think Neil and Dave did a good job. I don't think anybody realizes how close that came to utter disaster. In retrospect, that was probably as dangerous as Apollo 13. Not as time consuming, but if they had run out of reaction control fuel in stopping their spinning, they would have been dead." Wally Schirra felt the same way about it: "The decisions that Neil and Dave made were all good decisions."

"Everybody second-guessed everybody," recalled astronaut Alan Bean, who was backing up John Young and Mike Collins on Gemini X with crewmate Clifton C. Williams at the time. "Don't forget, you're dealing with really competitive people. You almost had to find something wrong in the other guy's performance. It was part of the way it was."

Jim McDivitt, the commander of Gemini IV, was sitting in the viewing section of Mission Control when Dave Scott's alarming words reached Houston. Scott later flew with McDivitt on Apollo 9 (along with Rusty Schweikart), so Jim heard a lot about what had happened during Gemini VIII. "There was always the thought," McDivitt remarked, "that Neil could have done this or could have done that or he could have done something else, but when you are going around in circles up there. . . . I think he did fine. He and Dave got it figured out."

During the crisis, Dick Gordon rubbed elbows with CapCom Jim Lovell, as did his Gemini VIII backup crewmate Pete Conrad. "I'm sure there were people who said their training should have allowed Neil and Dave to do it differently," Gordon has noted. "But Dave and Neil were real close to it, on the verge of disaster. They did what they had to do to get out of it."

Mike Collins was at his home in Nassau Bay but drove over to Mission Control as soon as he heard about the problem. "Given the rapidity of events, and given the red herring of everyone thinking the trouble would be with the Agena, I thought that they certainly responded more than adequately. There was Monday morning quarterbacking on everything at NASA, but I don't remember Neil and Dave, either officially or unofficially, being subject to a lot of criticism. I don't think they deserved a lot of criticism."

Buzz Aldrin, who was then preparing as backup pilot for Gemini IX, in retrospect has agreed that it is only with twenty-twenty hindsight that anyone can criticize anything that Neil did during the emergency. On the other hand, Aldrin has offered the following false conjecture: "I think there may have been a slim chance that they could have avoided activating one ring of their reentry system. [Again, it was not possible to energize the RCS rings individually.] It's very good that they didn't activate both of them. [Actually, they did.]."

John Glenn had left the space program well before Gemini VIII, but he followed the mission closely. The first American to orbit the Earth considers any criticism of Armstrong's performance in Gemini VIII to be nonsense: "You'll never hear it from me. I don't think anybody was as experienced a pilot as Neil was at that time. He assessed when it was getting beyond his control, and he assessed it right."

After the Gemini VII/VI missions, Chris Kraft had reluctantly turned over his duties as flight director in Mission Control to John Hodge and Gene Kranz, men he had trained, so that he could focus on the upcoming Apollo flights. Limited to the role of director of flight operations for Gemini VIII, he found himself sitting nervously on a step behind the back row of consoles at Mission Control during the Gemini VIII emergency. There he feverishly conferred with his old friend from NACA Langley, Bob Gilruth, the MSC director. In Kraft's estimation, "Armstrong's touch was as fine as any astronaut's," an impression totally reinforced by what Kraft had observed that evening as Neil gingerly piloted Gemini VIII to the world's first-ever spacecraft docking. When communications with the spacecraft resumed over Hawaii, Kraft remembered hearing Neil's voice, "amazingly calm," telling them that Gemini VIII was rolling to the left and he couldn't get the thrusters turned off. Only later did Kraft and the rest of Mission Control learn that Armstrong and Scott were being tossed around and beginning to suffer from grayed-out vision. "It was clearly a life-threatening situation in space," Kraft has acknowledged, "the worst we'd ever encountered.

"Gilruth and I, we said, 'My God, Neil must be having trouble with the stick!' It never occurred to us that he had a stuck thruster. If we had heard about the problem when they were still docked, we would have told them to do exactly what they did, 'Get off that thing!' "

Gene Kranz was just taking over as flight director from John Hodge during a shift change in Mission Control when Scott's urgent report came in over the radio. In retrospect, according to Kranz, "It would have been tough for the controller in a very dynamic situation to track that the solid-on one was the problem. But he might have done it.

"Then again," Kranz conceded, "we were talking about a rookie Flight Control team that hadn't flown many missions, and this was our first Agena mission. I think we would have picked up on the fact that the Agena was not the source of the problem. If so, we could have told the crew that we believed we had a 'hard-on' jet. But it would have taken a while to do that. I don't know if we would have been able to help the crew materially."

Rather than blaming the crew for any measure of failure, Kranz places the blame on himself and on the other flight directors and planners in Houston: "I was damn impressed with Neil, as was virtually everyone that had anything to do with the program." In the debriefing he gave to his flight controllers after the Gemini VIII mission, Kranz asserted: "The crew reacted as they were trained, and they reacted wrong because we trained them wrong. We failed to realize that when two spacecraft are docked they must be considered as one spacecraft, one integrated power system, one integrated control system, and a single structure. . . . We were lucky, too damned lucky, and we must never forget this mission's lesson." In retrospect, treating docked spacecraft as a single system was, in Kranz's judgment, one of the most important lessons to come from the entire Gemini program: "It had a profound effect on our future success as flight controllers." It was a lesson that proved invaluable when the second potentially fatal in-flight emergency happened, in 1970 during Apollo 13.

In total agreement with Kranz about where the fault lay, Chris Kraft has asserted, "We tricked the astronauts on that one. I think Neil and Dave did absolutely what I would have had them do. As for criticizing them afterwards for doing that? I guess maybe a few astronauts might have said, 'I'm better than that.' But they're only fooling themselves."

No one was ever a tougher, more honest critic of his technical piloting performance than Armstrong was himself: "I always felt as though if I had been a little smarter I would have been able to figure out the right diagnosis and been able to come up with something more quickly than I did. But I didn't. I did what I thought I had to do and recognized the consequence of that. You do the best you can."

Following his return to Houston, he found that, just a day or two before their launch, there had been a problem with the environmental control system in the spacecraft. This resulted in technicians pulling out the system to replace one or two parts. Curiously, the wiring for the damaged control system was part of the same cable that operated what turned out to be the faulty rocket. "So my guess," says Neil, "was that, sometime during that process, the technicians did something that put a nick in that cable, which allowed it to short. To my knowledge, they were never able to isolate that problem. Of course, the back end of the spacecraft—the adapter—did not come back to Earth with you. So if it really had been something in the back section of Gemini VIII, we never had a chance to examine it."

Much more vigorously than Neil, Dave Scott has defended the wisdom of what he and his commander did in space: "There was never any doubt in my mind that we had done everything right. Otherwise we would never have survived."

NASA "would have pored over the telemetry records they had from every station," Armstrong speculates. "It's conceivable that what happened to us would forever have remained a mystery." Dave Scott concurs, "They wouldn't have known what happened because they wouldn't have gotten any downlink. They wouldn't have known it was the Gemini because they never would have gotten any data, because it would have been turning too fast."

Such a mysterious tragedy "would have caused a big glitch in the program," especially coming so soon after the deaths of Bassett and See, Chris Kraft has speculated. "It would have taken us a long time to figure out what happened, if we ever would have." Without knowing what happened and why, it would have been very difficult to proceed on into the Apollo program. Then, if the Apollo fire, too, had still occurred, just ten months later, killing three more astronauts, national support for the manned space program would likely have vanished, along with prospects for a Moon landing. As Dave Scott has said, "If we had not recovered from the spin, it could have been a showstopper."

Turning out as well as it did, the broader political repercussions of the Gemini VIII flight were minor. "In the flight, both of them came across as being pretty much what we thought of them before," Mike Collins has explained. "There was certainly nothing in the aftermath that affected their crew assignments, absolutely not. And there would have been if they'd screwed up big-time." Astronaut Bill Anders, whose first mission was to be Apollo 8's historic circumlunar flight in December 1968, agreed: "Not only was Neil quick-thinking, he certainly wasn't shy about doing things that well could have worked against him." According to Chris Kraft, the way Armstrong handled himself during the emergency gave NASA "even greater confidence in Neil's abilities."

Two weeks after the flight, the Gemini VIII Mission Evaluation Team "positively ruled out" pilot error as a factor in the emergency. In revealing the team's findings, Bob Gilruth commented, "In fact, the crew demonstrated remarkable piloting skill in overcoming this very serious problem and bringing the spacecraft to a safe landing." There was no question that Armstrong would be given another assignment as a mission commander.

Most NASA people felt that Armstrong and Scott deserved the approbation, though Walt Cunningham would later issue a disgruntled statement: "Of course, Neil and Dave received the usual medals . . . Scott's career as the fair-haired boy of the third group of astronauts was unaffected. Both performed well over the remainder of their careers, but at the same time their very progress ignored the fact that their peers—and many others at the space center—felt they had botched their first mission." Most unfairly, Cunningham complained that Neil "parlayed a busted Gemini VIII flight into the Buck Rogers grand prize mission, the first lunar landing."

As for the medals the two men received, NASA did, indeed, present both with its Distinguished Service Medal. From the air force Dave also received a Distinguished Flying Cross, a lesser honor than the service's Distinguished Service Medal, which could have been presented to him. Major Scott also received a promotion to lieutenant colonel, whereas Neil received a $678 raise that brought his salary to $21,653, making him, thanks to his twelve years in the civil service system, the highest paid astronaut. Still, there was no ticker-tape parade or dinner with the wives at the White House, as there had been for some of the Mercury Seven or for Gemini IV's Jim McDivitt and Ed White.

As depressed as he was about his mission being cut short, Armstrong himself could not be so sure about his prospects: "I think if it had turned out that we, in fact, had made a mistake—a little one or a big one—that would have been a serious issue. Dave and I couldn't identify serious mistakes that we made, but we recognized that maybe we did make some. So I'm sure there was a concern that it might affect us someway in the future."

Like any pilot who loved to fly, Neil would have liked to have jumped in a spacecraft and gone back up again as soon as possible. All he could do was, as he put it, "get right back into the cycle." On March 21, 1966, just two days after he arrived back from Gemini VIII, NASA named him the backup commander and William Anders the backup pilot for Gemini XI, a rendezvous and docking flight made by Pete Conrad and Dick Gordon six months later.

It would be his last crew assignment prior to Apollo.

Armstrong's paternal grandfather, Willis Armstrong.

"Grandma Laura" Koenig.

Martin August Engel was mourned by his only child, Viola.

Caroline Katter Engel Korspeter.

Viola Engel Armstrong, making her first communion at age six
(*left*) and as a young teenager (*right*).

Wedding portrait of Stephen (*left*) and Viola (*seated*).
Stephen's younger sister, Mary Barbara, was maid of honor;
Guy Briggs, best man. October 8, 1929.

Viola with baby Neil, six weeks old, in
Warren, Ohio, September 1930.

Dean, Neil, and June Armstrong, 1936.

Neil's first birthday, August 5, 1931.

Upper Sandusky's Wolf Patrol (Ohio Boy Scout Troop 25).
Top row, left to right: Jim Kraus, Gene Blue, Dick Tucker, Jack
Stecher, Neil Armstrong. Bottom row: Kotcho Solacoff and
Jack Strasser. October 1943.

The Mississippi Moonshiners (*left to right*) Jerre Maxson, trombone; Neil Armstrong, baritone; Bob Gustafson, trombone; and Jim Mougey, clarinet.

Midshipman Second Class Armstrong, with his grandmother Caroline Korspeter, took leave in Ohio, spring 1950.

Twenty-year-old Ensign Neil Armstrong climbs into a Panther jet for a mission over North Korea.

Armstrong's leather aviator jacket displays the "Screaming Eagle," the symbol of Fighter Squadron 51.

During the *Essex* cruise, Armstrong (*front row, third from left*) was among fourteen VF-51 pilots who made 100 or more carrier landings: Bill Bowers, Bob Kaps, Neil, Wiley Scott, Bill Mackey, Danny Marshall, Bob Rostine; (*back row*) Tom Hayward, Skipper Ernie Beauchamp, Benny Sevilla, Don McNaught, Ernie Russell, Frank Jones, and Herschel Gott.

In the *Essex* ready room, Neil, "Wam" Mackey, and Ken "K.C." Kramer prepare to launch with the Air Group Commander Marshall Beebe (*second from left*).

Armstrong enjoys a lighter moment with fellow VF-51 aviator Hersh Gott.

Armstrong was serving below deck when a Banshee jet fatally crashed into fully fueled planes parked aboard the *Essex* on Sunday evening, September 16, 1951.

At the High-Speed Flight Station, Armstrong astride an innovative flight simulator dubbed the "Iron Cross."

Armstrong flew all four of the "Century Series" aircraft: the North American F-100 Super Sabre (*lower center*), McDonnell F-101 Voodoo (*top center*), Convair F-102 Voodoo (*right*), and Lockheed F-104 Starfighter (*left*).

The X-15 launching from a B-52 aircraft at 45,000 feet.

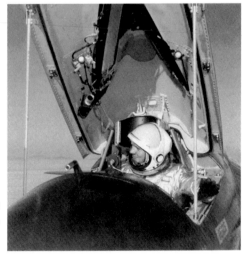

Armstrong in the cockpit of the X-15-1, December 1961.

Twenty-seven-year-old Janet Shearon Armstrong
makes the best of her mountain cabin kitchen,
Juniper Hills, California, 1961.

(*left*) Neil holds Karen, "Muffie," during a family outing in 1959; (*right*) Karen,
Christmas 1961, weeks before her death.

CHAPTER 20

The Astronaut's Wife

To the 7,000 folks back in Wapakoneta, their native son was a "space hero" whether the Gemini VIII spacecraft made its scheduled fifty-five orbits or only managed the seven that it flew. On Wednesday April 13, 1966, three weeks after his townsfolk had nervously sat around their TV sets and radios well past their regular bedtimes awaiting news of their boy's splashdown in the Pacific, the little Ohio burg played host to 15,000 attendees of the "Blastoff!" a gala homecoming in Neil's honor.

Armstrong was in no mood to celebrate, but, "Wapakoneta made the request, NASA put its seal of approval on it, and the event was on." For his old friends and neighbors, the astronaut put on his best face. So did wife Janet: "I didn't know these people," but "it was a happy event for the town. It was just one of the things we had to do."

Though it was a raw early-spring day, the smiling couple rode with their two boys in an open convertible from the small Lima, Ohio, airport to the Auglaize County Fairgrounds. Following a brief press conference, the parade then drove into Wapakoneta proper, through its flag-bedecked downtown business district to Blume High School, where Neil had graduated in 1947. In the high school gymnasium, to a luncheon crowd of 1,500 lucky invitees and ticket holders, Neil thrilled everyone by saying, "You are my people, and I am proud of you." Among the gifts he received during the ceremonies was a small statue of a lion, a leather attaché case, a silver tray, and life memberships in the Elks Lodge and local senior citizens club. A local columnist wrote that Neil accepted the gifts with "boyish modesty and blushes," reciprocating with small, framed American flags (as well as an Ohio flag) that had circled the globe with him aboard Gemini VIII. The prodigal son termed the homecoming "magnificent" and repeatedly told the crowds that the reception was "more than I deserve." Asked whether he was afraid for his life during Gemini VIII, he admitted that the stuck thruster had scared him, "but no more than on some previous occasions when I was pilot of an X-15 test flight."

Janet relates, "He was surprised at how much attention and admiration there was, and the number of people that were out there. I was, too. He probably wished that it could have gone away. He had to make the best of it."

Neil's parents beamed with pride from ear to ear. For Steve, a thirty-seven-year veteran employee of the State of Ohio, it was a tremendous honor to show off his family to government officials, including his boss in the Department of Mental Hygiene and Correction, Martin Janis, and Governor James Rhodes, like Steve a lifelong Republican. During his speech at the high school, the governor announced that the state would be joining Auglaize County in building a $200,000 airport to be named for Neil.

But Steve's elation could not match the radiant glow of Viola Armstrong. "Those dear people," Viola later wrote, "they did everything they could possibly think of to make it a lovely day. They were so good. Neil thanked everybody for everything that they had done. They [NASA] had a nice little movie for him to show, which is always a saving grace for the boys, so they can tell a little bit about their flight—you know, in color."

For Viola, the happy outcome of her son's Gemini VIII flight was, as always, a vindication of her Christian faith. Not that her own experience of the emergency had not terrified her. After watching the launch in person at the Cape, she and Steve had returned in the company of Janet's mother and that of Mr. and Mrs. Gerald Child, some friends of Neil's from Tacoma, Washington, to watch the television coverage in their Cocoa Beach motel room. When the networks reported that the docking had been made successfully, the group relaxed and went to dinner in the motel restaurant. While they were eating, the motel manager came and tapped Steve on the shoulder. Taking him to the side, he whispered to Neil's father that trouble had developed with the flight. The boys were all right, but it looked like their mission would need to be aborted. The manager advised the Armstrong party to leave quietly by way of the back door so as to escape the gaggle of reporters already positioned out front. According to Viola, "We did this immediately, only to find two or three newsmen at our door. They were poking their microphones in our faces and asking, 'What do you have to say, Mr. and Mrs. Armstrong?' " By then, the NASA protocol officer who had been assigned to them for the day had come to the rescue. He told them to say only, "Indeed, we know nothing yet, thank you."

Back home in her church in Wapakoneta that evening, a Lenten service was under way when a gentleman who had been listening to a radio out in the parking lot rushed down the aisle to tell the pastor about Neil's trouble. After asking the congregation "to pray unceasingly," the pastor then put through a call to the Florida motel where the Armstrongs were known to be staying. After much persuasion with the long-distance operator, he talked with Steve and Viola and led them individually in prayer. According to Viola, "It was a very touching situation. Fortunately for me, I had had myself very close to God as long as I can remember and in these hours of real trouble, He was very near to me. It made it much easier, for I was not talking to a stranger . . . Our prayers were answered, and about one-thirty the next morning our boys were safely recovered."

If not for NASA's unwritten rule that wives best not be at the Cape for launches, Janet Armstrong could have been in Florida that awful night. Instead, she and her sister Carolyn Trude were at home in El Lago, caring for Janet's young boys while playing host to a handful of houseguests.

In its bureaucratic paternalism, NASA equated keeping the wives away from the launch with "protecting" them. God forbid, if a disaster occurred at the launchpad, no one at NASA wanted a wife to experience personal tragedy in the VIP stands in view of a television audience of millions.

For the astronauts themselves, the rationale for keeping the wives at home was different. Bluntly put, Deke Slayton did not want the wives at the Cape. In the nervous days leading up to launch, a wife's presence could only divert her husband's attention. No astronaut wanted to risk Deke's ire and the chance of it carrying over into future crew assignments. "Florida was an off-limits playground," astronaut Gene Cernan has explained. "If you wanted to bring your wife and kids to Florida, you had to get advance approval from Deke and let the other astronauts know. There were plenty of pretty women imagining love with a space hero," Cernan has candidly admitted, "and some of them would give anything to sleep with an astronaut, a temptation that some astronauts found too great to ignore."

Some wives suspected their husbands were having extramarital affairs; a few wives might have known it with certainty. Members of the press who covered the NASA beat knew about a few of the indiscretions, but such things just were not reported in 1960s America. Still, circumstances must have been difficult for *Life* magazine's Dodie Hamblin. "I think *Life* treated the men and their families with kid gloves," Hamblin later observed. "So did most of the press. These guys were heroes. . . . I knew, of course, about some very shaky marriages, some womanizing, some drinking, and never reported it. The guys wouldn't have let me, and neither would NASA," not to mention the editors of her own magazine.

Infidelity was not something that Janet spent much time or energy worrying about. Staying at home alone was also nothing new to her. "When the men are preparing for a flight," Janet explained in an interview with Hamblin in March 1969, "they are really home hardly at all. They come on weekends and even then they have work to do. We're lucky if they have a chance to come in and sit down and say hello before they go off again a day later. Having them for eight hours is a privilege during times like this."

As for the dangers in Neil's line of work: "Certainly I realize that there are risks involved in his profession. I suppose we spend years trying to prepare ourselves for a possible tragedy, because the presence of danger is there. But I have a tremendous amount of confidence in the space program. I know that Neil has confidence, and so have I."

Yet the pressures of Neil's first space shot in March 1966 had been different, more extreme. For Gemini VIII, television cameras had not been allowed inside her home, but they were strategically positioned to start filming whenever she went outside. Right in her living room sat a ubiquitous *Life* magazine photographer. Janet realized that she was constantly on display, as were all of the wives of astronauts during a space mission.

"When Neil and Dave got in trouble," Janet recalled in 1969, "the first thing I thought was, 'I want to go see Lurton.' I didn't call. I didn't say anything to the children except that I would be back later. When I got over there and things settled down, I wanted to come home, but I didn't want to have to face all the press, so I waited a little longer until everything was really in satisfactory shape as far as the men were concerned. When we knew that they were down and that they were safe, then I felt that I could at least go by the reporters. It was dark and there were so many floodlights on. I was so petrified that I just walked right on through them."

But in 1969 Janet purposefully left out the most troubling part of her sojourn that evening. Initially she had set out, not for the Scott home, but for Mission Control. As soon as the trouble with Gemini VIII was known, NASA had turned off the squawk boxes the agency supplied to astronaut families, leaving her and Lurton Scott in the dark as to what was happening. The NASA public affairs officer assigned to the Armstrong home drove an insistent Janet to the Manned Spacecraft Center. There she was stopped at the front door of the control center. "I was denied entrance, and I was furious," Janet recalls. Only then did she drive to the Scotts'.

"Don't you ever do that to me again!" Janet later told Deke Slayton, on the eve of Apollo 11. "If there is a problem, I want to be in Mission Control, and if you don't let me in, I will blast this to the world!" As for turning off the squawk boxes, Janet understood: "NASA did not know who was in our homes listening to the squawk boxes. There might have been information that would be leaked to the public that NASA did not want leaked in a critical situation, which is why they had a policy for terminating communications in our homes during a crisis. This was totally understandable for security reasons." What was not understandable was why an astronaut's wife would not be allowed into a secure place to follow what was going on inside Mission Control. "Okay, the men there would have felt bad if something awful happened to our husbands and it might have been difficult for them to see us there, but my comment to Deke was, 'Well, what about the wives?'"

Life's version of Janet's experience that night was even more fictional than Janet's sanitized tale. In its initial story about the Gemini VIII flight, *Life* ran a dramatic picture of Janet down on her knees, "listening but not watching" as she leaned over a living room TV set. According to the caption, the picture was taken just as "the word came that the astronauts had been picked up and were back in good shape." The caption quoted Janet accurately as saying, "I simply knew they were going to make it. But also I am a fatalist." The truth ended there.

"The picture published in *Life* magazine with me kneeling at the TV was because the squawk box was there." (The shot was taken in her home before the squawk box was turned off, not at the Scotts', where she was when the word came that the astronauts were okay.) "I was on my knees there with my eyes closed trying to concentrate on what was being said, but it came out that I was in a praying position and blah, blah, blah. Well, that's not true."

Given the tragic deaths of Elliot See and Charlie Bassett just days before Gemini VIII, NASA should have been prepared to show far greater consideration for the astronauts' wives. See and Armstrong, the two civilians chosen by NASA for the New Nine back in 1962, had become quite close working together as the backup crew for Gemini V. In that role, they had spent a lot of time together, as had Janet with Elliot's wife Marilyn. Not since Chet Cheshire back in Korea had Neil grown so close personally to another man. "Elliot was a hard worker, diligent. He really worked hard on Gemini V. He had good ideas and would express them. He may not have had the same personality as most of the astronauts, but being of a little bit different personality is not necessarily bad. I heard from others that they thought his piloting—particularly his instrument skills—were not as good as they should have been. I flew with him a good bit, and I don't recall anything that was of substantial concern to me."

The deaths of Elliot and fellow Gemini XI crew member Charlie Bassett had occurred as they were coming in for a landing at St. Louis's Lambert Field in a T-38 airplane. The two men had flown up from Houston, accompanied by Tom Stafford and Gene Cernan, their backup crew, in another T-38, in order for the four of them to get in some practice time on McDonnell's rendezvous simulator. Approaching the field in bad weather and low cloud cover, both planes overshot the runway. Stafford climbed straight out of the fog, circled, and landed safely. Hoping to keep the field in sight, See banked to the left to stay below the clouds. His T-38 slipped too low. The aircraft smashed into Building 101, the same building in which McDonnell technicians were working on the Gemini IX spacecraft. Elliot and Charlie died instantly; no one else was killed.

For certain astronauts, the circumstances of Elliot's death only confirmed their dubious opinion of his astronaut status. Neil never saw it that way: "It's difficult to try and blame him for his own death, and I certainly wouldn't do that. When you're doing a low go-around underneath low clouds it's hard to be sure . . . It's easy to say, well, what he should have done was gone back up through the clouds and made another approach. There might have been other considerations that we're not even aware of. I would not begin to say that his death proves the first thing about his qualifications as an astronaut."

Armstrong also knew Bassett, and Janet knew his wife Jeannie, but not nearly as well as they knew the Sees. "Charlie was a very affable fellow," Neil relates. "He had a good reputation and was in my branch in the Astronaut Office. I had worked with him some. It's always hard to lose friends, but it was a common occurrence in the world I lived in."

On March 2, 1966, two weeks to the day before the launch of Gemini VIII, Neil and Janet joined a large group of mourners, most of them NASA employees, at two separate memorial services held for their deceased comrades. Elliot's funeral took place at Seabrook Methodist Church at ten in the morning, Charlie's at Webster Presbyterian Church at one-thirty in the afternoon. The following day, with every one of the astronauts present, the two astronauts were buried in Arlington National Cemetery outside Washington, DC. NASA's attention to the emotional state of their astronaut corps seemed virtually nonexistent. "I don't have any knowledge of them having such concerns," Armstrong recalls of the days between the death of his close friend and his own command of the most complicated space mission ever tried.

Such had been NASA protocol back in 1964, when astronaut Theodore C. Freeman had fatally crashed his T-38 trainer near Houston during a routine proficiency flight. The day was Halloween. Freeman ran into a flock of geese while coming in for a landing. A goose shattered his aircraft's canopy. Pieces of Plexiglas flew into the engine ducts, causing both engines to flame out. Freeman, a superb test pilot, tried to eject, but he was too low. He became the first U.S. astronaut to lose his life.

First on the scene at the Freeman home was a reporter from one of the Houston papers. Hearing the news that she had just become a widow, Faith Freeman became inconsolable.

Just six months before the Freeman tragedy, Janet and Neil faced their own trial by fire. That April night Janet awoke first to the smell of smoke and quickly shook Neil awake. He jumped up to investigate the source. Seconds later came Neil's shouts that the house was on fire and for Janet to call the fire department.

In the days before fully automated telephone exchange systems, this meant that Janet had to connect long distance from El Lago to Clear Lake. Getting no response from the operator, who, at three o'clock in the morning, had fallen asleep, she tried dialing Zenith 12000. In many parts of the country, this was the universal number for emergencies, but not in the Houston area. She then unsuccessfully tried dialing 116, a Los Angeles emergency code that she remembered from a first-aid class she had taken while living in Juniper Hills.

Desperate for help, Janet's thoughts turned to her next-door neighbors and friends, Ed and Pat White.

The Whites and the Armstrongs had arrived together in Houston in the fall of 1962 as members of the New Nine. After living in rentals for over a year, the two families bought property together in the El Lago development, "one of a handful of planned communities that had sprung up around the space center, scattered with ranch houses and crisscrossed with tidy streets." According to Neil, "We were looking for property in the area to the east of Clear Lake, down toward Seabrook. I don't remember who found the lots in El Lago, but Ed White and I both liked the area and we bought three contiguous lots and split the middle one in half so that we each had a lot and a half to build our house on."

Several other astronauts also lived in the area, as did a number of NASA managers. The Bormans, Youngs, and Staffords built homes in the El Lago subdivision, just down the block and around the corner from the Whites and Armstrongs. So, too, did the Freemans, after air force captain Ted Freeman was named one of the third group of astronauts in October 1963. Preferring a site on the water, Elliot See and his wife Marilyn built on Timber Cove, an estuary that separated them from El Lago. The Carpenters, Glenns, Grissoms, and Schirras already lived at Timber Cove. Together, the two neighborhoods amounted to a virtual astronaut colony.

Neil and Janet naturally grew quite close to their next-door neighbors, the Whites. "We saw each other often," Neil states. "I don't remember us socializing together a lot, but Ed and I were both gone an awful lot of the time, and Pat and Janet spent of lot of time together. We had a swimming pool and they didn't. We invited their kids, Eddie III and Bonnie, to use our pool anytime they wanted."

Separating the two backyards was a six-foot-tall wooden fence. Ed and Pat, who were sleeping with their windows open as well as their bedroom door, easily heard Janet through their master bathroom window. As Janet explains, "The reason the children weren't asphyxiated was the fact that our air conditioning wasn't working and it was a warm night and I had closed the doors and opened the windows."

Still to this day, Janet vividly recalls the image of Ed White clearing her six-foot fence: "He took one leap and he was over." Privately, Neil questions whether his brave friend, as superbly athletic as Ed was, literally bounded over the high fence: "Ed certainly had the ability to do it. He came very close to qualifying for the Olympic team in the high hurdles, so maybe he did." On the other hand, "We had a door on the fence. It was not an obvious door; you had to know where it was."

By whatever expeditious manner he did it, Ed White flew to the rescue with a water hose. Janet ran around to the front waiting for Neil to hand Mark out of the baby's bedroom window. "But no," Janet recalled, "Neil didn't do that! They were little windows, and Neil would have had to break one of them. He brought Mark back down the hall, back to our bedroom and out. He was standing out there calling for somebody to come and get Mark, because Mark was—what, ten months old—and Neil couldn't put him down because he was afraid he would crawl into the swimming pool and drown."

By this time, sirens were heard in the distance, as Pat White had managed to turn in the alarm. The living room wall of the house was glowing red, and window glass was beginning to crack. Ed passed the hose to Janet so that he could collect Mark from Neil then hand the child over the fence to Pat so he could get busy with another hose. The heat was now so intense that Janet had to hose down the concrete just to be able to stand on it in her bare feet. Parked in the garage, the fiberglass body of Neil's new Corvette—a vehicle that a local Chevy dealer had offered to all the astronauts at a heavily discounted price—began to melt.

Neil made a second trip into the fire, to save Rick: "The first time I just held my breath the whole time; the second time I had to get down lower and put a wet towel over my face. I was still trying to hold my breath. I couldn't completely. When you take a whiff of that thick smoke, it's terrible." If Rick had been screaming or making any sort of noise, it could have helped his father navigate his way through the ink-black smoke, but Neil does not remember hearing anything but the crackling of the fire. He would later say to Janet that the twenty-five feet he traversed to save Rick was "the longest journey" he ever made in his life, because he feared what he might find when he got there. But six-year-old Rick was fine. Neil took the wet towel from his own face, put it over his eldest son's, and scrambled out into the backyard with the boy in his arms. Catching his breath as best he could, Neil asked Ed to help him push the cars out of the superheated garage. Then both men picked up the hoses and continued their firefighting.

Once she knew her men had made it out safe and sound, Janet was able to laugh and joke a bit with the neighbors, who "couldn't sleep through all of this." Watching her house turn to cinders, she mimicked the actor in a popular television commercial who moaned, "I've got an Excedrin headache." But then she remembered Super. That night, as always, the pet had been sleeping in Rick's room. To lose Super, given his role in bolstering Rick's spirits after the loss of his little sister, would be devastating. A considerate neighbor put together a small hunting party. In a few minutes, Super was found alive and well.

The volunteer firefighters began arriving some eight minutes after Pat White's telephone call and took the rest of the night to drench the flames. Janet remembers, "It was a terrible mess afterwards." Several of the firemen stayed on for a few more hours, helping to carry anything that was salvageable over to the Whites' yard and carport. "We really made a mess of their whole place!" Janet recalls. The Armstrongs lived with the Whites for a few days before moving everything worth rescuing into a nearby rental home. Janet remembers Ed looking at the bottom of his feet the day after the fire and noticing an array of nasty cuts that he couldn't remember sustaining. Checking their own soles, Janet and Neil also found mysterious cuts, sores, and bruises.

The wire service story that appeared in newspapers around the country reflected only a pale shadow of the perilous drama:

> *Seabrook, Tex., April 24, 1964 (UPI)—The suburban home of Neil A. Armstrong, an astronaut, was badly damaged by fire early today, but he and his wife and two small children escaped without injury. His wife, Janet Elizabeth, said she and Mr. Armstrong awoke around 3:45 A.M. this morning and found flames eating across the roof of their home. There was no estimate of damage.*

Janet harbored no illusions: "We could have easily all been consumed by the smoke. It was real, real sickening." Even Neil characterized the danger in stark terms: "It could have been catastrophic . . . Had we started to become asphyxiated before we woke up, then we probably would not have made it."

If danger was a constant for Janet, so was a fatalistic attitude: "I never cried. I never felt down in the dumps over the things that we had lost, and we had lost a lot of things. I was just so darn grateful that we were all unharmed. Mark had a little burn on his finger, which we can't ever to this day figure out how he got because he wasn't really in any fire area at all . . . We were so fortunate not to injure or lose any of our children. My heart just goes out to people who do lose children." The loss of family photographs, particularly pictures of Karen, was deeply felt. Those few, salvageable shots of her became even more precious.

If they had been in their new home for longer than just four months, the losses would have multiplied. According to Janet, "The fire destroyed our dining room table and a beautiful glass-front hutch. All the crystal inside was shattered by fire hoses. Fortunately, we had minimum furniture in the living room. We had just bought brand-new bedroom furniture for Ricky's room and our room and some other furniture." They had insurance, but they still lost money.

"I feel very deeply for anyone who has a fire," Janet commiserates, "because maybe things aren't burned, but there is smoke damage to your clothes and to everything. Everything I was currently wearing was wrapped up waiting to be ironed on the ironing board. So I just didn't have anything to wear for a few days. I'll never forget how grateful I was to all the neighbors and people I didn't even know who brought toys over for the kids. In a couple of hours—oh, less than that—we had a playpen to put Mark in and pretty soon we had a crib and we had diapers. Everybody went through their attics and said, 'Here, we don't need this anymore, you take it,' shoes and all kinds of things. They were just marvelous. I have an attic full of things," Janet said in 1969, "that I'm saving to do for somebody else like that."

It took Neil and Janet "a good six months" to compile an inventory of what they had lost, a process compounded by the fact that so many of their possessions had remained in packed cartons since the move from California in November 1962.

For some of the cartons, Neil needed no inventory. These contained his prized boyhood collection of airplane models, as well as all of his handwritten notebooks filled with drawings of aircraft and aircraft design specifications plus issue upon issue of old aircraft magazines that he had bought in places like Brading's drugstore with his hard-earned money.

"His models, we saved those," Janet explained in 1969. "They weren't all burned up. He saves them for gifts now . . . Priceless! They all got melted and twisted. You can tell what it used to be, but you don't know how it got that way."

The same might be said of the original design specifications of the Armstrongs' El Lago home. "It was not a 'spec' home," Neil explains. "It was custom-built. The builder used a designer draftsman rather than an architect. This was a man who drew up what we wanted in terms of the floor plan, exterior effects, and the general overall look of the house. A number of my colleagues had used the technique in building their homes. It was very good quality construction for the amount of money that it cost, which was twelve dollars a square foot for a brick home with tile baths."

Armstrong determined that the loss of the house "could have been catastrophic but it wasn't, and at that point it was just an inconvenience that required a lot of time being spent on things which were not very productive, like getting into another house, staying there, and renting furniture until we could get back into our own house and have it rebuilt."

Back in the late 1960s Janet constructed her narrative about the El Lago home in the first-person singular: "*I* had just gone through the bit of building a house, carrying a baby around and the trips back and forth. After *I* built the house the first time—and Neil was gone most of the time during that—*I* vowed *I'*d never build another house! And here we were, going through the same thing again! But it was an experience, to say the least.

"We couldn't afford not to [rebuild on the same lot]. By the time we went to rebuild, the building costs had gone up so high that they rebuilt the same house for us, minus the slab, for an increase in price. It was a different builder this time, a fire specialist. They built completely differently, from the roof down instead of from the ground up."

As Neil would later do as part of the NASA teams that investigated the Apollo 13 accident in 1970 and the Space Shuttle *Challenger* explosion in 1986, he did his best in 1964 to learn why his home had caught on fire, in order to make sure it did not happen again.

"We had a large combination living-family room with cathedral ceilings and beams, and the walls were paneled. This was drywall-framed construction where they built drywall walls and then put the paneling over the drywall. After a couple of months in the house, the paneling was warping and curling up and the joints were not fitting right anymore. The builders had sealed the front of the paneling before they painted the front side, but they did not put any sealer on the backside, so moisture was warping the boards. When we noticed that, we had the builder come over. We said to him, 'Look what's happening here.' The builder said, 'Oh yes, it shouldn't be that way. We goofed, so we'll fix it.' In order to take the panels down they used a nail set and knocked the finishing nails through the back of the board so the board would just fall off. This time they put up seal paneling. After the fire, the inspectors found the cause immediately. What had happened is when they knocked in one of those nails, they knocked it into a wire. It wasn't a 'hard short'; it was a 'trickle short' with a little skin of insulation in-between, so there was a small current flowing for some months and built up the temperature in that location. There was no way to know until it had built up enough temperature there to ignite."

It wasn't until Christmas 1964 that their new home was ready. "Because of our fire," Janet recollects, "they were able to sell quite a few detector systems to homeowners in the area," including the Armstrongs themselves, as well as next-door-neighbors Ed White, Ted and Faith Freeman, and Elliot and Marilyn See.

Life is full of ironies. So is death. In less than three years time, all three of these vital young men would be killed—Freeman and See in fiery airplane crashes and good neighbor Ed White in the Apollo 1 launchpad fire.

•   •   •

"People are always asking me what it is like to be married to an astronaut," Janet told *Life* magazine during interviews conducted from 1966 through 1969. "What it's like for *me* to be the wife of *Neil Armstrong* is the more appropriate question. I'm married to Neil Armstrong, and being an astronaut happens to be part of his job. To me, to the children, to our families and close friends, he will always be Neil Armstrong, a husband and father of two boys, who has to cope with the problems of urban living, home ownership, family problems, just like everybody else does."

Janet did not coddle Neil: "As his wife I do keep his clothes clean for him. I try to keep his suits pressed. I occasionally polish his shoes, although he usually has to do that himself. I send his shirts out to the laundry because they come back all nice and folded and are easy for him to grab and put in the little suitcase that he carries. Many wives, I know, pack their husbands' bags. But long ago I quit doing that. I always packed too many things. I always added an extra shirt or an extra this or that. He knows better than I do what fits in a very limited space. He likes to help in the kitchen when there is time. In the winter, when I have to teach swimming at mealtime, I leave a note on the refrigerator door telling him what is in the oven for dinner. He is very good about getting it out and serving himself and the boys. Overall, he's very easy to live with. I really think I'm awfully lucky.

"It never, never shows in Neil that he's had a very distressed day. He does not bring his worries home. I don't like to ask him questions about his work," Janet related, "because he lives with it too much already. But I love it when someone else asks him about his work, and I can sit and listen to it all."

Based on her experience during Gemini VIII, Janet understood the dovetailing pressures on both spouses: "It kind of all works hand in hand, because they, the men, are so busy, and we, the wives, are so busy. Of course, we women have to do it in different ways. We certainly feel the pressure. It has to be dealt with in some way . . . You rush around very hard and fast before a flight as you know everything will be mostly under someone else's control for those important days." Then, as the actual countdown to launch begins, time stands still: "You get so intently involved, and there is always a strain. It is a strain on many, many people, and it is definitely a strain on the wife and the family.

"The only way we wives can participate, really participate, in what the men are doing," Janet explained, "is to know as much as we can about it in advance and then follow it closely on radio and television and through the communications with the ground." "If [the primary flight crew wives] don't listen [to NASA's squawk box]," Janet felt, "[they] miss the fun part, the humor that the men have, which helps to lighten your day and share their flight with them. You want to know every little thing that happens, everything they say.

"The way we do it at home is by listening to the local radio station, which has very good coverage. But invariably when they are having a transmission from the spacecraft, the children are in need of something, right then and there. Of course, it's even more of a conflict when your own husband is flying." Mark, her youngest, especially "notices that I am not giving him the proper attention and he is a very demanding child as far as attention goes . . . so I might as well quit fighting it."

Janet wanted both of her sons to have an appreciation of what their father was doing and of the remarkable events going on around them but worried, "I think I try a little extra hard to make sure they understand what is happening, and in so doing I have probably antagonized the whole situation. Instead of just letting them be!"

Both Janet and Neil worked hard to keep their boys grounded: "You don't want your children to go around with their thumbs under their armpits and saying, 'I'm an astronaut's son.' For this reason we try to make everything we do very common and everyday. We feel that is very important for them not to be favored by their classmates. We want them to grow up and have a regular life—a normal life. Kids are kids, and you want them to be kids, and yet this program has demanded an awful lot of our children. When you put your children in public, they really have to be very sophisticated children."

As she anticipated in the early months of 1969 what all the family would be going through for Apollo 11, she recorded for Dodie Hamblin her extended reflections of the Armstrong family's frenetic pace of life:

Something that occurred to me the other day when I was driving the car made me think of the compelling force that I have spoken to you about. . . . I was in a hurry and found myself pushing the speed limit as I was going down the freeway. I found that when I came to a red light, another car, which I had passed long ago, ended up at the same red light that I did. Here we were, two people—one person in a tremendous hurry, the other person not pushing the speed limit—and here we were together. . . . I couldn't help feel that this is just a small example of how we feel before a flight, or at least the way I feel before a flight.

Janet's mantra became, "Living in the present is most important. We take our lives day by day. As for planning and organizing for the future, it is very difficult in our lives—in my life, at least—because I find I have a husband whose schedule is changing day by day, sometimes minute by minute, and I never know whether he's coming or going, particularly during flight time when he's on a crew. It's very difficult for the wife to try and keep up.

"I think it's of prime importance that you are able to understand yourself," Janet concluded, underscoring her ongoing quest during the second half of the 1960s to carve out and maintain her own identity:

> Trying to maintain one's own identity as a wife, I feel, is very healthy for family situations. I think the wife needs a challenge—at least I, as a wife, need to be challenged. If I'm not challenged, I'm not accomplishing anything, and I'd like to feel that ninety percent of the time I am accomplishing something, whether it be with the children or with my own interests. I feel that I am a better person for it. . . . I feel I can be a better person to my children, to my husband, and to my community.

The pressure on all the astronauts' wives was extraordinary. Each bore a heavy burden, trying as they did to appear before the public as Mrs. Astronaut and the All-American Mother. They knew what NASA and even the White House expected of them. For an astronaut's wife, deciding what to wear was about much more than just a woman's sense of style or even her vanity. It was about maintaining the wholesome and sanctified image of the entire U.S. space program, and of America itself.

Some of the women delighted in the role. They enjoyed primping for the reporters. They loved attending all the parties and charity balls, the ones validated by the presence of the astronauts and only incidentally by their wives. Others, like Janet Armstrong, disliked social trappings to the point of avoidance.

Privately, Janet and many of the other wives also disliked the patronizing attitude of NASA leadership. For example, Deputy Administrator Dr. George Mueller occasionally came down to Houston for special meetings to which all the astronauts' wives were "invited." "It would be like a coffee," relates Janet. "We would meet over in the NASA auditorium. We would get all dressed up and we would have to put our gloves on to get, what I felt was, lectured: 'Keep a stiff upper lip, girls.' How else were you going to 'win' this unless you are 'proud, thrilled, and happy'? By the time we got to the Apollo program that's how it was. Well, it wasn't a joke, but what were we going to say? 'We were proud, we were thrilled, and we were happy.' Another successful flight had happened on the way to a goal.

"Our lives were dedicated to a cause, to try to reach the goal of putting a man on the Moon by the end of 1969. It was an all-out effort on everyone's agenda. It wasn't just our astronaut families that had put our lives on hold; thousand of families were in the same mode."

As for the notion of speaking more honestly to the press about her being barred from Mission Control during the Gemini VIII crisis or about anything else that troubled her about NASA and the space program back in the 1960s, Janet never felt inclined to do it. "That was none of their business," she expresses today. "What advantage would there have been in that? The press would have not understood and would have blown things all out of proportion."

NASA might have been wise to have established early on a formal counseling program for its astronauts' families. Given that thirteen of the twenty-one marriages involving astronauts who were married when they went to the Moon later ended in divorce or separation, it seems obvious that a number of couples could have benefited.

Sadly, some husbands did not recognize their own wife's anxiety or general unhappiness with her personal situation—or they chose not to recognize it. In his extremely candid autobiography, Gene Cernan, the veteran of three spaceflights (Gemini IX, Apollo 10, and Apollo 17), regretfully admitted that many years passed before he learned that his wife Barbara had been so frightened by staying home alone early on during their time in Houston that she stayed up half the night crying. According to Cernan, "There is no doubt that I was so overwhelmed and excited, caught up with being an astronaut, that when I came home for a weekend, all I wanted to talk about was our training and the program. It was, 'My God, let me tell you what I did,' rather than asking, 'What did you do this week?' Looking back now, I realize my family suffered because of my tunnel vision."

Cernan blames himself for failing to pay closer attention to the needs of his wife, but notes that "while everything had been planned in detail for the new astronauts, NASA did not have a survival handbook for our wives. That was a dreadful oversight, and one for which our families paid a heavy price. I guess NASA thought that since we were mostly military families, we were used to the long separations and tightly structured environment of service life, and that wives historically learned to make do with the hardships. They were wrong." Gene and Barbara's marriage survived from their wedding in 1961 through the entirety of Cernan's years in the space program, but in 1980, when their only child, daughter Tracy, turned seventeen, the couple separated. The following summer, they divorced.

Janet never actively participated in any wives' clubs, not even when Neil was with the NACA in California. She had never been a military wife, as Neil was already a reserve officer by the time they had married, and he had resigned his commission shortly thereafter. Janet was more of a loner, as Neil was.

In the coming years, Janet's struggle for identity would only intensify, because, after Apollo 11, she was no longer just *any* astronaut's wife, she was forever more the wife of the first man on the Moon.

The wonder is not that Janet and Neil eventually divorced. It is that she survived as Mrs. Neil Armstrong as long as she did, until a divorce that she initiated ended in 1994 a marriage that had lasted thirty-eight years.

CHAPTER 21

For All America

Even before he completed his debriefings on the Gemini VIII flight in late March 1966, Armstrong was named backup commander for Gemini XI. So quickly and thoroughly did he get into his training for the new role that he was not even able to stay overnight with his family in Wapakoneta the April day that his hometown staged its gala celebration in his honor.

The Gemini IX and Gemini X missions took place within a span of seven weeks in June and July 1966, repeating the pattern of a relatively easy rendezvous followed by a problematic docking. The Agena intended for Gemini IX never made it into space. It spiraled deep into the Atlantic Ocean after its Atlas booster failed shortly after launch. Astronauts Tom Stafford and Gene Cernan waited for another day, but on June 3, 1966, what they got as their target vehicle was not a second Agena but the barebones "augmented target docking adapter" once considered for Gemini VIII. After completing their rendezvous, Stafford and Cernan discovered that the ATDA's shroud had not jettisoned. That made docking impossible. The crew of Gemini IX instead performed a number of different rendezvous maneuvers.

For the Gemini X flight of July 18 to 21, 1966, Armstrong served as a CapCom in Houston. This time the docking worked, as commander John Young nestled his machine to a solid hookup with a brand-new Agena. This was the first time that a manned spacecraft had fully embraced a target vehicle since Armstrong's Gemini VIII flight and the first time it ever *stayed* embraced. Later in the mission, pilot Mike Collins performed a remarkable EVA lasting an hour and a half. Given the variety of significant problems that had been plaguing all previous American space walks, Collins's successful EVA came as an extremely welcome result.

For Armstrong, training as the backup commander for Gemini XI was more about teaching than learning. "This was my third run-through: Gemini V, VIII, and now XI. On the other hand, I had a new right-seat guy with me. Bill Anders was my pilot on the backup crew, and he had not been through any of this before, so everything was new to him. I probably still did quite a few of those basic things so Bill would get up to speed."

What most interested and concerned Armstrong about Gemini XI were those untested aspects of the mission, particularly regarding pilot maneuvers. Rendezvous with the Agena was supposed to occur on the spacecraft's very first revolution about the planet, a maneuver that simulated the type of rendezvous that might be used by a lunar module with a command module after the LM returned from the surface of the Moon. Some of the mission planners called it a "brute force" technique, since the spacecraft would be approaching the target vehicle at very high speed, whereas all earlier rendezvous flights had closed in on the target rather leisurely, waiting until the start of the fourth orbit before beginning to station keep.

"There was a lot of concern that it wasn't going to be successful," Gemini XI pilot Dick Gordon remembers. "For the Apollo application, the desire was to rendezvous as rapidly as possible because the lifetime of the LM's ascent stage was quite limited in terms of its fuel supply. It was a dynamic situation all the way. We had only a two-second launch window, the shortest launch window ever, because we had to launch just when the Agena was overhead. Otherwise, we wouldn't have been able to do it in the first orbit. Then the rendezvous calculations had to be made much more rapidly. As the backup commander, Neil supported all of the work that went into that very, very well."

The other major novelty in Gemini XI was the experimental tethering of the Gemini spacecraft with the Agena via a nearly 100-foot Dacron cord. One goal of the tether experiment, according to Armstrong, was to "find out if you could keep two vehicles in formation without any fuel input or control action." Another goal was to see whether tethering enhanced the stability of two rendezvousing spacecraft, thereby lessening the risk of their bumping into each other.

In the summer leading up to the launch in September 1966, Armstrong and Anders helped Pete Conrad and Dick Gordon, the prime crew, work on the techniques required to carry out all the aspects of the Gemini XI mission. Much of that time, the four men spent together in a beach house on the Cape. According to Neil, "Kennedy Space Center had been built on a big piece of ground, some of which had gone through condemnation proceedings to allow government acquisition of the land. There were some private homes in various places that became government property. Several houses ran along the beach north of the Apollo launchpad. One of them NASA maintained for the astronauts. In our training for Gemini XI, the four of us found this to be a convenient place to go to discuss problems. We'd go out on the beach and work out trajectory procedures and rendezvous procedures by drawing diagrams on the sand and walking around our drawings and essentially acting out the procedure and working out the difficult parts that we didn't quite understand. This was a very relaxing but a useful endeavor. Sometimes we'd have our cook from the regular astronaut quarters put together a picnic lunch and we'd take it out there with us, spend a few hours, with no telephone to bother us, and we'd really concentrate on something. That was really good."

Gemini XI launched on September 12, 1966. In the words of Mike Collins, it turned out to be "a very nice flight, indeed." The brute-force rendezvous technique worked well. The spacecraft shattered the 475-mile-high world altitude record set just two months before by John Young and Collins in Gemini X when it rose to an orbital apogee of some 850 miles. In the process, Conrad and Gordon snapped some truly spectacular color photographs of the planet and its curvature, including one astonishing picture of the entire Persian Gulf region.

The tether exercise caused several nervous moments. Dick Gordon's connecting the tether from the Gemini to the Agena during his first EVA turned into a major athletic contest. "Ride 'em, cowboy!" Conrad shouted to his partner at one point, as Gordon, nearly blind from sweat, sat perched upon the nose of the spacecraft trying to connect the tether to the target vehicle to which it was docked. Conrad ordered Dick to come back in after being out for only 30 of the EVA's planned 107 minutes, so tired and overheated did Gordon appear to become during the exercise. Even releasing the 100-foot tether from its stowage container inside the Gemini spacecraft proved to be a chore, as the Dacron line got hung up on a patch of Velcro. Linked between the two orbiting spacecraft, the line rotated oddly, occasionally causing such oscillations that Conrad needed to steady the vehicle with his controls. As Armstrong remembers, the astronauts had "a lot of difficulty achieving stable orientations while tethered, though they were eventually able to get stable situations while in the spin-up mode." After being hogtied to the Agena for three hours, Conrad and Gordon happily put an end to the puzzling experiment by jettisoning the docking bar. The tether was not tried on any subsequent flights.

Neil followed the Gemini XI mission from the CapCom station at Mission Control in Houston. With the flight's successful conclusion on September 15, 1966, and following his participation in several of the debriefings, Neil's responsibilities in the Gemini program came to an end.

There was one last Gemini flight, Gemini XII, from November 11 to 15, 1966. Jim Lovell, the commander, and Buzz Aldrin, the pilot, put a great finishing touch to the proud Gemini program by carrying out an impressive rendezvous and docking flight involving fifty-nine revolutions of the planet. The most notable achievement of the flight was Aldrin's very successful EVA informed by simulated EVA experience in a large water tank at the Manned Spacecraft Center. For over five hours Buzz made what earlier space walker Mike Collins called "a cool and methodical demonstration" of how an effective space walk should be made by making proper use of new handholds, footrests, and other anchoring devices that NASA had newly installed on the Gemini and Agena spacecraft.

Armstrong has always sided with the majority of U.S. space program analysts who have believed that Gemini was a vital bridge between Mercury and Apollo. "I believe that Gemini was timely and synergistic," Armstrong asserts. "It provided millions of hours of real experience in the preparation of space vehicles for flight and the processing of those vehicles through the apparatus at Cape Kennedy. Further, the Gemini experience required the development of the procedures required for the launch of multiple vehicles—the Gemini plus the Agena. It provided the flight experiences— especially for rendezvous—that were critical for us to understand. Gemini allowed us to work out communications procedures with multiple craft and gave us innumerable opportunities to increase the knowledge, experience, and confidence level of people throughout the space program. Gemini was just a wonderful spacecraft. I was a strong booster of Gemini."

Indeed, all of the specified goals of Gemini had been achieved, and then some: demonstration of the ability to rendezvous and dock with a target vehicle; demonstration of the value of a manned spacecraft for scientific and technological experiments; performance of work by astronauts in space; use of a powered, fueled satellite to provide primary and secondary propulsion for a docked spacecraft; long-duration spaceflights without extraordinary ill effects on the astronauts; and precision landing of a spacecraft. Major records set during the Gemini program included the longest manned spaceflight (330 hours and 35 minutes), the highest altitude (851 miles), and the longest EVA (5 hours and 28 minutes). By the time Lovell and Aldrin reentered the atmosphere, bringing Gemini XII and the entire program to a close, time spent in space by a piloted U.S. spacecraft stood at 1,993 hours.

It chagrined Neil Armstrong to know that his abbreviated Gemini VIII flight accounted for only some ten hours of them.

Such disappointment was trivial to the tragic personal losses that Neil and Janet continued to suffer. On June 8, 1966, two days after the splashdown of Tom Stafford and Gene Cernan in Gemini IX, Neil's boss and best friend from his days back at Edwards, Joe Walker, was killed in a freak midair collision over the Mojave. It happened when Walker's F-104N Starfighter inexplicably flew too close to a plane with which he was flying in formation—the XB-70A Valkyrie, a $500 million experimental bomber that North American Aviation had designed for Mach 3–plus speeds—and became caught in the mammoth plane's extraordinarily powerful wingtip vortex. Walker died instantly. One of the Valkyrie pilots, air force major Carl S. Cross, died in the wreckage of the bomber. The other XB-70A pilot, Al White, a test pilot for North American, survived via the plane's ejection capsule, but not without some serious injuries. Magnifying the tragedy was that the deaths came during what amounted to a publicity shoot for General Electric.

In Houston, Armstrong got a phone call from Edwards shortly after the accident happened. It had only been three months since the fatal crash in St. Louis that had killed his good friend Elliot See in the company of Charlie Bassett. Squeezed between those two fatal airplane accidents, Neil had survived his own near-disaster in the dizzying whirligig otherwise known as Gemini VIII. Returning to Lancaster to attend yet another emotionally charged funeral was almost too much to bear, but Neil and Janet were among the 700 persons who attended Walker's memorial service and burial. "All my adult life had been interrupted by the loss of friends," Neil remarks.

By the autumn of 1966, the Armstrongs were definitely in need of a vacation. At the behest of President Lyndon Johnson, they got one the likes of which no astronaut couple could ever forget.

In early October 1966, prior to the flight of Lovell and Aldrin in Gemini XII, Neil and Janet took off in a Convair 580 transport on a twenty-four-day goodwill tour of Latin America. Touring with Armstrong was Dick Gordon, just off his Gemini XI flight, and Dr. George Low, the former deputy director for manned spaceflight at NASA Headquarters who a few months earlier had become head of Apollo Applications at MSC. Joining them was Janet, Gordon's wife, Barbara, and Low's wife, Mary R., and Dr. George Armstrong (no relation to Neil), chief of MSC's Space Physiology Branch. Representatives from sponsor agencies included Ashley Hewitt and Gerry Whittington (protocol, State Department); Brian Duff and Fred Asselin (public affairs, NASA); and Si Bourgin, Harry Caicedo, Skip Lambert, and Joe Santos (United States Information Agency).

The entourage traveled 15,000 miles through eleven countries and made appearances in fourteen major cities. Everywhere the astronauts went, throngs of humanity lined the streets. Crowds rushed them. Throughout Latin America, they found the people "spontaneous, friendly, and extremely warm."

This trip was Neil's first brush with the iconic staus that would later change his life so dramatically. In Colombia, the second country visited, "the reception was overwhelming," George Low wrote in his journal. In Quito, the capital of Ecuador, the people "were not satisfied to stay on the sidewalks" and gave the motorcade "just barely enough room for the cars to pass through." In São Paolo, Brazil, the entourage saw people hanging out of nearly every window. In Santiago, Chile, little old ladies clapped their hands overhead and yelled *"Viva!"* More than 2,500 guests showed up at a formal dinner reception in Rio de Janeiro, each one of whom expected to shake hands with the astronauts. At the University of Brasilia, 1,500 people crowded into a 500-seat auditorium to hear the astronauts speak. Over the course of the three-and-a-half-week journey, untold millions got a look at the visiting American astronauts. "Whenever possible," Low wrote, "Neil and Dick were out of their cars shaking hands, signing autographs, and fostering a very personal relationship." All over South America, the tour made front-page headlines and national television, as when the president of Venezuela, Raul Leoni, and his children welcomed the Americans at La Casona, the presidential palace on the outskirts of Caracas.

Venezuela, Colombia, Ecuador, Peru, and Bolivia mounted heavy security precautions. In La Paz, Bolivia, armed troops stood every quarter mile from the airport to the center of town. In Brazil, Paraguay, and Uruguay, there was almost no military security, but a police escort performed crowd control. In a few places, like Buenos Aires, crowds overwhelmed the visiting Americans. In several instances, the men from the State Department, USIA, and NASA were forced to handle security.

Other than being mobbed regularly by autograph seekers, there were surprisingly few incidents. During the astronauts' presentation at the University of Brasilia, eleven days into the tour, a group of students raised a banner: "Peace on earth first, leave Vietnam." Low wrote about the experience, "Here we were quite concerned as to whether we would get out in one piece, but it turned out that the crowd was very well behaved."

The tour first ran into organized antagonism in Montevideo, the capital of Uruguay, a country that prided itself on possessing the most democratic form of government in South America. Every city block or two, somebody rushed the motorcade, yelling, "Murderers, get out of Vietnam!" or some similar slogan. Interpreter Fernando Van Reigersberg felt quite sure that the hostilities were part of an "organized campaign to embarrass us."

In Panama City, the last stop, "People lined the streets," Low wrote, "but the reception was very cool. There was no applause; there were generally only cold stares. It may be the general feeling hanging over from the difficulties of Panama two years ago [in 1964, when a diplomatic squabble over the flying of both the U.S. and Panamanian flags in the Canal Zone deteriorated into a riot]; or it may be the fact that every rooftop along the motorcade route was covered with armed soldiers." Ironically, the only place the Americans found "the usual warm greetings" was in the Canal Zone, at Balboa High School, where all the trouble had started in early 1964.

For the government Convair turboprop, trouble surfaced en route from Dulles Airport outside Washington, DC, to Caracas, Venezuela. Violent turbulence threw Dick Gordon, among others, to the ceiling, disturbed much of the luggage, and splashed a passenger's Bloody Mary all over the cabin. That inauspicious beginning was nothing compared to the wild ride into Asunción, Paraguay. "The pilots were on the radio," Armstrong relates, " 'Well, the weather at Asunción is getting a little iffy.' Two hours went by and we were still in the clouds. We were coming down lower and lower trying to get a visual. Finally we broke down out of the clouds, and the mountains were all around us. We had a Paraguayan fellow traveling with us from São Paolo to help orient us culturally. But he wasn't supposed to be there to navigate the airplane! Looking out of the window, he saw a lake that he recognized and he said, 'I know that place!' The crew used him to help direct us in."

Armstrong proceeded to greet local dignitaries with a few words in their native Guarani, an ancient language of tribal peoples. The words that Neil uttered sounded like "Ro-voo-ah ro-zhoo-a-guari para-guay-pay," meaning simply, "We are happy to be in Paraguay."

Armstrong's burgeoning talent for language impressed all of his traveling companions, including fellow astronaut Dick Gordon, who knew no

Spanish other than "Quiero presentarle a mi esposa," which he learned to introduce his wife, or "escotch y agua," to ask for the occasional scotch and water. As soon as Neil heard that he would be making the Latin America trip, he had enrolled in a Spanish conversation class, as had Gordon's wife Barbara. Aboard the Convair, Neil conversed with Fernando Van Reigersberg. "Fernando was Dutch," Armstrong explains, "but he had lived in Algeria as a boy. He had been President Kennedy's interpreter when he went to Latin America." Although Armstrong cited Van Reigersberg for laying "the groundwork for everything we needed to know in all the different [eleven] countries," Neil, before embarking on the tour, had spent many evenings with a set of encyclopedias.

Armstrong peppered his speeches with references to South American heroes such as Simón Bolívar and especially to the continent's aviation pioneers. Neil knew that, in the view of most Brazilians, their countryman Alberto Santos-Dumont was the true Father of Aviation, not the Wright brothers. Neil's rather detailed knowledge of the career of the great Brazilian aviator (most of whose flying was done in Europe) informed his gracious remarks during the welcoming ceremony at the Santos-Dumont Airport in Rio de Janeiro.

At the Venezuelan Science Academy, Columbian Association of Engineers, Centro Columbo Americano, Peruvian Instituto Geofisica, Brazilian Academy of Sciences, and Argentine Commission for Space Research, the astronauts narrated a film outlining key elements of their Gemini missions. In a subsequent slide show, they illustrated rendezvous, docking, EVA, the burn out of orbit, and reentry. Even these technical audiences were stirred by high-orbit perspectives of the Earth's surface, especially shots of Lake Titicaca in Bolivia, the Andes in Ecuador, an avalanche in Peru, and the mouth of the Amazon River. Dr. George Armstrong then summarized the medical results of the Gemini flights, followed by George Low offering a final series of slides outlining the upcoming Apollo program.

Over and over again, Gordon responded to questions about how it felt to be outside the spacecraft and why his visor fogged up during his EVA. Regular questions for Neil included: "Did you fear death during your spaceflight?" "Did flying in space change your belief in God or your view of the world?" Typical for Neil, he gave brief, cryptic responses to this sort of broad questioning, preferring to focus on the engineering, technology, and science of his time in space.

Armstrong's successful presentations were not what most impressed George Low about Neil. Prior to the trip, Armstrong and Low had barely known each other. Low had been a research engineer at NACA Lewis in Cleveland, where Neil had started his career as a test pilot, and "we had crossed paths occasionally." When Neil did get to know him better in Houston, Armstrong thought Low's abilities were "really very strong. He was thoughtful but pragmatic, and he had many creative ideas of his own. He was not an immovable type. He listened."

The admiration was mutual. "Neil had a knack of making short little speeches in response to toasts and when getting medals, in response to questions of any kind," Low recalled. "He never failed to choose the right words." In his travel journal Low concluded, "All I can say is that I am impressed. Neil also made a very significant effort in learning Spanish, and even learning Guarani for Paraguay, and this, of course, made a tremendous hit with the people."

Given the important role that George Low would come to play in future discussions about Apollo crew assignments, and in the spring of 1969 about which astronaut should be the first to step down off the LM and onto the Moon's surface, it is clear that his extremely positive evaluation of Armstrong cannot be overlooked as an influential factor in Neil's subsequent fortunes as an astronaut.

Low was not the only person in a leadership position to view Armstrong as the right sort of individual to represent America, at home and abroad. Inside the State Department, USIA, and NASA, politically minded officials felt that the goodwill tour through Latin America had struck a blow for "the American way." Low had it on authority that, when Soviet cosmonaut Yuri Gagarin toured Latin America in 1962, Gagarin had come off as a space hero but as nothing more. "Our visit was looked upon as an official visit by a team of scientists as well as space heroes," Low reported to friends back in Houston and Washington. "Perhaps this made little difference to the population in general, but it was noted by the officials we met, by the scientific community, and by the press." An important factor in this sentiment was due "to the astronauts' complete ability to answer all questions, and the realization that they were engineers and scientists as well as test pilots. . . . [It is] a powerful tool that the United States can use in our international relations, pursued for the purpose of peace."

PART SIX

APOLLO

As the day clock was ticking for takeoff, would you every night, or most nights, just go out quietly and look at the Moon? I mean did it become something like "my goodness"?

No, I never did that.

—NEIL ARMSTRONG IN RESPONSE TO QUESTION
POSED BY HISTORIAN DOUGLAS BRINKLEY
DURING AN INTERVIEW IN HOUSTON, TEXAS,
SEPTEMBER 19, 2001

CHAPTER 22

Out of the Ashes

By New Year's Day 1967, many observers of the U.S. manned space program believed that President Kennedy's "by the end of the decade" deadline for landing a man on the Moon might be achieved a couple of years ahead of schedule. The reasons for optimism were very good ones. The Gemini program had finished on a roll. Most of the Apollo spacecraft hardware was well on its way to being built. The powerful Saturn rocket that was to boost the Apollo spacecraft on its way to the Moon was getting closer and closer to being operational. True, a few astronauts had died in airplane crashes, but nothing about the space program itself had been at fault in the unfortunate deaths. Everything about the program appeared to be proceeding. Beating the Russians to the Moon seemed a safer and safer bet. Then, not a full month into 1967, a devastating accident occurred at Kennedy Space Center in Florida. The tragedy made it abundantly clear just how dear a price had to be paid to pursue such a bold adventure into the unknown.

The accident occurred in the twilight of what had been a gorgeous Friday, January 27, 1967. Between 6:31 and 6:32 P.M. EST, a fire flashed through the Apollo Block I command module as it sat atop its uprated Saturn IB rocket on Pad 34. In the cockpit were Apollo 1 astronauts Gus Grissom, Roger Chaffee, and Ed White, the Armstrongs' neighbor. The crew was going through a dress rehearsal for a launch that was not scheduled to occur for three more weeks, when a stray spark erupted into an inferno. Seconds later, all three men were dead. Upon hearing the news, it must have seemed to Neil and Janet Armstrong that nothing good ever happened at this time of year. When the clock struck midnight a few hours after the carnage, it was the couple's eleventh wedding anniversary, a day forever etched in their consciousness as the day Muffie died.

The immediate cause of the launchpad fire was just as mundane and

303

trivial as the nail-in-the-paneling problem that had caused the Armstrongs' home to burn down less than three years earlier. An electrical wire on the floor of the spacecraft's lower equipment bay became frayed, probably due to the procession of technicians in and out of the spacecraft in the days before the test. A spark from the frayed wire jumped into some combustible material, likely foam padding or Velcro patches. In the 100 percent oxygen atmosphere, even a momentary flicker—which in the open air would have ignited only into a small and easily controllable flame—became a firebomb. In the choking white heat, the three astronauts died from asphyxiation in a matter of seconds, their respiratory systems not waiting for their bodies to be incinerated in the 2,500-degree F. furnace.

For Ed White and his confreres, there was no chance for escape. For a brief, horrible moment, the astronauts surely realized what was happening to them. Roger Chaffee, a navy aviator who had flown photoreconnaissance missions during the Cuban Missile Crisis of October 1962, yelled first through his radio, "Fire in the spacecraft!" followed by White's "Fire in the cockpit!" and then again by Chaffee's "We're on fire! Get us out of here!"

Fifteen seconds after Chaffee's first words, the Apollo 1 command module blew apart from the pressure of the intense heat. The explosion was so forceful that members of the launchpad crew who were stationed up on gantry level eight got blasted off their feet. NASA systems technicians, even after donning gas masks and extinguishing part of the blaze, could not see through the smoke and flames to make their way through the ripped-apart spacecraft to the astronauts. Their only choice was to force open the spacecraft's complicated hatch. A primitive design, the Block I hatch amounted to two hatches pressure-sealed and attached by several dozen bolts.

It took the technicians several minutes to pry open the bolted-down hatch even partway. Rescuers initially thought that the astronauts had been cremated until pad leader Donald Babbitt shined his flashlight onto the remains of the three men. Two of the astronauts, Grissom and White, were clearly reaching in desperation for the hatch. Amazingly, Chaffee was still sitting almost in repose in his couch. The highly trained team of astronauts, to the bitter end, had done things by the book. Procedures for the emergency escape drill called for Chaffee, the junior crewman, to stay in his seat while the commander and pilot undid the hatch.

Armstrong was away from home when the Apollo fire occurred. He was at the White House as part of a delegation of astronauts that included Gordon

Cooper, Dick Gordon, Jim Lovell, and Scott Carpenter to witness the signing of an international agreement known by the complicated title Treaty on Principles Governing the Activities of States in the Exploration and Use of Outer Space. The astronauts called it the "non-staking-a-claim treaty" because it precluded land claims on the Moon, Mars, or any other heavenly body. The treaty—signed simultaneously in Washington, London, and Moscow and still in effect today—outlawed the militarization of space. Its Article Five assured the safe and cordial return of any astronauts (or cosmonauts) making an unexpected landing within the legal domain of another country, as had nearly occurred during two American space missions: Scott Carpenter's May 1962 Mercury 7 flight; and Gemini VIII, when Neil had thought the spacecraft's emergency trajectory might bring himself and Scott down in China.

Following the signing of the Outer Space Treaty was a reception in the Green Room of the White House. Among the dignitaries in attendance were ambassadors Anatoly Dobrynin of the Soviet Union, Patrick Dean of Great Britain, and Kurt Waldheim of Austria. Most of Washington's political heavyweights were there, including Everett Dirksen, the Senate minority leader, and Democratic senators Eugene McCarthy, Albert Gore Sr., and Walter Mondale. (In the weeks ahead, Mondale would lead the criticism of NASA in the congressional investigation of the Apollo fire.) President Johnson and wife Lady Bird hosted the event; it was the first time that Armstrong had seen LBJ in person since Neil had demonstrated the low L/D landing approach in an F5D at Edwards in 1962, when Johnson was still vice president. Loquacious Hubert H. Humphrey, the vice president, glibly mingled, whereas Secretary of State Dean Rusk and the American ambassador to the United Nations, Averill Harriman, socialized more studiously.

The five astronauts actively "worked the crowd," as per NASA directive. Armstrong remembers that the event ended precisely at 6:45 P.M., and that he and the other astronauts (except for Carpenter, who left immediately for the airport) took taxis to the Georgetown Inn on Wisconsin Avenue, where they had already checked in before heading to the White House.

The moment they entered their hotel rooms on the fifth and top floor of the Georgetown Inn, which was at about 7:15 P.M., the four astronauts saw the red message light on their telephones. The front desk relayed to Neil the urgent need to call the Manned Spacecraft Center. Dialing the number he was given—a number that he did not recognize—he reached what turned out to be the Apollo program office. The man on the phone in Houston shouted to Neil, "The details are sketchy, but there was a fire on Pad 34 tonight. A bad fire. It is probable the crew did not survive." The anonymous NASA employee then told Neil what Cooper, Gordon, and Lovell were also hearing at approximately the same instant: "It won't be long before the media gets word. When they do, they'll pounce on anyone connected to the agency. It is strongly suggested that you four disappear until we get further word to you. Don't leave the hotel tonight."

Replacing the phones on their cradles, the four astronauts headed into the hallway to find out what the others had heard. In the meantime, the owner of the Georgetown Inn, Collins Bird, a man whose hotel often hosted astronauts and NASA program leaders, had picked up on the bad news from Bob Gilruth, as the MSC director came into the hotel immediately after the White House event. The considerate hotelier arranged for the astronauts to occupy a large suite just steps from their fifth-floor rooms.

Before congregating in the suite, each astronaut tried to call home. Neil could not reach Janet. Astronaut Alan Bean had telephoned Janet shortly after the accident and told her to get over to the Whites'. Pat White was not home when Janet arrived; she was picking up her daughter Bonnie from ballet class. Janet was waiting near the Whites' carport when mother, daughter, and son Eddie drove into the driveway. Contrary to the portrayal of this incident in previous books and in a memorable episode of the 1998 HBO miniseries *From the Earth to the Moon,* Janet "did not know anything when I went over there. I only knew there was a problem. When Pat and her children arrived, I helped them in with some groceries. All I could say was 'There's been a problem. I don't know what it is,' and I didn't."

Remembering how the press got to Ted Freeman's wife first with the news of his death, NASA sent over one of its astronauts to tell Pat the horrible news. The unhappy messenger was Bill Anders. "I had been in a simulation and just gotten home," Anders remembers. "I was out in my yard, about three blocks from where the Armstrongs and Whites lived, and I got a call from Al Bean, whom Deke had assigned to tell me that there had been a fire and that Gus, Roger, and Ed had been killed. I was to go down to the Whites' and tell Pat about it before she heard it on television. I got a quick summary of what happened and then went over and knocked on the door. Pat came to the door and Jan was there. I think Jan already suspected, but Janet also knew that NASA preferred that one of the guys tell her. Pat was distraught."

"After Bill got there and told Pat," Janet remembers, "a number of other people arrived: Bill's wife Valerie, the Bormans, and I think also the Staffords. We stayed there until three or four o'clock in the morning, and I went back and forth between the houses to check on the kids. We all sat there and talked about death and what it meant to each one of us. It was an interesting conversation, a unique time to share ourselves."

Back in their suite at the Georgetown Inn, Neil and his fellow astronauts had tried to eat some dinner. They had no trouble drinking down a bottle of scotch. Late into the night, they talked about what must have happened to cause such a disaster down at the Cape.

None of the astronauts liked the Block I spacecraft that North American Aviation had built for NASA, the early version of the Apollo command module that was to be test-flown in Earth orbit prior to any lunar mission. Certainly not Gus Grissom, who after one checkout run at the manufacturer's plant in Downey, California, had left a lemon on top of the module. As the long night in the Georgetown Inn wore on, the topic of conversation, as Jim Lovell remembers, moved "from concern for the future of the program, to predictions about whether it would now be possible to get to the Moon before the end of the decade, to resentment of NASA for pushing the program so hard just to make that [JFK] artificial deadline, to rage at NASA for building that piece of crap spacecraft in the first place and refusing to listen to the astronauts when they told the agency bosses they were going to have to spend the money to rebuild it right."

Lovell and Gordon confirm that Neil spoke the least of the four men. "I don't blame people for anything," Neil relates. "These types of things, in the world we are living in, happen, and you should expect them to happen. You just try your best to avoid them. And if they do happen, you hope you have the right kind of procedures, equipment, knowledge, and skill to survive them. I've never been a blamer."

As for the deaths of Grissom, Chaffee, and especially his good friend and neighbor Ed White, "I suppose you're much more likely to accept a loss of a friend in flight, but it really hurt to lose them in a ground test." According to Neil, "that was an indictment of ourselves. It happened because we didn't do the right thing somehow. That's doubly, doubly traumatic. That's not the way you want it to happen. Not that it's any less noble. It just hurts. . . . When certain things happen in flight, there is just nothing you can do to handle them. You are doing what you want to be doing at the time, so injuries and even deaths are easier to accept than in a ground test, where there should be escapes available for any accident that occurs. But in this case, there weren't." As to why all the brainpower at NASA and in the aerospace industry missed the danger of ground testing the spacecraft in a 100 percent oxygen-rich environment, "Well, it was *some* bad oversight.

We'd been getting away with it for a period of time, as we had tested that way all through the Gemini program, and I guess we just became too complacent."

Four days after the fire, two separate funerals were held in honor of the three fallen astronauts. The date was January 31, the very same day of the year that Neil and Janet had buried their beloved daughter back in California five years earlier.

Naturally, Neil and Janet attended both of the funerals; Neil's mother came to Houston to watch her grandsons. The first funeral, for Grissom and Chaffee, took place with utmost gravity and military dignity at Arlington National Cemetery. So angry and upset were Grissom's parents and Chaffee's father with what they feared had been a needless accident that they greeted President Johnson very coldly when he came over to express his sympathies. The funeral for Ed White took place later the same day inside the Old Cadet Chapel at West Point, as both Ed and his father (who was still alive) had graduated from the U.S. Military Academy overlooking the Hudson River. Neil served as one of the pallbearers, along with four other members of what had been the New Nine: Borman, Conrad, Lovell, and Stafford. Buzz Aldrin, from the third class of astronauts, also served as a pallbearer for White's body. Ed had performed America's first space walk back in June 1965, on Gemini IV. Buzz had performed its most recent, just ten weeks earlier, on Gemini XII.

Not until many years later did Neil give any thought whatsoever to the ironic combination of tragedies that linked his house fire in April 1964 with the Apollo fire in January 1967: Ed White helping the Armstrongs fight the flames and save their children; Ed then being killed in a fire in which there was no one, with no way, to help him or his crewmates; the Apollo fire occuring literally on the eve of the Armstrongs' wedding anniversary and that of Karen's death; Janet being the one that had to prepare Pat White for the news that her husband had just been killed; White, Grissom, and Chaffee being buried on the same calendar day that Muffie was put in the ground. When asked why the irony escaped him at the time, Neil today responds, "It *is* a remarkable coincidence. Ed was able to help me save the situation, but I was not in a position to be able to help him."

The day after the launchpad fire, Dr. Robert Seamans, NASA's deputy administrator, speaking for Administrator James Webb, announced the formation of an accident investigation board. Armstrong's name was not on the list, Apollo 1 being one of the few major accidents in U.S. space program history that Neil would not be asked to help investigate. "I was involved in doing other things [flying helicopters and practicing lunar landing simulations]," Neil remembers, "and was immersed in my job."

The only astronaut to serve on the panel was Frank Borman. The assertive commander of Gemini VII performed exceptionally well, both as a technical expert who worked behind the scenes to identify the precise causes of the fire and as a NASA spokesman answering questions from the press and testifying before House and Senate space committees.

In contrast to the independent investigation formulated by the Reagan White House in 1986 following the Space Shuttle *Challenger* explosion, a body on which Armstrong would serve as vice chairman, the Johnson administration allowed NASA to keep the Apollo fire investigation entirely in-house. Panel chair Floyd L. Thompson, the sixty-nine-year-old director of NASA's Langley Research Center, served with five other NASA officials, one air force official, and one official from the U.S. Bureau of Standards.

With NASA controlling the investigation, progress came swiftly. Within twenty-four hours of the inferno, Thompson and his committee were on hand at Pad 34. Not having to face a daily media circus, the Apollo 204 Review Board, as it was formally called, quickly found what had caused the accident. By April 5, 1967, after only ten weeks on the job, most of it on site at Kennedy Space Center, Thompson's panel submitted its formal report. According to its terse engineering prose, an arc from faulty electrical wiring in an equipment bay inside the command module had started the fire. In the 100 percent oxygen atmosphere, the crew had died of asphyxia caused by inhalation of toxic gases. The board report concluded with a list of eleven major recommendations for hardware and operational changes.

It would take NASA two years to fix all the problems with Apollo. A special Apollo Configuration Control Board, chaired by George Low, eventually oversaw the completion of 1,341 design changes for the spacecraft. Never again would a grounded spacecraft risk the highly explosive 100 percent oxygen-rich atmosphere. On the launchpad, astronauts would breathe a mixture of 60 percent oxygen and 40 percent nitrogen. The nitrogen would be bled off as the spacecraft ascended.

"We were given the gift of time," Armstrong notes. "We didn't want that gift, but we were given months and months to not only fix the spacecraft, but also rethink all our previous decisions, plans, and strategies, and change a lot of things for the better. We got that added benefit, but we regret the price we had to pay." Neil's Apollo 11 command module pilot Mike Collins agrees: "It gave everyone not working on fire-related matters a breather, a period to catch up on their work."

In retrospect, some key space program officials, including Chris Kraft, even believe that if the launchpad fire had not happened, the overall goal of landing on the Moon may never have been reached, so important was it for NASA to go back and rethink the Apollo procedures and really produce a top-notch spacecraft. Armstrong's perspective on this "what if" has always been more judicious: "The operative word is 'may.' It 'may' have happened that Apollo had not been able to reach its goal."

What is clearer historically is that when Apollo did get back on track, it was again going full speed. Not that it was ever a runaway, but in the closing years of the decade the train did have to barrel through some scheduled stops in order to make it to the Moon on time.

The Apollo fire investigation board issued its formal report on a Friday, April 5, 1967. Early the next Monday morning, Deke Slayton called to-gether a group of his astronauts. The men assembled in a small conference room on the third floor of Building 4 at the Manned Spacecraft Center. "Deke had a lot of meetings that would come down on a pretty regular basis," Armstrong recalls. "He'd chew us out, or praise us, or both, or have a little heart to heart with us about this or that."

This meeting was different. It was not a full pilots' meeting. Slayton had invited only eighteen of his astronauts to attend, though NASA's astronaut corps now numbered nearly fifty. None of the new scientist-astronauts, such as Harrison Schmitt or Owen Garriott, were there. Only one of the original Mercury astronauts, Wally Schirra, sat at the conference table. All the rest came from the second and third groups of astronauts. Five of the men who were present, all of them from the third group, had not yet flown in space. They were Bill Anders, Gene Cernan, Walt Cunningham, Donn Eisele, and Clifton C. "C.C." Williams. (Major Williams would be killed a few months later, in December 1967, when his T-38 airplane crashed into a swamp in the Florida panhandle. Although he was flying an almost brand-new aircraft, ei-ther a tool or loose material was floating in the aileron control system of Williams's plane, resulting in an uncontrollable rolling situation during the cruise portion of his flight from Kennedy Space Center to Ellington AFB. Williams ejected at too low of an altitude to survive.) The other thirteen were all veterans of at least one Gemini flight: John Young (Gemini III and X), Jim McDivitt (Gemini IV), Pete Conrad (Gemini V and XI), Schirra (Gemini VI), Tom Stafford (Gemini VI and Gemini IX), Frank Borman and Jim Lovell (Gemini VII and XII), Armstrong and Dave Scott (Gemini

VIII), Mike Collins (Gemini X), Dick Gordon (Gemini XI), and Buzz Aldrin (Gemini XII).

"Father Slayton," as some of the men jokingly called the chief of the Astronaut Office behind his back, was not one for beating around the bush. Slayton told them straight out: "The guys who are going to fly the first lunar missions are the guys in this room."

"Tom Stafford hunched forward and nodded his head," Gene Cernan observed. "Neil Armstrong, who eventually would be most affected by the announcement, showed no emotion." Unlike the astronauts who had not yet been in space, and who felt lucky to be included in the elite group, it came as no surprise to Armstrong or to any of the other spaceflight veterans that they were on Deke's list for the Apollo missions. After all, as Neil has said with no immodesty intended, "Who else was around that would be flying those flights? I think it was more of a confidence-building thing for Deke to be telling us."

Yet not even Neil missed the significance of Slayton's words. Every astronaut around the conference table knew that he had just qualified as a finalist in "an unofficial and largely unspoken competition in which the prize was the ultimate flight test, the first lunar landing." At this early stage of the contest, it was anybody's guess who would get the job, but if the private thoughts of the eighteen astronauts present that April morning had been surveyed, the smart money would have been spread out almost evenly across the seven men from the New Nine who had already served as a commander for a Gemini flight. That meant McDivitt, Borman, Stafford, Young, Conrad, Lovell, or Armstrong. The oldest astronaut in the program, Wally Schirra, would not have been a good bet, not necessarily because of his age (Schirra was forty-four, whereas Borman and Lovell were thirty-nine, McDivitt was thirty-seven, and the other four were thirty-six), but because Wally had upset Slayton by complaining about the nature of the Apollo 2 mission to which he had originally been assigned back in 1966. Deke responded by moving Schirra's crew (Eisele and Cunningham) out of the prime role for Apollo 2 to the backup crew for Grissom, White, and Chaffee in Apollo 1.

At the meeting, Slayton laid out the course of the entire Apollo program. The first manned Apollo mission, the one delayed by the fatal fire, would take place in approximately a year and a half, after a series of major equipment tests. NASA was now calling this first manned mission Apollo 7. In honor of Grissom, White, and Chaffee, there would be no other Apollo 1. There was also to be no Apollo 2 or 3. Slayton told his astronauts that the upcoming Apollo flights would proceed from type A through type J. The A mission, to be performed by the unmanned flights of Apollo 4 and Apollo 6, would test the three-stage Saturn V launch rocket as well as the reentry capabilities of the command module. The B mission, involving Apollo 5, would be an unmanned test of the lunar module. The C mission—which Apollo 7, the first manned flight, was to satisfy—would test the Apollo command and service modules (CSM), the Apollo crew accommodations, and the Apollo navigation systems in Earth orbit. The D mission would test the combined operations of the CSM and the lunar module (LM), also in Earth orbit. The E mission would also test the combined operations but do it in deep space. The F mission amounted to a full-dress rehearsal for the lunar landing, while the G mission would be the landing itself. Following the first landing came the H mission, with a more complete instrument package aboard the LM for improved lunar surface exploration, followed by the I mission, originally conceived as lunar-orbit-only flights with remote-sensing packages inside the CSM and no lander. NASA had made no plans beyond the J mission, which repeated the H mission but with a lander capable of staying on the lunar surface for a longer period of time.

Slayton then named the first three Apollo crews. To the surprise of some, Deke called on Schirra to command Apollo 7. Joining Wally was his established crew of Eisele and Cunningham. (After being named commander, Schirra announced that Apollo 7 would be his last mission prior to his retirement from NASA.) Backing up Wally's crew would be Tom Stafford, John Young, and Gene Cernan. After Schirra's crew had been moved out of Apollo 2 to serve as backup for Apollo 1 back in 1966, Stafford's crew had become the backup for Jim McDivitt's Apollo 2 crew. Now, however, McDivitt was to become commander for Apollo 8, the proposed first test of the lunar module. Serving on McDivitt's Apollo 8 crew were Dave Scott and Rusty Schweikart, with Pete Conrad, Dick Gordon, and C. C. Williams serving as backups. (Al Bean would replace Williams on Conrad's crew after Williams's death in December 1967.) Comprising the crew for Apollo 9, which was to be a manned test of the CSM and LM in high Earth orbit, was Frank Borman, Mike Collins, and Bill Anders. Armstrong, Jim Lovell, and Buzz Aldrin would serve as the Apollo 9 backup crew.

This took the Apollo crew assignments up through the D mission, Slayton told his astronauts. For Armstrong, it was clear that his command of an Apollo mission could come no sooner than Apollo 11, as an astronaut had never moved from a backup crew (in Neil's case, backup on Apollo 9) to the very next prime crew (Apollo 10). Considering that missions E and F, according to the master plan, would have to be accomplished before NASA moved on to the actual Moon landing, which was the G mission, it appeared at the time of Slayton's pronouncement that the historic first step onto the surface of another heavenly body would not happen at least until Apollo 12. If Neil ended up getting the command for Apollo 11, he would be flying the dress rehearsal for the landing, not the landing itself.

CHAPTER 23

Wingless on Luna

Armstrong had begun to study the problem of how to land a flying machine on the Moon some seven and a half years before he became the commander of Apollo 11. "We knew that the lunar gravity was substantially different [roughly one-sixth that of Earth's]," Armstrong recalls of the engineering work begun at Edwards following President Kennedy's commitment in May 1961. "We knew that all our aerodynamic knowledge was not applicable in a vacuum. We knew that the flying characteristics of such a vehicle were going to be substantially different from anything we were accustomed to."

The notion of attacking the unique stability and control problems of a machine flying in the absence of an atmosphere, through an entirely different gravity field, "That was a natural thing for us, because in-flight simulation was our thing at Edwards," Armstrong relates. "We did lots and lots of in-flight simulations, trying to duplicate other vehicles, or duplicate trajectories, making something fly like something else."

The assistant director of research at the Flight Research Center, Hubert M. "Jake" Drake, got the small group organized. Back in the early 1950s, Drake had played a similar catalytic role in conceptualizing ways to attain speeds of Mach 3 and altitudes over 100,000 feet in a research airplane, an initiative that led to the hypersonic X-15 program. Attacking the problem of a lunar landing research vehicle along with Drake were research engineers and frequent collaborators Gene Matranga, Donald Bellman, and Armstrong, the only test pilot involved.

The first idea that the Drake group considered was some form of helicopter, because of the helicopter's abilities to hover and to take off and land vertically. Unfortunately, according to Neil, helicopters "could neither replicate the consequences of lunar gravity nor the handling characteristics of reaction system machines."

Another idea that the Drake group entertained was to suspend a small lunar landing research vehicle beneath some sort of giant gantry and "fly" the vehicle tethered. Independently, a pair of researchers at NASA Langley in Virginia, Hewitt Phillips and Donald Hewes, later developed this idea into a useful simulator called the Lunar Landing Research Facility (LLRF). The mockup could not actually fly. Tethered to an overhead trestle, it moved in limited ways and was not the realistic flying machine that the FRC group sought. An even safer option was to go the route of an electronic, fixed-based simulator. Ultimately, NASA used all three methods—helicopters, Langley's LLRF, and different electronic fixed-base simulators—to study the problems of lunar landing and to train Apollo astronauts.

Seeking to simulate as exactly as possible what Armstrong would later call flying "wingless on Luna," Drake's group opted for a bolder, more innovative scheme, one based on VTOL technology. VTOL referred to "vertical takeoff and landing." It was a new and potentially revolutionary technology in which an aircraft equipped with translatable engines (like the Harrier jet that the British eventually built) flew with some helicopter-like traits.

"There were dozens of experimental VTOL machines during the late fifties and early sixties," Armstrong relates, "and each of them had a unique attitude control system." The person who was building the best-known VTOL test rigs at the time was British engineer A. A. Griffith. As Armstrong began his last semester at Purdue in 1954, stories appeared in the aviation and popular press about Griffith's pioneering vertical takeoff and landing device. It was hard not to pay attention to the weird-looking machine. Its pilot sat in a control station atop an entirely open-air framework of tubing, a calliope of "puff pipes" for attitude control arranged all around him. The bizarre contraption earned the nickname the "Flying Bedstead." Others called it the "Pipe Rack."

"We were aware of that work, certainly to the extent that it was covered in *Aviation Week*," Armstrong states. "However, since lunar gravity simulation was the foundation of our concept, and the British Flying Bedstead had no such system, the most value to us of such a craft was its reaction control system. An Earth-based VTOL had to be able to handle the winds, wind shears, and gusts of our atmosphere. A lunar landing machine had no such need. Of course, an Earth-based flying simulator would have some of those problems. That was our challenge—to build something simulating lunar conditions that could fly that way here on Earth."

The Drake group's only known contender for attitude control of a lunar flyer was a reaction system using small rockets. At the High-Speed Flight Station in the late 1950s, as mentioned in a previous chapter, researchers had devised a test rig known as the Iron Cross. The rig investigated the basic handling qualities and control needs of a reaction control system for use in the X-15. Unlike the Flying Bedstead, the Iron Cross did not actually fly, but it did employ nitrogen gas jets, which provided control moments for testing in simulated near-vacuum maneuvers.

The basic concept for a lunar landing research vehicle that the Drake group arrived at in mid-1961 was to mount a jet engine in a gimbal placed underneath the test vehicle so that the thrust produced by the jet always pointed upward. The jet would lift the test vehicle to the desired test altitude, whereupon the pilot would throttle back the engine to support five-sixths of the vehicle's weight, simulating the Moon's one-sixth gravity. The vehicle's rate of descent and horizontal movement would be handled by firing two throttle-able hydrogen peroxide lift rockets. An array of smaller hydrogen peroxide thrusters would give the pilot attitude control in pitch, yaw, and roll. If the primary jet engine failed, auxiliary thrust rockets could take over the lift function, temporarily stabilizing the machine. What was so radical about the concept was that aerodynamics—the science on which all flying on Earth was done—played absolutely no part. In this sense, the lunar landing test vehicle that Armstrong helped to conceptualize in 1961 was the first flying machine ever designed for operation in the realm of another heavenly body, yet one that could also fly right here on Earth.

"Our first idea," according to Armstrong, "was to have the mockup of the lander carried on another, larger vehicle and make that larger vehicle something that created the conditions that duplicated the lunar gravity and the lunar vacuum. Our thought was, when the actual vehicle got built—and at that point no one knew what the Apollo configuration would be—we could put something like it on top of this carrier and pilot-astronauts could fly it just like they would over the Moon. They could do it at Edwards or wherever, and learn how such a machine flew. Then we decided it was going to be a pretty complicated project, and that what we should do first was build a little one-man device that just investigated the qualities and requirements of flying in a lunar environment. With that, a database would grow from which we could build the bigger vehicle carrying the mockup of the real spacecraft."

Through the summer and fall of 1961, the Drake team devised such a craft. According to Neil, "It looked like a big Campbell Soup can sitting on top of legs, with a gimbaled engine underneath it."

Unknown to the Drake group, another team of engineers was also busy in late 1961 exploring the design of a free-flight lunar landing simulator. The news that this team worked at Bell Aerosystems in Buffalo, New York, came as no surprise. The descendant of the company that had built the X-1 and so many of the other early X-series aircraft, Bell Aerosystems was the only American aircraft manufacturer with any significant experience in the design and construction of VTOL aircraft using jet lift for takeoff and landing. Jake Drake heard about the Bell initiative from a NASA Headquarters official in the fall of 1961. "We've just had a proposal from some people at Bell for a machine to do what you're talking about doing," the official told Drake. "You ought to go talk to them." According to Gene Matranga, "We talked to them, and they had not only thought about, they were much further down the road to a practical solution to the problem."

Immediately Drake invited Kenneth L. Levin and John Ryken, two of the principal Bell engineers at work on the concept (a third was John G. Allen Jr.), to Edwards for consultation. Subsequently, Bellman and Matranga traveled to Bell, where they rode the company's Model 47 helicopters on simulated lunar descents. Armstrong did not make the trip, because he had heavy responsibilities at the time in the X-15 and Dyna-Soar programs. It was also shortly before his daughter died. What the FRC engineers saw at Bell confirmed their strong suspicion that helicopters just could not fly the descent trajectories and sink rates that came close to what was expected for a lunar lander. Helicopters could approximate a variety of final descent trajectories, but to do that often required their flying for substantial periods inside the so-called Dead Man's Curve, the terminal phase of a descent trajectory where it would be impossible to abort safely without crashing into the surface.

NASA contracted with Bell to draw up blueprints for a small, relatively inexpensive lunar landing test vehicle whose design would be independent of the actual Apollo configuration, which it had to be, since the Apollo configuration had not yet been decided upon. Bell's job was to lay out a machine with which NASA could investigate the inherent problems of lunar descent from altitudes up to 2,000 feet with vertical velocities of up to 200 feet per second. Results from the $2.5-million study, NASA felt, could significantly help in the design of the Apollo spacecraft, a much larger contract that North American Aviation, Inc., had been awarded the previous autumn.

Not until July 1962 did NASA settle on how to go to the Moon. When JFK boldly called for the Moon landing, a great many qualified engineers and scientists envisioned getting there and back in one brute rocket ship. That was how Jules Verne and most other visionaries had seen it happening. A gargantuan rocket roughly the size—and no doubt the weight—of the Empire State Building would take off from Earth, fly to the Moon, back down rear end first to a landing, and blast off for home. It was a mission mode that advocates called Direct Ascent. A new rocket with twelve million pounds of thrust, by far the most powerful booster ever built, would take astronauts directly from the Earth to the Moon, with no stops in between. The name of the proposed monster was the Nova.

A second major option for the lunar landing—and one that many space-flight experts, including NASA's rocketmeister Dr. Wernher von Braun, came to favor—was Earth Orbit Rendezvous, or EOR. According to this plan, a number of the smaller Saturn-class boosters being designed by the von Braun team at Marshall Space Flight Center in Alabama would launch components of the to-be-lunar-bound spacecraft into Earth orbit, where those parts would be assembled and fueled for a trip to the Moon and back. The main advantage of EOR was that it required far less complicated booster rockets, ones already nearing the end of their development. Just two or three of von Braun's early Saturns would do the job. Another benefit of EOR was long-term: in the process of going to the Moon, the U.S. space program would build a platform in Earth orbit that could easily be converted into a space station.

To the surprise of many experts, NASA selected neither Direct Ascent nor Earth Orbit Rendezvous. On July 11, 1962, officials announced that a concept known as Lunar Orbit Rendezvous would be America's way to the Moon. Lunar Orbit Rendezvous, or LOR, was the only mission mode under consideration that called for a customized lunar excursion module to make the landing.

The LOR decision was made over the strenuous objections of President Kennedy's science adviser, Dr. Jerome Wiesner. Like other skeptics, Wiesner felt that LOR was too risky to try. If rendezvous had to be part of the lunar mission, he felt that it should be attempted only in Earth orbit. If rendezvous failed there, the threatened astronauts could be brought home simply by allowing the orbit of their spacecraft to decay. If a rendezvous around the Moon failed, the astronauts would be too far away to be saved. Nothing could be done. The specter of dead astronauts sailing around the Moon haunted those who were responsible for the Apollo program and made objective evaluation of its merits unusually difficult.

In the end, NASA's mission planners determined that LOR was no more dangerous than the other two schemes, likely even less dangerous, and that it enjoyed several critical advantages. It required less fuel, only half the payload, and somewhat less new technology. It did not require the monstrous Nova, and it called for only one launch from Earth, whereas the once-favored EOR required at least two. Trying to bring down a behemoth like the upper stage of a Nova onto the cratered lunar surface would be next to impossible, as every analysis came to show. Even if a landing with Nova could somehow be managed, there would still be the problem of the astronauts getting down to the lunar surface from atop such a giant structure, for, even after all of its rocket staging, the spacecraft that landed would still be about the size of the Washington Monument. Engineers had even looked into the design of a transport elevator for the spacecraft for that purpose. A Moon landing via EOR looked only marginally easier. The ship leaving for the Moon after Earth orbit rendezvous would be smaller than the battleship-sized Nova, but it would still be a very ponderous stack of machinery to eyeball down to a pinpoint landing. After months of study, with absolutely no satisfactory answers to the landing dilemmas of Direct Ascent or EOR appearing, there was no choice but to go with LOR.

The greatest technological advantage of LOR was that it turned the lander into a "module." Only the small, lightweight lunar module (LM), not the entire Apollo spacecraft, would have to land on the Moon. Also, because the lander was to be discarded after use and would not be needed to return to Earth, NASA could customize the LM's design for maneuvering flight in the lunar environment and for a soft, controlled lunar landing, and for nothing else. In fact, the beauty of LOR was that NASA could tailor *all* of the modules of the Apollo spacecraft independently—the command module (CM), service module (SM), and LM. The modularity extended to the LM itself. It would be a two-stage vehicle. The entire LM would descend to the surface using a throttle-able rocket engine. But the lower module, holding the landing legs, descent engine, and associated fuel tanks, would remain on the lunar surface and act as the launch platform for the upper or ascent stage, with its separate fixed-thrust engine, associated tankage, attitude control rockets, and, of course, cockpit.

Most important, LOR was the only mission mode by which the Moon landing could be achieved by Kennedy's deadline of decade's end. For NASA, that was the clincher. The phrase Armstrong remembers is that "LOR saves two years and two billion dollars."

The promise of the preliminary LLRV design played a very small but not inconsequential role in the LOR decision. The key people making the decision in favor of LOR at NASA were Associate Administrator Robert C. Seamans Jr.; Brainerd Holmes, the head of the Office of Manned Space Flight; George Low, Holmes's director of spacecraft and flight missions; and Joseph F. Shea, head of the Office of Manned Space Flight Systems. They made the decision in personal consultation with Bob Gilruth, director of the Manned Spacecraft Center, and Wernher von Braun, director of the Marshall Space Flight Center.

Von Braun's preference for LOR had surprised his own staff. At the end of a daylong briefing given to Joe Shea at NASA Marshall on June 7, 1962, the immigrant German rocketeer had announced, "We at the Marshall Space Flight Center readily admit that when first exposed to the proposal of the Lunar Orbit Rendezvous Mode we were a bit skeptical—particularly of the aspect of having the astronauts execute a complicated rendezvous maneuver at a distance of 240,000 miles from the Earth where any rescue possibility appeared remote. In the meantime, however, we have spent a great deal of time and effort studying the [different modes], and we have come to the conclusion that this particular disadvantage is far outweighed by [its] advantages."

Overnight, a landing module became one of the most critical systems, if not *the* most critical system, in the entire Apollo program. The big Saturn V rocket could propel astronauts inside their snug command module into lunar orbit, but unless a special lander went along also, there would be no way for them to land. And Apollo was all about *landing*.

Immediately, serious work on the LM began. In November 1962, the Grumman Corporation of Long Island, New York, won the contract. The evolutionary path to a finished LM turned out to be torturous. The cabin volume was changed from spherical to cylindrical. The landing legs were reduced in number from five to four. The window area was substantially reduced. The seats were removed, meaning that the two-man crew of the LM would stand, like trolley conductors. Not only did the new standing arrangement move the pilots' eyes closer to the "windshield," improving visibility, it also reduced the weight of the overall structure, which was a crucial factor in everything related to the LM design. But it also meant that a cable restraint system had to be devised to keep the pilots in the proper position inside the cabin and hold them secure during the impact of touchdown.

A long string of test failures—propulsion leaks, ascent-engine instabilities, stress corrosion of various aluminum alloy parts, electric battery problems—kept the Grumman team busy fixing and refining its extraordinary machine for nearly seven years. Not until March 1969 was even the first LM ready to test-fly. It took place in Earth orbit, as the primary task of Apollo 9. Throughout most of its developmental life, everyone called the vehicle the "LEM," until May 1966 when a memo from the NASA Project Designation Committee officiously changed the name simply to "LM." Apparently, the word "excursion" sounded too much like a vacation rather than a deeply serious enterprise for human space exploration. In the vernacular, people still pronounced the acronym, not as two individual letters, but as if the vowel were still there.

With the LOR decision in hand, the requirements for the Flight Research Center's lunar landing research vehicle became much more explicit. Strictly by chance, the characteristics, size, and inertias of the original LLRV design were very much like what Grumman soon realized it needed to build into the LM. "Bell already had a design for the LLRV," Gene Matranga relates, "but went through a very quick redesign when the concept of the lunar landing changed to LOR. As it turned out, the revised machine wound up being a better solution to the problem."

Bell Aerosystems began fabricating two LLRVs (of the same exact design) in February 1963; NASA wanted the vehicles ready in sixteen months' time. On April 15, 1964, the machines arrived at Edwards, as requested, disassembled and in boxes, because FRC technicians wanted to install their own research instruments and believed they could complete the craft more expeditiously than could Bell. President Lyndon Johnson saw an assembled LLRV on a visit to Edwards in mid-June 1963; the politician must have chuckled at its Rube Goldberg appearance. Standing ten feet tall and weighing 3,700 pounds, the LLRV had four aluminum truss legs that spread out across some thirteen feet. The pilot sat out in the open air, behind a Plexiglas shield. He sat in a specially designed rocket ejection seat built by Weber Aircraft, one of the least known of the American ejection seat manufacturers, yet one of the largest. Weber's seat was so effective that it operated successfully even at "zero-zero," the lowest point in an ejection envelope, and could do so safely even if the LLRV was moving downward at a rate as high as thirty feet per second. No ejection seat ever performed better, which was a good thing given that it would have to be used more than once in the LLRV program.

The first pilot to fly the LLRV was Neil's former boss Joe Walker. Walker made the inaugural flight on October 30, 1964, the day after astronaut Ted Freeman's fatal accident outside Houston in his T-38 trainer. The inaugural flight consisted of three brief takeoffs and landings totaling just under a minute of flight time. Prudently, Walker took the machine no higher than ten feet and used only the main jet (a General Electric CF-700-2V turbofan engine producing 4,200 pounds of thrust) for lift. He did not activate the two lift rockets, but he did briefly fire all sixteen of the small hydrogen peroxide control rockets (grouped in pairs of two) for attitude control. Walker compared taking off in the machine to rising up in an elevator, except for the hissing sound produced by the strange and grotesque piece of hardware when he fired short bursts of the reaction controls. When that happened, a cloud of peroxide steam nearly enveloped the craft, giving rise to another nickname, "the belching spider." Fellow FRC test pilot Donald Mallick and Emil "Jack" Kleuver, an army test pilot on loan to NASA, later flew the machine, Mallick making the most LLRV flights of all, over seventy.

Between 1964 and the end of the LLRV test program in late 1966, some 200 research flights were carried out at Edwards. Pilots could operate the vehicle in one of two modes. They could fly it as a "conventional" VTOL with the jet engine locked in position and providing all the lift; pilots called this the "Earth mode." Or they could fly it in the "lunar mode" in which the engine could be adjusted in flight to reduce the apparent weight of the LLRV to its lunar equivalent. In the lunar mode, as stated earlier, lift was provided by a pair of controllable 500-pound-thrust rockets (noncombustion rockets using a 90 percent solution of hydrogen peroxide as fuel) that were fixed to the fuselage outside the gimbal ring. Operating in the lunar mode, the pilot could modulate the angle and thrust of the engine to compensate for aerodynamic drag in all axes. Generally, the pilots preferred flying the Earth, or VTOL, mode. As Armstrong notes, "In the lunar simulation mode, uncomfortably large attitudes were required for reasonable decelerations." On the other hand, the sensitive throttle for the rocket engine made *altitude* control much better in lunar simulation.

As strange as it all was, the LLRV compensated for its Earthbound existence in some very clever ways and closely duplicated what it was like to fly over the Moon, though its highest altitude reached just under 800 feet, and its longest flight lasted something less than nine and half minutes. Amazingly, no serious accidents occurred during the entirety of the Flight Research Center's LLRV program.

Armstrong had left Edwards for Houston in September 1962, so he was unable to stay as informed about the LLRV program as he would have liked. "I did go to Edwards a few times and talked with Joe Walker. I was aware of some of the difficulties they were encountering in developing a satisfactory flight control system for the vehicle. I would have liked to have been more involved, but I was loaded with other responsibilities at the time." Gene Matranga confirms that Neil stayed a part of the LLRV program. "Neil got tabbed by the Houston people to be the engineering pilot focal point," he remembers, "making sure that the things we were doing met the needs of the astronauts." But Neil made it to Edwards only once to see the machine fly. NASA did not want him or any of the other astronauts to fly the contrary and risky machine. Still, as Matranga relates, "Neil made sure that we were doing the things that Houston wanted us to do."

Ground simulators offered considerable help. As Neil explains, "Traversing large pitch or roll angles required more time or larger control power. It was expected that control characteristics ideal on Earth might be not at all acceptable on the Moon." As a result of hundreds of hours in the simulators, the astronauts found that good control could be obtained with "on-off" rockets that had been mechanized for rate command—that is, for the vehicle's angular rate (or rate of change) proportional to control deflection—but they were still, in Neil's words, having "some difficulty in making precise landings and eliminating residual velocities at touchdown, probably due to a pilot's natural reluctance to make large attitude changes at low altitudes."

The Lunar Landing Research Facility at Langley was an imposing 250-foot-high, 400-foot-long gantry structure that had become operational in June 1965 at a cost of nearly $4 million. Armstrong considered the LLRF "an engineer's delight." "It worked surprisingly well," says Armstrong. "The flying volume—180 feet high, 360 feet long, and 42 feet wide—was limiting, but adequate to give pilots a substantive introduction to lunar flight characteristics." To make the simulated landings more authentic, its Langley designers filled the base of the huge eight-legged, red-and-white structure with dirt and modeled it to resemble the Moon's surface. Often testing at night, they erected floodlights at the proper angles to simulate lunar light and installed a black screen at the far end of the gantry to mimic the airless lunar "sky." Technicians climbed into the fake craters and sprayed them with black enamel so that the astronauts could experience the shadows that they would see during the actual Moon landing.

Though "the engineers at Langley did some wonderful work trying to create a flexible [cable and pulley] system that allowed it to feel like a real flying spacecraft," control for pitch and roll could be, in Neil's words, "excessively sluggish." "The LLRF was a clever device," in Armstrong's judgment. "You could do things in it that you would not want to try in a free-flying vehicle, because you could be saved from yourself."

In 1964, the Astronaut Office looked around to see what VTOL machines might be available as possible lunar landing simulators. Deke Slayton asked Armstrong specifically to look into the potential of the Bell X-14A. This was a small and versatile aircraft that employed the same vectored-thrust and reaction-control arrangement used by the British Harrier. Houston knew that engineers at NASA's Ames Research Center in Northern California were using the X-14A to simulate lunar descent trajectories, so Armstrong flew out for a visit. In February 1964, he made ten evaluation flights to see if the X-14A had any applicability to lunar landing simulations. Neil concluded that, while a pilot could simulate a lunar trajectory in the X-14A, the attitude changes required were that of an Earth-gravity VTOL machine and could not replicate lunar motions. In that sense, it flew more like a helicopter than it did a lunar module. The X-14A also had a problem with ground effects. When a helicopter descended toward the ground in hovering flight, the amount of power it required to stay aloft got smaller; however, with the X-14A (and many other VTOLs) the effect was the reverse. The closer to the ground it got, the more throttle it took. Reingestion of hot exhaust gases near the surface caused disconcerting instabilities and a reduction in thrust. Also, so much movement in the throttle developed in the final phase of descent that smooth touchdowns were a rarity. "It was hoped and expected that the actual lunar lander would have little ground effect," Armstrong explains, "somewhere between the helicopter and the VTOL." For that degree of accurate simulation, another class of training vehicle was required.

"Having no flying machines to simulate lunar control characteristics was frustrating the Astronaut Office," Armstrong recalls. The only effective alternative was to try the Flight Research Center's LLRV, however risky some people in NASA considered the highly unusual free-flight vehicle. Heading the program at Houston to convert the LLRV into an astronaut trainer was Dick Day, the simulations expert from the Flight Research Center who back in 1962 had helped Neil to become an astronaut.

The decision to turn the LLRV into a trainer, or LLTV, came early in 1966, just prior to Armstrong's Gemini VIII flight. By this time, Grumman had come a long way to finalizing the design of the LM, whose first test flight, designated Apollo 5, was scheduled for January 1968 (but did not occur until Apollo 9 in March 1969). Building an actual LM that could fly on Earth like the LLRV was possible but, according to Armstrong, would have been "prohibitively time consuming and expensive." As it was, the LLRV, although it predated the LM by five years, was not all that different in physical size and control rocket geometry from what had become Grumman's actual vehicle. Relatively quickly and inexpensively, NASA got Bell to produce an advanced version of the LLRV that even more closely matched the characteristics of the LM.

The decision to build LLTVs brought Neil back squarely into lunar landing studies. In the summer of 1966, as he was preparing for his backup role in Gemini XI, Houston ordered three LLTVs at a cost of roughly $2.5 million each. At the same time, the Manned Spacecraft Center requested that the Flight Research Center prepare its two LLRVs for shipping to Houston as soon as the FRC engineers were done with them. Even before he left on the Latin America tour, Neil participated in discussions with Bell on what was needed in the LLTV design. With MSC test pilot Joseph S. Algranti, he went to Edwards in August 1966 to check out the LLRV. (Algranti had checked out in the LLRV several months earlier.) Although he did not fly the machine during that visit, Neil did fly LM trajectories in a helicopter with Algranti. Upon returning from the Latin American tour, he became routinely involved in LLTV matters. He was on the scene when LLRV number one arrived in Houston from Edwards on December 12, 1966. When FRC test pilot Jack Kleuver came to Houston to verify that the machine was working, Armstrong observed. When Algranti and his fellow MSC test pilot H. E. "Bud" Ream made the first familiarization flights with it at Ellington AFB near the Manned Spacecraft Center, Neil watched the operation and studied their ground rules. He spent January 5 to 7, 1967, with Algranti in Buffalo, participating in the LLTV Design Engineering Inspection at Bell. A few days later, he and Algranti were off to Edwards to review the final results of the LLRV program. While in California, Neil flew some LM trajectories in a Bell H-13 helicopter. He also witnessed an LLRV flight piloted by Jack Kleuver. Immediately after attending the funerals for the Apollo 1 crew at Arlington National Cemetery and West Point in late January, Armstrong and Buzz Aldrin flew in a T-38 directly to Langley Field in order to make simulated lunar landings on the LLRF. It was Neil's first time on Langley's gadget and it would not be his last. On February 7, 1967, he and Buzz flew a T-38 to Los Angeles to be custom-fitted for an LLRV ejection seat at Weber Aircraft. Later in the month, he went again to Los Angeles, this time to North American (and with Bill Anders), to review the design for the tunnel through which the astronauts would move back and forth between the Apollo command and service module (CSM) and the LM. In March 1967, he traveled to the West Coast once more, to Los Angeles and to San Diego, where he reviewed the LM landing radar program at Ryan Aircraft. During these months, he also got in a good bit of helicopter time in order to get ready for training in the LLTV. Little wonder that when NASA assembled its Apollo fire investigation panel, Armstrong was nowhere in the picture. He was too deeply immersed in matters related to lunar landings.

Helping transform the research vehicle into a training vehicle was a challenge for which Armstrong as an engineer, test pilot, and astronaut was extremely well suited. Back in 1961, he had contributed to the machine's original concept. Bell built the LLTV essentially on the same structure as the LLRV, but now the main goal was to replicate as closely as possible the trajectory and control systems of the LM. Certain flying characteristics of the LM could not be replicated, however. Most notably, it was impractical, if not impossible, to design the LLTV so that it provided the rate of descent that the LM had.

Another goal was to make the LLTV as much like the LM in terms of critical design features. For example, Bell built the new LLTVs with an enclosed cockpit that enjoyed LM-like visibility. To match the LM configuration, it also moved the control panel from the center of the cockpit to the right side and set up the same array of visual displays. The LLTV was given a three-axis sidearm control stick very comparable to what Grumman was placing into the LM (rather than the conventional aircraft-type center stick for pitch and roll control and rudder pedals for yaw control that had been in the LLRV), and a rate-command/attitude-hold control system closely approximating the handling characteristics anticipated for the LM. The LLTV also incorporated a compensation system that sensed any aerodynamically induced forces and moments and provided automatic correction through the engine and attitude rocket system. In this way, the motions of the LLTV even more closely approximated flight in a vacuum. Several improvements were made in the electronics system to take advantage of the same miniaturized, lightweight components that were being used in the LM. Other improvements included an improved ejection seat, more peroxide for the rockets to increase their duration, a slightly upgraded jet engine, and a modified attitude to be more like the LM.

Armstrong was involved in the LLTV Design Engineering Inspection at Bell, so, in his words, he "must have more or less agreed with all the Bell proposals for the Bell LLTV—at least I had the chance to give my input." In Neil's view, "it was very necessary to have the LLTV control system replicate the LM. It was not necessary, nor was it attempted, to provide simulations of the LM environmental systems, communications systems, guidance systems, et cetera. The LLRV had had a number of system reliability and component problems, and many of the LLTV changes were intended to improve those areas."

Not all the changes from the LLRV to the LLTV were universally considered to be improvements, at least not by the team of FRC engineers who had made the LLRV program so successful at Edwards. In trying to make the training vehicle as much like the LM as possible, Gene Matranga asserts that Bell eventually added some systems that actually made the machine less reliable to fly. Most notably, Bell changed from an analog "fly-by-wire" (FBW) control system to a digital system, because that was the type being used in the LM. Unfortunately, "dead periods" existed within the circuitry of the digital system during which the pilot could not sense the loss of electrical power. In January 1971, just such an electrical system failure caused NASA test pilot Stuart Present to lose control (the switchover to battery backup power did not work), forcing him to eject and the LLTV to crash hard into the ground at Ellington, destroying the vehicle.

Not just the three new LLTVs were used for astronaut training; so too were the two older LLRVs. The Manned Spacecraft Center modified the existing machines into trainers, dubbing them LLTV A1 and LLTV A2. The three new machines, the first of which arrived from the Bell factory in December 1967, became LLTV B1, B2, and B3. Before the astronauts were allowed to fly any of them, they received a couple months' flight instruction from Joe Algranti and Bud Ream, the MSC test pilots who had gone out to Edwards to learn how to "master" the LLRV. The astronauts that Slayton designated as potential LM crewmen, including Armstrong, then went to helicopter school for three weeks, to Langley's LLRF for a week, and finally to fifteen hours in a ground simulator before they got their first chance to fly an LLTV, always at nearby Ellington. As Neil had already gone to navy helicopter school in 1963 and had built up quite a bit of "helo" time over the next four years, all he had to do as far as helicopters were concerned was brush up on his skills prior to his LLRV checkout.

"The helicopter wasn't a good simulation of the lunar module control at all," Armstrong explains. "Had it been, we would have configured a helicopter such that it could duplicate lunar flying. That could have been done with a great deal less risk than flying the LLRV or LLTV. But we never could come up with anything that worked at all well. The natural requirements of helicopter aerodynamics preclude you from duplicating the lunar module characteristics. Nevertheless, the helicopter was valuable to understand the trajectories and visual fields and the rates. You could precisely duplicate the flight paths that you wanted. It's just that the control you were using to do that was not at all the same."

Astronaut Bill Anders, who also flew the LLTV several times, wonders in retrospect why NASA did not think through its helicopter training for the astronauts more thoroughly: "That was, in a sense, almost bad training, flying helicopters. If you had a helicopter on the Moon, you would be fooled at first because the helicopter's mass would be the same but it would have one-sixth the weight and one-sixth the lift. When you tilted it up, it would have one-sixth the retarding force, so therefore you are probably going to go six times beyond the landing point. Flying on the Moon was literally a different world."

Frank Borman and Jim Lovell agreed. Borman, who flew the LLTV only once, on May 6, 1968, called flying it "a hairy deal." "From my standpoint it was a dicey training aid." Lovell: "Even though the LLTV and a helicopter operated entirely opposite in terms of controls, they still had you doing all this practicing in helicopters. Add to that all of the different safety factors you had to worry about—the ejection seat, the throttle, how to fly the thing, go up to two hundred feet and have two minutes of fuel and that was it. It made me worry about flying it."

An important thing to say about Armstrong, in the view of both Anders and Lovell, is that Neil was the kind of experienced engineering test pilot who did an outstanding job thinking through what it took to fly in the unusual lunar environment and not letting his helicopter training dominate his piloting decisions. "Neil's first experiences in the LLTV were probably not typical of the rest of us," Anders relates. "It's not that he had less helicopter time. It's that Neil always thought these things through. If it required something counterintuitive or otherwise against the grain, he figured it out. The guys who flew more intuitively or who relied too much on their helicopter experience would have tumbled into craters or landed on rocks if they had tried to land on the Moon. In my view, the LLTV was a much undersung hero of the Apollo program."

Eventually, all prime and backup commanders of Apollo lunar landing missions practiced on the LLTV. As the program went on, there was not enough LLTV time available and the backup commanders were cut short. The commanders usually flew a total of twenty-two flights, the backup commanders maybe a dozen. The astronauts who flew the LLTV besides Armstrong were Borman, Anders, Conrad, Scott, Lovell, Young, Shepard, Cernan, Gordon, and Haise.

Neil's initial LLTV flight came on March 27, 1967, when the machine first came to Ellington Field; he made two flights in LLTV A1 that day. Algranti and Ream also flew the LLTV that month, but due to a combination of technical problems the machine was not flown for the remainder of the year. (None of the three new LLTVs were ready for flight testing until the summer of 1968.) When the LLTV came back on line, Armstrong was the first to get checked out in the machine (again, LLTV A1), followed by checkouts for Anders, Conrad, and Borman. Neil's logbooks show that, between March 27, 1968, and April 25, 1968, he made ten flights in the converted LLRV. In Neil's opinion, "The LLTV proved to be an excellent simulator and was highly regarded by the astronauts as necessary to lunar landing preparation."

Yet the LLTV was also a highly dangerous machine to fly. "Without wings," as Buzz Aldrin has noted, "it could not glide to a safe landing if the main engine or the thrusters failed. And to train on it properly, an astronaut had to fly at altitudes up to 500 feet. At that height a glitch could be fatal." Armstrong found out just how unforgiving the vexatious machine could be on Monday afternoon, May 6, 1968, just fourteen months before the Apollo 11 landing.

"I wouldn't call it routine, because nothing with an LLTV was routine, but I was making *typical* landing trajectories during the flight that afternoon, and as I approached the final phase of one of them, in the final 100 feet of descent going into landing, I noted that my control was degrading. Quickly, control was nonexistent. The vehicle began to turn. We had no secondary control system that we could energize—no emergency system with which we could recover control. So it became obvious as the aircraft reached thirty degrees of banking that I wasn't going to be able to stop it. I had a very limited time left to escape the vehicle, so I ejected, using the rocket-powered seat. The ejection was somewhere over fifty feet of altitude, pretty low, but the rocket propelled me up fairly high. The vehicle crashed first, and I drifted in the parachute away from the flames and dropped successfully in the middle of a patch of weeds out in the center of Ellington Air Force Base."

During the explosive ejection, the first he had experienced since abandoning his crippled Panther jet over Korea seventeen years earlier, Neil accidentally bit hard into his tongue. That was his only injury, except for a bad case of chiggers from the weeds. "It's hard to compare against combat when a big shell from an aircraft just misses you. That's close too, but the LLRV accident was indeed one of the close ones."

To NASA Headquarters, Houston sent the following priority telegram about the accident:

LLRV #1 CRASHED MAY 6, 1968, AT 1328 CDT AT EAFB, TEXAS. PILOT, NEIL A. ARMSTRONG, NASA.MSC ASTRONAUT, EJECTED AFTER APPARENT LOSS OF CONTROL. ARMSTRONG INCURRED MINOR LACERATION TO TONGUE, VEHICLE WAS ON STANDARD LUNAR LANDING TRAINING MISSION. ESTIMATED ALTITUDE AT TIME OF EJECTION 200 FEET. LLRV #1 TOTAL LOSS—FIRST ESTIMATE $1.5 MILLION. PROBABLE CAUSE—NOT KNOWN AT THIS TIME. PROGRAM DELAY PROBABLE. LLRV #2 WILL NOT COMMENCE FLIGHT STATUS UNTIL ACCIDENT INVESTIGATION HAS BEEN COMPLETED AND CAUSE DETERMINED (LLTV'S HAVE NOT COMPLETED GROUND TEST PHASE AND THEREFORE ARE NOT APPLICABLE). BOARD OF INVESTIGATION APPOINTED BY DIRECTOR MSC.

Chairing the accident investigation board was Joe Algranti. Serving with him were Bill Anders and Pete Conrad, both of whom had also begun to fly the LLTV. (Conrad was a member only temporarily, until replaced by the FRC's Don Mallick.) The statement in the telegram that Neil's ejection took place from an estimated height of 200 feet was either in error or purposefully exaggerated to soothe fears in Washington about the dangers of flying the vehicle.

Those who observed the accident or who subsequently heard about it felt that Armstrong was very lucky to be alive. According to Chris Kraft, the frightening films he watched of the accident showed that Neil escaped death by just two-fifths of a second. "Winds were gusting that day," Kraft describes, "something that can't happen on the airless Moon, but Armstrong was fully in control for the first five minutes. He took it up several hundred feet and was ready to practice a nearly vertical descent and landing. Then the machine suddenly dropped. He steadied it and climbed back up another two hundred feet. Then the LLTV began to bounce around in the sky. It pitched down, then up, then sideways. Its stabilization had failed and it was clearly out of control. A ground controller radioed Neil to bail out. He activated the ejection seat with only a fractional second of margin. Neil's parachute opened just before he hit the ground. He wasn't hurt, but the LLTV was demolished in a fireball."

Buzz Aldrin was not at Ellington, either, to see the accident, but he, too, understood it to be a near fatality: "When the machine began to wobble and spin during [Neil's] descent from 210 feet to the runway, he fought to regain control with the thrusters, but the platform sagged badly to one side and lurched into a spin. He had maybe a second to decide. If the trainer had tipped completely over and he had fired his ejection seat, the rocket charge would have propelled him headfirst into the concrete below. Neil held on as long as he could, not wanting to abandon an expensive piece of hardware. At the last possible moment, he realized the thruster system had completely malfunctioned, and he pulled his ejection handles. He was blasted up several hundred feet, and his parachute opened just before he struck the grass at the side of the runway. Neil was shaken up pretty badly, and the LLRV exploded on impact."

The cause of the accident was a poorly designed thruster system that allowed Armstrong's propellant to leak out. Loss of helium pressure in the propellant tanks caused the attitude rockets to shut down, producing loss of control. "There was very little time to analyze alternatives at that point," Neil explains. "It was just because I was so close to the ground. So, again, it was a time when you had to make a quick decision. You 'departed.' "

The fact that NASA was flying the vehicle in such windy conditions was a major contributing factor. At Edwards, the FRC engineers had put a fifteen-knot limit on wind speed for LLRV flying, but the Houston staff felt they had to raise it to thirty knots in order to be able to use the machine on a regular basis. The FRC's Gene Matranga feels that this is what really got Neil in trouble: "That afternoon there was a higher wind than we normally dealt with. Neil was using more attitude control fuel than had been budgeted because of the higher winds and the attitude rockets were firing much more continuously. The way we had designed the system, the fuel would go down so far, and then there was a standpipe that allowed you to have fuel saved for the lift rockets in case you had to use the lift rockets to recover the vehicle if the jet engine failed. The gentleman at Ellington who was responsible for watching the fuel consumption apparently froze at the switch. Neil should have shut off the lift rockets and saved his fuel for the attitude rockets and go back to the jet engine. Nobody warned Neil of that. What happened was the helium pressure, which sat on the top of the fuel to pressurize the system, was expended very rapidly, and Neil wound up having fuel but no pressurizing gas, because the lift rockets were in the open position. In essence, he had no control. He had to jump out."

Interestingly, back before the LLRVs came to Houston, Armstrong had been present at Edwards to observe ground tests in which the FRC engineers, in association with technicians from Weber Aircraft, tested the lightweight ejection seat (less than 100 pounds) at different angles. Neil watched as the seat fired a human-sized dummy into the air and then saw that dummy smash hard into the ground after too few swings on its parachute.

"Neil didn't think much of that," Matranga laughs. "He wasn't terribly thrilled. But, as it turned out, that seat saved his life."

After his accident on May 6, 1968, Armstrong behaved, typically, as if absolutely nothing out of the ordinary had just happened. Upon returning from a late lunch, astronaut Al Bean returned to the Astronaut Office and saw Neil at work at his desk in the office the two men shared. A little later, Bean went out in the hallway and walked over to a group of colleagues who were talking; he thought he heard them say that somebody had just crashed the LLTV. According to Bean, "I'm saying, 'What happened?' and they said, 'Well, the wind was high and Neil ran out of fuel and bailed out at the last minute and the ejection seat worked and he lived through it.' I said, 'When did this happen?' They said, 'It just happened an hour ago.' 'An hour ago!' I said, 'That's bullshit! I just came out of my office and Neil's there at his desk. He's in his flight suit, but he's in there shuffling some papers.' And they said, 'No, it was Neil.' I said, 'Wait a minute!' So I go back in the office. Neil looked up and I said, 'I just heard the funniest story!' He said, 'What?' I said, 'I heard that you bailed out of the LLTV an hour ago.' He thought a second and said, 'Yeah, I did.' I said, 'What happened?' He said, 'I lost control and had to bail out of the darn thing.' "

Bean continues his story: "So, I went back down and told the other guys. Nobody gave a thought to rush down there and ask Neil about it. If it had been Pete Conrad, everybody would have rushed down there, because Pete would have regaled them with a great story. I don't think it was that Neil was so extraordinarily cooler than the other guys. But, offhand, I can't think of another person, let alone another astronaut, who would have just gone back to his office after ejecting a fraction of a second before getting killed. He never got up at an all-pilots meeting and told us anything about it. That was an incident that colored my opinion about Neil ever since. He was so different than other people."

Neil's reaction to hearing Al Bean's story is just as circumspect as his behavior in the story itself: "That is true, I did go back to the office. I mean, what are you going to do? It's one of those sad days when you lose a machine."

Once more, as had been the case in his Gemini VIII flight, Armstrong rightfully came out of the experience with an enhanced reputation for being able to handle an emergency situation—and this time there was no Monday morning quarterbacking.

"The LLTV was widely regarded—and properly so—as a high-risk vehicle," Armstrong admits, "and one with which the management felt very uncomfortable. But the pilots universally, although they may have not liked the vehicle or liked flying it, they all agreed that it was the best simulation we had and gave us by far the highest confidence about what it was like to fly in the lunar environment."

Houston grounded the LLTV pending the findings not only of the MSC's accident investigation team but also of a special review board appointed by Dr. Thomas O. Paine, the man who succeeded James Webb as NASA administrator in late 1968 following the election of Richard M. Nixon. Chaired by General Samuel C. Phillips, the chief manager of the Apollo program under Dr. George Mueller, the committee at headquarters studied the impact of Armstrong's crash on the overall Apollo program, particularly the LM. By mid-October 1968, the two reports were out, urging LLTV design and management improvements, yet clearing the program to continue.

Four minutes into a planned six-minute flight on December 8, 1968, MSC chief test pilot Joe Algranti was forced to "punch out" from LLTV 1 when large lateral-control oscillation developed as he descended from a maximum altitude of 550 feet. Ejecting at 200 feet, Algranti, who had flown the LLTV more than thirty times, landed by parachute uninjured, while the $1.8-million vehicle crashed and burned several hundred feet away. Once again, Houston convened an accident investigation board, headed this time by astronaut Wally Schirra.

MSC director Bob Gilruth and MSC's Director of Flight Operations Chris Kraft both felt that it was only a matter of time before an astronaut would be killed in the blasted instrument. "Gilruth and I were ready to eliminate it completely," Kraft notes, "but the astronauts were adamant. They wanted the training it offered."

LLTV flying resumed in April 1969, even before Schirra's accident investigation panel turned in its report. When nothing went wrong in the first few flights involving only MSC test pilots, routine training flights for the astronauts began again. Yet Kraft knew they were pressing their luck. One day in the late spring of 1969, he asked Armstrong to stop by his office, hoping that Neil would give him some tidbit that Kraft could turn into a negative report about the LLTV. Neil did not provide it. "It's absolutely essential," the commander of the upcoming Apollo 11 mission told him. "By far the best training for landing on the Moon." "It's dangerous, damn it!" Kraft snapped back. "Yes, it is," said Neil. "I know you're worried, but I have to support it. It's just darned good training."

Kraft gave in, but he didn't give up. Even after the lunar landings began, either he or Gilruth "grilled every returning astronaut, hoping to find some way to get the LLTV grounded forever." They lost every time, because the astronauts wanted it. "To a man," Kraft recalls, "they said it was the best training they received and was essential to landing on the Moon. So with our fingers crossed, we let them keep it." The last astronaut to fly it was Gene Cernan on November 13, 1972, three weeks before the launch of Apollo 17, the final landing mission.

For three straight days in mid-June 1969, less than a month before the launch of Apollo 11, Armstrong flew one of the new LLTVs while Kraft and other NASA managers held their breath. Over the course of those three days (the fourteenth through the sixteenth), he took the LLTV up for lunar descents eight separate times. In all, he made a grand total of nineteen flights in the converted LLRVs and eight flights in the new LLTVs. No other astronaut before or after Armstrong flew the vehicle so much; for the record, Aldrin never flew the machine.* To observing newsmen after one of his flights, Neil remarked, "We are very pleased with the way it flies. I think it does an excellent job of capturing the handling characteristics. We're getting a very high level of confidence in the overall landing maneuver."

To this day, Armstrong remains convinced that the LLTV was "absolutely required to prepare yourself properly for the lunar landing." If he had not felt this way back in 1968 and 1969, given how contrary and risky he knew the machine was, he would have said, in the best interest of the overall program, "let's quit it." Considering his collaboration with his colleagues at Edwards in conceptualizing and developing the original LLRV, "it is human nature to defend the things that you've been involved in the creation of. But I really believe that my motivation to recommend using it was always proper."

Gene Matranga puts the capstone on the significance of the landing simulator for the pilot of the first Moon landing: "Psychologically, it didn't hurt that the LLRV/LLTV was harder to fly than the LM. That pleasant surprise had to bolster any astronaut's confidence on his way down to the lunar surface."

---

* According to Aldrin, "I didn't see any need to become qualified in flying the bedstead. I appreciated what it was, but I didn't see any need to risk so many people in the machine. Clearly, Neil had to make up his mind as to what was absolutely needed to make the landing and he felt this training was essential. I agreed with his decision to fly it." Aldrin to author, Albuquerque, NM, Mar. 17, 2003, p. 19.

CHAPTER 24

Amiable Strangers

The trio of Frank Borman, Jim Lovell, and Bill Anders were farther away from home than any human beings had ever been. Gradually slowing from a top speed of approximately 25,000 miles per hour, the crew of Apollo 8 had just passed the invisible milestone where the gravity of the planet and its natural satellite balanced out. The rest of the way Apollo 8 would be "falling" toward the Moon.

It was midafternoon, Monday, December 23, 1968, just following the crew's live television transmission of a grainy yet very recognizable view of the Earth from over 200,000 miles away, or more than four-fifths of the way to the Moon. In Houston's Mission Control, a new shift of flight controllers, the so-called Maroon Team under flight director Milton L. Windler, was preparing for the spacecraft to reach the critical point in its trajectory where the astronauts could insert their spacecraft into humankind's first lunar orbit. If the burn failed, Apollo 8 would by default swing around the Moon on a slingshot path back toward Earth.

Armstrong stood in the back of Mission Control, quietly pondering the upcoming lunar orbit insertion. As the backup commander for Apollo 8, Armstrong had spent every moment of the last two and half days deeply involved with the details of the circumlunar flight. At the Cape on the morning of the launch on December 21, Neil had awakened at 3:00 A.M. so he could eat breakfast with the prime crew. Not much for eating filet mignon and scrambled eggs in the middle of the night, he only had coffee, black and unsugared, like he learned to drink it back in the navy. When breakfast was over and Borman, Lovell, and Anders were painstakingly suiting up, Neil hustled over to Launchpad 39A. It was customary for one or two members of the backup crew to monitor the prelaunch sequence from inside the cockpit and to set and check all the switches.

Launch came just a few minutes later than scheduled, at 7:51 A.M. Eastern Standard Time. The first manned flight of the Saturn V "Moon Rocket" was something to behold. Neil watched the slow, fiery ascent of the gigantic booster from the big window inside Launch Control Center in the company of Buzz Aldrin and Fred W. Haise Jr., his fellow backup crew members.

Into the early afternoon, Armstrong monitored the progress of the flight, through its two Earth orbits, through its translunar injection, and well on its way toward the Moon. Then, along with Aldrin and Haise, Neil boarded a NASA Gulfstream and headed back to Houston, arriving there at about 7:00 P.M. In the plane with them were their three wives, Janet, Joan Aldrin, and Mary Haise. The women had watched the launch from the VIP viewing stands, providing moral support for Susan Borman, Marilyn Lovell, and Valerie Anders, who were also in attendance at the historic launch.

After a quick trip home to El Lago to shower and change clothes, Neil drove over to Mission Control. Though he stayed there late, the next morning, a Sunday, he returned early: "I was in Mission Control all the time I could be. If I was not at the CapCom spot next to Jerry Carr, Mike Collins, or Ken Mattingly, I'd be off talking to FIDO [Flight Dynamics Officer] or people in Experiments or GNC [Guidance, Navigation, and Control]. Sometimes they'd have questions for me about what the crew would be doing at this point in the flight or how the crew would be looking at a particular problem."

Spotting Armstrong in the big room full of consoles, Deke Slayton approached with a pressing topic: Neil's next assignment.

Of course, no one at this point in time could be sure what the mission for Apollo 11 would be. For Apollo 11 to become the first lunar landing mission not only would Apollo 8 need to complete its bold around-the-Moon flight successfully, but Apollo 9 and Apollo 10 would also have to come off without a hitch. If something, anything, went wrong, the G mission, the first landing, could easily fall back to Apollo 12 or even to Apollo 13. If the deadline got too tight, NASA might even move the landing up to Apollo 10. In the wake of Apollo 8's audacity, even something as daring as that lived in the realm of possibility. Still, Armstrong's assignment to Apollo 11 looked fortuitous. He left the brief meeting with Slayton knowing there was a chance that he was going to be commanding the first Moon landing attempt.

It took an extraordinary turn of events for the Apollo missions to line up the way they did. In the original schedule that Slayton in April 1967 had first outlined to the Apollo astronauts, there was to be no such circumlunar flight. Following the first manned Apollo flight, or C mission—handled in October 1968 by Schirra, Eisele, and Cunningham in Apollo 7—the D mission was supposed to test the combined operations of the CSM and LM in Earth orbit. But Grumman's LM was not ready to fly. Wanting to keep the momentum of the program going, a few risk takers in NASA, notably George Low, proposed a radical stopgap. Since the LM was not yet ready, why not expedite the flight sequence by flying the CSM around the Moon?

The idea was so bold that NASA leadership in Washington strongly resisted it. Armstrong remembers, "It took a while to convince the headquarters people that this was doable and safe. There had only been two Saturn V flights, both unmanned. The first one [Apollo 4, November 9, 1967] had gone pretty well. It experienced a small pogo—a potentially serious vibration in a rocket caused by combustion instability—and it had some other small problems. The second Saturn flight [Apollo 6, April 4, 1968] was not a disaster, but it was far from a successful operation. It had major pogo. It also experienced a premature engine shutdown. So for NASA management to agree and say, 'On the next Saturn V, we're not only going to put men on it, we are also going to send them around the Moon,' that was enormously bold."

Yet as soon as Apollo 7 in October 1968 proved to be an unqualified success, that is exactly what NASA management decided to do. The fact that the Soviet Union in September 1968 had just sent Zond 5 on a lunar flyby, and was preparing Zond 6 for the same sort of flight in November, helped cure the indecision. Zond was known to be large enough to carry a cosmonaut, and the idea in the American mind ever since Sputnik was that the Soviets would do everything they could to keep upstaging America in space, so we better not risk waiting around. Inside NASA, the intrepid move of a circumlunar flight met with significantly less than universal acceptance. "I cannot imagine NASA management in any subsequent period of time being willing to take that kind of a step," Armstrong has asserted. In this case, geopolitical circumstances dictated NASA's willingness.

Armstrong supported the radical redirection of Apollo 8, as did virtually all of the astronauts, but not until he was convinced that the problems with the Saturn V were fixed: "There was a process during which technical people from the Saturn V program convinced everyone that they understood the problems, they were fixing them, and the problems wouldn't happen again. And as long as NASA was going to put any astronauts at risk riding on that big monster, we might as well do something as useful as we can, because the time schedule was becoming an overbearing issue. To get the job done by the end of the decade, we needed to take giant steps and really make lots of progress on each flight, and this was the only way.

"Now, had the lunar module been available on schedule, the idea of a circumlunar flight probably would never have come up. We no doubt would have gone ahead with the combined CSM-LM flight into high Earth orbit, which was in keeping with the original sequence of flight plans. As it was, there was not much time to get all our ducks in a row and get really serious about all the navigation issues and data processing that Apollo 8 required. Those became of paramount importance, to be really confident that we could do it. We did not have all that figured out at the time the circumlunar decision was made, but we sure had the motivation to get it done."

On that Monday afternoon, December 23, 1968, as things were settling down following the end of the TV transmission from Apollo 8, Armstrong and Slayton retired to one of the back rooms at the Mission Control Center for what would prove to be a historic conversation.

"Deke laid out his thinking about Apollo 11 and asked how I felt about having Mike Collins and Buzz Aldrin as my crew. We talked about it a little bit, and I didn't have any problem with that. And Deke said that Buzz wasn't necessarily so easy to work with, and I said, 'Well, I've been working with him the last few months [in the backup role for Apollo 8] and everything seems to be going all right.' But I knew what Deke was saying. Then he said he wanted to make Jim Lovell available for Apollo 11 even though it would be a little bit out of sequence, but that's what he'd do, if that is what I thought I needed. I would have been happy to get Lovell. Jim was a very reliable guy, very steady. I had a lot of confidence in him. It would have been highly unusual for the crew assignment to have worked out this way, but Deke offered the possibility that it would be Jim Lovell and Mike Collins as my crew."

Armstrong wanted a little time to think about it. He took only until the next day, Christmas Eve, to give Deke his answer. By then, the crew of Apollo 8, with Jim Lovell piloting the command module, was in orbit around the Moon. Lovell would never learn that if Armstrong's answer had been different he would have become a member of the Apollo 11 crew. "Jim had already been commander of Gemini XII," Neil states, "and I thought he deserved his own command. I thought it would be not right of me to pull Lovell out of line for a command, so he ended up with Apollo 13. To this day, he doesn't know anything about that. I have never related these conversations that I had with Slayton to anyone. As far as I know, Buzz doesn't know about them, either, unless Deke talked to him about them." What

Armstrong's taking of Lovell for Apollo 11 would have meant for Aldrin was that he would have been pushed back to a later crew, probably in exchange for Lovell, to the ill-fated Apollo 13.

Neil answered Slayton in the way he did because, one, he had had no trouble working with Buzz, and, two, Lovell deserved his own command. A third aspect of his thinking was more complicated. If Lovell came on board Apollo 11, it would be best to give him the same job he had on Apollo 8, that of command module pilot. The trouble was that Mike Collins was a CMP specialist. Mike had trained as such for the crew of Apollo 8 before being forced off that mission due to a bone spur growing between two cervical vertebrae, requiring neck surgery. If Collins was to be a part of Apollo 11, as Slayton and Armstrong both felt he deserved to be, Mike was best prepared to fly the command module.

Armstrong reasoned: "Aldrin had been the command module pilot for the Apollo 8 backup crew. I felt uncomfortable with Mike being the lunar module pilot for Apollo 11, because the command module pilot was the number-two guy in a crew and the lunar module pilot was number three. I had a little difficulty in my own mind putting Aldrin above Collins. In talking with Deke, we decided, because the CMP had such significant responsibilities for flying the command module solo and being able to do rendezvous by himself and so forth, that Mike was best to be in that position." In other words, Lovell could not justifiably be put in the number-three slot as the lunar module pilot, but Aldrin could. The decision was made to go with Collins and Aldrin.

One might wonder how Fred Haise felt about the development—after all, Haise was part of Neil's backup crew on Apollo 8 as the LM pilot. "Deke didn't think that Fred was quite ready for a prime crew," Armstrong recalls. "We had talked a little bit about the mission, and Deke said it could be a lunar module landing attempt—*could be*—though I thought that was a bit remote at that point." If Haise had been put on Neil's Apollo 11 crew, then Aldrin would have remained in the job of CM pilot.

The critical factor was that Slayton wanted to get Collins back in the sequence. "He'd been out for a while due to his neck," Neil states, "and Deke wanted to get him back. Deke was always trying to get all the feeds into the sequence that he could so that he would have maximum flexibility in covering all the missions. I was not aware of any disappointment on Fred Haise's part, though certainly there could have been."

Prior to their assignment as backup for Apollo 8, Armstrong had not had much interaction with either Aldrin or Haise. They had never served on a crew together before. Neil had worked on Gemini XI at the same time that Lovell and Aldrin were working on Gemini XII, so Neil and Buzz were at the Cape together a lot and saw each other frequently even though they were doing different things. Fred Haise he had seen even less. As part of his collateral responsibilities, Haise worked a lot on the lunar modules, and it was clear to Neil that Fred knew a lot about that area: "I was comfortable with him, although we did not have a lunar module on Apollo 8, so that expertise wasn't applicable." Haise became the LM pilot for the Apollo 11 backup crew. Providing the rest of the backup crew was Apollo 8's Jim Lovell, the backup commander, and Bill Anders, the backup command module pilot. Following Apollo 8, Frank Borman had decided to retire as an active astronaut.

All in all, Armstrong was quite content with the meeting of minds between himself and Slayton that Mike Collins and Buzz Aldrin would serve with him on Apollo 11.

That Christmas Eve was extraordinary, not just for Armstrong but for everyone who was glued to their television sets watching the live transmission from Apollo 8 in lunar orbit. It was a Christmas Eve the likes of which people would remember for the rest of their lives.

During their live broadcast that evening, Borman, Lovell, and Anders took turns reading the first ten verses of the Book of Genesis while television viewers watched wondrous pictures of the Moon's surface passing surreally underneath, in an almost godlike view. The astronauts next pointed their lightweight TV camera back at the home planet to show the awesome and delicate beauty of a waxing Earth "rising" gloriously above the lunar surface. Only when seen in such stark contrast to the Moon's dead surface and amid the infinite blackness of space could people the world over fully appreciate the extraordinarily fragile oasis of life that was "Spaceship Earth." American poet Archibald MacLeish wrote: "To see the Earth as it truly is, small and blue and beautiful in that eternal silence where it floats, is to see ourselves as riders on the Earth together, brothers on that bright loveliness in the eternal cold—brothers who know they are truly brothers."

The astronauts concluded their lunar vigil with the hopeful message "Merry Christmas and God bless all of you, all of you on the good Earth." A few hours later, at 1:10 A.M. EST on Christmas morning, Apollo 8 ignited its service propulsion system (SPS), the main rocket engine of the command and service module, and accelerated out of lunar orbit. Delighted to be homeward bound, Lovell remarked as the spacecraft came around the back side of the Moon, "Please be informed, there is a Santa Claus."

Apollo 8 splashed down safely on the morning of December 27, six days and three hours, two Earth orbits, and ten lunar orbits after launch. It had been a truly historic flight. Not only were Borman, Lovell, and Anders the first humans to break the bonds of Earth's gravity, their journey proved that astronauts could travel the nearly quarter of a million miles separating the home planet from its nearest neighbor. Their mission proved that course-correction maneuvers could be done out of line of sight and out of communications with Earth, that a craft could be tracked from an immense distance, and that it could successfully orbit the Moon and return.

"It was a remarkably trouble-free flight," Armstrong comments, "considering all the difficulties that we might have anticipated could happen in the first lunar flight. It really came off superbly well."

The year 1968 had been extraordinarily traumatic for America, not that 1967 had been much better. The paroxysms started in January 1968 when North Korea seized the USS *Pueblo,* claiming the American ship had violated its territorial waters while spying. (When it was seized, the ship was off Wonsan, the port city that Armstrong knew well from his months of combat off the eastern coast of North Korea.) A week after the *Pueblo* incident, the Vietcong launched a massive series of surprise attacks in South Vietnam. Known as the Tet Offensive, the bloody attacks made it abundantly clear that the war in Vietnam was not going to end anytime soon. Then in March, the world learned of the My Lai massacre, in which American soldiers killed at least 175 Vietnamese woman and children, a tragedy that seriously aggravated public feelings against the war. On the last day of the same month, a war-weary and broken president, Lyndon Johnson, announced that he would not seek or accept the nomination of his party for reelection.

The convulsions were just beginning. In April, student protesters at Columbia University in New York City took over campus administration buildings and shut down the college. In a span of nine weeks that spring, two of the country's leading antiwar and civil rights spokesmen were assassinated: Martin Luther King Jr., in Memphis, Tennessee, and Senator Robert F. Kennedy in Los Angeles, after winning the Democratic presidential primary in California. At the Democratic National Convention in Chicago that August, Mayor Richard Daly's police department clashed with angry crowds of demonstrators as antiwar candidate Eugene McCarthy went down to defeat at the hands of Hubert H. Humphrey's supporters. Two months later, on the victory stand at the Olympic Games in Mexico City, sprinters Tommie Smith and John Carlos, two African-American athletes who had won gold and bronze medals respectively, raised their gloved fists in a black power salute in support of civil rights and antiwar causes.

Internationally, the disquiet of 1968 was just as bad. Israel and Jordan clashed in a border dispute. Violence ignited between Protestants and Catholics in Northern Ireland, initiating "The Troubles," which the following year would bring the country to the brink of civil war. In Paris, a coalition of protesting students and workers nearly brought down the French government. Soviet tanks rolled into Czechoslovakia, then part of the USSR-led Warsaw Pact, ending a brief period of liberalization known as the Prague Spring. On the eve of the Olympics, a student demonstration at La Plaza de las Tres Culturas in Mexico City ended in a bloodbath that killed hundreds.

Amidst such chaos and upheaval, spending billions on trips to the Moon, in the view of many people, seemed a terribly misguided and misplaced priority. A popular saying began: "If we can go to the Moon, why can't we" and finished with any of a number of universally wholesome objectives: end injustice, eradicate poverty, cure cancer, abolish war, clean up the environment.

So noisy did the anti-Establishment outcries become in 1968 that no astronaut, however apolitical, including Armstrong, could have lived unaware of the criticisms being directed at NASA and the space program. To the limited extent the astronauts engaged the critics, they valued what they were doing in space, in immediate terms by beating the Russians to the Moon and, more permanently, in terms of civilization taking its inevitable step off the planet. "We were aware of the controversies," Armstrong comments. "I doubt that they had any pronounced or even noticeable effect on the performance of any of the guys on any of our flights. We were just doing our jobs—trying to, anyway, and happy to be doing them."

Even amid the clamor, criticism, and declining support for the space program, evidenced for more than two years in polling numbers and in congressional votes, the astronauts remained the object of the American public's adulation. "I don't know that I gave much thought to what turned out to be the public's extraordinary reaction to Apollo 8," Armstrong admits. "Not that I was surprised by it, because breaking the chains of the Earth's gravity for the first time and going to another world was extremely important—in many ways more important than the achievements of Apollo 11. But we were enveloped in an aura of public interest all the time, and in a way we got hardened to it."

•   •   •

Learning that they were to be a part of Apollo 11 was not one of the presents Mike Collins and Buzz Aldrin opened on Christmas morning 1968. The two men did not find out about their assignment, in fact, until the Monday after New Year's. On January 4, 1969, Slayton called the two men into his office where Armstrong was already on hand and told them they were being named the prime crew for Apollo 11. Neil recalls that Deke said it was "conceivable and may work out that this will be the first lunar landing attempt." Deke then added that he wanted them to conduct their preparation for the flight on the assumption that the landing was going to happen, so that, if it did, they would be totally ready to carry it out.

"We responded accordingly," Aldrin remarks, "trying to maintain a façade of business as usual while adrenaline sped through our bodies." "We thought it was great," Armstrong states. "It was going to be a great flight whatever the mission profile turned out to be." The possibility of being part of the first landing crew "must have been in everybody's mind to some extent, but I don't remember ever focusing on it. I was happy just being there and doing whatever jobs I got."

NASA announced the Apollo 11 crew to the public five days later, on January 9. The announcement came following ceremonies in which the Apollo 8 crewmen were awarded medals from President Johnson at the White House and received standing ovations at a joint meeting of Congress attended by the president's cabinet, the Supreme Court justices, and the diplomatic corps. Before Congress, Apollo 8 commander Frank Borman described the mission as a "triumph of mankind," not just an American triumph. Armstrong, Collins, and Aldrin were not present in Washington when, as many newspapers put it, the "Moon Team Is Named." They did appear at an Apollo 11 press briefing in Houston the next day. "Our intent is to train to make a lunar landing." Slayton told the reporters. "Whether we do or not will depend upon how the D mission goes and how the F mission goes. We could be flying one of those missions on Apollo 11 instead of the lunar mission. But these are the first guys who will be concentrating the greatest extent on getting a landing done."

Mike Collins later called himself, Armstrong, and Aldrin "amiable strangers," a phrase by all accounts that can be applied justifiably to no other crew. This makes Apollo 11 unique not only in terms of its historic mission but also in terms of how unusually the crew related to one another, to their colleagues in NASA, and even to the outside world.

Michael Collins was easily the trio's most lighthearted member. His up-bringing was also the most cosmopolitan, thanks to his father's distin-guished military career. The son of an army attaché in Rome, Mike was born in the Celestial City on October 31, 1930, in an apartment just off Via Veneto overlooking the Borghese Gardens. His father, General James L. Collins, had fought with General John J. Pershing in the Philippines and in the 1916 Mexican campaign against Pancho Villa. In France during World War I, Collins Sr., then an aide to "Black Jack" Pershing, won the Silver Star. Young Michael's uncle, J. Lawton Collins, became even more renowned as a soldier. As "Lightning Joe" Collins, he fought as one of Gen-eral Dwight Eisenhower's corps commanders in Europe during the Second World War. Following the war, Lightning Joe became the army chief of staff.

Like Armstrong, Mike moved around a lot as a boy. An army brat, he never had a hometown to speak of. When he was a year and a half old, his parents returned to the States, where his father posted in Oklahoma. From there, the family moved to Governors Island in New York Bay, to Fort Hoyle outside Baltimore, followed by stops at Fort Hays, Ohio, near Columbus, in San Antonio, Texas, and in San Juan, Puerto Rico.

Also as with Armstrong, the itinerant life of his family did not affect him at all adversely. San Antonio, he felt, had "something extra going for it." At Fort Hoyle near the Chesapeake Bay, "There were horses to ride, and woods to tramp through and, best of all, fishing [with] crabs for bait." In San Juan, where his father was commanding general of a military department that included not only Puerto Rico but some of the Virgin Islands and parts of the West Indies, the family lived in what reputedly was the second-oldest house in the Western Hemisphere, over four hundred years old. "It was an immense place," Collins remembers, "with extraordinary 'play places' for a boy ten years old. A house of ill-repute was right there [outside the enclosed military area]. The girls used to toss me money if I would come down and talk to them, but I never would. I was scared to death. I'm afraid a lot of their profits got converted into ice cream cones for me."

Mike had three siblings. The oldest was James L. Collins Jr., thirteen years older. Mike was not yet five when his brother went off to West Point, graduating in 1939. In World War II, James was a field artillery battalion commander who won the Purple Heart, Bronze Star, Silver Star, Distin-guished Service Medal, and Legion of Merit. In 1965 he became a brigadier general. Mike's two sisters, Virginia and Agnes, were six and ten years older than he and not of a mind to traipse around with their precocious little brother. So he spent a lot of time playing by himself, enlivening his imagination. His mother, Virginia Stewart Collins, was a cultured, educated woman whose Scottish-English family had come to America prior to the American Revolution. Her lasting influence over her youngest child included her love of books and admiration for the beauty of the English language.

In 1942, following the Japanese attack on Pearl Harbor, the family moved to Washington, DC, where it remained for the duration of the war. Mike was sent off to an Episcopal preparatory school, St. Albans, adjacent to Washington's National Cathedral. A tall, skinny, athletic boy, he captained the school's wrestling team and played guard on the football team. His grades were only slightly above average. "I was just a normal, active, troublesome kid. I liked airplanes and kites and climbing trees and falling out of them. I didn't like school much. I usually looked sleepy in the classroom, and the school yearbook poked fun at me about that. I was an altar boy at the cathedral and I had to get up for the 6:30 A.M. service; I never did seem to catch up on sleep. Reading was something else, though. I discovered books when I was about eleven, and it was just like somebody had turned on the light or opened the door."

All the kids liked him, as did his teachers, even though he was usually the prime suspect in whatever mischief took place, playing his innocence to humorous effect. He had a gift for leadership, for getting along with others, for thinking clearly, and for expressing himself with "intellectual precision."

Given the family's military tradition, Collins might have been pressured to go into the army when he graduated high school in 1948. Yet to the extent that his father exerted any influence on him, it was to keep him away from military service. "He was a very independent cuss himself," Mike asserts, "and he raised his kids to think independently. He didn't want me to do something just because it seemed the thing to do. My mother liked the field of diplomacy as a profession better than the military; I think she was trying to steer me subtly toward foreign service with the State Department. I can recall thinking I might want to be a doctor. In the end I chose West Point because I wanted to go to college and I knew West Point was a first-class education. Also it was free. You don't get rich in the service."

In a class of 527 cadets, Collins finished 185th, which was in the top third (or 28th percentile). Graduating in 1952, he was in the same class as Ed White. Frank Borman was two years ahead of him, Buzz Aldrin one year behind. With typical humorous modesty, Collins admits that his academic record was respectable but not stellar: "I do about as well in liberal arts as I do in the sciences, and I don't do particularly well in any of them. I'd rather *do something* than study about it or talk about it."

As a West Point graduate, he was committed to four years of active duty. "I chose the air force because it sounded more exciting and innovative [than the army]." By 1956, First Lieutenant Collins was a part of a fighter squadron flying F-86s in Chambley, France, and had gotten to very much like what he was doing. In fighter pilots, he found kindred spirits. "I *like* fighter pilots, I really do," Collins exclaimed to *Life* reporter Dodie Hamblin in an interview prior to the Apollo 11 mission in 1969.

He also got very much to like a slim, dark, attractive woman he met one night at the Chambley officers' mess. Spotting her at the bar, Mike walked over and said, "Hi, I'm Mike Collins. Do you live here?" The young woman, twenty-one years old, was Patricia Finnegan. The oldest of eight children, Pat had grown up in suburban Boston within a staunchly Roman Catholic family full of lawyers and politicians. After graduating from all-girls Emmanuel College, where she majored in English, she did social work with Aid to Dependent Children, working mostly with unwed mothers. Two and a half years later, wishing to see a little of the world but not having the money to travel very comfortably, Pat took a job that sent her to France with the air force service club. Before meeting Mike at Chambley, she had dated a doctor and a dentist. As soon as Mike spoke to her, she knew he was different: "He loved to eat and he understood French food and introduced me to a lot of things that I wouldn't have tried by myself. Some of the Americans were joining wine study clubs, but Mike didn't have to. He had learned a lot about wines from his father, and he had studied up on vineyards so he could tell wonderful stories about them. In fact he could talk about everything. He knew books; he knew poetry; he was interested in theater. He was bright about technical things, and he was lots and lots of fun. I couldn't get over all this combination in one man."

What Pat Finnegan most liked about Mike Collins was his approach to life: "It was, and still is, that everything will be okay; that everything will work out."

Quickly overcoming the matter of religion—Pat was ultra-Catholic, Mike was nominally Episcopalian—the young couple got engaged. Mike's letter to Pat's father in Boston, Joseph Finnegan, ran six sentences long. "Never," Joe Finnegan later told Pat and Mike when giving his approval to their marriage, "had [I] seen such a good lawyer's brief in six sentences."

Plans for a June 1956 wedding did not work out. The Hungarian Revolution intervened, and Mike's squadron was redeployed to Germany. The marriage waited until the summer of 1957.

Deciding to make the air force his career, Collins determined to become a test pilot. He considered it not only a way to stay settled and stateside but as the ultimate job in flying. "You can be irresponsible and you may get away with it being a fighter pilot; but you most certainly cannot as a test pilot. Fighter pilots can be impetuous; test pilots can't. They have to be more mature, a little bit smarter. They have to give more thought to what they're doing, or they're going to—well, maybe not kill themselves, but, even worse, they'll come to wrong conclusions about airplanes and others will kill themselves later when the aircraft reach squadron service. They have to be more deliberate, better trained—and they're not as much fun as fighter pilots."

While still based in Europe, Collins applied for the air force test pilot school at Edwards. Not until 1961 (the year that Chuck Yeager returned to Edwards as deputy director of the flight test operation, prior to Yeager's becoming the school's commandant the following year) did the school admit him. With the Space Age under way and the X-15 and Mercury spacecraft now flying, the school had just changed its name to the USAF Aerospace Research Pilot School (ARPS) and begun to build a program designed to train U.S. military test pilots for spaceflight. Collins became part of ARPS Class III. With him in Class III were Charlie Bassett, the astronaut killed with Elliot See in 1966, and Joe Engle, who eventually became the only person to fly into space in two different *winged* vehicles, the X-15 and the Space Shuttle. In the ARPS class right behind him were Ted Freeman, Jim Irwin, and Dave Scott. In all, twenty-six graduates of the air force test pilot school came to earn astronaut's wings by flying in the Gemini, Apollo, or Space Shuttle programs.

When NASA named its third group of astronauts in June 1963, Collins was one of them, specializing in pressure suits and extravehicular activity. For the December 1965 flight of Gemini VII, he served as Jim Lovell's backup. Mike's first spaceflight came in July 1966 on Gemini X, an exciting mission that achieved a successful docking with the Agena target vehicle during which Collins performed a space walk that retrieved a micrometeorite package that Dave Scott on Gemini VIII had been unable to bring back due to the spacecraft's in-flight emergency. Mike's first Apollo assignment was backup to Walt Cunninghan on the second Apollo flight. In the shakeup after the launchpad fire, Collins was to be the command module pilot for what became Apollo 8. Due to a dangerous bone spur in his spinal column, however, which required surgery in June 1968, he was replaced on Apollo 8 by Jim Lovell. Thanks to a very successful surgery and rapid recovery, he got paired with Armstrong and Aldrin for Apollo 11.

If all of this sounds like a whirlwind ride for Collins, from a fighter pilot who had a hard time getting into test pilot school to the astronaut who was serving as the command module pilot for the first lunar landing, all in less than eight years, it was exactly that.

Having progressed so far so fast, having grown up in such interesting surroundings, having had such supportive parents, and having had the very good fortune to have met and married such an intelligent and beautiful wife, it was no wonder that Mike Collins was an optimist, if not an eternal one: "I'm not *always* convinced that everything is going to work out well. On the other hand, there's nothing wrong in acting as if things will work out. I mean, if I tell my wife I believe in the Easter Bunny—well, why not? Either he exists or he doesn't, and I choose to believe. But if you really cornered me, I'd have to admit reluctantly that there is no Easter Bunny. Maybe."

Collins was the sort of man whom Armstrong naturally liked. He was good humored and liked to joke; yet he was very thoughtful, articulate, and learned. Long after the Apollo 11 mission, Mike would comment: "A closer relationship, while certainly not necessary for the success or happy completion of a spaceflight, would seem more 'normal' to me. Even as a self-acknowledged loner, I feel a bit freakish about our tendency as a crew to transfer only essential information, rather than thoughts or feelings."

Born January 30, 1930, in Glen Ridge, New Jersey,* Edwin Eugene Aldrin Jr. was the third child and only son of a man who was himself quite remote and distant—not to mention resolute and hard to please. The senior Aldrin (born 1896) had been a pilot in the army air corps during World War I. He had served as an aide to General Billy Mitchell, the outspoken and abrasive advocate of a separate U.S. air force who came before army court-martial in 1925. He was a highly educated man. Before going into the military, Gene Aldrin had studied physics at Clark University under Dr. Robert H. Goddard, the father of American rocketry. In 1918, he earned a master's degree at MIT in electrical engineering, writing a fifty-five-

---

* Buzz Aldrin's birthplace has frequently been given to be Montclair, New Jersey. In fact, he was born on the Glen Ridge wing of a hospital whose central body rested in Montclair. His birth certificate lists Glen Ridge as his birthplace.

page thesis under Professor A. E. Kennelly on the behavior of electrically heated wires, a topic with applications to telephone transmission, internal combustion engines, and aviation instrumentation. He later returned to MIT on military assignment, finishing a doctor of science (ScD) degree in 1928. Resigning from the air corps in 1928, Aldrin Sr. became a stockbroker. At the top of the bull market in August 1929, just three months before the Wall Street crash, he somehow had the clairvoyance to sell all his stock and purchase a large three-story, seven-bedroom house on a corner of Princeton Place in Montclair, New Jersey, eighteen miles northwest of Manhattan.

Gene Aldrin met his wife Marion while serving under General Mitchell in the Philippines, where he was in charge of putting together airplanes out of spare parts left over from World War I. Propitiously, at least for the son she would bear, Marion's maiden name was Moon. The perfectly groomed, blond, blue-eyed daughter of a strict Methodist minister who served as a chaplain in the army, Marion Gaddys Moon Aldrin possessed an independent spirit that often conflicted with her husband's own strong determination. Prior to Buzz, she gave birth to two daughters, Madeline, four years older, and Fay Ann, a year and a half older. Being the only boy, the two sisters called him "Brother." Little Fay Ann, just learning to speak, could not quite manage the word, which came out as "Buzzer." The nickname got shortened to Buzz.

Whereas the key to understanding Armstrong's personality lay primarily in understanding his relationship with his mother, the secret to understanding Buzz Aldrin rests in his feelings about his father. Buzz's autobiographical 1973 book *Return to Earth,* best known for its candid account of his battle with alcoholism and depression in the years immediately following the Apollo 11 flight, represents his growing up as a classic case of a boy desperately seeking the elusive love and approval of a strong father.

Settling his family in Montclair, Gene Aldrin became an executive with Standard Oil of New Jersey. He was rarely home. In fact, he became famous for being one of the country's first executives to compile many tens of thousands of miles of business travel by airplane. He even made a few trips by airship, including one memorable crossing of the Atlantic in the famous German zeppelin *Hindenburg.* (According to Buzz, his father told friends after making the dirigible flight that it was neither safe nor practical.) In the early 1930s, Aldrin Sr. piloted a flight in a Standard Oil Lockheed Vega over the Alps from Germany to Italy; on board with him was his wife and a mechanic. During the flight of Italian general Italo Balbo into the World's Fair in Chicago in 1933, Gene handled the American logistics. For that service to General Balbo, the Mussolini government made Gene Aldrin a commendatore, or commander, in Italy's National Order of Merit, the country's highest honor. Leaving Standard Oil in 1938, he became an independent aviation consultant. Among his professional associations were Charles Lindbergh, Howard Hughes, and Jimmy Doolittle.

With so much talk about aviation in the Aldrin home, Buzz naturally took an interest in flying, but not always to his father's complete satisfaction. He took his first airplane ride when he was two when his father piloted a company Lockheed Vega to Florida. Buzz remembered for his 1973 book: "My father must have been distressed to see his only son throwing up for most of his first plane ride." Along with Buzz on that ride was the family's African-American housekeeper, Alice. According to Buzz, Alice was his "best friend." The two of them shared the third floor of the Aldrin house. "Her enthusiasm for my world made it grow, and more by demonstration than by words she taught me tolerance."

Buzz's relationship with his sisters, living on the floor down below, was not very close. Older sister Madeline left her active little brother to his own playful occupations, while Fay Ann and Buzz mostly quarreled and picked at each other. Both girls teased him for not doing as well in school as they. One gets the definite impression that Buzz spent a lot of time alone. He worshiped the Lone Ranger for his independence and great sense of justice. Buzz liked sports but preferred those that were solitary, notably pole vaulting and scuba diving. For seven straight summers, from ages nine to fifteen, he went off to boys' camp at Trout Lake in southern Maine. Sometimes his parents would make a visit, but mostly they spent their summers at the New Jersey shore. "The eight weeks raced by each summer and I was never once homesick. I look back on my experience at camp as being quite instrumental in leading me toward what I call competitive appreciation for associating with other people: having standards set for you, set by other people, or standards you would set for yourself."

His ambition to excel grew by leaps and bounds. Small for his age, he picked a number of fights, hoping to prove something by getting a black eye. In pickup football games around his neighborhood, he played with older boys, impressing them with his energy and aggressiveness. At camp, he did his utmost to win individual awards, and he won many, including a trophy when he was eleven for the best all-around camper. Once he became serious about academic matters during the ninth grade, he was "crushed" whenever he received a grade as low as a B. At his father's insistence, he sat out of football during his junior year so as to continue producing the even higher grades he would need to be accepted into a military academy. When he returned to the football team as a senior, they won the New Jersey state championship. Although still small for his age, Aldrin played center, opposing the much bigger defensive linemen.

Buzz's father, however distant, loomed larger over him than any football opponent. "My father never gave direct instructions nor stated goals, but what was expected was somehow made clear. I also knew he was more important than most of my friends' fathers."

When the United States entered World War II, Buzz was eleven. Aldrin Sr. returned to duty as a full colonel. In the South Pacific, he worked as inspector general of the Thirteenth Air Force. Activated at New Caledonia in the Coral Sea in early 1943, the Thirteenth staged out of tropical jungles on more than forty remote islands, thus earning the nickname the "Jungle Air Force." Later, in Europe, Gene Aldrin studied antisubmarine warfare. Buzz remembers that visits home "were always short and, it seemed to me, rather remote." When the war ended, his father was serving as chief of the All Weather Flying Center at Wright Field in Ohio.

Immediately following Buzz's graduation from Montclair High School in 1947, his dad enrolled him in a military preparatory "poop school," Severn School in Maryland, not far from Annapolis, home of the U.S. Naval Academy. Without Buzz's knowledge, his father was laying the groundwork for his son's admission to Annapolis. Even when Buzz told him that he much preferred the U.S. Military Academy at West Point, his father persisted. "I advocated the Naval Academy," Gene Aldrin remarked later, "because they had more technical studies, engineering studies, and also because in my experience the navy took care of its people better." His father even told Buzz's mother, "As a matter of fact, I think Buzz prefers Annapolis." That Aldrin Sr. preferred Annapolis was really all that mattered. Gene Aldrin secured a principal appointment to the naval academy for his son from New Jersey's Republican senator Albert W. Hawkes.

But Buzz would not take his sights off West Point. "Whether the fact that my sister was dating a guy from West Point had anything to do with my preference, or that I got seasick, or that I felt that ships were a diversion from airplanes, I'm not sure. Somehow I just felt more aligned towards the army air corps and West Point. When news of the principal appointment to Annapolis came through, my father and I had a brief confrontation during which I stubbornly insisted that he go back to Senator Hawkes and say that my choice was West Point." Very reluctantly, his father gave in, but only after the idea of Buzz's going to West Point got assimilated into Gene Aldrin's adjusted mental scheme for his son's future.

At West Point, Buzz's quest for excellence continued. At the end of his plebe year, as he notes proudly in his autobiography, he ranked first in his class. That summer, at Camp Buckner, a military reserve some ten miles from West Point, Aldrin received the assignment to be a company commander. As for the standardization and regimentation in West Point's system of education, Aldrin liked its clarity: "To me, the beauty of the system was that you knew exactly where you were at all times. You could measure your progress. You also knew what was expected of you from day to day. You did your lessons, went to class, and performed." Such clarity existed in the Aldrin home only when Buzz found ways to satisfy his father, which was extremely rare. When Buzz graduated from West Point third in his class, his father wanted to know who finished first and second.

During the summer preceding Buzz's senior year at West Point, Gene Aldrin had "recommended" that his son apply for one of the prestigious Rhodes scholarships. Only those candidates with demonstrated excellence of mind and in qualities of person were seriously considered for the honor, which took them to Oxford University for two years of advanced studies. In the United States, a lengthy screening process annually sorted through hundreds of nominees until the field was reduced to thirty-two winners. In a building on the campus of Princeton University, Buzz interviewed for the Rhodes scholarship. He was not accepted.

"I fully expected my father to be disappointed and was not at all prepared for his immediate rationalization. 'I didn't really want it anyway,' he said, 'because it would do virtually nothing for [your] military career.' " Then, "Dad and I agreed that following West Point I would enter the air force." Father and son disagreed, however, over what type of flying Buzz should do.

Once again, Buzz's determination won out. His parents were in the viewing stands the autumn day in 1951 that Buzz earned his wings after completing fighter training in Bryan, Texas. After the ceremony, as a surprise for his father, Buzz arranged for one of his instructors to take his dad up in a T-33. "He was still lobbying for me to change to multiengine aircraft and I wanted him to sense some of the independence of the fighters," Buzz relates. "He was pleased with the flight but somewhat unimpressed." No matter what Buzz did, it never seemed to be quite good enough.

Aldrin fought in Korea with the 51st Fighter Wing; his outfit, flying the F-86 interceptor, arrived in Seoul the day after Christmas 1951. That same day, as cold winds hit nearly 100 miles per hour in the Sea of Japan, Neil Armstrong on the carrier *Essex* left Yokosuka for his third round of combat flying over North Korea. By the time the final cease-fire was negotiated in July 1952, Aldrin had flown a total of sixty-six missions. He had three encounters in his Sabre jet with Soviet MiGs. In the first, on May 14, in his own words, he "simply flew up behind the enemy and shot him down." It might have been "a singularly undramatic experience: no dogfight, no maneuvers, no excitement," but it was one that Aldrin's gun camera caught on film, the first such pictures of the Korean War showing an enemy pilot bailing out. *Life* magazine ran the pictures the following week.

Buzz's second encounter with a MiG, on June 7, was more daring, even reckless, though for that Aldrin was not responsible. With two of the planes in his formation of four having aborted their flight due to engine trouble, Aldrin tried to catch up in his F-86E with a preceding formation of faster F-86Fs. The planes led him into what turned out to be an unauthorized mission against an enemy airfield some fifty miles north of the Yalu River inside Manchuria. Near the forbidden target Buzz engaged and shot down his second MiG. Now over two hundred miles from base, he barely made it back. Debriefing with the renegade squadron of F-86Fs, something that was customary for a pilot to do after joining up with another formation, Buzz never told anyone else about the foray into Manchuria.

Aldrin's third and final encounter with MiG aircraft came shortly before the armistice. Observing several of the Russian jets heading north, he ineffectively fired several bursts at them from long distance. Buzz did not leave Korea until December 1952. For the last six months of his combat tour, he flew escort missions up and down the coast, being careful never to infringe on the twelve-mile limit that by treaty was now ensuring the legitimacy of North Korea's boundary.

Back in the States, Aldrin reported to Nevada's Nellis Air Force Base as a gunnery instructor. The following year, 1955, he applied and received a three-month assignment to Squadron Officer School at Maxwell Air Force Base in Montgomery, Alabama. In between, on December 29, 1954, Buzz married a bright and articulate young woman with a master's degree from Columbia University named Joan Archer, the daughter of one of his parents' friends. Joan came to think of her husband as "a curious mixture of magnificent confidence bordering on conceit, and humility." One of his classmates at Maxwell, a captain that Buzz respected a great deal, felt similarly, and one day took Buzz aside to tell him so. "He said, in effect, that I was too competitive, too insensitive to others, too determined to be the best, and that if I didn't watch it I'd end up with a reputation as a hotshot egotist." With "tears streaming down my cheeks," Buzz thanked the captain.

When a baby boy, James Michael Aldrin, was born to the newlyweds nine months later, Buzz's father displayed a rare moment of delight while having a celebratory drink of bourbon with his son. "It was one of the few times I can remember," Buzz remarks, "when my normally stern and disciplined father was literally fidgety with happiness." The only comparable father-son experience occurred when Buzz was nine years old. He was heading out the front door for his first trip to summer camp when his father stopped him, took him into one of the ground-floor bedrooms, sat him on the bed, and explained to him "the engineering wonders of pipes." According to Buzz, "the subject of the birds and the bees was woefully imprecise to my father compared with the exactness of fitting pipes together."

Finishing the officers' school at Maxwell, the Aldrins went to Colorado Springs, where Buzz served as aide to General Don Z. Zimmerman, dean of faculty at the new U.S. Air Force Academy. They stayed there, and loved the place, until General Zimmerman moved on to a job in the Pentagon. Then, in August 1956, Buzz joined the 36th Fighter-Day Wing, stationed in Bitburg, Germany. For the next three years, the Aldrins lived in Germany. While Buzz was busy flying the F-100, the most sophisticated fighter in the air force, and practicing nuclear strikes against targets behind what was then called the Iron Curtain, Joan gave birth to two more children, Janice Rose on August 16, 1957, and Andrew John on June 17, 1958.

One of the friends Buzz made at Bitburg was Ed White. In 1958, when White completed his time at Bitburg, Ed enrolled at the University of Michigan for graduate work in aeronautics. By now Aldrin had set his sights on the air force's experimental test pilot school at Edwards, but he believed that getting more education before going there, like Ed White was doing, would be the "perfect combination" to achieve whatever his future career goals might be. "I knew I needed more formal education," Buzz stated. "Not because I wanted to know more for the sake of knowing; I needed knowledge that I could put to useful work."

He asked the air force to send him to MIT, the school from which his father had earned a doctor of science degree some thirty years earlier. His first term in the fall of 1959 Buzz took from a bed in the Chelsea Naval Hospital, the military hospital closest to MIT. While touring southern Italy before returning from Bitburg, he and Joan had drunk some house wine that gave them both bad cases of infectious hepatitis. "I had nothing to do but study," Aldrin recalls. "It paid off because when the first-semester grades were posted in December, I was first in our class of air force officers."

In three years' time, Buzz finished a doctor of science degree (not a PhD, as has often been indicated). The title of his 259-page thesis was "Line of Sight Guidance Techniques for Manned Orbital Rendezvous." "I wanted to choose a subject which would have practical application to the air force, but which might also apply to astronautics." Wanting to contribute to the problem from the pilot's viewpoint, Aldrin zeroed in on the idea of what he called "man-controlling" rendezvous. "I knew there were computers and other sophisticated means of rendezvous being planned, but what if they failed at the last minute? Success would depend on the amount of knowledge the astronaut had about man-controlled rendezvous."

Buzz had a difficult time getting his thesis committee to approve his work. The members of the committee were Walter Wrigley, the thesis adviser and professor of instrumentation and aeronautics; Robert L. Halfman, associate professor of aeronautics and astronautics; Myron A. Hoffman, assistant professor of aeronautics and astronautics; and Norman E. Sears, group leader, Apollo Space Guidance Analysis Division, MIT Instrumentation Laboratory. Wrigley, a protégé of Dr. Charles Stark Draper and, like Draper, a specialist on inertial navigation, had serious questions about Buzz's emphasis on the need for piloting abilities to control spacecraft in precise maneuvers. So, too, did the thesis's outside reader, astronautics professor Dr. Richard Batten, who felt that Aldrin was not paying enough attention to the advantages of automated and computerized control systems.

For Buzz, passing the doctoral examination was a "very humbling" experience. "I did not know how to please academia. I took the written examination twice before doing it well enough to suit my advisers, and the oral exam was nearly my Waterloo. Deliberative, precise, and theoretical, Aldrin was not exactly quick on the verbal uptake," Buzz has explained. "But one day I emerged drenched with sweat—and victorious." Securing committee approval was even more difficult than Buzz knew at the time. Professor Batten, for one, refused to sign the approval form until the thesis underwent significant revision. "They wanted me to revise," Buzz admits, "and I agreed to do it, but my time had run out and I had an air force assignment [at its Space Systems Division in Los Angeles]. Then the air force assignment got me into the astronaut business and the folks at MIT kind of gave up expecting revisions of my thesis."

Buzz dedicated his thesis to "the crew of this country's present and future manned space programs. If only I could join them in their exciting endeavors!" In fact, he had already tried to become one of them. In the spring of 1962, as he was starting work on his doctorate, Aldrin had applied for the second class of astronauts, the one to which his friend Ed White and his future Apollo 11 commander Neil Armstrong was selected. At that point, flight test experience was still required, so Buzz tried for a waiver. "I knew darned well I wouldn't get it, but I wanted the application in the record."

By the time NASA announced that it would be selecting a third class of astronauts, Buzz had orders to work on Defense Department experiments that would be flying aboard the Gemini spacecraft, but he got to Houston another way. Passing the battery of psychological and the physical tests (there was some concern about his liver function due to the hepatitis), Major Edwin E. Aldrin Jr. became one of the fourteen astronauts announced to the public on October 17, 1963, the same class as Mike Collins.

Assigned early in his training to mission planning, Aldrin became a member of the MSC panel on rendezvous and reentry. Strangely, in his view, all of the important work on rendezvous, Buzz's specialty at MIT, was in the hands of another panel, one focused on trajectories and orbits. Buzz made the "tactical error" of pointing out "the absurdity of this arrangement." Several of his peers started referring to him as "Dr. Rendezvous." Apt though it was due to his MIT degree, the sobriquet was not meant to be flattering. Asked whether any of his fellow astronauts felt disdainful of his advanced degree, Aldrin today answers, "I think, yes." Buzz understood fully well that the term "Dr. Rendezvous" was used behind his back to make fun of him: "They were doing that, there's no doubt about it."

It is doubtful that Armstrong ever used the term, though he was certainly aware of it. "Buzz was very able in rendezvous matters. He knew more about that than anybody else in the Astronaut Office. He didn't hide that fact, but he didn't take advantage of it either, from my observations."

As an astronaut, Aldrin exhibited the same curious combination of ambitiousness and naïveté, of maneuvering and total directness, that characterized his earlier life. Unsure how Deke Slayton selected crews, Buzz asked a number of other astronauts how it all worked. When he did not get satisfactory answers from the fellows, largely because none of them really knew either, Buzz decided to go right to Slayton and ask. As crew after crew for the Gemini flights were announced in 1965 and 1966 without his name being included, Aldrin grew too frustrated to hold back. Dave Scott, like Aldrin, a Class of 1963 astronaut, got put on the crew with Armstrong for Gemini VIII. Gene Cernan, another member of his class, got the prime assignment for Gemini IX. Mike Collins, another classmate, teamed up with John Young for Gemini X. Aldrin lamented to Deke, "I understand the rendezvous business as well if not better than any of the others . . . I also told him that I had no idea at all how the selections were made, but that I felt it was honest to at least state that I had some pretty good qualifications. When I finished, there was a moment of awkward silence before Deke politely said he'd take the matter under consideration. What I had done, in my characteristic directness, was break an unstated ethic. I had been brash. I didn't think of it as a brash thing to do, but apparently that is how it was greeted by the NASA hierarchy."

When Buzz got the backup assignment behind Cernan for Gemini X, his heart sank. For someone who claims total ignorance of how Slayton scheduled crews, he fathomed that "under prevailing custom I would skip two flights and be on the prime crew of Gemini XIII." With the program to end with Gemini XII, there would be no Gemini XIII.

The tragic deaths in February 1966 of Elliot See and Charlie Bassett, the original crew for Gemini IX, altered the order and gave Aldrin his chance to fly. Jim Lovell and Buzz moved up from backup Gemini X to backup Gemini IX. With all the other shifts of assignment going on, that inked Lovell and Aldrin into the slots as the prime crew for Gemini XII, the program finale. The backyard of the Aldrin home in Nassau Bay connected to the backyard of Charlie and Jeannie Bassett. The two families and their children had become good friends. Knowing that Buzz was uncomfortable with the fact that he was, in essence, going to be making a Gemini flight because of the death of her husband, Jeannie Bassett one day took Buzz aside and, according to Buzz, reassured him that "Charlie felt you should have been in it all along. I know he'd be pleased."

Buzz went on to make one of the most successful flights in the Gemini program, featuring his remarkable five-hour EVA.

Armstrong still did not know Aldrin very well when the two men, along with Jim Lovell, were assigned as backup for Apollo 9, the prime crew for which was originally Frank Borman, Mike Collins, and Bill Anders. Eventually, when NASA decided to make Apollo 8 the circumlunar mission, Apollo 9 became Apollo 8, and Apollo 8, scheduled as the first flight to go with the LM, became Apollo 9. Mike Collins's back surgery then shifted the crew assignments. Lovell replaced Collins on Apollo 8, and Fred Haise took Lovell's place on the backup crew with Armstrong and Aldrin. In

Aldrin's view, it was automatic that Buzz would stay with Armstrong when their turn came for a prime crew, probably as Apollo 11. Yet, as we have seen, that was not really the case. Slayton gave Armstrong the option of replacing Aldrin with Lovell, a choice that Neil, after much thought, did not make.

There is good reason to think that Slayton had originally teamed Aldrin with Armstrong on the backup crew for Apollo 9 (which became Apollo 8) because he felt that the other commanders would not work as well with Buzz as Neil would. Deke recognized that Aldrin's personality grated on several of the other astronauts. For example, Frank Borman became "quite annoyed" when Aldrin took it upon himself to volunteer some suggestions to him during one preflight conference. According to Buzz, "Frank shot back that he didn't need any suggestions from me." In front of a number of responsible people, including Armstrong, Borman said, "Goddamn it, Aldrin, you have a reputation for screwing up other peoples' missions with this nitpicking planning. I don't want you screwing up my mission."

"I'm not sure I recognized at that point in time what might be considered eccentricities," Armstrong relates. "Buzz and I had both flown in Korea, and his flying skills, I was sure, were good. His intelligence was high. He was a creative thinker, and he was willing to make suggestions. It seemed to me that he was a fine person to work with. I really didn't have any qualms with him at that point."

"There was a hell of a difference between those three men," said Guenter Wendt, the head of the White Room Crew at the Cape. As the chief technician responsible for the final sealing of the astronauts into their capsule, Wendt (nicknamed "The Launchpad Führer" for his German accent and Teutonic exactness) saw all the Apollo crews in action over the course of many training and launch days, and he never saw anything like the crew of Apollo 11. "Although they were totally competent, they just didn't seem to gel as a team. Usually when a mission crew was named, they stuck together like glue. You saw one, you saw all three, together. But these three, they never did. When they drove up to the pad for tests, it was always in three separate cars. If we broke for lunch, they always drove away separately. There did not seem to be much camaraderie between the three men. I've always said that they were the first crew who weren't really a crew."

Aldrin does not quarrel in the least with Mike Collins's terse description of the Apollo 11 crew.

"Buzz, do you think that the phrase amiable strangers is apt?"

"Yes, I do. In the group of fourteen new astronauts from 1963, there wasn't anything that particularly drew me to Mike, and Neil and I hardly knew one another."

"Does that sort of distant relationship between one another make the crew of Apollo 11 historically unique?"

"Oh, yes, it really does. There was a distinct pairing, or tripling, in most of the other crews. . . . I don't consider myself the most compatible 'joiner.' I always put more emphasis, rather than on building a team, on the bigger picture."

Armstrong looks at the most famous triad in the history of space exploration quite a bit differently, as if he is not even sure what Collins means by the phrase "amiable strangers." "In general," Neil affirms, "all the crews I was on worked very well together. There were certainly slight differences, but the experiences were more alike than unlike each other in terms of the relative compatibility and cooperative nature, helping each other, and making sure everything got done." Tongue in cheek, Armstrong puts the lid on the subject by saying, "As an old navy guy, I think I did remarkably well in getting along with two air force guys."

CHAPTER 25

First Out

The very first question asked by a reporter at the Houston press conference introducing the crew of Apollo 11 on January 9, 1969, got right to the issue: "Which of you gentlemen will be the first man to step out onto the lunar surface?" As the mission commander, Armstrong began to answer, "I think I can . . ." then stopped himself in midsentence and turned to Deke Slayton, the director for flight crew operations, and asked plaintively, "You want to take a crack at it?" Slayton took over: "I don't think we've really decided that question yet. We've done a large amount of simulating, and I think which one steps out will be dependent upon some further simulations that this particular crew runs."

Somewhat uncharacteristically, Armstrong did not let the matter go without elaborating on the spot: "I'd like to say from my point of view that it would be the person whose activities for that time period would fit in best with the overall objectives on the lunar surface at that time. It's not based on individual desire; it's based on how the job can best be accomplished on the lunar surface and, since those lunar surface time lines are in a somewhat preliminary state and we have not yet had the opportunity to exercise them in simulation at this time, we have not decided yet on the order of exit from the spacecraft. I can say that the current plan, the preliminary plan, is fairly well laid out, that is, what activities take place on the lunar surface. The current plan involves one man on the lunar surface for approximately three quarters of an hour prior to the second man's emergence. Now which person is which has not yet been decided up to this point." Following up, the naïve reporter asked whether the order of the astronauts out of the LM would be decided before the mission. "Oh, yes," Armstrong answered. "It will be decided based on the simulations prior to the mission. Every step will be firmly decided prior to flight."

Thus emerged a critical issue in the life of Neil Armstrong, one that has provoked questioning, speculation, and controversy from 1969 to the present. How exactly did NASA decide which of the two astronauts inside the LM would be the first to step out onto the Moon?

Whereas several of his fellow astronauts over the years since 1969 have remarked on how personally desirous Buzz Aldrin was to be the first man on the Moon, Aldrin himself states that he experienced qualms about even being part of the first lunar landing team. "If I had had a choice," Aldrin wrote in *Return to Earth*, "I would have preferred to go on a later lunar flight. Not only would there be considerably less public attention, but the flight would be more complicated, more adventurous, and a far greater test of my abilities than the first landing." Buzz told no one about his preference at the time, other than his wife Joan, because within the astronaut corps declining a flight was "tantamount to sacrilege." "No one had ever refused a flight," Buzz states. "If I, as one individual, refused, both Mike and Neil would likely be taken off the flight. And if I did such a thing, I would so impair my position that I'd probably never be assigned to a subsequent flight."

On the other hand, Buzz's autobiography shows that he was tremendously excited by the news that he was going to be part of Apollo 11. Emerging from Slayton's office, he "telephoned Joan early and asked her to come and pick him up." In the car on the way home, Buzz told his wife, "I am going to land on the Moon." The day of the Houston news conference introducing the crew, according to Joan's diary, "Buzz spent much time explaining to me the various methods planned for obtaining rocks from the Moon."

Through the first months of 1969, there is no doubt that Aldrin believed he would be the first to step out onto the lunar surface. As Buzz explains, "Throughout the short history of the space program, beginning with Ed White's space walk and continuing on all subsequent flights, the commander of the flight remained in the spacecraft while his partner did the moving around. I had never given it much thought and had presumed that I would leave the LM and step onto the Moon ahead of Neil."

Newspaper stories reinforced this thinking. In late February 1969, the *Chicago Daily News, New Orleans Times-Picayune,* and other leading metropolitan papers ran a story by space-beat correspondent Arthur J. Snider whose headline read "Aldrin to Be First Man on the Moon." During the Apollo 9 mission a few weeks later (March 3 to 13, 1969), Dr. George E. Mueller, NASA's associate administrator for manned space flight, told a number of people, including some reporters, that Aldrin would be the first out on Apollo 11.

Buzz felt confident about the situation until he heard rumors of a literally different "outcome" in the days following Apollo 9's splashdown. The key task for Apollo 9 during its complicated ten-day flight (done in Earth rather than lunar orbit) had been to put men (Jim McDivitt and Rusty Schweickart) into a LM (nicknamed *Spider*) for the first time, separate them from the CSM (flown by Dave Scott), and get them to complete a rendezvous, one that simulated the maneuvers of an actual lunar landing mission. Although NASA would persist in its plan to have Apollo 10, scheduled for May 1969, make a full-dress rehearsal of a landing (in actual flight around the Moon), most of the mission planners felt, after the unqualified success of Apollo 9, that Apollo 11 would, indeed, be the first attempt to land. The matter of which astronaut would step out first became a subject of real import as it had not been when the Apollo 11 crew was first announced back in January.

In the days following the Apollo 9 success, Aldrin heard through the MSC grapevine that it had been decided that Armstrong would go out first rather than he. Initially, the news only puzzled him. When he heard that NASA wanted Neil to do it because he was a civilian, however, Buzz became angry: "Such a move, I thought, was an insult to the service. I understood that my country wanted to make this moment look like a triumph for all mankind in the cause of peace, but the implication was that the military service, by being denied the right to be first, was some sort of warmonger. As to any differences between Neil and myself, there simply were none. Neil had learned to fly in the service, just as I had. Well before he was chosen for the astronaut corps, he had left the service and become a civilian. When I was selected I had just completed my doctoral studies at MIT. My salary was paid by the air force, but it had been ten years since I had served in any capacity other than maintaining my flying hours."

For a few days, a chagrined Aldrin mulled over the situation, consulting only with his wife. Feeling that "the subject was potentially too explosive for even the subtlest maneuvering," Buzz decided to take the direct approach. He went to Neil.

If Aldrin expected a definitive resolution from Armstrong, he was sadly mistaken. "Neil, who can be enigmatic if he wishes, was just that," Buzz recalls. "Clearly, the matter was weighing on him as well, but I thought by now we knew and liked each other enough to discuss the matter candidly." In *Return to Earth*, Aldrin wrote that Neil, "equivocated a minute or so, then with a coolness I had not known he possessed he said that the decision was quite historical and he didn't want to rule out the possibility of going first."

Aldrin has since claimed that the description of this incident in his autobiography was exaggerated by his 1973 coauthor Wayne Warga. "If I had
been given the pen and paper, I probably wouldn't have written it that way.
I understood that it was typical not to get anything decisive on this from
Neil, particularly when it was really not his decision to make. His observation about the historical significance of stepping out first, which he did
make, was perfectly valid, and I understood it as such. It was also clear to me
that Neil did not want to discuss the matter further. There was absolutely no
indication from him of, 'Yes, I think you're right. I think I'll push someone
to make a decision.' There was no indication at all that that was going to
happen."

Aldrin tried in vain to curb his mounting frustration, "all the time struggling not be angry with Neil." Buzz then approached a few of his fellow astronauts, particularly those like Alan Bean and Gene Cernan whom he
imagined might be sympathetic because they were in the same position as
he, as lunar module pilots for Apollo 10 and Apollo 12. "I felt that I owed it
to the people who were following me," Aldrin explains, "because whatever
was decided for Apollo 11 was going to be a precedent for all the rest of the
crews. I felt that consulting some of the other guys, maybe they had a
thought or two about it that they would share since it was going to affect
them, too."

Instead of a constructive reaction to his overtures, however, Aldrin's private conversations led to the general notion that Buzz was lobbying behind
the scenes to be first. According to Gene Cernan, Aldrin had "worked himself into a frenzy" over who was going to be the first man to walk on the
Moon. "He came flapping into my office at the Manned Spacecraft Center
one day like an angry stork, laden with charts and graphs and statistics, arguing what he considered to be obvious—that he, the lunar module pilot,
and not Neil Armstrong, should be the first down the ladder on Apollo 11.
Since I shared an office with Neil, who was away training that day, I found
Aldrin's arguments both offensive and ridiculous. Ever since learning that
Apollo 11 would attempt the first Moon landing, Buzz had pursued this peculiar effort to sneak his way into history, and was met at every turn by angry
stares and muttered insults from his fellow astronauts. How Neil put up
with such nonsense for so long before ordering Buzz to stop making a fool
of himself is beyond me."

Apollo 11 crewmate Mike Collins recalls a similar incident. "Once Buzz
tentatively approached me about the injustice of the situation," Collins remembers, "but I quickly turned him off. I had enough problems without

getting into the middle of *that* one. . . . Although Buzz never came out and said it in so many words, I think his basic beef was that Neil was going to be the first to set foot on the Moon." With Collins and the other astronauts whom he approached, Aldrin did not make the case that he should be first out because he could do a better job of articulating the cosmic significance of the historic moment. "It's a good question why Buzz didn't get into those areas," Collins relates, "because he was presenting his own case and he should therefore have presented all facets of his own case, but I don't recall that he ever got into anything like that. Why he didn't—whether it was because he didn't believe it, or didn't think of it—I don't know. But, as I recall, everything Buzz presented—as most things with Buzz—was very technical, related to the checklist, the procedures, and so on."

Aldrin insists that his fellow astronauts misinterpreted his motive. "I didn't really want to be first," claims Buzz, "but I knew that we had to have a decision." On the other hand, Buzz admits that he was bothered to know that "every navy carrier test pilot was going to be in there charging hard for everything they could possibly get. It was a little different when you were an egghead from MIT like me."

With highly unflattering talk building inside the MSC about what many believed to be an Aldrin lobbying campaign, Slayton tried to put an end to it. Deke dropped by Buzz's office to say that it would probably be Neil who would be out first. At least Slayton gave Buzz a more palatable reason for the pecking order. "Neil was a member of the second group of astronauts, the group ahead of the group to which I belonged," Aldrin relates. "As such, it was only right that he step onto the Moon first, as Columbus and other historical expedition commanders had done. . . . For the decision to have been the other way, to have the commander sitting up there watching the junior guy go out, kicking up the dust, picking up the contingency sample, saying the famous words and all that, the mission would have been so criticized by all sorts of people. It would have been so inappropriate."

According to Aldrin, he was okay with Slayton saying it would be Neil; what had frustrated him all along were the effects of everyone's not knowing. "Whether or not I was going to be the first to step onto the Moon was personally no great issue. From a technical standpoint, the great achievement was making the first lunar landing, and two of us would be doing that. We all expected the actual surface activities to be relatively easy, a deduction based on detailed study and on the space walks of the Gemini program. It would probably even be simpler than the Gemini space walks because they were made in zero gravity and the lunar surface has one-sixth the

Earth's gravity. It might even seem a bit familiar." Buzz fully understood that "the larger share of acclaim and attention would go to whichever of us actually made the step," and, according to his own testimony, that was fine with him if it was to be Neil, because he was not after the acclaim. What he did resent, however, was how "the decision was stalled and stalled, until finally it was the subject of gossip, speculation, and awkward encounters" in which friends, family, and reporters kept asking him, "Who is going to be first?" Armstrong possessed the type of stoic personality that easily handled such ambiguity and uncertainty, whereas Aldrin did not.

The only "awkward encounter" that Aldrin has ever specified, however, is the one that he had with his father. One night soon after hearing from Deke Slayton on the matter, Buzz related the order of egress in a telephone conversation. The senior Aldrin "was instantly angry," Buzz explains, "and said he intended to do something about it. It took a great deal of persuasion, but I finally got him to promise he'd stay out of it." The promise was not delivered, however, until after Gene Aldrin had worked his connections, contacting a number of influential friends with connections to NASA and the Pentagon.

Emotionally hobbled by his father's intrusion, Buzz felt compelled to make one last appeal for clarity: "I went finally to George Low, director of the Apollo program office, and explained what I had heard. I said I believed I understood their need for careful consideration and added I'd happily go along with whatever was decided. It was no huge problem for me personally, but it would be in the best interest of both morale and training if their decision would be made as soon as possible." Low assured Aldrin that it would.

Monday, April 14, 1969, ended what the *New York Times* called "weeks of speculation" as to whether it would be Armstrong or Aldrin to first set foot on the Moon. At an MSC press conference, George Low indicated that "plans called for Mr. Armstrong to be the first man out after the Moon landing. . . . A few minutes later, Colonel Aldrin will follow Mr. Armstrong down the ladder." One editorial cartoon from the day after the announcement showed Armstrong and Aldrin at the open hatch of their landing craft as comically confused Alphonse and Gaston characters, both men graciously saying that the other should go ahead first while all the time trying to shove their way ahead of each other.

It is Aldrin's understanding that NASA, in the end, decided on the order of the astronauts' egress based solely on the LM's interior design and the physical positions of the two astronauts inside the LM's cockpit. It was an engineering rationale that seemed to make total sense and which came closer to satisfying Aldrin's sensibilities. According to Buzz, after the initial coolness, the two men began to "speculate together" as to how the decision should be made. "Our conclusion," Aldrin explains, "was that the decision as to who would be first would be determined by the allocation of tasks on the lunar surface and by our physical positions inside the LM itself. Unless something changed, as LM pilot I'd be on the right, a pilot's usual position, and Neil would be on the left, next to the hatch opening. It was not practical, and it was an added complication to change positions with Neil after the landing. And that, to the best of my knowledge, is how the matter was finally decided." Aldrin claims that, as soon as the announcement was made, he was okay with the situation. Mike Collins remembers otherwise: "Buzz's attitude took a noticeable turn in the direction of gloom and introspection shortly thereafter." So do many other NASA officials, including the head of launch preparations at the Cape, Guenter Wendt: "Buzz had it in mind that he should be the first one to exit the LM and place the historic footprint in the lunar soil. He alienated a lot of people, management and astronauts alike, arguing his case. Neil, the mission's commander, just plugged along, nose to the grindstone, trying to stay focused on the job."

Typically for Armstrong, Neil, in the weeks leading up to the "first out" decision, had not spoken about the matter with anyone, not even with members of his family. "Neil was recently in Wapakoneta for the funeral of his grandfather [William Korspeter]," Stephen Armstrong told a local reporter just after hearing the exciting news. "We talked about the flight, but he didn't say anything about being first on the Moon." Interestingly, Neil's father went on to say to the newspaperman, "I always thought Aldrin would be the first, because Neil is the commander."

Armstrong's own version of the "first out" decision differs from Aldrin's narrative in several salient respects. First of all, Neil relates that he was never as concerned about the matter as Aldrin came to believe Neil was, as intimated in Buzz's autobiography when he said that "the matter was weighing on him as well." As for the answer that Neil first gave to reporters back at the initial Apollo 11 news conference in January 1969, Neil explains, "I started to answer and then realized that it wasn't my prerogative to answer that question because we had not done the work at that point to determine what the procedure would be. I think Deke answered the question properly. He said that we were going to have to do some work to figure it out, which was true. At that time I didn't have any knowledge about the issue, either. As a matter of fact, I wasn't very concerned about it. That wasn't an issue in my mind. I had no preconceived notions at that point who it would be."

As for the conversation described by Aldrin (or Aldrin's writer), "I can't remember the exact conversation," asserts Armstrong today. "I can recall one point in time—and I don't know if this was the same time—when he asked me what I thought about it and my reply was, 'I'm not going to take a position on that. It's for our simulations and other people to decide.' The reality was that it was not something that I thought was really very important. It has always been surprising to me that there was such an intense public interest about stepping onto the lunar surface, let alone who did it first. In my mind the important thing was that we got four aluminum legs safely down on the surface of the Moon while we were still inside the craft. To me, there wasn't a lot of difference between having ten feet of aluminum leg between the bottom of the spacecraft in which we were standing and the surface of the Moon and having one inch of neoprene rubber or plastic on the bottom of our boots touching the lunar surface. That didn't seem to me to be a big issue, but it clearly was important to the public at large."

As unlikely as the statement would sound if it was expressed by anyone with less focus on the job and more concern with astronaut politics, Armstrong claims that he knew nothing at the time about any conversations that Aldrin was having with other astronauts about how NASA was deciding who should be first out. Neil was also oblivious of any behind-the-scenes campaigning being done on Buzz's behalf by the intemperate Gene Aldrin. "I was not aware of any of that at the time," Neil comments. "I didn't know that was going on, and I really can't say anything about it."

Not even Armstrong, though, could be unaware of the newspaper stories about him that hit the stands a few weeks before the Apollo 11 launch. With headlines such as "Did Moonman Pull Rank?" and "Armstrong Demands First-on-Moon Role," these stories reported that Armstrong had used his "commander's prerogative" to become the first man on the Moon, thereby reversing the traditional practice in the manned space program of having the number-two man make the EVA.

The source for the stories was Paul Haney, a former public affairs officer at the Manned Spacecraft Center who had just resigned from NASA to take a job as a space correspondent for a British TV network. Based on the practice in Gemini, Haney informed reporters that "the lunar module pilot, not the commander, was supposed to be the first on the Moon." For almost three years, that had been NASA's plan, "regardless of personalities."

Asked if he thought Armstrong had "pulled rank" on Aldrin, Haney remarked, "It shouldn't be that he pulled rank, but I think he was not unaware of the importance of the first man who stepped onto the Moon and looked at it very carefully and decided that perhaps it should be the commander's prerogative. Precisely why the change, I don't know, but I do know it caused quite an upset. Both Armstrong and Aldrin talked to me to see if I couldn't do something about the disquieting stories cropping up over the change in roles."

How and why Haney instigated the story, almost all of it untrue (including Neil's talking to Haney), is unknown. Perhaps the public affairs officer was disgruntled with NASA after being reassigned from MSC to NASA Headquarters in the spring of 1969. The most generous explanation is that Haney simply did not know better. Armstrong himself passed off the stories as a combination of misunderstanding and creative journalism: "There were journalists who were aware that the copilots had always been the ones to do the EVAs on Gemini, and their expectation might have been similar for Apollo."

The story was too negative for NASA not to issue a comment. In a press statement, George Low explained that preliminary studies, indeed, had been made with the lunar module pilot as the first man on the Moon, but after dozens of rehearsals of lunar surface activities, the flight training crew at the Manned Spacecraft Center had come forward with a definitive recommendation in favor of the commander going out first. "The only firm plan ever made was the one we're going to go with," Low said. Deke Slayton echoed Low's statement, declaring that the decision to have Armstrong make the first step was a management decision that in no way involved Armstrong or any of the other astronauts. Asked directly at a July 5, 1969 news conference in Houston (a press briefing at which Paul Haney was also in attendance) whether he exercised his commander's prerogative to step out first on the Moon, Armstrong answered: "In the one article I read about this, the gentleman said that I *may* have, or *could have,* done that, or something to that effect. The facts are that my recommendation was never asked for or given."

"In the Gemini program," Neil relates, "the copilot had always been the guy who did the EVA, and that was principally because the commander was always so loaded with jobs that it was impractical to try to have the commander do all the work necessary to prepare himself to do it. The copilot had much more time available and it was a much more logical thing for him to do. When we first did simulations on the ground for the Apollo surface activity, that was the way we tried to do it, probably just as a result of the Gemini experience. We tried doing it the same way. Accordingly, Buzz may have felt that, because that's the way it had been done in Gemini, that's the way it should be done, and it would be his responsibility to do it. He may have thought that it was important to him." However, as more and more ground simulations were done, it became clearer and clearer to everyone that it would be easier and safer for the commander to leave the LM first.

"We did a lot of simulations," Neil recalls. "Buzz and I both actively did simulations in a mockup of the lunar module. We went through the complete package of procedures. It wasn't just who went out of the hatch first, it was how you did it. It was not obvious what the proper way to exit through the door of the LM was, because it was quite complicated. There were a lot of considerations. In the procedures you needed to organize all the connections and hoses and the positions you'd take inside the LM. And when you were pressurized in the suit, you were like Frankenstein's monster. You were big, bulky, and bumbling and not very adept." If an astronaut was not careful, he could bump into circuits and switches inside the LM that could do real damage to the spacecraft's systems.

In the end, the ground simulations showed that the technique of having the right-hand pilot, which was Aldrin, go out first just did not work very well. According to Neil, "I think that most people felt that there was an inherent risk involved in the LM pilot stepping around the commander and going out the hatch first that was avoidable doing it the other way." When the key people in charge of the simulations, notably MSC engineers George Franklin and Raymond Zedekar, concluded that the risk was far less when the commander went out first, the mission planners scratched the Gemini procedures and wrote new ones for Apollo. "And that's the way we did it," Armstrong states. "On subsequent Apollo flights, where it wouldn't matter symbolically and historically which astronaut came out first, they all did it exactly the same way, with the commander stepping out first."

Whether Aldrin actually agreed with this finding from the lunar landing mockup simulations is not totally clear; it is only clear that he found NASA's technical reasoning much more acceptable than the idea that Armstrong should be first out because he was a civilian.

But could the men in charge of the ground simulations have reached a different conclusion if they had approached the matter with different direction from their superiors? In the opinion of Alan Bean, the lunar module pilot for Apollo 12, the argument that the commander absolutely needed to go out first because of the hatch design and interior layout of the LM was not just overblown, it was a rationalization.

"No, no, here's what you could have done if you were Buzz or myself," Bean explains. "*Before* you put on your bulky EVA backpack, you're standing in there and you can move wherever you want. Buzz moves from right to left and puts on his stuff over there, and Neil moves from left to right and puts on his stuff where Buzz had been. Then they exchange backpacks; Buzz takes Neil's backpack off the rack and hands it over to him, and Neil hands Buzz's backpack to Buzz. 'I want to get out the door, let's change.' It was a nothing thing. No matter what NASA said at the time, Buzz could have gotten out first easily; it was all about where you put your backpack on."

What Bean suggests is that NASA used the technicalities of hatch design and LM interior layout as a way of shutting the door on the entire "first out" controversy—and calming down an upset Aldrin in the process: "My opinion is, they were looking for technical reasons because they didn't want to say directly to Buzz or anyone else that 'we just want Neil to go out first.'

"Look, NASA knew both these guys," Bean exclaims. "Slayton probably approached Neil at some point early on and said to him, 'Look, we picked you to command this mission and we want the commander to go out first.' Neil wouldn't have told anyone about that sort of conversation, if it happened, but Deke very easily could have come to him and said, 'I don't want us to talk about this to anyone, but I want you out there first. And I don't want us to ever mention this again.' Knowing Deke and knowing Neil, neither of them ever would, or ever did, talk about it, as far as I know." *

A version of Bean's conjectural scenario did, in fact, take place. What is more, the technicalities of hatch design and LM interior layout were, indeed, *not* the primary matters that those in charge of the Manned Space Program were thinking about when it came to who was going to be first out.

Sometime in the middle of March 1969, in the heady days following the successful completion of Apollo 9 when it was becoming clear that Apollo 11 would likely be the first Moon landing, an informal meeting took place between the four men in Houston who had the most authority over the Apollo program. Getting their heads together were Deke Slayton, the director of flight crew operations; Bob Gilruth, the MSC director; George

---

* In his posthumously published 2001 autobiography, *Deke!*, Slayton states that if Gus Grissom had not been killed in the Apollo fire, he would have chosen Grissom to be the first man on the Moon.

Low, the Apollo program manager (and the official who had traveled throughout South America with Armstrong in 1966); and Chris Kraft, the director of flight operations.

"Everything was happening so fast during this time period," Chris Kraft relates. "But right around the time of Apollo 9, George Low and I had the same revelation. Just the two of us, George and I, had a discussion about it. I wasn't close enough to the crew training to know, but my people had been telling me—and George always knew everything about everything—that the way things looked, it was going to be Aldrin out of the LM first on Apollo 11 because he was the lunar module pilot and he was doing all the training with the scientists and with the experiments package that was going to be put on the Moon, and Buzz knew about all that in detail. It looked like the lunar module pilot was going to be the first man on the Moon. And I said to myself, 'Good God, we can't let that happen!' " Either on his own or at Kraft's inciting, Low had come to the same conclusion.

"When we realized that," Kraft continues, "we called a meeting specifically to discuss the matter. For things like this in that time period, it was usually just the four of us that got together—Gilruth, Slayton, Low, and myself. I don't think either Gilruth or Slayton felt as strongly about it as George and I did, but they didn't disagree with us, either.

"Look, we just knew damn well that the first guy on the Moon was going to be a Lindbergh. We said that to ourselves, 'He's going to be a Lindbergh.' George and I had talked about that, and we said it to Gilruth and to Slayton: 'He's going to be like Lindbergh. He's going to be the guy for time immemorial that's going to be known as the guy that set foot on the Moon first. And who do we want that to be? The first man on the Moon would be a legend, an American hero beyond Lucky Lindbergh, beyond any soldier or politician or inventor.'

"It should be Neil Armstrong.

"Neil was Neil. Calm, quiet, and absolute confidence. We all knew that he was the Lindbergh type. He had no ego. He was not of a mind that, 'Hey, I'm going to be the first man on the Moon!' That was never what Neil had in his head. The most Neil had ever said about it might have been that he wanted to be the first test pilot on the Moon or the first flier to land on the Moon. If you would have said to him, 'You are going to be the most famous human being on Earth for the rest of your life,' he would have answered. 'Then I don't want to be the first man on the Moon.' But he probably knew it was his obligation to do so. On the other hand, Aldrin desperately wanted the honor and wasn't quiet in letting it be known. Neil had said nothing. It wasn't his nature to push himself into any spotlight. He was much like Bob Gilruth himself, content to do the job and then go home.

"Not once did we criticize Buzz for his strongly held positions or for his ambition. The unspoken feeling was that we admired him and that we wanted people to speak their mind. But did we think Buzz was the man who would be our best representative to the world, the man who would be legend? We didn't. We had two men to choose from, and Neil Armstrong, reticent, soft-spoken, and heroic, was our only choice.

"It was unanimous. Collectively, we said, 'Change it.' 'Change it so the lunar module pilot is no longer going to be the first one out.' Bob Gilruth passed our decision to George Mueller and Sam Phillips at NASA Headquarters, and Deke told the crew. In our meeting, we had told Deke to do that. He did not argue with us. He did it, and I'm sure he did it in his most diplomatic way.

"Buzz Aldrin was crushed, but he seemed to take it stoically. Neil Armstrong accepted his role with neither gloating nor surprise. He was the commander, and perhaps it should always have been the commander's assignment to go first onto the Moon. Buzz probably thought that he was a better-trained man for the EVA job and had more capabilities than Neil to do the job on the lunar surface—and frankly, he may have been right. In the end, Neil gave Buzz a lot of the responsibility for surface activities. He expected Buzz to do them well and knew that Buzz could do them better than he. But nothing about performing surface activities had anything to do with the reason why we made the decision about who should be first out."

At no time in talking over the situation from every angle did Slayton, Gilruth, Low, or Kraft express the first word about the LM's interior layout or its hatch design. As Kraft attests, that was "an engineering side to it that we hadn't considered. That was a fortuitous excuse." Slayton, in particular, wanted the decision explained in technical terms. "That was Deke," Kraft explains. "He didn't want to be known as the guy that had made the decision that Buzz was not going to do it and that Neil was."

In fact, none of the four men present at the March 1969 meeting ever felt very comfortable confessing the truth about what was said there. For example, in a memorandum for the record prepared by George Low in September 1972 following a personal meeting in his office with Buzz Aldrin, Low wrote, "Aldrin asked me whether the decision as to who would be the first man on the Moon had been made by NASA Houston, NASA Headquarters, or whether it was an externally imposed decision on NASA. I told him that this was a Bob Gilruth decision based on a Deke Slayton recommendation." Obviously, Low's version of events does not precisely match up with the story subsequently told in Chris Kraft's 2001 autobiography, *Flight: My Life in Mission Control.*

Understandably, it has been hard for Aldrin to let it all go. As late as 1972, Buzz was still bothered enough by it to ask George Low how the "first out" decision had actually been made. That can only mean that Buzz was not totally convinced that the technical reasons he had been given back in 1969 were really as determinative as he and the rest of the world had been led to believe. No doubt part of the reason for Buzz's subsequent emotional distress and alcohol abuse lies in how difficult it was for him, the son of Gene Aldrin, to be the second man on the Moon.

Buzz never knew the first thing about the Gilruth-Slayton-Low-Kraft meeting until Chris Kraft wrote about it in his autobiography, nor did Armstrong. Even after becoming aware of the behind-the-scenes, nontechnical factors in the decision making, Neil has remained convinced that engineering considerations related to the interior layout of the LM played a primary role in determining who should be the first man out: "It just seems to me that the fact that all six Moon landings were done the same way is pretty strong evidence that that was the proper way to do it. Otherwise, they would have changed it. I can't imagine the other commanders, especially someone like Al Shepard [commander of Apollo 14], agreeing to something if it wasn't the right way to do it. Knowing their nature, the other commanders would have done it or certainly attempted to do it differently, if they had thought there was a better way. I would have felt the same about it myself."

CHAPTER 26

Dialectics of a Moon Mission

Buzz Aldrin's concern over who should be the first out did nothing to help the working relationship of the Apollo 11 crew. At the same time his sour feelings never seriously impaired the crew's training for its historic mission because Armstrong's stoic personality did not allow it to. If the commander had been a confrontational sort like Frank Borman or Alan Shepard, the situation with Aldrin might easily have turned highly injurious to the mission.

"Neil would have regarded that kind of infighting as sort of beneath him," explains Mike Collins. Even if he had known about the behind-the-scenes campaigning by Buzz's father, "Neil was not the sort that would have gotten into the fray and presented counterarguments. He always rose above internecine warfare of that kind." Not only that, as Collins testifies. "I never heard Neil say a bad thing about Buzz. Never. I mean, what Neil thought about Buzz, God only knows. But their working relationship, as I saw it, was always extremely polite and, from Neil to Buzz, in no way critical."

The training for the first Moon landing was intense enough to challenge the patience and goodwill of the entire NASA team, not just the Apollo 11 crew. Not only did the astronauts need to be made ready, so too did the entire NASA ground apparatus, including the Mission Control Center, the tracking network, the quarantine facility to house a crew that might bring back lunar "bugs," not to mention the Saturn V rocket, Command Module No. 107, and Lunar Module No. 5. Armstrong, Collins, and Aldrin trained fourteen-hour days, six days a week for six full months. They often worked another eight hours on Sundays.

Beginning January 15, 1969, until July 15, 1969, the day before the launch, the crew of Apollo 11 logged a total of 3,521 actual training hours. That equates to 126 hours per week, or 42 hours per crew member, in specified training programs and exercises. Roughly another 20 hours per week were taken up by reading, studying, doing paperwork, poring over mission plans and procedures, talking to colleagues, traveling to training facilities, suiting up and getting suits off, and other routine work. Armstrong and Aldrin logged 1,298 and 1,297 training hours, respectively, while Collins recorded some 370 hours less. Half of Collins's hours came inside the CSM simulator, where he worked physically apart from Armstrong and Aldrin (though for special integrated simulations all three astronauts in the two different simulators would be connected to Mission Control). On the other hand, there were very few hours when Neil and Buzz were not working side by side. Nearly a third of their training time was inside the cramped quarters of the LM simulator, practicing the Moon landing they were about to make as a duo.

The overriding objective of Apollo 11 was to get the Moon landing done. Training for surface activities represented less than 14 percent of the astronauts' time. That included preparing Armstrong and Aldrin to collect geological samples and to set up all the planned lunar surface experiments, as well as to learn how to handle the Extravehicular Mobile Unit (EMU). This vital piece of equipment, the EMU, was composed of all the protective apparel and paraphernalia worn during lunar surface work, including suit, helmet, gloves, outer boots, backpack, remote control, hoses, cables, liquid-cooled garment (LCG), outer visor, and so forth. During EMU training, the astronauts "checked out" every part of this assembly.

"We practiced the lunar surface work until we were reasonably confident in our ability to carry out the surface plan," Armstrong states. "If the descent and the final approach to landing were rated a nine on a ten-point scale of difficulty, I would put the surface work down at a two. Not that there weren't some high risks involved with it, because there were. Certainly, we were completely dependent on the integrity of our pressure suits, and there were significant questions about the thermal environment—whether we would have overheating problems, because it was going to be warm out there on the lunar surface, over 200 degrees Fahrenheit. We did some of our surface simulation work in the altitude chamber, with thermal simulation, and those had worked well. So we reached a confidence level that it was going to work fine. I didn't have a lot of concern whether we were getting enough lunar surface practice because we got plenty of practice on operating defective equipment. The only real concerns involved the unknowns that we couldn't simulate, because we didn't know what they were.

"In the end, the ground simulations proved to be pretty good even though the lunar gravity conditions could not be matched," Armstrong continues. "The suits were pressurized and, when suits were inflated, they carried a lot of the weight, so the fact that we were going around with a hundred pounds or so of equipment on our backs wasn't a problem. As for simulating the nature of the lunar terrain itself, despite photographs and data from the Surveyor spacecraft that had made soft landings on the Moon, no one knew precisely what the lunar surface would be like. Our guess was okay but not very much like the actual surface when we got there."

Ever since the selection of the New Nine in 1962, "All of us were exposed over several years to Geology 101. We had very fine instructors who were very knowledgeable about astrogeology and selenology, the astronomical study of the Moon. We went to Hawaii, to Iceland, great places to focus on volcanic rocks. The assumption was that on the Moon we would encounter tectonic formations principally, or remnants of volcanic and tectonic lava flows, that sort of thing. I was very tempted to sneak a piece of limestone up there with us on Apollo 11 and bring it back as a sample. That would have upset a lot of apple carts! But we didn't do it."

Harrison "Jack" Schmitt, a Harvard-trained geologist who had worked for the U.S. Geological Survey in New Mexico, Montana, and Alaska, did a lot to prepare Armstrong and Aldrin for their lunar rock collecting. "Jack worked diligently and endlessly to make things a bit easier for us and tell us what was important," Neil relates.

"There was little chance for Neil and Buzz to be trained in a systematic way," Jack Schmitt explains. "Some of the geologists in NASA claimed that by the end of the training the astronauts received the equivalent of a master's degree in geology. Well, even if they did, that's not what you wanted. You wanted people to be able to be very focused on a particular set of tasks that had to be done, and you wanted them as knowledgeable as you could possibly make them in a short amount of time about the relevant geological aspects of their mission."

Armstrong agrees that his geological training could have been more effective: "I don't think we had much specific geological preparation for Apollo 11 itself, which differs from some of the later flights when crews were going into specific areas of the Moon with very specific geological goals. We were going into a mare, a lunar 'sea,' an area where the principal feature would just be the regolith and the accumulation of debris on the surface around the craters."

Another reality for Apollo 11 was that Armstrong and Aldrin would not have much time to spend out on the lunar surface. "That was principally dictated by the fact that we didn't know how long our supply of water for the cooling of our suits would last," Armstrong explains. "Neither that nor our metabolic rate could be duplicated on Earth in a lunar gravity. The only way you could try to do it was in the zero-g airplane, the KC-135, but the flight times in those were so limited that we could not get realistic data. So it was just an unknown. The mission planners wanted to be conservative in their estimate. As it turned out, we were able to stay out a little bit longer than our plan stipulated. After getting back in the craft we drained the water tanks to see how much water remained. From that we got a useful data point against the time that we had been out."

Though Armstrong enjoyed geology, he found the nature of the discipline a bit puzzling: "The geologists had a wonderful theory they called the 'theory of least astonishment.' According to the theory, when you ran into a particular rock formation, you hypothesized how it might have occurred and created as many scenarios as you could think of as to how it might have gotten there. But the scenario that was the least astonishing was the one you were supposed to accept as the basis for further analysis. I found that fascinating. It was an approach to logic that I had never experienced in engineering." Yet it is precisely Armstrong's engineering approach that Jack Schmitt connects with Neil's geologic capabilities, citing Neil's collection of rock samples as "the *best* that anybody did on the Moon."

All of the Apollo training was important, but no aspect of it was more critical to mission success than the work done in the flight simulators. "They taught us to fly these incredible machines with subtleties and complexities that even their flying counterparts did not possess," Mike Collins explains. "Their job was to duplicate, insofar as they could, the spacecraft and the space environment."

The two main simulators were the command module simulator, built (as the CSM itself was) by North American, and the lunar module simulator, built by the LM designer, Grumman. Collins spent the lion's share of time in the former, Armstrong and Aldrin in the latter. Apollo 10 and Apollo 16 astronaut John Young dubbed the command module simulator "The Great Train Wreck" for its jumbled array of differently shaped boxes and compartments built around a full-size mockup of the command module's interior, down to the identical dials, controls, switches, equipment, and even color schemes in the genuine article. With all of the controls and instruments hooked up to a bank of computers in a back room as well as to consoles in Mission Control, the CSM simulator was dynamic and totally inter-active. Looking out the windows as they were making their "flights," the as-tronauts saw rough displays of the Earth, sky, Moon, and stars. "Here the fidelity broke down," as Collins notes, explaining that, for training pur-poses, "It didn't matter that in the simulator the star Antares was not pre-cisely its true shade of red, only that it be in the proper position for a measurement with the sextant."

"On balance, the simulations were quite good," echoes Armstrong. "They would certainly be better today with the improvements in technology that have occurred over the past thirty-five years, but for the time they were certainly the best, most advanced simulators ever constructed anywhere. They did a good enough job to give us the level of confidence that we needed, and I think that is evident by the fact that six out of six lunar land-ings that were attempted all turned out successfully."

During his Apollo 11 training, Armstrong spent 164 hours in the CSM simulator, which was only about one-third of the time that Collins, the CM pilot, spent in it. Naturally, given his primary responsibility in the mission, Neil spent considerably more time practicing lunar landings, 383 hours in the LM simulator and 34 in the LLTV or LLRF, for a total of 417 hours of Moon landing simulation. His grand total of 581 hours in a simulator equates to over 72 days—more than 10 full weeks—of 8-hour days in a sim-ulator. Aldrin compiled even more time in simulators than did Neil: 18 more in the CM simulator and 28 more in the LM simulator. Unlike Neil, Buzz did not fly either the LLTV or LLRF during the six-month-long prepa-ration for Apollo 11.

"You are trying to build simulators to be exactly like the real thing, but they never are able to get it to the degree of reality that it flies as easily as a real machine." In the case of a Moon landing, they could not simulate such difficulties as a cloud of dust agitated by the LM's descent rockets. "If you could fly the simulations with confidence," Neil remarks, "then you could be quite confident that you'd be able to handle the real vehicle.

"People who had not been involved in simulator development during their career usually just tried to 'win.' They tried to operate perfectly all the time and avoid simulator problems. I did the opposite. I tried actively to en-courage simulator problems so I could investigate and learn from them.

"I'm sure that some of the guys were well aware of my approach," surely more so following what has become a rather notorious incident involving Armstrong and Aldrin's particularly taxing "run" in the LM simulator. The source for the story is Mike Collins.

"Neil and Buzz had been descending in the LM [simulator] when some catastrophe had overtaken them, and they had been ordered by Houston to abort. Neil, for some reason, either questioned the advice or was just slow to act on it, but in any event, the computer printout showed that the LM had descended below the altitude of the lunar surface before starting to climb again. In plain English, Neil had crashed the LM and destroyed the machine, himself, and Buzz.

"That night in the crew quarters Buzz was incensed and kept me up far past my bedtime complaining about it. I could not discern whether he was concerned about his actual safety in flight, should Neil repeat this error, or whether he was simply embarrassed to have crashed in front of a roomful of experts in Mission Control. But no matter, Buzz was in fine voice, and as the scotch bottle emptied and his complaints became louder and more specific, Neil suddenly appeared in his pajamas, tousle-haired and coldly indignant, and joined the fray. Politely I excused myself and gratefully crept off to bed, not wishing to intrude in an intercrew clash of technique or personality.

"Neil and Buzz continued their discussion far into the night, but the next morning at breakfast neither appeared changed, ruffled, nonplussed, or pissed off, so I assume it was a frank and beneficial discussion, as they say in the State Department. It was the only such outburst in our training cycle."

Aldrin's version of the late-night exchange is a little different. "The three of us often ate dinner quite late in our quarters. Afterwards, Mike and I sat around having a drink and talking while Neil had gone off to bed. Mike said something like, 'Well, how did it go? What did you guys do in the simulator today?' and I said, 'Well, we lost control during an abort.' [Neil insists that Mission Control did not order an abort.] Now just how loud I said that, I can't really say. But what I said, I felt was between the two of us, between Mike and me. I didn't feel I needed to express my feelings about this to Neil, because that was just not Neil's and my relationship. In the normal course of what we were doing, I did not critique him. But Mike asked me a question about the simulation, so I told him what happened. It was a surprise to both of us when Neil came out of his bedroom and said, 'You guys are making too much noise. I'm trying to sleep.' " Neil did not say a word at the time to defend what he had done in the simulation, why he chose not to abort. "That wouldn't have been Neil," explains Aldrin.

What Aldrin was explaining to Collins when Neil came out to quiet them down was that "I thought we were playing a game and we should make an attempt to do everything we could to win the game, and the sooner we did it when we saw that things were going bad for us, the better off we'd be and

the more in keeping with what we'd actually do in a real situation like that."
The most important thing in every situation, Aldrin said to Collins, was not
to crash. "I felt analyzing this and that system and whatever was not playing
the game properly as far as the simulator people were concerned. If they
threw a failure at us and we were losing control of the LM, would we in real
flight actually go on and land? I'm not sure we would. The same way that if
something disabled the commander, or disabled the primary guidance, or
disabled the landing radar, why, we wouldn't land on the first try, we'd abort
and come back. Clearly, there was a difference between Neil and I in how
we reacted to the simulation. Neil had his reason for doing what he did. It
was between him and the simulator people to decide what he got out of that.
As for me, I was there to support what was going on in the training, almost
as an observer. Thus my answer to Mike's question about my evaluation of
what had happened."

Some versions of the simulation story that have been told over the years
suggest that Aldrin also urged Armstrong to abort, but Neil states, "I don't
recall that Buzz asked me to abort—ever—I don't remember that. What I
do remember is that the descent trajectory that we were on during the simulation and the information we had available to us had become seriously de-
graded, and I thought that it was a great time to test the Mission Control
center, 'Okay, guys, let's see what you can do with this.'

"I knew that I could abort at any time—and probably successfully—but
then you lose the mission, the rest of the simulation. This was a chance to
test the control center. Buzz took that as a black mark against us. He thought
it was a mark against his ability to perform, a mark against both of us and
against our crew ability. I didn't look at it that way at all. It was a complete
difference of opinion, and he expressed his concern to me later that night."

As for precisely what went on during that late-night exchange between
him and Aldrin, "I don't really remember the details of that, but I do remember that Buzz expressed his displeasure. He had a different way of looking at the sims. He never liked to crash in a real simulation, while I thought it
was a learning experience for all of us. Not just for the crew but also for the
control center personnel. We were all in it together."

Interestingly, this story of the simulation-that-Armstrong-would-not-
abort is reminiscent of Neil's April 1962 flight in the X-15, the one in which
his aircraft ballooned up and ended up dangerously over Pasadena. In
both cases, Neil was trying to promote technological learning through di-
alectical experimentation. "If we couldn't come up with a solution or the
ground controllers couldn't come up with a solution, that was an indication

to me that, for one, I needed to understand that part of the flight trajectory better." As a matter of fact, as a result of his crashing into the lunar surface during the particular simulation under review, Neil "constructed a plot of altitude versus descent rate with bands on it that I hadn't had before, so that I could tell when I was getting into a questionable area. If I had aborted when everyone wanted me to, I probably would not have bothered to even make that." At the same time, the "botched" simulation caused the flight director and his people to reevaluate how they had analyzed the situation. "I'm sure they improved their approach to understanding it, too, and knowing when they were getting into a dangerous area," Armstrong states. "So it did serve a valuable purpose. I was a little disappointed that we didn't figure it out soon enough, but you learn through the process. These were the most extensive simulations I had ever encountered—and they needed to be. The Moon landing was a bigger project, a more extensive project, with more people involved, than any of us had ever encountered."

Four months into training, Apollo 10 flew to the Moon. Launched on May 18, 1969, with a crew composed of three veterans of Gemini rendezvous missions—commander Tom Stafford, command module pilot John Young, and lunar module pilot Gene Cernan—the eight-day mission was a very successful full-dress rehearsal of the Moon landing. Apollo 10 achieved a number of space firsts, including the first CSM-LM operations in the cislunar and lunar environment, the first CSM-LM docking in translunar trajectory, the first LM undocking in lunar orbit, the first LM staging in lunar orbit, and the first manned LM-CSM docking in lunar orbit. About the only thing Apollo 10 did not accomplish was the lunar landing itself, though its LM—nicknamed *Snoopy*—did swoop down to within a mere 50,000 feet of the proposed Apollo 11 landing site before shooting back to orbit and redocking with *Charlie Brown,* the command module.

Apollo 10 aided preparations for Apollo 11 in a number of ways. First, as Armstrong explains, "There was the matter of lunar module handling qualities, LM responsiveness, and LM engine operations. These had been studied initially in Earth orbit during Apollo 9, with Jim McDivitt doing some very good work. We had a good, solid foundation from Apollo 9, but we were very interested in learning everything we could from Apollo 10 and the experiences of Tom Stafford and Gene Cernan in operating the LM and in how well they were able to control the machine's attitude in flight. We wanted to know, for example, how similar or different was flying the actual

LM from flying the simulator and from flying the LLTV? Could we expect it to be like our experience on the ground had led us to believe it would be? What were the characteristics of the engine operation? We wanted to learn anything we could about that, and Apollo 10 turned out to be very helpful there; it told us a lot."

There was also the matter of the lunar environment itself, especially the possibly significant gravitational effects that mascons might have on the flight paths of the Apollo 11 spacecraft. "I was very interested in additional information about the mascons based on the Apollo 10 experience," relates Armstrong. Mascons were areas beneath the visible lunar surface, generally in the mares, that because the interior rock was of greater density than that of the surrounding area, exerted a slightly higher gravitational force. From the flights of the five unmanned Lunar Orbiter spacecraft of 1966 and 1967 (all of them enormously successful), telemetry data indicated that the Moon's gravitational pull was not uniform. Perturbations likely caused by mascons had led to slight dips in the paths of the Lunar Orbiters. Data from the circumlunar flight of Apollo 8 left the mascon effects in question.

"So, clearly, the guys who were trying to map these gravity anomalies were very interested in all the data they could get concerning these perturbations to the orbit," Armstrong states. "The fact that Apollo 10, flying the same orbit that we were going to be flying, was documenting the influence of the mass concentrations on our own exact trajectory was very important to us, because mascons could affect how well we would be able to get to our desired landing point. Naturally, we wanted do that as accurately as we could.*

----

* Even after Apollo 10, some of the Apollo mission planners were still concerned about the effects of mascons. For example, Howard W. "Bill" Tindall Jr., the chief of Apollo data priority coordination and one of the unsung geniuses at the MSC in Houston, asked two days before the launch of Apollo 11 in one of his highly respected internal memoranda known as "Tindallgrams," "What do we do if one of those big damn lumps of gold is buried so near the LM that it screws up our gravity alignment on the lunar surface?" If that was the case, Tindall worried, the LM's alignments could be in error, resulting in the processing of mistaken ground trajectory data during the flight of the LM's ascent stage back to a docking with the command module in lunar orbit. Just in case "the various far-flung experts," as Tindall called them, were wrong in their prediction that mascons would have no significant effect on the lunar surface gravity alignments, Tindall recommended a series of measures to ensure that the LM's two different computer guidance systems, known as AGS (Abort Guidance System) and PNGS (Primary Navigation, Guidance, and Control System, pronounced *pings*) could be effectively aligned. Howard W. Tindall Jr., Apollo Data Priority Coordination, to [a long list of individuals at the MSC], "Subject: How we will handle the effects of mascons on the LM lunar surface gravity alignments," July 14, 1969, NASA Manned Spacecraft Center, copy in Historical Archives, University of Houston—Clear Lake. There is a CD that contains most of the "Tindallgrams."

"Stafford and Cernan did a superb job flying almost precisely the same track over the lunar surface that Apollo 11 would be flying. They took superb pictures of the descent and landing areas all the way down to before the time of engine ignition. So that was very useful. As a result of all the fine photographs from Apollo 10, Buzz and I developed a very high level of confidence in our ability to recognize our flight path and principal landmarks along the way. By the time we launched in July, we knew all the principal landmarks on our descent path by heart and, equally importantly, we knew all the landmarks on our way prior to the point at which we would ignite our descent engines. That was important as a cross-check, to be able to determine that we were, in fact, geographically—or more precisely, selenographically—over the exact place we wanted to be over—and as close to the scheduled time on the flight plan as possible."

Finally, the success of Apollo 10 meant that Apollo 11 would certainly be the first landing mission. The only uncertainty was the date of the launch. A few weeks after Apollo 10, Deke Slayton asked Armstrong, "Well, how do you feel? What's your assessment of how you stand? Are you ready?" Armstrong answered: "Well, Deke, it would be nice to have another month of training, but I cannot in honesty say that I think we have to have it. I think we can be ready for a July launch window." It is Armstrong's assumption that Slayton, on the basis of that conversation, went to his gathering with Bob Gilruth, George Low, and Chris Kraft and announced, "Well, I've talked to Neil, and he says they are going to be ready."

On June 11, 1969, NASA announced that the Apollo 11 astronauts had received the go-ahead for the landing attempt. Their launch would come on July 16 with the historic landing scheduled for Sunday afternoon, July 20.

The conscientious, highly professional, and vigorous manner in which Armstrong, Collins, and Aldrin pursued every item on their six-month training agenda gave NASA great confidence in the crew. Yet the Apollo 11 mission was replete with unknowns, uncertainties, and unexplored risks—some technological, others human. How would individual astronauts perform in the clutch, during a crisis moment when some instinct or impulse of personality might supersede the rational mind? In Commander Neil Armstrong, NASA managers took a calculated risk that, in order to achieve the landing, he might push the envelope, his luck, or his abilities a little too far.

NASA established its "mission rules" as a system of preventive checks. The genesis of the concept had come early in the Mercury program from

Chris Kraft, Walt Williams, Bob Gilruth, and other veteran engineers who together had made the transition from NACA aeronautical flight research to the NASA Space Task Group. Early on, they decided they had better formally record every one of their important thoughts and observations about the Mercury capsule, about the Redstone (and later Atlas) rocket that was to launch Mercury, about each flight control system, and every possible flight situation. As Kraft relates, "We noted a large number of what-ifs, too, along with what to do about them. Then we printed the whole bunch in a booklet and called it our mission rules." It was an unprecedented type of publication based on some unprecedented thinking.

As Gemini came on the heels of Mercury, and Apollo in his chariot took over from Gemini's twins, the booklets of mission rules became *books* of mission rules. In preparation for Apollo 11, it took many months for teams of mission planners, flight directors, simulation experts, engineers, and astronauts to talk over, debate, write down, review, redraft, and finalize the rules for what was to be the first Moon landing. The first complete set of rules for Apollo 11 was not published until May 16, 1969, two months before launch. Rules were then updated weekly as ongoing simulations revealed where new rules or changes to rules had to be made.

The mission rules book for Apollo 11 came to span more than 330 pages, evolving from "Initial Rules" (white paper, May 16, 1969) through an "A Revision" (pink paper, June 20, 1969), "B Revision" (yellow paper, July 3, 1969), and ending in the "C Revision" (blue paper, July 11, 1969). Each revision came printed on a different color paper so that the flight directors could see that their flight controllers had incorporated the changes properly into their books. Even though the C Revision came out only five days before the launch, it was not the end to the changes. On the day of the launch (July 16) itself, Flight inserted seven "write-in" changes to the rules. One of the last-minute changes, unknown to the crew of Apollo 11 itself, stated that there was no need to abort the landing if the LM's onboard computer experienced a specific series of program alarms.

Inside the mission rules book were thirty-one topical sections and three appendices. The longest section was section two, "Flight Operations Rules," concerning the overall policy for mission conduct, the treatment of risk by mission phases, and redundancy management. In the other thirty sections could be found all the rules for launch, for trajectory and guidance, for communications, for engine burns, for docking, for EVA, for electrical systems, and for aeromedical emergencies. There were rules to cover every conceivable problem, situation, and contingency.

Shorthand written instructions laid out how each contingency was to be handled by everyone involved. For example, in section twenty-two of the document pertaining to "LM Electrical Power," more than two dozen rules covered what should happen in the event that the lunar module experienced electrical power problems anytime during its descent to the surface, while on the surface, or when leaving the surface of the Moon. A mission rule from part five of section three of the book required an abort if the radar data was not obtained before the LM descended to 10,000 feet. In each section of the mission rules book there was a summary of all the "Go/NoGo" situations (or "Stay/NoStay" situations, in the case of whether to stay or abort immediately after landing on the lunar surface). This was the plain-spoken and impossible-to-mistake terminology used by the flight director in a final systems check to make sure that his controllers were confident about proceeding on to the next phase of the mission.

Another very critical mission rule—one that became a matter of grave urgency during the descent of Armstrong and Aldrin to the lunar surface—stated that once the warning light came on inside the LM showing a low level of fuel for descent, the astronauts had one minute either to commit to the landing or abort.

So many mission rules were written for Apollo 11 and for the subsequent Apollo missions that they had to be organized according to a numerical code. To wit, Item 11 under Rule 5-90 dictated that "powered descent will be terminated for the following primary guidance system failures—105, 214, 402 (continuing), 430, 607, 1103, 1107, 1204, 1206, 1302, 1501, and 1502." There was no way any single person could remember all the mission rules, let alone the number and content of every computer program alarm; it would have been like memorizing the dictionary. During a spaceflight, flight controllers had to keep their copies of the rules book very close by.

For many of the rules, there was a defined margin, some leeway, a little give. Yet, not until all mission rule requirements were met to the satisfaction of the flight director—known in Houston's Mission Control simply as "Flight"—could any vital decision about the flight be made and acted upon. Some mission rules could be interpreted so as to leave an ultimate decision in the hands of the astronauts, but that sort of independent, on-the-spot judgment was not something that NASA managers wanted to encourage, not even for someone as solidly dependable and experienced as Armstrong.

According to Gene Kranz, one of Mission Control's flight directors, "Buzz Aldrin was the crewman usually involved in discussing mission rules, demonstrating his knowledge of a variety of subjects, and generally dominating the crew side of the conversations. Neil Armstrong seemed more the observer than the participant, but when you looked at his eyes, you knew he was the commander and had all the pieces assembled in his mind. I don't think he ever raised his voice. He just saved his energy for when it was needed. He would listen to our discussions, and if there was any controversy, he and Aldrin would try out our ideas in the simulators and then give feedback through Charlie Duke to the controllers. [Astronaut Duke served as one of the CapComs for Apollo 11.] Mike Collins used a different tactic. He worked directly with the Trench and system guys." ("The Trench" was the nickname for the men in Mission Control who worked as the flight dynamics team, led by the Flight Dynamics Officer, or FIDO.)

Armstrong accepts Kranz's characterization: "It is true that Buzz was talkative and very involved in conversations, and I was probably more reserved. I think that was just our nature."

Almost all the mission rules were written down and formally agreed upon; a very few were not. The most important unwritten rules for Apollo 11 concerned the landing.

"To get a handshake on the unwritten rules for the landing," Kranz remembers, "I had a final strategy session before simulation startup with Neil, Buzz, Mike, and Charlie Duke. It was in this session that I outlined the landing strategy. We had only two consecutive orbits to try to land on the Moon. If we had problems on the first orbit, we would delay to the second. If we still had problems, we would start the lunar descent to buy five additional minutes to solve the problem. If we couldn't come up with answers, we would abort the landing and start a rendezvous to recover the LM, then jettison it and head back home. If problems surfaced beyond five minutes, we would try to land and then lift off from the surface after a brief stay. We would try for the landing even if we could only touch down and then lift off two hours later when the CSM passed overhead in lunar orbit with proper conditions for rendezvous.

"I knew Armstrong never said much," Kranz continues, "but I expected him to be vocal on the mission rule strategy. He wasn't. At that time he was silent. It took time to get used to his silence. As we went through the rules, Neil would generally smile and/or nod. I believe that he had set his own rules for the landing, I just wanted to know what they were. My gut feeling said he would press on, accepting any risk as long as there was even a remote chance to land. I believed we were well in sync, since I had a similar set of rules. I would let the crew continue as long as there was a chance."

Again, Armstrong today does not quarrel with Kranz's interpretation: "I had high respect for mission rules and how they were developed and their usefulness and the advantage of everyone agreeing on what was the proper thing to do. But I would admit that if everything seemed to be going well and there was a mission rule that interrupted and said we have to do such and such, I would have been willing to use my commander's prerogative on the scene and overrule the mission rule if I thought that was the safest route. After all, aborts were not very well understood phenomenon—no one had ever done an abort. You were shutting off engines, firing pyrotechnic separation devices, igniting other engines in midflight. Doing all of that in close proximity to the lunar surface was not something in which I had a great deal of confidence.

"There is some truth to what Gene is saying, but I wouldn't go as far as to say that even if there was only a *remote* chance to land . . . I wouldn't have accepted that. I would have said, as long as there is a *good* chance of landing, I would proceed." Not that Armstrong ever explicitly verbalized his perspective on this crucial matter to Kranz or anyone else. "I probably didn't, unless it came out in the context of a specific rule which I thought was irrational for some reason. Then I might have argued against it."

Like Kranz, a nervous Chris Kraft was also bothered by the fact that he could not be sure what Armstrong might do to override mission rules and force a lunar landing to happen. "In the last month, we'd had Neil in Mission Control to go over the rules for lunar descent, landing, surface operations, and takeoff," Kraft explains. "Mission rules could leave the ultimate decision to the astronaut, but that wasn't something we encouraged. Now I wanted to make certain that all of us understood exactly where we were. We got down to the finest details—descent-engine performance, computer bugs that we knew about, landmarks on the lunar surface, even talking through the most unlikely events we could imagine during the landing.

"The computer and the landing radar got particular attention. We'd be sending last-minute updates to the computer on the lunar module's trajectory, its engine performance, and location over the Moon. Until *Eagle* was about ten thousand feet high, its altitude was based on Earth radars, and its guidance system could be off by hundreds of thousands of feet. Then the LM's own landing radar was supposed to kick in and provide accurate readings.

"That led to some heated discussion. Neil worried that an overzealous flight controller would abort a good descent, based on faulty information. 'I'm going to be in a better position to know what's happening than the people back in Houston,' Neil said over and over.

"And I'm not going to tolerate any unnecessary risks," Kraft retorted. "That's why we have mission rules."

Arguing about the specifics of the landing radar, Kraft insisted that if the landing radar failed, an abort was mandatory: "I didn't trust the ability of an astronaut, not even one as tried and tested as Neil Armstrong, to accurately estimate his altitude over a cratered lunar surface. It was unfamiliar terrain, and nobody knew the exact size of the landmarks that would normally be used for reference." Finally, Kraft and Armstrong agreed. "That mission rule stayed as written," Kraft recalls. "But I could tell from Neil's frown that he wasn't convinced. I wondered then if he'd overrule all of us in lunar orbit and try to land without a radar system.

"Those conversations came back to me when I saw Neil a few days before the launch," Kraft relates. " 'What can we do?' I asked Neil. 'Is there anything we've missed?' 'No, Chris, we're ready. It's all done except the countdown.' He was right. If there was anything undone, none of us could say what it was. . . . We had come to this last point, and for a moment I felt my legs shake."

Because he, too, was worried that the crew might take unnecessary risks in order to make the landing, Dr. Thomas Paine, the NASA administrator, even got into the act. In the week before the launch, he made a point of speaking to Armstrong. According to Neil, Paine told him, "If we didn't get a chance to land and came back, he would give us the chance to go again, on the very next flight. I believe he meant it at that point."

The truth was, Paine told every subsequent Apollo crew the very same thing. It was his way of encouraging the crews not to try anything stupid, thinking it would be their only chance. If Apollo 11's landing had been aborted, Armstrong was ready to take the NASA administrator up on his offer. "Had that circumstance happened, my guess is I would have said, 'Yeah, let's go again.' We were all trained. The requirements would not be burdensome at all to go through the same process. We'd love to have another flight, and we would have done it."

Armstrong, Collins, and Aldrin trained up to the very last moment. This fact led to a concern that was picked up on—and mostly misinterpreted—by the news media, that the astronauts were being rushed to get in all of the training necessary for the flight. "The reason that was of concern," Armstrong explained to reporters at the time, was because "the final training for a crew is the last thing that takes place." Before final training of a crew can take place, "the procedures must be developed in the simulations after they are completely set up and ready to 'fly' with all the pertinent checklists and so on. These were the intermediate, pacing items leading to the final training. There was a good deal of concern in our own minds and the minds of many in the organization that all these things for the descent to and ascent from the surface would fall into place in time." By the time they left Houston in late June for their final days of training at Cape Kennedy, the crew, in Neil's words, felt "very fortunate" that all the mission rules, techniques, and checklists had, in fact, been worked out and were fully based on a thorough series of highly integrated flight simulations.

The crew moved into their astronaut living quarters at the Cape on June 26. Beginning at the stroke of midnight on the twenty-seventh, they participated in a weeklong trial countdown. Simulated launch came on the morning of July 3 precisely at 9:32 A.M., the exact time scheduled for the real launch. Before the trial started, the three men entered a strict physical quarantine that was to last for two weeks before the flight and endure for three more weeks after the flight. The quarantine was invoked in order to limit the astronauts' exposure to infectious organisms. Dr. Charles E. Berry, chief astronaut physician, gave them their last head-to-toe going-over the day the simulated countdown began. Besides checking on their health (Dr. Berry reported to the press that the crew was "in excellent physical shape" and looked "amazingly relaxed"), the doctor wanted to catalog all organisms that were apparently normal to the three men's systems. A growing fear from the scientific community that hostile, alien organisms might accompany the astronauts and their rock samples back to Earth—a concern hyped by the publication of the sensational Michael Crichton novel *The Andromeda Strain,* a June 1969 Book-of-the-Month Club selection—had persuaded (even *forced*) NASA to take every possible preventive measure against contamination from extraterrestrial life.

"The National Academy of Sciences was given the task of evaluating the potential danger from lunar contaminants on the Earth," Armstrong recalls. "The scientists said that the chances were extremely unlikely, but NASA in consultation with the academy decided to have a contamination facility and put us in a quarantine after the mission for a period of time equal to the expected incubation time of any disease that could provide an epidemic. That period lasted for twenty-one days from the time we left the surface of the Moon."

On July 5, the crew of Apollo 11 returned to Houston from Florida for a media day. First up in the morning was a full press conference staged in the movie theater inside the MSC visitors' center. After that came sessions with the wire services, another with a group of magazine writers, and finally, interviews separately filmed with each of the three television networks for broadcast that evening. Before it was over, the three astronauts endured a fourteen-hour day answering questions from several hundred international reporters and journalists, a gaggle that included, according to author Norman Mailer, attending the day's events with credentials from *Life* magazine, "some of the worst word-sculptors ever assembled in southeastern Texas."

Armstrong, Collins, and Aldrin arrived at the morning press conference wearing gas masks. Knowing how silly they looked—like "razorback hogs," as Mailer described them—the three men grinned in embarrassment but with apparent good humor as they walked onstage. A few jokers in the audience had donned white hospital masks to share the crew's embarrassment and poke fun at NASA for the extremes of its biological wariness.

Onstage Neil, Mike, and Buzz sat in a three-sided plastic box roughly twelve feet wide, ten feet deep, and ten feet high. To ensure that no contagion from the journalists circulated into the breathing space of the astronauts, blowers located to the rear of the plastic booth blew air from behind the Apollo crew out into the audience. Once safely within the confines of their hygienic box, the astronauts took off their masks and sat down in easy chairs before a large walnut-brown desk emblazoned with NASA's emblematic "meatball" and the Apollo 11 seal: an eagle, the symbol of America, coming in for a landing on the lunar surface; its talons bearing an olive branch, a symbol of peace. (Originally, the astronauts had the eagle carrying the olive branch in its beak, but Bob Gilruth repositioned the olive branch from the eagle's mouth to its claws so as to make the eagle appear more peaceful and benign. The Apollo 11 crew, especially Aldrin, disagreed with Gilruth, but did not press their case.) To the rear of the astronauts' protective booth stood an American flag, a conspicuous reminder of the congressional mandate that Apollo 11 plant the standard into the lunar soil. Mailer called the restrained jeering at Old Glory "a splash of derision" at the entire Apollo show, already sufficiently American without yet another American flag on display.

The atmosphere in the theater felt decidedly strange. Convening to talk about a trip to the Moon still seemed a little fantastical. Naturally the astronauts were a little edgy, too, among the crowd of reporters, some of whom, as Mailer described, were so ignorant of science and engineering that they were "not just certain where laxatives ended and physics began."

Brian Duff, a NASA public affairs officer, opened by reading a statement from Dr. Charles Berry explaining the import of hygiene precautions. Duff warned journalists to "stay behind the ropes" demarcating the prescribed minimum of fifty feet from the Apollo crew.

"The astronauts walked with the easy saunter of athletes," Mailer related. "They were comfortable in motion. As men being scrutinized by other men they had little to worry about. Still, they did not strut. Like all good professional athletes, they had the modesty of knowing you could be good and still lose. Therefore they looked to enjoy the snouts [i.e., the gas masks] they were wearing, they waved at reporter friends they recognized, they grinned."

As mission commander, Armstrong spoke first. Mailer, like everyone else present, sensed that Neil was "ill at ease." What Mailer might not have known was that Armstrong often paused in formal conversation, searching for the right words.

"We're here today to talk a little bit about the forthcoming flight, Apollo 11, hopefully the culmination of the Apollo national objective. We are here to be able to talk about this attempt because of the success of four previous Apollo command flights and a number of unmanned flights. Each of those flights contributed in a great way to this flight. Each and every flight took a large number of new objectives and large hurdles, and left us with just a very few additions—the final descent-to-the-lunar-surface work—to be completed. We're very grateful to those large efforts of people here at MSC and across the nation who made those first flights successful, and made it possible for us to sit here today and discuss Apollo 11 with you. I'll ask Mike first to talk about the differences you might see in the command module activities on the flight."

As usual, Neil was brief—a total of six sentences, 149 words. Collins talked for a little longer—ten sentences, 273 words. Mike emphasized that he was going to be alone in the command module much longer than any previous CM pilot and that rendezvous was going to happen for the first time between a stationary LM, down on the lunar surface, and a CSM "whizzing around the Moon." Last but certainly not least in terms of how much he said—twenty sentences, 490 words—came Aldrin. Buzz outlined a complete lunar descent and landing; to be fair, those critical elements of

Apollo 11 did involve so much that was new that it did take quite a bit longer to describe them.

According to Armstrong today, "the media attention would have been a burden if we really had had the time to notice it. Fortunately we didn't have to fight that battle ourselves. Deke was probably the principal person in building barriers that allowed us to get our training done and then negotiating with NASA's public affairs branch to give the press a few opportunities to photograph our training activities in certain selected venues. During our simulated lunar surface activity, for example, they allowed the press in so they could cover that. NASA set that up specially where we had lights and platforms and other props. But as far as the media's interest affecting what we were doing, we didn't have to worry that much about answering questions or posing for pictures. We just did our work. Even when the press was there, we did the same thing we'd be doing if they weren't there."

At the morning press conference on July 5, the Apollo 11 crew responded to a total of thirty-seven questions. Armstrong answered twenty-seven of them. Nine of the newsmen specifically asked for Neil to answer their questions; the other eighteen questions were of a nature that Armstrong, as commander, felt it was his responsibility to answer. Twice, Neil turned and asked Buzz to respond to a question directed specifically at Neil; on two other occasions, Buzz, unsolicited, added to Neil's comments. Collins, like Aldrin, answered only three questions directed at him. A few questions called for responses from all three astronauts. It was an overall pattern that would long outlast the Apollo program. People most wanted to hear from the commander, the First Man who would step out onto the Moon.

Armstrong announced for the first time the nicknames for the Apollo command and lunar modules: "Yes, we do intend to use call signs other than those you may have heard in simulation. The call sign for the lunar module will be 'Eagle.' The call sign for the command module will be 'Columbia.' Both names were suggested by a number of people, very many. A large number of other names were also submitted for our consideration, many of which were quite good. We selected these as being representative of the flight, the nation's hope. Columbia is a national symbol. Columbia stands on top of our Capitol and, as you all know, it was the name of Jules Verne's spacecraft that went to the Moon in his novel of one hundred years ago."

Actually, Verne named his Moon rocket *Columbiad*, a fact that Armstrong knew from his own reading of the book, done in his late teens. "We thought that *Columbia* was better," Neil explains today. "*Columbia* was well known in the American lexicon. It had been a candidate for the name of our country, so it was a natural."

"Was Verne one of your favorite authors?"

"No, I don't think so, but I had certainly read the book. Verne's story definitely had a role in our deliberations." The entire crew participated in naming the spacecraft. "We had a lot of those little things, which we considered to be nonoperational decisions. Many of them were kind of a pain to have to deal with, but we had to do it." Choosing *Columbia* and *Eagle* was one of the few nonoperational decisions they actually enjoyed.

Neil states that Mike Collins more than himself or Aldrin played the major role in choosing both the call names: "Mike was certainly as convincing as anyone that these would be the names to use. We all participated, but Mike was especially thoughtful about it. Some of his ideas were the principal ones." Aldrin remembers it a little differently: "Neil and I asked Mike to choose a name for the command ship. He replied instantly; he'd done his thinking in advance and had chosen *Columbia.* Neil and I considered a long list of possibilities for naming our LM and settled on *Eagle,* the symbol of America."

Naturally, the press, eleven days before Apollo 11's launch, was curious as to what Armstrong would say when he first stepped out of the LM and onto the Moon. "For Neil Armstrong," a reporter rose to his feet to ask. "By the nature of your assignment if you carry it out successfully, you're destined to become a historical personage of some consequence. I'm wondering if, in that light, you have decided on something suitably historical and memorable to say when you perform this symbolic act of stepping down on the Moon for the first time?"

Not even those few who knew Armstrong personally or who exercised authority over the manned space program had been able to get Neil to disclose any of his thoughts about the historic first words he would utter from afoot on the lunar surface. At one point, the internal pressures inside of NASA motivated Julian Scheer, the chief of NASA's public affairs office, to write a terse internal memo that asked, in effect, did King Ferdinand and Queen Isabella of Spain tell Christopher Columbus what to say when he reached the New World? Among the rumors that Aldrin heard at the time was that Simon Bourgin, a United States Information Agency official in frequent contact with the astronauts—and who allegedly had advised Frank Borman to read from Genesis during Apollo 8—tried to advise Armstrong. If Bourgin did make any suggestions, they had no effect on Neil.

George Low had tried. In late June, when Armstrong was brought to

Mission Control for the final run-through of the mission rules for the lunar landing, Low broke in, "Have you thought about what you're going to say, Neil, when you step off the ladder?" According to Chris Kraft, who was part of the conversation, Neil was quiet for a moment and then answered, enigmatically true to form, "Sure, George, I've been thinking about it." Then, characteristically, Neil changed the subject. "Tell everybody thanks for all of us. We know how hard everybody's been working."

Kraft remembers that Low was "taken aback" by Neil's refusal to share any of his thoughts on the matter; Kraft himself was not surprised by it. "There was no way Neil was going to tell George Low or myself or anyone else," Kraft relates. "I wouldn't have asked Neil that question, to be perfectly honest, because I figured it was his business. But George was one of those guys who wanted to know what everybody was up to so, if necessary, he could tell people what they ought to do. George also probably had a better feel for the worldwide impact and symbolic meaning of Apollo." Low thought about pressing Armstrong but chose not to. Kraft never gave it another thought: "Whatever Neil said would be something that none of us were likely ever to forget. He'd say the right thing."

In response to the reporter's question about choosing his first words from on the lunar surface, Armstrong simply answered, "No, I haven't." As hard as it may be to believe, that was the plain truth. "The most important part of the flight in my mind was the landing," Armstrong explains today. "I thought that if there was any statement to have any importance, it would be whatever occurred right after landing, when the engine stopped. I had given some thought to what we would call the landing site. I had also thought about what I would say right at the landing; I thought it was the one that history might note. But not even that was something that I had given a great deal of thought to, because, statistics aside, my gut feeling was that, whereas we had a ninety percent chance of returning safely to Earth, our chances were only even money of actually making the landing."

In fact, Neil had already chosen Tranquility Base as the name of the spot on the Sea of Tranquility where he and Aldrin would land; privately, he had told Charlie Duke about the name, since Duke would serve as CapCom during the landing and Neil did not want Charlie to be caught unawares when Neil used the phrase immediately upon touchdown. "In the absence of official names for the various locations and landmarks on the lunar surface," he told the press, "we have chosen to use some unofficial names for our recognition purposes and for our training purposes, and we'll continue to do that." No one else in NASA besides Charlie Duke knew about Tranquility Base until *Eagle* landed.

A special high-level government committee had decided that Armstrong and Aldrin should leave three items on the surface as symbolic of humankind's arrival. The first was a plaque mounted on the leg of the LM that held the ladder down which the astronauts would climb. This plaque depicted the Earth's two hemispheres; on it was inscribed the statement, HERE MEN FROM THE PLANET EARTH SET FOOT UPON THE MOON, JULY 1969 A.D. WE CAME IN PEACE FOR ALL MANKIND. The second item was a small disk, less than one and a half inches in diameter, upon which had been electronically recorded a microminiaturized photo-print of goodwill letters from various heads of states around the world. The third item was the American flag.

"I would like to ask Neil Armstrong if he agrees with the congressional mandate which specifies that the U.S. flag and only the U.S. flag will be implanted on the Moon on Apollo 11," a foreign reporter asked at the prelaunch press conference on July 5.

"Well, I suspect that if we asked all the people in the audience and all of us up here," answered Neil, "all of us would give different ideas on what they would like to take to the Moon and think should be taken, everyone within his own experience. I don't think that there is any question what our job is. Our job is to fly the spacecraft as best as we can. We never would suggest that it is our responsibility to suggest what the U.S. posture on the Moon should be. That decision has been made where it should be made, namely in the Congress of this country. I wouldn't presume to question it.

"Some people thought a United Nations flag should be there," Armstrong explains today, "and some people thought there should be flags of a lot of nations. In the end, it was decided by Congress that this was a United States project. We were not going to make any territorial claim, but we ought to let people know that we were here and put up a U.S. flag. My job was to get the flag there. I was less concerned about whether that was the right artifact to place. I let other, wiser minds than mine make those kinds of decisions."

Later at the press conference, Armstrong responded to another question from a foreign correspondent as to whether there was not some legal importance to the United States' landing first on the Moon. As so often was the case, there was a simple eloquence in the offhanded directness of Neil's answer: "I think we might refer to this plaque again, in the last line. It says we came in peace for all mankind. I think that is precisely what we mean."

Reporters tried hard—and mostly in vain—to get Armstrong to philosophize about the historical significance of the Moon landing. "What particular gain do you see in going to the Moon for yourselves as human beings, for your country, and for mankind as a whole?" "Do you think that eventually the Moon will become part of the civilized world just as the Antarctic is now, which was also once a removed and unacceptable place?"

"First, let me repeat something that you have all heard before, but probably addresses itself to your question," Armstrong answered. "That is, the objective of this flight is precisely to take man to the Moon, make a landing there, and return. That is the objective. There are a number of peripheral secondary objectives including some of those you mentioned early in the question that we hope very highly to achieve in great depth. But the primary objective is the ability to demonstrate that man, in fact, can do this kind of job. How we'll use that information in the centuries to come, only history can tell. I hope that we're wise enough to use the information that we get on these early flights to the maximum advantage possible, and I would think that in the light of our experience over the past decade that we can indeed hope for that kind of result."

Nor did the journalists have much luck in provoking Armstrong into giving anything other than unemotional, engineering answers about the grave risks inherent to the flight.

"What would, according to you, be the most dangerous phase of the flight of Apollo 11?"

"Well, as in any flight, the things that give one most concern are those which have not been done previously, things that are new. I would hope that in our initial statement that we gave to you an idea, at least, of what the new things on this flight are. Now, there are other things that we always concern ourselves about greatly, and those are the situations where we have no alternative method to do the job, where we have only one. You, when you ride in an airliner across the Atlantic, depend on the wing of the airplane to stay on the fuselage; without it, you could not have made the trip, see? We have on recent flights had some of those kinds of situations. In our earlier lunar flights, the rocket engine for the service module must operate for us to return from the Moon. There are no alternatives. Similarly, in this flight, we have several situations like that. The LM engine must operate to accelerate us from the Moon's surface into lunar orbit, and the service module engine, of course, must operate again to return us to Earth. As we go farther and farther into spaceflight, there will be more and more of the single-point systems that must operate. We have a very high confidence level in those systems, incidentally."

"What will your plans be in the extremely unlikely event that the lunar module does not come up off the lunar surface?"

"Well, that's an unpleasant thing to think about and we've chosen not to think about that up to the present time. We don't think that's at all a likely situation. It's simply a possible one, but at the present time we're left without recourse should that occur."

"What is the longest time, if the ascent stage doesn't fire . . . I think Mike Collins said in an earlier interview that he would then have to just leave and go back to the Earth. What is the longest time you can wait between the not-firing and the time when Mike Collins would have to go back, the time you would have to work on the LM or fix whatever was wrong or try to fix it?"

"I don't have the numbers. Probably it would be a matter of a couple of days."

It was such seemingly passionless answers to questions about the human dimensions of spaceflight and about the historical and existential meanings of going to the Moon that piqued Norman Mailer's razor-sharp acumen for disdainful insight. Like other reporters, the Pulitzer Prize–winning author of *The Naked and the Dead* and *Armies of the Night* wanted more from Armstrong, a lot more. Mailer wrote that Armstrong "surrendered words about as happily as a hound allowed meat to be pulled out of his teeth"; that Armstrong "answered with his characteristic mixture of modesty and technical arrogance, of apology and tight-lipped superiority"; that Armstrong had "the sly privacy of a man whose thoughts may never be read"; that Armstrong, like a trapped animal, seemed to be looking for "a way to drift clear of any room like this where he was trapped with psyche-eaters, psyche-gorgers, and the duty of responding to questions heard some hundred of times." At the same time, Armstrong was "a professional" who had "learned how to contend in a practical way with the necessary language," always choosing words and phrases that "protected him."

It intrigued Mailer (in narrating his book, *Of a Fire on the Moon,* Mailer called himself Aquarius, in reference to the hopeful spirit of a future Age of Aquarius) that Armstrong exuded such an "extraordinarily remote," almost mystical quality that made him appear different from other men. "He was a presence in the room," Mailer noted, "as much a spirit as a man. One hardly knew if he were the spirit of the high thermal currents or that spirit of neutrality which rises to the top in bureaucratic situations, or both. . . . Indeed, contradictions lay subtly upon him—it was not unlike looking at a bewildering nest of leaves: some are autumn fallings, some the green of early spring." Of all the astronauts, Armstrong seemed "the man nearest to being saintly." As a speaker, Neil was "all but limp." Still, the overall impression Armstrong made on Mailer was not unremarkable. "Certainly the knowledge he was an astronaut restored his stature," Mailer realized, "yet even if he had been a junior executive accepting an award, Armstrong would have presented a quality which was arresting. . . . He would have been more extraordinary in fact if he had been just a salesman making a modest inept dull little speech, for then one would have been forced to wonder how he had ever gotten his job, how he could sell even one item, how in fact he got out of the bed in the morning. Something particularly innocent or subtly sinister was in the gentle remote air. If he had been a young boy selling subscriptions at the door, one grandmother might have warned her granddaughter never to let him in the house; another would have commented, 'That boy will go very far.' "

Mailer continued his dogged pursuit of the puzzle-that-was-Armstrong into the press conference organized exclusively for the magazine writers and beyond that into the studio where NBC filmed its interview of the astronauts. As the journalists kept pushing hard for the crew of Apollo 11 to disclose personal feelings and emotions, Mailer watched and listened as Armstrong entrenched himself ever deeper in his engineer's protective cloak, the armor of "a shining knight of technology." Armstrong replied in "a mild and honest voice" to a question about the role of intuition in his flying by remarking that intuition had "never been my strong suit" and by asserting, like a logical positivist, Mailer noted, that the best approach to any problem was to "interpret it properly, then attack it."

Armstrong had mastered "computerese." Instead of saying "we," Neil convoluted the English language and said, "A joint exercise has demonstrated." Instead of saying "other choices," he referred to "peripheral secondary objectives." Rather than "doing our best," it was "obtaining maximum advantage possible." To "turn on" and "turn off" became "enable" and "disable." Mailer, who had rejected in disgust his own college education as an engineer, saw in Neil's vernacular proof not only that "the more natural forms of English had not been built for the computer" but that Armstrong represented "either the end of the old or the first of the new men."

"If not me, another," Neil stated, to Mailer's mind disclaiming "large reactions, large ideas" behind media comparisons of his own journey as commander of Apollo 11 to Christopher Columbus's adventure in 1492. Armstrong's concern was "directed mainly to doing the job," one that could be done by no fewer than ten other astronauts. And hundreds of people were backing up his crew in Houston, at the Cape, at the other NASA centers, and tens of thousands had been working in industrial firms all around the country to enable Apollo to blaze its course. "It's their success more than ours," Neil humbly told the media.

Armstrong was no common hero, Mailer realized. "If they would insist on making him a hero," the author noted, "he would be a hero on terms he alone would make clear."

From Collins and Aldrin, the reporters were able to get a few remarks about family and personal background (Buzz mentioned the family jewelry he was taking with him to the Moon). Nothing of the sort came from Armstrong. "Will you take personal mementos to the Moon, Neil?"

"If I had a choice, I would take more fuel."

"Will you keep a piece of the Moon for yourself?"

"At this time, no plans have been made" came the stiff response.

"Will you lose your private life after this achievement?"

"I think a private life is possible within the context of such an achievement."

Neil left them with very few opportunities for discursive follow-ups. When the rare chance came, a member of the media rushed through the hole like a fullback plunging off-tackle to the goal line. Following a comment from Neil about the economic benefits to the nation of the space program, a writer jumped in to ask, "So, are we going to the Moon only for economic reasons, only to get out of an expensive hole of a sluggish economy? Don't you see any philosophical reason why we might be going?"

It was exactly the sort of open-ended question that Armstrong had tried hard all day—in fact, all his life—not to answer. Yet it was a question that Neil could not avoid without looking like a "spiritual neuter," to use Mailer's phrase. "I think we're going to the Moon," Armstrong offered tentatively, "because it's in the nature of the human being to face challenges. It's by the nature of his deep inner soul. We're required to do these things just as salmon swim upstream."

What precisely was in Armstrong's own deep inner soul about the Moon landing, or about anything else that happened in his life—his true feelings about his father, his religious beliefs, the effects of little Karen's death—was hardly laid bare by the remark, or by any other verbal statement he ever made. It was just not his way. Perhaps, his extraordinarily judicious restraint of expression was a deeply inculcated outcome of the avoidance strategy he had developed in childhood. Or perhaps it derived, as his first wife Janet today hesitantly suggests, from a feeling of social inferiority based on his humble family background in rural Ohio.

What Armstrong on the eve of becoming the First Man did not and would not define or explain about himself, others now sought, almost desperately in the days before the launch, to explain and define for him. All the humanistic and cosmic meanings that he would not fill in, others felt compelled to fill in for him. On the eve of humankind's great adventure to set foot on another heavenly body, Armstrong had become like an oracle of ancient times, a medium, wise, prophetic, mysterious, by which fortunes and misfortunes were told, deities consulted, prayers answered.

Not until he constructed his own myth out of Armstrong could the creative mind of Norman Mailer be satisfied. It did not matter that Mailer would never meet Neil face to face, never once talk to him directly, never ask him a single question of his own. Mailer, too, had sat the before the oracle, "the most saintly of the astronauts," someone who was "simply not like other men," who was "apparently in communion with some string in the universe others did not think to play." It was up to Mailer, up to Aquarius, to decode Armstrong.

Like Mailer, we were to be the author of our own Moon landing.

Mailer conjured the makings of his own Armstrong while sitting in on NBC correspondent Frank McGee's interview with Neil near the end of the day on July 5. In the interview McGee referred to a story in *Life* by Dodie Hamblin in which Armstrong told of the recurring boyhood dream in which he hovered over the ground. Mailer had read Hamblin's story when it appeared but dismissed its importance until he heard Armstrong, after a day filled with Neil's engineer-speak, corroborate that, indeed, as a boy, he had such dreams. Mailer was taken with the beauty of the dream: "It was beautiful because it might soon prove to be prophetic, beautiful because it was profound and it was mysterious, beautiful because it was appropriate to a man who would land on the moon." For Mailer, it was a type of epiphany, one by which he could construct "The Psychology of Astronauts" and interpret the entire Space Age: "It was therefore a dream on which one might found a new theory of the dream, for any theory incapable of explaining this visitor of the night would have to be inadequate, unless it were ready to declare that levitation, breath, and the moon were not proper provinces of the dream."

The idea that such a nonwhimsical man as Armstrong, as a young boy, dreamed of flight "intoxicated" Mailer, "for it dramatized how much at odds might be the extremes of Armstrong's personality." On the one hand, consciously, Armstrong, the archetypal astronaut-engineer, was grounded in the "conventional," the "practical," the "technical," and the "hardworking." He resided at the very "center of the suburban middle class." On the other hand, what Armstrong and the other astronauts were doing in space was "enterprising beyond the limits of the imagination." Their drive and ambition simply had to have a subconscious element.

It was in this union of opposites, the impenetrable fusion of the conscious and the unconscious, that one found in the modern technological age "a new psychological constitution to man." More than any of the other astronauts, Neil's personality stemmed from the core of that "magnetic human force called Americanism, Protestantism, or Waspitude." He was the Lancelot of the silent majority, "the Wasp emerging from human history in order to take us to the stars." Never mind that Mailer knew almost nothing about Armstrong's family background, personal history, married life, religious beliefs, friends, or genuine psychological state. Aquarius's object was not to understand Armstrong; it was to understand the comings and wrong-goings of humankind in the twentieth century:

> On the one hand to dwell in the very center of technological reality . . . yet to inhabit—if only in one's dreams—that other world where death, metaphysics and the unanswerable questions of eternity must reside, was to suggest natures so divided that they could have been the most miserable and unbalanced of men if they did not contain in their huge contradictions some of the profound and accelerating opposites of the country itself. The century would seek to dominate nature as it had never been dominated, would attack the idea of war, poverty and natural catastrophe as never before. The century would create death, devastation and pollution as never before. Yet the century was now attached to the idea that man must take his conception of life out to the stars.
>
> So, in turn, the astronauts had personalities of unequaled banality and apocalyptic dignity. So they suggested in their contradictions the power of the century to live with its own incredible contradictions and yet release some of the untold energies of the earth. A century devoted to the rationality of technique was also a century so irrational as to open in every mind the real possibility of global destruction. It was the first century in history which

presented to sane and sober minds the end of its span. It was a world half
convinced of the future death of our species yet half aroused by the apoca-
lyptic notion that an exceptional future still lay before us. So it was a century
which moved with the most magnificent display of power into directions it
could not comprehend. The itch was to accelerate—the metaphysical direc-
tion unknown.

There was no denying the brilliance of Mailer's exposé. Yet Mailer really
did not care about Armstrong, the man, on a personal level, only as a vessel
into which the author could pour his own mental energy and profundity.
What Mailer wrote in his chapter "The Psychology of Astronauts" was
highly provocative and insightful as social criticism, but as history, biography, or real psychology, it shed considerably more heat than light.

The mythologizing and iconography had only just begun. Fifteen days
after the press conference, Armstrong would step onto the Moon. He
would no longer be just a man, not for any of us. He would be First Man.

PART SEVEN

ONE GIANT LEAP

He who would bring back the wealth of the Indies, must carry the wealth of the Indies with him.

—INSCRIPTION ON THE FAÇADE OF
UNION STATION, WASHINGTON DC

Did he take something of Karen with him to the Moon? Oh, I dearly hope so.

—JUNE ARMSTRONG HOFFMAN

CHAPTER 27

Outward Bound

For Armstrong, Collins, and Aldrin, going into space actually commenced back in the crew quarters three and a half hours before liftoff, shortly after 6:00 A.M., when technicians snapped the astronauts' helmets down onto their neck rings and locked them into place. From that moment on, the crew of the first Moon landing breathed no outside air. They heard no human voice other than that piped in electronically through the barrier of their pressure suits. They saw the world only through the veneer of their faceplates, and could smell, hear, feel, or taste nothing but that which modern technology manufactured for them inside their protective cocoon.

For Armstrong, the isolation was more familiar than it was for his mates. As a test pilot back at Edwards, he had grown accustomed to the confinement of pressurized flight suits. In comparison to the partial pressure suits and headgear he had donned for flying zooms in the F-104 or going to the edge of space in the X-15, the Apollo suit was downright roomy and easy to maneuver.

Still, as the crew of Apollo 11 left the Manned Spacecraft Operations Building at 6:27 A.M. and paraded in their protective yellow galoshes into the air-conditioned transfer van that was to transport them eight miles to Launchpad 39A, every tissue of their being, every nerve fiber, every brain cell, every recess of their inner space, acknowledged that they had left the ordinary, commonsense realm of nature and had entered the totally artificial environment that would sustain them in outer space.

As best as they could manage for the past weeks and months, the three astronauts had ignored the steady buildup around their mission. "We were running on a pretty fast track," relates Armstrong. "There were so many things to do, and reading newspapers and watching television was not high on our list."

Going into the mission, Neil, Mike, and Buzz possessed great confi-

405

dence in the Saturn rocket, but one could never be sure about any rocket's performance—not even the massive machine designed by von Braun's accomplished team of rocketeers at NASA's Marshall Space Flight Center in Alabama. "It was certainly a very high-performance machine," Armstrong asserts. "It was not perfect, though. Indeed, in the flight after ours, there would be problems." A lightning strike thirty-six seconds after Apollo 12's liftoff resulted in a complete, albeit temporary, electrical failure inside the spacecraft. The failure was not the fault of the rocket except for the fact that an ionized plume from the rocket made the entire vehicle more electromagnetically attractive.

Another concern about the rocket lay in the fact that the Saturn V had come to life so quickly. The phenomenally fast pace of its development resulted from the strategy of "all-up testing," a new NASA R&D philosophy championed by Dr. George Mueller, the associate administrator for manned space flight. Mueller put the development of the Saturn V on the fast track by having the rocket tested from the very start with all three of its stages "live" and ready to go, rather than having the stages incrementally tested one at a time and then mating the three of them together only after each had proven itself independently.

The von Braun team was not a big fan of all-up testing—nor was Neil Armstrong: "I viewed it as a good approach for unmanned tests but as a somewhat dangerous approach in manned flight. I'd been brought up in step-by-step testing; that was the old NACA/NASA method of doing things. I knew the value of the incremental approach, and this one was quite different. All-up testing was a subject of conversation among the astronauts, particularly at four o'clock in the morning when we were inside the spacecraft running some test in order to make the schedule for an upcoming all-up test on the pad. On the other hand, the development of the Saturn V tended to be more operational than research oriented, so the motivations were different." Without all-up testing, Neil recognized, Kennedy's end-of-the-decade deadline for the Moon landing just could not be met. Still, it was not the surest way to assure the development of a sound rocket, particularly one that was such a vast and complex piece of novel machinery—producing an enormous 7.6 million pounds of thrust.

By the time the crew sat on top of the monumentally powerful rocket waiting for it to fire, they were past pondering its dangers. Moreover, there was always the chance that something minor would go wrong at the last minute in one of the several hundred subsystems associated with the rocket, the spacecraft, or the launch complex and cancel the launch. "These things were canceled more often than they were launched," Neil explains. "We'd climb out, go back, and get ready for another day." That possibility—perhaps probability—"softened the intensity" of an astronaut's emotions, Neil relates, as he headed to the launchpad.

The first astronaut into *Columbia* the morning of the launch was not Armstrong, Collins, or Aldrin; it was Fred Haise, Collins's backup as command module pilot. "Freddo," as he was known, preceded the crew into the spacecraft by some ninety minutes in order to run through a 417-step checklist designed to ensure that every switch was set in its proper position. At 6:54 A.M. local time, Haise and the rest of the pad "close-out crew" gave the spacecraft their thumbs-up. Having taken the elevator up the 320 feet to the level of the waiting spacecraft, Armstrong grasped the overhead handrail of the capsule with both hands and swung himself through the hatch. Prior to climbing in, Neil received a small gift from Guenter Wendt, the pad leader: it was a crescent moon that Wendt had carved out of Styrofoam and covered with metal foil. Wendt told him "it's a key to the Moon," and a smiling Neil asked Wendt to hold on to the token for him until he got back. In exchange Neil gave Wendt a small card he had been keeping under the wristband of his Omega watch. It was a printed ticket for a ride in a "space taxi," reading "good between any two planets."

Inside the command module Armstrong settled into the commander's seat to the far left. Five minutes later, after pad technician Joe Schmitt hooked up Neil's lines and hoses for communication, respiration, and all the rest, Collins, the command module pilot, climbed into the right seat, followed by Aldrin, the lunar module pilot, in the center. (Aldrin was in the center seat because he had trained for that position on Apollo 8. Collins had been out for a while with his neck spur, so rather than retrain Buzz for ascent, NASA just left him in the center and trained Mike for the right seat.)

To Neil's left hand was the abort handle. One twist of the handle would trigger the solid rocket escape tower that was attached to the top of the command module to blast Apollo 11 clear of trouble. In the Gemini program, the spacecraft had possessed ejection seats rather than an escape tower, but the Gemini's Titan booster used hypergolic fuels that could not explode the way the Saturn could, and would—in a huge fireball—because the Saturn was fueled with kerosene, hydrogen, and oxygen. With Apollo, ejection seats could not have worked because they would not throw the astronauts far enough away from a Saturn explosion. Armstrong does not recall second-guessing the wisdom of the Apollo escape-tower system: "It gave us the only chance we would have had, and we certainly wanted to have some option for any emergency that might happen." As for the possibility of an abort, "I felt our training was excellent and adequate to handle almost any situation that we could envision in booster malfunctions. We would know what to do. We thought we had a very high probability of being successful in an abort throughout the launch sequence."

The Saturn V's ascent was especially suited to Neil's background in research, in that the booster rocket was controllable from the cockpit: "You could not fly the earlier models of the Saturn rocket from the spacecraft. Had there been a failure on the Saturn's inertial system on Apollo 9, for example, McDivitt, Scott, and Schweickart would have had to splash down into the Atlantic or maybe land in Africa, with a high risk of physical injury. For our flight we had added an alternate guidance system in the command module's gear so that if there were a failure of some kind on the Saturn we could switch to the alternate systems and fly the rocket from the spacecraft.

"I never had much to do with booster development, but I was very interested in getting this guidance capability," Neil relates. Back in 1959 and 1960 at Edwards (as mentioned in an earlier chapter), Armstrong and research engineer Ed Holleman had conducted a study that showed the feasibility of flying a large booster manually. Many simulations were done at Edwards and at the Johnsville centrifuge in Pennsylvania to confirm that the effects of acceleration on a pilot doing the "guiding task" from atop a rocket were not traumatic. If the autopilot went out, the pilot could fly the booster into orbit manually just as a pilot could fly a large supersonic airplane to altitude. Though ready for Apollo 10, the alternative guidance system did not fly until Apollo 11.

"It's nice to see one of your ideas become reality," Neil states, "but it was fortunate that the concept never had to prove itself."

The powered ascent of Apollo 11 from its launchpad into orbit involved a number of discrete phases, and within each of these phases there were discrete changes in abort technique. "You have to do things right away and do them properly, so that was the focus," Armstrong explains. "It was a complete concentration on getting through each phase and being ready to do the proper thing if anything went wrong in the next phase." His most important cues during the fiery ascent came, in his words, from "a combination of looking at the attitude indicator, following the flight performance on the computer, and listening to indications over the radio as to which phase you were in or were about to enter."

•   •   •

In the time it took for just a small fraction of the heavy automobile traffic to crawl its way clear of Cape Kennedy's environs, Apollo 11 went around the world one and a half times and was on its way to the Moon. On the front lawn of their Ohio home, Neil's parents had already been interviewed by a small horde of media: "Mr. Armstrong, what did you think of that launch?" and "Mrs. Armstrong, what were your feelings when you saw that rocket disappear into the sky?" Viola exclaimed, "I'm thankful beyond words." Projecting her religious beliefs onto her son as she always did, she asserted, "Neil believes God is up there with all three of those boys. I believe that, and Neil believes that." Steve remarked, "It's a tremendous, most happy time. We'll stay glued to the television for the entire flight." Viola's mother, eighty-two-year-old Caroline Korspeter, remarked before the TV cameras: "I think it's dangerous. I told Neil to look around and not to step out if it didn't look good. He said he wouldn't."

Back on the Banana River, Janet Armstrong and her boys stayed on the yacht listening to transmissions from the spacecraft on a NASA squawk box until the crowds dispersed. Though greatly relieved the launch had gone off smoothly, at Janet's request no bottles of champagne or boxes of cigars were opened on board; she preferred that celebrating be reserved for after the mission when the men were home safely. Before departing Patrick Air Force Base, south of Cocoa Beach, for home, Janet agreed to meet briefly with journalists. "We couldn't see the rocket right away," Rick shyly reported, "and I was kind of worried at first. All of a sudden, we could see it and it was beautiful." Janet told the press, "It was a tremendous sight. I was just thrilled," though her main feeling was simply relief that the launch had gone off safely. "This, too, shall pass" was what she was actually thinking. She had gotten almost no sleep the night before. Overly tired, she tossed and turned until her wakeup call came at 4:00 A.M.—the same time that Neil, Mike, and Buzz got up. On the yacht, Janet kept saying to people, "I wish they would hurry up and get this off so I can get some sleep!" At one point the boat's skipper asked her if all the years of living through the anxious moments of test flights and space shots had not begun to affect her. Pointing to a few streaks of gray in her hair, Janet replied, laughing, "I haven't aged a day."

When she got home to Houston late that afternoon, the press waited in her yard. "I don't feel historic," Janet succinctly told them, ushering her boys into the house. What she and the boys mainly felt was worn out. Rick did not participate in his Little League All-Star game that night: "I think you're too tired," his mother told him, and Rick did not argue. Not playing baseball was another part of the price the boy paid for his father's going to the Moon.

The vigil for the crew had just begun. It would be two and a half more days before the astronauts even made it to lunar orbit, a day after that before Neil and Buzz descended to the landing, and four days beyond that before they returned to Earth.

So much could still go wrong.

At 10:58 Houston time, two hours and twenty-six minutes after liftoff, Mission Control gave Apollo 11 the "go" for TLI. In the patois of spaceflight, TLI meant "translunar injection"—leaving Earth orbit and heading into deep space. The astronauts accomplished TLI by firing the Saturn V's third-stage engine, the only stage still attached to the command service module. This burn, lasting some five and a half minutes, accelerated Apollo 11 to over 24,200 miles per hour, the speed required to escape the hold of Earth's gravity.

Everything from the moment of the launch to this point had gone very well. "That Saturn gave us a magnificent ride," Armstrong reported after leaving Earth orbit. "We have no complaints with any of three stages of that ride. It was beautiful."

Privately, Armstrong would have liked the ride to have been smoother: "In the first stage, the Saturn V noise was enormous, particularly when we were at low altitude because we got the noise from seven and a half million pounds of thrust plus the echo of that noise off the ground that reinforced it. After about thirty seconds, we flew out of that echo noise and the volume went down substantially. But in that first thirty seconds it was very difficult to hear anything over the radio—even inside the helmet with the earphones. It was considerably louder than the Titan. In the first stage, it was also a lot rougher ride than the Titan. It seemed to be vibrating in all three axes simultaneously." During the worst of it, which came shortly after liftoff, Armstrong's heart rate rose to 110 beats per minute, compared to Collins's 99 and Aldrin's 88—all within the satisfactory range. Neil's heart rate always seemed a little higher than most of the other astronauts', though the cardiac numbers for all three members of the Apollo 11 crew were lower than what they had been during their Gemini launches, which for Armstrong had been 146 beats per minute, for Collins 125, and for Aldrin 110.

With the burnout of the first stage, the flight smoothed out and quieted down considerably, so much so that the astronauts could not feel any vibration or even hear the engines running. Rocketing upward on the second and third stages of the Saturn proved superior to any stage of the Titan. Mike Collins later described the herky-jerky early ascent of the Saturn V: "It was like a nervous novice driving a wide car down a narrow alley and jerking the wheel back and forth spasmodically." Then on the upper stages the Saturn V turned into "a gentle giant," with the climb out of the atmosphere as "smooth as glass, as quiet and serene as a rocket ride can be."

Out their windows the astronauts could see nothing until three minutes into their ride, when the spacecraft reached sixty miles high. At that altitude, the Apollo 11 crew jettisoned their unused escape rocket and let loose the protective shield that had been covering the command module. Still pointing straight up, however, there was nothing for the crew to see except for what Collins called "a small patch of blue sky that gradually darkens to the jet black of space."

Earth orbit was achieved twelve minutes into the flight when the first burn of the Saturn's single third-stage engine pushed the Apollo 11 spacecraft (while over the Canary Islands tracking station in the eastern Atlantic) up to the required speed of 17,500 miles per hour. In an ellipse described in astronaut shorthand as 102.5 by 99.7 nautical miles, the trio now had an orbit and a half in which to make sure all their equipment was operating properly before they reignited their third-stage engine and committed themselves to leaving the Earth's gravitational field.

According to Armstrong, "The purpose of doing the orbit and a half was twofold. One, it allowed a little more flexibility in launch time, and second, it gave us the opportunity to check out all the principal systems of the spacecraft—the command module, not the lunar module—prior to leaving the Earth's orbit on a translunar trajectory. So systems checkout was the principal reason that we were in this holding orbit, and the responsibility was shared between the crew on board and the people on the ground. The people on the ground could see a good bit more detail of systems operations and the orbit and a half gave them a long enough time to look at it. If something went wrong on the spacecraft, we would have the time to decide whether we should forget the whole thing and abort."

Initially, the crew found only brief moments to take in the spectacular view of the Earth below. Their first sunrise one hour and nineteen minutes into the flight prompted a hunt for the Swedish-made Hasselblad camera. "Look at that horizon!" Collins exclaimed. Neil replied, "Isn't that something?!" Mike continued, "Damn, that's pretty. It's unreal." "Get a picture of that," Neil urged. But the camera could not be found. "I've lost a Hasselblad," Collins jested. "Has anyone seen a Hasselblad floating by? It couldn't have gone very far, big son of a gun like that. . . . Everybody look for a floating Hasselblad. I see a pen floating loose down here, too. Is anybody missing a ballpoint pen? . . . I mean, felt tip. . . . I've looked everywhere over here for that Hasselblad, and I just don't see it." "It's too late for sunrise now, anyway," Neil noted. "But you want to get it before TLI," warned Aldrin, because the acceleration of the spacecraft out of orbit could launch the bandit camera into someone's head, or worse, into the spacecraft's control panel. "Let me go on a little expedition here," Collins said. In less than fifteen seconds he found the camera floating in the aft bulkhead. "Beautiful," said Neil.

For the first time since their respective Gemini flights, Armstrong, Collins, and Aldrin again experienced the wonder of weightlessness, though there was too much to do to make ready for TLI to enjoy it—if enjoying it was even what would happen. In weightlessness, the fluid in the inner ear sloshed freely. Motion sickness could happen more easily in the Apollo spacecraft than in the Gemini because Apollo was more commodious. On the way to the Moon in Apollo 8, Frank Borman got ill from the motion, causing quite a stir in Mission Control. The mission planners for the subsequent Apollo flights told the crews to move around as slowly and gingerly as possible and not to wiggle their heads back and forth too much, until they got used to being in weightless conditions. Armstrong was intently aware of the potential problem. One hour and seventeen minutes into the flight, he asked Mike and Buzz: "How does zero g feel? Your head feel funny, anybody, or anything like that?" Mike answered, "No. It just feels like we're going around upside down." Buzz: "I don't even feel that."

According to Neil, "We were very fortunate that none of the crew came down with the malady at any point in the flight. [The same was true for he and Dave Scott in Gemini VIII.] I don't know how you predict that. Some of the people that were best known to have an iron gut ended up getting space sickness. No one was sure at the time what exactly was causing it. They were trying various things." As for his own proclivity for nausea, "I was sensitive to motion sickness when I was small, in automobiles and boats. I grew out of it, but I could still make myself queasy by doing a lot of aerobatics. So I was a candidate. But, curiously, the predisposition does not correlate with what goes on in space. Space sickness does not correlate to motion sickness on Earth. It involves sensitivity to other motion situations."

Convinced that the ship was ready to leave Earth orbit, Mission Control gave Apollo 11 the go for TLI some two hours and fifteen minutes after the spacecraft reached orbit. Flight procedures required that the crew, for their protection during the burn, put their helmets and gloves back on; the idea was that if the Saturn third stage, known as the S-IVB, exploded, the astronauts might benefit from some protection inside their sealed pressure suits. "The problem with that thinking," as Collins has explained it, was that "any explosion massive enough to crack our ship's hull would also result in multiple equipment failures, and we would never get back in one piece. Still, a rule was a rule, so we sat there, helmet and gloves on, ready to be propelled to another planet."

Privately Armstrong also questioned the rationale for putting the helmets and gloves back on: "There was the viewpoint that whenever you were in powered flight you were being exposed to more risk than when you were just in free-floating flight. However, the disadvantage of helmets and gloves was that you were less able, less mobile, and less facile. You couldn't hear or see as well, so you actually gave up a lot of safety when you had the helmets and gloves on. It was always a balance trying to figure out what was absolutely required."

Approaching the point for translunar injection halfway around its second Earth orbit, a preprogrammed sequence fired the Saturn's third-stage engine for one final time, accelerating Apollo 11 to the escape velocity. The TLI burn took just under six minutes. At the moment of ignition, the spacecraft was over the Pacific Ocean; circling more than ninety miles beneath it, a formation of KC-135 aircraft—converted air force tankers carrying a large array of electronic gear—relayed telemetry data from the spacecraft back to Houston. The data indicated that the Saturn V had performed its last job well. Speeding away from the home planet at a rate of six miles per second—faster than a rifle bullet—the astronauts discovered the true meaning of "outward bound."

The trip out started far busier for Collins than it did for Armstrong or Aldrin. As command module pilot, it was Mike's job (assisted by Neil and Buzz) to separate *Columbia* from the S-IVB and turn the command service module around. Mike would then maneuver the CSM into a docking with *Eagle,* the lunar module, which, to survive the launch—with its spindly legs, thrusters and antennae stuck out at odd angles, and extremely fragile pressure shell of a body—had flown up to this point tightly secured inside a strong boxlike container attached atop the S-IVB. It was a critical maneuver in the flight plan. "If the separation and docking did not work," Aldrin has explained, "we would return to Earth. There was also the possibility of an in-space collision and the subsequent decompression of our cabin, so we were still in our spacesuits as Mike separated us from the Saturn third stage."

Neither Aldrin nor Armstrong felt any great apprehension about the maneuver. "Mike did this docking maneuver," Neil relates, "as he would need to make a similar docking with the LM after we returned from the lunar surface. This had been done before on both Apollo 8 and 9, so I was pretty confident about Mike being able to pull it off without any problems."

The maneuver came off perfectly. Explosive bolts blew apart the upper section of the large container, giving access to the LM in its garage atop the rocket. Collins controlled rocket thrusters that moved the CSM out and away some one hundred feet from the landing craft. Turning the spacecraft around, he inched forward gently to a successful head-to-head docking. *Columbia* and *Eagle* were now mated; when the time came, Neil and Buzz could enter the LM through an internal tunnel and hatch arrangement. To complete the separation maneuver, the LM had to be released from its mounting points and the CSM/LM stack had to be backed away from the S-IVB. Then all that remained was to slingshot the S-IVB out of the way. A command sent over to the S-IVB from Apollo 11 caused it to dump all of its leftover fuel, resulting in a propulsive reaction that sent the rocket tumbling off on a long solar-orbit trajectory that would keep it far out of Apollo 11's way.

The time was 1:43 P.M. CDT, which was Houston time, only five hours and eleven minutes into the flight. Apollo 11 was traveling at 12,914 feet per second and approaching 22,000 nautical miles from Earth.

Well in excess of five hours was an awfully long time to be living inside a bulky, sweaty space suit. With the separation, docking, and evasive post-TLI maneuvers behind them, the astronauts stripped down and pulled on their considerably more comfortable two-piece white Teflon fabric jumpsuits. In weightlessness, some things were easier to do than in a gravity field, but three men changing out of space suits—in a compartment equivalent in interior space to a small station wagon—was not one of them. Undressing, folding their stiff heavy suits into storage bags, and then stuffing the filled bags under the couch of the spacecraft was a laborious process that, in Aldrin's words, brought about "a great deal of confusion, with parts and pieces floating about the cabin as we tried to keep logistics under control."

Collins compared it to "three albino whales inside a small tank, banging into the instrument panel despite our best efforts to move slowly. . . . Every time we pushed against the spacecraft our bodies tended to carom off in some unwanted direction and we had to muscle them back into place."

With their clothes finally off, the crew blissfully removed the gadgets affixed to their private parts. Because the astronauts might need to urinate or have a bowel movement before their suits could be taken off, devices for excreting had been connected to them preliminary to suiting up. Aldrin recalls the nitty-gritty details: "We rubbed our behinds with a special salve and pulled on what were euphemistically called fecal-containment garments." The modified diaper kept the odor of despoiled briefs to a minimum, and the salve kept the men's rear ends from chafing too badly. Urinating was accomplished through prophylactic-like devices from which a connector led to a sack resembling a bikini secured around the hips. To function without leaking, the rubber condom catheter had to fit quite snugly, an uncomfortable reality for male plumbing that the crew joked about privately. Once cleaned up and in their jumpsuits with fresh underwear, going to the bathroom was easier and more palatable. Feces got stowed in special containers, and urine was vented out of the spacecraft where it crystallized into bright particles before vanishing from view.

Safely, and now comfortably and hygienically, on their way Moonward, the astronauts relaxed for the first time. As Collins explains, there was no way to prepare oneself for the novel, Twilight Zone–like experience of cislunar space, the region between the Earth and the Moon: "Unlike the roller-coaster ride of the Earth orbit, we are entering a slow-motion domain where time and distance seem to have more meaning than speed. To get a sensation of traveling fast, you must see something whizzing by: the telephone poles along the highway, another airplane crossing your path. . . . In space, objects are too far from each other to blur or whiz, except during a rendezvous or a landing and in those cases the approach is made slowly, very slowly. But if I can't sense speed out my window, I can certainly gauge distance, as the Earth gets smaller and smaller. Finally the whole disk can be seen."

This cosmic vision of "Spaceship Earth" would deeply move every lunar astronaut. "It was a slowly changing panorama as you went from just the horizon to a large arc, to a larger and larger arc, and finally a whole sphere," Armstrong describes. "And depending on what the flight attitude requirements of the vehicle were at any given moment, you may not have been able to see all of that all the time. But we certainly saw the Earth become a sphere. I don't know if we all saw it at the same instant, nor do I remember the exact instant that it occurred. It was a striking event, leaving the planet and realizing that there was no logical reason that you were ever going to fall back to that planet at some point. It was a commitment to excellence, in terms of what you had to do to get back."

Looking back at what would come to be known as the "Whole Earth," Armstrong reveled in his knowledge of geography, a subject at which he had excelled since boyhood. He radioed at three hours and fifty-three minutes into the flight, "You might be interested that out of our left-hand window right now, I can observe the entire continent of North America, Alaska, and over the Pole, down to the Yucatán Peninsula, Cuba, northern part of South America, and then I run out of window." An hour later, he continued the lesson, adding weather reports: "The weather was good just about every-where. There was one cyclonic depression in northern Canada, in the Athabasca, probably east of the Athabasca area. Greenland was clear, and it appeared to be we were seeing just the icecap in Greenland. All North At-lantic was pretty good; and Europe and northern Africa seemed to be clear. Most of the United States was clear. There was what looked like a low front stretching from the center of the country up across north of the Great Lakes and into Newfoundland." Kidding Neil about his geographical expertise, Collins facetiously reported, "I didn't know what I was looking at, but I sure did like it."

In order to make sure that the spacecraft's pipes did not freeze on one side while tank pressures increased from too much heat on the other, Apollo 11 began a slow rotation to ensure that solar rays were absorbed as evenly as possible by all sides of the spacecraft. "We were like a chicken on a barbecue spit," Collins explained. "If we stopped in one position for too long, all kinds of bad things could happen." Visually, the rotisserie action resulted in an incredible panorama, with stunning views of the Sun, Moon, and Earth cycling into the spacecraft's windows every two minutes. Aiding the sightseeing was a simple viewing device called a monocular—half of a set of binoculars. Using it like a magnifying glass, the astronauts took turns getting close looks at different features of their home planet.

It has since become one of the legends of spaceflight that there are only two man-made objects on Earth that can be seen from outer space—the Great Wall of China and the gigantic Fort Peck Dam in Montana. "I would challenge both," Neil states. In cislunar space, "We could see the conti-nents; we could see Greenland. Greenland stood out, just as it does on the globe in your library, all white. Antarctica we couldn't see because there were clouds over it. Africa was quite visible, and we could see sun glint off of a lake. It might have been Lake Chad. . . . But I do not believe that, at least with my eyes, there was any man-made object that could be seen. I have not yet found anyone who has told me they've seen the Great Wall of China even from Earth orbit. I'm not going to say there aren't people, but I personally haven't talked to them. I've asked various people, particularly [Space] Shuttle guys, that have been many orbits around China in the daytime, and the ones I've talked to didn't see it."

Whether it was with the naked eye or with the monocular, Neil could not help but contemplate how fragile the Earth looked: "I don't know why you have that impression, but it is so small. It's very colorful, you know. You see an ocean and gaseous layer, a little bit—just a tiny bit—of atmosphere around it, and compared with all the other celestial objects, which in many cases are much more massive and more terrifying, it just looks like it couldn't put up a very good defense against a celestial onslaught." Buzz and Mike felt likewise, with Buzz thinking how crazy it was for the globe to be so politically and culturally divided: "From space it has an almost benign quality. Intellectually one could realize there were wars under way on Earth, but emotionally it was impossible to understand such things. The thought occurred and reoccurred that wars are generally fought for territory or are disputes over borders; from space the arbitrary borders established on Earth cannot be seen."

Their first urge for serious sightseeing satisfied, the astronauts moved to satiate their belly hunger. Nutritionally, it was important for them during the voyage to consume a sufficient amount of water and calories per day (between 1,700 and 2,500 calories), whether the food in its various dehydrated and freeze-dried preparations was savory or not. Already before their first full meal—scheduled for midafternoon of the first day, following the slingshot of the S-IVB and getting out of their suits—the crew munched down a sandwich or two, made from four types of tubed spread: ham salad, tuna salad, chicken salad, and cheddar cheese. They also made the first raid into their snack pantry, filled with peanut cubes, caramel candy, bacon bites, barbecue beef bites, as well as dried apricots, peaches, and pears.

For the first time in a U.S. spaceflight, the beverage list included not just juice and water but also coffee: fifteen black coffees (for Neil), fifteen with sugar (for Mike), and fifteen with cream and sugar (for Buzz). As blasphemous as it may sound, the juice aboard Apollo 11 was not Tang, the famous orange juice made from powder that its manufacturer, General Foods, advertised as the special drink of the astronauts. "I can't speak for the other flights," Aldrin confesses, "but before ours, the three of us dutifully sampled the orange drink and instead chose a grapefruit-orange mixture as our citrus drink. If Tang was on our flight I was unaware of it."

To get water, the astronauts grabbed one of two six-foot flexible tubes that were attached to spigots—one for cold water, one for hot. At the end of each tube was a pistol probe with a push button. If the astronaut wanted a cold drink, he held the probe in his mouth, pushed the button, and out came a mouthful of water. If he was preparing food, he stuck the hot water gun into a plastic bag and squirted three blasts into it. Massaging the rehydrating food into an edible form, he ate most entrées by sucking them through a tube. Unfortunately, the device designed to ventilate hydrogen from the water before it passed from the gun to the food bag did not function well. Considerable gas came with the water and got into the food to be swallowed by the astronauts, bloating them and giving them stomach gas. "At one point on the trip back to Earth it got so bad," Aldrin jokes, "that we could have shut down our attitude-control thrusters and done the job ourselves!"

The fare turned out to be appetizing enough, if bland. Based on a successful experiment first tried on Apollo 8, one of the dishes enjoyed by Apollo 11—a turkey dinner with gravy and dressing—could be eaten (after mixing with hot water) with a spoon. Also in the spacecraft's pantry were "wet packs" that could be eaten just as they were, including a meal of ham and potatoes. Sometimes the crew all ate the same meal—as they did for lunch on day two of the mission, when they had hot dogs (the first genuine frankfurters to be launched into space), applesauce, chocolate pudding, and the citrus-drink-that-was-not-Tang. Other times, they ate individualized meals that had been prepared by the Manned Spacecraft Center's chief of food and nutrition, Dr. Malcolm C. Smith Jr., after he had consulted with the astronauts' wives about their husbands' likes and dislikes. Neil's favorite meal, according to the NASA's public affairs officer who regularly gave reports on what the astronauts were eating and drinking, was spaghetti with meat sauce, scalloped potatoes, pineapple fruitcake cubes, and grape punch. Aldrin fell in love with shrimp cocktails: "The shrimp were chosen one by one to be sure they would be tiny enough to squeeze out of the food packet, and they were delicious." Collins especially liked the cream of chicken soup and the salmon salad. They were "really delicious by anyone's standards. . . . Ah, this salmon salad! I'll rate it four spoons any day!"

Eleven hours into the flight—stomachs full and housekeeping duties taken care of—the crew was ready for its first sleep period. In fact, at

7:52 P.M. CDT, two hours before the scheduled time, Houston wished its tired crew good night and signed off. The urge to sleep had actually come on the astronauts quite a bit earlier. Just two hours into the flight, before preparations for TLI began, Neil yawned to his mates, "Gee, I almost went to sleep then," to which Collins replied, "Me, too. I'm taking a little rest. . . . You need to get out the alarm clock." Buzz said, "It's going to be a long day. . . . Wake me up at TLI, somebody." For the next nine hours, they fought sporadic drowsiness until it was time to sleep.

Collins took the first watch. As much thinking as had been done to pre-plan every detail of the Apollo 11 mission, there was no way to simulate sleeping three-dimensionally in weightless conditions. "Although you could install the sleep devices in a spacecraft mockup here on Earth," relates Armstrong, "you couldn't sleep in them here on Earth. It required a weight-less condition for that. I don't recall us having any difficulty, however. How we established the places for the 3-D cots, I also don't remember, but we all seemed to find our own all the time. All of the sleeping arrangements were identical in configuration, so the disadvantages of one spot might be that one was closer to noise or light or something like that. But I don't remember any discussion of dissatisfaction with any individual location. I think all the Apollo 11 crew slept well."

The three-dimensional cots referred to by Armstrong were light mesh hammocks, very much like sleeping bags, which were stretched and an-chored beneath the left and right couches—the center couch having been folded down, still covering the crews' space suits. "It kept our arms from floating around and from inadvertently actuating switches," Neil explains. The man on watch—Collins the first night out—slept not in a hammock but floated above the left couch, a lap belt keeping him from floating off and with a miniature headset taped to his ear in case Houston called during the "night." "It was a strange but pleasant sensation to doze off with no pres-sure points falling anywhere on your body," Collins relates. It was like being "suspended by a cobweb's light touch—just floating and falling all the way to the Moon." Buzz got to experience the feeling, but Neil did not, as he al-ways slept in his hammock.

With adrenaline levels still fairly high from the excitement of liftoff and TLI, the men slept only five and a half hours that first night. When CapCom Bruce McCandless of Mission Control's Green Team (headed by Flight Di-rector Cliff Charlesworth) called to wake the crew at 7:48 CDT, all three were already alert. As the astronauts went over their "postsleep checklist," following updates on the flight plan and on consumables, McCandless gave them a brief review of the morning news, much of which concerned the world's enthusiastic reaction to their successful launch.

The very first news item relayed to the crew that morning concerned the flight of the Soviet Union's Luna 15: according to the story read to the astronauts, the USSR's robotic spacecraft had just reached the Moon and started around it. What had happened was this. In a last-ditch effort to steal thunder from America's Moon landing, the Russians had launched the small unmanned spacecraft toward the Moon on July 13, three days prior to Apollo 11's liftoff; its objective was not just to land on the Moon but to scoop up a sample of lunar soil and return it to Earth before Apollo 11 got back. Newspapers in the United States editorialized (accurately) that the Russians were purposefully trying to upstage the Americans with their "mystery probe" and speculated (inaccurately) that they might also be trying to interfere technically with the American flight. U.S. space officials worried that Soviet operations and communications with Luna 15 (Soviet designation Ў e-8-5) might, in fact, interfere with Apollo—over the years that had happened occasionally when the Russians operated at or near NASA's radio frequencies.

MSC's Chris Kraft spoke critically of Luna 15 at a NASA press conference on July 14. Then Kraft telephoned Colonel Frank Borman, the Apollo 8 commander, who was just back from a nine-day tour of the USSR, the first U.S. astronaut ever to visit the country. "The best thing to do is just ask 'em," Borman told Kraft. So, with Nixon's permission, over the famed hotline used by President Kennedy and Soviet premier Nikita Khrushchev to avert nuclear holocaust during the Cuban Missile Crisis of 1962, Borman sent a message to the head of the USSR Academy of Sciences, sixty-eight-year-old Mstislav V. Keldysh. Dr. Keldysh was a leading Soviet academician and the chief of his country's Institute of Applied Mathematics. For over fifteen years, Keldysh had been one of Russian's lead officials in the area of missile and spacecraft design. Borman had met Keldysh during Borman's trip to Moscow. His message asked Keldysh for the exact orbital parameters of the Russian probe. Keldysh complied, assuring Borman, "The orbit of probe Luna 15 does not intersect the trajectory of Apollo 11 spacecraft announced by you in flight program."

True to his word, nothing about Luna 15, in fact, would bother Apollo. Not just that, the Soviet mission failed miserably. Instead of landing on the Moon as scheduled, Luna 15 crashed into the Moon on July 21, the day after Apollo 11's successful landing. Tass, the Soviet news agency, asserted that Luna 15 had "reached the Moon's surface" after flying fifty-two revolutions around it, but American and British sources quickly confirmed that the robotic craft had in fact crashed.

As for the Apollo 11 crew itself, they were never very worried about the Soviet probe. Collins later remarked that the chances of the Russians being able to fly a trajectory that intersected with either *Columbia* or with *Eagle* were "equivalent to my high school football team beating the Miami Dolphins." Armstrong and Aldrin felt similarly. "I wasn't thinking about Luna 15," Neil asserts. "I had too many of my own things to think about."

As for being aware of the Soviet Union's *manned* lunar program, neither the Apollo 11 crew nor any other American astronauts knew much more about it than could be read in the trade press. "I don't remember receiving any classified briefings on the Soviet program," Armstrong comments. "In general, NASA had an unclassified program, and we were seldom burdened with classified information about 'the other side.' That made it substantially easier for us to remember what we could and could not say."

Actually, no one outside the deep dark core of the Soviet space program knew just how far the USSR was falling short of launching cosmonauts to the Moon, or whether the Soviets were even pushing a manned lunar program. Not confirmed until many years later was a powerful explosion—the most powerful in the history of rocketry—on the launchpad at the Baikonur Cosmodrome in Kazakhstan on July 3, 1969, just nine days before the launch of Luna 15 and thirteen days before the liftoff of Apollo 11. On that day, the Soviets were test firing a Moon rocket of their own: a mammoth booster designated the N-1. If the unmanned test launch of the N-1 worked, the Soviets were prepared to press on with their clandestine manned lunar program, a program that Kremlin leadership had always insisted they did not have. Seconds after the launch, however, the N-1 rocket collapsed back onto its pad and exploded—by some estimates with a strength equivalent to 250 tons of TNT, not quite the power of a nuclear explosion, but still formidable. Somehow no one was killed in the carnage, but the launchpad was completely destroyed and the steppe surrounding it "literally strewn with dead animals and birds." Not until November 1969 did rumors of the Soviet accident surface in the Western press; by then, American intelligence knew about it. Photos taken in early August 1969 by U.S. spy satellites flying as part of the ultra-secret CORONA photoreconnaissance program clearly showed the ruin at Baikonur.

For all practical purposes, the N-1 disaster spelled the end of the Soviet Moon program; Luna 15 was a last-gasp effort to salvage a minor victory from the Moon race. Not until after the fall of the Soviet Union in August 1991 did participants in the Soviet Moon program even admit their program existed, let alone that the N-1 disaster had occurred. All evidence of the N-1's very existence had been destroyed, with some of its casings even being used as outlying buildings at the Baikonur installation.

Armstrong did not learn about the N-1 accident until many years later: "I don't remember any briefings on it during my astronaut days."

Another news item read to Apollo 11 by Mission Control that morning said that "Vice President Spiro T. Agnew has called for putting a man on Mars by the year 2000, but Democratic leaders replied that priority must go to needs on Earth. Agnew, the ranking government official at the Apollo 11 blastoff Wednesday, apparently was speaking for himself and not necessarily for the Nixon administration." "Right on, Spiro!" was Mike Collin's off-air reaction. For three men going to the Moon, it could not have seemed that much more fantastical that a future group of astronauts might, in the reasonably near future, be voyaging to the Red Planet. True, political support for NASA had been declining in the second half of the 1960s, but, in the heady summer days of 1969, there was reason to think that the situation would improve. There was no way to know just how lame the support for space exploration would grow under the direction of the Nixon administration and how, for the rest of the century, there would be absolutely no chance for a manned Mars program—or even for a continuation of a manned lunar program beyond 1972.

The major flight event of day two came at 10:17 A.M. CDT when a three-second burn refined the course of Apollo 11 and tested the CSM engine, which would be needed to get the spacecraft in and out of lunar orbit. At the moment of that slight midcourse correction, Armstrong and his mates were 108,594 miles from Earth—over two-fifths of the way to the Moon—and traveling at a velocity of only 5,057 feet per second. Still in the pull of Earth's gravity, the speed of Apollo 11 would decrease steadily until it was less than 40,000 miles from the Moon—by which point the spacecraft had slowed from its top velocity of approximately 25,000 mph to a mere 2,000 mph. Then as the Moon's pull became dominant, it would speed up again.

Much of the astronauts' time during their midflight coast was taken up with the various minor tasks required to keep the CSM operating properly: purging fuel cells, charging batteries, dumping waste water, changing carbon dioxide canisters, preparing food, chlorinating drinking water, and so forth. Collins did most of the routine housekeeping so Armstrong and Aldrin could stay focused on reviewing the details of the landing to come—going over checklists, rehearsing landing procedures. "The flight plan to the Moon had several blank pages," Aldrin remembers, "periods in which we had nothing to do. Yet I have no recollection at all of being idle. I don't think any of us was. . . . Everything had to be stowed or sealed away or anchored to one of the many panels by Velcro. We each had little cloth pouches in which we kept various frequently used items, such as pens, sunglasses and, for me [as well as for Neil], a slide rule. As often or not, one or two of us would be scrambling around on the floor searching for a missing pair of sunglasses, the monocular, a film pack, or a toothbrush." Even during the rare times when they were not performing some manual task, the astronauts were thinking about what was to come next. With Neil in command, there was little idle conversation and small talk—and what there was did not come from him.

During rest periods they did relax to some music. It was played on a small portable tape recorder carried on the flight primarily for the purpose of recording crew comments and observations. Neil and Mike requested some specific music be preloaded onto the cassette tape; Buzz did not, later saying he "was much too busy to be bothered with selecting music and deferred to Neil and Mike, who chose mostly easy listening music."

Neil asked specifically for two recordings. One was Antonin Dvorak's once wildly popular *New World Symphony*, an 1895 composition by the Czech immigrant to the United States that helped legitimize American music to the rest of a dubious world. Neil had played the piece when he was in the Purdue concert band, and he liked it. As the Moon was a new world, it also seemed appropriate to him.

The other was a little-known piece by composer Dr. Samuel J. Hoffman (1904–1968), entitled *Music out of the Moon*. The featured instrument in the Hoffman composition was the theremin, an unusual device (named for Russian engineer and inventor Leo Theremin—known in his homeland as Lev Sergeivich Termen [1836–1933]) that generated tones electronically by a musician controlling the distance between his hands and two metal rods serving as antenna. (The 1945 Alfred Hitchcock film *Spellbound* and the 1951 science-fiction classic *The Day the Earth Stood Still* were scored with the haunting electronic sounds of the theremin.) *Life* magazine reported after the flight that Neil selected *Music out of the Moon* for sentimental reasons, and that he chose a time to broadcast it back to Earth so his wife Janet would hear it and know he was thinking of her. Early in their marriage up in the rustic cabin at Juniper Hills, the couple had allegedly fallen in love with the theremin music. When Neil was flying experimental aircraft at Edwards, Janet listened to the recording by the hour, *Life* said. It was one of the many items that had been lost in their 1964 house fire. Someone found a copy of the album for Neil and taped part of it for the flight.

Both Neil and Janet remember the music, but not quite in the way *Life* reported. "I can remember liking the theremin," Janet recalls, "and may have said 'I love that music,' probably because it was unusual music in those days—different. However, to say that I played it all the time is incorrect." The only record player that the couple owned while in Juniper Hills was an old Victrola that was in the cabin when they bought it, the kind with a crank-operated turntable. "I did know that, when the music was played in space, Neil selected it, because the music was so unusual and no one else would have known it. It was nice to think he was thinking of me and was able to take a moment to relax and reflect on the flight. In a sense it was a bit of the 'home' touch to the people of the world that these were real people up there, no robots flying the spacecraft. Good PR." Neil remembers the music even less sentimentally: "I did have the theremin music, which I liked. I don't remember whether Janet liked it or not and do not know if she ever played it at home. I included it because *Music out of the Moon* seemed appropriate for the flight. I do not remember that it had anything to do with Janet."

The highlight of day two was the first live television broadcast from Apollo 11, which was scheduled to begin at 7:30 P.M. EDT. Actually, it was the third TV transmission overall from the flight; the first two were conducted to check out camera functions, the picture quality of both interior and exterior shots, and the strength of signal coming into and out of the Goldstone tracking station in California. That way any glitches could be fixed before several million people around the world tuned in to see the broadcast on Thursday evening.

The first fuzzy picture to appear on everyone's screen was a shot looking back at the home planet, which Armstrong described as "just a little more than a half Earth." In plain but wondrous language, Neil pointed out the "definite blue cast" of the oceans, the "white bands of major cloud formations over the Pacific," "the browns in the landforms," and "some greens showing along the northwestern coast of the United States and northwestern coast of Canada." He explained that at their current distance—some

139,000 nautical miles—the depth of the colors was not as great as what they had enjoyed while in Earth orbit or even at 50,000 miles out. Collins humorously turned the camera around in his hands a full 180 degrees, saying, "Okay, world, hold on to your hat. I'm going to turn you upside down." Mike rotated the camera a second time, a little more smoothly, then told Charlie Duke, the CapCom for Flight Director Gene Kranz's White Team, "I'm making myself seasick, Charlie, I'll just put you back right-side-up where you belong."

For thirty-six minutes, the astronauts put on a show. The model of spontaneity, Collins disavowed the use of cue cards, Aldrin did a few zero-g push-ups, and Neil even stood on his head. (Collins: "Neil's standing on his head again. He's trying to make me nervous.") Head chef Collins also demonstrated how to make chicken stew when traveling at a speed of 4,400 feet per second. Neil relates that most of the telecast seemed improvised but Aldrin notes that "we went to great lengths" to make it look that way. "The fact is they were carefully planned in advance and for me the exact words were written down on little cards stuck on to the panel in front of us." Neil used no written aids, having thought through what he wanted to do and say only shortly before the TV transmission.

The transmission ended emotionally with Neil saying, "As we pan back out to the distance at which we see the Earth, it's Apollo 11 signing off." The crew then spent the next three hours taking care of additional housekeeping items and participating fruitlessly in a telescope experiment during which they were unable to spot a bluish-green laser light being shot at them from the McDonald Observatory near El Paso. Though the sleep period was scheduled to begin shortly before 9:00 P.M. CDT, none of them fell asleep until after 11:30, this time with Aldrin in the floating "watch" position. The sleep period was scheduled to be a long one, lasting ten hours. Data from the flight surgeon indicated that "the crew slept rather well all night"—so well, in fact, that Mission Control let them have an extra hour before waking them up to perform such chores as charging batteries, dumping wastewater, and checking fuel and oxygen reserves.

In the preliminary flight plan, Aldrin and Armstrong were not scheduled to make their first inspection trip into *Eagle* until Apollo 11 reached lunar orbit around midday of day three, but Aldrin lobbied successfully with the mission planners to enter the LM a day early in order to make sure the lander had suffered no damage during launch and the long flight out. The sojourn began a little after 4:00 P.M. CDT, about twenty minutes into what NASA considered at the time the clearest TV transmission from space ever made. Collins did the honors of opening the hatch. Armstrong squeezed through the thirty-inch-wide tunnel and floated in through the top of the LM, followed by Aldrin. Both Neil and Buzz remember the down-up-up-down trip into *Eagle* as one of the oddest sensations of their entire Moon trip, crawling from the floor to the ceiling of the command module only to find themselves descending headfirst from the ceiling of the docked LM. "Though slightly disorienting," Buzz states, "it was intriguing to move about my chores, knowing all the time that just a few feet away everyone else was, by my reckoning, upside down."

Though Neil was the first one to take a look inside *Eagle,* it was Buzz as lunar module pilot who began preparing the LM for its separation from *Columbia* that was to come forty-five hours later. Buzz and Neil took the movie camera and television camera along with them, sending back the first pictures from inside the LM. Mission Control knew that the transmission was coming, but it surprised the TV networks, which were not expecting the next pictures from Apollo 11 until 7:30 P.M. EDT, the same time as the previous evening. Scurrying to make the necessary technical connections, CBS, for example, went on air with Cronkite and sidekick Wally Schirra at 5:50 P.M. The first images—being broadcast live to the United States, Japan, western Europe, and much of South America—showed Aldrin taking an equipment inventory in the LM. Later, Buzz gave the international television audience a look at the space suit and life support equipment that he and Neil would wear on the Moon.

No account of the flight of Apollo 11 would be complete without coming to grips with subsequent tales that the crew saw a UFO.

According to the story—which over the past thirty-plus years has been told and retold in so many different versions that it is in fact wrong to call it *one* story—the astronauts on their way to the Moon saw something, perhaps several things, they could not identify, ranging from mysterious lights to actual formations of spaceships. One version has "a mass of intelligent energy" tailing the spacecraft all the way from the Earth to the Moon. Another has "a bright object resembling a giant snowman," which later "proved" to be two UFOs, racing across Apollo 11's path as it reached lunar orbit. Still another has Collins spotting a UFO as he was photographing the LM's ascent from the surface. Allegedly, close analysis of the Apollo 11 film and photographs verified the presence of UFOs, but NASA, the Pentagon, and the entirety of the U.S. government all conspired to cover up the evidence, going so far as editing out major portions of Apollo 11's onboard and air-to-ground audio recordings. Most incredible of all, the story has made the rounds that just as Armstrong started down the ladder to make his historic first step off the LM and onto the Moon, he saw something on the lunar surface that made him scramble back into the LM, only venturing out again several minutes later after Mission Control calmed him down and insisted that he and Aldrin make their Moon walk.

In broad sociocultural perspective, it is not at all surprising to find that people fascinated with UFOs and the possibility of extraterrestrial life have projected their anticipations onto the astronauts and their missions. The sighting of "flying saucers" became an epidemic in the years following World War II, perhaps because, as one historian has tried to explain it, the specter of Armageddon brought on by the appearance of the atomic bomb spawned "at once an appetite for vicarious scientific adventure and a need to externalize fear." So crazy had the belief in UFOs become in the late 1940s that the U.S. Air Force began to amass hundreds of case studies and firsthand personal testimonies about UFOs from pilots and common folk alike, in what came to be called the "Blue Book investigations"; in the end, the air force's conclusions satisfied no one. The UFO craze crested in the late 1950s and early 1960s with the birth of the Space Age, heightened by the launch of the first satellites and space capsules. Any comment about a possible unidentified flying object, especially if made by a pilot, set off another string of reported sightings. Stories circulated that NASA test pilot Joe Walker, in April 1962, filmed five cylindrical and disk-shaped objects from his X-15 aircraft; that two radar technicians, in April 1964, watched UFOs following an unmanned Gemini capsule; that NASA installed a special instrument on Gemini IV to detect UFOs; that Borman and Lovell on Gemini VII and Conrad and Gordon on Gemini XI had spotted "bogeys." Whatever it was that was originally factual behind the reports quickly got lost amid the illusions, gross exaggerations, and outright fabrications that fed the public's growing appetite for news about UFOs.

It would have been astounding if something as epochal as the first Moon landing had not generated a fresh and intense new round of UFO stories even more untruthful, hyperbolic, and stubbornly persistent than what came before. On the Internet today, a search involving the words "Apollo 11" and "UFO" results in 5,410 hits, "Apollo" and "UFO" in 61,700 hits, "astronaut" and "UFO" in 46,000 hits; "pilot" and "UFO" in 136,000 hits; and "UFO" alone in 4.46 million hits. Just for "Neil Armstrong" and "UFO," one gets directed to 3,180 different Web sites; for Buzz Aldrin,

1,700 sites; for Mike Collins only 349. Clearly, it is important to those who want to believe in alien intelligence that the First Man, even more so than his two crewmates (or any other astronaut), spotted a UFO.

As is true for many a fanciful story, the stories about Apollo 11's UFO "sightings" have a kernel of truth. The first alleged sighting came early on day one just as the burn for TLI was starting:

00:02:44:37 elapsed time

Collins: *Flashes out window number five. I'm not sure whether that's— it could be lightning or it could be something to do with the engine. . . . Continual flashes. . . . Look out the window. If you're—if it looks like what I see out window 5, you don't want to look at it* [laughter].

Armstrong: *I don't see anything.*

Aldrin: *Why?* [in response to Collins's statement]

Collins: *These flashes out there . . .*

Armstrong: *Oh, I see a little flashing out there, yes.*

Collins: *You see that? Buzz is usually looking . . . Just watch window 5 for a second. See it?*

Aldrin: *Yes, yes. Damn! Everything's—just kind of sparks flying out there.*

Why Collins jokingly said to his crewmates, "you don't want to look at it," can only be interpreted to mean that he worried that, if they did look, and saw what he saw, they all might feel it necessary to report that they had seen something they could not identify. And reporting anything that sounded like a UFO was not something the astronauts wanted to do. So, they said nothing to the ground about the flashing lights, even though, as Aldrin recalls, they saw the flashes "at least two or three different times," and not just on the outbound flight.

The first time that an American astronaut said he saw something strange in space was in 1962 when John Glenn in *Friendship 7* spotted what he called "fireflies" ("I see a big mass of some very small particles that are brilliantly lit up like they're luminescent. . . . they look like little stars. . . . They swirl around the capsule"). As it turned out, Glenn's fireflies were ice flakes falling off the skin of the Mercury 6 space capsule, but that discovery was not made until Carpenter's Mercury 7 flight. By that time, the idea had circulated in the popular mind that Glenn might have run into some alien life form.

Armstrong, Collins, and Aldrin knew all about John Glenn's fireflies—as well as about every other phenomenon, physical, optical, or otherwise, that they and their fellow astronauts had experienced in the twenty manned spaceflights prior to Apollo—but what the flashes were that seemed to appear outside their windows less than three hours into their own flight they did not know.

After the astronauts were back safely on Earth, Aldrin had the most to say about the flashing lights; not surprisingly, Armstrong had the least. So anxious was Buzz to tell someone about them that he did not wait until the astrophysics part of the Apollo debriefing; he volunteered the information right in the middle of the debriefing about the astronauts' *food.*

"The food guys couldn't have cared less," Buzz laughs today. "It wasn't their subject, and the astrophysics guys never listened to the food debriefing, so nothing happened. At the time we were in quarantine, so I finally called up somebody but was told, 'They are all on travel.' Later, I was able to talk to somebody and together we began to understand what it was. I forget how many weeks later, someone from astrophysics finally called and said, 'We're getting more curious about this, and we're wondering if you could help us with an experiment. We've designed something and would you come over and put your head in this thing for us,' and I said, 'No, thanks!' "

The phenomenon of the flashing lights was unusual enough that NASA briefed the next crew about it. When Apollo 12 went up, they too saw the lights; in fact, they came back and reported, "Guess what? We see them with our eyes closed!"

The flashing lights turned out to be a phenomenon that occurred in the especially dark conditions of outer space *inside the human eyeball.* "I thought I was seeing something within the cabin and outside of my body," Buzz relates today, and so did Mike. From his few remarks to his mates about the flashes at the time, it is not clear that Neil was so sure they were not just optical phenomena—and typical of Neil, he was never fast about drawing conclusions except when he had to.

What the Apollo 11 crew eventually found out was that there was a threshold—an optical threshold tied to a psychological threshold—where a person had to *want* to look and see the flashing lights or he just would not observe them. Experts have since explained that some astronauts have such a sensitive threshold that they see the flashes even when flying in near space below the Van Allen radiation belt. "But six people had gone outside the Van Allen Belt before we did [the crews of Apollo 8 and 10]," Aldrin notes, "and they hadn't seen any flashes." So, the crew of Apollo 11 was involved in another "first."

Less significantly from the point of view of science, but of import for those who want to believe in UFOs, was a second "sighting" that the crew could not explain—or at least be 100 percent sure of their explanation.

It took place the evening of the third day—the day of the first sojourn into the LM—shortly after 9:00 P.M. Aldrin apparently saw it first: "I found myself idly staring out of the window of the *Columbia* and saw something that looked a bit unusual. It appeared brighter than any star and not quite the pinpoint of light that stars are. It was also moving relative to the stars. I pointed this out to Mike and Neil, and the three of us were beset with curiosity. With the help of the monocular we guessed that whatever it was, it was only a hundred miles or so away. Looking at it through the sextant we found it occasionally formed a cylinder, but when the sextant's focus was adjusted it had a sort of illuminated 'L' look to it. There was a straight line, maybe a little bump in it, and then a little something off to the side. It had a shape of some sort—we all agreed on that—but exactly what it was we couldn't pin down."

The crew fretted, "What are we going to say about this?" Aldrin remembers, "We sure as hell were not going to talk about it to the ground, because all that would do is raise a curiosity and if that got out, someone might say NASA needed to be commanded to abandon the mission, because we had aliens going along! Our reticence to be outspoken while it was happening was because we were just prudent. We didn't want to do anything that gave the UFO nuts any ammunition at all, because enough wild things had been said over the years about astronauts seeing strange things."

At first the crew speculated that what they were seeing was the shell of the Saturn S-IVB that had been slingshot away more than two days earlier. After the S-IVB's propulsive maneuver, the astronauts had seen it traveling well out of their way, on a trajectory that would miss the Moon and send it into solar orbit. (On later Apollo missions, NASA intentionally maneuvered the S-IVB to impact the Moon for the purpose of taking seismographic readings, but it did not do that on Apollo 11.) So, at two days, twelve hours, forty-five minutes, and forty-six seconds of elapsed time into the flight, Neil radioed, "Houston, Apollo 11. Do you have any idea where the S-IVB is with respect to us?" The answer came back some three minutes later: "Apollo 11, Houston. The S-IVB is about 6,000 nautical miles away from you. Over." "Okay. Thank you," replied Neil.

The astronauts scratched their heads. At far closer than 6,000 miles, the object in sight could not be the S-IVB, but rather one of the four panels that had enclosed the LM's launch garage. When the LM was extracted for face-to-face mating with the command module, the side panels had sprung off in different directions. Analytical studies had indicated the most likely trajectories for the four ejected panels, but NASA could not track the panels because there were no transponders on them.

The Apollo 11 crew was convinced that what they saw was one of the panels. According to Aldrin, "We could see it for about forty-five seconds at a time as the ship rotated, and we watched it off and on for about an hour. . . . Its course appeared in no way to conflict with ours, and as it presented no danger we dropped the matter there," and went to sleep. Nothing more was said about the sighting until one portion of NASA's classified debriefing. Armstrong is confident that no one in NASA suggested what they should or should not say in the future about the UFO. What was to be said was left to the individual crew member.

In Armstrong's mind today, there is still no doubt that what they all saw was a detached part of their own spacecraft. "We did watch a slow blinking light some substantial distance away from us. Mission Control eventually concluded—and I agree—that it was one of the Saturn LM adapter panels. These panels were enormous and would have been given a rotation in the process of their ejection from the S-IVB. The reflection from these panels would, therefore, be similar to blinking. I do not know why we did not see the other three panels, but I suspect that the one that was directly down from the Sun from us would have provided the brightest reflection."

How the panel had kept up with the Apollo 11 spacecraft for over two days—and in fact, was out in front of it—was a simple matter of Newtonian physics. "When the SLA panels were ejected," Neil explains, "they had a very slight outward relative velocity, but their velocity along the flight path was essentially identical to that of the CSM-LM combination. The panels, therefore, having no atmospheric drag to slow them, traveled at the CSM-LM speed, but developed an ever-increasing lateral separation from it." As for why the S-IVB was so far *behind* the spacecraft, that was explained by the fact that the S-IVB was traveling along the same velocity vector but after separation was traveling slightly slower than the CSM-LM. Over a couple days' time, a sizable distance developed between the two.

No matter the thoroughness of the scientific explanation, however, the fact of the matter is that Apollo 11 did see what technically has to be called an unidentified flying object. "When somebody asks, 'Did you see a UFO?' Aldrin admits, "technically we should say we did. But given all the misstatements that would come forth from that, I'll only tell the story if I'm given enough time. I'll tell a complete story to somebody with the idea that, once they understand the whole story, they won't make a big thing of it. I'll try to manage the information in the right way. But immediately after Apollo 11 we all thought it was so, 'No, no, no.' "

The third night out the Apollo 11 astronauts rested more fitfully—they knew that when they awoke, day four was going to be different. As Collins would later say, it was time for the crew "to lay their little pink bodies on the line." Stopping their rotisserie motion and getting into lunar orbit was not automatic. If the spacecraft did not slow down sufficiently it would sail on by the Moon in a gigantic arc and make a looping return back to the vicinity of the Earth.

Arousing the astronauts that morning at 7:32 A.M. CDT, Mission Control again started the day by reading them the morning news. "First off, it looks like it's going to be impossible to get away from the fact that you guys are dominating all the news back here on Earth," said Bruce McCandless, taking his turn as CapCom. "Even *Pravda* in Russia is headlining the mission and calls Neil 'The Czar of the Ship.' I think maybe they got the wrong mission. . . . Back here in Houston, your three wives and children got together for lunch yesterday at Buzz's house. And, according to Pat, it turned out to be a gabfest. The children swam and did some high jumping over Buzz's bamboo pole."

McCandless mentioned that a Houston astrologer by the name of Ruby Graham was reading all signs as right for Apollo 11's trip to the Moon: "She says that Neil is clever, Mike has good judgment, and Buzz can work out intricate problems. She also says Neil tends to see the world through rose-colored glasses, but he is always ready to help the afflicted or distressed. Neil, you are also supposed to have 'intuition that enables you to interpret life with feeling.' " Armstrong offered no comment, as the word of an astrologer held no interest for him—nor offered any real understanding of his personality.

With their spacecraft now only 12,486 miles from the Moon, the dawning of a spectacular and eerie view made it clear that the moment of truth would soon be at hand. With the Sun directly behind the Moon and backlighting the planetoid, Apollo 11 was flying through a giant solar eclipse, a massive lunar shadow, with the Sun's corona cascading brilliantly around the edges of what was now a huge dark object completely filling their windows. The Earthshine shone so brightly from behind them that it cast the lunar surface as three-dimensional. Grabbing their cameras, the astronauts took numerous shots of the sensational effect, but the highly unusual lighting conditions impacted the quality of the pictures.

Only six men in history had ever seen the Moon look anything like this, but neither the crew of Apollo 8 nor Apollo 10 had done more than contemplate setting down in such a forlorn-looking place. Apollo 11 had to do it. Even Collins, the one who did not have to land, privately felt a foreboding—the "cool, magnificent sphere" hanging there "ominously," "a formidable presence without sound or motion," issuing "no invitation to invade its domain." Despite the fact that the crew had spent years studying photographs from the Ranger, Lunar Orbiter, and Surveyor spacecraft, as well as from Apollo 8 and 10, it was "nevertheless a shock to actually see the Moon at firsthand," Collins later wrote. "The first thing that springs to mind is the vivid contrast between the Earth and the Moon. One has to see the second planet up close to truly appreciate the first. I'm sure that to a geologist the Moon is a fascinating place, but this monotonous rock pile, this withered, sun-seared peach pit out my window offers absolutely no competition to the gem it orbits. Ah, the Earth, with its verdant valleys, its misty waterfalls . . . I'd just like to get our job done and get out of here."

Inside the spacecraft at the time, the astronauts searched with much less success for the right adjectives to describe for the public the incredible phenomenon they were seeing. In talking to the ground, Armstrong did his best to keep reports tangible and unemotional, but it was hard even for him to hold back the superlatives. "The view of the Moon that we've been having recently is really spectacular," Neil reported. "It fills about three-quarters of the hatch window and, of course, we can see the entire circumference, even though part of it is in complete shadow and part of it's in Earthshine. It's a view worth the price of the trip."

But the trip was not about looking at the Moon, it was about landing on it—and that could not happen unless Apollo 11 managed to get into a proper parking orbit from which the LM could make its descent. The vital first step in that process was making a very precise burn called "LOI-1," the basic Lunar Orbit Insertion.

03:03:30:46   CapCom: *Eleven, this is Houston. You are Go for*
                          LOI. Over.

03:03:30:53   Aldrin: *Roger. Go for LOI.*

The burn involved firing the service propulsion system engine for just under six minutes, braking Apollo 11 down to a speed that allowed the Moon's gravity to trap the spacecraft and reel it into orbit. As Mike Collins's explanation makes clear, it was a moment of truth: "We need to reduce our speed by 2,000 mph, from 5,000 down to 3,000, and will do this by burning our service propulsion system engine for six minutes. We are extra careful, paying painful attention to each entry on their checklist." A lot of help with the burn came from the onboard computer and from Mission Control, but it was up to the astronauts to get it right: "If just one digit slips in our computer, and it is the worst possible digit, we could turn around backward and blast ourselves into an orbit headed for the Sun."

From every indication, it seemed that the LOI burn went well, but Mission Control could not know with certainty until the vehicle swung its way around the back side of the Moon and Houston, twenty-three minutes later, could once again communicate with it.

"We don't know if all is going well with Apollo 11," Walter Cronkite intoned on CBS's live coverage, which began at 1:30 P.M. EDT, "because it is behind the Moon and out of contact with Earth for the first time. Eight minutes ago they fired their large service propulsion system engine to go into orbit around the Moon. We'll know about that in the next fifteen minutes or so. That's when they come around the Moon and again acquire contact with the Earth and they can report. We hope that they are successfully in orbit around the Moon and that the rest of the historic mission can go as well as the first three days."

Inside Mission Control, a few isolated conversations were taking place, but not very many; most people were waiting in silence for the "acquisition of signal," or AOS. On TV, Cronkite accentuated the drama, noting, "It is quiet around the world as the world waits to see if Apollo 11 is in a successful Moon orbit."

The anxiety ended when Houston heard a faint, indistinct signal from the spacecraft, at exactly the moment it was expected:

03:04:15:47   CapCom: *Apollo 11, Apollo 11, this is Houston. Do you*
                          read? Over.

03:04:15:59	CapCom:	*Apollo 11, Apollo 11, this is Houston. Do you read? Over.*
03:04:16:11	Apollo 11:	[indistinct signal]
03:04:16:59	Apollo 11:	*Houston, Apollo 11. Over.*
03:04:17:00	CapCom:	*Apollo 11, Apollo 11, this is Houston. We are reading you weakly. Go ahead. Over.*

Sounding about as elated as he ever got when communicating with the ground from the cockpit of a flying machine, Neil immediately provided Houston with a status report on the burn. Running through a long string of numbers on burn time and residuals,* when Houston then asked to "send the whole thing again, please," Neil exclaimed, "It was like—like perfect!"

Twenty minutes before Apollo came coasting around the Moon and back into contact with Houston, the astronauts thrilled at achieving precisely their intended orbit:

03:03:58:10	Armstrong:	*That was a beautiful burn.*
03:03:58:12	Collins:	*Goddamn, I guess!†*
03:03:58:37	Armstrong:	*All right, let's— Okay, now we've got some things to do . . .*
03:03:58:48	Aldrin:	*Okay, let's do them.*
03:03:59:08	Collins:	*Well, I don't know if we're sixty miles or not, but at least we haven't hit that mother.*
03:03:59:11	Aldrin:	*Look at that! Look at that! 169.6* [nautical miles] *by 60.9* [nautical miles].

---

* Performing a timed burn with Apollo's SPS rocket engine could produce a substantial acceleration (or deceleration) if the engine shutoff was not precise. It was critically important to know what these differences in speed, or "residuals," amounted to, so as correct them. Corrections were made, not by firing the main engine again—that could add to the problem—but by briefly firing (the astronauts called it "tickling") the spacecraft's smaller maneuvering thrusters.

† This transcript excerpt as well as the two that follow in the text were from the onboard recorder and were not transmitted to Earth. The astronauts were careful about uttering profanity when they knew that what they were saying was being transmitted home.

03:03:59:15	Collins:	*Beautiful, beautiful, beautiful, beautiful! You want to write that down or something? Write it down just for the hell of it: 170 by 60. Like gangbusters.*
03:03:59:28	Aldrin:	*We only missed by a couple tenths of a mile.*
03:03:59:36	Collins:	*Hello, Moon!*

All across the Moon's rocky back side, the part never visible from Earth and densely pockmarked by 4.6 billion years of meteoroid bombardment, Aldrin and Collins had excitedly pointed out one spectacular feature after another, while the "Ice Commander," as a few astronauts privately had come to call Armstrong, was more restrained in expressing what was his own genuine enthusiasm:

03:04:05:32	Aldrin:	*Oh, golly, let me have that camera back. There's a huge, magnificent crater over here. I wish we had the other lens on but, God, that's a big beauty. You want to look at that guy, Neil?*
03:04:05:43	Armstrong:	*Yes, I see him. . . . You want to get the other lens on?*
03:04:06:07	Collins:	*Don't you want to get the Earth coming up? It's going to be nine minutes.*
03:04:06:11	Aldrin:	*Yes. Let's take some pictures here first.*
03:04:06:15	Collins:	*Well, don't miss that first one. . . .*
03:04:06:27	Armstrong:	*You're going to have plenty of passes.*
03:04:06:30	Aldrin:	*Yes, right.*
03:04:06:33	Collins:	*Plenty of Earthrises, I guess.*
03:04:06:37	Armstrong:	*Yes, we are. Boy, look at that . . . crater. You can probably see him right there. . . . What a spectacular view!*
03:04:08:48	Collins:	*Fantastic. Look back there behind us. Sure looks like a gigantic crater. Look at the mountains going around it. My gosh, they're monsters!*
03:04:09:58	Armstrong:	*See that real big—*

03:04:10:01	Collins:	*Yes, there's a moose down here you just wouldn't believe. There's the biggest one yet. God, it's huge! It's enormous! It's so big I can't even get it in the window. You want to look at that?! That's the biggest one that you ever seen in your life, Neil? God, look at this central mountain peak! Isn't that a huge one?*
03:04:11:01	Aldrin:	*Yes, there's a big mother over here, too.*
03:04:11:07	Collins:	*Come on now, Buzz, don't refer to them as big mothers. Give them some scientific name . . . Golly damn, a geologist up here would just go crazy.*

In lunar orbit, the crew tried to settle an informal controversy that had arisen from the two previous circumlunar flights. To the Apollo 8 crew, the surface of the Moon appeared to be gray, whereas it looked mostly brown to Apollo 10. As soon as they had a chance, Neil, Mike, and Buzz looked to settle the issue. "Plaster of Paris gray to me," Collins remarked even before they got into orbit. "Well, I have to vote with the 10 crew," Aldrin said shortly after LOI. "Looks tan to me," Armstrong offered. "But when I first saw it, at the other Sun angle, it really looked gray," Buzz continued, and his mates agreed, though they expatiated about the Moon's color throughout several orbits. Ultimately, the controversy was settled in no one's favor. Lighting conditions made all the difference. The color of the Moon shifted almost hourly from charcoal, near dawn or dusk, to a rosy tan at midday.

The first time Armstrong had a chance to survey his approach to the landing site he took it. "Apollo 11 is getting its first view of the landing approach," he reported to Mission Control at 11:55 A.M. Houston time. "This time we are going over the Taruntius crater, and the pictures and maps brought back by Apollo 8 and 10 have given us a very good preview of what to look at here. It looks very much like the pictures, but like the difference between watching a real football game and watching it on TV. There's no substitute for actually being here." Houston responded: "We concur, and we surely wish we could see it firsthand."

Apollo 11's first television transmission from lunar orbit started at 3:56 P.M. EDT. As it was a Saturday afternoon in July, many Americans tuned to the broadcast after watching the baseball *Game of the Week* on NBC TV, which that day pitted the Baltimore Orioles against the Boston Red Sox at Fenway Park. (The Red Sox won the game 5–3, but the Orioles ultimately won the American League pennant but lost the World Series to the New York "Miracle" Mets.)

Given that an orbit circularization burn was scheduled for 5:44 EDT that afternoon, the astronauts were in no mood for a television performance; in fact, as Neil made clear to Mission Control, if they had their druthers, they would not have had a TV show then at all.

03:05:34:24	CapCom:	*Eleven, this is Houston.* [The CapCom at AOS after the LOI burn and through the first pass over the landing site was Bruce McCandless.] *We have about six minutes remaining until LOS* [loss of signal]*, and in order that we may configure our ground lines, we'd like to know if you're still planning to have the TV up with the beginning of the next pass. Over.*
03:05:34:48	Armstrong:	*Roger, Houston. We'll try to have it ready.*
03:05:34:50	CapCom:	*This is Houston. We are inquiring if it is your plan to. Over.*
03:05:35:00	Armstrong:	*It never was our plan to, but it's in the flight plan, so I guess we'll do it.*
03:05:35:07	CapCom:	*Houston. Roger. Out.*

The broadcast lasted for thirty-five minutes. Focusing the camera first out of a side window and then out of the hatch window as the spacecraft passed from west to east nearly one hundred miles above the lunar surface, the astronauts took the worldwide TV audience on a guided tour of the Moon's visible side. Like airline pilots pointing out the Grand Canyon or Hoover Dam down below, they talked their way along the path that Neil and Buzz would be taking in the LM in less than twenty-four hours. Neil indicated the "PDI point," where powered descent would be initiated, then Collins and Aldrin spontaneously took turns noting every significant landmark that would be guiding *Eagle* down to its touchdown: the twin peaks of Mount Marilyn, named by Jim Lovell during Apollo 8 after his wife; the large Maskelyne Crater; the small hills dubbed Boothill and Duke Island that would be passed over just twenty seconds into descent; the washbasin that was Maskelyne W; the rilles labeled Sidewinder and Diamondback because they twisted across the surface like desert snakes; the Gashes; the Last Ridge; and finally, the landing site on the Sea of Tranquility, which was then barely into the darkness.

It was the first time that the astronauts themselves caught a glimpse of the landing site, as on the previous orbit the spot had lay hidden, beyond the "terminator" line where the astronauts would pass from light into darkness. This time around, the spot was just barely visible, brightened by Earthshine.

Everyone at home and in the spacecraft strained with Neil to take a close look. Collins, for one, did not especially like what he saw, though he kept it to himself: "It is just past dawn in the Sea of Tranquility and the Sun's rays are intersecting the landing site at a very shallow angle. Under these conditions the craters on the surface cast long, jagged shadows, and to me the entire region looks distinctly forbidding. I don't see anyplace smooth enough to park a baby buggy, much less a Lunar Module."

Crossing the terminator, the crew trained its TV camera back though the window for a last look at the landing site before sign-off. "And as the Moon sinks slowly in the west," the witty Collins remarked, "Apollo 11 bids good day to you."

An hour and thirteen minutes later, Apollo 11 fired the SPS engine for the second time that afternoon. Even more than with the first burn, precise timing was critical. "If we overburned for as little as two seconds," Aldrin explains, "we'd be on an impact course with the other side of the Moon." Concentration was intense as the astronauts, in coordination with Mission Control, made a systematic series of star checks, inertial platform alignments, and navigational calculations with the onboard computer. Collins used a stopwatch to make sure it lasted seventeen seconds, no more and no less. The burn came off perfectly. Apollo 11's orbit dropped and stabilized from an orbit of 168.8 miles by 61.3 nautical miles, in astronomical terms an "eccentric" orbit, to one that was 66.1 by 54.4 miles, close to a perfect ellipse. It was a high degree of precision that excited even the commander:

03:08:13:47	Armstrong:	*66.1 by 54.4—now you can't beat that.*
03:08:13:52	Collins:	*That's right downtown.*
03:08:14:00	Aldrin:	*We're more elliptic now, huh?*
03:08:14:05	Collins:	*That's about as close as you're going to get.*

With Apollo 11 now snug in its orbit, it was time to prepare the LM for its designated job. Powering it up, completing a long list of communications checks, and presetting a number of switches was scheduled to take Neil and Buzz a period of three hours, but it took them thirty minutes less thanks to Aldrin's preparatory work in the module the previous day. By 8:30 P.M. Houston time *Eagle* was ready. So were the two astronauts, who reluctantly headed back into *Columbia* for their fourth night's sleep inside the spacecraft, the first in orbit about the Moon. The commander and his lunar module pilot carefully organized all the equipment and clothing they would need in the morning. Then they covered the windows to keep out not only direct light from the Sun but also the Moonshine—far brighter than we see on Earth—and began to settle into their sleeping positions:

03:13:52:25	Aldrin:	*Why don't you guys sleep underneath tonight? I'll sleep top deck.*
03:13:52:34	Armstrong:	*You're going to sleep underneath tonight, aren't you?*
03:13:52:36	Aldrin:	*Yes, that's right; I remember.*
03:13:52:40	Collins:	*Unless you'd rather sleep up top, Buzz. I like . . . You guys ought to get a good night's sleep, going in that damn LM. How about . . . Which would you prefer? . . . Take your druthers.*

Knowing of Neil's preference that he sleep before the landing attempt, Buzz eased, as Neil did, into one of the floating hammocks. Dousing the cabin lights, Collins put the punctuation on the day: "Well, I thought today went pretty well. If tomorrow and the next day are like today, we'll be safe."

At three minutes after midnight, the on-duty PAO at Mission Control reported to the press, many of whom would themselves not get much sleep that night or the next, "The Apollo 11 crew is currently in their rest period, but we've received no indication that any of the crew members are actually sleeping." Aldrin recalls sleeping fitfully; Neil remembers sleeping soundly, but not for very long. Houston's wakeup call came at 6:00 A.M. By midmorning Aldrin and Armstrong would need to be inside the LM ready to separate *Eagle* from *Columbia* for its trip down to the Moon.

CHAPTER 28

The Landing

The drama that was Apollo 11 unfolded in five acts almost as if Aeschylus or Shakespeare had staged it. Act One launched the protagonists—those "amiable strangers"—toward their lunar destiny. Act Two moved them inexorably into the brave new world of the outward bound. Bereft of the safety and security of their home planet, the astronauts probed the vastness of deep space, an alien environment into which only six human beings had ever before ventured. In that cold and unforgiving world, the intrepid crew journeyed with seeming nonchalance for three days and three nights. As it always did in classical theater, the climax came in Act Three: two of the chosen ones left a vigilant third behind, entered their fragile landing craft, and headed down to the Moon's cratered surface. In itself, that was the astronaut's Holy Grail. Not that stepping onto another heavenly body for the first time, the essential element of Act Four, or returning to Earth safely, the denouement of Act Five, were without grave risk, high adventure, and cosmic symbolism. But the critical turning point—certainly in Neil Armstrong's life story—was piloting the LM down to the landing.

It was as if everything in Neil's life as a flier led to confronting this supreme challenge: the young boy repeatedly hand-tossing model planes to see how far they could fly; the teenager easing the little rental plane down over the telephone lines bounding his hometown's grass airfield; the aviator flaring in over open water to drop his hurtling machine onto the pitching deck of an aircraft carrier; the test pilot coming down so low onto the desert floor that he could almost count the Joshua trees; the astronaut thrusting up, down, and sideways in a flying bedstead.

As was true even for seasoned pilots, not every one of Neil's landings had been good ones. The rough ground of an Ohio farm field had left his Purdue University airplane in such bad shape that the machine had to be trucked back to West Lafayette in pieces aboard his grandfather's hay wagon. His porpoising after touchdown at Edwards had broken the X-1B's nose gear. Then there was the day he stuck the T-33 deep in the mud while doing touch-and-go's on a not-so-dry lake with Yeager, and the time he fouled the runway at Nellis when the arresting hook of his F-104 snared an anchor chain and sent big chunks of steel careening here and yon. Twice in his career, the machines he piloted became so dysfunctional that coaxing the craft down to a landing proved impossible, and his only choice was to eject.

Indeed, going back all the way to his boyhood fall from a backyard tree, most of the high drama in Armstrong's life lay more in his "comings down" than his "goings up." Not that his ascents did not take extreme concentration and skill. Still, it was the descents that ultimately posed the greatest challenge and danger—and defined his destiny.

The day of the first Moon landing was a Sunday for Americans, Europeans, Africans, and some Asians, a fact that did not pass unnoticed by millions of devout believers; in fact, of all the lunar landings, only Apollo 11 landed on the Christian Sabbath.

Getting up at 5:30 A.M., even earlier than her son did that morning, Viola Armstrong put on a bathrobe and went outside to water her flowers before the reporters could get to her. Then she dressed for a 7:30 church service. She wanted to be home in plenty of time to follow on television her son's separation from the command module.

All around the world the devout prayed for Apollo 11. The worship service at the Nixon White House was dedicated to the mission: astronaut Frank Borman read once more from the Book of Genesis, reprising the narration that he and his fellow Apollo 8 crew members had performed so memorably from lunar orbit the previous Christmas Eve. A few days previous to the Apollo 11 launch, one of the people attending the worship service, H. R. "Bob" Haldeman, the White House chief of staff and Nixon's primary aide and gatekeeper, had arranged for journalist William Safire, a senior speechwriter for Nixon, to draft statements for use by the president in case something major went wrong during the mission. One of Safire's statements covered the hypothetical scenario of the astronauts managing to land on the Moon but then not being able to get off it.

> *In Event of Moon Disaster:*
>   *Fate has ordained that the men who went to the moon to explore in peace will stay on the moon to rest in peace.*

These brave men, Neil Armstrong and Edwin Aldrin, know that there is no hope for their recovery. But they also know that there is hope for mankind in their sacrifice.

These two men are laying down their lives in mankind's most noble goal: the search for truth and understanding.

They will be mourned by their families and friends; they will be mourned by their nation; they will be mourned by the people of the world; they will be mourned by a Mother Earth that dared send two of her sons into the un-known.

In their exploration, they stirred the people of the world to feel as one; in their sacrifice, they bind more tightly the brotherhood of man.

In ancient days, men looked at stars and saw their heroes in the constellations. In modern times, we do much the same, but our heroes are epic men of flesh and blood.

Others will follow, and surely find their way home. Man's search will not be denied. But these men were the first, and they will remain the foremost in our hearts.

For every human being who looks up at the moon in the nights to come will know that there is some corner of another world that is forever mankind.

In his memo to Haldeman, Safire also recommended that, prior to issuing the statement, the president "should telephone each of the widows-to-be." After the statement and at the point when NASA ended communication with the men, "a clergyman should adopt the same procedure as a burial at sea, commending their souls to the deepest-of-the-deep, concluding with the Lord's Prayer." Sitting that morning in the White House chapel, Bob Haldeman's mind could not have helped but wander to the Safire statements resting in a locked drawer of his office desk.

At 10:05 A.M. EDT, following a five-minute progress report on the Apollo 11 mission from anchorman Walter Cronkite (Cronkite's first TV appearance that morning), CBS aired a religious broadcast, *Nearer to Thee*. The program featured a discussion of the religious meaning of Apollo 11 by a theologian, a sculptor, an aerospace executive, and a physicist. The voice of CBS correspondent Charles Kuralt followed promptly at eleven, beginning the live coverage of what the network called *Man on the Moon: The Epic Journey of Apollo 11*. Providing a voice-over to dramatic pictures of the Earth and the Moon that had been taken by the previous Apollo flights and by the unmanned Lunar Orbiter spacecraft, Kuralt also took Genesis as Apollo's spiritual theme yet elucidated its cosmic meaning with insights

from modern science, including the Big Bang Theory. Kuralt, who in the
coming years would become one of Armstrong's favorite TV journalists for
his wistful human-interest stories drawn from the back roads and small
towns of America, set a humanistic tone for the universal achievement to
unfold that day. His essay reflected nearly perfectly how Armstrong himself
felt about the Moon, its history, and its sibling relationship with the Earth:

> *In the beginning God created the heavens and the Earth. And the Earth
> was without form and void. And darkness was on the face of the deep. Some
> five billion years ago, whirling and condensing in that darkness, was a cloud
> of interstellar hydrogen, four hundred degrees below zero, eight million miles
> from end to end. This was our solar system waiting to be born.*
>
> *A hundred million years passed. And God said, "Let there be light." And
> there was light at the center of that whirling cloud as a protostar began to
> form, its gravitational pull attracting larger and larger mass—rotating faster
> and faster. And in that condensation and heat the Sun was born—in fire out
> of cold—ever smaller and ever more brilliant, ringed with those satellites
> that were to be its planets. Two protoplanets—the Earth and the Moon—
> now separate gaseous eddies mutually trapped in their gravitational pull,
> moving in tandem orbit around the Sun and growing more dense. Through
> space and time the increasing gravitation of the system drew in more and
> more debris, the heavier elements converging in those burning clouds to
> form molten cores at their centers.*
>
> *And more millions of years passed. The Earth and the Moon drew slowly
> apart, their rotation about each other gradually decreasing in the expanding
> universe. By now, most of the dust in the solar system had disappeared, ei-
> ther swept up by the planets, or condensed into solid particles of varying
> size—meteoroids that roamed in eccentric orbits through the vastness of
> space. Millions of these wandering objects showered onto these new planets,
> disappearing into their molten surfaces, leaving no trace of their impact.*
>
> *And time passed. The Moon, being smaller than the Earth, began to cool
> first and its outer crust to harden. But this hardening was interrupted by gi-
> gantic asteroids colliding with the Moon and breaking through the crust,
> opening fissures that released seas of molten lava from within, flooding vast
> areas of the lunar landscape. As the molten seas flowed outward and over
> the torn surface they formed the plains or mares. Impact debris projecting
> above the flows became the mountains of the Moon.*
>
> *And, with time, the crust would cool again and, as it cooled, fissures
> opened, wrinkles and ridges formed. And volcanic pressures under that sur-*

face raised great domes that would later collapse leaving craterlike forma-
tions when the eruptions subsided. Most of the lunar craters though were
probably being formed by bombardments that had been going on from the
Moon's earliest beginnings: a continuous shower of meteoroids upon the
lunar surface, some of the larger ones breaking through the crust and releas-
ing lava from below.

Millennium upon millennium, this cosmic rain persisted. Through bil-
lions of years, meteorite debris has been collecting upon the surface of the
Moon. Even the level areas caused by the lava flows are now deeply buried.
Nearly every square foot of this outer layer is pitted with impact craters of its
own. Seven hundred thousand years ago came perhaps the most recent large
alteration of the lunar surface. A gigantic meteoroid struck the southern
mountainous region, creating the Crater Tycho with an explosive force that
scattered material in a radiating pattern nearly halfway around the Moon.
Some of this material was driven out into space and into the Earth's gravita-
tional pull, penetrating our atmosphere and falling to Earth among the life
on our planet at the time.

As we look back through space and time at the origin of the Moon, we
may be in part contemplating our own beginnings. Were it not for the Moon
and its effects on the creation of the Earth, man might not be on this planet
at all, gazing into that luminescent face on countless nights, or be reaching
out for it on this day.

Switching from Kuralt's taped segment to the CBS anchor desk live in
New York City, the venerable Cronkite—personally equipped with ten separate notebooks full of pertinent facts about Apollo 11 and the U.S. space
program—referred to the upcoming Moon landing as "a giant step," not realizing, of course, that, in less than twelve hours, similar words uttered by
the First Man would be heard and forever remembered by a worldwide
multitude.

Armstrong and Aldrin had been together inside *Eagle* for less than thirty
minutes by the time CBS began its comprehensive coverage at 11:00 A.M.
Nervous anticipation of what was to come had made it difficult for the astronauts to perform even mundane tasks that morning. Buzz remembers:
"The activity of three men in space must, of necessity, be a cooperative
venture. By now we had worked out various routines for living together,
but in our excitement this particular morning the system came unglued."

The rhythm that had been devised for eating, with one man pulling a food packet out, another snipping the packet, and the third liquefying his food with the water gun, got a little out of whack. Attaching new fecal-containment garments, urine catheters, and collection bags prior to suiting up proved especially unpleasant. Nerves frayed as the three men took turns dressing inside the CSM's navigation bay, a space large enough for only one man to change clothes, requiring another man to stand by to help with buttons, clasps, and zippers. Besides Armstrong and Aldrin, Collins also had to suit up in case something went wrong with the undocking.

Suiting up for spaceflight was always done meticulously, but never more so than on the morning of the landing. Neil and Buzz would need to be in their pressure suits for over thirty hours. The first garment they had carefully squeezed into was liquid-cooled underwear. Resembling long johns, the mesh garments held hundreds of small transparent plastic tubes. On the Moon, cooling water pumped from the astronauts' backpacks would circulate through the tubes, but until the mission progressed to that point the tight undergarments only added to the general discomfort and claustrophobia of being outfitted for space. Aldrin, with only his underwear on, was first into the LM because he wanted to make some initial checks. A half hour later a fully suited Armstrong crawled his way into the module. With Neil inside, Buzz returned to the CSM navigation bay to finish suiting up, then immediately reentered the LM. He and Neil sealed their side of the hatch, with Mike doing the same on the other side.

Inside *Eagle,* Neil and Buzz powered up several more systems preliminary to deploying the LM's spiderlike landing gear. Successful extension of the gear came just before noon EDT. Because a number of communication and equipment checks still had to be made, it took another hour and forty-six minutes before the LM was ready to be detached by a firing of *Columbia*'s engine. Characteristically, Collins and Aldrin did most of the talking over the radio. "How's the czar over there?" Mike asked from the command module. "He's so quiet." "Just hanging on—and punching," came Neil's answer, referring to inputs he was making on the LM's primary computer in readiness for separation. "You cats take it easy on the lunar surface," Collins told them shortly before he threw the switch to release them. "If I hear you huffing and puffing, I'm going to start bitching at you."

04:04:10:44	Collins:	*We got just about a minute to go. You guys all set?*
04:04:10:48	Armstrong:	*Yes, I think we're about ready. . . . We're all set when you are, Mike.*

04:04:11:51	Collins:	*Fifteen seconds. . . . Okay, there you go. Beautiful!*
04:04:12:10	Aldrin:	*Looks like a good SEP.*
04:04:12:10	Collins:	*Looks good to me.*

His nose pressed against a window, Collins watched them drift away and waited for word from Neil about the efficacy of the two spacecrafts' relative motion. It was a good idea not to drift too far apart until Mike gave the LM a very close visual going-over; it was critical to make sure that all four legs of the landing gear were down and in place. To help Mike with the inspection, Neil performed a little pirouette, turning the vehicle around a full rotation. A few months before launch, Mike had made a special trip to the Grumman factory on Long Island just to see what the LM looked like with its gear properly deployed. In particular, it was important for Collins to take a close look at the six-foot-long touchdown sensor prongs that extended from the LM's left, right, and rear footpads. He also needed to confirm that the footpad on the front gear, the only one without a sensor, was in the correct position. That leg held the ladder down which the astronauts would climb to the lunar surface. Originally that leg, too, had a landing sensor, but it was removed after Armstrong and Aldrin indicated that there was some chance they might trip over it when climbing down. "It was another piece of metal that was there around the ladder where you were coming down," Neil explains, "and we asked, 'Why do we need that there? We have three others.' "

04:04:12:59	Armstrong:	*Okay. I've killed my rate, Mike, so you drift out to the distance you like and then stop your rate. . . . Starting my yaw. . . . There's sure a better visual in the simulator.*
04:04:13:38	Collins:	*Okay, I picked up a little roll; I'm going to get rid of it.*
04:04:14:22	Armstrong:	*Okay with you if I start my pitch, or do you think you're not far enough away yet, Mike?*
04:04:14:31	Collins:	*I'd prefer you stand by just a couple of seconds, Neil.*
04:04:14:34	Armstrong:	*Okay, I'll wait for when you're ready, when you think you've got your rates killed perfectly.*

04:04:14:39	Collins:	*Okay. I'm still holding.*
04:04:15:26	Collins:	*Okay, looks pretty good to me now.*
04:04:15:30	Armstrong:	*Okay.*
04:04:16:34	Collins:	*Just like in the simulator, you're drifting off to one side and down below a little bit.*
04:04:16:39	Armstrong:	*Yes.*
04:04:17:06	Collins:	*The gear are looking good; I've seen three of them.*
04:04:17:11	Armstrong:	*The MESA is not down, right?*
04:04:17:14	Collins:	*Say again.*
04:04:17:15	Armstrong:	*The MESA's still up?*[The Modular Equipment Storage Assembly, or MESA, folded up against the side of the LM near the front (sensorless) landing leg. The MESA contained a television camera, boxes in which collected rocks would be put, and various tools. Once on the lunar surface, Neil would pull a D-ring that released the MESA and swung it down into an accessible position. Here Armstrong was expressing his concern that the MESA might have come down during the separation maneuver.]
04:04:17:19	Collins:	*Yes.*
04:04:17:20	Armstrong:	*Good.*
04:04:17:49	Collins:	*Now you're looking good.*
04:04:17:59	Armstrong:	*Roger. Eagle's undocked. The Eagle has wings.*

It was a bird unlike any that had ever flown, and the teasing Collins could not stop himself from poking fun at the LM's appearance: "I think you have a fine-looking flying machine there, *Eagle,* despite the fact that you are upside down."

"*Someone's* upside down," Neil joked back.

Inside the LM, now flying less than sixty-three nautical miles above the Moon, Neil and Buzz were not seated; they stood upright. Grumman's chief engineer, Thomas J. Kelly, reflects back on why getting rid of the seats was such an advantage: "Without the bulky seats, the usable volume of the LM cabin became much greater. Seats were not required because the LM's mission was relatively brief and the astronauts were at zero gravity while flying or at Moon gravity [one-sixth Earth's] while on the surface. Even LM rocket firings did not exceed one-third g." Some form of astronaut restraint was needed, so Grumman anchored foot restraints into the deck of the cabin and devised a spring-loaded cable and pulley arrangement that clipped onto the astronaut's belt. If they needed to brace themselves further, Neil and Buzz could grab handholds and armrests located at mid-body nearby. Best of all, the astronauts standing erect meant that the windows of the LM could be smaller (triangularly shaped) and more light-weight while at the same time giving the astronauts an excellent vantage point from which to peer down out of the spacecraft to the landing zone.

Before *Eagle* could begin its landing approach, Neil and Buzz needed to lower its orbit down to the vicinity of 50,000 feet. Flying feet first and face-down relative to the lunar surface, they accomplished this by igniting the LM descent engine, its first firing of the mission. This burn, known as Descent Orbit Insertion, occurred fifty-six minutes after separation from *Columbia*, at 3:08 EDT. DOI took place while both spacecraft were on the back side of the Moon and out of contact with Earth. Lasting 28.5 seconds, the burn dropped *Eagle* into a coasting path that took it down on the front side of the Moon where the landing would be made.* As the descent proceeded, Neil and Buzz checked their range rate so they could return to *Columbia* via the LM's abort guidance system should the craft's primary navigation system fail or something else major go wrong.

With the DOI burn accomplished, *Eagle* was now considerably lower than *Columbia* and thus orbiting at a faster speed. This put the LM out in front of *Columbia*'s orbit by about one minute. As *Columbia* was in a higher orbit and at an angle that brought it in direct line with the Earth, *Columbia*'s carrier signal arrived first in Houston, about three minutes earlier than *Eagle*'s. In both cases, less than a minute after acquisition of signal came the return of voice contact.

---

* Beginning with Apollo 14, the DOI burn was performed with the CSM engine while the LM was still attached. This change was necessitated by the additional weight of the later lunar modules: they had the lunar rover onboard and stored more oxygen and dried food for longer stays on the lunar surface. Using command module fuel for the DOI maneuver also saved some of the LM's fuel.

04:06:15:02	CapCom:	Columbia, *Houston*. [The CapCom was Charlie Duke.] *We're standing by, over.* [Long pause.] Columbia, *Houston. Over.*
04:06:15:41	Collins:	Houston, Columbia. *Reading you loud and clear. How me?*
04:06:15:43	CapCom:	*Rog. Five-by, Mike.* [In communications shorthand, "five-by-five" meant "loud and clear." *How did it* [the DOI burn] *go? Over.*
04:06:15:49	Collins:	*Listen, babe. Everything is going just swimmingly. Beautiful.*
04:06:15:52	CapCom:	*Great. We're standing by for* Eagle.
04:06:15:57	Collins:	*Okay. He's coming along.*

A minute and a half later, Aldrin's voice was heard in Houston:

| *04:06:17:27* | Aldrin: | *Houston,* Eagle. *How do you read?* |
| *04:06:17:29* | CapCom: | *Five-by,* Eagle. *We're standing by for your burn report. Over.* |

Aldrin reported that DOI had come off extremely well, and that it had put *Eagle* into almost the exact, predetermined perilune from which it was to start its final, powered descent. If all went well from this point, in less than thirty minutes, the lunar module would touch down.

Prior to initiating final descent, it was important for Armstrong and Aldrin to check out their onboard guidance and navigation systems. The LM possessed two unique and independent systems. The first was the Primary Navigation, Guidance, and Control System (PNGS), or "pings" for short. This small digital computer, located in the panel in front of and between the astronauts, processed data from a built-in inertial platform—one that was held in a constant position by the action of gyroscopes that sensed movement and kept the platform from tipping in any direction. Finely tuned to the position of distant stars, PNGS flashed yellow-green numbers on a digital display that indicated the LM's position.

The second system was the Abort Guidance System (AGS). Rather than basing its navigation on an inertial platform, the spacecraft itself, however it was flying, served as AGS's measuring table, with body-mounted accelerometers providing the flight data. Both PNGS and AGS integrated accelerations that estimated the spacecraft's velocities, with PNGS generally producing considerably more accurate data. Ideally, the mathematics inherent to the two systems—both involving the measurement of angles changing over time—produced the same answers as to where the spacecraft was and where it was heading, but inevitably errors crept into the measurements. If tiny errors were allowed to compound, gross errors in computing the LM's course and location could result.

After DOI and prior to initiating powered descent (PDI), Neil and Buzz ran a number of cross-checks between the two systems. Close agreement was essential to prevent PNGS from initiating an undesired path. The primary cause of error in PNGS was platform drift, a constant concern for any inertial system. Drift needed to be corrected by realignment of the platform via computer-aided celestial navigation, followed by mechanical reorientation by the motors and gears connected to the gyroscope.

During their outbound flight, Apollo 11 performed a number of platform alignments, but these took time and required the spacecraft to be kept relatively still. In the half-orbit prior to DOI when they were busy doing other things, Neil and Buzz made a gross check on the accuracy of their previous alignment. "The way we did that," Armstrong explains, "was by telling the spacecraft to get in an attitude so our sextant was looking directly at the Sun. If our crosshairs were in the center of the Sun, we knew the platform had not drifted. If the crosshairs were an eighth or a quarter out of the Sun's center, we knew the alignment was still okay." Neil performed the Sun check shortly before PDI. Though it had been a few hours since the last alignment, he found that the platform was still aligned satisfactorily, with only a fraction of a degree of drift. "I figured for the next thirty to forty-five minutes, the time it would take us to land, it was probably okay."

Platform drift was not the only worry relevant to LM navigation. Both PNGS and AGS had to be "on" during the descent, and this could prove to be a problem if the astronauts did not keep everything about the operation of the two systems straight. While only PNGS could help the astronauts make a successful descent to the lunar surface, AGS had to be waiting and ready to navigate an emergency return to the command module; in the final seconds before touchdown, AGS also could take over from PNGS if it failed. According to Armstrong, "We couldn't land on AGS unless we got right down close to the surface, because you couldn't navigate the trajectory with it." Yet both systems needed to be energized and running, because the crew might have to switch instantaneously from PNGS to AGS. "That doesn't mean that the two systems were both driving the spacecraft simultaneously," Neil explains. "Both were operating as independent systems, and only one was selected to actually be controlling the spacecraft. We also had information coming out of both that was important to compare."

In Apollo 10, as Armstrong well knew, Tom Stafford and Gene Cernan experienced some wild gyrations in their LM, nicknamed *Snoopy,* when AGS and PNGS got crossed up. In the midst of simulating an abort, the astronauts, while some 47,000 feet above the lunar surface and on their way back up to the command module, switched their navigational control from PNGS to AGS. In doing so, however, Stafford did not realize that Cernan had already flipped the AGS switch from AUTO to HOLD ALTITUDE and flipped the switch himself. This put it back in AUTO and caused the lunar module to go "bouncing, diving, and spinning all over the place." Set in the automatic mode, the abort computer was only doing what it was designed to do: in the mind of AGS, *Snoopy* was heading in the wrong direction and had to be immediately turned around so that it could power its way up to a rendezvous with its command module (*Charlie Brown,* with John Young aboard). Fortunately, Stafford and Cernan managed to switch back to manual and regain control without damaging their spacecraft, but it was the sort of systems mixup that Armstrong and Aldrin knew they had to avoid at all cost.

Another major concern involved the fuel supply. Recognizing exactly when it was they were to reach the point where powered descent should begin was extremely important from the point of view of fuel consumption: if Neil and Buzz started down from too high out, *Eagle* would run out of fuel before it was in a position to make a safe landing. "I don't remember exactly what the altitude limits were," Neil comments, "but they must have been in the range of plus or minus four thousand feet."

Calculating that altitude was almost as much art as science. A standard altimeter could not tell the astronauts when they reached their perilune because an altimeter was an instrument that determined altitude based on changes in atmospheric pressure and the Moon has no atmosphere. The LM did have a radar altimeter, but from the cockpit perspective that instrument pointed down and forward. Early in the descent when the LM's vertical axis was nearly horizontal—meaning that the pilots were facing downward—the radar altimeter pointed up and away from the lunar surface and could not provide any landing data. (It would have produced very poor radar data from that height anyway, as landing radar was not reliable above about 30,000 feet.) Guesstimating their PDI point from the height of the lunar mountains protruding below them was impossible, because, while Neil and Buzz could roughly figure out the heights of the mountains at the edges of the lunar sphere, they could not judge them in its middle.

The technique devised by Armstrong during training to determine the PDI point (Neil did this in association with Floyd Bennett, a talented engineer in MSC's guidance section) was a relatively simple one. It involved a direct, naked-eye check of the lunar surface combined with what Armstrong calls some "barnyard math."

"We used the equation $v = r\,\Omega$," Neil explains, "where r was the altitude that you wanted to know, Ω was the LM's angular rate, and v was the LM's velocity. We knew very well what our velocity was based on radar tracking from Earth and from our own navigation system, so to figure out altitude all we needed was our angular rate. Going into the mission, we knew we could determine that by watching a point on the ground." Early in the descent phase, the LM flew with its windows facing down (and the LM's back end forward), which made it easy for Armstrong to spot major landmarks on their way down. The facedown attitude was also useful for solving the altitude equation. On the double-paned window on Neil's side of the LM there was a vertical line with horizontal marks on it. As the LM flew facedown, Neil used a stopwatch to time the number of seconds it took to move from mark A to mark B on the window line. By that he calculated the spacecraft's angular rate. With him in the cabin Neil had a chart that he used to compare tracking rates with expected values at various positions along the orbit. Differences between his visual observations and the expected values allowed him to estimate both the altitude of the LM's perilune and the time at which they would reach it. "It was a simple technique and easy to do," Neil relates. "It was a valuable exercise to confirm that we were in fact at a good altitude to start the powered descent."

04:06:26:29	Armstrong:	*Our radar checks indicate 50,000-foot perilune. Our visual checks are steadying out at about 53,000.*
04:06:26:37	CapCom:	*Roger, copy.*

A minute and half later, Houston told *Eagle*, "You're Go for powered descent." Before Mission Control gave them the green light, as Neil explains, "all the guys in the trenches at Mission Control who were looking at

ONE GIANT LEAP

all the various systems and subsystems made sure that the pressures, temperatures, valves, and so forth were all checking out okay." Mission rules allowed the descent to continue even if some minor instrumentation was not functioning with 100 percent efficiency, but generally the flight directors required everything to be working very well before PDI commenced. "They looked at most everything in somewhat more detail, or at least with more time, than we could," Armstrong reflects. "They had more eyes looking at the information." What ground control could not know very precisely, however, was the LM's altitude. "The barnyard math was something I came up with myself and did on my own. I'm not sure if any of the other astronauts even used it. I'm sure I told them about it."

Collins relayed the "Go for PDI" to his mates because *Eagle* was still incommunicado. Then even after swinging back around to the front side of the Moon, communications unexpectedly remained broken. "We had a small dish antenna mounted on top of the LM, which was a good antenna," Armstrong notes. "It was steerable, but it had to be pointed very close to Earth to get much signal. We also had an omnidirectional antenna. The omni was just a blade antenna like a person has on his automobile; it was not very accurate or very powerful. It was important to get the dish antenna pointed directly at Earth, but it was not particularly easy to do when you were lying horizontal. If you were off in yaw angle just a little bit, you could easily lose the signal."

04:06:28:34	Collins:	Eagle, *this is* Columbia. *You're Go for PDI, and they recommend you yaw right ten degrees and try the high gain again.*
04:06:28:48	Aldrin:	*Rog. We read you.*
04:06:28:51	CapCom:	Eagle, *Houston. We read you now. You're Go for PDI.*

It took almost five minutes for Neil and Buzz to make final preparations for powered descent. "We had to get the computer into the right program," Neil explains, "and make sure that all the switches and circuit breakers and everything else was ready to make the systems work and make the engines run for the powered descent." Buzz's focus was exclusively on readouts from the navigational computers, while Neil's was on assuring that everything from engine performance to attitude control was working the way it was supposed to. As *Eagle* started down, the duo activated the sixteen-millimeter film camera that was mounted above the right-hand window next to Buzz; pointing forward and downward, the camera was to film every foot of the historic descent.

Back on planet Earth, tension began to crescendo as network television coverage prepared for PDI and counting down the minutes to touchdown. On air with CBS, Cronkite said to sidekick Wally Schirra, "One minute to ignition, and thirteen minutes to landing. I don't know whether we could take the tension if they decided to go around again."

In Wapakoneta Viola Armstrong, watching Cronkite while clutching a sofa pillow to her breast, showed her generosity of spirit in these anxious moments by thinking of the lonely vigil of Mike Collins. "The tension rose to a peak each step of the way," recalled Viola. "The tense period between the separation of the Lem [sic] from *Columbia,* when Buzz and Neil left Mike, really pulled on my heartstrings. We felt sorry for him because he was alone and could not go along with the other two. We were so proud of him because he was so faithful."

PDI came at 4:05 P.M. EDT. Strapped into restraining belts and cables that worked like shock absorbers, neither Neil nor Buzz felt the motion, so they looked quickly at their computer to make sure the engine was in fact firing. For the first twenty-six seconds—a quantity that programmers of the LM propulsion system called "zoom time"—the two astronauts kept the engine firing at merely 10 percent of maximum thrust. The gentle power gave the guidance computer the leeway it needed to sense when the lunar module was in the proper geometric position to go full throttle. "Basically, you liked to be at a pretty high thrust for good fuel efficiency," Armstrong notes. "But if something was wrong and you were at too high of a throttle for too long, you couldn't sync to your target. So there was a strategy for the throttle profile—for throttling the engine to start at point A and end up at point B with a relative maximum efficiency."

As power from the engine grew, the motion became noticeable to the astronauts; even though the LM was falling at a rate of thirty feet per second, it seemed no more dramatic than a trip down several floors in a quiet hotel elevator. As they fell, Armstrong watched his instruments for proper readings while Aldrin made sure that the numbers from PNGS and AGS were correlating with preestablished figures written onto a stack of note cards that Buzz had placed between Neil and himself.

By his own admission, Buzz chattered the entire way down, "like a magpie," as he continually read out numbers from the computers, whereas very little was heard from Neil in the minutes leading up to landing.

If Neil had had his way, nothing from either one of them would have been heard by the *outside* world. Late in training Armstrong had asked about the possibility of keeping all the talking in the LM during the last minutes of descent off the radio, so as to minimize distractions. Mission Control quickly rejected the notion because it wanted to hear what was being said; the flight directors wanted their teams at the consoles to be fully informed. The idea was that one of the many experts on the ground might be able to help out the crew even in the very last seconds if a problem popped up. "Whenever I wanted to talk to the outside world," states Neil, "normally I used the push-to-talk mode," meaning he squeezed a switch. "We had a voice-activated [VOX] position as well, and I think Buzz used that during the descent."

In the first minutes after PDI, while flying with the engine forward and windows down, Neil tracked his surface landmarks in order to confirm *Eagle*'s pathway and its timing down along it. Three minutes into descent, he noticed they were passing over the crater known as Maskaleyne W. a few seconds early:

04:06:36:03	Armstrong:	*Okay, we went by the three-minute point early. A little off.*
04:06:36:11	Aldrin:	*Rate of descent looks good. Attitude—right about on.*
04:06:36:16	Armstrong:	*Our position-checks downrange show us to be a little long.*

Neither Neil nor Buzz could be sure why they were over the crater a little early. They guessed that PDI must have started a little bit late. "Our downrange position appeared to be good at the minus-three and minus-one minute points prior to ignition," Neil reported during Apollo 11's postflight debriefing. On a chart placed in front of them, he had premarked where PDI was supposed to start but, when PDI actually began, things were too hectic for him to pay careful attention to precisely where it had happened. "I did not accurately catch the ignition point because I was watching the engine performance. But it appeared to be reasonable, certainly in the right ballpark. Our cross-range position was difficult to tell accurately because of the skewed yaw attitude that we were obliged to maintain for communications. However, the downrange position-marks on my window after ignition indicated that we were long." From one mark to another represented two or three seconds farther downrange, with every second corresponding to roughly a mile of distance. "The fact that throttle-down essentially came on time, rather than being delayed, indicated that the computer was a little confused as to what our downrange position was. Had the computer known where it was, it would have throttled down later to kill a little velocity. Landmark visibility was very good. We had no difficulty determining our position throughout all the facedown phase of powered descent." *

The reason for the slight delay in starting PDI was not analyzed by NASA until after the mission: what it involved were very small perturbations in the motion of the lunar module—in engineering terms, small delta-v inputs—that had occurred back at the instant the LM and CSM had separated. Very likely, residual pressure in the tunnel between the two modules had given *Eagle* a little extra "kick," a force resulting, some eighty minutes (and over one orbit) later, in a velocity-induced positional error that put *Eagle* a sizable distance away from where it was supposed to be. Incomplete venting of the tunnel was not considered a serious matter before Apollo 11, but it was afterwards. In all subsequent Apollo missions, Mission Control made sure to double-check the status of the tunnel pressure before approving the LM's undocking.

Armstrong had no time to worry that his descent path was taking him a little long, topographically speaking. "It wasn't a sure thing that we were going to be long because we didn't know how accurately the markings on the window would turn out be. Anyway, it wasn't a big deal as to exactly where we were going to set down. There wasn't going to be any welcoming committee there anyway."

His first indication that *Eagle* might be overflying its landing spot came just as he began to turn the LM into a faceup, feet-forward position. The reason for moving into this unusual position (via a yawing maneuver that took a little more time than expected) was to get the LM's radar antenna pointing down at the Moon. "We needed to get landing radar into the equation pretty soon because Earth didn't know how close we were and we didn't

---

* Armstrong has always discussed the landmark tracking as if he and Aldrin were doing it together, but that was not the case. "I appreciate the 'we,'" Aldrin has commented, "but Neil did the tracking, because I wasn't looking out the window. I could have cared less about the landmarks. If it wasn't in the computer displays, I didn't see it." Aldrin quoted in "The First Lunar Landing," *Apollo Lunar Surface Journal*, ed. Eric M. Jones, p. 13.

want to get too close to the lunar surface before we got that radar. If we found there was a big difference between where we were and where we were supposed to be, we might have to make some rather wild maneuvers to try and get us back on a proper trajectory, and we wanted to avoid that. So it was a matter of rolling over so that our landing radar was getting contact. It was a Doppler radar that gave three components of velocity and altitude, a pretty unique device." As it turned out, it was good that the radar was working because it showed an altitude of 33,500 feet, some 2,900 feet lower than what PNGS was indicating because PNGS was programmed into the mean surface height, not the actual height above the surface at any one place.

Completing the roll, what the crew saw right out in front of them was their home planet in all the rare beauty and security it represented. "We got the Earth right out our front window," Buzz said to Neil, looking up from the computer. "Sure enough," was the limit of Neil's response.

With a reliable radar reading coming in, Neil prepared for the onboard computer to pitch the LM over so that it would be almost upright. As that happened, he would get a great view of the landmarks down below, leading like roadside signs down what the astronauts (in reference to the main north-south route from New York to Florida pre-dating the 1950s–1960s construction of the Interstate Highway System) had been calling "U.S. Highway 1," the pathway to the landing site on the Sea of Tranquility.

It was at that instant—at 04:06:38:22 elapsed time—that a yellow caution light came on and the first of what turned out to be several computer program alarms sounded inside the LM. With only the slightest touch of urgency in his voice, Neil squeezed his comm switch and told Houston: "Program alarm," adding three seconds later after moving his eyes down to the computer display, "It's a 1202." "Give us a reading on the 1202 program alarm," Neil quickly asked, not knowing which of the dozens of alarms 1202 represented.

It took Mission Control only fifteen seconds to respond: "We got you . . . we're Go on that alarm." The problem with the computer was not a critical one. *Eagle*'s descent could continue.

"We had gone that far and we wanted to land," Neil asserts. "We didn't want to practice aborts. We were focusing our attention on doing what was required in order to complete the landing."

What caused the 1202 alarm was an overload in the onboard computer incited by the inflow of the just-arriving landing radar data. Fortunately, one of the brilliant young minds in the Houston control room—that belonging to twenty-six-year-old Steve Bales, the GUIDO (pronounced *gido,* with a long *i*) or lead specialist in LM navigation and computer software on Flight Director Gene Kranz's White Team—very quickly determined that the landing would not be jeopardized by the overflow, because the computer had been programmed to recognize landing radar data as being of secondary importance. The computer would ignore that data whenever there were more important computations to make.

Two more times in the next four minutes, the same computer alarm, 1202, flashed on, the second time just after Armstrong had "throttled down" to reduce his engine thrust for the final approach to landing. At that moment, *Eagle* was only 3,000 feet above the lunar surface.

Seven seconds after the third 1202 alarm, the situation grew more intense when a new alarm came on—a 1201.

04:06:42:15	Aldrin:	*Program alarm—1201.*
04:06:42:22	Armstrong:	*1201!* [Pause] *Okay, 2,000 at 50.* [This meant that the LM was now 2,000 feet above the lunar surface and dropping at a rate of 50 feet per second, which was significantly slower than previously in the descent.]

It took Mission Control only an instant to realize that the 1201 alarm, like the 1202, was not in itself a dangerous problem.

04:06:42:25	CapCom:	*Roger, 1201 alarm. We're Go. Same type. We're Go.*

The massive international television audience that was tuned in to the coverage of Apollo 11 had no idea what the alarms meant. On CBS, an oblivious Cronkite told his viewers after hearing the crew's reference to the 1201 alarm, "These are space communications, simply for readout purposes." Schirra said nothing to correct the newsman.

One can imagine how sensational the live coverage would have been if on-air commentators such as Cronkite had had an inkling of the alarm call's significance. Even in the years after Apollo 11, people telling the story of the mission have exaggerated the sounding of the alarms into an urgent life-or-death drama. In a sense, even Aldrin has done this by writing in his 1973 autobiography:

At six thousand feet above the lunar surface a yellow caution light came on and we encountered one of the few potentially serious problems in the entire flight, a problem which might have caused us to abort, had it not been for a man on the ground [Steve Bales] who really knew his job. When the yellow program alarm light came on, we routinely asked the computer to define its problem. The coded answer it gave was that the machine was overloaded; it was being asked to do too much in too little time. It turned out that the men at MIT, who had designed the landing computer program that interrogated the landing radar, had never talked to the men who designed the rendezvous radar program. The combination overloaded our onboard computer. The problem had never come up in the simulators because we were using special-purpose computers. Back in Houston, not to mention on board the Eagle, *hearts shot up into throats while we waited to learn what would happen.*

Armstrong never felt this way about the alarms. For him, they were mainly a distraction that only endangered the landing slightly by prompting him to turn his eyes away from his landmarks. "We were getting good velocities and good altitudes; the principal source of my confidence at that point was the navigation was working fine. There were no anomalies other than the fact that the computer was saying, 'Hey, I've got a problem.' Everything else was working right and seemed to be calculating fine. There were no anomalies in the information that was being presented, and nothing was jiggling or acting erratic. Everything was very steady and working just like you would expect it to work if the computer were not complaining.

"My inclination was just to keep going ahead as long as everything looked like it was fine. There had never been an abort from this situation, and aborting at this point at rather low altitude would not have been a low-risk maneuver. I didn't want to do that unless I was absolutely out of all other alternatives—and I wasn't out of alternatives at this point.

"So going ahead looked like the very best thing to me. But I was listening to the ground because I had great respect for the information and help it could provide. When you get that close, why go put yourself intentionally in what was expected to be a dangerous situation—an abort—just because you had a warning light saying you might have a problem."

Armstrong gave no thought at the time as to how worried Aldrin might have been about the alarms. "Buzz was trying to get all the information he could out of the ground and trying to come up with a position that would be helpful," explains Neil. "I didn't have a bit of complaint about any of the information he was providing. I am not sure how he felt about it. I don't know if he had the same confidence level that I did that we should keep going."

Neil would have been less distracted by the computer alarms if he had known more about a simulation that had been conducted at Mission Control just a few days before the launch. The mastermind behind the "sim" was Richard Koos, the so-called SimSup, or simulation supervisor, at the Manned Spacecraft Center. A thin guy who wore wire-rimmed glasses, Dick Koos had been with the Army Missile Command at Fort Bliss, Texas, before joining the Space Task Group in 1959. Previously an expert in computer guidance for guided missiles, for Projects Mercury and Gemini Koos became one of Houston's foremost authorities in the computer simulation of spaceflight missions. For Apollo, it was his job to cook up the most intense training sessions imaginable and put every aspect of the vital relationship between a crew in flight and the ground team at Mission Control through trials by fire.

Late in the afternoon of July 5, eleven days prior to launch, Koos had told his technicians to load "Case No. 26" into the simulators. The exercise was not done to educate the astronauts, because the crew sitting inside the LM simulator that afternoon was Dave Scott and Jim Irwin, the backup crew for Apollo 12. The purpose of the simulation was to throw Flight Director Gene Kranz's White Team a wicked curveball. The White Team was the unit that was to be at the consoles inside Mission Control during the landing of Apollo 11, and Koos knew that the only way to train its members for their high-pressure duties was to put them through the wringer. A sly grin on his face, SimSup told his team, "Okay, everyone on your toes. We have never run this case, so it is going to take a helluva lot of precise timing on our part. This one must go by the numbers, so stand by for my call-outs. If we screw it up, I hope you got a bunch of change 'cause we'll end up buying the beer!"

Three minutes into the landing sequence, the devilish SimSup played his wild card: "Okay, gang, let's sock it to them and see what they know about computer program alarms."

The first alarm put to Kranz's team was code 1201, one of the very ones Apollo 11 would ultimately face. Steve Bales, the LM computer system expert, had no idea what it was. Hurriedly paging through a quarter-inch-thick handbook containing a glossary of LM software, Bales read out "1201— Executive Overflow—no vacant areas." What this meant, Bales knew, was that the onboard computer was overloaded with data, but the ramifications of the overload were unknown.

Gene Kranz vividly recalls the thought process that led Mission Control to abort the simulated landing: "Bales had no mission rules on program alarms. Everything still seemed to be working; the alarm did not make sense. As he watched, another series of alarms were displayed. Punching up his backroom loop, Bales called Jack Garman, his software expert. 'Jack, what the hell is going on with those program alarms? Do you see anything wrong?' Steve was counting the seconds, waiting for Garman's response, happy that the crew had not called for an answer. Garman's response did not help. 'It's a BAILOUT alarm. The computer is busier than hell for some reason, it has run out of time to get all the work done.' Bales did not need to consult the rules; he had written every computer rule. But there were no rules on computer program alarms. Where in the hell had the alarm come from? Bales felt naked, vulnerable, rapidly moving into uncharted territory. The computer on the LM was designed to operate within certain well-defined limits—it could do only so much, and bad things could happen if it were pushed to do things it didn't have the time or capacity to do.

"Staring at the displays and plot boards, Steve desperately sought a way out of the dilemma. The computer was telling him something was not getting done, and he wondered what in the hell it was. After another burst of alarms, Steve called, 'Jack, I'm getting behind the power curve, whatever is happening ain't any good. I can't find a damn thing wrong, but the computer keeps going through software restarts and sending alarms. I think it's time to abort!'"

Seconds later, Kranz called the abort. Charlie Duke, who was serving as the CapCom for the simulation just as he would be serving as the CapCom for the actual landing, told astronauts Scott and Irwin inside the LM to carry out the abort, which they accomplished successfully.

The exercise over, SimSup strongly expressed his unhappiness with the outcome in the debrief: "THIS WAS NOT AN ABORT. YOU SHOULD HAVE CONTINUED THE LANDING. The 1201 computer alarm said the computer was operating to an internal priority scheme. If the guidance was working, the control jets firing, and the crew displays updating, then all the mission-critical tasks were getting done." Turning to Bales, Koos told GUIDO in a more fatherly tone, "Steve, I was listening to you talk to your back room and I thought you had it nailed. I thought you were going to keep going, but then for some reason you went off on a tangent and decided to abort. You sure shocked the hell out of me!" Then, addressing Kranz, Koos made his last stinging point. "You violated the most fundamental rule of

Mission Control. You must have *two* cues before aborting. You called for an abort with only one!"

Immediately after the debrief Bales pulled his team together in order to figure out where they had gone wrong. Later that evening, he telephoned Kranz at home: "Koos was right, Gene, and I'm damn glad he gave us the run."

The next day, July 6, Koos put them through four additional hours of training exclusively on program alarms. At the end of a thorough analysis of computer performance and response times during a host of different alarm conditions, an enterprise that took until July 11, Bales added a new rule to what was already a long list of reasons to abort the lunar landing. The rule, numbered "5–90, Item 11," read: "Powered descent will be terminated for the following primary guidance system program alarms—105, 214, 402 (continuing), 430, 607, 1103, 1107, 1204, 1206, 1302, 1501, and 1502."

Program alarms 1201 and 1202 did not make Bales's list. In the unlikely event that one or the other popped up during the main event, the lesson from SimSup would not be forgotten.

When Armstrong and Aldrin reported the first program alarm at 4:10 P.M. EST, Bales and his team of LM computer experts were busy in a back room of the control center studying the data just coming in from the landing radar. It took a few seconds before Jack Garman brought the alarm call to Bales's attention. "Stand by, Flight," GUIDO told Kranz over the flight director's communication loop. Charlie Duke quickly echoed that the alarm was a 1202. Then musing aloud, Duke said almost incredulously, "It's the same one we had in training." Instantaneously, the coincidence dawned on Kranz: "These were the same exact alarms that brought us to the wrong conclusion, an abort command, in the final training run when SimSup won the last round. This time we won't be stampeded."

Mission Control knew that each alarm had to be accounted for, because if an alarm stayed on, the onboard computer could grind to a halt, possibly forcing an abort. But in and of themselves, without additional trouble, neither alarm 1202 nor the later-occurring 1201 required an abort. "We're Go on that alarm," Bales told Kranz as quickly but clearly as he could from the back room after the alarm came up the first time. "He's taking in the radar data." When 1202 came up again, Bales responded even more quickly. "We are Go. Tell him we will monitor his altitude data. I think that is why he is getting the alarm." When the new 1201 alarm popped up, it brought the same speedy response from Bales: "Go . . . same type . . . We're Go."

Despite Mission Control's decisiveness in keeping the landing going, it would have been helpful to Armstrong and Aldrin if they had experienced the program alarm *simulation* themselves, as part of their own training. "We did have some computer alarms in the simulations we were put through, but not these particular ones," Armstrong notes. "I can't tell you how many alarms there were, but there were quite a number—maybe a hundred. I didn't have all those program alarms committed to memory, and I'm glad I didn't." Knowledge of so many alarms would have just cluttered his brain with a type of information he did not absolutely need to know—as long as the guys at Mission Control knew what to do if any of the myriad program alarms sounded.

Still, one would imagine that someone would have thought to brief the Apollo 11 crew about any important results from simulations that occurred after they left Houston for the Cape, or at least have mentioned them informally to both Neil and Buzz. But the astronauts' recollection is that this never happened.

"Neil, in the days before launch, did anyone, perhaps Charlie Duke, tell you about a simulation back in Houston involving LM computer overloads that might happen during the last minutes of the descent?"

"I had heard or remembered somewhere that such failures had been put into the simulator."

"But had you been told that Mission Control in this case had unnecessarily aborted the simulated landing and then figured out afterwards that an abort was not commanded if such-and-such a computer program alarm went off but there was no other problem? You don't recall hearing about that?"

"I don't."

"Would that have made a difference in how you reacted to the alarms when they actually occurred in Apollo 11?"

"Well, it would have been helpful to have known that."

Aldrin categorically does not remember hearing anything at all about the last-minute simulation: "I didn't know anything about it until I heard about it a year or two after the flight. That was the first I knew that anyone had experienced that in any training." On the other hand, Buzz feels that Neil must have heard something about it before the launch: "I believe that people briefed Neil on that, so Neil knew that there was something like that that could come up."

"So, Buzz, when the program alarms hit the two of you during the landing,

Neil had some recognition that this was a possibility and that it had been worked on in a simulation, but you didn't know anything about it?"

"That's right. I didn't know anything about it. And that was not a good situation. I should have known where the flag was on that. I should have known a few other things. But that's the communication reticence that existed with Neil, and I didn't know how to change that."

"But wouldn't it have been good if you had both known the results of that simulation, so you could both react the most reasonably if such a program alarm actually occurred?"

"I agree, but I didn't find out about it until a year or so after. Then, it was too late to make an issue of it, because it would have brought up things in somebody's methods that were not enhancing, and I sure didn't want to do that."

As it was, the principal effect of the actual computer alarms on Armstrong was that he gave more of his time and attention to the alarms than he would have liked: "I had the obligation to make sure that I understood what was happening and that we weren't overlooking something that was important; so in that sense, yes, sure, it was a distraction, and it did take some time. The alarms as they came prevented me from concentrating on focusing on the landmarks. Had I been able to spend more time looking out the window and identifying landmarks, I might have had a better position on just precisely where our landing location was." But never during the alarms did Neil think he might have to abort, because he knew instinctively as an experienced test pilot and well-trained astronaut that such alarms did not command an abort if everything else about his flying machine was in order. "In my mind, the operative indicator was how the airplane was flying and the information that was on the panel. If everything was going well, going how you expected it to go . . . I wasn't going to be intimidated by one computer yellow light."

As Neil shifted his focus to the lunar surface they were fast approaching, he didn't see craters or patterns of craters that he recognized, but, under the circumstances, it wasn't a big concern. For hours on end during training, Neil had studied different maps of the Moon, pored over dozens of Lunar Orbiter pictures of the surface, and scrutinized a score of high-resolution photographs taken by Apollo 10 marking the way, landmark by landmark, down to the Sea of Tranquility. "The landmarks that I was looking at out there were not ones that I had studied or remembered well enough to know just where we were, but I was pragmatic about it. I didn't find it surprising or worrisome that we ended up some other place. Anyway, it would have been surprising on the first try for a lunar landing if we had ended up anywhere very close to where we wanted to be. I didn't count on that at all. From an objective point of view, I didn't particularly care where we landed as long as it was a decent area that wasn't dangerous. It didn't make a lot of difference where it was. I thought we might just have to find somebody's backyard to land in."

Because his attention had been directed toward clearing the program alarms, not until the LM got below 2,000 feet was Armstrong actually able to look outside without interruption at the landing area. What he saw as they dropped the next 1,500 feet was not good:

04:06:42:58	Aldrin:	*Thirty-five degrees, thirty-five degrees. Seven hundred fifty* [feet]. *Coming down at twenty-three* [feet per second].
04:06:43:05	Armstrong:	*Okay.*
04:06:43:06	Aldrin:	*Seven hundred* [feet], *twenty-one* [feet per second] *down, thirty-three degrees.*
04:06:43:08	Armstrong:	*Pretty rocky area.*

The onboard computer was taking them right toward the near slope of a crater the size of a football field. Later designated West Crater, it was surrounded by a large boulder field. Some of the hefty rocks in it were the size of Volkswagens.

"Initially, I felt that it might be a good landing area if we could stop just short of that crater, because it would have more scientific value to be close to a large crater. The slope on the side of the big crater was substantial, however, and I didn't think we should be trying to land on a steep slope.

"Then I thought that I could probably avoid the big rocks in the boulder field but, never having landed this craft before, I didn't know how well I'd be able to maneuver in and between them to a particular landing point. Trying to get into a pretty tight spot probably wouldn't be fun. Also the area was coming up quickly, and it soon became obvious that I could not stop short enough to find a safe landing spot; it was not the place where I wanted to be landing. Better to have a larger, more open area without the imminent dangers on all sides."

04:06:43:10 Aldrin: *Six hundred feet, down at nineteen. Five hundred forty feet, down at thirty. Down at fifteen.*

04:06:43:15 Armstrong: *I'm going to . . .*

Approaching 500 feet, Armstrong took over manually. The first thing he did was tip the vehicle over to approximately zero pitch, thereby slowing the descent. By pitching nearly upright, he also maintained his forward speed—some 50 to 60 feet per second—so that, like a helicopter pilot, he could fly beyond the crater.

Now that Armstrong was headed beyond the crater, he needed to pick a good spot to land, a potentially difficult enterprise given the very peculiar lighting conditions affecting the Moon's surface, which there had been no way on Earth to simulate. "It was a great concern," Neil recalls, "that as we got close to the Moon, the reflected light off the surface would be so strong, no matter what angle we came in on, that a lot of our vision would be wiped out, seriously affecting our depth perception."

Fortunately, NASA's mission planners had given plenty of forethought to the photometrics involved. They had concluded that, for optimum depth perception, *Eagle* needed to land at a time of "day" and at an angle that produced the longest possible shadows. Where there were no shadows, the Moon looked flat, but where shadows were long, the Moon looked fully three-dimensional. An astronaut could then perceive depth on the lunar surface very well: he could detect differences in elevation; he could easily identify the accented shapes and forms of peaks, valleys, craters, ridges, and rims. The ideal condition occurred for the trajectory of the LM when the Sun was 12.5 degrees above the horizon. That was the time when Armstrong and Aldrin would have adequate light over the area and still strong depth-of-field definition: "We could pick out bumps and craters and things like that so you could pick out a level landing area."

With Armstrong able to see quite well out into the area beyond the crater, bringing the LM down became a matter of Neil's piloting abilities, pure and simple. It was here that Neil's time in the LLTV really paid off, for he needed to bring the *Eagle* to a touchdown point not simply by hovering and dropping vertically but by sweeping down for another 1,500 feet at a relatively fast speed. "In the Lunar Lander Training Vehicle I had done some of that sort of maneuvering. It was a matter of using those types of techniques and traversing over the ground. If I had had a little more experience in the machine, I might have been a little more aggressive with how fast I tried to get over the crater, but it didn't seem prudent to be making any very large moves in terms of attitude. I just didn't have enough flying experience in the machine in those conditions to know how well it was going to react and how comfortable I would be with it. Fortunately the LM flew better than I expected. So I certainly could have gotten away with being a little more aggressive to moving more smartly over and away from the bad area into the better area, which might of saved us a little fuel."

Normally in flying, "landing long" was not a bad idea, especially when the landing was to take place on a runway where the condition ahead was known for a substantial distance. But when the landing was to occur on the rocky, pitted surface of the Moon, landing long brought in more unknowns than landing "short" in an area where the pilot had already seen the hazards involved. "If you don't like what you see," Aldrin explains, "there are four classes of alternatives: left, right, down or short, or go over. Overwhelmingly, the less traumatic one is to go over, even though there may be some question, 'Well, if I go over, then I don't know where it is. Whereas if I land short, then I know where it is. I'm not on it, I'm in front of it.' As I try to reconstruct it, going right is a hairy thing; going left is a hairy thing; and coming down and stopping short . . . You might drive yourself into a . . . You know, it's just a bad deal." Armstrong concurs: "You might get down there and find, 'Jesus, I've got a terrible situation.' " "So the natural thing to do," Aldrin continues, "is to fly over." "Extend it," adds Neil. "We had to pick a spot, and we didn't know how much visibility we would lose as we got closer down to the surface. We wanted to pick a spot that was pretty good while we still had about a hundred and fifty feet of altitude."

04:06:43:46	Aldrin:	*Three hundred feet* [altitude], *down three and a half* [feet per second], *forty-seven* [feet per second] *forward. Slow it up. One and a half down. Ease her down.*
04:06:43:57	Armstrong:	*Okay, how's the fuel?*
04:06:44:00	Aldrin:	*Take it down.*
04:06:44:02	Armstrong:	*Okay. Here's a . . . Looks like a good area here.*
04:06:44:04	Aldrin:	*I got the shadow out there.*

Seeing the LM's shadow was helpful because it was an added visual cue of how high they were. Buzz estimates today that he first saw the shadow at around 260 feet: "I would have thought that, at two hundred sixty feet, the shadow would have been way the hell out there, quite long, but it wasn't. I could tell that we had our gear down and that we had an ascent and a descent stage. Had I looked sooner, I'm sure I could have something identified as a shadow at four hundred feet, maybe higher. Anyway, at the lower altitude, it was a cue that was useful but, of course, you had to have it out your window," which Neil did not. During the final stages of the approach, Armstrong was flying with the LM rotated to the left. As a result, the spacecraft structure over the hatch was blocking his view of the LM's shadow.

Dropping between 200 feet and 160 feet, Armstrong found where he wanted to land, on a smooth spot just beyond another, smaller crater that lay past West Crater:

04:06:44:18	Aldrin:	*Eleven forward. Coming down nicely. Two hundred feet, four and a half down.*
04:06:44:23	Armstrong:	*Gonna be right over that crater.*
04:06:44:25	Aldrin:	*Five and a half down.*
04:06:44:27	Armstrong:	*I got a good spot.*
04:06:44:31	Aldrin:	*One hundred and sixty feet, six and a half down. Five and a half down, nine forward. You're looking good.*

What Neil could see below him was a layer of curiously moving lunar dust being kicked up by the LM's descent engine; in fact, the LM's shadow that Buzz was seeing was being cast upon this dust layer rather than on the Moon's surface itself. According to Neil: "We started losing visibility when we got a little below a hundred feet. We started picking up dust—and not just normal dust clouds like we would experience here on Earth. Dust from the lunar surface formed a blanket that moved out and away from the lunar module in all directions. This sheet of moving dust obscured the surface almost completely, though some of the biggest boulders stuck up through it. This very fast, almost horizontally moving sheet of dust did not billow up at all; it just moved out and away in a straight radial sheet.

"As we got lower, the visibility continued to decrease," Neil relates. "I don't think the visual altitude determination was severely hurt by the blow-ing dust, but the thing that was confusing to me was that it was hard to judge our lateral and downrange velocities. Some of the larger rocks were sticking up and out of the moving dust, and you had to look through the dust layer to pick up the stationary rocks and then base your translational velocity deci-sions on that. I found that to be quite difficult. I spent more time trying to arrest translational velocity than I thought would be necessary.

"Then, after finding the area to land, it was all about lowering the LM down relatively slowly and keeping from inducing any substantial forward or sideward motions. Once I got below fifty feet, even though we were run-ning out of fuel, I thought we'd be all right. I felt the lander could stand the impact because of the collapsible foam inside of the landing legs. I didn't *want* to drop from that height, but once I got below fifty feet I felt pretty confident we would be all right."

From Houston's point of view, the situation was, in fact, critical—the drama at the control consoles over the fuel supply palpable and gripping.

Back at a height of 270 feet, just prior to Buzz's seeing the LM's shadow, Armstrong had asked, "How's the fuel?" When the LM was down to 160 feet, Bob Carlton, Kranz's control systems engineer on the White Team, re-ported over the flight director loop that the LM's fuel supply had reached "Low Level." This meant that the propellant in the tanks of the LM had fallen below the point where it could be measured, like a gas gauge in an au-tomobile showing empty but the car still running. Kranz asserted later, "I never dreamed we would still be flying this close to empty."

At just under 100 feet, Aldrin had called "Quantity light," indicating that only 5 percent of the original fuel load remained. At Mission Control, this event started a ninety-four-second countdown to a "bingo" fuel call. When "bingo" was called at the end of those ninety-four seconds, Armstrong at his rate of descent would have only twenty seconds to land. If Neil felt he could not land in that amount of time, he would have to abort immediately—something by the time he had gotten to 100 feet he had no thought of actu-ally doing.

At 75 feet, Bob Carlton reported to Kranz that only sixty seconds re-mained before bingo. Charlie Duke repeated Carlton's call so Neil and Buzz could hear it. As Kranz remembers, "There was no response from the crew. They were too busy. I got the feeling they were going for broke. I had this feeling ever since they took over manual control: 'They are the right ones for the job.' I crossed myself and said, 'Please, God.'"

According to Armstrong, "If we were still at a hundred feet or more, then we would certainly have to abort. But if we were down lower than that, then the safest thing for us to do was to continue. We were very aware of the fuel situation. We heard Charlie make the bingo call and we had the quantity light go on in the cockpit, but we were past both of those. I knew we were pretty low by this time. But below one hundred feet was not a time you would want to abort."

At 04:06:45:07 mission elapsed time, Aldrin read out, "Sixty feet, down two and half. Two forward, two forward. That's good." "Two forward" was good because Armstrong wanted to be moving forward when he landed so he could be sure of not backing into a hole that he had not noticed or had forgotten about. "Not at touchdown but all the way through the final approach I liked to have a little forward motion because once you were going straight down you couldn't see where you were. You couldn't see what was immediately below you. You wanted to get pretty close to the ground so that you knew it was a pretty good area. Then you could stop the forward motion and let it settle."

04:06:45:13   Aldrin: *Forty feet, down two and a half. Picking up some dust. Thirty feet, two and a half down.* [Garbled] *shadow.* Four forward, four forward. Drifting to the right a little.*

"Stand by for thirty seconds. Thirty seconds," came Carlton's next call, Duke echoed it on the uplink. In Mission Control, the silence became deafening; Kranz said, "You could hear a feather drop." Everyone at the consoles and in the observation rooms swallowed hard as they strained to hear what would come next, *Eagle*'s landing or Carlton's next fuel call.

At the controls of the LM, Neil was not terribly worried about his fuel. "Typically in the LLTV it wasn't unusual to land with fifteen seconds left of fuel—we did it all the time. It looked to me like everything was manageable. It would have been nice if I'd had another minute of fuel to fiddle around a little bit longer. I knew we were getting short; I knew we had to get it on the

---

* Experts who have listened many times to the flight recordings cannot make out with certainty what word Aldrin used here. Buzz believes he might have said "Faint shadow," referring to a fuzzy edge of a shadow on the streaking dust layer. Others suggest it sounds more like "Great shadow."

ground, and I knew we had to get it below fifty feet. But I wasn't panic-stricken about the fuel."

04:06:45:26 Aldrin: *Twenty feet, down a half. Drifting forward just a little bit. Good. Okay. Contact light.*

The contact light went on the instant that one or more of the LM's sensory probes hanging down from three of the four footpads touched the lunar surface.

So focused was Neil on what he needed to be doing to touch down safely that he neither heard Aldrin expressly call "Contact light" nor did he see the blue contact light flash on. His plan had been to shut the descent engine down as soon as the contact light came on, but he did not manage to do it. "I heard Buzz say something about contact. But when he did, we were still over this moving sheet of sand, and I wasn't completely confident at that point that we had really touched. The indicator light might have been an anomaly or something, so I wanted to feel my way down a little closer. We might have actually touched down before I shut the engine down—it was very close anyway. The only danger with that was that if we had gotten the engine belt too close to the surface when it was running, it was possible we could have damaged the engine. We wouldn't have gotten an explosion, so it wasn't something I was concerned about. But looking back on it, I guess there was a possibility that something bad could have happened. If we had landed right on top of a rock with the engine belt still sticking out, that would not have been good."

04:06:45:41 Armstrong: *Shutdown.*

04:06:45:42 Aldrin: *Okay. Engine stop.*

It was a very gentle touchdown, so soft that it was hard for the astronauts to tell when they were actually fully down. "There was no tendency toward tipping over that I could feel," Neil declares. "It just settled down like a helicopter." In actuality, it might have been helpful to land a little harder, as later Apollo crews would purposefully do. "You always try to make a soft touchdown," Neil explains, "but by landing a little harder, engaging the clasps on the landing legs and compressing more foam, the bottom of the LM would have been a little closer to the ground and we wouldn't have had to jump so far up and down the ladder. So there was probably some merit to landing a little bit hard."

04:06:45:57   CapCom: *We copy you down,* Eagle.

04:06:45:58   Armstrong: *Houston, Tranquility Base here. The* Eagle *has landed.*

Aldrin knew that Neil was going to call the landing site Tranquility Base, but Neil had not told him when he was going to say it. The same was true for Charlie Duke. Neil had told Charlie in advance of the launch about the name, but when Charlie heard it for the first time at the moment of the landing, the normally smooth-talking South Carolinian turned a little tongue-tied:

04:06:46:06   CapCom: *Roger, Twan . . .* [correcting himself] *Tranquility. We copy you on the ground. You got a bunch of guys about to turn blue. We're breathing again. Thanks a lot.*

04:06:46:16   Aldrin: *Thank you.*

04:06:46:18   CapCom: *You're looking good here.*

In retrospect it seems clear that the matter of *Eagle*'s fuel supply was never quite as dire as Mission Control thought at the time—or as historians have made it out to be in their accounts of the Apollo 11 mission. Post-flight analysis indicated that Armstrong and Aldrin landed with about 770 pounds of fuel remaining. Of this total, about 100 pounds would have been unusable. The remainder would have been enough for about fifty seconds of additional hovering flight. That was some 500 pounds less usable fuel than what would be left for any of the five subsequent Apollo landings.

Armstrong has heard various theories regarding the actual fuel situation: "I don't know if there's any way to know how much fuel was left. The fuel tank bottom was spherical, and it's very difficult to have any kind of a quantity measuring system in the bottom of a spherical surface. It's very difficult to know how much was in there, particularly if the fluid in there was wandering around. The port was supposed to tell us at typical thrust settings when we would have about thirty seconds of fuel left. I don't know how accurate that was; if there was sloshing, you wouldn't know whether that light went on too early or too late.

"The important thing was that we were close enough to the surface that it didn't really matter. We wouldn't have lost our attitude control if we had run out of fuel. The engine would have quit but, from the distance we were at, we would have settled to the ground safely enough."

Touchdown came at 4:17:39 P.M. EDT, Sunday, July 20, 1969 (20:17:39 Greenwich Mean Time). The instant humanity realized that a safe and successful landing had occurred—millions of Americans by watching Cronkite on TV exclaim, amid an uncharacteristic personal loss for words, "Whew, boy! Man on the Moon!"—jubilation broke out. As Cronkite himself did, people everywhere felt a tremendous emotional release. They sat speechless or wildly applauded. They laughed with tears running down their cheeks. They shouted, whooped, hollered, and cheered. They shook hands and hugged one another, clinked glasses and proposed toasts. Men lit up celebratory cigars, children banged drums, teenagers lit off firecrackers. The sincerely devout offered prayers and gave quiet thanks. In a few parts of the world, some residents remarked, "Well, the Americans finally did it." But in every corner of the globe, most people, no matter their nationality, ethnicity, or religion, felt that the Moon landing was *their* achievement and exclaimed, "We did it!" Naturally, in the United States, there was a special sense of pride and accomplishment. From Alaska to the Florida Keys, from Penobscot Bay to Pearl Harbor, a nation's multitude thanked God for the blessing of living in a country where such a lofty goal could be set and then actually achieved according to plan. Even those who were unhappy with their country, as many, many were in the anguished days of the Vietnam War, felt how extraordinary it was to be living in an age that experienced the wonder of a Moon landing.

That evening at Arlington National Cemetery outside Washington an anonymous someone placed a small bouquet of flowers on the grave of John F. Kennedy, without whom (even though his reasons for doing so were mostly political) there would have been no Moon landing program. The note on the bouquet read: "Mr. President, the *Eagle* has landed."

Inside the LM 240,000 miles away, Armstrong and Aldrin, in the rarefied moments after touchdown, did their best to suppress whatever emotions they felt. To their excitement the two astronauts gave in only long enough to shake hands and pat each other on the shoulder—in retrospect, it is perhaps surprising they even took time to do that.

It was a defining moment of Armstrong's life and possibly of humankind in the twentieth century, but for the first two men on the Moon there was no time for enjoying the moment.

"So far, so good," was the only reaction Neil remembers having. Turning back to his checklist, all he said to Buzz was "Okay, let's get on with it."

CHAPTER 29

One Small Step

For Viola Armstrong, her son's touching down on the Moon was among life's most holy moments: "We were told that most of the world was watching, at least over fifty percent, pulling for them, and praying for them. If I told you that I could feel the power of millions of prayers, you might not believe me, and I could not blame you. But waves of these prayers were coming to me, and I was being gently and firmly supported by God's invisible strength.

"We watched them with keen interest, listening to Cronkite's every word. We were as still as death, the boys were so near the surface of the Moon. The spot where they intended to stop was so rugged with boulders and deep craters, so Neil took over the controls and safely guided their LM to smoother and safer grounds before landing. They gently touched down. At our house there was dead silence. We heard Neil's voice saying, 'Houston, Tranquility Base here. The *Eagle* has landed.' Prayers of thanksgiving were in our hearts, and our reverend, Pastor Weber, offered them upward. We listened so intently.

"I'm sure that never in their lives had they been so excited. Their hearts were racing a mile a minute. Neil's heartbeat had risen from a normal 77 to 156. This heavenly body had illumined our Earth for millions of years, but remained untouched by human hands. This is where they were—250,000 miles away from home."

Outside of Neil's parents' home in Wapakoneta, TV reporters had interviewed Viola and Steve shortly after the landing:

VIOLA: I was afraid that the floor of the Moon was going to be so unsafe for them. I was worried that they might sink in too deep. But no, they didn't. So it was wonderful.

REPORTER: Mr. Armstrong, what were your feelings?

STEVE: I was really concerned the way I understood that Neil had guided the craft to another area. And that would signify that the original was not exactly as they had planned.

REPORTER: What about his voice? Did it sound any different? Or did it sound calm and normal to you?

VIOLA: I could tell that he was pleased and tickled and thrilled. He was much like he always has been.

STEVE: I had the same feeling, that it was the same old Neil.

In El Lago at home with her two boys, Janet Armstrong's experience of the landing, and her reaction to it, was distinctly different from her in-laws', in particular her mother-in-law's, as one might guess, given that the two women's personalities lay, in Janet's own words, "at opposite ends of the spectrum." For one thing, Janet preferred not to watch the television coverage. Instead, she hovered near one of two NASA squawk boxes. She had placed one of the boxes in her living room for all of her houseguests to hear and the other back in her master bedroom so she could listen privately.

"Watching TV was not something that I did during the flight. Now it's true that we watched TV during the landing, for the landing, and while the men were walking on the lunar surface, because that was a good way to hear and see, because they had the cameras there. The speculation by the TV commentators—the drama of things that could happen if there was a problem along the way—I didn't need to hear all that. That just drove me nuts. That's exactly what had happened in Gemini VIII; there was speculation. Well, they didn't know! What I wanted to know, I wanted to *really* know."

Even more so than at Steve and Viola's, Janet's house was packed full of neighbors and guests, not all of them invited. Her sisters Carolyn Trude and Nancy "Nan" Thiessen were there, the latter with her husband Scotty, an IBM district manager for Cleveland and Pittsburgh, and their children. A big guy, Scotty ran interference whenever Janet needed to get through the swarm of reporters waiting outside the house. Inside were the ubiquitous folks from *Life* magazine, notably Dodie Hamblin. Neil's brother Dean and his wife Marilyn and their son Jay were there; the couple's two daughters had stayed back at home in Anderson, Indiana. A local Catholic priest, Father Eugene Cargill, was there at Janet's invitation. Though she herself was neither Catholic nor a formally religious woman, Janet felt that Father

Cargill "was just a wonderful man. I didn't care whether he was Catholic or whatever. He was just a good person, a people person I appreciated having there," especially if something went wrong during the landing. Janet's mother had come to Houston for the launch but afterwards returned home to Southern California because, in Janet's words, there was going to be "too much confusion in the house for her."

People came and went throughout the day. Neil's mate from Korea, Ken Danneberg, the intelligence officer for Fighter Squadron 51, now a successful oilman, popped in from Denver totally unannounced, as did a few others. Figuring "I probably won't remember all that's going on tonight," Janet stuck a clipboard on her front door with a sign-up sheet and a ballpoint pen hanging from it. Otherwise, if people arrived, she would not have known it. "I was paying attention to the flight, and that was most important. It was not a social occasion as far as I was concerned. Well, it was and it wasn't. It was a great tense time."

As always, the other astronauts and their wives came around to lend the families of the crew their emotional support. Barbara Young, Marilyn Lovell, Tom Stafford, Bill Anders, and Ron Evans were among the many who stopped in for a visit.

"People in the program would go from one crew member's house to another," Janet explains. "Sometimes you'd split up. It's like when Apollo 8 flew. I went to Fred Haise's house and Neil went to the Lovells'. We welcomed other people, especially the guys. They were wonderful at explaining what was going on if we didn't understand."

Janet was quite savvy about the mission, not that she tried to fathom the intricacies of such technical details as AGS and PNGS. In her bedroom, she kept maps of the Moon and other technical material that Neil had given her. She studied graphs indicating the stages of the powered descent, and pencil in hand she checked off landmarks—Dry Gulch, Apollo Ridge, Twin Peaks (better known as Mount Marilyn)—as radio communications made clear that *Eagle* was passing over them. One indication of her dedication to the science of flight was that just after NASA named the Apollo 11 crew she took some pilot training, in part so that when her family was flying in the Beech Bonanza that Neil had just bought a part-ownership in she would have a better idea of how to bring the plane down in an emergency. Not necessarily seeking to gain a license, she also sought to better understand and communicate what her husband was doing before the press and to her boys.

"Rick was twelve, five years older than Mark. He was interested, but

Mark was too young. Mark doesn't remember much about it—any of it."
At the time the little boy repeated, "My daddy's going to the Moon. It will take him three days to get there. I want to go to the Moon someday with my daddy."

Janet remembers "talking to Neil just before he left for the Apollo flight, asking him to talk to the boys and explain to them what he was doing. . . . I said to Neil, there is a possibility you might not come back. It was right in front of the boys when I said that. I said, 'I'd like *you* to tell the boys.'

"I don't think that went very far. . . . Rick didn't ask many questions because he couldn't bring himself to ask.

"I don't know what he might have said to them. . . . Rick would have understood; Mark probably wouldn't have understood. He was off in another world."

For the boys on the day of the landing, with their house so full of people, it was a big party. Because her sisters and sister-in-law were there, Janet had help. "I had people in the house. I didn't really have to worry too much about the boys. They would go swimming, and people would watch them. They had some friends over. I tried to keep life as normal as possible for them, but that day probably wasn't very normal."

During the crew's TV transmissions during the outbound journey, she would urge, "Mark, hurry up. We're going to see Daddy." When Neil's arm came into view on the screen, she quickly pointed it out: "That must be Daddy right there. There he is! There he is!" But while Rick stayed very attentive, Mark was preoccupied with other things, like a baby bird he had found in the yard earlier that morning. Later seeing her six-year-old covered with dirt, Janet asked, "*Where* have you been?" "I was behind the dresser thing in the garage," Mark replied. "I had to get him. Do you have some bird food?"

With all the preparations for houseguests, Janet had barely slept the night before the landing. Instead of going out to dinner with her family and guests, Janet chose to stay home alone, sending Rick with the family and Mark to a friend's house. When he timidly asked permission to camp overnight in his friend's backyard tent, Janet surprised him by granting him permission. "You mean I can?" he asked. Janet knew she wouldn't be sleeping either that night or the following one when the men made their EVA. "I caught some catnaps here and there, but you know, my sleep wasn't really important at that point."

No doubt the pressure of it all wore on her, and she lit cigarette after cigarette to ease the tension. The afternoon before the landing, when Mission Control seemed to be a little late in reporting the acquisition of *Columbia*'s signal, Janet banged her fist on a coffee table.

By the time PDI came, it had already become a very long day in the Armstrong home. For the terrors of the landing, Janet again needed to be alone, so she retired to the privacy of her bedroom. Bill Anders decided to join her. Bill and Janet together had given Pat White the bad news that awful night in January 1967 when her husband Ed died in the Apollo fire, and Bill felt he should stay with Janet right through the touchdown. Rick, a very intelligent and sensitive boy, also wanted to be with his mother. She and Rick had been following the NASA flight map step by step, now with Anders's help. Rick settled on the floor near the squawk box, while Janet and Bill sat on the foot of the bed. (Long after the Moon landing, this led to one of Bill Anders's favorite quips, "Where was I when the first Moon landing occurred? I was in bed with Janet Armstrong!") But Janet was too nervous to stay seated. She hunched down on her knees next to Rick, putting her arm around her son tightly as *Eagle* dropped its final 250 feet.

What Janet recalls about her emotions at the moment of the landing was issuing a big sigh of relief. Other people came in, hugged her, kissed her, and offered her congratulations. Returning to the living room, she and her entire company enjoyed a celebratory drink. Yet Janet was still wary. The worry was far from over.

"I really wasn't too concerned about the landing. I felt Neil could do that, if at all possible. But, God, you didn't know if that ascent engine was going to fire the next day. If you listened to the TV, as I did later that evening, the drama was on the landing. Well, forget the landing! Are they going to be able to get off of there?!"

A beaming Dean Armstrong, a cocktail in hand in his brother's living room that Sunday afternoon, knew exactly what Neil would say when asked how difficult it had been for him to make the Moon landing: "When we ask him about it later, he'll say, 'a piece of cake.' "

To his uncle's humorous comment, a proud Rick Armstrong added, with just a tinge of hurt in his voice, "Usually when you ask him something, he just doesn't answer."

In retrospect, two items may seem curious about Apollo 11's technical situation immediately following touchdown. First, no one in NASA knew exactly where *Eagle* had landed. "One would have thought that their radar would have been good enough to pinpoint us more quickly than it did," remarks Neil. When a spacecraft was in a trajectory or when it was in orbit, with all the optical and radar measurements being taken, both the ground and the crew had a pretty good idea of where the flight vehicle was, but it was a different problem when the object was sitting in one spot and all that anyone was getting was the same single measurement over and over again. "There was an uncertainty in that that was bigger than I would have guessed it would have been."

04:07:02:03   Armstrong: *Houston, the guys that said we wouldn't be able to tell precisely where we are, are the winners today. We were a little busy worrying about our program alarms and things like that in the part of the descent where we would normally be picking out our landing spot, and aside from a good look at several of the craters we came over in the final descent, I haven't been able to pick out the things on the horizon as a reference as yet.*

Up in *Columbia,* which was passing over Tranquility Base at a height of sixty miles, Collins peered hard through his sextant trying to spot the LM. Over his radio he had heard the whole thing and rightfully felt he shared in the achievement. "Tranquility Base, it sure sounded great from up here," Mike had radioed to his mates. "You guys did a fantastic job." "Thank you," Neil replied warmly. "Just keep that orbiting base ready for us up there." "Will do," answered Collins. With his right eye straining through his eyepiece, Mike had tracked them as long as he could during their descent until they disappeared from his view as a "miniscule dot" about 115 miles from the landing site. Now even with the ground sending up tracking numbers for him to input on his DSKY (display-keyboard) unit so that the command module's guidance computer could accurately point his sextant, it frustrated Mike that he could not see them.

04:07:07:13   Collins: [To Houston] *Do you have any idea whether they landed left or right of centerline? Just a little bit long—is that all you know?*

04:07:07:19   CapCom (Charlie Duke): *Apparently that's about all we can tell, over.*

The limited information provided by Houston was no help to Mike: "I can't see a darn thing but craters. Big craters, little craters, rounded ones, sharp ones, but no LM anywhere among them. The sextant is a powerful optical instrument, magnifying everything it sees twenty-eight times, but the price it pays for this magnification is a very narrow field of view, only 1.8 degrees wide (corresponding to 0.6 miles on the ground), so that it is almost like looking down a gun barrel. The LM might be close by, and I swing the sextant back and forth in a frantic search for it, but in the very limited time I have, it is possible to study only a square mile or so of lunar surface, and this time it is the wrong mile."

Collins never did locate *Eagle* down on the surface, not on any of his passes, which was more of a concern to Mike than it was to anyone else. The main concern at Mission Control over the LM's exact location did not come from the geologists—they were happy enough that Apollo 11 had landed anywhere in the mare. "They just wanted us to get out there and get some stuff!" Yet the question of where exactly the LM had come down did bother Mission Control, as Neil explains: "A lot of people were interested in where we landed, particularly those people who were involved in the descent guidance trajectory controls. After all, in later flights, we were going to try to go to specific spots on the surface and we needed to get all the information we could regarding methods that might help precision. However, not knowing exactly where the LM had landed did not affect what we did very much. Nor did people on the ground think that this was a disastrous occurrence. But the fact was, they didn't know exactly where we were and they did want to know if they could."

Related to the question of where exactly they had landed was the mystery of how mascons might have affected *Eagle*'s pathway down to the surface. Though NASA had figured out how perturbations caused by mascons in the vicinity of the Moon's equator might affect a spacecraft, at the time of Apollo 11, as Armstrong notes, "Perturbations by the mascons were still a concern." NASA was "trying to reduce the error from these uncertainties to the point that we could have increasing confidence about going to a particular point on the surface."

Much more pressing in the first few minutes of landing than not knowing the LM's exact location was the question of whether Neil and Buzz should even be staying on the surface for any time at all. There was always a chance that some spacecraft system was not operating properly, requiring a quick takeoff by *Eagle*'s ascent stage. "If we had problems that indicated that it was not safe to continue staying on the surface," Neil relates, "we would have had to make an immediate takeoff."

Within the lifetime of the electrical power system on the LM, there were three early times that the LM could lift off and get into a satisfactory trajectory to rendezvous with the command module. The first of these times, designated T-1, came a mere two minutes after landing. T-2 followed eight minutes later, with T-3 not coming until *Columbia* completed another orbit in two hours' time. If there was an emergency that absolutely forced *Eagle* to leave at any other time than these three, it would be up to Armstrong and Aldrin in the LM and Collins in the CSM to find some way, any way, to get in a decent position for joining up.

From a quick initial look at the LM systems, everything seemed to be okay. Gene Kranz's White Team quickly assented to a "Stay/NoStay" decision, which Charlie Duke passed on to Neil and Buzz.

04:06:47:06   CapCom: *Eagle, you are Stay for T-1.*

04:06:47:12   Armstrong: *Roger. Understand. Stay for T-1.*

Five minutes later, after more checks of spacecraft systems had been made, Duke relayed to *Eagle,* "You are Stay for T-2." The astronauts were going to remain on the Moon at least until the final Stay/NoStay decision.

A major technical concern in the first minutes after landing was the possibility that too much pressure was building up in the LM's fuel lines due to the high daylight temperature on the lunar surface. "Those fuel lines were not a new subject," Armstrong remembers. In the last days before launch, hydraulics experts had discussed with the crew what could happen if the tanks became too hot and lines overpressurized. "If we closed all valves and trapped fluid in certain lines," Neil explains, "then we were sitting on a two-hundred-degree surface of sunlight with a lot of reflected heat coming up towards the bottom of the LM, and it's heating up the pipes. The fluid pressure might really build in that line, and then we'd have a problem. It was a thing we talked about before launch in terms of optimum procedures, and we knew it was something to pay attention to when we landed, but it wasn't an uncontrollable situation. We had a couple of options of how to handle the situation, and we knew the guys on the ground were going to be doing their job, so we were not too concerned about it."

Just as predicted, immediately after engine shutdown, there was a sharp rise in pressure inside the fuel lines of the LM's descent engine. "Within two minutes after landing," as Neil tells it, "we vented both fuel and oxidizer tanks as planned. But the pressure still subsequently rose, probably due to evaporation of residual propellant in the tank as a consequence of the high surface temperature. Then we vented again. The ground was getting a different reading than we were, due to a different transducer location; I think theirs was in a trapped line. It was my view that the worst that could happen was a line or a tank could split open. As we would no longer be using the descent stage, it was less than a serious problem, in my opinion. I wasn't too worried about it."

Houston considered the situation dangerous, however. If fuel sprayed onto what was still a hot descent engine, a fire could result, though unlikely in a vacuum. Fortunately, the venting eased the pressure and the problem soon resolved itself.

For Armstrong and Aldrin there certainly was no time to savor the landing. Even after getting the stays for T-1 and T-2, even before they could look out at their windows and take their first close look at the lunar landscape, they had to go through a complete dress rehearsal for the next day's takeoff from the lunar surface. According to Neil, "The intention was to go through all the procedures for a normal takeoff and find out if they all worked okay. This required aligning the LM platform [its inertial reference], which was a first because no one had ever done a *surface* platform alignment before. We used gravity to establish the local vertical and a star 'shot' to establish an azimuth; in that way we got the platform aligned and ready for takeoff. Even though everyone considered it a simulation, we still went through all the systems checks just the way we would have if we had been going to make a real takeoff."

As Neil looked at it, the simulation run time allowed Mission Control to make a thorough evaluation of mission progress. "Our data resources on the lunar surface were limited. If we found there was some problem, we needed to maximize the time available for the people at Mission Control to work the problem and figure out what we might do about it. So I think it was a good strategy to get that simulated takeoff out of the way, first thing."

Only after Collins passed overhead a second time and Buzz and Neil could cease their simulated countdown following the Stay for T-3 did the two LM crewmen breathe easier: "We relaxed a little bit once we got through all the systems checks and found that everything was working okay, that the LM was fine, that we had no reason to believe that we had any major problems on our hands, and that we were going to be able to go ahead with our planned activities. There was certainly a degree of relaxation there."

During the first two hours on the Moon, while Aldrin was painstakingly communicating back to Earth a variety of measurements and alignments that he was making for navigational purposes, Armstrong took his first opportunities to describe what he saw outside:

04:07:03:55 Armstrong: *The area out the left-hand window is a relatively level plain cratered with a fairly large number of craters of the five-to-fifty-foot variety, and some ridges that are small, twenty, thirty feet high, I would guess, and literally thousands of little, one- and two-foot craters around the area. We see some angular blocks out several hundred feet in front of us that are probably two feet in size and have angular edges. There is a hill in view, just about on the ground track ahead of us. Difficult to estimate, but might be a half a mile or a mile.*

04:07:04:54 CapCom: *Roger, Tranquility. We copy, over.*

04:07:05:02 Collins: *Sounds like it looks a lot better than it did yesterday at that very low Sun angle. It looked rough as a [corn] cob then.*

04:07:05:11 Armstrong: *It really was rough, Mike. Over the targeted landing area, it was extremely rough, cratered, and large numbers of rocks that were probably—some, many—larger than five or ten feet in size.*

04:07:05:32 Collins: *When in doubt, land long.*

04:07:05:38 Armstrong: *That's what we did.*

Neil then returned to documenting the Moon's color: "I'd say the color of the local surface is very comparable to that we observed from orbit at this Sun angle—about ten degrees Sun angle. It's pretty much without color. It's gray, and it's very white, chalky gray, as you look into the zero-phase line. And it's considerably darker gray, more like ashen gray, as you look out ninety degrees to the Sun. Some of the surface rocks in close here that have been fractured or disturbed by the rocket-engine plume are coated with this light gray on the outside, but where they've been broken, they display a very dark gray interior, and it looks like it could be country basalt."

"Whatever I saw, I wasn't going to be too disappointed," Aldrin said in a 1991 interview for Eric M. Jones's *Apollo Lunar Surface Journal*. "I think both of us were trying to just describe what we saw whenever we had a little free time." Armstrong added during that same interview, "Anything that might be helpful to the science teams on the ground. They'd been waiting a long time for this information."

According to the flight plan, the takeoff simulation was followed by meal time and then, officially, by a four-hour rest period. Aldrin recalls, "It was called a rest period, but it was also a built-in time pad in case we had to make an extra lunar orbit before landing, or if there was any kind of difficulty which might delay the landing. Since we landed on schedule and weren't overly tired, as we had thought we might be, we opted to skip the four-hour rest period. We were too excited to sleep anyway."

The idea of skipping the rest period had actually been fully discussed and strategized about prior to the launch. "From our early discussions of how we would organize our time line of activities," Neil relates, "we concluded that the best thing to do, if everything was going well, was to go ahead outside as soon as we could and do the surface work before we took our sleep period. We recognized that the chances for even getting down safely—having things go well enough with all the systems to allow a landing—were problematical. If we scheduled the surface activity immediately for as soon as we could after *Columbia*'s first revolution and after the practice takeoff and so on—immediately after that—and then didn't make it on time, the public and the press would crucify us. That was just the reality of the world. So we tried to finesse things by saying that we were going to sleep and then we would do the EVA.

"But we never had any plan to do it that way. We had discussed it with Slayton and Kraft—and a few other people. My recollection was that they all thought it was a reasonable thing to do. And so everyone agreed we'd do it that way if we could. We knew it would create a change that people weren't expecting, but we thought that was the better of the two evils."

With everything in order, at 5:00 P.M. Eastern time, Armstrong radioed a recommendation that they plan to start the EVA earlier than originally scheduled. Aware of the prearranged deal, Charlie Duke, just about ready to pass over the CapCom duties to astronaut Owen Garriott of the Maroon Team, took only a few seconds to get approval:

04:08:39:07	Armstrong:	*Houston, Tranquility.*
04:08:39:09	Duke:	*Go, Tranquility. Over.*
04:08:39:14	Armstrong:	*Our recommendation at this point is planning an EVA, with your concurrence, starting about eight o'clock this evening, Houston time. That is about three hours from now.*
04:08:39:31	Duke:	*Stand by.*
04:08:39:35	Armstrong:	*Well, we'll give you some time to think about that.*
04:08:39:40	Duke:	*Tranquility Base, Houston. We thought about it. We will support it. We're Go at that time. Over.*
04:08:39:48	Armstrong:	*Roger.*

They did eat a meal as scheduled, but not before Aldrin first reached into his Personal Preference Kit, or PPK, and pulled out two small packages given to him by his Presbyterian minister, Reverend Dean Woodruff, back in Houston. One package contained a vial of wine, the other a wafer. Pouring the wine into a small chalice that he also pulled from his kit, he prepared to take Holy Communion.

At 04:09:25:38 mission elapsed time, Buzz radioed, "Houston, this is the LM pilot speaking. I would like to request a few moments of silence. I would like to invite each person listening in, wherever or whoever he may be, to contemplate the events of the last few hours and to give thanks in his own individual way." Then, with his mike off, Buzz read to himself from a small card on which he had written the portion of the Book of John (John 15:5) traditionally used in the Presbyterian communion ceremony.

I am the vine, you are the branches,
  He who abides in me, and I in him, will bear much fruit,
  For apart from me, you can do nothing.

It had been Buzz's intention to read the beautiful passage back to Earth, but at the last minute Slayton had advised him not to do it and Buzz reluctantly agreed. Apollo 8's Christmas Eve reading from Genesis had generated sufficient controversy to make the space agency shy away from overt religious messages. Madalyn Murray O'Hair, the celebrated American atheist, had sued the federal government over the Bible reading by Borman, Lovell, and Anders. By the time of Apollo 11, O'Hair had added a complaint that NASA was purposefully withholding "facts" about Armstrong being an atheist. Though the U.S. Supreme Court eventually rejected O'Hair's lawsuit, NASA understandably did not want to risk getting embroiled in another battle of this type. Regrettably to NASA, the word of Aldrin's religious ceremony quickly made its way to the press. CBS's Cronkite passed advance word to his viewers: "Buzz Aldrin did take something most unusual with him today, and it has become public—made public by the pastor at his church outside of Houston. He took part of the Communion bread loaf, so that during his evening meal tonight he will, in a sense, share communion with the people of his church, by having a bit of that bread up there on the surface of the Moon. The first Communion on the Moon."

Characteristically, Neil greeted Buzz's religious ritual with polite silence. "He had told me he planned a little celebratory communion," Neil recalls, "and he asked if I had any problems with that, and I said, 'No, go right ahead.' I had plenty of things to keep busy with. I just let him do his own thing."

As for Mrs. O'Hair's assertion pertaining to Armstrong's religious beliefs or lack thereof, Neil really never knew much, or cared much, about it. "I can't say I was very familiar with that. I don't remember that ever being mentioned to me until sometime in the aftermath of the mission."

After eating their meal and performing a few housekeeping chores, the astronauts turned all their attention to gearing up for the EVA. No matter how much they had practiced their EVA preparation inside the LM mockup back in Houston, doing it for real was much more difficult and time-consuming. "When you do simulations of EVA Prep," Neil explained in NASA's technical debriefing following the mission, "you have a clean cockpit and you have all the things that you're going to use there in the cockpit and nothing else. But in reality, you have a lot of checklists, data, food packages, stowage places filled with odds and ends, binoculars,* stopwatches,

---

* Armstrong misspoke here, as there were no binoculars on board. Rather, the LM was equipped with a monocular, made from one half of a set of commercial binoculars made by a German company, Leitz, and modified by instrument experts at the Manned Spacecraft Center. Neil and Buzz used the monocular both before and after their EVA. It thus ranks as the first telescopic viewing device (10 x 40 power) used on another celestial body.

and assorted things, each of which you feel obliged to evaluate as to whether its stowage position is satisfactory for EVA and whether you might want to change anything from the preflight plans. . . . We followed the EVA preparation checklist pretty much to the letter, just the way we had done during training exercises—that is, the hookups and where we put equipment—and the checks were done precisely as per our checklist. That was all good. It was these other little things that you didn't think about and didn't consider that took more time than we thought."

It took an hour and a half before Buzz and Neil were ready to start the EVA prep procedures and then three hours to do the preps, which were expected to take two hours. Much of the time involved getting their backpacks on, donning helmets and gloves, and getting everything configured for going outside. "We had tried to simulate the care with which we were going to perform each operation. When you are putting together the suit and making all the connections, you are really putting your life on the line with those connections, so you try to take the proper amount of time and care to make sure they are done properly. We had tried to simulate that. I don't know that we timed them necessarily, if so, I don't remember the numbers. But doing it for real on the lunar surface took quite a bit longer."

One of the main reasons why it took so long was because it was so cramped inside the LM. Aldrin recalls: "We felt like two fullbacks trying to change positions inside a Cub Scout pup tent. We also had to be very careful of our movements. Weight in the LM was an even more critical factor than in the *Columbia*. The LM structure was so thin one of us could have taken a pencil and jammed it through the side of the ship."

The tight fit confirmed for Neil—though he did not think about it at the time—that it did in fact make much better sense to stay where they were for suiting up and have the commander go out of the hatch first rather than do a two-step around each other just so the lunar module pilot could make the first egress. "It was pretty close in there with the suits inflated. It was certainly a larger cockpit than the Gemini, so there was more room than I was used to. Nevertheless, in Gemini we were strapped down and couldn't move around except during EVA periods. In the LM you were free to roam around, but you had to be very careful and move slowly. It was very easy to bump things. That backpack [Portable Life Support System, or PLSS, pronounced "Pliss"] was sticking out behind you almost a foot and it had a hard surface; if you made a quick motion, you could easily bang into something." And things were, in fact, banged into. For example, the outer knob of an ascent engine-arming circuit breaker broke off, which Buzz was able to depress prior to liftoff with a felt-tipped pen. "We were certainly very aware of the cumbersome nature of operating in our suits," Neil concludes.

Proceeding with great care, the two men used all the estimated time for suiting up and then some. Then it also took longer than anticipated to get the cooling units in their PLSS backpacks operating and even more time than expected to depressurize the LM for egress. According to Neil, "We had to depressurize the cabin and we wanted to protect the lunar surface from Earth germs so we had filters on all the vents. We had never done the tests with the filters on and it took a much longer time to depressurize the cabin than we had anticipated." They were ready to swing open the hatch and for Neil to step out onto the surface an hour later than estimated, though that was still five hours ahead of the original schedule.

Opening the hatch proved to be a chore. "It was an effort in patience more than anything else," Neil explains. "It was a pretty good-sized hatch—five or six hundred square inches or something like that. So when we got the cabin pressure down to a very low psi, it took something like two hundred pounds of pressure to open that up. You can't put two hundred pounds of pressure into pulling on a handle very easily—not in those cumbersome suits. So we had to wait until we got to a very low-pressure difference between the inside of the door and the outside of the door before it would break free. We tried a number of times to open it up, but we didn't want to bend or break anything. Mostly it was Buzz doing the pulling because the door opened his direction; it was easier for him to pull toward himself than it was for me to push."

The hatch finally opened, Neil began backing through a fairly tiny opening. Peering down and around, Buzz helped navigate. According to Neil, "Egress required you go through the hatch backward, feet first. The technique was to get the door wide open and face the rear of the lunar module cabin, then kneel down and slide backwards, allowing your feet to go out through the hatch first. Then you had to get around the backpack. The backpack extended quite a long way above your back. You needed to get quite low but then you also had things on the front of you that you didn't want to damage. So it was a matter of doing that kind of awkward procedure with as much care as possible so as not to damage."

"Having said that, getting through the hatch proved to be no more difficult than a lot of other maneuvers that we had been required to do back in the Gemini spacecraft or in the Apollo command module, so it worked well. To my knowledge all the crew on all the Apollo flights used the same approach, and as far as I know there was never any significant damage."

So intent was Armstrong on his egress technique that when he got out onto the small porch of the LM, he forgot to pull the lanyard just north of the ladder rigged to deploy the swing-action Modular Equipment Storage Assembly. The MESA lanyard also activated the television camera that was to transmit to Earth images of Neil's descent down the ladder and his first step onto the lunar surface. Quickly noticing the omission, Houston reminded him about it, and Neil moved back a bit to pull the deployment handle.

The television camera was black and white. "We did have a color camera in the command module," explains Neil, "but it was quite big and bulky and for the LM we were very concerned about weight. Principally, weight and electrical power were the factors that required the much smaller black-and-white-image orthicon TV camera." Essentially, the orthicon was a pickup tube that used a low-velocity electron beam to scan a photoactive mosaic.

"When I first exited the lunar module out onto the porch and pulled the handle to release the MESA table, as I remember it, Buzz turned a circuit breaker powering the camera. I asked Houston if they were getting a picture and they said, yes, they were, but it was upside down. I was the most surprised guy probably of anybody listening to that conversation, because I did not expect them to get a picture [none had been obtained during any preflight simulation]."

Standing at the top of the ladder seemed not at all precarious. "You are so light up there and you fall so slowly that, if you have anything to hold on to anywhere, you are going to be able to control yourself. So I was not ever concerned about falling from the ladder."

In the CapCom seat, astronaut Bruce McCandless had taken over from Owen Garriott for the EVA:

04:13:22:48   McCandless: *Okay, Neil, we can see you coming down the ladder now.*

04:13:22:59   Armstrong: *Okay, I just checked getting back up to that first step, Buzz. The strut isn't collapsed too far, but it's adequate to get back up.*

04:13:23:10   McCandless: *Roger. We copy.*

04:13:23:25	Armstrong:	*It takes a pretty good little jump* [to get back up to the first rung].
04:13:23:38	Armstrong:	*I'm at the foot of the ladder. The LM footpads are only depressed in the surface about one or two inches, although the surface appears to be very, very fine-grained as you get close to it. It's almost like a powder.* [The] *ground mass is very fine.*
04:13:24:13	Armstrong:	*I'm going to step off the LM now.*

Every one of the global millions who watched what next happened on their television sets will never forget the moment that Armstrong took his first step out onto the surface of the Moon. Watching the shadowy black-and-white TV pictures coming back from a quarter of a million miles away, it seemed like an eternity before Neil, his right hand on the ladder, finally stepped off onto the Moon, leading with his booted left foot.

The historic first step took place at 10:56:15 P.M. EDT, which was 02:56:15 Greenwich Mean Time. In terms of mission elapsed time, the step came, according to NASA's official press statement, at four days, thirteen hours, twenty-four minutes, and twenty seconds.

In the United States, the largest share of the television audience, including everyone at the Armstrong homes in Wapakoneta and El Lago, were watching CBS and listening to Cronkite, who for one of the very few times in his broadcasting career was virtually speechless. Having taken his eye-glasses off, and rubbing tears from his eyes, Cronkite declared, "Armstrong is on the Moon! Neil Armstrong, a thirty-eight-year-old American, standing on the surface of the Moon! On this July twentieth, nineteen hundred and sixty-nine."

What also so impressed Cronkite, as it did everybody else, was that the world was watching something that was happening so far away, at a place no human being had ever been before, via a live television feed. "Boy! Look at those pictures!" the veteran newsman exclaimed. "It's a little shadowy, but he [Neil] said he expected that in the shadow of the lunar module."

Television pictures afforded the audience the virtual sensibility of being there with Armstrong when he stepped out onto the Moon. Without them, the human experience of the First Man's first step would still have been meaningful, sensational, and immortal, yet surely very different. "How different it is hard to say," Neil reflects today. "The pictures were surreal, not because the situation was actually surreal, but just because the television technique and picture quality gave it sort of a superimposed unreal image." As dangerous as it is to say today given all the ridiculous conspiracy theories over the past four decades about the Moon landing having been a faked telecast from a remote movie studio location somewhere out in the Arizona or Nevada desert, even Armstrong must confess, "I have to say that it almost looked contrived.

"That certainly wasn't planned. Had we had the ability to make a much clearer picture, we certainly would have opted to do so." The only way that Neil and Buzz could have improved the TV picture with the orthicon camera system was to move from the small antenna to the large S-band erectable antenna that was stored on the LM. "It is possible that with the big antenna [a dish model] we might have produced a better picture, I don't know. We might have accomplished that.

"From a technical standpoint, the TV was still valuable," Armstrong recalls, "to various individuals in and around NASA." But no piece of information carried a greater worth, or was more closely guarded, than what words Armstrong would say when he stepped out onto the lunar surface. No one knew, not even his crewmates. Buzz recalls: "On the way to the Moon, Mike and I had asked Neil what he was going to say when he stepped out on the Moon. He had replied that he was still thinking it over."

Armstrong maintains he spent no time thinking about what he would say until sometime after he had successfully executed the landing.

At 04:13:24:48 mission elapsed time, which was a few seconds before 10:57 P.M. EDT, Neil spoke his eternally famous words*:

That's one small step for man, one giant leap for mankind.

In El Lago, Janet reportedly said as Neil was coming down the ladder, "I can't believe it's really happening," then when Neil stepped off, "That's the big step!" As he began to walk upon the Moon, she coaxed him, "Be de-

---

* Because of the Moon's position relative to the Earth at the moment of Armstrong's "one small step" statement, the TV downlink used by NASA came from Honeysuckle Station outside Canberra, Australia; previously the *Eagle*'s TV signal had been coming from the Goldstone tracking station in California. Much of the TV downlink for the remainder of Apollo 11's EVA came from the big radio astronomy telescope at Parkes, in New South Wales, Australia. The story of the Australian role in the first Moon landing's navigation and communications has been detailed in Hamish Lindsay's book *Tracking Apollo to the Moon*. The story of what happened at Parkes observatory and in the surrounding rural town during the Apollo 11 mission has been marvelously (and humorously) depicted—albeit with a lot of harmless inaccuracy—in the 2001 Australian film *The Dish*.

scriptive now, Neil." In Wapakoneta, Viola, clutching the arms of her chair ever so tightly, thanked God that her son was not sinking into the lunar dust, a fear that many people still harbored even after the LM had landed.

In El Lago, Janet kept telling her company that she had absolutely no idea what her husband would say when he stepped onto the Moon. An hour earlier, she had jested, as everyone grew more impatient for Neil and Buzz to begin the EVA, "It's taking them so long because Neil's trying to decide about the first words he's going to say when he steps out on the Moon. Decisions, decisions, decisions!"

Janet's joke was not too far from the truth, as Neil testifies: "Once on the surface and realizing that the moment was at hand, fortunately I had some hours to think about it after getting there. My own view was that it was a very simplistic statement: what can you say when you step off of something? Well, something about a step. It just sort of evolved during the period that I was doing the procedures of the practice takeoff and the EVA prep and all the other activities that were on our flight schedule at that time. I didn't think it was particularly important, but other people obviously did. Even so, I have never thought that I picked a particularly enlightening statement. It was a very simple statement."

Then there was the matter of the missing "a"—the fact that Neil fully intended to say, "That's one small step for *a* man," but, in the rush of the moment, forgot to say, or just did not say, the "a."

In terms of memory, "I can't recapture it. For people who have listened to me for hours on the radio communication tapes, they know I left a lot of syllables out. It was not unusual for me to do that. I'm not particularly articulate. Perhaps it was a suppressed sound that didn't get picked up by the voice mike. As I have listened to it, it doesn't sound like there was time there for the word to be there. On the other hand, I think that reasonable people will realize that I didn't intentionally make an inane statement, and that certainly the 'a' was intended, because that's the only way the statement makes any sense. So I would hope that history would grant me leeway for dropping the syllable and understand that it was certainly intended, even if it wasn't said—although it actually might have been."

When asked how he prefers for historians to quote his statement, Neil answers only somewhat facetiously, "They can put it in parentheses."

"As for what I did say on the Moon, I took a small step—so that part of it came real easy. Then it wasn't much of a jump to say what you could compare that with."

One theory is that Armstrong came across the idea for his statement while reading J. R. R. Tolkien's *The Hobbit*. In one scene of the book, the protagonist Bilbo Baggins, while invisible, jumps over the villainous Gollum in a leap that Tolkien described as "not a great leap for a man, but a leap in the dark." Reinforcing this suggestion is the fact that Armstrong, when he moved his family to a farm in Lebanon, Ohio, after leaving NASA in 1971, named his farm Rivendell, which is the name of the idyllic secluded valley of Tolkien's fictional Middle Earth in *Lord of the Rings* and the abode ("the last homely house") of noble Elrond, who is half elf and half human. In the *Rings* trilogy Rivendell is the last place where elves live before leaving Middle Earth and returning to "the immortal lands" over the sea. Adding spice to this theory is the fact, known to many of Neil's friends, that in the 1990s Neil also based his e-mail address on a Tolkien theme.

Regrettably for Tolkien fans, Armstrong's reading of the classic books could not have influenced what he said when he stepped onto the lunar surface in 1969. Indeed, he did come to read *The Hobbit* and *Lord of the Rings*, but not until well after Apollo 11. "My boys made me read the series years later when we were living on the farm. I read all the books, but I don't remember bumping into anything even then that made me think about what I had said."

A far less chimerical theory is that a high NASA official gave him the idea. This hypothesis is based on the existence of an April 19, 1969, memorandum from Willis Shapley, an associate deputy administrator at NASA Headquarters, to Dr. George Mueller, head of the Office of Manned Space Flight. Shapley's three-page memo, entitled "Symbolic Items for the First Lunar Landing," addressed what sorts of items should be left on the Moon by the Apollo 11 crew as well as what commemorative articles should be taken to the lunar surface and returned. Early in the memo, in talking about what sort of message the Moon landing should present to the world, Shapley wrote: "The intended overall impression of the symbolic activities and of the manner in which they are presented to the world should be to signalize [sic] the first lunar landing as an historic step forward for all mankind that has been accomplished by the United States of America. . . . The 'forward step for all mankind' aspect of the landing should be symbolized primarily by a suitable inscription to be left on the Moon and by statements made on Earth, and also perhaps by leaving on the Moon miniature flags of all nations." As the story goes, Mueller passed this memo on to Deke Slayton who shared it with Armstrong, thus planting the seed for the idea that led to Neil's historic statement.

The problem is, Armstrong has absolutely no recall of the memo. As hauntingly similar as the phrase "forward step for all mankind" seems to be, he does not remember getting a copy of it or ever hearing about it. It seems to be another example—like Cronkite's TV comment about "a giant leap" on the morning of the landing—of a similar statement having been made independently of the thought process behind Armstrong's own words.

"My guess is that you can take almost any statement, and if you look around for a while, you can find other statements that were made similarly by other people."

One example of that is President Kennedy's quotation, "Ask not what your country can do for you, ask what you can do for your country." A statement very much like Kennedy's was made by Warren Harding when he was running for president—and before that, by Oliver Wendell Holmes. Following the Russian launch of Sputnik in October 1957, President Eisenhower, in fact, used the phrase, "a giant leap into outer space," but Armstrong had no previous conscious knowledge of that statement, either.

"So, in your mind, Neil, there was never any particular context for your coming up with the phrase? It did not connect back to any other quotation or experience?"

"Not that I know of or can recall. But you never know subliminally in your brain where things come from. But it certainly wasn't conscious. When an idea runs for the first time through your own mind, it comes out as an original thought."

For the first few minutes after stepping off the LM, Armstrong kept his exploring close to the ladder. He was intrigued by the peculiar properties of the lunar dust. He told Houston: "The surface is fine and powdery. I can kick it up loosely with my toe. It does adhere in fine layers, like powdered charcoal, to the sole and sides of my boots. I only go in a small fraction of an inch, maybe an eighth of an inch, but I can see the footprints of my boots and the treads in the fine, sandy particles." As was expected, motion posed no problem. "It's even perhaps easier than the simulations of one-sixth g that we performed in the various simulations on the ground. It's absolutely no trouble to walk around."

Back in Ohio, his mother took immense pleasure in seeing Neil move without the slightest sign of difficulty. "He seemed to have a buoyancy," she later wrote, "almost floating as he walked . . . I knew his suit was bulky, and I hoped so much that he would not fall. Falling could cause a puncture, and a puncture could cause his life-support to fail. I knew this was dangerous."

Still in close proximity to the LM, Neil saw that the descent engine had not left a crater of any marked size. "It has about one foot clearance on the ground. We're essentially on a very level place here. I can see some evidence of [exhaust-induced erosion] rays emanating from the descent engine, but a very insignificant amount."

He was anxious to have the mission's photographic camera, a 70-millimeter Hasselblad, sent down to him. To do that, Buzz, just inside the hatch, needed to hook the camera to a device known as the Lunar Equipment Conveyor, or LEC.* The astronauts nicknamed it the "Brooklyn Clothesline" because it worked pretty much the same way as the line in New York apartment buildings used to hang out and dry wash. The idea for the LEC came along not so much to solve the problem of bringing the camera and other things down from the LM but for taking things back up from the lunar surface at the conclusion of the EVA. "We had done some practice sessions on the final segment of the lunar surface work where we brought all the rock boxes, cameras, and various equipment that needed to go inside. It was very cumbersome. We found it very difficult to manhandle all that stuff around and get it in the proper position so that the other person—the top man—could pick it up. I think it was my suggestion that we try the clothesline technique. So we did that, and it seemed to work out all right."

Unhooking the camera from the LEC, Armstrong set it in the bracketing framework of the Remote Control Unit, or RCU, which was built according to his own design right into the front of his suit. Neil believes that whoever had comprised the first crew, facing such practical problems, would have come up with something very similar, because the Hasselblad was a rather large camera.

"It was not an automatic camera; everything was manual—shutter speed, f-stop, focus, everything. It was very obvious that it was a two-handed operation and that if you were doing anything else at the time you needed

---

* Only recently, Eric M. Jones, the Australia-based editor of the *Apollo Lunar Surface Journal,* has discovered evidence that, during Armstrong's historic climb down the ladder, Neil had the Lunar Equipment Conveyor hooked to his suit and that Aldrin was playing it out as a safety tether. (Jones provides the evidence for his conjecture at http://www.nasa.gov/alsj/all/alltether.html.) To Jones, Armstrong has written, "You make a persuasive case about the LEC, but I cannot remember the detail well enough to confirm or dissent." Eric M. Jones, e-mail to author, Mar. 27, 2005.

another hand. Secondly, there was the problem of when you were doing other things with other equipment, what were you to do with the camera? You didn't want to set it down in the dirt. So it was just immediately obvious that we needed something else. I suggested, why don't we put a mounting bracket for it on the backpack control unit, which was mounted on our chests. That would be a convenient place to locate it. We would be able to see the marks on the camera, and we could probably take many of the pictures we wanted right from the bracket location, essentially making our bodies into a bipod to hold the camera. That seemed to work out well. Everybody ended up using that technique."

As soon he got the camera mounted, Armstrong was so intent on taking a few pictures that he neglected to scoop up the contingency sample of lunar dirt, a higher priority item that he was supposed to accomplish first in case something went wrong and he quickly needed to get back into the LM. NASA did not want to get all the way to the Moon and then not be able to bring back any lunar sample for scientific study. Houston had to remind Neil, never one to be rushed, a couple of times to get the sample.

"First thing you are at the surface. The camera is all ready after you get that mounted. It was very easy to take a few pictures. They were very important, too, but, of course, the contingency sample guys wanted to make sure that that was the first thing we got done. It was going to take somewhat more effort to get that sample—to get the equipment and the container for that sample—than it was to get a few pictures. My thought was just that I was going to get a few quick pictures—a panoramic sequence of the LM's surroundings—while I was there, and then I was going to get the sample."

| 04:13:30:53 | Armstrong: | *I'll step out and take some of my first pictures here.* |
| 04:13:31:05 | McCandless: | *Roger, Neil, we're reading you loud and clear. We see you getting some pictures and the contingency sample.* |

COMM BREAK

| 04:13:32:19 | McCandless: | *Neil, this is Houston. Did you copy about the contingency sample? Over.* |
| 04:13:32:26 | Armstrong: | *Roger. I'm going to get to that just as soon as I finish these . . . this picture series.* |

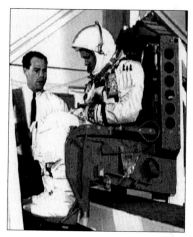

Astronaut Armstrong undergoes weight and balance tests in the Pyrotechnic Installation Building, Kennedy Space Center, February 1966.

Armstrong and Dave Scott designed their own logo for the Gemini VIII mission, a light spectrum emanating from the mythological twins Castor and Pollux.

Command pilot Armstrong (*foreground*) and David R. Scott, pilot, walk up the ramp at Pad 19 for the Gemini VIII launch, March 16, 1966.

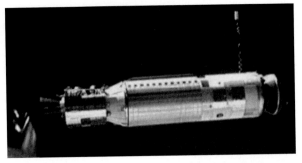

View of the Agena target-docking vehicle as seen from Gemini VIII prior to history's first docking in space.

Scott (*left*) and Armstrong stand on the deck of their recovery ship, the destroyer USS *Leonard F. Mason*.

Neil holds up his newsprint likeness during the Wapakoneta celebration of his Gemini VIII flight.

The "amiable strangers" of Apollo 11: (*left to right*) Armstrong, Collins, and Aldrin.

The official Apollo 11 portrait, signed later by each of the crew members.

Armstrong flies the LLTV, June 16, 1969, exactly one month prior to the Apollo 11 launch date.

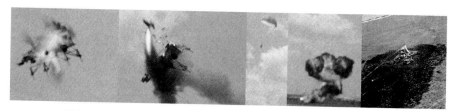

Triggering his malfunctioning LLTV's rocket-powered ejection seat, Armstrong parachutes to safety, May 6, 1968.

Wearing an Extravehicular Mobility Unit, Armstrong simulates collection of a lunar surface sample, Manned Spacecraft Center, Houston, April 18, 1969.

Armstrong examines a geologic field sample, Sierra Blanca, Texas, February 1969.

The "neutral strangers": Neil and Buzz train in Houston, April 22, 1969.

A rare quiet moment at home for the Armstrong family—Janet, Neil, Mark, and Rick—during the buildup to the Apollo 11 launch.

Five days before launch, Neil and Buzz work LM simulations at the Cape.

During the pre-launch breakfast, Deke Slayton maps recovery ship locations for the early phases of the Apollo 11 mission.

Neil's space suit in its lunar surface configuration included a Liquid Cooled Garment (*left*) and EVA gloves and Moon boots (*right*).

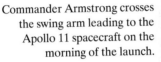

Commander Armstrong crosses the swing arm leading to the Apollo 11 spacecraft on the morning of the launch.

Steve and Viola Armstrong gaze proudly at a scale-model replica of the Saturn V Moon rocket.

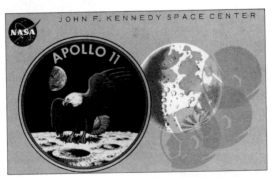

For the July 16, 1969 launch, Kennedy Space Center's director Dr. Kurt H. Debus issued press credentials depicting the Apollo 11 mission crest, the Moon, and the three astronauts' helmeted silhouettes.

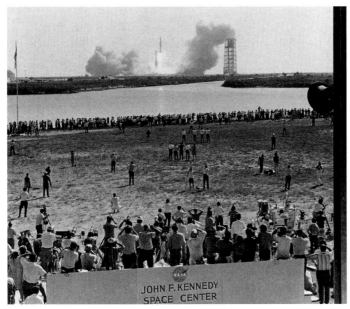

The press witnesses Apollo 11/Saturn V clearing the tower at
Launch Complex 39.

Apollo 11 roars upward just
after pitchover.

Janet Armstrong watches the
Apollo 11 launch.

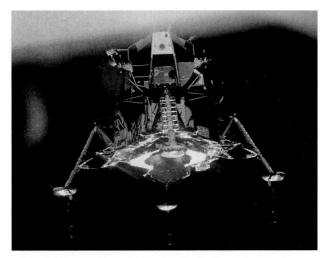

"The Eagle has wings": *Eagle*, shortly after its undocking from *Columbia*.

Armstrong's Moonwalk is documented by just five still photographs:

1. The iconic image of Neil reflected in Buzz's visor.

2. Neil's back and legs visible from his position in front of Buzz.

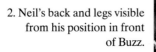

3. This underexposed picture of the Ascent Stage shows Neil at the MESA.

4. Neil's legs as he stands below the LM porch.

5. A Hasselblad pan shot by Buzz yields the only full-body view of Neil on the Lunar Surface.

Mission Control observes the Apollo 11 astronauts' historic Moonwalk.

Deployment of the U.S. flag by Armstrong and Aldrin was caught by the sixteen-millimeter film camera mounted in the LM window.

President Richard M. Nixon telephones his congratulations to the Moonwalkers.

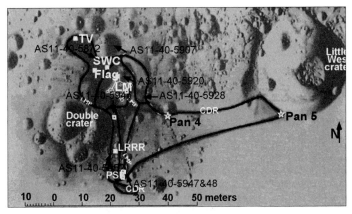

"Where the guys walked": a traverse map of the Apollo 11 EVA.

Back in the LM, Buzz snapped
Neil while in his "Snoopy" cap.

"Spaceship Earth" over the LM on the Sea of Tranquility.

Eagle approaches *Columbia* during rendezvous.

"Task Accomplished . . . July 1969."
Mission Control celebrates after splashdown.

Columbia, scarred from the heat of reentry, is recovered by USS *Hornet*'s navy frogmen.

During recovery, the astronauts wore Biological Containment Garments (BIGs) designed to save the world from "Moon germs."

The slogan "Hornet + 3" adorned the astronauts' Mobile Quarantine Facility, as well as the tiered cake decorated in their honor.

Collins, Aldrin, and Armstrong parade through New York City,
August 13, 1969.

Collins, Armstrong, and
Aldrin with U.S. Postmaster
General Winton M. Blount
unveiling the commemorative
Apollo 11 ten-cent air mail
stamp, September 9, 1969.

The Apollo 11 crew donned
panchos and sombreros on
the Mexico City leg of the
GIANTSTEP goodwill tour,
September 29, 1969.

Professor Armstrong teaching engineering at the University of Cincinnati, 1974.

Armstrong became the national spokesperson for the
Chrysler Corporation, 1979.

The Apollo 11 crew reunited on the thirtieth anniversary of their mission, 1999.

Neil, with wife Carol, returns to
Launch Pad 39A, this time to
observe the launch of Space
Shuttle *Columbia* (STS-83),
April 4, 1987.

Neil, with Carol, maintains his active flight status on a Cessna 421, October 2003.

COMM BREAK

04:13:33:25   Aldrin: *Okay. Going to get the contingency sample there, Neil?*

04:13:33:27   Armstrong: *Right.*

04:13:33:30   Aldrin: *Okay. That's good.*

In the technical debrief following the mission, Neil explained his conservative reasoning for changing the order of doing these first two things by saying that he was at first standing in the shadow of the LM, where good pictures could be taken. "I wanted to get that camera down and hooked up while I was over there in the shadow because, to do the contingency sample, I was going to have to stow the LEC and go over into the area out of the shadow. Since I wanted to do it on the right side [north of the ladder] where the [movie] camera was mounted [in Buzz's window], I was going to have to make a trip of about ten or fifteen feet before I started the contingency sample. That's the reason we [I] changed the order." Subsequent Moon landing crews, building on Apollo 11's experience, would consider moving ten or fifteen feet a trivial distance, but not the First Man. Having been on the lunar surface for all of eight minutes at this point, everything about his initial movements were done incrementally and with great caution.

To take the contingency sample Neil had to assemble a pooper-scooper-like device with a collapsible handle that had a removable bag at the end. After he scooped up a small amount of soil sample, he deposited the bag inside a special strap-on pocket on his right thigh. Digging into the top surface was no problem at all, as the soil was very loose. Though the contingency sample did not require him to take anything from any real depth, he did try digging an inch or more into the surface only to find that it quickly became very hard. He also made sure to get a couple of small rocks into his bag before closing it up. He also conducted a little soil mechanics experiment by pushing the handle-end of his sampler down into the surface from four to six inches.

His sample completed, Neil took a moment just to gaze out at the lunar landscape. "It has a stark beauty of its own," he reported. "It's much like the high desert of the United States. It's different, but it's very pretty out here." Then, still thinking about what he could do to experiment, he detached the ring that had been holding the collection bag on to the contingency sample and threw it sidearm to see how far it would go. "Didn't know you could throw so far," Aldrin teased, watching out his window. Chuckling, Neil answered, "You can really throw things a long way up here!" Curiously, Neil today has no recollection of making the throw, the Moon's first pitch. "I don't remember that."

   "You don't remember doing that at all?"

   "No, not at all."

Sixteen minutes into the EVA, it was time for Aldrin to egress, something he was just itching to do:

04:13:38:41	Aldrin:	*Okay, are you ready for me to come out?*
04:13:38:42	Armstrong:	*Yeah. Just stand by a second. I'll move this* [LEC] *over the handrail.* [Long pause] *Okay.*
04:13:39:07	Aldrin:	*All right. That's got it. Are you ready?*
04:13:39:11	Armstrong:	*All set. Okay, you saw what difficulties I was having. I'll try to watch your PLSS from underneath here.*

Standing southwest of the ladder, Neil used the Hasselblad to snap a series of remarkable photographs of Buzz slowly emerging from the hatch, studiously coming down the ladder, kneeling on the porch, moving down to the last rung, jumping down to the footpad, and hopping off onto the lunar surface. These are the pictures that people would later see and forever remember in terms of the first human stepping onto the Moon: Buzz doing it rather than Neil, for whom no photographs from below could be taken because he went out first. Actually, Buzz climbed down to the last rung twice before stepping off—the first time just as rehearsal.

04:13:41:28	Aldrin:	*Okay. Now I want to go back up and partially close the hatch.* [Long pause] *Making sure not to lock it on my way out!*
04:13:41:53	Armstrong:	[Laughing] *A particularly good thought.*

Not that the two men were actually worried that they could lock themselves out, as the hatch could be opened from the outside, if necessary. According to Neil, "That was just a joke, perhaps to avoid somebody saying, 'Were you born in a barn?' " Aldrin's reason for partially closing the hatch was apparently to prevent radiative cooling of the LM cabin:

04:13:41:56   Aldrin: *That's our home for the next couple of hours, and*
                                    we want to take good care of it.

As a matter of fact, though Buzz and Neil did not think of it at the time, there *was* a way that they could have locked themselves out, if the hatch's pressure valve had somehow gone awry and started repressurizing. "Did we really ever investigate that problem?" Aldrin has asked, chuckling. "It probably would have been a good idea to use a brick or a camera to keep it from closing. Somebody must have thought through that. . . . We had a handle [on the outside] to unlatch it, but, considering the difficulty we had, if you had a couple of psi [in the cabin], you'd never get it open. Well, you'd get it open, but you'd never get the bent hatch closed again!"

Down on the surface, it was at this moment that Buzz referred to the Moon's unique beauty as "magnificent desolation." Leaning toward Buzz so close that their helmets almost touched, Neil clapped his gloved hand on his mate's shoulder. According to Buzz's autobiography, Neil then said to him, "Isn't it fun?" But Neil insists today that " 'fine' is definitely what I said," in reference to the very fine powder that the two astronauts were still in the midst of examining.

After that, they moved off their separate ways and began testing their mobility. Though their substantial number of hours in one-sixth g had not been spent moving very far or very fast, inside the LM they had been standing, bending, and leaning and, in Neil's words, had "a pretty good appreciation of what the one-sixth g environment felt like before we ever got out."

What they were not accustomed to were major and very rapid body movements. In ground simulations and in the one-sixth g airplane, they had practiced a number of different possible lunar gaits. In one of the ground simulations, Neil remembers, "You were suspended sideways against an incline plane and walked sideways while hooked to an assembly of cables." Although a truer feeling came in the one-sixth g airplane—a converted KC-135, flying parabolas—that only gave them a few seconds each flight to polish their techniques.

During the EVA, it was Aldrin's job specifically to test all the different lunar gaits. These included a "loping gait" (Neil's preference) in which the astronaut alternated feet, pushed off with each step, and floated forward before planting the next foot; a "skipping stride," in which he kept one foot always forward, hit with the trailing foot just a fraction of a second before the lead foot, then pushed off with each foot, launching into the next glide; as well as a "kangaroo hop," which few Apollo astronauts ever employed, except playfully, because its movements were so stilted.

With their big backpack and heavy suit on, the astronauts would have weighed 360 pounds apiece on Earth; on the Moon, in one-sixth gravity, they each weighed merely sixty pounds. Since they felt so lightweight, special care in all movements did need to be taken, primarily because of their backpacks, whose mass effects on their balance, they quickly discovered, pitched their walk slightly forward. When looking out in any direction toward the horizon, both men felt a bit disoriented. Because the Moon was so much smaller a sphere than Earth, the planetoid curved much more visibly down and away than they were accustomed to. Also, because the terrain varied a good bit relative to their ability to move over it, they had to be constantly alert. "On Earth, you only worry about one or two steps ahead," Buzz has recalled. "On the Moon, you have to keep a good eye out four or five steps ahead." Mostly, the two astronauts, trained as they were to be very conservative in their EVA mobility, walked flat-footed, with one foot always firmly planted into the lunar surface.

Armstrong did try making some fairly high jumps straight up off the ground. What he found was a tendency to tip over backwards upon landing. "One time I came close to falling and decided that was enough of that." After he and Buzz stretched out the TV cable so the television camera could be moved to its position some fifty feet away from the LM, Neil also tripped over the cable a couple of times. "The TV cable was coiled in storage, so when we stretched it out we had a spiral on the ground that was lifting up, and with the low gravity that was accentuated a little bit. It was very easy to trip over that cable, which I did a few times." Exacerbating the problem was the fact that the astronauts really could not see their feet very well. "Because of our suits, it was hard to see anything right below you. It was hard to see your feet; they were pretty far down there." The fact that the cables got dusty almost immediately also contributed to the problem.

Sometime during this initial stretching of their lunar muscles, Aldrin contributed his own "first" on the Moon. Always forthright, Buzz relates: "My kidneys, which have never been of the strongest, sent me a message of distress. Neil might have been the first man to step on the Moon, but I was the first to pee in his pants on the Moon. I was, of course, linked up with the urine-collection device, but it was a unique feeling. The whole world was watching, but I was the only one who knew what they were really witnessing."

It is not known when or where, or whether, Armstrong experienced a similar call from nature while he was on the lunar surface. If he did, it is definitely not something he would ever have told anyone about.

Sewn to each man's left gauntlet was an ordered checklist of EVA tasks. Even though Neil and Buzz, through repeated simulations, knew from memory the order of events, they still used the checklists consistently, as professional pilots did, no matter how well they knew the procedures.

The astronauts' next task (another late addition) was unveiling the commemorative plaque that was mounted on the ladder leg of the LM. "For those who haven't read the plaque," Neil said to the world at 04:13:52:40 elapsed time, "we'll read the plaque that's on the front landing gear of this LM. First, there's two hemispheres, one showing each of the two hemispheres of the Earth. Underneath it says, 'Here Men from the Planet Earth first set foot upon the Moon, July 1969 A.D. We came in peace for all mankind.' It has the crew members' signatures and the signature of the president of the United States."

Though the crew played no role in developing the plaque or its inscription, they were happy to endorse the message and to put their signatures on it. Aldrin, who would later formally change his name to Buzz, felt that the plaque was one place that required his formal assignation, "Edwin E."

Another item that was not on their checklist but that NASA wanted accomplished fairly early during their EVA was the planting of the American flag. As discussed earlier, the decision to erect an American flag on the Moon had been controversial. Armstrong remembers: "There was substantial discussion before the flight on what the flag should be. It was questioned as to whether it should be an American flag or a United Nations flag." Once it was decided (with no input from the crew) that it should be the American flag, Neil, a former Eagle Scout, did give some thought as to *how* the flag should be displayed. "I thought the flag should just be draped down, that it should fall down the flagpole like it would here on Earth. It shouldn't be made to stand out or put into any rigid framework, which it ultimately was. I soon decided that this had gotten to be such a big issue, outside of my realm and point of view, that it didn't pay for me to even worry about it. It was going to be other people's decision, and whatever they decided was okay. I wasn't going to have any voice in that."

While he and Buzz had trained in minute detail to execute virtually every other assigned task during the EVA, they had done no training at all for the flag ceremony, as it, too, like the unveiling of the plaque, was a late addition. As it turned out, planting the flag (some thirty feet in front of the LM) took a lot more effort than anyone had imagined—so much more that the whole thing nearly turned into a public relations disaster.

First there was difficulty with the small telescoping arm that was attached as a crossbar to the top end of the flagpole; its function was to keep the flag (measuring three feet by five feet) extended and perpendicular in the still, windless lunar atmosphere. Armstrong and Aldrin were able quickly enough to lock the arm in its 90-degree position, but as hard as they tried, they could not get the telescope to extend fully. Thus, instead of the flag turning out flat and fully stretched, it had what Buzz has called "a unique permanent wave." Then, to the dismay of the two men, fully aware that the whole world was watching them through the TV camera they had just set up, they could not get the staff of the flagpole to penetrate deeply enough into the soil to support itself in an upright position. "We had trouble getting it into the surface," recalls Neil. "It ran into the subsurface crust." With the pole sticking barely six inches into the Moon, all the two men could think about was the dreaded possibility that the American flag might collapse into the lunar dust right in front of the global television audience.

Fortunately, the pole, with its funny curly flag, stayed standing. With his camera, Neil took the memorable picture of Aldrin saluting the flag. According to Aldrin, he and Neil were just about to change positions and transfer the camera so that Buzz could take a picture of him when Mission Control radioed that President Nixon was on the line and wanted to talk to them. This distracted them from taking the picture, Buzz relates, so a photo of Neil never got taken.

However, the sequence of events as evidenced in the NASA communications transcript shows that the first word of Nixon's call did not come to the astronauts until *well* after Neil took the picture of Aldrin saluting the flag; the picture was taken during a break in communications very shortly after 04:14:10:33 elapsed time whereas the news that Nixon wanted to talk to them came at 04:14:15:47. During most of that five-minute-and-fourteen-second interval, the two men were no longer even together. Following the flag planting, Armstrong moved back to the LM, the camera still with him. There, at the MESA, he prepared to collect his first rock samples. Aldrin moved out westward from the LM a distance of some fifty feet before rejoining Neil at the MESA.

04:14:15:47	McCandless:	*Tranquility Base, this is Houston. Could we get both of you on the [TV] camera for a minute, please?*
04:14:16:00	Aldrin:	*Say again, Houston.*
04:14:16:03	Armstrong:	*He wants us on camera.*
04:14:16:03	McCandless:	*We'd like to get both of you in the field-of-view of the camera for a minute. [Pause] Neil and Buzz, the president of the United States is in his office now and would like to say a few words to you. Over.*
04:14:16:23	Armstrong:	*That would be an honor.*
04:14:16:25	McCandless:	*All right. Go ahead, Mr. President. This is Houston. Out.*
04:14:16:30	Nixon:	*Hello, Neil and Buzz. I'm talking to you by telephone from the Oval Room at the White House, and this certainly has to be the most historic telephone call ever made. I just can't tell you how proud we all are of what you have done. For every American, this has to be the proudest day of our lives. And for all people all over the world, I am sure they, too, join with Americans in recognizing what an immense feat this is. Because of what you have done, the heavens have become a part of man's world. And as you talk to us from the Sea of Tranquility, it inspires us to redouble our efforts to bring peace and tranquility to Earth. For one priceless moment in the whole history of man, all the people on this Earth are truly one—one in their pride in what you have done, and one in our prayers that you will return safely to Earth.*
04:14:17:44	Armstrong:	*Thank you, Mr. President. It's a great honor and privilege for us to be here representing not only the United States but men of peace of all nations, and with interests and the curiosity and with the vision*

		for the future. It's an honor for us to be able to par- *ticipate here today.*
04:14:18:12	Nixon:	*And thank you very much, and I look forward. . . .* *All of us look forward to seeing you on the* Hornet [Apollo 11's recovery ship] *on Thursday.*
04:14:18:21	Aldrin:	*I look forward to that very much, sir.*

A long pause indicated that Nixon had finished. The astronauts saluted—Buzz for the second time during the conversation—and then they both headed back to the MESA.

There is no question that President Nixon's phone call came as a surprise to Aldrin. In his autobiography, Buzz recalled: "My heart rate, which had been low throughout the entire flight, suddenly jumped. Later Neil said he had known the president might be speaking with us while we were on the Moon, but no one had told me. I hadn't even considered the possibility. The conversation was short and, for me, awkward. I felt it somehow incumbent on me to make some profound statement, for which I had made no preparation whatsoever. I took the handiest possible refuge. Neil was the commander of the flight, so I let him do the responding. I conveniently concluded that any observation I might make would look as though I was butting into the conversation, so I kept silent."

Armstrong attests, "Deke had told me shortly before the flight that we might expect some special communication. He didn't say it would be the president necessarily, but just to expect some special communication that would come through the CapCom. It was just a heads-up, to tell me that something might come through that seems unusual, but Deke didn't tell me exactly what it was. I didn't know it was going to be the president, and I'm not sure Deke knew exactly who or what it was going to be, either, but apparently he had gotten wind of something, maybe through Bob Gilruth. If I'd known it was going to be the president, I might of tried to conjure some kind of an appropriate statement, but I didn't know."

A written comment from Viola supports Neil's assertion that he did not know in advance that Nixon would call. "I have never asked Neil if he knew the president was planning to call, but I must admit that I could sense our son was emotionally shaken. I could hear the tremor in his voice. God love him, and Buzz too, how could they be otherwise? It truly was a touching time for all of us watching. The tears were trickling down our cheeks."

Aldrin has plainly stated in the years since Apollo 11 his desire to have been given the courtesy of the same heads-up that Neil got—specifically from his own commander. "I don't think I even thought about it," Armstrong states today. "Whatever it was, it was going to be a surprise. And maybe it wasn't even going to happen."

Without question, it was a highly unusual relationship between two men who had to work so closely together—one of amiable (read neutral)—strangers. But the strangeness went in both directions, not just from Neil to Buzz.

Consider the fact that, while Armstrong took dozens of wonderful photographs of Aldrin, Buzz took not a single explicit picture of Neil. The only pictures of Neil were one with a reflection of him in Aldrin's helmet visor in a picture Neil took, or a very few where Neil was standing in the dark shadow of the LM with his back to the camera or only partially shown.*

It is one of the minor tragedies of Apollo 11 that posterity benefits from no photos of the First Man on the Moon. Not of him saluting the American flag. Not of him climbing down the ladder. Not of him stepping on the Moon. Not of him standing by the LM. Not of him with the Earth in the background. Not of him next to a crater. Not of him directly anywhere. Sure, there are the grainy, shadowy, black-and-white TV pictures of Armstrong on the Moon, and they are remarkable and forever memorable. There are also a number of frames from the 16mm movie camera. But, very regrettably, there are no high-resolution color photographic images of the First Man with the spectacular detail provided by the Hasselblad.

Why not? The answer, according to Aldrin, was that he simply did not think to take any—except at that moment when they were planting the American flag and President Nixon's call allegedly ended what would have been a Buzz-at-Neil photo shoot.

In his autobiography, Aldrin excuses what he failed to do. "As the sequence of lunar operations evolved, Neil had the camera most of the time, and *the majority of the pictures taken on the Moon that include an astronaut are of me* [author's emphasis]. It wasn't until we were back on Earth and in the Lunar Receiving Laboratory looking over the pictures that we realized

---

* Besides the famous picture that has his reflection in Aldrin's visor, Armstrong is shown on the lunar surface in pictures 5886, 5895, 5903, and 5916. In all but 5886, Neil is either in deep shadow or only partially shown. Photo 5895 shows Neil's legs and 5916 shows the back of his suit from close-up (it is a frame from one of Buzz's pans). Another image, AS11-40-5894, would have provided a good view of Armstrong at the MESA, if only the exposure would have been more appropriate.

there were *few pictures of Neil.* My fault perhaps, but we had never simulated this during our training."

"We didn't spend any time worrying about who took what pictures," Armstrong graciously recalls. "It didn't occur to me that it made any difference, as long as they were good.

"I don't think Buzz had any reason to take my picture, and it never occurred to me that he should. I have always said that Buzz was the far more photogenic of the crew."

At the same time, Armstrong does offer real clarification of the situation pertaining to cameras and the photographic plan for surface activities during Apollo 11. "We always had a plan for when we were going to transfer the camera. He was going to take some pictures, and I was going to take some. And I think roughly we did it approximately like the plan called for in terms of the camera transfer. I had the camera for a large fraction of the time and I had more assigned photographic responsibilities, but Buzz did have the camera some of the time and did take pictures. It was in the flight plan."

Besides the Hasselblad that Neil mounted on his chest bracket shortly after the EVA began, another Hasselblad was kept in the LM as a spare in case the first camera malfunctioned. This camera—an intravehicular (IV) Hasselblad—did not have the reflective outer shell (that kept the EVA camera from overheating) and didn't have a reseau plate for putting calibration crosses on the images; it was never brought out. The only other still-photo camera that was used on the surface was the Apollo Lunar Surface Close-Up Camera (ALSCC), a stereoscopic camera—often called the "Gold camera," as its proponent was Dr. Thomas Gold, a prominent Cornell University astronomer—that had been specially designed for taking extreme close-ups of lunar soils and rocks.*

The Gold camera was solely Neil's responsibility, and Aldrin does not recall taking any pictures with it. But Buzz definitely took a number of pictures of his own choosing with the EVA Hasselblad. This means Neil painstakingly took the camera off his chest bracket and handed it directly

---

* The man who pushed the use of the ALSCC stereoscopic camera on Apollo 11 was Dr. Thomas "Tommy" Gold (1920–2004), a brilliant Viennese gadfly of an astronomer who taught at Cornell University. "I didn't know Professor Gold," relates Armstrong. "He got his device on Apollo 11 pretty much at the last minute. It was an inconvenience and a new addition that we had to work into the timeline, and we felt uncomfortable with the situation. Nevertheless, we took some pictures with his stereo camera. I took some pictures of some small rocks with it that I thought would be of particular interest to him." NAA to author, Sept. 19, 2003, p. 16.

and carefully over to Aldrin. Buzz does not recall whether he, in turn, ever put the camera into his own bracket; he believes he did not but rather kept it mostly in his right hand.* Buzz does remember taking pictures, though. He took two complete 360-degree panoramas. He took pictures of the distant Earth. He took pictures of the LM. He took the famous shots of footprints (his own) in the lunar dust. But he took no purposeful shots of Neil. Not one. To be fair, all of the photos Buzz took were planned photo tasks of his; taking a picture of Neil was not part of them.

"I should have taken it upon myself to do that," Aldrin offers today. "But, you know, when I look back at where I am now, and what I'm aware of now, compared to where I was, I hate to use the word, but I was *intimidated* by the enormity of the situation. At the time there was certainly a gun-barrel vision of focusing in on what you were supposed to be doing rather than being innovative and creative. Right there was an opportunity where I could have been creative and wasn't."

But Buzz had found other opportunities to be creative. "When I saw what my footprint looked like, I said to myself, 'Golly, we ought to take a picture of that, but I'd better take a picture before and after.' That was split-second. Then there was another instance when, 'Gee, that footprint looks awful lonesome. Let's have the boot, too. Yeah, but then, if I do that, I won't see the footprint.' So I took a picture with the boot slightly away from it. The rest of my picture taking was documenting going around the LM. Neil took most of the panoramas, both with the TV camera when he was first out there and then with the Hasselblad. It was just a matter of who had what when, and there was just not the opportunity for me ever to do that.

"When I got back and someone said, 'There's not any of Neil,' I thought, 'What in the hell can I do now?' I felt so bad about that. And then to have somebody say that might have been intentional. . . . How do you come up with a nonconfrontational argument against that? I mean, that was just such a divisive observation, and Neil and I were never in the least divisive. We really were intimidated by the situation we found ourselves in on the Moon, hesitant and with an unclear idea of what to do next."

Not even Apollo 11 crewmate Mike Collins realized it until well after the mission. "Stupid me, stupid me. We came back, the pictures got devel-

---

* In the first Armstrong-to-Aldrin camera transfer, Neil put the Hasselblad on the MESA at about 4:14:12:32 as Neil got ready to do the bulk sample. Buzz got the camera off the MESA at about 4:14:25:09. The second Neil-to-Buzz transfer came at 4:44:43:18 and the TV image of it is very inconclusive about how the transfer was made. This appears to have been the moment when Neil handed the camera carefully to Buzz.

oped—they came back from the NASA photo lab. I loved them. I thought they were terrific. I thought they were great. I mean, the clarity of them, the composition, the colors, everything. I thought they were just magnificent. Never once did it occur to me, 'Which one of them is that?' It's just some guy in a pressure suit. It was not until later that people said, 'That's Buzz,' and 'That's Buzz,' and 'That's Buzz,' and the only Neil was the one where he was in Buzz's visor. But even then, I attributed it to technical stuff—you know, the timeline, who was carrying what piece of equipment, what they were supposed to be doing at given time, experiments they were running on the surface, and so forth."

Flight Director Gene Kranz only shakes his head sadly trying to come up with an answer: "I don't have an explanation. In recent years I have been speaking to about 100,000 people a year. I do sixty to seventy public appearance engagements. And the only picture I can put up on the screen of Neil is his reflection in Buzz's facemask. I find that shocking. That's something to me that's unacceptable. But, you know, life isn't fair."

For years even someone as close to the pulse of the Manned Space Program as Chris Kraft failed to realize that there were no pictures of Neil on the Moon. When asked about the riddle, Kraft answered: "I can't answer that. I was taken aback by it when I first recognized it was so, but I can't give you any reason why it didn't happen. I think it would be an unfair judgment that Buzz intentionally did not want to take any pictures of him. No, no, no. I don't think Aldrin would have been that devious. I would not accuse him of that."

Nor would Mike Collins.

"It never once entered your mind, Mike, that Buzz might have not taken a picture of Neil on purpose?"

"Never. I mean, I'm not saying it couldn't be true. I'm just saying I'm a naïve person. It never entered my mind that there was some nefarious plot on Buzz's part to exclude Neil from the photo-documentation of the first lunar landing. It just never occurred to me. Maybe it should have."

According to Chris Kraft and others involved in Apollo 11's mission planning, "There were all kinds of scientific reasons to take pictures and all kinds of plans to take pictures of the lunar landscape, but I don't think there was ever any game plan to have them take a picture of each other like you would do at the beach. I don't recall that ever being discussed."

Interestingly, when asked whether he thought Armstrong while on the Moon had been oblivious of the fact that Aldrin was not taking any pictures of him, Kraft asserted: "Yes, yes. I don't think Neil cared. He may today, because he might like to have a picture of himself on the Moon, but I don't think it crossed his mind at the time."

In Apollo 12 astronaut Alan Bean's view, the rather extensive photographic training the astronauts underwent for the mission should have led to pictures of both men. "Don't forget, they had practiced their photography over and over again. It wasn't that they just did this for the first time on the Moon. They practiced this in ground simulation over the course of several different days. In training you looked at all this film you had shot. Deke Slayton, for one, would have noticed if Neil wasn't showing up in any of the pictures."

Al Bean stops short of suggesting why Buzz failed to take pictures of Neil.

"Obviously one possibility is that Buzz just wasn't thinking about taking a picture of Neil, and he wasn't realizing that he wasn't thinking about it."

"That's a possibility."

"But there is also the possibility that he was *thinking about it and that is why there aren't any pictures of Neil."*

"That's a possibility, too."

"That he was thinking, 'Neil may be the first on the Moon, but I'm not taking any pictures of him.'"

"That's a possibility, too. I don't know. We don't know. And we *should know,* because I think it's important to the long-range issue."

"What makes it an important long-range issue?"

"Because there should be a bunch of good pictures of Neil. This was such an historic event. I mean, think about it: I'm going along on the boat with Christopher Columbus. He's carrying the camera at the moment, but I'm his first mate. We all know what should happen. Nobody knows the answer why it didn't."

But Al Bean does possess a crystal clear idea as to the motivation of Armstrong's silence, during and after the mission, to Buzz on the matter: "He was interested in doing the job. Neil was probably saying to himself all through his training, 'I've got to make this landing safe; I've got to get out and do a good EVA; and I've got to get us back to the command module.'

"I got that way myself on my Apollo 12 flight. I didn't think about people back home. I just thought about trying to be a good astronaut and doing my job. And Neil was even more focused than I was—more than most astronauts were.

"It would have been normal for Neil to be this way—for him to focus on the flying, on the jobs that really made the historic mission successful." Within such a tight mental framework, the idea of a personal photograph not being taken would have been totally trivial.

Gene Cernan sees it similarly. "Certainly Neil realized the significance of the moment, but he was not going to be so arrogant as to say, 'Here, Buzz, take a picture of me.' What I can imagine Neil thinking was, 'Oh well, we don't have time to take a picture of me, so I'll take a few pictures of Buzz to show everyone we were here.'

"Myself, if I had been in Neil's place, I would have said, 'Buzz, take a picture of me—quick.' "

At the conclusion of the telephone conversation with President Nixon, Armstrong immediately returned to the MESA to gear up for his primary geological work. Up to this point the only lunar material that had been collected was the contingency sample. Now he needed to get to work on what was known as the bulk sample. "The general area in which I did that work was to the left forward quadrant of the lunar module. For the bulk sample, we were trying to get a variety of different kinds of rock forms, but the primary focus was just to get enough volume—try to make it a volume of some good stuff but mostly just get volume because lots of experimenters around the world would be getting pieces of this stuff and doing experiments with them."

Over a period of about fourteen minutes, Armstrong made some twenty-three scoops. "We didn't have to be too careful in getting that part. I got out the sample bags and put the material—both rocks and soil—in the bulk sample containers. That worked all right, but the containers were a little contrary in terms of getting them sealed properly. It was a vacuum-packed kind of seal designed so that the inside of the samples would stay uncontaminated. Otherwise, when the lunar materials were brought back to Earth, air would get in through the seal and contaminate the rocks. So the sampling container was not as easy to open and close as was the average shoebox; it was a bit more of a challenge. Having said that, I can't remember that there was any particular difficulty in doing it. It just took a little more time than expected." Part of the reason for that was the area in which Neil was working was in deep shadow, making it hard to see. More significantly, in one-sixth gravity he couldn't apply as much force as he had been able to do in training in full Earth gravity.

In all, Apollo 11 brought back nearly 48 pounds (21.7 kilograms) of rock and soil samples, the great majority scooped up by Armstrong. Overall in the Apollo program, 841.6 pounds (381.69 kilograms) of Moon rock were returned. Understandably, given the unknown of the first landing mission and the heavy emphasis on making a successful landing and return, the load brought back by Apollo 11 was the lightest of all the landing missions. The last, Apollo 17, brought back more than five times the weight in rocks that Apollo 11 did—over 243 pounds (110.5 kilograms).

Mostly the rocks brought back from the Sea of Tranquility were basalt: a dense, dark-gray, fine-grained igneous rock composed chiefly of calcium-rich plagioclase feldspar and pyroxene; on Earth, basalt is the commonest type of solidified lava. The oldest basalts brought back by Apollo 11 had been formed some 3.7 billion years ago. Later flights brought back a greater variety of specimens, including lighter-colored igneous rocks that were even older, called gabbros and anorthosite.

Some critics in the years following Apollo 11 were disappointed that the Moon rocks proved less valuable in unlocking as many secrets of the universe as hoped, but not Armstrong. "I have never been disappointed about the rocks. I am persuaded that they produced an extraordinary proof of the constituency of the regolith, the layer of loose rock atop the lunar mantle. They also demonstrated the different kinds of rock types, while confirming their plutonic character, their deep igneous or magmatic origin. Many of the rock types also revealed evidence of valuable metallic ores.

"The geology community had hoped we would provide what they called 'documented samples,' that is, samples whose emplacement was photographed prior to and after lifting the samples. Time did not permit our doing as much of that as we had hoped. Without documenting photographs, I selected and collected a number of different rock types of various sizes, perhaps as large as softballs, but mostly somewhat smaller. Samples of the ground mass were extracted from the surface using a scoop as per the plan. I do not remember what the relative weights of volumes of the types of samples were, rocks versus soil, but they were probably about equal."

Less than 10 percent of the Moon rocks collected by the Apollo missions have yet even been studied, Armstrong emphasizes today. By 1975, the total 841.6-pound mass of Moon rocks collected by all the Apollo missions had been split into 35,600 samples, with only 11 pounds (5 kilograms) of them consigned for public viewing in museums around the world. By 1997, only 42.5 pounds (19.3 kilograms), or a little over 5 percent of the total, had been allocated for scientific study. "Today geologists are still actively studying the

Moon rocks and writing scientific papers about them," Neil notes. Several of the samples have become so famous within the international geoscience community that they are recognizable by their given names, such as the "Genesis Rock," "The Black and White Breccia," "Big Bertha," "Rusty Rock," "Great Scott," and "The First Apollo 11 Sample Analyzed." Well over 90 percent of the samples have been placed untouched in archival reserve for the benefit of posterity.

Besides the rock sampling, the astronauts had a number of experiments to conduct, and precious little time to conduct them, as surface activity for Apollo 11 was limited to two hours and forty minutes. There were six experiments in all, each one selected by a NASA scientific panel after rigorous peer review.

The most generic of the experiments was a soil mechanics investigation with core samples (taken primarily by Aldrin) measuring soil density, grain size, strength, and compressibility as a function of depth. Near the end of the EVA, Buzz hammered a couple of core tubes into the surface, the Moon's tightly locked soil grains yielding only about six inches. The objective here was not just to improve scientific knowledge of the Moon, but to provide engineering data toward the design of an astronaut-carrying lunar vehicle, the later Lunar Rover, which motored electrically across the Moon's hills and dales like a dune buggy starting with Apollo 15.

The Solar Wind Composition Experiment was designed to trap evidence of the flux of electrically charged particles emitted by the Sun. With Armstrong's help, it took Aldrin five minutes to deploy the solar wind instrument (a small banner of thin aluminum foil 11.7 inches [30 centimeters] wide by 54.6 inches [140 centimeters] that unrolled downwards from a reel to face the Sun) early in the EVA, starting at 04:13:58:32 elapsed time. This was right after he and Neil had unveiled the plaque on the LM ladder leg. Exposed on the lunar surface for a total of seventy-seven minutes, the foil collector effectively entrapped ions of helium, neon, and argon, expanding scientists' knowledge of the origin of the solar system, the history of planetary atmospheres, and solar wind dynamics.

The other five experiments came as part of EASEP, the Early Apollo Scientific Experiment Package. Actually, EASEP consisted of two units about the size of small backpacks. The PSEP, or Passive Seismometer Experiment, deployed by Aldrin, was designed to analyze lunar structure and to detect moonquakes. Supplemental to it was a lunar dust detector experiment—attached to the back side of the PSEP—that monitored the effects of lunar dust on all the EASEP experiments.

At the same time Aldrin was deploying the seismic experiment (from 04:15:53:00 to 04:16:09:50, a duration of roughly seventeen minutes), Armstrong assembled the LRRR, or "LR-cubed." Designed to measure precisely the distance between the Moon and Earth, the LRRR device consisted of a series of corner-cube reflectors, essentially a special mirror that reflected an incoming light beam back in the direction it came—in this case from a laser aimed at the Sea of Tranquility from inside a large telescope at the University of California's Lick Observatory, east of San Jose. Though the laser beam remained tightly focused over a very large distance, by the time it traveled the quarter of a million miles from Earth, its signal was widely dispersed, to a signal something in the range of two miles in diameter. To maximize reception of the signal, it was necessary for Armstrong to align the reflector quite accurately.

Speaking in the collective although the LR-cubed setup was all his, Neil recalls: "We wanted to make sure that all the mirrors were pointed at Earth, and we wanted to make certain that the reflector was mounted on a fairly stable surface where it wouldn't be likely to get shifted later. We aligned it with the local vertical by means of a circular bubble—like the bubble in a level, except it was in a circle—so once you got the bubble in the middle of the circle the platform was level. Then we also had to align the whole platform by turning it until the mirrors were pointed directly at the Earth. For that we used simply a shadow stick—a gnomon—where the shadow made by the stick created the alignment. Always on the Earth when we had practiced it, this bubble was fairly stable; it would meander to a point, adjust, and stop. To our great surprise in the lunar gravity environment the bubble just kept circling around. It was just a matter of the low gravity there."

Mysteriously, the bubble (actually its inverse, the shape of a concave dish) finally did stabilize. Not only did the laser reflector experiment work, it ended up being one of the most scientifically productive of all the Apollo experiments, deployed not just on Apollo 11 but on Apollo 14 and 15 as well. Together, the three LRRR instruments deployed by the Apollo missions produced many important measurements. These included an improved knowledge of the Moon's orbit, of variations in the Moon's rotation, of the rate at which the Moon is receding from Earth (currently 1.5 inches or 3.8 centimeters per year), as well as of the Earth's own rotation rate and precession of its spin axis. Scientists in the United States and abroad have used data from the laser reflectors to test Einstein's theory of relativity. For those few misguided souls who still cling to the belief that the Moon landings never happened, examination of the results of five decades of LRRR experiments should evidence how delusional their rejection of the Moon landing really is.

Armstrong recalls the decision against utilizing the large S-band dish antenna, which was stowed in LM Quad 1 to the right of the ladder. "We didn't have to erect it as the signal for the LM antenna was strong enough to transmit the TV to Earth." From a mission efficiency viewpoint, Neil was happy that the S-band antenna, which was roughly eight feet across, did not need to be deployed. It took about twenty minutes to assemble and he and Buzz were already running thirty minutes behind schedule. On the other hand, "It was really fun putting that thing together. I would have enjoyed doing it if I had had to, and finding out if it really worked. I'd done that quite a few times on the ground, and I was always amazed watching that thing bloom like a flower."

According to Armstrong, the overall plan for the entire EVA was well conceived. "We had a plan. We had a substantial number of events to complete that were all in a proper order. We had built that plan based on the relative importance of the different events and the convenience and practicality of doing them in a certain order. We'd gone through a lot of simulations and developed the plan over a period of time. We knew it forwards, backwards, and blindfolded. That wasn't going to be any trouble. I didn't feel any restriction against violating a plan or drifting away from a plan somehow if the situation warranted."

The most noteworthy change in the plan came late in the EVA when Armstrong decided he wanted to go over and take a look at the sizable crater about sixty-five yards east of the LM (thus known today to Apollo 11 afficionados as East Crater). "When I went over to look at the crater, that was something that wasn't on the plan, but I didn't know the crater was going to be there. I thought seeing and photographing it was a worthwhile addition, although I did have to give up some documented-sample time to do that. But it looked to me like that could be a piece of evidence that people would be interested in." There were guidelines but no specific mission rules as to how far away from the LM a crew member could go. If he or Buzz strayed too far from the LM, Mission Control would have definitely reined them back in. "In fact, I had some personal reservations in taking the time to go over and snap a picture of the crater. But I thought it was of sufficient interest that it was worth getting."

With EVA time running out, Neil hustled to get to the crater and back. Based on subsequent analysis of the TV footage showing him running there and back (he used a loping, foot-to-foot stride), his speed appears to have been about 2 miles (3.2 kilometers) per hour. Later crews achieved speeds of over 3 miles (5 kilometers) per hour, but they benefited from additional gait training as well as more time on the Moon to try out their running skills. In all, Neil's little expedition took three minutes and fifteen seconds. While there he took eight Hasselblad shots showing various features of East Crater. What most interested him about the crater once he got there were the outcroppings in its sidewalls: "Not spectacular outcroppings, but they certainly showed that there was a certain layering in there that I thought might be of interest to the geology guys."

The moment Armstrong had headed toward the crater, Houston informed Buzz that it was time for him to start thinking about heading back into the LM.

| 04:15:11:15 | McCandless: | *Buzz, this is Houston. You've got about ten minutes now prior to commencing your EVA termination activities. Over.* |
| 04:15:11:31 | Aldrin: | *Roger. I understand.* |

Neil would follow Aldrin up the ladder some ten minutes later. Before either headed up the ladder, though, they needed to finish up and cap the final core samples, and Neil, with a pair of long-handled tongs, had to complete his final rock sampling. Everything that was to be returned to Earth needed to be brought to the ladder for loading. That included the camera film magazines, the solar wind experiment, and all the rock boxes.

As Armstrong explained in a postmission press conference, "There was just far too little time to do the variety of things that we would have liked to have done. There were rocks in a boulder field that we had photographed out of Buzz's window before going out that were three to four feet in size. Very likely they were pieces of lunar bedrock. It would have been very interesting to go over and get some samples of those. There were just too many interesting things to do.

"When you are in a new environment, everything around you is new and different and you have the tendency to look a little more carefully at 'What is this?' and 'Is this important?' or 'Let me look at it from a different angle,' which you would never do in a simulation. In a simulation, you just picked up the rock and threw it in the pot.

"So it doesn't surprise me that it took us somewhat longer to get through things. We didn't have that presidential call either—that was never in our simulations. And there were questions coming from the ground. We were responding to those, which took a little extra time. No one was asking us questions when we went through this in our practice sessions.

"It would have been nice from our point of view to have had more time to ourselves so that we could have gone out and looked around a little bit. But a lot of people had needs based on whatever discipline they belonged to, and these people had spent a lot of time getting ready to have their experiments done. I felt that we had a substantial obligation to try to honor those needs as best we could, and in a most timely fashion. I didn't mind breaking the rules if it seemed like the right thing to do.

"I do remember thinking, 'Gee I'd like to stay out a little longer, because there are other things I would like to look at and do.' It wasn't an overpowering urge. It was just something that I felt, that I'd like to stay out longer. But I recognized that they wanted us to go back in." Back on Earth, it was approaching 1:00 A.M. EDT.

04:15:24:00	Aldrin:	*. . . and I'll head on up the ladder? . . . Okay. Adios, amigo.*
04:15:24:56	Armstrong:	*Okay.*
04:15:24:58	Aldrin:	*Anything more before I head on up, Bruce?*
04:15:25:04	McCandless:	*Negative. Head on up the ladder, Buzz.*

According to the mission plan, Armstrong was supposed to take the time to dust off Buzz's suit before Buzz went back inside the LM, but the act of hygiene was forgotten, perhaps because it seemed pointless. "The dust was so fine that you couldn't have got rid of all of it," explains Neil. There was a hypothesis going into the mission that, if a lot of dust was brought back on their suits into the LM, the suits could actually ignite. "I don't know how seriously that was considered by anyone. But dust in an oxygen environment can be flammable. It was not something that had been presented to us as being a serious concern."

Armstrong's last tasks on the lunar surface were labor intensive and physically demanding. To prevent contamination, the NASA contractor that built the rock boxes had cleaned their hinges rather than leaving them lubricated.

To close their lids, Neil had to apply thirty-two pounds of force. After struggling to close the bulk sample box, it took "just about everything I could do," "an inordinate amount of force," to close the documented sample, his second box. Low gravity made for an added difficulty: the boxes felt very light and tended to skid away. In order to close the boxes, Neil placed them on the MESA table, a surface that was not very rigid. Just holding the box securely enough in place to apply the necessary force on the sealing handles caused him considerable trouble. Then he had to carry the rock boxes one by one over to the LEC, hook them to the "Brooklyn clothesline" running from the porch of the LM up to the hatch, and, with Buzz's help, hoist them up.

In Houston, a cardiac monitor showed that Neil's heart rate rose during the EVA close-out period to 160 beats per minute, the typical heart rate of an Indy car driver at the start of the Indianapolis 500. Five minutes before he was to head up the ladder, Houston made a disguised request for Neil to slow down for a moment, by asking him to report on the status of the tank pressure and oxygen in his EMU.

More concerned about getting every necessary object inside the LM, the astronauts almost forgot to leave a small packet of memorial items on the lunar surface. Aldrin recalls the near-oversight: "We were so busy that I was halfway up the ladder before Neil asked me if I had remembered to leave the mementos we had brought along. I had completely forgotten. What we had hoped to make into a brief ceremony, had there been time, ended almost as an afterthought. I reached into my shoulder pocket, pulled the packet out and tossed it onto the surface." The packet contained two Soviet-made medals, in honor of deceased cosmonauts Yuri Gagarin, the first human to orbit the Earth, who died in a MiG-15 accident in March 1967; and Vladimir Komarov, killed a month after Gagarin at the conclusion of his Soyuz 1 flight when his spacecraft's descent parachute failed to open. Also in the packet was an Apollo 1 patch commemorating Gus Grissom, Ed White, and Roger Chaffee. Also inside was a small gold olive-branch pin, symbolic of the peaceful nature of the American Moon landing program. The token was identical to the pins that the three Apollo 11 astronauts were carrying as gifts for their wives.

04:15:36:38	Armstrong:	*How about that package out of your sleeve? Get that?*
04:15:36:53	Aldrin:	*No.*

04:15:36:55   Armstrong: *Okay, I'll get it when I get up there to the porch.*

04:15:37:02   Aldrin: *Want it now?*

04:15:37:06   Armstrong: *Guess so.*

"I don't think we really wanted to talk totally open about what it was," Aldrin relates. "So it was sort of guarded. I knew what Neil was talking about." Aldrin's packet landed just to Neil's right. Armstrong straightened it out a little, to get some of the dust off of it, by moving it with his foot.

Immediately after doing that, at 1:09 A.M. EDT (04:15:37:32 elapsed time), Neil climbed onto the LM footpad, put his arms on the ladder arms, and, pushing with his legs and pulling his arms, jumped all the way up to the third rung of the ladder.

"The technique I used was one in which I did a deep knee bend with both legs and got my torso down absolutely as close to the footpad as I could. I then sprang vertically up and guided myself with my hands by use of the handrails. That's how I got to the third step, which I guess was easily five or six feet above the ground."

Characteristically, the engineer was experimenting, not showboating. "It was just curiosity. You could have really jumped high if you didn't have that suit on. But the suit's weight. . . . You didn't really feel the weight of the suit because it was pressurized from the inside, so the interior pressure was holding most of the weight of the suit up. But when you jumped you had to carry that, and our lunar weight was sixty-two pounds or something like that. So if you are a sixty-two-pound man, how high can you jump? If you are unencumbered in a real stiff suit, you can probably jump pretty high. I just wanted to get an idea of how high could you go if you took a good leap up."

Armstrong's leap up the ladder probably stands as a lunar record, as subsequent Apollo astronauts were usually carrying something in their hands or arms when they ascended. If Neil had missed the step while making the jump—and the steps were slippery from lunar dust—there was only a slight chance he could have hurt himself. With his hands on the rails, a position both he and Buzz had checked, he could have easily guided himself to a soft landing. In addition, if Neil had fallen, he would have had no trouble getting up, having practiced that in the water tank back at the Manned Spacecraft Center. It was very unlikely that Aldrin would have had to come back down to the surface to help him up.

Aldrin's ingress a few minutes earlier had proven relatively easy, considering that the bulky PLSS necessitated that the astronaut arch his back so as to afford the least profile going in. Navigating solo, Aldrin first brought his knees inside the cockpit, then he moved from a kneeling to an upright position. Before turning around, he had to ensure adequate allowance for the switches and other equipment immediately behind him.

Neil's ingress, which took one minute and twenty-six seconds from the time he climbed on the LM footpad, benefited from Aldrin's guidance:

04:15:38:08	Aldrin:	*Just keep your head down. Now start arching your back. That's good. Plenty of room. Okay now, all right, arch your back a little, your head up against* [garbled]. *Roll right just a little bit. Head down. Getting in in good shape.*
04:15:38:26	Armstrong:	*Thank you. . . . Am I bumping now?*
04:15:38:33	Aldrin:	*No, you're clear. You're rubbing up against me a little bit.*
04:15:38:36	Armstrong:	*Okay.*
04:15:38:38	Aldrin:	*Turn right. That's right. A little to the left . . . Okay. Now move your foot and I'll get the hatch . . .*
04:15:38:58	Armstrong:	*Okay!*
04:15:39:13	Aldrin:	*Okay. The hatch is closed and latched . . . and verified secured.*

The time between the hatch opening and its closing was two hours, thirty-one minutes, and forty seconds. Earth time upon closure was 1:11 A.M. EDT. Humankind's first direct sojourn onto the surface of the Moon was over in less time than it took to watch a football game or Broadway play.

On CBS, Eric Sevareid and Walter Cronkite tried to sum up the momentous events. "Man has landed and man has taken his first steps. What is there to add to that?" Cronkite asked. Sevareid answered: "At this hour one can only subtract. I don't know what one can add now. We've seen some kind of 'birth' here. And I'm sure that to many, many people the first scene of Armstrong emerging must have seemed like a birth. One's image of this clumsy creature, half-blind, maneuvering with great awkwardness at first, and slowly learning to use its legs, until, in a rather short time it's running.

"And in this new world, this new reality. And the quickness of the adjustment of the human body, and the nervous system. The weight of gravity on Earth. Just the other day they were at the Cape; then weightlessness of several days; and then to the Moon's one-sixth gravity. And somehow the body adjusts with that speed and in totally different elements. This is what overwhelms you.

"And Armstrong's words. He sounded very laconic, unemotional. His mother said as she heard them on the air that he was thrilled. And I think we'd have to take a mother's word for that. And then when they moved around, you sensed their feeling of joy up there. I never expected to see them bound, did you? Everything we've been told was that they would move with great care. Foot after foot with great deliberation. We were told they might fall. And here they were, like children playing hopscotch."

"Like colts almost," Cronkite interjected.

"Like colts finding their legs, exactly. I must say, as somebody who loves the English language, I have such a great gratitude that the first voices that came from another celestial body were in the English tongue, which I feel is the richest language of all. I think it is the greatest vocabulary. And maybe only one million people or so on the Earth speak and understand it. But I never expected to hear that word 'pretty.' He said it was 'pretty.' What we thought was cold and desolate and forbidding—somehow they found a strange beauty there that I suppose they can never really describe to us. So we'll never know."

Cronkite: "It may not be a beauty that one can pass on to future beholders, either. These first men on the Moon can see something that men who follow will miss."

Sevareid: "We're always going to feel, somehow, strangers to these men. They will, in effect, be a bit stranger, even to their own wives and children. Disappeared into another life that we can't follow. I wonder what their life will be like, now. The Moon has treated them well, so far. How people on Earth will treat these men, the rest of their lives, that gives me more foreboding, I think, than anything else."

One of the gaps in the record of Apollo 11 concerns the personal items and mementos Armstrong and his crewmates took with them to the Moon. All three men had a Personal Preference Kit stowed on board for them at launch. A PPK was a beta-cloth pouch about the size of a large brown lunch sack, with a pull-string opening at the top, coated with fireproof Teflon.

Exactly how many PPK pouches were taken by each Apollo 11 astronaut to the Moon is unknown. Apparently at least one belonging to each stayed for the entire flight in the left side lower equipment stowage compartment of the command module; these CM PPKs could weigh no more than five pounds per astronaut. At least two other PPKs, one for Neil and one for Buzz, were stowed inside the LM, in compartment cabinets located underneath the control and display panels to the right and left of Aldrin's and Armstrong's flight stations, respectively. These LM PPKs—it is likely there were only two of them, one for each of them—were limited to half a pound per astronaut. Anything in excess of those amounts would have required a special waiver from the manager of the Apollo Spacecraft Program Office, Dr. George Low. (The weights of Apollo 11's PPKs are unknown.) Sometime before or after the flight, Neil, Mike, and Buzz agreed to authenticate all items on board Apollo 11 as "carried to the Moon," whether they went to the lunar surface or stayed in the CSM, so as not to devalue the symbolic importance of the items carried by Collins only in lunar orbit.

None of the three astronauts has ever shared an inventory of the souvenirs that were in those six bags. (In addition to the bags mentioned above, the astronauts also took another PPK for frequently used personal items, such as pens, razors, and sunglasses.) What is known about them has been based solely on what the astronauts over the years have said or written and on what they have released and identified from their private holdings for sale or display. In Armstrong's case, this has amounted to almost nothing, since Neil has never spoken about what he took to the Moon—and, unlike Buzz and Mike, has never put any of his items up for auction.

All attempts to discover the contents of the PPKs have failed. Even before the launch of Apollo 11, rumors circulated, but NASA refused to shed any light upon the subject. "The astronauts don't have to tell anyone around here what is in those kits because they are their own personal items," one MSC official declared prior to the Apollo 11 launch. It was not quite the whole truth. As astronaut Alan Bean has explained, "You had to make a list, so that Deke Slayton and everybody could have it. But as long as it didn't get too heavy, you could carry lots of stuff."

Janet Armstrong, in reply to a persistent newsman on hand for her public greeting two hours after her husband landed on the Moon, admitted that Neil had taken something to the Moon for her, but she refused to reveal what it was. On air with CBS, Cronkite quickly commented on the news clip: "While we heard a minute ago from Janet Armstrong that Neil had taken a little packet of something memorable for her along with him, we know that the others have as well. And they're also being secretive about what it is, as all of the astronauts have from the first flight of Alan Shepard in 1961."

Indeed, it was NASA's policy to keep the astronauts' personal belongings strictly confidential. Souvenir items carried by Shepard and other Mercury astronauts did not even have to be manifested formally. When PPKs came into existence during Project Gemini (when they were known as APKs, or Astronaut Preference Kits), only the astronauts themselves and Deke Slayton as head of the Astronaut Office had access to their manifest. Aldrin remembers how loose the PPK procedure actually was: "NASA had requested that we furnish them with a list of everything we were taking, and we quickly obliged. It was of such small import that NASA's official compilation of what I took was not even deemed worthy of being typed up. The confirming list they gave me back was handwritten and complete."

Changes to the relaxed souvenir policy, as well as to the physical makeup of the PPKs, came only after two scandals broke in 1971. The first was a minor scandal involving a reported deal—never consummated—between the Apollo 14 astronauts and the Franklin Mint in Philadelphia. The story, which angered some members of Congress, involved the Franklin Mint's plan to melt down pure silver medallions "carried to the Moon" by the Apollo 14 crew, then sell for profit a large quantity of medallions incorporating traces of the original silver.

The second scandal generated significant negative publicity, brought on by revelations of an unfortunate decision by the Apollo 15 astronauts. In exchange for transporting one hundred first-day postal covers, German stamp dealer Hermann Sieger paid each of the three astronauts $6,000, depositing the money into individual Swiss bank accounts as trust funds for the astronauts' children. Instead of withholding sale of the covers until after the Apollo program was over, which was the astronauts' understanding of how the deal would be handled, Sieger immediately began selling them—for $1,500 each. When all one hundred were sold, the dealer would enjoy a total return equivalent in today's dollars to some three-quarters of a million. Much more bothersome in the mind of the American public were reports that the Apollo 15 astronauts had carried three hundred additional covers for themselves. Critics assumed that the men were planning to sell theirs off as well. The story infuriated Congress and led NASA to conduct an internal investigation, one that turned into something of a witch hunt and resulted in a firm reprimand for the astronauts. It was a sad and complicated affair, with the three astronauts—Dave Scott, Al Worden, and Jim Irwin—unfairly bearing the brunt of the blame for a questionable practice involving personal mementos that had been going on ever since the early days of Mercury.*

So cautious was NASA about releasing what its astronauts carried as souvenirs that it is not known with certainty even today what Apollo 11 was carrying in its OFK, or Official Flight Kit. An OFK manifest for Apollo 11 was never released publicly, and none has ever been located. The only proof that one even existed is a 1974 memorandum from NASA Associate Administrator Rocco A. Petrone to NASA Administrator Dr. James C. Fletcher dealing with the proposed future distribution of American flags flown on U.S. space missions, stating that an OFK had flown on Apollo 11. (The memo informed Fletcher that the remaining U.S. flags that had been flown on Apollo 11 and not yet given away were being reserved for future U.S. presidents and vice presidents only.)

Apollo 11's OFK might not even have been an actual bag or pouch. It is possible that OFK items for the first Moon landing were simply stowed in one or more of the cabinets inside the command module. A NASA document from 1972 would later indicate that "the total weight of this kit shall not exceed 53.3 pounds per mission." Clearly, the contents of the OFK comprised a much larger stash of souvenir items than what went into the astronauts' PPKs. As official NASA souvenirs, OFK items were meant for distribution, either by the astronauts or by leading NASA officials, to VIPs and organizations. As none of these items were transferred over to the LM prior to its separation in lunar orbit, it seems clear that nothing from the OFK, whether one physically existed or not, was carried to the surface.

Thus, the only items taken to the surface of the Moon was whatever was in the PPKs that had been stowed in the LM—and we do not know what was in them. To wit:

---

* By the time the first Space Shuttle launched in 1981, NASA was grudgingly accommodating legitimate press requests for PPK manifests, but only after its own people had cleared every item and completed a thorough postflight inventory. Even today, Freedom of Information Act requests for PPK manifests are fulfilled with a copy of an October 22, 1968, letter from Deke Slayton, who died in 1993, stating that the contents of PPKs were not to be made public. In that memo to NASA Headquarters, Slayton wrote: "The only list of PPK contents is retained by me. I certify to the Mission Director on each mission that the contents meet flammability and toxicity requirements and are noncontroversial in nature. We do not intend to make this list available to anyone else at any time. It is the crew's prerogative to discuss the contents after the flight if they wish. Since these items are personal in nature, we do not feel that NASA has any other official prerogative on the issue." Slayton to NASA Headquarters, Attn: Mr. Julian Scheer, Oct. 22, 1968. Carbon copies of this memo were sent to George Mueller, Bob Gilruth, and Alan Shepard.

- Four hundred fifty silver medallions that had been minted by the Robbins Company of Massachusetts. These had been divided equally between the three astronauts and stowed in their PPKs. How many of the medallions were in the PPKs that were stowed aboard the *Eagle* and taken down to the surface, however, is unknown.
- Three gold medallions, also minted by the Robbins Company, one for each astronaut. One can assume that these medals were in the LM PPKs.
- An unknown number of miniature (4 x 6-inch) flags of the United States; of the fifty U.S. states, District of Columbia, and U.S. territories; of the nations of the world; and of the United Nations. According to a NASA press release of July 3, 1969, "These flags will be carried in the lunar module and brought back to Earth. They will not be deployed on the Moon. The small flags are to be carried in a plastic vacuum cloth and stowed in a beta cloth pouch with a Teflon outer wrap." What this seems to mean is that all these miniature flags were stowed aboard the LM in a special, third PPK that did not belong to either Neil or Buzz. As part of the OFK kept inside the command module, there were a great many additional miniature American flags. There were also two full-size (5 x 8-foot) American flags, which were to be presented to the two houses of Congress upon return to Earth. These exact flags had been flown over the U.S. Capitol prior to the Apollo 11 mission and were to be flown again there after the mission. It is also known that Aldrin carried miniature U.S. flags in his PPK, some of which he later sold. As Buzz has only specified that these flags were "carried to the Moon," it is not certain whether they went to Tranquility Base or just stayed in orbit.
- A commemorative Apollo 11 envelope issued by the U.S. Post Department. On it was a newly issued ten-cent stamp also commemorating Apollo 11. It is not known whether these items were in Neil's or in Buzz's LM PPK. While on the lunar surface, they were supposed to cancel the cover, but they forgot to do so. (That was not done until July 24 when the crew was together in the quarantine facility. Nonetheless, the cancellation read July 20.) In the command module, in either Collins's PPK or the OFK, the crew also brought along the die from which the commemorative stamp had been printed. In his CM PPK, Aldrin carried 101 philatelic covers on behalf of the Manned Spacecraft Center's Stamp Club. Another 113 envelopes, perhaps more, were also carried onboard the command module, some in PPKs, but most of them in the OFK. Each member of the crew signed all of the covers carried. In later years,

Aldrin and Collins initialed some of their covers, in the upper left corner, and some were put up for sale. No one has ever seen a cover initialed by Armstrong, because he has never initialed one.

- An unknown number of Apollo 11 "beta cloth" patches, so named by their manufacturer, Owen-Corning Fiberglass of Ashton, Rhode Island, because they were made of tightly woven and fireproof glass fiber and worn only by the astronauts. Each astronaut may have had a small number of beta patches in his PPK, but how many of them went to the surface, if any, is unknown.
- An unknown number of embroidered Apollo 11 patches. Most of these were likely part of the OFK, but a few might have been taken in PPKs, though few if any of them traveled to the lunar surface.
- Three gold olive-branch pins, exact replicas of the gold olive branch in the packet that Aldrin tossed down at the last minute to the lunar surface during the EVA. After the flight, the crew presented the pins to their wives as gifts. Presumably, each LM astronaut carried his own wife's pin in his respective PPK, with either Neil or Buzz carrying the pin that Collins was to give his wife Patricia.
- A vial filled with wine and a miniature chalice, in Aldrin's LM PPK.
- Pieces of jewelry for his wife and family, in Aldrin's LM PPK.

As for Armstrong specifically, he has never released any information about the contents of his PPK. He agreed to do so for publication in this book, but reported that he was unable to find the manifest among his many papers. All he had to say about what he took with him to the Moon was, "In my PPK I had some Apollo 11 medallions, some jewelry for my wife and mother [simply the gold olive branch pin for each], and some things for other people." He is most clear about, and most proud of, the pieces of the historic Wright Flyer that he took to the Moon. Under a special arrangement with the U.S. Air Force Museum in Dayton, he took in his LM PPK a piece of wood from the Wright brothers' 1903 airplane's left propeller and a piece of muslin fabric (8 x 13 inches) from its upper left wing.

Armstrong also took along his college fraternity pin from Purdue, which he later donated for display at Phi Delta Theta's headquarters in Oxford, Ohio. Contrary to published stories, he did not take Janet's Alpha Chi Omega sorority pin.

"I didn't bring anything else for myself," Neil states today. "At least not that I can remember." As for Janet, the only thing taken to the Moon for her was the olive branch pin. "He didn't ask me if I wanted to send anything."

Perhaps surprisingly, Armstrong took nothing else for family members—not even for his two boys, a fact that still distresses Janet. "I assumed he had taken things to give to the boys later, but I don't believe he has ever given them anything.

"Neil can be thoughtful, but he does not give much time to being thoughtful, or at least to expressing it."

Another loved one that Neil apparently did not remember by taking anything of hers to the Moon was his daughter Karen. What could have made the first Moon landing more meaningful "for all mankind" than a father honoring the cherished memory of his beloved little girl, by taking a picture of the child, dead now over seven years (she would have been a ten-year-old), one of her toys, an article of her clothing, a lock of hair? Astronaut Gene Cernan, just before he left the lunar surface on Apollo 17, had done something touching for his healthy nine-year-old daughter Tracy: at the end of his final EVA, Gene had signed her name in the dust.

What if Neil had done something like that but had never told anyone about it, not even Janet, because it was of such an intensely personal nature? How much more would posterity—fathers and mothers, sons and daughters—value and esteem the character and actions of the First Man? It would have elevated the Moon landing to an even higher level of significance. Among those who feel so are Neil's sister June, who knows her brother as well as anyone. "Did he take something of Karen with him to the Moon?" ran June's rhetorical question. "Oh, I dearly hope so."

CHAPTER 30

Return to Earth

Neil had always worried most about the final descent to the Moon landing. "The unknowns were rampant. The systems in this mode had only been tested on Earth and never in the real environment. There were just a thousand things to worry about in the final descent. It was hardest for the systems, and it was hardest for the crew. . . . It was the thing I most worried about, because it was so difficult.

"Walking around on the surface, on a ten-point scale, I deemed a one. The lunar descent on that scale was probably a thirteen."

Somewhere in between was what it took to pilot the ascent stage of the LM back to a reunion with Mike Collins. That little tender piece of flying, though perhaps only a five or six on the scale of difficulty, was a ten-plus on the scale of the mission's ultimate success. If that ascent to docking, for whatever reason, did not work out, nothing about Apollo 11's remarkable performance up to this point, or about the dedicated efforts of four hundred thousand talented people who had endeavored to get Apollo 11 to the Moon, could be regarded as anything but a tragedy. The first Moon landing would have happened, but the astronauts who accomplished it would never return home. Nor would their bodies.

Back inside *Eagle* with the hatch closed, Armstrong and Aldrin repressurized their cabin, doffed their PLSSs, and looked at control panel readings to ensure the safety of the LM. They started to fill up a trash bag with unnecessary gear to be left on the lunar surface to save weight. From a historical perspective, the "trash" included a lot of valuable items. "There was a full truckload of equipment inside that cockpit at the end of the EVA," Armstrong relates. "It was just a bunch of stuff." The astronauts again hooked up to the LM's environmental control system, and they took their helmets and visors off, partly so the two tired and hungry men could eat.

Before their meal, they used up the rest of their film. The EVA Hasselblad had been purposefully left outside after retrieving its finished film magazines. They trained the spare Hasselblad that had remained in the LM through the portals, snapping pictures of the American flag, the TV stand, and the faraway Earth. (The EVA Hasselblad photos are distinctive in the absence of grid-patterned reseau crosses.) Buzz finally got around to taking pictures of Neil, two of them, showing the commander, tired and relieved, in what the astronauts had come to call their "Snoopy cap," the stretchable black and white cap with foam ear covers that looked like the head and ears of the famous canine from Charles Schulz's *Peanuts* cartoon. Neil returned the favor, taking one shot of Buzz.

While they were eating, a delighted Slayton sent his congratulations in the masculine style germane to the astronauts corps:

04:18:00:02	Slayton:	*Just want to let you guys know that, since you're an hour and a half over your timeline and we're all taking a day off tomorrow, we're going to leave you. See you later.*
04:18:00:13	Armstrong:	*I don't blame you a bit.*
04:18:00:16	Slayton:	*That's a real great day, guys. I really enjoyed it.*
04:18:00:23	Armstrong:	*Thank you. You couldn't have enjoyed it as much as we did.*
04:18:00:26	Slayton:	*Roger.*
04:18:00:28	Aldrin:	*It was great.*
04:18:00:30	Slayton:	*Sure wish you'd hurry up and get that trash out of there, though.*
04:18:00:34	Armstrong:	*Yes, we're just about to do it.*

To achieve jettison, the astronauts had to depressurize their cabin once again, refitting their helmets so they could open the hatch. It was almost like performing another EVA prep, though this prep took less than twenty minutes and did not involve any hose-swapping or donning of the PLSSs.

In an act some might regard as lunar littering, they threw it all out. First came the PLSSs, their cooling water drained into a plastic bag that was then stowed. "We could get down far enough in our pressurized suits to reach the backpacks with our gloves and then tossed them rather than kicked them out as later crews did," Neil offers. "Each PLSS bounced on the porch before it went down," adds Aldrin.

On TV, both backpacks could be seen tumbling down. The exact moment they hit the ground was detected back on Earth thanks to the seismometer experiment Buzz had put out during the EVA.

04:18:18:31	McCandless:	*Roger, Tranquility. We observed your equipment jettison on TV, and the passive seismic experiment recorded shocks when each PLSS hit the surface. Over.*
04:18:18:47	Armstrong:	*You can't get away with anything anymore, can you?*
04:15:18:51	McCandless:	*No, indeed.*

Neil tossed out both pairs of dust-covered boots, a bagful of empty food packages, and the LM urine and fecal containment bags. He threw out the spare Hasselblad, minus the exposed film. He jettisoned the lithium hydroxide canister that he and Buzz had changed out as planned to refresh the LM's environmental control system (the canister had been in use since they powered up the LM in orbit prior to descent). According to Aldrin, "We were able to jettison everything without any problems. I didn't notice Neil having any difficulty giving the packages the heave-ho."

"Only one thing did not make it all the way down onto the surface," Neil reports. "That was a small part of the left-hand-side storage container, which did not make it off the porch. That was the last item jettisoned.

"I was glad that we were able to get rid of a lot of these things and finish the jettison before we started our sleep period. With all that stuff in the cockpit, there really was no place for people to relax."

Though less cluttered, the cockpit was hardly clean. It was incredible how much dust the men had picked up while out on the surface. When they returned to zero g, some of it began to float around inside the cabin. It even affected the way they sounded due to the angularity of the Moon particles they had breathed into their noses and sinuses. Neil remembers, "We were aware of a new scent in the air of the cabin that clearly came from all the lunar material that had accumulated on and in our clothes. I remember commenting that we had the scent of wet ashes." "There was a hint of something," Buzz recalls, "like it was going to catch fire."

Members of the science and engineering teams at Mission Control were itching to ask Neil and Buzz questions about what they had seen during the EVA. "I guess we can take a couple of them now," Armstrong offered. After answering eight or nine questions, though, Neil was ready to take a break. When asked for a more lengthy and detailed description of the geology they had observed, Neil put a stop to it. "Yeah, let's . . . We'll postpone our answer to that one until tomorrow. Okay?"

At 2:50 A.M. CDT, July 21, Mission Control finally signed off and told the men to get a good night's sleep. Up in *Columbia,* Collins had fallen soundly asleep shortly after hearing his mates had gotten back into the LM okay.

Armstrong and Aldrin had been up for nearly twenty-two hours. "I couldn't tell if I was tired or not," Neil relates. "It would be hard to determine that in those circumstances unless you were really, really tired. The adrenaline had been pumping for quite a while."

What Neil and Buzz felt mostly was relief. "There are always some regrets that you didn't do more or accomplish everything that you wanted, but we had gotten a pretty fair share of stuff done. There is always the great satisfaction of getting things behind you and getting things accomplished. That satisfaction outweighed any regrets we might have had. Also, we were thinking, 'That's another couple hundred pages of checklist items we no longer have to remember and worry about.' "

It was their first and only night's sleep in the LM, and it was not at all pleasant. According to Neil, "The floor was adequate for one person—not to stretch out, but to lay halfway between a fetal position and a stretched-out position. That was where Buzz slept. The only other place to rest was the engine cover, which was a circular table some two and a half feet in diameter. To support my legs from it we configured a sling from one of our waist tethers. We attached that to a pipe structure that was hanging down. It was a good structure to hang a sling from, so I stuck my legs in there and kept the center part of my body on the engine cover. That kept my legs suspended. Behind the cover there was a flat shelf where I could sort of rest my head. It was a jerry-rigged operation and not very comfortable."

Neither man slept well. Compounding their uncomfortable sleeping positions was the fact they were sleeping with their helmets and gloves on to protect their lungs from all the dust they had brought in. The filtered oxygen from the LM's environment control system was significantly cleaner than the air circulating in the cabin.

Then there was the temperature. Even though it was over 200 degrees Fahrenheit outside the LM, it was quite cold inside—something in the range of 61 to 62 degrees F. "When we put the window covers on so that it would be relatively dark inside," Armstrong explains, "the temperature got quite brisk in the cockpit."

Another factor was the light. On the LM's control panels were several warning lights and illuminated display switches that could not be dimmed. Also, "We were all settled down when we realized that we still had a light source coming from something outside." Although they had the window shades down, they had forgotten about the Alignment Optical Telescope (AOT). "It was pointed right about at Earth and the Earth was very bright. That was coming right through the telescope into the cockpit." Neil and Buzz tied a kind of cover over the top of the instrument, but it did not prevent the light from shining through.

Most bothersome, at least to Neil atop the engine cover, was the noise. A loud glycol or water pump seriously interfered with his sleep. "It had to be in a different [lunar gravity] environment to work properly, so we had never heard this thing run."

Scheduled to sleep for seven hours, Neil may have gotten two restful ones, right at the very end. One hour into the rest period, medical telemetry indicated he was only dozing; during the next four hours, his heart rate occasionally dropped into the fifties—the "sleep range"—but jumped right back up. (As there was only one medical monitor on board the LM, there was no record of Buzz's physiological status.) "The quality of sleep was poor in my case," asserts Neil. "I'd say the same thing," adds Buzz, though he admits he had it better than his cabin mate. "I had the better sleeping place. I found that it was relatively comfortable on the floor, either on my back with my feet up against the side, or with my knees bent and feet on the floor. Also, I could roll over on one side or the other."

As the commander struggled to slumber, he thought through the geology question he had promised to answer. He did not overly worry that lack of rest might affect his flying of the LM the next day. "What was painfully obvious was that I didn't really have any choice. The schedule was there, and I had to perform. I had to do it." The obstacle was hardly a first. "One night. Most people can get by with a low amount of sleep—for several nights, actually," he told himself. "I had relaxed and slept well generally in the command module. Mike said things like, 'This part of the flight is easy. All these other guys have done it and haven't had any trouble. So just relax and enjoy it and save yourself for when you need to be bright eyed.' And I took it to heart."

Ron Evans, the capsule communicator for the night shift, made the wake-up call to the LM crew at 9:32 A.M. CDT. Liftoff from the Moon, after a stay totaling twenty-one hours, was scheduled to occur shortly after noon.

Most of the intervening time was taken up going over checklists in preparation for the ascent, taking star sightings, establishing the proper state vector for the flight up, inputting computer code, and tracking the command module for one last hack on the LM's precise landing location. The only significant change to the checklist was Houston wanting the LM's rendezvous radar turned off during the ascent. As CapCom Evans told the crew, "We think that this will take care of some of the overflow of program alarms that you were getting during descent."

The science experts on the ground were also anxious to hear more from Neil and Buzz about what they had observed on the lunar surface. Neil was now ready to tell them. "I was excited about the experience myself and was honored and willing to share it with the guys, who I knew were really interested in what was going on. This was a very exciting day for some of those guys; they had been working for many years on what might be found. All of a sudden they had a chance to get real information. It was important to them."

Armstrong's observations that morning impressed everyone with their incisiveness and clarity. "I don't remember writing notes. I think it was just so fresh in my memory that it wasn't hard to re-create what I'd just seen."

"Houston, Tranquility Base is going to give you a few comments with regard to the geology question of last night.

"We landed in a relatively smooth crater field of elongate secondary . . . [correcting himself] circular secondary craters, most of which have raised rims, irrespective of their size. That's not universally true. There are a few of the smaller craters around which do not have a discernible rim. The groundmass throughout the area is a very fine sand to a silt. I'd say the thing that would be most like it on Earth is powdered graphite. Immersed in this groundmass are a wide variety of rock shapes, sizes, textures—round and angular—many with varying consistencies. As I've said, I've seen what looked to be plain basalt and vesicular basalt. Others with no crystals, some with small white phenocrysts, maybe one to less than five percent.

"And we are in a boulder field where the boulders range generally up to two feet with a few larger than that. Now, some of the boulders are lying on top of the surface, some are partially exposed and some are just barely exposed. And in our traverse around on the surface—and particularly working with the scoop—we've run into boulders below the surface; it was probably buried under several inches of the groundmass.

"I suspect this boulder field may have some of its origin with this large, sharp-edged, blocky-rim crater that we passed over in final descent. Now, yesterday, I said that was about the size of a football field, and I have to admit it was a little hard to measure coming in. But I thought that it might just fit in the Astrodome as we came by it. And the rocks in the vicinity of this blocky-rim crater are much larger than these in this area. Some are ten feet or so and perhaps bigger, and they are very thickly populated out to about one crater diameter beyond the crater rim. Beyond that, there is some diminishing, and even out in this area [around the LM], the blocks seem to run out in rows and irregular patterns, and then there are paths between them where there are considerably less surface evidence of hard rocks. Over."

Heading into the countdown for lunar liftoff, Neil's mind-set was that of a typical test pilot: pragmatic and hard-nosed. "The LM's ascent engine was a single chamber. The tanks and the propellants and the oxidizer were what they were. We did have various means of controlling the circuitry to the valves—opening the flow of propellants to the engine. So that was an alternative. I had proposed many months earlier—maybe even years earlier—that we just put a big manual valve in there to open those propellant valves rather than, or in addition to, having all the electronic circuitry. But management didn't think that that was up to NASA's standards of sophistication. So I really knew that circuitry very well. But it wasn't really a problem, because if we fired the engine and it didn't fire, we weren't out of time. We had a lot of time to think about the problem to figure out what else we could do. When pilots really get worried is when they run out of options and run out of time simultaneously.

"The ascent was a very simple trajectory. We were on PNGS. If we had PNGS malfunction we could have gone to AGS and got into a safe orbit—at least in that point in time we thought we could. How could Houston help? Maybe if PNGS was acting up or there were questions, they would certainly have been able to do more analysis of the problem down there than we could. We were in a pretty good position. We were on the eastern side of the Moon and we were moving west, so during that ascent phase we were going right through the center of the Moon and should be getting pretty good data from Earth's radars there. Maybe they could tell us that we needed to switch to AGS. But other than that, there was not a lot that they could do. They were going to be watching other things, too—systems problems, batteries, environmental systems, and various things. I'm sure if they saw anything funny they would want to know about it and we would have to work out what should be done. But the ascent trajectory itself was pretty straightforward. All through our rendezvous we were calculating the different trajectory changes—the burns—we needed to make. They were doing the same thing using different sources of information on Earth."

At 05:04:04:51 elapsed time, Ron Evans cleared them for takeoff. "Understand," Aldrin answered. "We're number one on the runway." Some seventeen minutes later, at 12:37 P.M. CDT, it was time for that single, nonredundant engine to fire for its first time. Next to the landing itself, there was no more tense moment in the entire Apollo 11 mission—correct that: in the history of the entire U.S. manned space program.

On CBS, Cronkite uttered to Schirra, "I don't suppose we've been this nervous since back in the early days of Mercury."

In Wapakoneta, even the ever-faithful Viola questioned whether things would work out. "What if that burner would not ignite? What if it simply would not ignite? I was silently in deep concentration with our Lord. It seemed to take a while for the boys to get ready to leave. They seemed to be making sure they were doing it all just right. There were many last things to do."

In El Lago, Janet naturally had the very same fears. Exhausted by the pressure and exhilaration of it all, she desperately wanted the next moments to be over.

05:04:21:54	Aldrin:	*Nine, eight, seven, six, five, Abort Stage, Engine Arm, Ascent, Proceed.*

05:04:22:00　LAUNCH OCCURS

05:04:22:07	Aldrin:	[Static] [Garbled] *shadow. Beautiful.*

In his autobiography, Buzz eloquently described the liftoff: "The ascent stage of the LM separated from the descent stage with its chunky body and spindly legs, sending out a shower of brilliant insulation particles which had been ripped off from the ascent of the ascent engine."

05:04:22:09	Aldrin:	*Twenty-six, thirty-six feet per second up. Be advised for the pitchover.*
05:04:22:14	Armstrong:	*Pitchover.*

Again from Buzz: "There was no time to sightsee. I was concentrating intently on the computers, and Neil was studying the attitude indicator, but I looked up long enough to see the American flag fall over. Seconds after liftoff, the LM pitched forward about forty-five degrees, and though we had anticipated it would be an abrupt and maybe even a frightening maneuver, the straps and springs securing us in the LM cushioned the tilt so much and the acceleration was so great it was barely noticeable."

05:04:22:15	Aldrin:	*Very smooth. Balance couple, off. Very quiet ride. There's that one crater down there.* [This is not the crater they overflew during the landing; that crater was behind them and out of sight. In the pictures they took out of the window during ascent, the rim of the crater Buzz is referring to is visible on the horizon just to the right of the LM shadow.]
05:04:23:04	Evans:	*One minute and you're looking good.*
05:04:23:10	Aldrin:	*Roger.* [Pause] *A very quiet ride, just a little bit of wallowing back and forth. Not very much thruster activity.*
05:04:23:31	Evans:	*Roger. Mighty fine.*
05:04:23:37	Aldrin:	*Seven hundred* [feet per second horizontal velocity], *150* [feet per second vertical velocity] *up. Beautiful. Nine thousand feet* [altitude]. *AGS agrees* [with PNGS] *within a foot per second.*
05:04:23:59	Evans:	Eagle, *Houston. You're looking good at two* [minutes] . . .
05:04:24:06	Aldrin:	*And that's a thousand. One hundred seventy up. Beautiful. Fourteen thousand. And a foot per second again . . .*

Neil's mother was hardly the only person in tears as she heard Cronkite exclaim. "Oh, boy! Their words 'beautiful' . . . 'very smooth' . . . 'very quiet ride.' Armstrong and Aldrin, just short of twenty-four hours on the Moon's surface, on their way back now to rendezvous with Mike Collins orbiting the Moon."

For the past six months Mike Collins's "secret terror" had been that he might have to leave his mates on the Moon and return to Earth alone. "*Columbia* has no landing gear; I cannot help them if they fail to rise from the surface, or crash back into it." If either tragedy happened, Mike was coming home, but he knew he would be a marked man for life. "It would almost be better not to have that option," he sometimes thought.

The ascent stage had to fire for slightly over seven minutes to achieve the requisite altitude and speed to reach orbit. In the command module, Collins followed their progress very carefully. More than anyone, he knew the precariousness of "rendezvous day." As soon as he awoke that morning, there had been a "a multitude of things to keep me busy," including approximately 850 separate computer keystrokes, "eight hundred fifty chances for me to screw it up." If all went well with *Eagle,* then he would just serve "as a sturdy base-camp operator and let them find me in my constant circle. But if . . . if . . . if any one of a thousand things goes wrong with *Eagle,* then I become the hunter instead of the hunted." At the instant of LM liftoff, Mike was "like a nervous bride." He had been flying for seventeen years, had circled the Earth forty-four times in Gemini X, but had "never sweated out any flight" like he was sweating out the LM.

As *Eagle* rose upwards to meet him, Collins knew "One little hiccup and they are dead men. I hold my breath for the seven minutes it takes them to get into orbit." A Gemini veteran, he was "morbidly aware of how swiftly a rendezvous could turn sour. A titled gyro, a stubborn computer, a pilot's error—ah, it was that last one that troubled me the most. If Neil and Buzz limped up into a lopsided orbit, would I have enough fuel and enough moxie to catch them?" Next to him in the CM was a notebook outlining eighteen different variations of what he could try to intersect the LM if the module did not manage to get up to him on its own.

At *Eagle*'s controls, Armstrong drew not just on his Apollo training but also on his Gemini experience to fly to the proper rendezvous point. In terms of the piloting he needed to do and the thruster activities required, flying the LM to its rendezvous with *Columbia* was more like what he had done in Gemini VIII than unlike: the same relative strategy and techniques, the same size velocity changes. "That was one of the main reasons we felt comfortable in the situation."

The ascent was very different from the descent to landing. During much of the descent, the cockpit of the LM faced up; the crew was not able to see the lunar surface. Now, they were staring right at it. "Yes, we were looking at it now from very close range and going over it facedown where we could look at things very closely. The ascent also had a characteristic unlike any other portion of the flight. The attitude control rockets were being used to position the proper attitude of the lunar module. Normally to pitch up—to pitch the nose upward—you would fire the forward rockets upward and the aft rockets downward, both of which tended to rotate the vehicle upward. But in the ascent phase, any rockets that were pointed forward and firing actually slowed you down and fought against the action of the main ascent engine. So the forward-firing rockets were disabled for the ascent engine. To pitch the vehicle we only used half of the rockets—only the ones that were pointing downwards. The result of that, since the center of gravity was never quite on center, was those rockets would fire and move the vehicle upward. Then they would shut off, because the CG was offset, and we would be pushed the other way. Then they would kick in again. The whole thing was like a rocking chair going up and down through the entire ascent trajectory.

"That was different than Gemini. We had tried to implement the experience of this motion in the LM simulator, but because the simulator was a stationary object, you had no sensation of that rocking motion. That was quite an unusual characteristic. I didn't remember having it reported to me by the previous crews that had fired the ascent engine on Apollo 9 or 10. If they did report it, I had overlooked it somehow."

As was typical for Neil when he was piloting, he spoke sparingly during the ascent. Heading westward over the same landmarks they had been trying to identify when coming down, Neil remarked, "We're going right down U.S. 1." His only other comment was, "It's a pretty spectacular ride."

At one o'clock in the afternoon Houston time, July 22, a NASA public affairs officer reported that *Eagle* had achieved lunar orbit, one with an apolune of 47.2 nautical miles and a perilune of 9.1 miles. To move from this orbit below *Columbia* to a docking with it would take almost another three hours. Neil, Buzz, and Mike would all be busy with a long and detailed series of rendezvous procedures, navigational maneuvers, and backup checks. "Three hours may seem like a long time," Buzz remarks, "but we were too busy to notice." Mike recalls that his hands were full with the "arcane, almost black-magical manipulations" called for by his notebook full of rendezvous procedures.

Eagle needed to make three separate maneuvers to catch up with *Columbia.* The first, occurring at 1:53 P.M. CDT, took place on the back side of the Moon. Firing the LM's reaction control system (RCS) engines, Armstrong brought the spacecraft into a higher orbit that was just fifteen miles below the command module. An hour later, a second burn put the LM even more in plane with its target, reducing the altitude variations as it incrementally overtook the CSM.

Collins recalls their coming up the rest of the way. "The LM is fifteen miles below me now, and some forty miles behind. It is overtaking me at the comfortable rate of 120 feet per second. They are studying me with their radar and I am studying them with my sextant. At precisely the right moment, when I am up above them, twenty-seven degrees above the horizon, they make their move, thrusting toward me. 'We're burning,' Neil lets me know, and I congratulate him, 'That-a-boy!' We are on a collision course now; our trajectories are designed to cross 130 degrees of orbital travel later (in other words, slightly over one third of the way around in our next orbit). I have just passed 'over the hill,' and the next time the Earth pops up into view, I should be parked next to the LM. As we emerge into sunlight on the back side, the LM changes from a blinking light in my sextant to a visible bug, gliding golden and black across the crater fields below."

So close yet still so far away, the amiable strangers jested over the radio about their manner of reconvening:

05:07:22:11	Collins:	*Well, I see you don't have any landing gear.*
05:07:22:15	Armstrong:	*That's good . . . You're not confused on which end to dock with, are you?*

Continuing to close in, even the conversation between Neil and Buzz became more lighthearted:

05:07:25:31	Armstrong:	*One of those two bright spots is bound to be Mike.*
05:07:25:36	Aldrin:	*How about picking the closest one?*
05:07:25:44	Armstrong:	*Good idea.*

For Neil, the image of the command module passing so closely overhead brought back memories of his days as a fighter pilot:

05:07:28:23   Armstrong: *Looks like you're making a high-side pass on us, Michael.*

Buzz got his first good look at *Columbia* as well:

05:07:32:25   Aldrin: *Okay. I can see the shape of your vehicle now, Mike.*

05:07:32:42   Armstrong: *Oh, yes. . . . Got your high-gain [antenna] in sight. Your tracking light . . . whole vehicle shows. I see that you're pointed at me. Now, you're turning a little bit. Great.*

05:07:33:49   Collins: *Are you burning yet?*

05:07:33:50   Armstrong: *We're burning.*

"All that remains," Collins recalled, "was for them to brake to a halt using the correct schedule of range versus range rate. . . . While they are doing this, they must make certain they stay exactly on their prescribed approach path, slipping neither left nor right nor up nor down. . . . The sextant is useless this close in, so I close up shop in the lower equipment bay, transfer to the left couch, and wheel *Columbia* around to face the LM."

Peering out through his docking reticle, Mike marveled at the steady, centered approach of the LM as Neil and Buzz brought it home:

05:07:43:43   Collins: *I have 0.7 mile and I got you at thirty-one feet per second. Look good . . .*

05:07:44:15   Aldrin: *Yes, yes. We're in good shape, Mike. We're braking . . .*

05:07:46:13   Armstrong: *Okay, we're about eleven feet a second coming in at you.*

05:07:46:43   Collins: *That's good . . .*

Bigger and bigger the LM appeared in Collins's window, and it was hard for him to hold back the feeling of exultation. "For the first time since I was assigned to this incredible flight six months ago, for the first time I feel that it *is* going to happen." Inside *Eagle,* however, the commander and the lunar module pilot were nervously entertaining what still needed to be done— and what still could go wrong.

05:07:47:05	Aldrin:	*Hope we're not going to get a pitch straight down.*
05:07:47:16	Armstrong:	*We've got a pitch down and then a yaw to do . . . It flies good . . . Okay, if I pitch over, I'm going to be looking right into the Sun.*
05:07:50:09	Aldrin:	*I hope you know how to roll.*
05:07:50:11	Armstrong:	*Yes, I do.*
05:07:50:23	Aldrin:	*You want to end up with that window opposite his right window, so you don't want to roll right. Right?*
05:07:50:32	Armstrong:	*Yes.*
05:07:50:34	Aldrin:	*The only trouble is, it's towards—towards* [a] *ninety* [degree roll], *isn't it? . . . You could . . . You . . .*
05:07:50:58	Armstrong:	*If I roll 120—it'll roll left.*
05:07:51:06	Aldrin:	*Ninety, huh? . . . Sixty?*
05:07:51:21	Armstrong:	*Well, why don't I start to roll . . .*
05:07:51:24	Aldrin:	*Yes, I think if you roll up sixty . . .*
05:07:51:29	Armstrong:	*I'll be looking into his left window when I pitch up.*
05:07:51:32	Aldrin:	*I don't think so. If you did it right now you'd . . .*

With the LM only fifty feet away, technically the rendezvous was over. Neil having turned the LM around, *Eagle*'s drogue directly faced *Columbia*'s docking port. Collins could not contain his emotions when he caught a gorgeous view of Earthrise:

05:07:51:36	Collins:	*I got the Earth coming up already. It's fantastic!*

Houston broke in at this crucial moment to learn what was going on:

05:07:52:00	Evans:	Eagle *and* Columbia, *Houston. Standing by.*
05:07:52:05	Armstrong:	*Roger. We're station keeping.*

Neil's succinct answer and sharp tone made it clear the unwelcome intrusion was barely tolerable.

05:07:52:24	Aldrin:	*Pitch up . . . Pass right up a little. You got a better view . . . Bottom side . . . Move back.*
05:07:52:45	Collins:	*That's right.*
05:07:53:08	Armstrong:	*Okay, I'm getting about into the right attitude, I think . . .*
05:07:53:18	Aldrin:	*Yes.*
05:07:53:21	Armstrong:	*That roll's pretty far. I just don't know how much . . . So that's . . . Oh, it's going to go* BLOCK!

Although the alignment between *Eagle* and *Columbia* looked good, as the vehicles came together they experienced a potentially nasty phenomenon known as gimbal lock. Put simply, two of the three pivoting gimbals that were located between the inertial platform of the LM's guidance system and the spacecraft itself accidentally got into alignment and temporarily could not move, resulting in the loss of the platform's stability and the firing of some attitude jets. Armstrong recalls how it happened. "The docking technique was to have the lunar module stabilize itself in the vicinity of the command module and maneuver to a point where it would be convenient for the command module to go ahead with the docking. Then Mike would do the actual command module motion to engage the docking mechanism. In a way it's similar to how the Gemini spacecraft had docked with Agena, because Mike's position in the command module was just like the position of the commander of a Gemini. He's looking out his front window and through his docking reticle, a device that helped him make sure the vehicles were properly aligned. We, on the other hand, were looking up. The docking hatch was in the roof of the lunar module so we are looking upward through a small flat window in the roof.

"In trying to achieve the best attitude for the lunar module so that Mike could make an easy docking, I was looking through the top window and making the attitude corrections relative to the command module. Unfortunately, I neglected to be looking at the attitude indicator, which would have told me that we were getting close to gimbal lock. In the process of flying through the top window I flew it right into gimbal lock.

"Now the consequence of that was not very bad, particularly since we were finished flying the lunar module at that point. We weren't going to be in it anymore; we were going to leave it behind. There were alternatives for stabilizing the system and [we] were approximately in the right spot at that point for Mike to complete the docking.

"It's not something that you would do intentionally. But we didn't have any substantial motions or [tumbling] resulting from it."

Perhaps because Collins was controlling the actual docking from his end, and perhaps because Mike had waited so long, all alone, to master this critical final maneuver, his reaction to the gimbal lock was more extreme. As soon as the two spacecraft were engaged by the small capture latches, he flipped a switch that fired a nitrogen bottle to pull the two vehicles together. As soon as he flipped it, he got what he later called "the surprise of my life": "Instead of a docile little LM, suddenly I find myself attached to a wildly veering critter that seems to be trying to escape." Specifically, the LM yawed to his right, instigating a misalignment of about fifteen degrees. Working with his right hand to swing *Columbia* around, there was nothing he could do to stop the automatic retraction cycle designed to pull *Eagle* into a deep embrace. "All I can hope for is no damage to the equipment, so that if this retraction fails, I can release the LM and try again."

Wrestling with his controller, the two vehicles veered back into proper alignment. The docking was sealed. Later, when Neil and Buzz reentered the command module, Mike sought to explain. "That was a funny one. You know, I didn't feel a shock, and I thought things were pretty much steady. I went to retract there, and that's when all hell broke loose." Armstrong offered Mike his own explanation: "It seemed to happen at the time I put the plus-X thrust to it, and apparently it wasn't centered, because, somehow or other, I accidentally got off in attitude and then the attitude-hold system started firing." "I was sure busy there for a couple seconds," Mike declared.

It was 4:38 P.M. CDT. It then took well over an hour for Armstrong and Aldrin to disable the specified LM systems (some were left on), snare and stow floating items, and get *Eagle* into configuration for its final jettisoning.

At 6:20 P.M., Collins opened the hatch mechanism from the other side, and Neil and Buzz, still very dusty, made their way up, down, and into *Columbia*'s cockpit. "The first one through is Buzz, a big smile on his face," Collins noted. "I grab his head, a hand on each temple, and am about to give him a big smooch on the forehead, as a parent might greet an errant child; but then, embarrassed, I think better of it and grab his hand, and then Neil's. We cavort about a little bit, all smiles and giggles about our success, and then it's back to work as usual, as Neil and Buzz prepare the LM for its final journey." Viola later remarked, "My, what a feeling they must have had when they were back in the *Columbia* with Mike! How happy and thankful I'm sure they were . . . Our boys were together and on their way home."

On CBS, Cronkite brought the historic thirty-two hours to an end with the following thoughts that he had no doubt prepared in advance:

> *Man has finally visited the Moon after all the ages of waiting and wait-ing. Two Americans with the alliterative names of Armstrong and Aldrin have spent just under a full Earth day on the Moon. They picked at it and sampled it, and they deployed experiments on it, and they packed away some of it to pack with them and bring home.*
>
> *Above the men on the Moon, satellite over satellite, orbited the third member of the Apollo team, Michael Collins. His bittersweet mission was to guide and watch over the Command Service Module whose power and guidance system provided the only means of getting home, and it still does.*
>
> *Now at this point in the journey with the lunar lander reunited with the mother ship and the astronauts preparing for the rocket burn which will send them back home here, certain times and images remain that I've noted here: 4:17:40 P.M., seventeen minutes and forty seconds after four Eastern time, yesterday—Sunday, July 20, 1969—the moment the Lunar Module touched down on the Moon's surface; 10:56 P.M., Sunday, the moment that Arm-strong's foot first touched the lunar crust; and 1:54 P.M. today, the instant of liftoff from that newly named Tranquility Base camp.*
>
> *There were the ghostly television pictures we all saw of Aldrin and Arm-strong on the Moon. Armstrong's first words, "That's one small step for a man, a giant leap for mankind." And Aldrin's two-word description, "Mag-nificent desolation . . ." And left behind, a plaque with the words: "Here Man from Planet Earth First Set Foot Upon the Moon. July 1969 A.D. We Came in Peace for All Mankind."*
>
> *And they left the flag of the United States flying there, too. [Naturally, the crew did not report that the flag had fallen over during liftoff.] Left behind were hundreds of thousands of dollars' worth of cameras and hard-ware and equipment, discarded for the return flight; a small disk with mes-sages microscopically reduced in size from the leaders of the world; an olive*

branch—symbolically at least; and two medals in memory of the three Americans and the two Russians who died in man's recent quest for the Moon.

All this comes rushing back to us now as we think of the round-trip Moon flight still in progress and still some critical maneuvers yet to perform.

And with this flight, man has really begun to move away from the Earth. But with this flight, some new challenges for mankind. A challenge to determine yet, whether in coming to the Moon, we turn our centuries-old friend in the sky into an enemy, that we invaded, conquered, exploited, and perhaps someday left as a desolate globe once more. Or will we make the most of it, as perhaps a way station on beyond the stars. Apollo 11 still has a long way to go—and so do we.

Thus concluded the longest continuous scheduled broadcast in the history of television.

Back in lunar orbit, Collins helped his mates transfer all their gold and spices into the mother ship, including the camera film and rock boxes, "shiny little metal caskets about two feet long." "Get ready for those million-dollar boxes," Buzz advised. "Got a lot of weight. Now watch it." Neil and Buzz then enclosed the boxes inside white fiberglass fabric containers that zipped up. That done, they tried to clear *Columbia* of Moon dust. They extracted from storage a small vacuum cleaner head, as directed by the microbe people. "The vacuum didn't take off much of the dust at all," Buzz states. "We got more off by dusting each other by hand, but even that didn't do the job."

Before closing the hatch, Neil and Buzz tidied things up in the LM. It was very hard to say good-bye to the machine. *Eagle* had done absolutely everything it had been asked to do, and then some.

At 6:42 P.M. CDT, it was time to send the LM on its way. "It was a fond farewell," Armstrong remembers. On all subsequent Apollo lunar missions, the LM would be purposefully impacted into the Moon for seismographical measurements, but not *Eagle*. It simply floated for the next few years as a piece of debris until its orbit deteriorated and the noble craft crashed ignominiously into the lunar surface. Buzz and Neil were both glad it was Collins who flipped the switches to release it. Settling into its own orbit some miles behind the command module, it seemed almost as if the little LM was trying to catch up and rejoin its masters.

"Neil, did NASA ever figure out where on the Moon that Eagle *hit?"*

"I don't know the answer. That is something I have wondered about myself."

"After impact how big could some of its pieces have been?"

"Not too large since the velocity would have been on the order of five thousand feet a second."

"When we someday return to the Moon, won't there be an interest in getting parts of the Eagle *back to Earth for museum exhibition?"*

"Yes, that's no doubt going to be true for any of the missions—any components from any of the spacecraft. I'm not good at predicting the results of a crash, and what might survive and what might not. But I think whatever's left would be of interest no matter what size."

During the subsequent meal, Collins started throwing question after question at his mates: "How was liftoff? How did liftoff feel? . . . Well, do the rocks—do the rocks all look the same? They're different? Good, great. I'm glad to hear it. . . . Luckily, you were able to get a little bit of everything. I mean, were the rocks . . . I mean, how did you—did you go around and just pick up rocks, put them in—in. . . . Great, great. Man, that's beautiful. . . . That's great. Fantastic! That'll keep the geologists jumping for years. . . . What was that thing that you said it was supposed to be concave but it was convex . . . ? But there's all different kinds of rocks, huh, or at least several different kinds? . . . Well, did—when you look—when you're walking around or just looking out the window of the LM, did it appear very homogenous? Everything sort of the same color and all, or did it look . . . ? It's that dark battleship gray like? . . . How big are the rocks that you just scurried around and picked up with tongs? Good gravy! Beautiful!"

At 11:10 P.M. Houston time, still Monday, July 21, Mission Control gave *Columbia* the go-ahead for Trans-Earth Injection. Collins later called TEI "the get us out of here, we don't want to be a permanent Moon satellite" maneuver. What it amounted to was a two-and-a-half-minute burn of the service propulsion engine that was to send them home by increasing their velocity to 6,188 miles per hour, the speed necessary to escape lunar orbit. If TEI did not go well, as Neil explains, "we would have been in for a long, lonely ride."

TEI took place on the back side of the Moon, out of contact with Earth. Along with Earth reentry, it was the only truly nervous moment left to face.

As complicated as the whole mission had been, what the astronauts had to make absolutely sure of when they did deorbit the Moon was that they were pointed in the right direction. They relieved the tension with humor:

05:15:14:12	Collins:	*I see a horizon. It looks like we are going forward* [laughter].
05:15:14:26	Armstrong:	*Shades of Gemini.*
05:07:14:29	Collins:	*It is most important that we be going forward* [more laughter]. *There's only one really bad mistake you can make there.*
05:15:14:50	Aldrin:	*Shades of Gemini retrofire. Are you sure we're* [laughter] . . . *no, let's see, the motors point this way and the gases escape that way, therefore imparting a thrust that-a-way.*
05:15:15:03	Collins:	*Yes, horizon looks good.*

Actually, there was a very remote chance that the astronauts could have shot themselves off in the wrong direction. "I wouldn't put it at zero," Armstrong admits. "There was certainly a chance—particularly when you are in the dark, without external references, and dependent on your instruments. Is it possible to get that attitude wrong? I would say it's possible. You've got three guys inside trying to make sure it wasn't wrong, so I think it's very unlikely. In the Russian space program, there was at least one occasion when a retrofire didn't have the proper alignment. Jim Lovell made the memorable statement, 'There is a Santa Claus,' when their Apollo 8 TEI went off properly. It's something that Mission Control always worried about because they can't see you on the far side and they don't have any data. They are completely in the dark, and that worries them a lot when they don't have any numbers in front of them."

As soon as the spacecraft peeked around the disk of the Moon half an hour later, Houston wanted to know what had happened:

| 05:15:35:14 | Duke: | *Hello Apollo 11. How did it go? Over.* |
| 05:15:35:22 | Collins: | *Time to open up the LRL* [Lunar Receiving Laboratory] *doors, Charlie.* |

05:15:35:25	Duke:	*Roger. We got you coming home. It's well stocked. . . . All your systems look real good to us. We'll keep you posted.*
05:15:36:27	Armstrong:	*Hey, Charlie boy, looking good here. That was a beautiful burn. They don't come any finer.*

As Collins recalls, all three men next took turns with the cameras, pointing them alternately at the Moon and the Earth. "The Moon from this side is full, a golden brown globe glorying in the sunshine. It is an optimistic, cheery view, but all the same, it is wonderful to look out the window and see it shrinking and the tiny Earth growing." Not only seeing it from this distance but knowing they were coming back home to it made the sight of Planet Earth "unforgettable."

The remainder of the two-and-a-half-day trip home was relatively routine. The first night's sleep after the reunion was the deepest and most satisfying of the entire trip, and lasted some eight and a half hours, until noon Houston time, Tuesday, July 22. The spacecraft passed the point where Earth's gravity took over and began drawing the astronauts progressively homeward—a point 38,800 nautical miles from the Moon and 174,000 from the Earth—shortly after they woke up. Later that afternoon, they made their only midcourse correction, slightly adjusting their flight path for the best trajectory into Earth orbit. By midafternoon of the next day, *Columbia* reached the midway point of the journey home, 101,000 nautical miles from splashdown. So relaxed was the crew and so uneventful their duties that they created a little mischief by playing over their radio to Houston a special tape of sound effects they had brought along. On it were sounds of dogs barking and of a speeding diesel locomotive.

What everyone back on Earth most remembered about the return home were the two evening prime-time color television transmissions. "The TV broadcasts served a useful purpose," Neil believes. "It was news, and I have always believed that when there is news, you should report it. We were in a good position to report what was really news, for which there was a great deal of interest. The only caveat that I would add is that I don't think you should ever jeopardize the safety of a flight in order to do television. You should do it only at such times that it doesn't interfere with your principal duties. I think we were successful at only having them at times when it was convenient. That was not always true on some other flights. On some the commander rightfully had to change the TV schedule and even cancel a transmission, because it just wasn't an appropriate time to be doing that."

In the final TV transmission from Apollo 11, each astronaut explained what the Moon landing meant to him within the grander scheme of things. At 7:03 P.M. EDT (07:09:32:24 elapsed time), Armstrong opened the broadcast:

> *Good evening. This is the commander of Apollo 11. A hundred years ago, Jules Verne wrote a book about a voyage to the Moon. His spaceship,* Columbia, *took off from Florida and landed in the Pacific Ocean after completing a trip to the Moon. It seems appropriate to us to share with you some of the reflections of the crew as the modern-day* Columbia *completes its rendezvous with the planet Earth and the same Pacific Ocean tomorrow. First, Mike Collins.*

At Mission Control, Janet and her boys, Pat Collins and her youngsters, as well as one of the Aldrin children, were taking in the show from the viewing room.

Mike Collins:

> *Roger. This trip of ours to the Moon may have looked, to you, simple or easy. I'd like to assure you that has not been the case. The Saturn V rocket which put us into orbit is an incredibly complicated piece of machinery, every piece of which worked flawlessly. This computer up above my head has a 38,000-word vocabulary, each word of which has been very carefully chosen to be of the utmost value to us, the crew. This switch, which I have in my hand now, has over 300 counterparts in the command module alone—this one single switch design. In addition to that, there are myriads of circuit breakers, levers, rods, and other associated controls. The SPS engine, our large rocket engine on the aft end of our service module, must have performed flawlessly or we would have been stranded in lunar orbit. The parachutes above my head must work perfectly tomorrow or we will plummet into the ocean. We have always had confidence that all this equipment will work, and work*

*properly, and we continue to have confidence that it will do so for the re-
mainder of the flight. All this is possible only through the blood, sweat, and
tears of a number of people. First, the American workmen who put these
pieces of machinery together in the factory. Second, the painstaking work
done by the various test teams during the assembly and retest after assembly.
And finally, the people at the Manned Spacecraft Center, both in management, in mission planning, in flight control, and last but not least, in
crew training. This operation is somewhat like the periscope of a submarine.
All you see is the three of us, but beneath the surface are thousands and
thousands of others, and to all those, I would like to say, thank you very
much.*

In Buzz's time on camera, he presented the first of his many future statements on behalf of the spirit of exploration:

*Good evening. I'd like to discuss with you a few of the more symbolic aspects
of the flight of our mission, Apollo 11. As we've been discussing the events
that have taken place in the past two or three days here on board our spacecraft, we've come to the conclusion that this has been far more than three
men on a voyage to the Moon; more still than the efforts of a government
and industry team; more even than the efforts of one nation. We feel that this
stands as a symbol of the insatiable curiosity of all mankind to explore the
unknown. Neil's statement the other day upon first setting foot on the surface of the Moon, 'This is a small step for a man, but a great leap for
mankind,' I believe sums up these feelings very nicely. We accepted the
challenge of going to the Moon; the acceptance of this challenge was inevitable. The relative ease with which we carried out our mission, I believe, is
a tribute to the timeliness of that acceptance. Today, I feel we're fully capable
of accepting expanded roles in the exploration of space. In retrospect, we
have all been particularly pleased with the call signs that we very laboriously
chose for our spacecraft,* Columbia *and* Eagle. *We've been particularly
pleased with the emblem of our flight, depicting the U.S. eagle bringing
the universal symbol of peace from the Earth, from the planet Earth, to the
Moon—that symbol being the olive branch. It was our overall crew choice
to deposit a replica of this symbol on the Moon. Personally, in reflecting
on the events of the past several days, a verse from Psalms come to mind to
me: "When I consider the heavens, the word of Thy fingers, the moon
and the stars which Thou hast ordained, what is man that Thou art mindful
of him."*

The man of the fewest words, Commander Armstrong, closed the broadcast eloquently. His mood was as reflective as it would ever be in public:

The responsibility for this flight lies first with history and with the giants of science who have preceded this effort; next with the American people, who have, through their will, indicated their desire; next, to four administrations and their Congresses, for implementing that will; and then to the agency and industry teams that built our spacecraft: the Saturn, the Columbia, *the* Eagle, *and the little EMU, the space suit and backpack that was our small spacecraft out on the lunar surface. We would like to give a special thanks to all those Americans who built the spacecraft, who did the construction, design, the tests, and put their hearts and all their abilities into those crafts. To those people tonight, we give a special thank-you. And to all the other people that are listening and watching tonight, God bless you. Good night from Apollo 11.*

For everyone who was watching at home in their living rooms that midsummer night's eve, these were proud moments. Wrapping up the broadcast on CBS, Cronkite called the crew's closing statements "a heartwarming vote of appreciation from those three astronauts who have done the incredible—gone to the Moon and walked upon it." Total success for Apollo 11 now hinged upon reentering the Earth's atmosphere, splashing down, and being safely recovered.

But back on Earth unforeseen danger threatened the final moments of Apollo 11. A bad storm was brewing over the Pacific that a couple of fast-thinking meteorologists saw was moving right over the splashdown point. At work in his "secure vault" at Hickam Air Force Base in Hawaii, Captain Hank Brandli, an air force officer charged with tracking weather systems for the top-secret National Reconnaissance Office's ultra-classified Corona spy satellite program, had detected the early formation of a deadly "Screaming Eagle" thunderstorm with tops at 50,000 feet forming over exactly where he knew the Apollo 11 astronauts were supposed to come down. Though his work was strictly classified, Brandli arranged to meet Captain Willard (Sam) Houston Jr., the commanding officer of Fleet Weather Central–Pearl Harbor, in a nearby parking lot, and then took the navy weatherman back to his vault. Shown the classified photographic images, Captain Houston convinced Rear Admiral Donald C. Davis, commander of Task Force 30, in charge of retrieving Apollo 11, that he needed to get NASA to change the landing site, which he did. Early on the morning of Thursday, July 24, the prime recovery ship, the USS *Hornet*, a carrier built in 1943, with President Nixon aboard, was ordered to move northwesterly a distance of some 250 miles to an area where the forecast was for calmer seas.

Columbia then had to change its inbound trajectory. "We used a slightly altered skip maneuver for reentry that moved our splashdown point the necessary distance. Otherwise, the entry part was routine." As always, Mission Control fretted about the possibility of a fundamental oversight:

08:01:31:33	Lovell:	*This is your friendly backup CMP. Have a good trip and . . . remember to come to in BEF [back end first].*
08:01:31:42	Collins:	*You better believe. Thank you kindly.*

At 11:35 Houston time on the twenty-fourth, Apollo 11 started down through the Earth's atmosphere. It slammed into the first fringes of air at some 400,000 feet when the spacecraft was northeast of Australia. Collins, at the controls, graphically detailed the reentry: "We are scheduled to hit our entry corridor at an angle of six and a half degrees below the horizon, at a speed of 36,194 feet per second, nearly 25,000 miles per hour. We are aimed at a spot eight miles southwest of Hawaii. We jettison our Service Module, our faithful storehouse still half full of oxygen, and turn around so that our heat shield is leading the way."

08:02:54:40	Aldrin:	*Houston, we got the service module going by. A little high and a little bit to the right.*
08:02:54:49	Lovell:	*Roger. Thank you.*
08:01:54:53	Aldrin:	*And it's rotating just like it should be.*

"Deceleration begins gradually and is heralded by the beginnings of a spectacular light show. We are in the center of a sheath of protoplasm, trailing a comet's tail of ionized particles and heat shield material. The ultimate black of space is gone, replaced by a wispy tunnel of colors: subtle lavenders, light blue-greens, little touches of violet, all surrounding a central core of orange-yellow." Dropping fast but feeling as if they are in a state of suspended animation, the three astronauts see the first earthly forms, a big bank of gorgeous stratocumulus clouds. Then their three huge drogue chutes blast open, "beautiful orange-and-white blossoms of reassurance." Soon the astronauts were able to make out the wide expanse of ocean below. At 08:03:09:45 elapsed time, Air Boss, the head of the interservice recovery team, radioed it had visual contact with the descending capsule. Dawn was just breaking over the southwestern Pacific.

Eight minutes and thirty-three seconds later, at 11:51 A.M. CDT, the spacecraft, with its chutes tilting in the wind, hit the water like a ton of bricks, forcing a grunt out of each astronaut. Armstrong radioed to Air Boss, "Everyone okay inside. Our checklist is complete. Awaiting swimmers." Air Boss verified an on-target landing, 940 nautical miles southwest of Honolulu and 230 miles south of Johnston Island. The *Hornet* was only thirteen miles away. Navy helicopters were in the immediate area.

Armstrong and his mates had each taken an anti-motion-sickness pill before reentry, only to discover they should have taken two.

"The seas weren't supposed to be too bad," Neil remembers, "but it was good preventive maintenance. Why take a chance?" The swell turned out to be worse than expected. Aldrin suffered most from the nausea: "Air Boss announced to us that the wave height was between three and four feet, but it looked more like thirteen or fourteen. And it felt like it too." Worse yet, the waves had turned the command module over, so it was floating small-end down. Mike owed Neil a beer, payment for Neil betting that the module would, in fact, topple over.

Technically, it was called the "stable two" position—the CM's hatch underwater and the astronauts hanging from their straps. Armstrong remembers, "It was unusual being upside down looking into the water while hanging from the straps. Everything looked completely different because gravity had now established an orientation that had been missing for a long time. All of a sudden you had a gravity vector that you could identify with, but it was not like anything you'd ever seen before! Everything looked like it was in the wrong spot."

Quickly the crew acted to put themselves aright, starting the motorized pumps to inflate three small spherical brown and white airbags that changed the spacecraft's buoyancy center of gravity and turned it back over big end down. It took almost ten minutes for the float motors to fill the bags.

Waiting for the team of three navy frogmen, they sat in silence, willing themselves not to be seasick, especially Aldrin. "It was one thing to land upside down," Buzz later remarked, "it would be quite another to scramble out of the spacecraft in front of television cameras tossing our cookies all over the place."

The swimmers attached the orange flotation collar, then opened the spacecraft's hatch; it was 12:20 P.M. CDT, 6:20 in the morning Hawaii time. The astronauts sensed they had been in the water for eternity, but only twenty-nine minutes had elapsed. Into the command module the head of the water rescue team, twenty-five-year-old Lieutenant Clancy Hatleberg, threw the Biological Containment Garments, or BIGs. Grayish-green in color, these were the rubberized, zippered, hooded, and visored containment suits meant to save the world from "Moon germs." Each rescue swimmer himself wore a special BIG topped by a side-filtered face mask. Swimming in the garment was nothing compared to the astronauts' having to put them on inside the command module. Dealing with gravity for the first time in eight days, they were so light-headed, and their feet and legs so swollen, they could barely stand, especially against eighteen-knot winds.

The BIGs finally donned, the astronauts squeezed through the small hatch; as the commander, Neil came out last. Before they were escorted one by one into the raft bobbing alongside, the frogmen sprayed them with a precautionary disinfectant against lunar microbes. Once inside the dinghy, they were then given cloths and two different doses of chemical detergent to continue the scrub-down. When they were finished, the frogmen tied the cloths to weights and dropped them into the ocean, as if banishing them to the deep would eliminate any chance of a biological Armageddon brought on by an Andromeda Strain. Supposedly the BIGs were airtight, but within minutes moisture began seeping into them. Virtually nothing was said by the astronauts during any of this, mostly because the visors and headgear of their BIGs made it almost impossible to be heard, especially with four helicopters beating their rotors overhead.

Again they sat, for fifteen minutes, until a helicopter got the order to drop down and pick them up. The *Hornet* was now in view, less than a quarter of a mile away. With TV cameras on board a couple of the helicopters, every moment of the recovery was being broadcast live around the world. Waiting for them inside the helicopter was Dr. William R. Carpentier, their flight surgeon from the Manned Spacecraft Center. They gave him the thumbs-up sign as they entered. He reminded them, "Don't take off your BIGs till we're on the ship, in the quarantine facility, and I've got all the swabs."

At 12:57 P.M CDT, the helicopter landed on the *Hornet*'s flight deck. A brass band was playing. Cheering sailors crowded on deck. A big grin on his face and his hands crossed atop a rail, President Nixon stood on the bridge along with Secretary of State William P. Rogers and NASA Administrator

Dr. Thomas O. Paine, who were accompanying the president on a twelve-day, round-the-world trip that included a stop in Vietnam.

The astronauts could barely see the hoopla. Still inside the chopper they rode one of the ship's elevators down to the hangar deck. Disembarking, they walked down a newly painted line through a cheering crowd of seamen and VIPs into the mobile quarantine facility—a thirty-five-foot-long modified house trailer—in which they were to remain until they arrived at the Lunar Receiving Laboratory in Houston on July 27.

Neil remembers what it was like landing on the ship and getting up on his feet. "I was wondering how physiologically well we might feel, but we all felt pretty good. We didn't have any seasickness kinds of problems." They were able to go right into the quarantine trailer where they immediately sat down in easy chairs to undergo the microbiology sampling and a preliminary medical exam by Dr. Carpentier.

They had time only for a quick shower before seeing the president. "There were the Nixon ceremonial activities to attend to," Neil reflects. "We needed to do [that] and get it behind us so that we could celebrate." Following the playing of the National Anthem, President Nixon, nearly dancing a jig of pleasure, addressed the astronauts via intercom at 2:00 P.M. CDT. Crouching behind a picture window at the back end of the trailer the three tired but exhilarated crew members arranged themselves, Neil to the president's left, Buzz to the right, and Mike in the middle.

> *Neil, Buzz, and Mike. I want you to know that I think I'm the luckiest man in the world. I say this not only because I have the honor of being the president of the United States, but particularly because I have the privilege of speaking for so many in welcoming you back to Earth. I could tell you about all the messages we received in Washington. Over one hundred foreign governments, emperors, and presidents and prime ministers and kings have sent the most warm messages that we have ever received. They represent over two billion people on this Earth—all of them who have had the opportunity through television to see what you have done. And then I also bring you messages from members of the Cabinet and members of the Senate and members of the House, and Space Agency.*
>
> *But most important, I made a telephone call yesterday. The toll wasn't, incidentally, as great as the one I made to you fellows on the Moon. I made that collect, just in case you didn't know. I called, in my view, three of the greatest ladies and most courageous ladies in the world today, your wives. And from Jan and Joan and Pat, I bring their love and their congratulations.*

*We think that it is just wonderful that they could have participated at least
through television in this return; we're only sorry they couldn't be here. And
also, I've got to let you in on a little secret—I made a date with them. I invited them to dinner on the thirteenth of August, right after you come out of
quarantine. It will be a state dinner held in Los Angeles. The governors of all
the fifty states will be there, the ambassadors, others from around the world
and in America. And they told me that you would come too. And all I want
to know—will you come? We want to honor you then.*

"We'll do anything you say. Just anything," answered Armstrong. After
brief banter with Nixon and with Frank Borman, NASA's special presidential adviser for Apollo 11, the president closed his remarks with one of
the most memorable phrases of his administration. He called the eight days
of Apollo 11 "the greatest week in the history of the world since the Creation." It proved to be a controversial statement, especially for many Christians, but not for Neil's mother watching in Ohio, who loved it. Neil himself
has always regarded Nixon's statement as hyperbolic: "It was an exciting
time. A lot of times when you are exuberant, you tend to be a little exaggerative."

On her front lawn in El Lago, Janet thanked all of the people who
helped make the flight successful: "We thank you for everything—your
prayers, your thoughts, just everything. And if anyone were to ask me how I
could describe this flight, I can only say that it was out of this world!"

In Wapakoneta, a crowd of newsmen waited for Viola and Steve to make
some comments. "I wanted to cry out and say, 'Oh, thank you dear heavenly
Father," Viola wrote later, "but when the words came out I said, 'Praise
God from whom all blessings flow!" I forget what Steve said, but I remember the TV man asking the questions grabbed our hand and said, 'Oh, thank
you, only six million people have just heard your voices.' That sent another
chill up my back." Later that afternoon, the local high school band marched
down Neil Armstrong Drive, playing some of Viola's favorite hymns. "That
was too much for me, my tears spilled all over. Stephen came to my rescue
and kissed me right in front of the entire group. We were so happy, we loved
everybody, and surely loved our God."

As the *Hornet* steamed toward Honolulu, the astronauts could not yet fully
relax, as there were still more postflight medical exams to undergo. One
thing the doctor spotted with Neil was an accumulation of fluid in one of his

ears; caused by the stress of reentry, it cleared up by the next day. With the doctors interested in how eight days in zero g had affected their bodies, it almost seemed like the mission was still occurring. "It was part of the deal to do that," Neil understood. "We knew it going in, and the tests weren't anything surprising, basically checking on the extent of the deterioration in our physical condition. We were glad we were in that position because it was confirmation that all that had gone before was okay. Of course, we were in isolation and couldn't see day or night outside."

With the tests over, an impromptu cocktail hour broke out inside the small living room of the mobile quarantine facility; Neil drank scotch. Then came a dinner of grilled steaks and baked potatoes.

That night, in soft beds with real pillows, the crew slept hard for nearly nine hours. Their rest was timed to restore a regular sleeping pattern, soon to be disrupted by the loss of six hours traveling east from Hawaii to Houston. Buzz remembers, "We kept right on taking our leisure until we were totally off schedule but more and more rested."

After a hearty breakfast of crêpes, link sausages, pecan rolls, and coffee, there was work to do. *Columbia* had been brought on board and its precious rock boxes and other treasures needed to be unloaded. Through a plastic tunnel Neil, Buzz, and Mike walked to their grizzled spacecraft, scarred as it now was from the heat of reentry, and with the help of John Hirasaki, a Japanese-American recovery engineer assigned to assist the crew while staying in the MQF, they took the boxes out of the back wall of the command module and loaded them in a special sterilization unit. A few hours later, the boxes were flown off the aircraft carrier to Houston.

That afternoon witnessed another shipboard ceremony. The captain, Carl J. Seiberlich, presented each of them a plaque, a set of inscribed drinking mugs, and caps with their names, "Apollo 11," and "USS Hornet." Food was sent in through the MQF's air-lock sterilizer, but, due to the quarantine precautions, the astronauts did not get to eat any of the large decorated cake. Commander Armstrong continued to act as the crew spokesman, as he would in all public events. Someone in the trailer innocently remarked, "And now it begins," a comment that would become the astronauts' refrain in the coming weeks.

For two nights the Apollo 11 crew stayed on the *Hornet,* an experience Neil alone was accustomed to from his days in the navy. He passed some of the time by playing a marathon game of gin rummy with Mike, while Buzz read or played solitaire. Under Hirasaki's direction, they also started autographing pictures earmarked for NASA and White House VIPs.

The scene was wild as they arrived at Pearl Harbor on Saturday morning, July 26. The first time Neil had steamed into Pearl was aboard the *Essex,* as a midshipman, eighteen years earlier. People were cheering, a band was playing, and flags were waving. A broomstick was flying from the *Hornet*'s mast, the symbol of a mission well done. But, as Neil relates, "We weren't in a very good position to see all that stuff." Commander of Pacific Forces Admiral John Sidney McCain Jr., the father and namesake of the future U.S. senator from Arizona, greeted the crew upon their arrival, as Nixon had on the *Hornet,* through the rear window of their trailer. "You lucky sons of bitches," he said. "I'd have given anything to go with you."

They stayed at Pearl only long enough to transfer to an airplane for their flight to Houston. Their trailer got lifted onto a flatbed truck and was then driven, at a speed of ten miles per hour, to nearby Hickam Field. The Apollo 11 crew could not understand why the truck had to be driven so slowly. Buzz remembers that they asked about the speed a number of times, but received no explanation. "Somebody somewhere had made the decision and that was that." Crowds of people lined the streets. A young boy crippled from polio ran alongside the truck much of the way.

Finally reaching Hickam, the MQF was loaded into the cavernous belly of a C-141 Starlifter transport. The long flight to Houston meant just that much more time inside the MQF. According to Neil, "It was pretty much like everything else. Here we were confined to a very small place—but a bigger place than we had been in for quite a while. We had more room. We had hot food. We had cocktail hour. We had lots of things to do. Anytime we had spare time there were lots of things we wanted to write down or talk about."

Arriving at Ellington Air Force Base in Houston around midnight, they got rolled onto another flatbed truck. The off-loading at Pearl and the loading at Hickam had both gone well, but, as Buzz recalls, not here. "First one method of getting onto the truck bed failed, then another wouldn't work, and finally on the third try in more than an hour, we bumped and swayed down onto the truck bed and were driven slowly into a brightly lit area and backed up window-first to another platform." At the window with the astronauts, Dr. Bill Carpentier gently quipped, "They can send men safely to the Moon and back, but they can't get the men off the airplane."

Finally safely on the back of the truck, they were driven across the tarmac to an awaiting crowd of several thousand people and a host of television cameras. The mayor of Houston, Louis Welch, addressed the astronauts, as did MSC head Bob Gilruth. "Everybody was assembled to greet us," Armstrong remembers, including the crew's wives and children. The astronauts spoke to their loved ones through special small red telephone hookups. Neil does not recall what he said specifically to Janet or the boys, or what they said to him, except "glad to have you back."

Not until 1:30 A.M. did the truck leave Ellington and head slowly down NASA Road 1 to the Manned Spacecraft Center. Regardless of the late hour, people were still clamoring in the street. It was not until around 2:30 that they arrived at the Lunar Receiving Laboratory, where they were to spend the rest of their twenty-one-day quarantine. With its special air-conditioning system, no air was supposed to escape from the LRL without passing through a number of filters and pumps.

The Lunar Receiving Laboratory was safe, secure, and quiet. Besides private bedrooms for each crew member, it had a kitchen and a dining area. It also had a large living room and recreation area where, besides a television, recent Hollywood movies were projected on a big screen.

Besides those who had been in the MQF, the population of the LRL included two cooks, a NASA public relations officer, another doctor who was a lab specialist, and a janitor. It was big enough to accommodate everyone without crowding the astronauts. NASA had even agreed to embed a journalist, John Macleish, who issued a stream of communiqués. (Before the flight, the Apollo 11 crew had complained unsuccessfully to Slayton about including any member of the press.) Accidental exposure to potential contamination in an adjoining laboratory dealing with the Moon rocks drew six more individuals into the merry band—including a very pretty twenty-four-year-old woman. Buzz remembers that the appearance of the first female in what had been an all-male group caused quite a stir, especially when it was learned she was assigned the room next to Collins's. "It turned out after her arrival that there was, well, something questionable about her contamination. The quarantined area had a special phone for families to call in and our lady arrival had not so much as entered when she got a telephone call from her boyfriend. We were all suspicious. Had she expected to be contaminated in advance?"

On that same phone, Neil made his first calls to his family. Viola remembered, "Praise the Lord, it was so good to hear his voice. I remember our conversation went something like this, 'Hello.' 'Hello, Mom, this is Neil.' 'Oh, honey, how are you?' 'Oh, I'm just fine. All three of us are just fine. It was wonderful. None of us got sick, and all of the machinery worked.' 'You said it was pretty up there.' 'Oh, it was fantastically beautiful. The surface is covered with a black dust, and it got all over our nice, clean white suits and wouldn't brush off.' 'I'm so sorry that Daddy isn't here. He just left for the farm.' 'Tell him we are okay.' 'Here is Grandma.' 'Hello, Neil, how are you?' 'Hello, Grandma, I'm fine. I'll be seeing you pretty soon. Take care.' 'I will. Neil, it is so good to hear your voice.' Then I said, 'I'll bet it felt great to take a good bath.' " (Viola then remembered Neil saying, "As a matter of fact, Mom, we haven't been permitted to take a bath yet. They did let us wash our faces, but we had to keep the water and the washcloth to be analyzed." Either Viola heard him wrong or Neil was putting her on, because all three astronauts took turns taking showers as soon as they got in the MQF.) "He continued, 'Well, I'll be seeing you pretty soon.' Then our exchange of 'loves and good-byes' and the call was over. My, my, we just thanked God in heaven right then and there."

Mike and Buzz eventually found the time inside the LRL almost insufferably boring, but not Neil; he welcomed the refuge from the turmoil now surrounding them. "We really needed that time to be able to do all of the debriefings and talk to all the various systems guys. The subsequent Apollo crews were very interested in this question and that question that had to do with their own mission planning—what they thought they might reasonably do and whether we had ideas on how they might improve their own flights. Mostly, the discussion revolved around what was doable on the surface, because that affected the planning substantially. So that time was very valuable to us personally, as well as to everyone else. Of course, we would have liked to have been with our families, and we were prevented from that. But we knew they were not far away. All the uncertainty was gone now."

The days in the LRL also gave them plenty of time to review batch after batch of mission photographs that were being developed and printed by a special MSC photo lab. "Those were dribbling in to us a few at a time," Neil recollects. "They would run one roll of film and, as soon as that was ready, they would get copies of them to us. As we went through the pictures themselves, a lot of questions also came up that the other flight crews were interested in having answers to. The photos helped them ask their questions and helped us answer them." Some of the debriefings required the astronauts to write out long pilot reports covering their special responsibilities in the mission; other debriefings were filmed in a room resembling a TV control booth, the astronauts sitting at a table opposite questioners behind a glass wall. The mission was documented down to the minutest detail, resulting in 527 pages of single-spaced transcripts.

On August 5, the LRL chef surprised Neil with a cake on his thirty-ninth birthday.

Near the end of their stay, each astronaut, as federal government employees, was asked to fill out an expense report for their flight to the Moon. Filled out for them to sign, the forms read: "From Houston, Tex., to Cape Kennedy, Fla., to the Moon, to the Pacific Ocean to Hawaii and return to Houston, Tex." The astronauts had traveled by "Government Aircraft, Government Spacecraft, USN Hornet, USAF Plane." Their total reimbursement was for $33.31.

Only one time during the quarantine did any tension simmer between the three astronauts. It came when Aldrin, during the debriefings, elaborated at extensive lengths on the phenomenon of the flashing lights that all three of them had seen during the outbound journey. Buzz sensed Neil's growing irritation. "Neil began to look doubtful and annoyed whenever the flashes were discussed. . . . When the feeling finally became apparent to me in the Lunar Receiving Laboratory, I quickly suppressed it. Although it was never stated officially, it went without saying that rivalries or arguments within the astronaut corps were not discussed in public because it would tarnish both our image as individuals and the image of the space program."

As busy as they were with the debriefings, day after day in seclusion gave Armstrong and his mates plenty of time to think about their future with the space program; one day Deke even directed them to consider whether or not they wanted to return to flight status. Neil thought it was too early to come to any conclusion, though he hoped he would be able to fly again.

The men also considered how all the glamour and publicity would affect their personal and professional lives, and the lives of their families. Just prior to reentry, Jim Lovell had warned the Apollo 11 astronauts, "Backup crew is still standing by. I just want to remind you that the most difficult part of your mission is going to be after recovery."

Armstrong understood Lovell's message, as he thinks back to it today: "We were not naïve, but we could never have guessed what the volume and intensity of public interest would turn out to be. It certainly was going to be more than anything any of us had experienced before in previous activities of flight. And it was."

Their quarantine blissfully came to an end at 9:00 on Sunday evening, August 10. By then, even Neil was very ready for it to be over. Going back to the restrictions the crew had been placed under days prior to the launch, they had been in physical seclusion for over a month. Outside the LRL, a

NASA staff car and driver waited to drive them home individually. The crew of Apollo 11 went their separate ways, but not for long.

Their short trips home that night presaged the astronauts' lot for years to come. The moment each car passed through the NASA gate, a different TV crew pulled behind to follow the famous passengers. Reporters and photographers awaited them in front of their residences.

Neil wanted none of it, certainly not then. As soon as his NASA car pulled into his driveway, he bolted for the front door. Janet was waiting to shut it quickly behind him.

Armstrong's life on the dark side of the Moon had begun.

CHAPTER 31

For All Mankind

A month or so before the launch of Apollo 11, Armstrong, at the request of *Life* magazine, reflected on the meaning of the Moon landing:

"It would be presumptuous of me to pick out a single thing that history will identify as a result of this mission. But I would say that it will enlighten the human race and help us all to comprehend that we are an important part of a much bigger universe than we can normally see from the front porch. I would hope that it will help individuals, the world over, to think in a proper perspective about the various endeavors of mankind as a whole. Perhaps going to the Moon and back in itself isn't all that important. But it is a big enough step to give people a new dimension in their thinking—a sort of enlightenment.

"After all, the Earth itself is a spacecraft. It's an odd kind of spacecraft, since it carries its crew on the outside instead of the inside. But it's pretty small. And it's cruising in an orbit around the Sun. It's cruising in an orbit around the center of a galaxy that's cruising in some unknown orbit, in some unknown direction and at some unspecified velocity, but with a tremendous rate of change, position, and environment.

"It's hard for us to get far enough away from this scene to see what's happening. If you're in the middle of a crowd, the crowd appears to extend in every direction as far as you can see. You have to step back and look down from the Washington Monument or something like that to see that you're really pretty close to the edge of the crowd, and that the whole picture is quite a bit different from the way it looks when you are in the middle of all those people.

"From our position on the Earth it is difficult to observe where the Earth is and where it's going, or what its future course might be. Hopefully, by getting a little farther away, both in the real sense and the figurative sense, we'll be able to make some people step back and reconsider their mission in the universe, to think of themselves as a group of people who constitute the crew of a spaceship going through the universe. If you're going to run a spaceship, you've got to be pretty cautious about how you use your resources, how you use your crew, and how you treat your spacecraft.

"Hopefully the trips we will be making in the next couple of decades will open up our eyes a little. When you are looking at the Earth from the lunar distance, its atmosphere is just unobservable. The atmosphere is so thin, and such a minute part of the Earth, that it can't be sensed at all. That should impress everyone. The atmosphere of the Earth is a small and valuable resource. We're going to have to learn how to conserve it and use it wisely. Down here in the crowd you are aware of the atmosphere and it seems adequate, so you don't worry about it too much. But from a different vantage point, perhaps it is possible to understand more easily why we should be worrying."

Few people ever accused Neil of being a philosopher. In the months following *Columbia*'s return to Earth, Armstrong and his two crewmates would be asked almost endlessly to express themselves about the Moon landing and its meaning for history and the global community. By all accounts, Neil, center stage, performed superbly well. Even today his first wife Janet, who accompanied him on all the immediate post–Apollo 11 goodwill trips, proudly relates that Neil was "never comfortable speaking . . . but he did it, and he did a great job of it."

Post-quarantine, Neil stayed at home one full day to take refuge from reporters. As a matter of courtesy, the legitimate press had agreed to leave all three of the astronauts alone until Wednesday, though casual onlookers and paparazzi continued to stake out the crew's homes. One carload of photographers pursued Aldrin and his wife, en route to buy him a new suit for what was to be a one-day, coast-to-coast Apollo 11 celebration tour, even after Aldrin diverted into Ellington Air Force Base. "It's an open base and we can't restrict anyone," said the gate guard. Neil spent that Monday indoors, catching up on personal mail, visiting with the family, and watching Janet get herself and the boys ready to join the cross-country trip. The next day he returned to his office at the Manned Spacecraft Center, where huge bags of mail awaited some reply.

That same afternoon the first postlanding press conference was held in the MSC auditorium. Computer program alarms, the fuel situation during the lunar descent, and the other problems involved in the landing dominated the questions, which then turned to Neil's unique experiences. Asked if there was ever a moment on the Moon when he was "just a little spellbound by what was going on," Neil replied with a smile, "about two and a half hours." Asked about the primary difficulty during the EVA, he offered, "We had the problems of a five-year-old boy in a candy store. There were just too many things to do." Asked what he thought about the imminent three-cities-in-one-day tour to New York, Chicago, and Los Angeles, Neil shook his head slowly and admitted it was "certainly the last thing we're prepared for."

At five A.M. the next morning, Wednesday, September 13, the Armstrong family of four, the Collins family of five, and the Aldrin family of five boarded the transport jet *Air Force 2,* which President Nixon had sent to Houston for the trip. Mike and Neil spent the flight preparing their speeches (Buzz's unease with extemporaneous speaking had motivated him to begin days in advance). At La Guardia Airport, Mayor John Lindsay and his wife greeted their honored guests, then flew them by helicopter to a pier near Wall Street in full view of a salute by a flotilla of fireboats. A string of open convertibles waited for them. Into the lead car went the three astronauts, followed by a security car, a car with the wives, another security car, a car with all eight of the astronauts' children, and yet another security car. Buzz remembers, "We were advised not to reach out to shake hands because we could be pulled from cars and couldn't be rescued easily."

Not even the revelry at the end of World War II or the parade for Lindbergh in 1927 matched in size the New York City celebration for the lunar astronauts. A blizzard of ticker tape enveloped their parade as it moved between the skyscrapers—the so-called Canyon of Heroes—through the Financial District, along Broadway and Park Avenue, past a Manhattan-record turnout of an estimated four million.

"I had never seen so many people in my life," Janet exclaims, remembering "people cheering and waving and dropping confetti that floated down from everywhere out of buildings, from out of the sky."

"They also threw out IBM punch cards," Neil adds. "Sometimes they threw a whole stack of punch cards from the eighty-seventh floor of a building, and, when they didn't come apart, it made like a brick. We had a couple of dents in our car from cards that didn't quite open."

At City Hall, the handsome Mayor Lindsay presented them with keys to the city, and all three astronauts made brief remarks, Buzz saying how the footprints he and Neil had left on the Moon belonged to all mankind, and presented the city with a framed picture Neil had taken on the Moon. Then onward they went to the United Nations, where they shook hands with Secretary-General U Thant. The crew received a book of commemorative stamps representing all the UN member nations. Neil was the only astronaut to speak.

As wild as the crowds were in New York, they were wilder in Chicago. By the time the parade of open limousines crept its way down Michigan Avenue and State Street to the Windy City's massive new Civic Center, Aldrin recalls, "we were covered with confetti and streamers and perspiring so much that they were glued to us. We were deaf from the shouting, and jaws ached from smiling." Following a public ceremony at Richard J. Daley's City Hall—where the rough-mannered boss mayor directed the astronauts' photo shoot by saying, "Hey you, over here"—the astronauts were surprised to find themselves, before heading to O'Hare International Airport, in Grant Park to address a gathering of some 15,000 young people.

"It was exciting to be in these cities as there was electricity in the air from the joy these people were expressing on behalf of the achievement," Janet notes. Neil explains, "That's probably the first time we had seen such large aggregations of people . . . *really* a lot of people. It was just one event after another, big parades, ending up with the Nixon state dinner in Beverly Hills."

Arriving at Los Angeles International Airport, the plane was met by Mayor Sam Yorty, then helicopters took the party to the posh Century Plaza Hotel. The children of the three astronauts would not be attending the black-tie affair, instead partaking of a spread of hamburgers, French fries, and chocolate malts in front of a color TV tuned to the live telecast.

President Nixon, his wife Patricia, and their two grown-up daughters Julie and Tricia hosted the astronauts and their wives in their presidential suite prior to joining dinner guests Mamie Eisenhower, widow of the former president; Esther Goddard, widow of rocket pioneer Robert Goddard; Chief Justice and Mrs. Warren E. Burger; former Vice President and Mrs. Hubert H. Humphrey (among the few Democrats invited); Arizona senator and 1964 Republican presidential nominee Barry Goldwater; and current Vice President Spiro Agnew and his wife. Government notables filled the high-domed and elegantly chandeliered banquet hall: NASA and other space program officials, more Cabinet members than sometimes attended Cabinet meetings, governors of forty-four states (including California governor Ronald Reagan), members of the Joint Chiefs of Staff, diplomatic corps members representing eighty-three nations, and a battery of Congressional leaders. U.S. and international aviation pioneers were represented by Jimmy Doolittle, the man who had headed the NACA when Neil began his government career in 1955, Wernher von Braun, and Willy Messerschmitt. From Hollywood and show business came entertainers Rudy Vallee, Gene Autry, Jimmy Stewart, Bob Hope, Red Skelton, Rosalind Russell, Art Linkletter, and a score of others. Evangelist Reverend Billy Graham was there. Howard Hughes and Charles Lindbergh had been invited, but neither aviator came out of his self-imposed seclusion to attend. Ironically, not a single member of the Kennedy family attended, indebted as was the occasion to the inspiration of former President John Kennedy. On July 18, the day Apollo 11 approached lunar orbit, Massachusetts Senator Edward "Ted" Kennedy following a party had plunged off a bridge at Chappaquiddick Island, near Martha's Vineyard, an accident that had killed twenty-eight-year-old campaign worker Mary Jo Kopechne.

While the Kennedys remained in seclusion, peace and antipoverty protestors did not, waging an orderly demonstration outside the hotel where a fleet of black limousines—glistening Cadillacs, Imperials, Continentals, and Rolls-Royces—sat in the parking lot. To the protestors the glory of Apollo 11 was temporary or shallow, or both. The mood of Vietnam-era America remained highly agitated, and these particular taxpayers were not eager to pick up the tab for Nixon's $43,000-plus gala, with its 1,440 guests, the menu including garden peas shelled by hand to prevent bruising. The president himself had approved the menu right down to the *claire de lune* dessert, a sphere of dimpled ice cream topped with a tiny American flag.

After the meal, Vice President Agnew, the chairman of the administration's National Aeronautics and Space Council, presented the three astronauts with the Medal of Freedom, the nation's highest civilian honor, for their participation in "a unique and profoundly important adventure . . . Their undertaking will be remembered as long as men wonder and dream and search for truth on this planet and among the stars." Flight controller Steve Bales, who, according to his citation that night, "made the decision to proceed with the lunar landing when computers failed just before *Eagle*'s landing on the Sea of Tranquility," earned a Medal of Freedom of his own. As factually misleading as that citation was, Bales's honor was an important symbolic gesture on behalf of the estimated 400,000 persons who had contributed to the Apollo program.

When it came Armstrong's turn to address the throng, he was, by all accounts, emotional: "Neil Armstrong choked back tears as he groped for words to tell America how the Apollo 11 astronauts feel about their country and the honor it has given them," opened the UPI wire coverage. And *Time* magazine reported, "Neil Armstrong's words to President Nixon in Los Angeles last week seemed all the more eloquent because they were unstudied, and because for once the usually phlegmatic voice of the first man on the Moon quavered with emotion."

"We were very privileged to leave on the Moon a plaque endorsed by you, Mr. President, saying, 'For all mankind.' Perhaps in the third millennium a wayward stranger will read the plaque at Tranquility Base. We'll let history mark that this was the age in which that became a fact. I was struck this morning in New York by a proudly waved but uncarefully scribbled sign. It said: 'Through you, we touched the Moon.' It was our privilege today to touch America. I suspect that perhaps the most warm, genuine feeling that all of us could receive came through the cheers and shouts and, most of all, the smiles of our fellow Americans. We hope and think that those people shared our belief that this is the beginning of a new era—the beginning of an era when man understands the universe around him, and the beginning of the era when man understands himself."

No one in the audience was prouder of Neil than his own family. "My parents were there as guests," Neil relates, "as well my grandmother and sister and brother and their families. I had very little time to see them, but they were there. It was an impressive occasion for everyone."

On Saturday, an estimated 250,000 gathered in Houston (a city of only 1.2 million in 1969)—"Spacetown USA"—to throw ticker tape, confetti, and enough "Moon certificates," fake $100 and $1,000 bills, to cover the streets in two to three feet of litter. The ultimate Texas barbecue was held in the Astrodome for a by-invitation-only crowd of 55,000. Placards in the grandstands read: "You've come a long way, baby. Welcome home," and "We're proud of y'all." Frank Sinatra served as master of ceremonies and entertained with singer Dionne Warwick and comedians Bill ("Jose Jimenez") Dana and Flip Wilson, all of them big stars in 1969.

The day before the parade, Neil, Mike, and Buzz had taped NBC's *Meet the Press* for Sunday morning broadcast, a morning they were also to appear live on CBS's *Face the Nation*. It was in that interview that Cronkite raised with Neil Madalyn Murray O'Hair's statements about his religious beliefs.

In regard to the crew's future as part of the U.S. space program, Neil answered: "Oh, I have no idea what the future is going to hold for each of us, Walter, but I know that the next ten years and the next several decades are going to be even more exciting than the past decade." Pressed for specifics, the commander of Apollo 11 continued, "We have always been poor prophets, Walter. We underestimate. We can do much more in ten years than we would expect. And if we judge that will probably be true, then I think in ten years we will be looking at the planets."

Presaging a recommendation early the following month by a presidentially appointed Space Task Group chaired by Vice President Agnew, Armstrong expounded, "I am quite certain that goals of the Mars variety are within our range, should we choose to decide to make that investment of our national resources. I think it is certainly possible, since a planetary trip always involves a long duration flight, that initial flights to the planets—that is, particularly circumplanetary, nonlanding, but exploratory flights—can be combined with Earth orbiting spacecraft [i.e., some sort of space station] to develop that long-term capability with the very same type of spacecraft. So that would certainly be a contender, in my view.

"We know how to go to Mars. Clearly, our recent unmanned observations of Mars [by Mariner 6 and 7] have shown that we know how to go there, and I think we can equally well return. There are some variations in the method that might be used."

Armstrong elaborated: "We might very well use an intermediate point [instead of flying directly from the Earth to Mars]. I meant to imply that the navigation and the method of the traverse—the geometry of the trajectory—is known." Asked by Howard Benedict of the Associated Press whether man can survive for months on end in space, Neil replied, "I should say, Howard, that I certainly enjoyed the entire trip, and I had no hesitation about living in that environment for a considerably longer period.

"I would like to take a trip of [up to two years], and perhaps a considerably larger vehicle would allow us to take the families along. . . . Certainly there is historical precedent . . . even [with] our present maritime vehicles."

To what had become the perennial Space Age question of how to balance the dreams of exploration with realities here on Earth, Neil raised the stakes for all: "We do have, and will continue to have, an unquenchable curiosity to understand our solar system, and I am quite sure, now that we believe that it is within our means to look, we will, and it is just a matter of time now of *when* you will do it, not *whether* you will do it.

"Now, assuming that it will be done at some point, it is just a question of what is the order. I think it is important to say that a spacecraft that is able to fly tomorrow, that is able to transfer itself around between planets, that same spacecraft can probably go to nearly any of the planets, with the same configuration, the same type of spacecraft. So such an exploring vehicle would not be limited just to what we know about Mars but be more a truth-searching vehicle that could go to any of the planets and find out things of substance." In other words, Armstrong was thinking of an interplanetary vehicle, no doubt unmanned, very much like the two Voyager spacecraft that would begin their "Grand Tour" of the planets in 1977.

Ending the program, correspondent David Schoumacher of CBS News asked all three astronauts whether—and when—they would return to space. Collins announced that Apollo 11 was his last flight; Aldrin antici-pated a future Apollo mission. Neil said, "I am available to serve in any ca-pacity that they feel I can contribute best. . . . I would certainly hope that my technical abilities are the things that I would use most."

Returning to Houston, Neil had a question that the governor of Colorado ultimately answered. "I was looking for a place to get away for a week's va-cation." That question got to Colorado governor John Love. The governor remembered a place in the remote southwestern part of the state where he had done some hunting. It was called Sleeping Indian Ranch and was owned by fifty-six-year-old Harry Combs, the chief of aircraft distributor Combs Gates Denver, Inc. (a subsidiary of Gates Aviation Corp.), who had attended the Apollo 11 launch with the governor.

Just weeks before his death in 2004, Harry Combs recalled the gover-nor's telephone call: " 'How would you like to have Neil Armstrong come stay at your ranch for a week?' And I said, 'It was yesterday when I'd like to have him!' And the governor said, 'He can't go to a dude ranch. They will mob him and murder him! I told the FBI I knew just the place.' "

Flying in to Sleeping Indian Ranch, near the Continental Divide, was, in very different ways, about as challenging as landing *Eagle* on the Sea of Tranquility. "My mountain landing strip was pretty tight—you could only fly in one way and you had to fly out the other. So, Neil showed up in his Bo-nanza with his family, and I was flagging him in wearing my cowboy outfit. I could just see his wife's hand just waving and shaking, all hysterical like. It was quite a trip in to the place!

"We gave them the whole top floor. It was just a rough little ranch, but it was gorgeous country. We were loaded with game—bear and deer—with a stream full of trout, and Neil enjoyed that. I took him and his boys up in the high country, where we saw bands of elk.

"Me and my wife kept absolutely still about it. If we had ever talked [to the neighbors], they would have ripped the thing right open. We took him into town for dinner and never let anybody know. People didn't recognize him. I remember a cop stopped us in the car—he pulled me over for making a wrong turn or something. He didn't notice it was Neil in there, and we never let on for a second."

A week of near-total relaxation in Colorado's mountain air bolstered Neil and Janet mentally and physically for the incredibly frenetic schedule to come. It began in Wapakoneta, where the good people of Armstrong's hometown were not about to be left out of the national celebration. The town's big day came—as it did for the residents of Montclair, New Jersey, Buzz's hometown, and of New Orleans, Mike's adopted hometown—on Saturday, September 6, 1969.

Wapakoneta's was by the far the largest of the hometown events. Area newspaper headlines previewed Neil's return: "Moonwalker Coming Home to Wapak," "Wapakoneta Bursting at the Seams," and "Wapak Wild! Hot Dogs Selling 3 for $1." More than five hundred police officers were brought in. Service stations ran out of gasoline. A local movie theater stayed open all night free of charge to give visitors a place to rest as they awaited the festivities. With Cleveland native Bob Hope serving as the parade's grand marshal (along with his wife Delores) and other special guests including TV star Ed McMahon and Dr. Albert B. Sabin, the developer of the oral polio vaccine, the arriving crowd numbered in excess of ten times that of the town's normal 7,000 population. (That compared to 15,000 that attended the Wapakoneta parade following Neil's Gemini VIII mission.) Neil's Purdue University Marching Band with its Golden Girl provided music. Ohio governor James Rhodes, whose attendance was prominent (overly so, in the view of some locals), sent one of his aides to help coordinate plans to the best advantage of Columbus.

The small town was wrapped almost entirely in red, white, and blue bunting. Streets along the parade route were renamed for their favorite son—"Lift-Off Lane," "Apollo Drive," "Eagle Boulevard"—in the tradition of "Neil Armstrong Drive," site of the senior Armstrongs' residence. Downtown headquarters, directed by Charles Brading Jr., the son of Neil's boyhood employer, welcomed visitors (and some 350 credentialed journalists) to "Tranquility Base." Heading the Neil Armstrong Homecoming VIP Committee was Fred Fisher, Neil's boyhood friend whose little sister was Neil's first Karen.

To this day, locals recall the events to minute detail. Ned Keiber remembers, "We, his classmates, didn't get to see the parade because we had to go out to the county fairground. It was tough because we were sitting in ninety-degree heat. When the parade arrived, we made two lines so when Neil got out of his car, we acted like security. He walked between our two lines, as did Bob Hope and Neil's mother and dad. Neil's dad shook hands with every single one of us. The whole parade just stopped and backed everything up. I never forgot that."

Bob Hope kept the crowd in stitches, Neil's good friend Arthur Frame remembered prior to his passing in 2003. "One of Hope's jokes was about how well Neil had adjusted since returning from space: 'But he keeps throwing his shoes out the window and eating his toothpaste.' " In another joke, addressed to Janet Armstrong, Hope quipped, "It must be tough to sleep with a man who keeps murmuring 'Buzz, Buzz.' "

Alma Lou-Shaw Kuffner, Neil's prom date, remembers that Neil, in addressing the crowd, was not nearly as stiff as he had been during his Gemini VIII homecoming, "Everyone wanted him to spout these great words of wisdom."

The Brading family drugstore, with young Neil Armstrong's signature on one of its interior walls, was a prime media destination. Charles Brading's executive homecoming committee presented Neil with a town roll mounted on a board from a cross-cut oak table donated by Grandma Korspeter. Governor Rhodes announced—though Neil himself had yet to be consulted—that the State of Ohio would be moving forward with plans to build a Neil Armstrong Museum in Wapakoneta.

Neil took it all in very good humor, content to repeat what he had told them during his visit back in 1966, "I'm proud to stand before you today and consider myself one of you." Then, to the delight of his mostly Ohio audience, he added that though news reports indicated that he and Buzz had not found anything "organic" on the lunar surface, "I think you know better now. There was a Buckeye on the Moon."

From Wapakoneta Neil and Janet flew to Washington, leaving the boys with Neil's parents. On Monday the ninth of September they attended NASA's Apollo 11 Splashdown Party at the Shoreham Hotel, preceded by the formal unveiling at the U.S. Post Department of the commemorative Moon landing stamp, the ten-cent stamp that Neil and Buzz canceled after they got back into *Columbia* on July 22. The following week the Armstrongs returned to Washington, where the Apollo 11 crew was to be honored at a midday joint session of Congress. Promptly at noon, the astronauts were led by a bipartisan delegation up to seats on the Speaker's rostrum. Following a long and loud standing ovation, Armstrong stepped first to the microphone:

"Mr. Speaker, Mr. President, members of Congress, distinguished guests:

"We are greatly honored that you have invited us here today. Only now have we completed our journey to land on and explore the Moon and return. It was here in these halls that our venture really began. Here the Space Act of 1958 was framed, the chartering document of the National Aeronautics and Space Administration. And here in the years that followed the key decisions that permitted the successive steps of Mercury and Gemini and Apollo were made.

"Your policies and the marvels of modern communication have permitted people around the world to share the excitement of our exploration. And, although you have been informed of the results of Apollo 11, we are particularly pleased to have this opportunity to complete our work by reporting to you and through you to the American people. My colleagues share the honor of presenting this report."

Neil then introduced Buzz, followed by Mike, to the great chamber. After their remarks, he took the podium to offer the crew's final thoughts:

"We landed on the Sea of Tranquility in the cool of the early lunar morning, when the long shadows would aid our perception. The Sun was only ten degrees above the horizon. While the Earth turned through nearly a full day during our stay, the Sun at Tranquility Base rose barely eleven degrees—a small fraction of the monthlong lunar day. There was a peculiar sensation of the duality of time—the swift rush of events that characterizes all our lives—and the ponderous parade which marks the aging of the universe.

"Both kinds of time were evident—the first by the routine events of the flight, whose planning and execution were detailed to fractions of a second—the latter by rocks around us, unchanged throughout the history of man—whose three-billion-year-old secrets made them the treasure we sought.

"The plaque on the *Eagle* which summarized our hopes bears this message: 'Here men from the planet Earth first set foot upon the Moon. July 1969 A.D. We came in peace for all mankind.'

"Those nineteen hundred and sixty-nine years had constituted the majority of the Age of Pisces, a twelfth of the great year that is measured by the thousand generations the precession of the Earth's axis requires to scribe a giant circle in the heavens.

"In the next twenty centuries, the Age of Aquarius of the great year, the age for which our young people have such high hopes, humanity may begin to understand its most baffling mystery: Where are we going?

"The Earth is, in fact, traveling many thousands of miles per hour in the direction of the constellation Hercules—to some unknown destination in the cosmos. Man must understand his universe in order to understand his destiny.

"Mystery, however, is a very necessary ingredient in our lives. Mystery creates wonder, and wonder is the basis for man's desire to understand. Who knows what mysteries will be solved in our lifetime, and what new riddles will become the challenge of the new generations?

"Science has not mastered prophecy. We predict too much for the next year yet far too little for the next ten. Responding to challenge is one of democracy's great strengths. Our successes in space lead us to hope that this strength can be used in the next decade in the solution of many of our planet's problems.

"Several weeks ago I enjoyed the warmth of reflection on the true meanings of the spirit of Apollo. I stood in the highlands of this nation, near the Continental Divide, introducing to my sons the wonders of nature, and pleasures of looking for deer and for elk. In their enthusiasm for the view, they frequently stumbled on the rocky trails, but when they looked only to their footing, they did not see the elk.

"To those of you who have advocated looking high, we owe our sincere gratitude, for you have granted us the opportunity to see some of the grandest views of the Creator. To those of you who have been our honest critics, we also thank, for you have reminded us that we dare not forget to watch the trail.

"We carried on Apollo 11 two flags of this Union that had flown over the Capital, one over the House of Representatives, one over the Senate. It is our privilege to return them now in these halls which exemplify man's highest purpose—to serve one's fellow man.

"We thank you on behalf of all the men of Apollo, for giving us the privilege of joining you in serving—for all mankind."

With thunderous applause, the U.S. Congress seemed poised to vote strong support for the future of the space program. That was not to be.

Instead, the astronauts were treated to a nadir of political influence. Standing in the Senate cloakroom prior to their appearance before the joint session, the three had decided to make a quick bathroom stop. The heroic crew of Apollo 11 were occupied at urinals when Democratic congressman L. Mendel Rivers of South Carolina, chairman of the Armed Services Committee and a key supporter of the space program, approached, pen and commemorative stamped envelopes in hand. Aldrin remembers, "We zipped up, lined up, signed our sincerest greetings, and returned to the cloakroom. Neil looked annoyed. Mike's face was red with embarrassment, and I was shaking my head in disbelief."

Immediately following their speeches, the trio was confronted with seven cameras and a complex of small lights manned by a grinning Japanese photographer charged with creating three-dimensional portraits in light and shadow. Unbeknownst to the astronauts, the Japanese embassy had commissioned busts of each one of the astronauts, statues that would be presented to the astronauts when they visited Japan during their forthcoming around-the-world tour in October.

Following the photo shoot, the wives and families of congressmen awaited the astronauts' narration of Apollo 11. Remembers Aldrin, "No one had previously mentioned this to any of us. My reaction was tempered by my elation of the moment, but both Mike and Neil were justifiably furious." Buzz recalls, "We raised hell" with NASA Headquarters for letting the session run for over two hours.

The next morning's State Department briefing afforded the crew's first details on their impending world tour of a minimum of twenty-three countries in forty-five days. Logistics of travel aboard Air Force Two would be managed by a "support team" of six PR officers from the space agency, a White House representative, two men from the United States Information Agency, two secretaries, a doctor, a baggage man, two full-time security officers, a photographer-cameraman, plus four men from the Voice of America.

The astronauts ranked their stated objective "to demonstrate goodwill to all people in the world and to stress that what we had done was for all mankind," over State Department and NASA agendas "to visit the American embassies anxious to score social coups." "We would take care of Americans in America," they insisted at the briefing.

The tour called "Giant Step" pledged to go "around the world to emphasize the willingness of the United States to share its space knowledge." The trip would kick off from Houston on September 29, then travel to Mexico City, Bogotá, Buenos Aires, Rio de Janeiro, Grand Canary Island, Madrid, Paris, Amsterdam, Brussels, Oslo, Cologne, Berlin, London, Rome, Belgrade, Ankara, Kinshasa (Congo), Tehran, Bombay, Dacca, Bangkok, Darwin (Australia), Sydney, Guam, Seoul, Tokyo, Honolulu, and back to Houston.

Neil did not keep a diary of the trip as George Low had for the Latin American tour three years earlier, but he did tape-record a travelogue.

On October 8 in Paris, France, Neil reported, "A representative of the Aero Club of France gave us their gold medal, which had previously only been given to the Wright Brothers and Charles Lindbergh from America and it had been given to no other crews from spaceflights. I responded with some remarks concerning recollection of that welcome by Charles Lindbergh."

Janet, who herself had "a wonderful trip" representing her country, has a particularly distinct memory of the visit to Belgium and the Netherlands, regarding meeting the two kings and two queens in one day: "That was really something. We had lunch with one and dinner with the next one. We were told you were never supposed to turn your back on a king or a queen. Well, Mike Collins got caught in a situation in Belgium where the king was ahead of him and the queen was behind him and Mike was in between and so he had to sidestep up twenty-five or thirty stairs in the palace. He was just so good about it. We all joked about that later." On the way back to the hotel, Collins reportedly said, "I think I broke my goddamn ankle!"

Attendance at a "typical press conference" numbered, as it did in Cologne and Bonn, Germany, on October 12, "a thousand or more people." The next day in Berlin assembled "an extremely large crowd estimated as two hundred thousand to three hundred thousand, but I expect it to be probably closer to a million. We proceeded upstairs to a gigantic reception for a thousand people. There was so many people and it was so poorly controlled that we detoured into a side room, waved to the assembled crowd from the balcony along with the mayor, and began our escape."

On October 14 in London, England, he noted, "We had canceled our two scheduled TV programs, with BBC and an independent network, and did only the press conference on television. Because of colds and laryngitis. . . . All the press reports [led] with our bleary eyes and sore throats."

About the cancellation of the television programs in London, Neil today recalls: "That ruffled a few feathers, but we had to keep from getting absolutely worn into the ground, and I thought we were getting there. I thought it was irresponsible to ask us to be on television for three hours," Aldrin remembers that Dr. Bill Carpentier "was conned into going on television" to state that the astronauts were "exhausted." It was "the only way out of big trouble" with the British TV networks.

One incident from the Congo on October 22–23 that Armstrong decided not to comment on in his journal was an embarrassing moment at the evening ball when Aldrin jumped from the dais and cut in on Miss Congo, who was dancing with her escort. Buzz later described what happened: "The bandleader noticed and picked up a faster beat. The dancers all moved back to watch. Neil, it turned out, disapproved of my obviously spontaneous participation. Nick Ruhe [from NASA public affairs] and [the State Department's] Bill Der Bung . . . thought it was a genuine and honest move. The newspapers loved it. Neil subsequently came around." Today Neil comments: "Some people would say that was great and others would say that it wasn't. That was one occasion when some people questioned whether that was really the right thing to be doing. I don't know myself whether it was really good or not. I wouldn't have done it, but I can't say that it was wrong to have done it."

It was not the only incident during the tour involving Aldrin, as he himself admitted in his autobiography. As early as the stop in Bogotá, Dr. Carpentier had prescribed anti-anxiety pills for Buzz. One night in Norway Buzz felt so depressed he had stayed in his room all evening while all the others, including his wife, went out to dinner. Buzz wrote that this was the only night of the trip that he drank too much, but the problem for him was "there was liquor everywhere," "bottles of scotch or gin in every hotel room, a jug of mimosas on the breakfast tray every morning." In Rome, attending "an elegant party right out of *La Dolce Vita* at Gina Lollobrigida's," minus Joan, Buzz did not return to their hotel room until after dawn and was "in the doghouse" for the rest of the day. Later, in Iran, the couple had "one of the more memorable fights" of their marriage; Buzz remembers, "I was informed either begin to stay at home more or plan to move out."

Both Collins and Armstrong knew that something serious was bothering their crewmate. "The trip produced some disturbing symptoms in Buzz," Mike has written, "causing him to withdraw into stony-faced silence from time to time," resulting in "obvious stress" to Joan. Neil today remembers different indications of an onset of depression but "wasn't smart enough to recognize the problem. . . . It bothered me then, and bothers me now, that I wasn't up to the job. I've thought to myself, Had I been more observant or more attentive, I might have noted something that could have helped Buzz's situation, and I failed to do that. It was sometime after the tour that he started having real problems."

Whether any of Buzz's depression was a carryover from how he felt about Neil being deemed the first man on the Moon is unclear, but there is no question that the situation still grated on him—and on his father. Back at the ceremonial unveiling of the ten-cent Apollo 11 stamp at the U.S. Post Office building in Washington just a few weeks earlier, Buzz had been chagrined to see that the stamp, which showed Neil stepping down onto the lunar surface, bore the caption "First Man on the Moon." Aldrin recalled in his autobiography, "Lord knows what prompted the caption under the stamp, but it caused me to feel rather useless and it positively infuriated my father . . . 'Men' would have been more accurate, and I must confess, my feelings were hurt."

Janet Armstrong feels that the fact that Neil made most of the toasts and did such an outstanding job as the crew's spokesman exacerbated Buzz's sense of being aggrieved. "It was hard to follow Neil—he always did so well. Buzz used notes and that bothered Buzz. He was not as comfortable speaking as Neil and Mike were. Neil was not comfortable speaking, either, but he did it, and he did a great job of it," as the tour continued from Tehran, where the astronauts visited the Shah of Iran, to Tokyo, where they were received by Emperor Hirohito.

Thus ended the astronauts' Giant Step forty-five-day world tour. After a fuel stop in Anchorage, Alaska, Air Force Two flew directly to the nation's capital. Shortly before landing at Dulles National, each astronaut received a memo parodying national protocols:

Your next stop is Washington, DC, USA. Here are a few helpful reminders. 1. The water is drinkable, although it is not the most popular native drink. 2. You can always expect student demonstrations. 3. Never turn your back on the President. 4. Never be seen with the Vice President. 5. If you leave your shoes outside the door, they will be stolen. 6. It is unsafe to walk on the street after dark. 7. Do not discuss the following sensitive issues with the natives: Vietnam War, Budget, Foreign Aid, Import-Exports. 8. Rate of exchange is .05 cents per one dollar (American).

On the White House lawn, with the Marine Band playing, President and Mrs. Nixon welcomed them home. That night the astronauts and their wives dined and slept at the White House. "The president was quite nice," Neil remembers. "He was very interested in everything we had to report about the tour, about the various leaders we had met, what their reaction was and what did they say. He had been trying for years to get a meeting with Romanian president Nicolae Ceausescu and after leaving the *Hornet* he was able to get an appointment. President Nixon said something to the effect, 'That meeting alone paid for everything we spent on the space program.'"

During dinner Nixon asked all three men in turn what they wanted to do next in their lives. Collins said he would like to continue doing goodwill work for the State Department, upon which, right at the table, Nixon instantly phoned Secretary of State William Rogers, asking him to get Mike set up. Aldrin told the president he felt he could contribute more by staying in technical work. When Nixon then asked the commander of Apollo 11 if he wouldn't like to serve somewhere as a goodwill ambassador, Neil politely said he, too, would be honored to serve as an ambassador, but he was not sure in what kind of role he could serve best. Nixon told him to think it over and requested a personal reply.

During Giant Step, between 100 million and 150 million people were estimated to have seen the astronauts, and as many as 25,000 of these actually shaking hands with them or receiving autographs. In the immediate aftermath of the trip, Armstrong certainly felt like it had done some good. Speaking to an audience at Ohio's Wittenberg College in November 1969, Neil said, "More can be gained from friendship than from technical knowledge," quite an admission coming from the devoted aeronautical engineer.

Armstrong next joined Bob Hope's Christmas 1969 USO tour to entertain the U.S. and allied troops in Vietnam, with stops along the way in Germany, Italy, Turkey, Taiwan, and Guam. Actresses Teresa Graves, Romy Schneider, Connie Stevens, Miss World 1969 (Eva Reuber-Staier), the "Golddiggers" showgirls, and Les Brown and His Band of Renown completed the cast.

Under Hope's tutelage, Armstrong, decked out in chino pants, a red sport shirt, and a jungle hat, often played the straight man:

Hope: *Your step on the Moon was the second most dangerous of the year.*

Neil: *Who took the most dangerous?*

Hope: *The girl who married Tiny Tim.* [Tiny Tim was a long-haired ukulele player with bad teeth and a very high-pitched voice who had become a pop icon because of his regular appearance on the TV show *Rowan and Martin's Laugh-In.*]

In his 1974 memoir *The Last Christmas Show,* Hope remembered the 1969 tour: "When Neil came out at the end of the shows for a question-and-answer free for all, the GIs wouldn't let him go. We had mikes set up in the audience and they bombarded him with questions. . . . Normally, when we finished a show, all the GIs would rush onstage to talk to the girls, get their autographs, and take their pictures. You know the sort of stuff—anything to get to stand next to a girl instead of another GI. Well, this time around, the soldiers rushed the stage to talk with Neil, even after the question-and-answer period. The poor girls just clumped around looking like the losers in a deodorant commercial." To that assertion by Hope, Neil responds: "I don't think so! He was always making jokes."

A few questions posed by the American soldiers tested Neil's mettle. At the show in Bangkok, where a four-minute standing ovation greeted the First Man, a young helicopter pilot stood up from the second row and demanded, "I wanna know why the U.S. is so interested in the Moon instead of the conflict in Vietnam." Neil waited patiently for the cheers and whistles to stop. Recalling his experiences as a Korean War veteran, Neil answered, "Well, that's a . . . that's a great question. The American . . . the nature of the American system is that it works on many levels in many areas to try to build peace on Earth, goodwill to men. And one of the advantages of the space activity is that it has promoted international understanding and enabled cooperative effort between countries on many levels and will continue to do so in the future."

During a show in Vietnam, another GI asked, "Mr. Armstrong, from your experience on the Moon and the knowledge that you have of it now, do you think it's possible that one day humans will live on the Moon?"

"Yes, I think they will. We will see a manned scientific base being built on the Moon. It'll be a scientific station manned by an international crew, very much like the Antarctic station. But there's a much more important question than whether man will be able to live on the Moon. We have to ask ourselves whether man will be able to live together down here on Earth."

Armstrong had a serious message for the soldiers: "I tried to use the occasion to have the troops in Vietnam consider increasing their education when they got back home. I tried to make the point that in today's world that this would be a good time for them to do it—many of them—before they got too many other commitments. That idea seemed to be well received, but in that situation those guys would have welcomed anyone. They were so hungry for news from home and for anything to cheer them up and take their mind away from the situation they were in. . . . I got a lot of letters."

The Christmas 1969 tour was spared "any [enemy] fire or even any explosions in the distance. Some of the places were fairly close to combat zones, but I don't remember any action." At Lai Khe, the troupe performed for the U.S. 1st Infantry Division, which had seen some of the heaviest fighting in the war to date. So battle-weary were the soldiers that, when Hope reiterated his personal assurances from President Nixon of a plan for peace, more than a scattering of boos arose, a startling precedent for Bob Hope, whose USO shows dated back to World War II.

For the first time, Neil faced scandalous publicity. Stories appeared in the gossip columns and even in *Parade* magazine that he and actress Connie Stevens had become romantically involved while on the USO tour, and that Neil had been, after their return, more than once spotted in the audience of Stevens's Las Vegas act. So rampant did the rumors become that Stevens called Neil to apologize. The truth of the matter was that the thirty-one-year-old singer-actress and the Apollo 11 astronaut had done nothing more intimate on the USO tour than play cards to pass the time. Learning of the rumors, Janet Armstrong anticipated a courtesy call from Stevens, but that never happened. "In retrospect," says Janet today, "it was probably the best way to handle the whole situation."

In May 1970, Armstrong traveled to the Soviet Union, as only the second American astronaut to make an official visit. "I was invited to give a paper to the thirteenth annual conference of the International Committee on Space Research." On May 24 he arrived at the Leningrad airport on a flight from Warsaw. A red carpet awaited him but no crowds, as the Soviet government had not released news of Armstrong's arrival.

Serving as his hosts were Georgy T. Beregovoy and Konstantin P. Feoktistov, the cosmonauts whose goodwill visit to America came two months after Apollo 11. (Feoktistov had flown the Voskhod I mission in 1964, and Beregovoy made the Soyuz III flight in 1968.) The Western press reported that at COSPAR he received a "tumultuous welcome from a predominantly Russian audience" and was "mobbed by scientists seeking autographs and wildly applauding when he took the rostrum."

After five days in Leningrad, he was given permission to visit Moscow. At the Kremlin, he met with Premier Alexei N. Kosygin for an hour. On behalf of President Nixon, Neil presented him with some chips of a Moon rock and a small Soviet flag that had been carried aboard Apollo 11, gifts that prompted Kosygin to lament, "What you have seen is something I'll never see," to which Armstrong replied, "Progress is so rapid, you may be surprised." The sixty-six-year-old Kosygin was insistent, perhaps because he knew far too well the multitude of problems, big and small, that had been keeping the Soviet lunar program so far behind the American: "I am convinced of my ability to predict the spread of human progress, and I still don't think I'll get to the Moon."

"Kosygin shook his finger at me and said, If our two countries are involved in armed conflict, it's not going to be *our* fault."

"The next morning there was a message at the hotel desk that there was a package for me; the security guys said, 'What do you think it is?' And I said, 'Well, it's probably a nice little package of caviar or bottle of vodka or something like that.' And they said, 'Oh, no, no, no.' I asked why not. They said, 'Mr. Kosygin is a temperance man.' I thought that couldn't be possible, not in Russia. Well, it was a lovely wooden case—furniture-quality case—with six bottles of cognac and six bottles of vodka!"

The great Russian aircraft designer Andrey N. Tupolev and his son Adrian "took me to the airfield hanger where they kept their supersonic TU-144—the "striking" Concorde lookalike. Apparently I was the first Westerner to see the airplane. The Tupolevs gave me a model of the TU-144, which Andrey Tupolev signed. When I got back, I gave that to the Smithsonian."

Viewing a display of czarist Russia's crown jewels at the Kremlin's Armory Museum, Armstrong's cosmonaut host Beregovoy joked that Neil had brought parts of a Moon rock to Russia and now it was time to reciprocate. "Pick one," the cosmonaut said. Armstrong pointed at one of the most dazzling. "Fine," said Georgy, "that will cost you $300 million." Replied Neil, "I think I'll wait until they sell it at half price."

Besides Beregovoy and Feoktistov, Armstrong met several other Soviet astronauts. In a secluded forest outside of Moscow, he spent the day at the Cosmonaut Training Center, which was part of the space complex of Zvezdyny Gorodok ("Star City"), Russia's version of Houston's Manned Spacecraft Center. His hostess there was Valentina Tereshkova, the first woman to fly in space. "I had sort of thought of her as a lady wrestler kind of person, but she wasn't that way at all. She was very small, petite, and charming." Neil toured their training facilities, simulators, and spacecraft mockups, "which struck me as being functional but a bit Victorian in nature." Tereshkova also took him to the office of the late Yuri Gagarin, whose personal effects had been preserved as a shrine to the first human space traveler. Neil's lecture was attended by "many of the cosmonauts. They asked the kinds of questions that pilots would ask."

Afterward "they brought two ladies up—one was Mrs. Gagarin and the other Mrs. Vladimir Komarov. Because we had left medallions on the lunar surface in their husbands' honor on the lunar surface, it was kind of a touching little ceremony." Neil told Soviet media he had been "most emotionally moved" by his meeting with the widows.

"That night the cosmonauts invited me to a dinner. There was much toasting going on. No women—this was a stag affair, so Valentina was not there. They presented me a very nice shotgun inscribed with my name on the stock—a twelve-gauge double-barrel side-by-side that the U.S. government permitted me to keep.

"After dinner, around midnight, Georgy Beregovoy, my host, invited me to his apartment for coffee. At one point Georgy talked a little bit on the phone, then someone called him and he went over and turned on his television set. It was the launch of Soyuz IX. It wasn't live; it was a tape of the launch that had occurred earlier in the day at Baikonur. And the occupant was Andrian G. Nikolayev, who was Valentina's husband, as well as Vitaly I. Sevastyanov. So I had spent the whole day with Tereshkova and the whole evening with all the colleagues of the two cosmonauts, and it was never mentioned once that they were having a launch that day. I concluded that Valentina was either awfully good at keeping a secret or she was dreadfully misinformed."

The launch went well or Neil would never have seen it. Vodka was brought out for toasts. Bergovoy smiled broadly when he told Armstrong, "This launch was in your honor!"

From July 1969 to June 1970, Armstrong traveled the half million miles to the Moon and back followed by nearly 100,000 miles on Earth. Such was his journey from the present to the future.

On May 18, 1970, NASA announced that Neil would be taking over as deputy associate administrator for aeronautics for the Office of Advanced Research and Technology (OART). In his new position, Neil would be returning to his first love—airplanes—and "responsible for the coordination and management of overall NASA research and technology work related to aeronautics and coordination between NASA, industry, and other government agencies with respect to aeronautics."

On July 1, following a three-week vacation, Armstrong raised his right hand and was sworn in by NASA Administrator Paine. A little over a year later, he would resign.

PART EIGHT

DARK SIDE OF THE MOON

*I think that people should be recognized for their
achievements and the value that adds to society's
progress. But it can be easily overdone. I think highly
of many people and their accomplishments, but I don't
believe that that should be paramount over the actual
achievements themselves. Celebrity shouldn't supersede
the things they've accomplished.*

—NEIL A. ARMSTRONG TO AUTHOR,
CINCINNATI, OH,
JUNE 2, 2004

*I recognize that I am portrayed as staying out of the pub-
lic eye, but from my perspective it doesn't seem that way,
because I do so many things, go so many places.
I give so many talks, I write so many papers, that, from
my point of view, it seems like I don't know how I could
do more. But I realize that, from another perspective,
outside, I'm only able to accept one percent of all the
requests that come in, so to them it seems like I'm not
doing anything. But I can't change that.*

—NEIL A. ARMSTRONG TO STEPHEN E. AMBROSE
AND DOUGLAS BRINKLEY, HOUSTON, TX,
SEPTEMBER 19, 2001

CHAPTER 32

Standing Ground

Following the Moon landing, Armstrong recalls, "I never asked the question about returning to spaceflight, but I began to believe that I wouldn't have another chance, although that never was explicitly stated." Both George Low and Bob Gilruth "said they would like me to consider going back to aeronautics and take a deputy associate administrator job in Washington. I was not convinced that that was a good thing for me. Probably because of all the time I had worked at the field centers, I more or less looked down at Washington jobs as not being in the real world."

Private-sector opportunities were plentiful, from business ventures, hotel and restaurant property development, to commercial banking. People suggested he run for political office, as fellow Ohio astronaut John Glenn had done. But Neil wanted to stay in engineering.

"Thinking it over, I concluded that the NASA aeronautics job was something I could do." Janet felt that Neil was not unhappy with the change: "He was a pilot, and he was always happier when he was flying." Still she worried, "he was not a desk job person" and that it "was going to be a real adjustment for him."

Armstrong's principal contribution to NASA aeronautics during his time in Washington was his support for the new technology of fly-by-wire. Until Neil became deputy associate administrator for aeronautics, no one at NASA Headquarters had given the radical concept of flying an airplane electronically (and with only one of its inputs being the pilot's controls) much credence. Neil stunned a team of Flight Research Center engineers when they visited his office in 1970 asking for modest funding to conduct flight research with an airplane installed with an *analog* fly-by-wire system. As NASA historian Michael H. Gorn has written, "To their surprise, Armstrong objected. Why analog technology?" he asked. Rather than a system of human impulses transmitted by mechanical linkages from the cockpit to the control surfaces, Neil proposed employing a more advanced system, one based on counting—on *digital* fly-by-wire (DFBW). The FRC engineers knew of no flight-qualified digital computer. "I just went to the Moon and back on one," said Armstrong. According to Gorn, "The visitors from the Flight Research Center admitted with embarrassment [that] they had not even thought of it."

Out of this initiative arose NASA's innovative F-8C Crusader DFBW flight test program, undertaken at Dryden Flight Research Center from 1972 to 1976. Proven reliable, DFBW untied the hands of high-speed aircraft designers, coaxing them to venture forward with radical new aerodynamic configurations, including airplanes possessing absolutely no innate stability of their own minus the computerized control system. DFBW stands as another major contribution to aeronautics, rather than space, that needs always to be associated with the First Man.

Neil's main frustration was not with his aeronautics job per se but with the ongoing "requests" from NASA, Congress, and the White House for "appearances on demand," which Neil came to find "a real burden." "I would say to NASA, 'Here's the proposal so tell me what you want me to do.' In general that was true for all public appearances while I was in government service. I didn't have a choice."

Many an evening was spent on the Washington dinner-party circuit. Recollects Janet, "We were able to meet a lot of Washington people. They enjoyed meeting Neil personally and congratulating him for what Apollo 11 accomplished for our country and the world. Since we were still on the government pay scale [Neil's annual salary was $36,000], there was not much money available. Dottie Blackman, the wife of Supreme Court Justice Harry Blackmun, was a fine seamstress and operated a dress store in Minnesota before their move to DC. She was a dear friend and helped with [evening] clothes."

Armstrong took every opportunity to fly airplanes, including NASA transports en route to the Ames, Lewis, Langley, or Dryden laboratories. "I was able to maintain my flight currency—not as current as I would have liked, but better than not at all. And being around the research programs involving the field centers gave me the opportunity to accept some invitations to fly other aircraft"—including England's Handley-Page 115, a small aircraft to test the Concorde supersonic transport's highly swept wing shape; Germany's large Akaflieg Braunschweig SB-8 sailplane, innovative for its use of structural composite materials; and England's Short

SC-1, an experimental VTOL machine, only two of which were built. When he got to the RAF airfield, however, the SC-1 was temporarily out of commission.

NASA's foremost aeronautical endeavor of the 1960s fell victim to politics when, on March 24, 1971, in one of the most dramatic roll calls in modern U.S. Senate history, fifty-one senators voted to deny further funding for the American supersonic transport program. "In our office, we didn't have any responsibility for the SST, but we followed it closely. I thought the prototype aircraft that Boeing was building would be a good research machine that we at NASA would want access to. Consequently I stayed relatively close to what was going on. I knew Bill [William M.] Magruder, [the national director of the SST program, first for the FAA and then for the Department of Transportation] very well and I had a lot of responsibilities in that area. Scott Crossfield was the SST guy for Eastern Airlines at the time, and I knew him, too. Different congressmen and senators [asked] for my opinion on SST matters. Wisconsin senator Gaylord Nelson, who had introduced legislation to prohibit the operation of any civil supersonic aircraft within the territorial jurisdiction of the United States until—and unless—sonic boom and stratospheric pollution from such aircraft could be reduced to zero, asked me a specific question about the subject [Armstrong was in favor of continuing the SST program] and my answer wasn't to his liking. Nonetheless, Nelson went right over to the floor of the Senate and immediately quoted me as saying just the opposite of what I had said. I was learning the ways of Washington."

The demise of the American SST had no bearing on Neil's decision, in August 1971, to resign from NASA for a teaching post at the University of Cincinnati. "I had always told people it was my intention to go back to the university. That was not a new thought for me. I didn't want to leave NASA precipitously, though it was never my intention to be in that bureaucracy job that long. I had met the president of the University of Cincinnati on several occasions. His name was Walter C. Langsam, a historian of early-twentieth-century Europe. Walter had talked to me and written me a couple of nice little notes saying how much he would like me to come to his university. Walter said, 'If you come, we will make you a full professor and you can do whatever you want.' I decided to accept the invitation. I had had a lot of university invitations by this point but most of them—far and away the majority of them—were invitations to be considered for university presidencies. I just wanted to be a professor."

Curiously, NASA offered little resistance to Armstrong's departure. The new Nixon-appointed NASA administrator, Dr. James C. Fletcher, issued the following statement: "It is with special regret that I accept Neil Armstrong's resignation, and I wish him well in his new duties at the University of Cincinnati. His contribution to the National Aeronautics and Space Administration went far beyond his role as an astronaut and as a commander of the first Moon landing. He joined the Agency as a research test pilot, and he leaves it as Deputy Administrator for Aeronautics. In all his duties he has served with distinction and dedication." Neil's time in civilian government service totaled sixteen and a half years. Fletcher indicated that Armstrong would serve as a part-time NASA consultant, something that Neil personally did not plan on doing or, in the end, actually did.

Some people in and around NASA thought that Neil must be "batty" for landing in a place like Cincinnati. An editorial in the *Cincinnati Enquirer* stated, "One would have to imagine the appointment of Christopher Columbus as a professor of navigation at, say, the University of Barcelona, or the appointment of Thomas Edison as a professor of electrical engineering at Rutgers, or the appointment of Napoleon as a professor of military science at the Sorbonne to grasp the significance of the University of Cincinnati's success in engaging the talents of Neil Armstrong as a professor of aerospace engineering." A cartoon in the same newspaper showed him standing behind a classroom lectern with a space helmet on his head and one student sitting at a desk whispering to another, "They say his lectures are out of this world." The unkindest comment from a local writer was that university officials "hoped" Neil "will pimp for UC," a comment for which the writer's newspaper later apologized in print.

Friends and associates recall Neil's interest over the years in writing an engineering textbook. Most suspected a geographic pull, which Neil flatly denies: "Returning to Ohio wasn't a consideration."

Even a professorship at one of the elite engineering schools—Caltech, MIT, Stanford, Georgia Tech, even Neil's alma mater, Purdue—would not have been as appealing. "I thought Cincinnati's was a pretty good department and it was small, about a dozen people," and unlikely to protest Neil's immediate full-tenure status without the customary year of probation. Department head Dr. Tom Davis was a fairly well known specialist in the burgeoning field of computational fluid dynamics (CFD). The program offered a PhD degree, though Neil's highest academic achievement was a master's, recently awarded at the University of Southern California after more than a ten-year stretch of off-and-on graduate work.* Asked by a reporter whether Armstrong wouldn't be the university's only full professor minus a doctorate, a UC spokesman responded, "We don't have any others that have been on the Moon, either."

Armstrong's title was university professor of aerospace engineering. Students called him "Professor Armstrong" or "Dr. Armstrong," even though the only doctorates that he had at this point were honorary (from Wittenberg University and Miami University in Ohio and his alma mater, Purdue).† The faculty naturally called him Neil. "I seemed to get along well with all the other members of the department. I don't know what their thoughts were about me, but I felt comfortable with all of them, and some I became quite good friends with."

Neil could have gotten away with a light teaching load, but that wasn't what he wanted. "I didn't want to get out of any of the teaching. I didn't even mind teaching core courses, though I didn't teach a lot of them. It was always a scramble to find enough guys to cover all the courses, so I did. I taught three quarters a year and took the summer off. I was usually there every day. I did travel some, but tried to make sure it didn't interfere with my normal full schedule of responsibilities."

Getting started in the classroom did not prove easy for such a famous person. Dave Burrus, a student in Armstrong's very first class, remembers

---

* Armstrong had started taking courses while a NACA test pilot, at a night school on Edwards AFB run by the University of Southern California. Under the direction of Professor Ken Springer, he had started his thesis, concerning a method for simulation of hypersonic flight, before he moved to Houston. After Neil left the Apollo program, Springer, still at USC, contacted him and asked if he wanted to finish up the thesis. Springer made it easy for him, "We have concluded," the professor said, "that, if you would give us a presentation on certain aspects of Apollo, we would consider that an acceptable substitute for finishing the thesis work you have done up to this point." Neil told him it would, in fact, be difficult to finish the thesis as originally conceived since all of the data had been generated in analog, and analog computers were not much available anymore. "To redo my research in digital would have been a very challenging thing for which I wasn't really qualified. So anyway, I prepared a paper and they deemed that acceptable for completion."

† Armstrong currently holds no less than nineteen honorary doctorates, including (besides the three mentioned above), Ohio State University (1971), University of Notre Dame (1971), University of Maryland–Heidelberg (1971), Butler University (1972), Drake University (1972), University of Dublin–Trinity College (1976), Brown University (1979), University of Cincinnati (1982), Lafayette College (1983), Virginia Polytechnic Institute and State University (1986), Weber State University (1988), Cranfield University (1996), Xavier University (1999), College of Mount St. Joseph (2000), Tufts University (2004), and University of Southern California (2005). Twelve of them conferred a Doctor of Science, two a Doctor of Engineering, one a Doctor of Laws, two a Doctor of Humane Letters, one a Doctor of Humanities, and one an LLD.

the scene: "The first day of class started out normal like any other. At the end of class when we opened the door to leave we found the hall packed with reporters. Chaos broke out almost immediately. I was the last student out the door. Professor Armstrong grabbed the door handle and slammed the door shut and would not come out.

"The reporters had no one to interview except the students," so Burrus obliged: "I guess he'll never be just another professor. I'm just afraid he'll get bugged and leave. He's the best thing that ever happened to this program." Other students were more antagonistic: "Why don't you guys leave him alone. He's just another person now, just another professor. Give him a break."

Neil remembers that first day. "It *was* very chaotic. I was just trying to get these guys started in a worthwhile class, and it was hard on them and hard on me. Just another example of how journalists aren't always very thoughtful."

Neither, apparently, were actresses. In 1974 Italian actress Gina Lollobrigida appeared unannounced at the door to his Baldwin Hall classroom, much to the delight of the students, but not to their teacher. "She came to town ostensibly to take pictures for a book she was doing, but it turned out that it wasn't for a book at all but rather for a magazine article [*Ladies' Home Journal,* August 1974]. I really liked Gina from my visits with her in Mexico and Italy [during the 1969 Giant Leap world tour], but I was really disappointed in her not being truthful about her objective."

Armstrong personally invented two courses for the department. The first was aircraft design. "I didn't come with a background in design, but no one was teaching that course and, since I had never been successful at being a designer, I thought I at least could teach it." The second was experimental flight mechanics, which basically concerned how professional flight-testing got done. Most students took both courses in the series. "They were the courses most important to me personally, and I thought they were interesting offerings that a lot of students might enjoy. Both of them were graduate courses, though they were available to upper-level undergraduates, generally seniors."

Students were surprised to find their celebrity professor such an excellent teacher. Though a serious lecturer and a demanding grader, near the end of an academic quarter he was known to relate some of his favorite flying stories.

"When we got to the first quiz, reality set in!" Neil remembers. "In the core courses I tried to be reasonable, but maybe I was a little tough there, too. But certainly in the upper-level courses I tried to make the tests challenging. I thought that graduate-level courses—even for undergraduates stepping up to the graduate level—shouldn't ever be considered as pushovers ... I was not a believer in the big final test—a one-shotter. I wasn't taught that way at Purdue. In the real world, though, you do have to face big final tests from time to time, and there's always a chance that if you have an off day at the wrong time it can really penalize you badly."

Armstrong ultimately failed to navigate the Byzantine labyrinth of university politics. "I really couldn't work the system. I had determined not to take any work from NASA; I wouldn't make proposals to them because I thought it might be viewed as taking advantage of my past association, which I wouldn't do. In retrospect, I was probably wrong about that. I probably should have been active, because I would have known exactly where to go to get some satisfying research projects done. It would have been easier in terms of funding sources had I taken that route."

Two major changes at the University of Cincinnati ultimately led, in 1980, to Armstrong's leaving the school. "It was burdened with lots of new rules," relates Armstrong of UC's shift from independent municipal university to state-school status. "In order to escape being bound to the rules of the faculty collective bargaining group, it was required that I be less than full-time. So a strategy some of us tried was going to half-time teaching and half-time in a research institute." In July 1975, the university approved George Rieveschl, a UC chemist famous for his invention of Benadryl, the first antihistamine; Edward A. Patrick, an electrical engineering professor; Dr. Henry Heimlich, Cincinnati's famous inventor of the Heimlich maneuver, who practiced medicine at the local Jewish hospital; and Armstrong coming together as the Institute of Engineering and Medicine.

Like others over the years who have been philosophically opposed to collective bargaining agreements, Armstrong "wanted to be valued on my own merits, not on some group's merits. Because I was involved by this time in professional societies, projects of various kinds, sometimes speaking engagements, I was looking for a way to legally circumvent this envelope of instructions that had been thrown over the top of us.

"Establishing the institute was not something that had been high on my priority list. It was just kind of a necessary evil. Once getting into the work, though, I did find some of it very interesting and tried to actively participate in it." What got the most publicity in the newspapers were reputed attempts to design a palm-sized artificial heart on the basis of the coolant pump that had been used in the Apollo space suit, and to develop a portable artificial lung from a modified version of the PLSS (Portable Life Support System). According to Armstrong, however, "the project was only intended to investigate methods of reducing damage to blood cells while being pumped. The press extrapolated and created some confusion in this matter.

"Yet the university's rules were still so cumbersome that I just went completely to half-time. Really it was half-time in name only—what it really amounted to was half pay," * and ultimately "a conflict of the instructions between my basic job as it had been offered to me by President Langsam and the new rules." Beyond that, "I could not expect the volume of requests coming my way to subside—some of which were good opportunities with good people and quality institutions. I realized that, in my situation, I couldn't remain in that kind of job. On the other hand, taking board of directors' positions provided a livelihood without obliging myself to spend all of my time with any one of them."

For Armstrong, his last years at the university were not especially stressful, "just irritating." In the autumn of 1979 he wrote a short note of resignation, effective the first of the year, to President Henry R. Winkler, Warren Bennis's successor after Langsam as UC president. Winkler reported to his board of trustees about the resignation: "Now, Neil's own personal career pursuits lead him into other activities. . . . I hope that he will always continue to look upon the University of Cincinnati as his academic home." To some colleagues, including Dr. Ron Houston, the head of the newly organized Institute of Applied Interdisciplinary Research, which subsumed the Institute of Engineering and Medicine in 1978 with Neil as its associate director, Armstrong's leaving was a mystery: "He didn't even say why he was leaving."

To the press Winkler intimated that Neil's financial situation might have played a role. "The resignation was necessary in light of his own personal plans and 'personal reasons.' I assume 'personal reasons' might include the economic status of his family." UC director of information services, Ken Service, surmised: "When you're the first man on the Moon and everyone's hanging on you, I guess you just get tired of it after a while."

In January 1979 Neil, after turning down any number of lucrative promotional offers, agreed to become a national spokesperson for the Chrysler Corporation.

---

* Armstrong's tax form for 1979 showed that he earned an income of $18,196 from the University of Cincinnati. From his own personal service corporation that year, he earned $168,000. Beyond that, he earned about $50,000 in fees for serving on boards of directors for various companies.

His first TV commercial for the American car manufacturer came during the telecast of that month's Super Bowl XIII, which Neil attended in Miami in the company of Chrysler execs. More TV spots aired the next day as did splashy print ads in fifty U.S. newspaper markets, showing Neil endorsing Chrysler's new five-year, 50,000-mile protection plan. At the 185-acre Warren County farm northwest of Lebanon, Ohio, that the Armstrongs had purchased after moving from Bethesda, a small fleet of Chrysler automobiles—a New Yorker, Fifth Edition, Cordoba, W200 four-wheel-drive pickup truck, two different front-wheel-drive Omnis, and a Plymouth Horizon—had been seen parked for days at a time. According to Janet, Neil had told Chrysler, " 'I need to try your product first.' "

The press asked questions: Why is Armstrong starting to do advertising now, after all this time? And why Chrysler, of all companies? Neil explains today: "In the Chrysler case, they were under severe attack and in financial difficulty, but they had been perhaps the preeminent engineering leader in automotive products in the United States, just very impressive. I was concerned about them and when their head of marketing approached me to take a role that was not just as a public spokesman but also as someone to be involved in their technical decision-making process, I became attracted to that. I visited Detroit, where I talked to Chrysler head Lee Iacocca and other leading company executives [one of them ironically named "Moon Mullins"]. I had a look at the projects they were working on. I got to know some of their people and concluded that it was something I should try.

"It wasn't an easy decision, because I hadn't done anything like it before. Yet I decided to try, on the basis of a three-year agreement. I loved the engineering aspects of the job, but I didn't think I was very competent in the role as a spokesman. I tried my best, but it wasn't something I was good at. I was always struggling to do it properly."

In the coming months Armstrong forged professional relationships with General Time Corp. (a subsidiary of Tally Industries) and the Bankers Association of America. He made promotional commitments on a case-by-case basis, in General Time's case by conceiving his involvement not as a commercial endorsement of the company's "Quartzmatic wristwatch" but rather a technological breakthrough. "The Quartz watch company had built the timer in the lunar module, so that was the connection there—the technology was good. As it turned out, the product quality was not as good as I thought it should be. As for the American Bankers Association, it was not a commercial organization, but rather did an institutional kind of advertising. We made a couple of ads, but it just didn't come together."

Armstrong's trial run as a public spokesman for select American—always *American*—products proved to be temporary, but corporate concerns became his primary focus for the rest of his professional life.

Simultaneous with leaving UC, Neil entered into a business partnership with his brother Dean and their second cousin Richard Teichgraber, owner of oil industry supplier International Petroleum Services of El Dorado, Kansas. Dean, formerly the head of a General Motors' Delco Remy transmission plant in Anderson, Indiana, became the IPS president; Neil became an IPS partner and the chairman of Cardwell International Ltd., a new subsidiary that made portable drilling rigs, half of them for overseas sale. "Neil has inroads with people we'd like to see," Teichgraber said at the time of Cardwell's formation. "Neil got us in to see the president of Mexico [Lopez Portillo]." Neil and his brother stayed involved with IPS/Cardwell for two years, at which time they sold their interests in the company. Dean later bought a Kansas bank.

By 1982, Neil had several different corporate involvements: "I think some people invited me on their boards precisely because I *didn't* have a business background, but I did have a technical background. So I accepted quite a few different board jobs. I turned down a lot more than I accepted."

The very first board on which Armstrong had agreed to serve, back in 1972, had been with Gates Learjet, then headed by Harry Combs. Chairing its technical committee and type-rated in the Learjet, Neil flew most of the new and experimental developments in the company's line of business jets. In February 1979, he took off in a new Learjet from First Flight airstrip at nearby Kill Devil (where the Wright brothers made history's first controlled and powered manned flight in December 1903) and climbed over the Atlantic Ocean to an altitude of 51,000 feet in a little over twelve minutes, setting new altitude and climb records for business jets.

In the spring of 1973 Neil joined the board of Cincinnati Gas & Electric: "CG&E was very much an engineering company, for power generation. We were getting into the nuclear power age and the company wanted more technical competence generally, so they asked me to join."

Armstrong links his connection with Cincinnati-based Taft Broadcasting to Taft's dynamic CEO and president Charles S. Mechem Jr., who was "one of the seven or eight Cincinnati people I invited as my guest to Gene Cernan's Apollo 17 flight [the first night Moon shot] in December 1972."

Mechem's recollection remains vivid: "Two-thirds of the way to the Cape, Neil said, 'Oh, boy! I've left my wallet with all my identification back in the motel room.' I was thinking, We're going to get to the first checkpoint, and the guard's going to say, 'Who are you?' and he's going to say, 'Neil Armstrong,' and the guard's going to say, 'Yeah, and I'm George Washington.'

"So we got to the first guard gate and the guard said, 'Oh, you're Neil Armstrong, aren't you?' And we go, 'Yes! Yes! He is!' "

Mechem gives a very clear impression of the strengths Armstrong brought to the corporate boardroom: "Typically you ask somebody to go on the board and they say, 'Terrific, when's the first meeting?' Well, it wasn't that way with Neil. After "probing as to why I wanted him and what he could bring to the board that didn't have anything to do with his being the first man on the Moon," Armstrong came on board.

"Neil fit in perfectly," Mechem declares, "because there was nobody quite like Neil."

Charlie remembers how "wonderfully compatible" Armstrong was "with our people." "We had this dinner party and afterwards everybody went up into the hospitality suite, and I went to bed, and the next morning, they said, 'Charlie! We were out on the balcony singing with Neil Armstrong!' "

Armstrong's celebrity led to an uproarious moment when, in the midst of photographing the Taft board of directors, the cameraman got behind the camera and said, "Mr. Armstrong, would you take one small step forward?"

"Once involved in something, Neil never gave up. We were playing golf one time in a corporate outing with Paul 'Bear' Bryant, the football coach of the Alabama Crimson Tide, someone who was also very competitive. On the seventeenth hole there was a fairway bunker about a hundred yards long. Neil pulled his drive into it, walked in, and dutifully took a swipe, moving the ball maybe five yards. He didn't say a word, just walked up, took another swipe, another five yards, maybe. Of course, Neil will never give up, ever. Paul and I were walking along, and Bear turned to me and huskily whispered, 'Is this the man who went to the Moon?' "

Then there was the time the Mechem and Armstrong families visited (Taft-owned) Kings Island upon the park's grand opening: " 'Neil, what rides would you like to go on?' And he said, 'Nothing that's too dangerous.' "

One connection inevitably led to another. For example, Armstrong joined United Airlines in January 1978. When a Chicago blizzard forced United to accommodate its inbound board members at the UAL flight attendants training school, Neil spent three days with E. Mandell "Dell" De Windt, the chairman and CEO of Cleveland's Eaton Corporation, who together with Eaton and United board member Nicholas Petrie, "conspired" until 1980 to get Neil to join the Eaton board. James Stover, CEO for Eaton following De Windt, asked Neil to join and chair a newly formed board of directors for their AIL Systems subsidiary located in Deer Park, New York, which made electronic warfare equipment (including defensive avionics systems for the B-1 bomber, tactical jamming systems, battlefield surveillance radar, laser guidance for missiles, and advanced microwave receivers). Neil and Jim Smith, president and CEO of AIL, were successful in taking the company private in 1977 and, in 2000, it merged with the EDO Corporation, which Neil chaired until his retirement from corporate life in 2002.

In March 1989, three years after the explosion of Space Shuttle *Challenger,* Armstrong joined Thiokol, who had made the Shuttle's solid-rocket boosters (SRBs). If it had not been for Armstrong's record of integrity, skeptics may have questioned the propriety of Neil's joining Thiokol, given that he had served as vice chair of the Rogers Commission that had investigated the *Challenger* accident. But no one ever suggested any conflict of interest. Remembers James R. Wilson, then Thiokol's chief financial officer: "We were this fragile entity recovering from the *Challenger* accident. Just the fact that Neil joined our board and loaned us his good name and reputation did an awful lot of good for our credibility in the marketplace with our customers."

Armstrong provided more than credibility for the Utah-based aerospace and defense contractor. With Neil's help, Thiokol managed not only to survive but also grow, in the expanded form of Cordant Technologies, into a manufacturer of solid-rocket motors, jet aircraft engine components, and high-performance fastening systems worth some $2.5 billion, with manufacturing facilities throughout the United States, Europe, and Asia. In 2000 Cordant was acquired in a cash deal by Alcoa, Inc., at which time the Thiokol board on which Neil had been serving for eleven years dissolved.

Reluctant to assess the value of any of the corporate contributions he has made over the past thirty years, Armstrong only says, "I felt that in most cases I understood the issues and usually then had a view on what was the proper position on that issue. . . . I felt comfortable in the boardroom."

For the first time in his life, Armstrong also made a good deal of money. Besides handsome compensation for his activities as a director, he was also receiving significant stock options and investing his money wisely. By the time he and Janet divorced in 1994, the couple was worth well over $2 million.

Though he never made a show of his philanthropy, Neil was regularly involved in promoting charitable causes, particularly in and around Ohio. In 1973, he headed the state's Easter Seal campaign. From 1978 to 1985, Armstrong was on the board of directors for the Countryside YMCA in Lebanon, Ohio. From 1976 to 1985, he served on the board of the Cincinnati Museum of Natural History, for the last five years as its chairman. From 1988 to 1991, he belonged to the President's Executive Council at the University of Cincinnati. To this day, he actively participates in the Commonwealth Club and Commercial Club of Cincinnati, having presided over both, in 1984–85 and 1996–97, respectively. In 1992–93 he sat on the Ohio Commission on Public Service. In 1982 he narrated the "Lincoln Portrait" with the Cincinnati Pops Orchestra.

According to Cincinnati Museum of Natural History director Devere Burt: "His game gave us instant credibility. Anywhere you went looking for money, you simply had to present the letterhead, 'Board Chairman Neil A. Armstrong.' "

For his college alma mater, Neil was perhaps the most active. He served on the board of governors for the Purdue University Foundation from 1979 to 1982, on the school's Engineering Visiting Committee from 1990 to 1995, and from 1990 to 1994 he cochaired with Gene Cernan the university's biggest-ever capital fund-raiser, Vision 21. Its goal set at a whopping $250 million, the campaign raised $85 million more, setting an American public university fund-raising record.

Dr. Stephen Beering, Purdue's president from 1983 to 2000, recalled Armstrong's essential contributions to Vision 21: "Neil was really the PR piece of it. He might say to an alumni group, 'You know, my landing on the Moon was really facilitated by my Purdue experiences—it goes back to my very first semester when I had a physics professor who had written our textbook and for the first Friday recitation I anticipated that I would need to regurgitate the assigned chapter. Instead, the professor said, 'I'm curious what you *thought* about this material.' At that moment I realized what Purdue was about: it was about teaching problem-solving, critical thinking, analyzing situations, and coming to conclusions that were in detail and original. When I was flying the LM down onto the Moon, that's exactly what I had to do—take my training but then solve problems, analyze situations, and find a practical solution for myself. Without Purdue, I couldn't have done it.'

"And whenever he was on campus, you could see in his eyes how much he enjoyed it. His pure joy showed just standing there with his arm around some band member at a football game. He was thrilled like a kid when he was asked to be the one to bang the big Boilermaker drum. 'I've never done that! I'd like to do it.' And he marched with the baritones, which he played back when he was in the band. Not for a moment did he act like a celebrity."

Armstrong was also involved in a few benevolent causes at the national level. From 1975 to 1977, he cochaired, with Jimmy Doolittle, the Charles A. Lindbergh Memorial Fund, which by the fiftieth anniversary of Lindbergh's historic flight, in May 1977, raised over $5 million for an endowment fund supporting young scientists, explorers, and conservationists. In 1977–78 Neil accepted an appointment to Jimmy Carter's President's Commission on White House Fellowships. In 1979 he served as the on-air host for *The Voyage of Charles Darwin,* a seven-part documentary broadcast on PBS. The National Honorary Council's USS *Constitution* Museum Association counted him as a member from 1996 to 2000.

Some have said that Neil does not have a political bone in his body: "I don't think I would agree in the sense that I have beliefs, I participate in the process, and I vote my conscience. But what is true is that I am not in any way drawn to the political world."

Both parties, Democratic and Republican, tried to lure him in. In April 1972, major Ohio newspapers headlined, "Armstrong Possible Chief of Nixon's Ohio Race." In July 1979, on the eve of Apollo 11's tenth anniversary, the stories were about the Republican Party trying to get Neil to take on Democratic senator John Glenn. "I've often been approached to run for various positions. But I have had no interest in that at all."

In terms of the American political tradition, Armstrong has always identified most strongly with the moderate roots of Jeffersonian Republicanism. "I tend to be more in favor of the states retaining their powers unless it's something only the federal government can do and it's in everyone's interest. I'm not persuaded that either of our current political parties is very right on the education issue. But it's not politic to express those views to anyone today. So I don't.

"Both political parties take credit for when the economy is going well and blame the other party for any failures in the economic system. Actually, I don't think either one has very much to do with the business cycle."

In terms of American foreign policy, Armstrong is a realist, not an idealist. "In Jefferson's time, we were relatively a small nation, certainly in assets, military strength, and financial power—we were still some time and distance away from becoming a power at all. Now for the past fifteen years we have found ourselves as the only so-called superpower, although it's very likely that China will challenge our position in the not-too-distant future. I don't believe we should be the world's policeman even though we are the only superpower. In that sense, I'm not a hawk. On the other hand, I think there is merit to speaking softly and carrying a big stick. How we use the stick, that's for people more thoughtful and experienced in international relations than I have ever been."

CHAPTER 33

To Engineer Is Human

"I am, and ever will be, a white-socks, pocket-protector nerdy engineer. And I take substantial pride in the accomplishments of my profession," so Armstrong declared in his February 2000 address to the National Press Club honoring the Top 20 Engineering Achievements of the Twentieth Century as determined by the National Academy of Engineering, an organization he had been elected to in 1978. Neil went on to say: "Science is about what is; engineering is about what can be."

Spaceflight ranked only twelfth on the NAE list. In regard to pure engineering achievement, however, Armstrong regarded human spaceflight as one of the greatest achievements of the century, if not *the* greatest.

Armstrong never lost touch with the U.S. space program. Back in April 1970, just as he was transferring from the astronaut corps to the aeronautics office, the Apollo 13 accident occurred. Halfway to the Moon, an oxygen tank exploded in the service module, causing another tank to leak as well. Commander Jim Lovell ordered his crew—Fred Haise and Jack Swigert—into the LM, where the three astronauts rationed the module's limited supply of oxygen and electricity long enough to slingshot back around the Moon and return home safely. The Apollo program could only continue when and if NASA discovered the cause of the accident, "a harsh reminder of the immense difficulty" in undertaking a manned Moon mission.

NASA asked Armstrong to serve on its internal investigation board under Dr. Edgar M. Cortright, the director of NASA's Langley Research Center. Neil aided F. B. Smith, NASA's assistant administrator for university affairs, with production of a detailed and accurate chronology of pertinent events from a review of telemetry records, air-to-ground communications transcripts, and crew and control center observations, as well as the flight plan and crew checklists. Other members of this panel were Tom B. Ballard from the Flight Instrument Division at Langley Research Center, M. P. Frank from the Flight Control Division in Houston, and John J. Williams, director of Spacecraft Operations at Kennedy Space Center.

After nearly two months of investigation, Cortright's Apollo 13 review board released its report on June 15, 1970. Typical of so many technological accidents, what happened to the spacecraft "was not the result of a chance malfunction in a statistical sense but, rather, it was the result of an unusual combination of mistakes coupled with a somewhat deficient and unforgiving system," a complicated label for what Chris Kraft has called "a stupid and preventable accident." Tank manufacturer Beech Aircraft Co. was supposed to have replaced a 28-volt thermostat switch that heated up the liquid oxygen with a 65-volt switch, but had failed to do it. The Apollo Program Office was not diligent in cross-checking its own orders, so it overlooked the omission.

One of the most questionable conclusions of Cortright's panel was its recommendation that the service module's entire tank needed to be re-designed—at a cost of $40 million. A number of Apollo managers thought the costly change was unnecessary since Apollo 13's problem pertained not to the tank but the thermostat. According to Kraft, "If it didn't look difficult, Cortright didn't look good. We argued, but Cortright wouldn't budge." In the following weeks, Kraft and Cortright fought it out all the way through NASA Headquarters. Privately, Armstrong was not on the side of the tank being replaced. Designing a new tank would be—and proved to be—a difficult engineering job, and, as Kraft argued, "ground tests couldn't possibly provide the kind of testing and flight experience we were throwing away." "After taking up the new job," Armstrong recalls, "I was released from active involvement in the Apollo 13 investigation," or he might have taken some active role in supporting Kraft's position.

Naturally, the public valued Armstrong's thoughts on U.S. space exploration, present and future. Newspapers quoted his commencement address at Ohio State University in June 1971: "My enthusiasm for the future of space travel, I think you'll grant is understandable. To stand on the surface of the Moon and look at the Earth high overhead leaves an impression not easily forgotten. Although our blue planet is very beautiful, it is very remote and apparently very small. You might suspect in such a situation, the observer might dismiss the Earth as relatively unimportant.

"However, exactly the opposite conclusion has been reached by each of the individuals who has had the opportunity to share that view. We have all been struck by the similarity to an oasis or island. More importantly, it is the only island that we know is a suitable home for man."

In the early 1970s Armstrong continued to consider environmental concerns about the health of the home planet: "The very success of the human species over eons of time now threatens our extinction. It is the drive that made for success that must now be curbed, redirected or released by expansion into a new world ecology. . . . If we can find people skillful enough to reach the Moon, we sure can find people to solve our environmental problems." In 1975, Neil accepted a position on the National Center for Resource Recovery board. Promoting recycling, Neil would quip, "You know, the purpose of all those Moon walks was to take the garbage out."

As a futurologist, Armstrong's vision was sometimes blurry. To a gathering of hardware dealers at the Mid America Show in Columbus, Ohio, in February 1972, he predicted, for example, that by using space technology "within our lifetime we will have eliminated the calamity of severe storms." More accurate was his notion of the day "when satellites will provide complete libraries of films and books to monitors in homes." To his credit, he often humorously related, "the future is not something I know a great deal about. But I did live in Washington for a time and learned that lack of knowledge about a subject is no impediment to talking about it."

When thinking historically, as he did in 1974 at the two hundredth anniversary of Harrodsburg, Kentucky, the early settlers' westward drive rated comparison with trips that took men to the Moon. "They were dissatisfied with taxation without representation, and we today cry a little bit about both of them. . . . Your town founder, Colonel James Harrod, took much longer to make the trip from Pennsylvania to Kentucky than we did going to the Moon, but I think he spent less money." Turning more serious, Armstrong told the crowd, "The need to build a new world is what lifts man's horizons in search of the future. Without these horizons, a man turns inward and is concerned only with himself. With them, he thinks more about tomorrow than today, more about society than himself." Addressing a Chicago meeting of the American Bar Association in 1977, Armstrong expressed his concern that a nation of laws had to be made to work: "Ancient Athens died, but her principles survive. And we ask, 'Is this the destiny of our nation, or might it just be possible that our nation can survive along with preservation of its principles?' "

Armstrong's far more typical reserve earned him the moniker "The Lunar Lindbergh" from some disgruntled members of the press. "Armstrong Has No Comment for Last Shot" one frustrated reporter complained in the buildup to Apollo 17 in December 1972, the last flight in the manned lunar program. The story became Neil's silence, and it quoted one unidentified NASA public relations man at the Cape for the launch saying, "He's a closed-mouth son of a bitch. If he's here [which he was], we're probably the last people in the world he would tell where he is and what his plans are." The story also included a critical quote from University of Cincinnati press officer Al Kuttner: "Since he's been here, he's only had one session with the press and there was a lot of arm twisting done to get that. He's not very easy to find. In fact, I don't even have his home phone number, and I don't know where he lives." There was also a statement from Armstrong's special secretary at the university, Ruta Bankovikis, identified only as "Miss Bankovikis," coolly saying in very formal English: "Mr. Armstrong does not wish to speak to reporters. He does not give exclusives. He does not give out interviews. It would be indiscreet of me to tell you where he is staying at Cape Kennedy while he watches the Moonshot."

"Invisiblest" headlined a Cincinnati paper's 1974 short feature story on Neil. An accompanying editorial cartoon showed a Mt. Rushmore–sized Armstrong in his NASA space suit with three gentlemen (one of them clearly a reporter) climbing up a ladder to talk to him. Reaching the top of the ladder, what the men saw inside his helmet was literally a brick wall. Any sort of public appearance generated headlines like "Armstrong Out of Seclusion," "Armstrong Stays Alone in His Private Orbit," "Neil Armstrong, Where Are You?," "Cincinnati's Invisible Hero," "The Hermit of Cincinnati," and "In Search of Neil Armstrong." Readers' posts to gossip columns such as "Will Neil Armstrong ever return to public life?" were answered "Not if he can help it."

Armstrong's resolute unwillingness to play any direct public role other than that of his own choosing proved especially frustrating to proponents of the U.S. space program, including some of his fellow astronauts. Gordon Cooper, for example, later criticized, "After his walk on the Moon . . . Neil came home, sat for a news conference or two, then quit NASA and became a recluse rather than take part in NASA's grand plan to milk the event for all the public goodwill possible. I think the next time Neil took a question at a press conference about his historic mission was at the thirtieth reunion of the flight, in July 1999. In this regard, Armstrong was the opposite of John

Glenn, who, come to think of it, would have been a *great* first man on the Moon." Even the fairer minded and more historically accurate Jim Lovell has expressed a similar sentiment: "Sometimes I chastise Neil for being too Lindbergh-like. I tell him, 'Neil, Charles Lindbergh flew across the Atlantic on private funds and had a private group build his airplane and everything else, so he had all the right to be as reclusive as he wanted. But you went to the Moon on public funds. The public taxpayers paid for your trip and gave you all that opportunity and fame, and there is a certain amount of return that is due them.' And Neil's answer to that is, 'I'd be harassed all the time if I weren't reclusive.' And he's probably right."

Yet, Armstrong did regularly speak out. "I've given a large number of press conferences. When I've visited other countries, I've usually given them. Every Apollo anniversary we hold press conferences. I feel no obligation to have a press conference just for the purpose of creating feature material which is not newsworthy; it's just human interest. I don't feel that that's required and, consequently, I try to avoid those kinds of situations.

"I've had some bad experiences with individual interviews where the journalist wasn't honest about what he was after. Once they report something erroneously, there is not much you can do that's effective in correcting it. So, a long time ago, I concluded that I just would not do individual interviews with journalists. They would be restricted to press conferences, because when there is a number of journalists present who are all hearing the same thing, they are much less inclined to tell it differently than they heard it."

"Man's Mars Landing Possible: Armstrong," *Cleveland Plain Dealer,* December 7, 1971: "I am a pilot not a prophet. . . . It is only a matter of will, resources, and justification."

"Armstrong Envisions Great Space Benefits for Earth," *Cincinnati Enquirer,* February 9, 1972: "I'm here today because the people here wanted to stay away from politics and controversy, and I'm the only guy they could find who is not a presidential candidate."

"Moon Walker Hopes for Return of Surface Transportation," *Cincinnati Enquirer,* April 5, 1974: "The airplane is about sixty times better than the automobile as far as pollution is concerned, and we're still working to make it better. The balance is to find an acceptable level of transportation without deterring the quality of life."

"First Man on Moon Says Space Ventures Paying Off," *The Spokesman Review* (Spokane, Washington), September 17, 1976: "There has been a synergistic growth from original advancements of the space program—such as miniaturization—which has spread into a number of different fields."

"Neil Armstrong Takes 'Citizen's Look at National Defense,' " *Western Star* (Lebanon, Ohio), May 3, 1978: "We have the advantage over the Soviet system . . . It is my hope that such a cumbersome system, plus the maturity of the Soviet leadership, can work to reduce any catastrophic initiative on their part. . . . If we are to have a government by the people, the people must be informed and responsible. I am optimistic that this can be achieved."

"Armstrong Says We Need Space," *Cincinnati Post,* May 14, 1978: "As we look ahead ten years, I would hope that we maintain the momentum of the past two decades, that we enjoy significant success with the Space Shuttle, that we initiate a new permanent space station, and that we provide the vista from a spacecraft to many, many new travelers."

"Disappointed Astronaut: Armstrong Urges More U.S. Space Efforts," *Cleveland Plain Dealer,* June 12, 1979: "The problem is that we may have suffered from too much success. The most disappointing thing is that we had a lot of ideas, but we were only able to get a few started."

"Space Shuttle May Snap Nation Out of Dumps: Armstrong," *Columbus* (Ohio) *Dispatch,* February 14, 1981: "The Shuttle is, in fact, the first spacecraft of commerce. . . . Our education system must encourage looking outward to the universe that is our home."

"Armstrong Wants Cutbacks Halted," Associated Press, December 9, 1981: "Government research has made America the world leader in aviation and we should not undermine that advantage by canceling aeronautical research." (House Subcommittee on Transportation, Aviation, and Materials.)

"Former Astronaut Supports 'Star Wars,' " *Florida Today,* October 19, 1985: "I find no difficulties, personally, with the ethics of providing a shield when the other fellow has a sword. The technology required to do that seems very challenging to me."

"Character: Our Next Frontier," *Cincinnati Post,* February 20, 1976: "Human character. This is the area where we've made the least progress—learning about the brain, about our behavior and the ways we relate to one another. I think that's the most important direction we can take in the next twenty years, basically to begin to understand ourselves."

"Seek Truth, Armstrong Urges," *Toledo Blade,* June 14, 1982: "Mark Twain said, 'Truth is mighty and will prevail.' There's nothing the matter with that except it ain't so. We hold that the pursuit of truth is meritorious for its own sake. Truth is seldom absolute. It's more often dependent on the perspective of the observer." (Commencement address, University of Cincinnati.)

Snapshots of Armstrong frequently appeared in the social section of Cincinnati newspapers on those occasions that he attended charity balls and other civic functions. Appearing semiregularly were feature stories and personality profiles written specifically about him or about him as part of the select group of men who had walked on the Moon, though he only rarely agreed to be interviewed for the piece.

When he severed the ring finger of his left hand in a freak accident at his Lebanon farm in November 1978, the injury and successful emergency microsurgery (by a special team at the Jewish Hospital in Louisville, Kentucky) inspired a fresh spate of headlines: "First Moon Man Hurt on Barn Door," "Louisville Surgery Team Rejoins Armstrong's Finger," "From Moon Walk to Microsurgery: Astronaut Praises Technique That Saved Finger," "Armstrong Blasts Off After Touchy Operation," and "One Small Tip: Moon Walker Leaves City with a Restored Finger." To the inevitable questions he received upon release from the hospital,* Neil declared with his dry wit, "I didn't think it was news for a man to travel about half a million miles through space unharmed and then rip his finger off when his wedding ring caught on a door as he jumped off the back of a truck. Like all of us, I suppose, I incur routine injuries along the way."

As the tenth anniversary of the first Moon landing approached, the press

---

* Contrary to some published reports, Armstrong did not drive himself, with his severed fingertip, to Cincinnati's Bethesda North Hospital; he traveled by life squad van. From there he was flown by a friend to the then-world-famous microsurgery unit at Louisville's Jewish Hospital. Drs. Joseph Kutz, Tse-Min Tsai, and Thomas Wolff performed the delicate surgery. Two major arteries and five veins had to be rejoined. Following the surgery, the finger became fully functional except for the last joint nearest the tip.

was reduced to begging: "Speak to Us, Neil," ran one editorial in a local paper. "You're a hero whether you like it or not," the plea concluded. Armstrong opted to hold a press conference—immediately dubbed "A giant leap for the press" when word surfaced that the "First Person on Moon Will Step Out of Anonymity." Yet the local *Cincinnati Enquirer* could do no better than "Armstrong Reticent Talking of Moon Walk 10 Years Later" and "The Search Goes On." In the following years, the legend of the lunar Lindbergh only grew, despite all he was actually doing and saying publicly, further fueled in January 1983 by nationally syndicated radio commentator Paul Harvey's labeling of Neil as a "recluse."

One notable activity that Neil successfully kept out of the press was his trip to the North Pole, which he made in April 1985 under the direction of the professional expedition leader and adventurer, California's Michael Chalmer Dunn, and in the company of the world-famous climber of Mt. Everest, Sir Edmund Hilary, Hilary's son Peter, and Pat Morrow, the first Canadian to reach Everest's summit. "I found the trip to the North Pole tremendously interesting," Armstrong recalled, "predominately because it was so different from everything we normally see in our usual life. It's so very different up there. It was well worth the troubles of the trip."

A month before he journeyed to the North Pole with the Hilary expedition, Neil had become a member of a fourteen-member commission named by President Ronald Reagan to "devise an aggressive civilian space agenda to carry America into the twenty-first century." Other members of the commission included U.N. ambassador Jeane J. Kirkpatrick, astronaut Dr. Kathryn D. Sullivan, space futurist Dr. Gerard K. O'Neill, Nobel laureate physicist Dr. Luis W. Alvarez, air force general Bernard A. Schriever, and Brigadier General Charles E. Yeager. Chairing the commission was Dr. Thomas O. Paine, the former NASA administrator.

"We worked off and on for several months, collected a lot of information from all kinds of different sources, had meetings and presentations, and then tried to develop a long-range plan for the nation's future in space." Early on, Chairman Paine (whom Armstrong knew well from the Apollo program and had always found very easy to work with) told the group to set their sights on fifty years out, to the year 2035, "though the fewer number of recommendations a commission makes, the more effective those recommendations will be and the more likely they will be implemented."

In May 1986, Bantam Books published a glossy 209-page book entitled *Pioneering the Space Frontier: The Report of the National Commission on Space,* illustrated by imaginative renderings of space artists Robert McCall,

Ron Miller, and William K. Hartmann. Supplementing the splashy written report was a fifty-minute videotaped program anchored by Armstrong's opening remarks. Among the panel's bold recommendations were calls for a permanent base on the Moon by 2006 and a human outpost on Mars by 2015.

"The recommendations of the Paine Commission are not today sitting on everyone's desk as something we remember and emulate. It's not referred to or even thought about very much," largely due to the tragic events of January 28, 1986, when STS 51-L, the Space Shuttle known as *Challenger,* disintegrated, killing commander Dick Scobee and pilot Mike Smith along with three mission specialists: flight test engineer Ellison Onizuka, the first American of Asian descent to fly in space; physicist Ron McNair, the second black American in space; and electrical engineer Judy Resnik, the second American woman in space. Dying with them were two payload specialists, Gregory Jarvis, a designer of satellites, and Christa McAuliffe, a high school social studies teacher from Concord, New Hampshire, who had been selected from a list of over eleven thousand applicants to be the first teacher in space. With the deaths of the *Challenger* 7, as they came to be known, representing as they did a microcosm of American society, the U.S. space program entered a deep and prolonged period of crisis and depression, obfuscating the dreams of the Paine Commission.

At Reagan's request, Armstrong joined the Presidential Commission on the Space Shuttle *Challenger* Accident. Reagan and former secretary of state William P. Rogers, who had agreed to chair the commission, both wanted Neil to serve as its vice chair. "The morning after the accident, I received information that the White House was trying to get in touch with me. I called the switchboard and after talking to one of the president's staff, I was put on the line with Mr. Reagan. It is very difficult to turn down a president.

"Our job was to get the report to the president in four months—a hundred and twenty days—from the time he gave us the job.

"Secretary Rogers seemed to be very interested in doing this job and doing it very diligently." Neil did not meet with him face to face, however, until the first time the commission met, on February 3, six days after the accident, in the New York City law offices of Rogers & Wells. Other members of the prestigious group were David Acheson, a former U.S. attorney for the District of Columbia and senior vice president for Communications Satellite Corp.; Eugene E. Covert, head of the Department of Aeronautics and Astronautics at MIT; Richard P. Feynman, a Nobel Prize winner in physics who taught at Caltech; Robert B. Hotz, former editor of *Aviation Week and Space Technology;* Major General Donald J. Kutyna, who formerly managed the DoD side of the Space Shuttle program and was then serving as the director of the air force's Space Systems and Command, Control and Communications; Sally K. Ride, the first U.S. woman astronaut in space; Robert W. Rummell, a member of the National Academy of Engineering and former vice president of TWA; Joseph F. Sutter, a Boeing executive vice president; Arthur B. C. Walker Jr., a professor of applied physics at Stanford University; and Albert D. Wheelon, an executive vice president at Hughes Aircraft. Completing the baker's dozen was General Chuck Yeager. Their swearing in (Covert and Yeager were the only absentees) took place in Washington on February 6.

In choosing Rogers as the chair and Armstrong as vice chair, Reagan girded the panel. "Bill Rogers was Mr. Outside, and he did that job very well," Neil commented. "He knew what the commission needed to have, and he knew the best ways to accommodate all the different constituents in this matter without jeopardizing the commission's work.

"Bill gave me the job of running the operational side of the committee, and then we formed some committees and put chairmen in the committees. I suggested that Donald Kutyna [active-duty military] be the head of the Accident Investigating Committee, because Don had been on accident boards before and he knew how they worked." "Neil was Mr. Inside," Kutyna remarks. "He really ran the commission."

Going in, Armstrong was privately concerned that the *Challenger* investigation would be conducted by an outside body and not by NASA, as with the Apollo 1 fire or the Apollo 13 accident. "As it happened, the hardcore investigators were out there doing their work anyway, and they weren't so much encumbered with having to deal with public hearings and other affairs that the commissioners were stuck with. So perhaps in the long run, being public didn't affect the investigation's timetable very much, but I had apprehensions about it in the first place."

Rogers's rationale for running the commission in a very public way was persuasive even to Armstrong. "At the start Bill talked to all of the commissioners about what his expectations were and some of the things he thought were very important. He thought it was very important, for example, for the commissioners to be aware of how public opinion was being expressed through the media. So he encouraged everyone to read the *Washington Post* and the *New York Times* every morning, stuff that I certainly wouldn't have thought of or encouraged. He understood that side of the equation.

"He was of a firm opinion—and I certainly agreed with this—that there ought to be one investigation, and that we had to find ways to placate the other constituencies out there that would like to be doing our job—or at least would like to be catching some of the limelight from it. So Bill was busy early on going over and talking with committee chairmen in the House and the Senate.

"So our compromise was that we, the commission, would report to Congress periodically. We would go over up to the Hill and testify to the progress of the investigation and what some of its difficult points were, some of the items we were making progress on, and what our outlooks were at that point. Then the legislators would get a certain amount of media coverage on what they were thinking and doing in Congress, but without it really affecting what was going on in the investigation.

"We had a lot more public hearings than I had ever been exposed to in any of the accident investigations that I had participated in before. So that was a new wrinkle for me. The fact that the investigation panel was a public entity had pluses and minuses. The pluses were that it did give us an opportunity to give a status report to the public at large as to what was happening, but it was also an opportunity for some people to play to the cameras."

As vice chair of the commission, Armstrong sat ex officio on all subcommittees. "I probably spent the most time on the accident itself, because my feeling was that, if we didn't get the accident pinned down precisely, then all the rest was for naught. So I wanted to be the closest to that.

"But each committee chair [Development and Production; Prelaunch Activities; Mission Planning and Operation; and Accident Analysis] established, with the help of their committee members, what kinds of matters they would be looking into, where they would go, and what kind of information they wanted to get. Then the commission staff headed by Dr. Alton G. Keel Jr., who came from the White House, and Thomas T. Reinhardt, an army major from the Office of Management of Budget, would put something together for each committee that would be sent out to Thiokol or North American or down to Huntsville. Each committee would set up their own schedule of hearings and presentations as well as site visits where they would look at hardware and get explained how things worked and see how things were put together. Each committee busied itself in the early months doing those kinds of things—getting a lot of data.

"From the Justice Department, we borrowed a system for keeping track of all the data and documents and filing them properly so that we could retrieve anything that we wanted at any time. So everything was both written down and computerized, which was good since the investigation generated almost 6,300 documents totaling more than 122,000 pages, as well as almost 12,000 pages of investigative and 2,800 pages of hearings transcript.

"We had several very good people on the staff, technically. There was a metallurgist from the National Transportation and Safety Board, Michael L. Marx, who was a great resource for us because metallurgical failures were involved in the burn-through of the Shuttle's solid rocket booster."

Armstrong did some of his own private investigating, seeking information or insights from some of the private contacts he had developed over thirty years in NASA and the aerospace industry. "On occasion I would talk to people privately. We had no such prohibitions from our chairman, so I didn't hesitate to do that."

Rogers specified, "We shouldn't be offering opinions before the commission had ruled on these matters. We shouldn't be giving individual opinions based on limited amounts of information. We shouldn't jump to conclusions, and we shouldn't be confusing the public by stating different positions. All contacts with the press were to be coordinated in advance, and there were a few times when commissioners were to talk to the press.

"Of course, we couldn't always get the commissioners to remember what the rules were! And the media was always trying to get us to speak out. I remember Andrea Mitchell from NBC News saying, 'Well, tell us this because it's interesting.' And I said, 'Ms. Mitchell, this commission is not about "interesting." This commission is about getting the answers.' We had a pretty good system of protecting the commissioners and keeping them out of the public eye."

Kutyna remembers another incident involving Vice Chair Armstrong and the press. "We had just flown in to Huntsville and the media was inside Marshall Space Flight Center headquarters, the von Braun building, waiting for us, anxious to get to Neil in particular. The reporters were chasing him down the hall and I said, 'I know! Let's get in the elevator! They will never get us there!' So we jumped into the elevator and, of course, a media guy reached his arm in and pushed the stop button. There was Neil cornered in the back of this elevator with forty microphones, just sweating bullets."

"I think we pretty much would have made the same conclusions without the public hearings. As for whether the investigation would have concluded any faster without them, because proof of our hypothesis [that "the cause of the *Challenger* accident was the failure of the pressure seal in the aft field joint of the right solid rocket motor . . . due to a faulty design unacceptably sensitive to a number of factors" including cold temperature] only came when we finally got that last piece of debris off the bottom of the ocean, the end result couldn't really be hurried up."

Transcripts of the public hearings into *Challenger* dated February 6 to May 2, 1986, illustrate the driving acumen behind Armstrong's investigative thinking:

> *February 6, to Arnold Aldrich, Shuttle program manager at Johnson Space Center, Houston, Texas: "Could I ask the source of the ice, what percentage was due to the ambient conditions and what was condensation on the vehicle that froze?"*

> *February 14, to Robert K. Lund, Thiokol vice president for engineering: "Clearly, you had a concern about temperature. Did you ever consider or take thought of controlling the temperature at the seals, or to changing the material of the seals to something that had different characteristics?"*

> *February 25, to Allan McDonald, director, Solid Rocket Motor Project and Thiokol's senior man at Kennedy Space Center: "Had Morton Thiokol to your knowledge ever informed NASA that the launch commit criteria were inadequate or did not in fact cover the kinds of conditions that you were concerned about?"*

> *March 21, to George Abbey, director of Flight Crew Operations, JSC: "I think I understand that we have a system of very complex information flow and a system that you've devised with checks and balances to make sure that information flow properly gets to the right people. Nevertheless, we have to face the fact that somehow it hasn't."*

The public hearings portion of the Rogers Commission investigation concluded with Armstrong's leading another tough line of questioning for a NASA official (Lawrence M. Weeks, Jesse Moore's deputy in NASA's office for space flight), but not before Chairman Rogers's confrontational summary: "Now, in answer to Mr. Armstrong's questions, I got the impression you didn't think there was anything wrong with the [NASA communications] system at all. Everybody knew what everybody else was doing, and I gather you don't think the system of communication should be changed. Is that right?"

When it was all over, Armstrong came out pleased with the commission's conclusions and recommendations. "I think the conclusions and findings were right on, and I think our descriptions of how the accident occurred were very close to precisely correct. There have been only a few contrary opinions or hypotheses, but none of them have stood the test of time."

One of the most stubborn contrary opinions—primarily by engineers at NASA's Marshall Space Flight Center in Alabama—is that instead of putting so much emphasis on frozen O-rings and on a flawed decision-making process to launch, the Rogers Commission should have taken a closer look at the effects of reusability on the external tank and solid rocket boosters—most specifically that, as a result of an assembly flaw at Cape Kennedy, the aft- and aft-center segments of *Challenger*'s guilty right-hand SRB were not mated together properly, were out of round, thereby creating the leaky joint and burn-through leading to the explosion.

As he did at the time, Armstrong supports the commission's conclusions as the proper ones. "We spent so much time at the Cape. We were there to see how they put the SRBs and ET together. We looked at what all the possible errors could be as they were joining the sections, right there at the Cape. We didn't discount the fact that there could be errors in assembly—and that the errors could be serious—but it was unanimous in the commission when we got to the end point, beyond a reasonable doubt of what had happened."

Armstrong played the key role in laying out the basis for the manner of thinking that went into the commission's final report. "I made the case to fellow commissioners that the effectiveness of our recommendations was going to be inversely proportional to their number. The fewer, the better. Second, let's make sure that we don't tell NASA to do something it can't do. Those were the two fundamental ground rules.

"Then we had a long session where everybody wrote down everything that they thought might be related to a recommendation. Everybody wrote down everything they could think of, and we put them all together. There were a lot of duplications, but we got them down to about sixty or seventy.

"Then I said, 'Okay, which of these are semiredundant or related? Is there any way we can combine these?' That way we finally got down to nine. The nine had subparts to them, but we arrived at nine fundamental recommendations. I would have liked it to be only five, but everybody had their own pet items that they wanted to make sure got in, which was a product of their own experience and investigative work for the past several months. So everyone felt fully invested in it.

"So we could only get down so far. Still in all, that's not bad. I've seen other reports, and they have a hundred recommendations. A report with a hundred recommendations doesn't mean anything.

"Two or three of our recommendations related to NASA as an organization. [Recommendation II concerned NASA management structure, and Recommendation V dealt with improved communications. Recommendation III involved criticality review and hazard analysis.] I think those were taken to heart. It seemed to me at the time that NASA was going to try to implement everything that was said."

As for Chuck Yeager, "He came once, for the first meeting. Chairman Rogers was very concerned that Yeager might not sign the final report because he had no basis for signing it, really. I believe Bill Rogers sent him a copy of the signature page to sign and return by mail."

As for Richard Feynman's famous Minority Report to the Space Shuttle Challenger Inquiry, contrary to stories that the commission tried hard to suppress its publication (because it was allegedly "anti-NASA"), Armstrong was okay with the colorful physicist expressing his unique take on the subject and attaching it to the commission's final report as an appendix, as long as Chairman Rogers was.

Armstrong knew the truth of what Richard Feynman wrote at the end of his Minority Report, because he had been living and breathing it ever since he first took flight in an airplane forty years earlier: "For a successful technology, reality must take precedence over public relations, for nature cannot be fooled."

On Saturday morning, February 1, 2003, a morning phone call from a friend drove Armstrong to the television in his study. Another Space Shuttle was lost. Just minutes before its scheduled landing at the Cape, STS-107, *Columbia,* had come to pieces over Texas, high in the Earth's atmosphere, following a sixteen-day mission to the International Space Station.

As soon as Neil heard reports that debris was being found, "I knew at that point the vehicle was lost. There was no chance." Another tragic loss of a crew of astronauts: Rick Husband, the commander; Willie McCool, the pilot; five mission specialists: Kalpana Chawla, Laurel Clark, Mike Anderson, David Brown, and Ilan Roman, payload specialist.

The seventy-three-year-old former test pilot and astronaut watched TV for the rest of the day as did millions of other deeply saddened Americans. The height at which the *Columbia* had been ripped apart was a little over thirty-nine miles. Neil could not help but ponder the irony that the Shuttle had broken up at almost exactly the same height as his highest flight in the X-15—207,500 feet.

A few reporters tried to reach him, and Neil agreed to do an interview with a woman from his hometown paper, the *Cincinnati Enquirer.* "People should not jump to conclusions about how this happened," he told her. "The first impression is usually wrong. These things take time. Nobody wants to know the answers more quickly than those who run the Shuttle program. They will be working with as much speed as possible.

"It is a sad day. You don't want to hear this. There is a great deal of grief."

This time around there was no phone call asking him to serve on a presidential panel; the investigation would be handled very differently—more internally within NASA. Instead the Bush White House telephoned to ask if Neil and Carol, Neil's second wife, would attend the memorial service for the *Columbia* crew, scheduled for Monday, February 3, at the Johnson Space Center in Houston, which they quickly agreed to do. The day that the country paid its respects to the lost astronauts was seventeen years to the day after Armstrong had arrived at Bill Rogers's New York office to begin the *Challenger* investigation.

"We like to think that we are immortal as a species and we will keep going. But if that's true, we are going to have to increase the number of options we have for survival.

"If our striving, if our decision to do it, is based on a threat like incoming asteroids, epidemic diseases, or other catastrophic scenarios like that, if that's what's driving us, then we will recognize and know why we are doing it. But it might be that we won't recognize we are doing it for other reasons, perhaps not even explicitly for science or for industrial development."

The United States should recognize "a lot of persuasive reasons why we could benefit from a return visit" to the Moon. "It's reachable. We know it's reachable. We know what it takes to do it. Long before the beginning of the Apollo program, sometime right after the birth of NASA in 1958, someone said that the Moon was the best space objective for mankind because if we could go to the Moon, we would have solved all the essential elements of spaceflight, which are leaving one gravitational system and going into another and landing on another body in a new environment. If you could do that, by the same token you could go anywhere. In that sense, I think travel back and forth between Earth and the Moon remains our first objective."

The idea of space tourism does not provide a reliable foundation, however, on which to build and coordinate a national space program, in Armstrong's view. "I am suspicious of space tourism being the winning model because, in my view, the reliability of the technology has not developed to the point where the model could survive after a few catastrophes, though I don't object to its advocates trying to build that kind of a model and trying to make it work.

"We know that we can go to Mars—we've done it with probes. It is my belief that we can go there with humans and that we could do it now. We could go straight away. We probably do need to know a little bit more about the radiation protection requirements for a trip of that duration. When you are away from a large body—either the Earth or the Moon—you don't have the protection. The Earth's atmosphere and magnetic field shields us. What there is of the lunar atmosphere provides some shielding. But in free space going to Mars, we are going to be encountering a radiation environment from a complete sphere and that is impacting us from all directions.

"We know a lot about what that flux is. But we don't have a high confidence level yet in our knowledge of just what the appropriate level of protection is for humans for that kind of environment, for that duration. That needs more study.

"Going back to the Moon makes sense, not as another 'flying-the-flag' project but rather as a slowly evolving, steady progression of scientific understanding and engineering knowledge."

In January 2004, President George W. Bush announced a "new vision" for the U.S. space program. The president proposed a commitment to a long-term human and robotic program to explore the solar system, starting with a return to the Moon that, in the view of the White House, "will ultimately enable future exploration of Mars and other destinations." Two months later, Armstrong, in Houston to accept the Rotary National Award for Space Achievement, lent his support to the Bush plan. "Our president has introduced a new initiative with renewed emphasis on the exploration of our solar system and expansion of human frontiers. This proposal has substantial merit and promise. Our economy can afford an effort of this magnitude, but the public must believe the benefits to society deserve the investment. We know the advancement of knowledge and the rate of progress is proportional to the risk encountered. . . . The success of the endeavor will also be dependent on the degrees to which the aerospace community, government, industry, and academia can coalesce their forces and converge on a common goal."

Later in 2004, Armstrong was asked to testify at congressional hearings on the Bush space plan, but prior commitments precluded it. He did do a voice-over narration of a NASA video report on the plan.

There have been many critics of the Bush plan both inside and outside the space community, but Neil's philosophy, even before knowing all of the details of the proposal, has been to favor anything that moves the technology forward. In June 2004, he commented: "I know that some people think going back to the Moon would be a mistake and that we should target Mars for a human landing right now. I don't argue against the merits of that, because I'm a Mars enthusiast myself. Nevertheless I think those of us in the aerospace world have to take the opportunities where we find them. I am a great believer in the fact that you make progress built on other progress."

To critics of the Bush initiative who fear the militarization of outer space, Armstrong offers: "We are party to an international treaty on uses of the Moon. I'm quite confident that those legal concerns, as well as other concerns, would express themselves before we got too far down any particular path of further militarization of space."

As for other nations of the world competing or cooperating with the United States in major space endeavors, Armstrong, like many in the U.S. space program, has mixed feelings. "Significant accomplishments by the Chinese would certainly be a factor in how the United States viewed its own program. I personally don't see the evidence of the Chinese having as far-reaching ambitions as some have surmised. Time will tell. For their space ambitions, the Chinese don't seem to have the secretive nature that the Soviets did. They essentially do announce what they are going to do. In recent years, some reports have said that the Chinese plan to send astronauts to the Moon as soon as possible and other reports saying that goal is longer term. They did an unmanned probe, but it's hard to tell. I have been invited to China on a number of occasions, but not by the space science people. I have not gone to China and not accepted any of its invitations."

It may seem ironic to many, but Neil Armstrong has never considered himself an *explorer:* "What I attended to was the progressive development of flight machinery. My exploration came totally as a by-product of that. I flew to the Moon not so much to go there but as part of developing the systems that would allow it to happen."

CHAPTER 34

The Astronaut as Icon

Not surprisingly, one of Armstrong's boyhood heroes was Charles A. Lindbergh. Neil first met Lindbergh along with his wife, Anne, at the launch of Apollo 8. "I was given the job of helping with touring him around and taking him and showing him the facilities. The night before the launch, I took him out to look at the Saturn V; it was all illuminated with the xenon lights. As Frank Borman's backup, I couldn't spend more than just a little time with him." At the launch, Janet also had a chance to meet the Lindberghs. "I thought Anne Morrow was just fabulous. I had read her book *Gift from the Sea.* Neil's mother had given me a copy after Karen's death. Anne's description of the Apollo 8 launch, published in *Life,* was in my mind the only one that was able to communicate what it was really like to see and feel a liftoff." Lindbergh himself was quoted as saying, "I have never experienced such a sense of power."

Lindbergh biographer A. Scott Berg has written, "Lindbergh accepted an invitation from Neil A. Armstrong to attend the launch of Apollo 11 . . . quietly attending the event with his son Jon." Neil does not specifically remember inviting the man whom friends called "Slim": "I might have. Once we got into quarantine, the crew couldn't be bothered anymore, so we never really knew who came and who didn't." Most likely, Armstrong did ask Lindbergh to come, because he attended, later calling the successful Moon landing a "fascinating, extraordinary, and beautifully executed mission." Lindbergh, however, refused President Nixon's invitation to accompany him to the USS *Hornet* for the astronauts' recovery, later explaining: "My declining was based on the fact that I spent close to a quarter century . . . achieving a position in which I could live, work, and travel under normal conditions." Apollo 11's splashdown would naturally "attract the greatest concentration of publicity in the history of the world."

Privately, Neil had the chance to talk with Slim "several times" following Apollo 11. "We both went to the Society of Experimental Test Pilots meeting in Los Angeles in late September 1969. He was being inducted as an honorary fellow, and we were seated next to each other at the banquet." The two fliers also corresponded, as Neil would later do with Anne Morrow before and after Neil came to cochair the Lindbergh Memorial Fund. Lindbergh posed to Neil the rhetorical question: "I wonder if you felt on the Moon's surface as I did after landing at Paris in 1927—that I would like to have had more chance to look around."

Following Lindbergh's death in 1974, when Armstrong was frequently asked to compare the historic flight of 1927 and the Moon landing, he'd note, "There are certain similarities in the two events."

It was Armstrong's conclusion, however, that "they are probably more unlike than alike—most important because General Lindbergh's achievement was very individual. There were a limited number of people involved—just a financier, some investors, and him. In the case of Apollo it was an effort of national will, one in which hundreds of thousands of people were involved. We faced different degrees of complexity, but I wouldn't make light of the general's accomplishment. He had mastered the technology of his day no less than we mastered ours. One reason his flight was so well received is that many different kinds of people were trying to accomplish the same thing. We pretty much had the Moon to ourselves."

The inevitable next question was an uncomfortable one for Neil: how the First Man and "Lucky Lindy" compared on the public adoration front. "I'm not called upon as much as I used to be," Neil remarked in 1976, "but enough so I do understand his predicament."

At the SETP banquet in September 1969, Lindbergh had offered Neil one, and only one, piece of advice: "He told me never to sign autographs.

"Unfortunately I didn't take his advice for thirty years, and I probably should have."

During the eight years he was at the University of Cincinnati, most of Armstrong's fan mail came through the campus post office, his only well-known address. "That was a bit of an uncomfortable thing for me because the majority of the correspondence that I received was from people I didn't know and the majority of that, ninety-eight percent of them, wanted something. Not more than two percent had anything at all to do with the university, so the university was forced to spend resources supporting all that mail, including a special secretary.* Generally we didn't get that kind of mail at home because most people didn't know our home address."

When he left the university, Neil soon realized that handling his mail on his own was an impossible burden. In February 1980 he rented a small office on Broadway in Lebanon, Ohio, then "I had my accountant put an ad in the paper, not with my name on it," for an administrative aide.† Vivian White of Lebanon had worked in the local real estate business for twenty-eight years as well as being a part-time secretary for the mayor of Lebanon. Vivian "worked out very well, a very good choice," in part because, as Vivian explains, "I don't ask! That has been my policy all along. You can tell what a private person he is, and I just made it a point that I don't ask him anything that I don't need to know to do my job.

"He didn't even have any furniture in the office when we started. We sat down at a folding card table and he asked me a few questions, and he just happened to ask me things that I knew!" Then "he and his son Mark carried my furniture down the street and put it in this bare office."

White worked full-time for about ten years; after that, she "cut back" to four and a half days a week. Armstrong's countless correspondents received form letters that he himself composed.

"For the first twelve to fifteen years, he would sign anything he was asked to sign, except a first-day cover. Sometimes a letter would come in and I would think, 'That name looks kind of familiar. I think this guy asked before.' So I would go back through the files and check to see if Neil had signed for this guy before. If so, I would just send it back unsigned. Then about 1993, he realized that his autographs were being sold over the Internet. Many of the signatures, he found, were forgeries. So he just quit signing. Still, we get letters saying, 'I know Mr. Armstrong doesn't sign anymore, but would you ask him to make an exception for me?' "

Since 1993, form letters under Vivian's signature have gone out in an-

---

* Three different secretaries worked for Armstrong while he was at the University of Cincinnati: Ruta Bankovikis (1971–73), Luanna Fisher (1974–76), and Elaine Moore (1977–79).

† The Armstrong office on Broadway in downtown Lebanon, Ohio, lasted for roughly six years, until 1986. After that, for a while, the office was at Neil's farm on Route 123 north of town. Then the office moved briefly to a building on the northern outskirts of Cincinnati. For the last dozen years, the mail has been handled at a Columbus Avenue office back in Lebanon. Letters always came to Armstrong through this entire twenty-five-year period though a Lebanon post office box number.

swer to 99 percent of the requests, which she categorizes into eleven boxes. First is "I want an autograph or an autographed picture," second, "I want a congratulatory letter for becoming an Eagle Scout." A third is individual youth requests for information about piloting or space exploration, a fourth for similar requests coming from entire classes. A fifth comes from students seeking astronaut qualifications. A sixth asks for donations or contributions for a charitable auction. A seventh responds to invitations for specific events, an eighth for requests for speaking engagements, a ninth for queries from authors wanting a foreword to their book. A tenth category handles media interview requests. Nearly all are declined via standardized letter. In the few instances that Armstrong accepts the invitation, he composes and signs a personal letter. If he chooses to answer someone's technical question, according to White, "he will write out his answer, I'll type it up and then put underneath it, 'Mr. Armstrong asked me to give you the following information,' and I sign it.

"We never answer personal questions—they're just too much an invasion of privacy." They go into "File Eleven," the wastebasket.

On the outbound journey to the Sea of Tranquility from aboard *Columbia,* Neil made sure to pass along a "hello to all my fellow Scouts at Farragut State Park in Idaho having a National Jamboree there this week; Apollo 11 would like to send them best wishes." For several years thereafter he took the time to write letters congratulating boys who had achieved the ultimate rank of Eagle Scout.

In the 1990s, Armstrong concluded that the practice had taken a disturbing turn: "Congratulatory letters should be from people who know the Scouts personally, who know what they've achieved and honestly want to congratulate them. When Scouts get letters from political potentates that have actually been written by staff members and signed by an autopen, perhaps it impresses the individual getting the award and receiving that message, but it's the wrong message. It's just something that the Scouts don't do right."

According to White, "In the first five months of 2003 alone, we received 950 letters asking for congratulatory letters for new Eagle Scouts. And he used to do this! But after people put his address on the Internet with the word he did this sort of thing, it just increased so much there was no way he could do it."

"Over the years I have done a lot of work on behalf of the Scouts," Neil relates, "but I have not done any of that in recent years." Much to the chagrin of the BSA, "I have no official association with them." As for congratulatory letters to Eagle Scouts, today he will only write them to young Cincinnati residents whom he personally knows.

Armstrong's belated decision to follow Charles Lindbergh's advice has provoked disappointment and even antagonism, mostly from profiteer, or more commonly, hobbyist "collectors" of autographs and space memorabilia.

One 2000 posting on collectSPACE.com, the Internet's leading resource and community Web site for space history enthusiasts and space artifact collectors, growled: "I realize that many astronauts have been generous with their signing of autographs. And that is wonderful. But some have been stingy from day one. But do they have the right to totally cut the general public off? I do not think so. I am sorry to say this, but, yes, they do owe us something. I am not suggesting that they should sign anything and everything rudely thrust in front of them, anytime, anyplace. Certainly not. They are our cherished American heroes and, yes, they do have a private life. But why can't there be some kind of middle ground? If an astronaut has a bad experience with an ugly collector, or is just plain tired of signing, by all means, take a break. But, please do not use that as an excuse to punish all of us by saying no forever."

Robert Pearlman, the founder of collectSPACE, relates four primary reasons why collectors feel that all astronauts, but Armstrong in particular, should sign autographs. Primarily, "Armstrong was granted the opportunity to go to the Moon by virtue of American taxpayers footing the bill, so he 'owes' us his signature." Pearlman and like-minded hobbyist collectors of space memorabilia rightfully reject this argument.

Pearlman explains the second argument of the "mad collector." "There are tales—some more substantiated than others—of dealers or accumulators discovering that Armstrong would reply through the mail with twenty five or thirty autographed photos when a teacher would request signatures for his/her classroom and thus these 'bad eggs' began faking educational affiliations. Likewise, some dealers would pay or invent children to request signatures on the theory it would improve their chances of a positive reply. Some collectors feel they do not deserve to be penalized for something that they never would dream to do."

Third, collectors suggest that Armstrong "could do a lot of good if he would only sign for a fee and donate the proceeds to a worthy cause."

Finally, perturbed collectors believe that it was Armstrong's disdain for "the autograph market" that provoked his stringent policy—which has served to drive the value of signed Armstrong items ever higher. On the

Internet or at an auction in 2005, collectors faced the following high price list:

- Index card: $250 to $350;
- 8 x 10 photo/lithograph, other than portrait, personalized: $600 to $800;
- 8 x 10 photo/lithograph, portrait, personalized: $600 to $1,200;
- 8 x 10 photo/lithograph, without personalization: $2,000 to $5,000;
- typewritten letter on NASA letterhead, signed: $600 to $800;
- handwritten letter and signed: $1,500 to $2,500;
- magazines, books, event programs, newspapers: $250 to $500;
- covers (stamped, canceled envelopes), not flown: $800 to $1,500;
- commercial art prints (by Calle or Rasmussen), may include other signatures: $2,200 to $3,500 (will vary greatly depending on what the photograph depicts).

According to Pearlman, any of these items—index cards the exception—have sold in the past decade for upwards of $10,000, prior ownership, market venue, and the degree of provenance all being influencing factors. Today, Neil Armstrong forgeries far outnumber the authentic examples. One estimate places the fake Armstrong signatures as high as 90 percent of the eBay catalog.

The ultimate Armstrong memento, Pearlman relates, would be a signed picture or letter that includes Neil's famous quote "one small step." For years it was believed that no authentic examples of such an item existed. Recently, "an authentic example," signed while Neil was still in quarantine, surfaced, and though it never sold, many thought it could easily reach $25,000, if not higher.

Armstrong categorically denounces any such item as a fake. "I know that to be false, because I have never, ever quoted myself. From day one, I never did that. So it doesn't exist anywhere. Not for my mom, not for the Smithsonian, not for anybody—there is not one anywhere. Not in quarantine or any other time. I never did one."

Without question, Armstrong's signature remains by far the most popularly sought after astronaut autograph. Enthusiasts call it "the holy grail" of autographs. Armstrong handwriting "experts" have even published articles on how the downstrokes to his "N" and "A" and other characteristics of his signature have changed over the years. Though not rare (given how many signatures Neil provided for the public for over twenty years), given the perceived value and the desire to possess his autograph, demand is high.

One unhappy result is that the hundreds of children and teenagers who write to Armstrong yearly of their own fascination with flying or space exploration are disappointed. Questions such as "How did you feel when you were cramped inside the lunar module?" and "What did you learn about yourself after the trip to the Moon?" never cease to fascinate. Though these are the people Armstrong might wish to exempt from his no-autograph policy, it is simply not possible. As a last resort, he has gone with Lindbergh's way.

On the third anniversary of Apollo 11 in July 1972, the Neil Armstrong Air and Space Museum opened in Wapakoneta right near the junction of Interstate 75 and U.S. Highway 33. The pride of Ohio governor James Rhodes, the facility began with half a million dollars earmarked by the state legislature even before the Apollo 11 mission was over—even before Armstrong's likeness made out of butter melted at that summer's Ohio State Fair. Its exterior designed to resemble a rising full Moon, the museum's grand opening featured an appearance by the twenty-six-year-old presidential daughter Tricia Nixon, who said, "Because of what you, Neil, have done, the heavens have become a part of our world." Before a crowd of five thousand, the blond Tricia then presented the museum with one of Apollo 11's Moon rocks: "It is a rock which symbolizes mankind's ability for great achievement to build a better America and a better world."

Armstrong's attendance at the grand opening was shrouded in rumor and uncertainty fueled by newspaper reports that his presence came at the behest of President Nixon, who didn't want his daughter embarrassed. Frequently during Miss Nixon's visit, she was overheard to say, "Daddy will be so pleased." Armstrong told the press, "This is not a homecoming for me. I'm just here to see the museum." After touring the exhibits, Neil indicated his preference for "the old displays," notably the Aeronca airplane in which he had learned to fly thirty-six years ago.

Armstrong put on a relatively happy face for the crowd that day, many of them old friends and neighbors, but he was not at all happy with how the entire museum project had come together: "I should have been asked. The policy I followed from the start had been that I neither encouraged nor prohibited the use of my name on public buildings, but I did not approve their use on any commercial or other nonpublic facility.

"If the organizing committee had asked me I'm sure I would have said okay, because it was in the town where my parents lived. Nevertheless, I would have been happier had they not used my name or, if they used my name, they would have used a different approach for the museum.

"I did try to support them in any way that I could by presenting them with such materials as I had available, either gifting or loaning items.

"From the outset I was uncomfortable because that museum was built as the 'Neil Armstrong Museum.' A number of people came to believe that it was my personal property and a business undertaking of mine. The Ohio Historical Society in Columbus was actually going to be overseeing the museum, and I told its director that I felt uncomfortable. I asked him as well as another member of the planning board if there was anything that could be done about the public image issue and to respond to me about what they thought. They said they would, but they did not."

Armstrong's relationship with the museum leadership has remained strained throughout the thirty-three years of the facility's existence. In the mid-1990s, for example, came the issue of a picture postcard of Neil as an astronaut on sale in the museum gift shop. The image came from an official NASA photograph, taken when he was a federal government employee. For him it was a question of ownership. The rights to the picture belong to the people, the same visitors, Neil believes, who "think I own the place." The seal of the Ohio Historical Society is displayed inside the main door, but according to Neil, "it's so low profile that most people don't notice it." Eventually, Armstrong relented on the matter of the picture, granting then museum director John Zwez "my permission on a limited-time basis."

As for the namesake Wapakoneta airport, "Again, they just didn't ask. It's a public airport so, had they asked, I probably would have said sure, okay. The problem is that there were businesses on that airport that took the name of the airport, like the 'Neil Armstrong Electronics Shop.' "

In the 1990s Armstrong had a run-in with Hallmark, the greeting card company.

"The Hallmark case was simple," Neil relates. "They put out a Christmas tree ornament. It had a little spaceman inside it. It also had a recording that played my voice, and it had my name on the box." Hallmark advertised the product by saying, "The Moon glows as the famous words spoken by Neil Armstrong when he stepped out on the Moon and into history." Unfortunately, Hallmark's people had not received or even asked his permission. Nor did the popular card company follow NASA's established procedures for such matters.

So in 1994 Neil sued Hallmark. Wendy Armstrong, the wife of his son Mark, served as his attorney. At the end of 1995, the two parties settled out of court: "Hallmark Cards announced today that it had settled a lawsuit with Apollo 11 astronaut Neil Armstrong over the use of his likeness in a Christmas ornament last year. Armstrong had claimed that his name and likeness was used without his permission on the ornament, which celebrated the twenty-fifth anniversary of the Apollo 11 landing. The size of the settlement was undisclosed, but said by one source to be substantial. Armstrong plans to donate the settlement from the Kansas City–based company, minus legal fees, to Purdue University, his alma mater." Purdue later confirmed that it received the money.

"NASA hadn't been very careful about the matter, either. Up to then, it had been pretty careless in the treatment of individual rights. Now, I get letters that correctly state what NASA's position is about getting my approval, and before that I never did. I get many such requests, some of which I've granted [some without charge and some for a fee] and some of which I haven't.

"In many cases where they are either nonprofit or government public-service announcements, I will approve them. At first, I wasn't very careful about keeping records of this and would just say, 'Yes, that's all right.' Then, after being exposed to the legal world, I recognized that you have to have all kinds of files of proof."

An even more loathsome legal matter concerned the sale of some of Neil's hair. In early 2005, the Lebanon, Ohio, barbershop that Neil had patronized for more than twenty years sold some of its famous client's locks for $3,000 to a Connecticut man who, according to Guinness World Records, had amassed the largest collection of hair from "historical celebrities." In a private conversation in the back of the shop, Neil asked his barber to either return the hair or donate the $3,000 to a charity of Armstrong's choosing. When neither result followed, Neil's attorney sent the barber a two-page letter, one that referenced an Ohio law protecting the names of its celebrities. Instead of settling the matter quietly, the barber sent the letter to local media. The strange story attracted international attention.

Christian leaders the world over gave voice to the idea that humankind's trip to the Moon was a "pilgrimage," a "spiritual quest," and that at the heart of all flying, all space exploration, was a religious truth.

NASA's master rocketeer and builder of the Saturn V, Wernher von

Braun, expressed the sentiment in 1969 for the scientific and technical community: "Astronomy and space exploration are teaching us that the good Lord is a much greater Lord, and Master of a greater kingdom. The fact that Christ carried out his mission on Earth does not limit his validity for a greater environment. It could very well be that the Lord would send his Son to other worlds, taking whatever steps are necessary to bring the Truth to His Creation."

Pope Paul VI expressed it for the Catholic world, referring to the Moon landing as "the ecstasy of this prophetic day."

The morning Apollo 11 launched, Reverend Herman Weber gave voice to it for Viola and for all American evangelicals from his pulpit in Wapakoneta's St. Paul United Church of Christ: "As Thou hast guided our astronauts in previous flights, so guide, we pray, Neil, the esteemed son of our proud community, and his partners, Buzz and Michael, and all others who are involved in this righteous Lunar flight in every station."

In a speech to his congregation days after the Moon landing, the Iowa minister to whom Viola later confided by letter that Neil had strayed from the truth of Jesus Christ, asked, "Could the external presence of Neil Armstrong, the courageous leader, be a symbol of the presence within of the strong arm of the Lord? . . . Their place was the Moon, their ship was the *Eagle,* which landed on a firm rock at a place called Tranquility Base. Could there possibly be a rock of ages which is a base for all tranquility, for all peace?"

Several theologians, Protestant and Catholic, concurred: "Armstrong's boots, grating on the crisp, dry surface of the Moon, have announced a new theological watershed. That earthly sound on an unearthly body will lead to a profound shift in the faith and basic attitudes of Christians and other believers, a fact that gradually will become apparent with coming generations. . . . It will cause an eventual, and inevitable, modification in the way man comprehends the man-God relationship—perhaps the most important keystone in his ego-structure and in his concept of his place in eternity."

These thinkers were of the mind that God put Neil Armstrong (but not Buzz?) on the Moon to show God's greatness in a new light; to reveal God's expansive presence; restore "proper balance" in humankind's outlook on life; and make people *believe* in God even more deeply than before. "Of course, we knew that the astronauts were religious men. They *had* to be religious. We wouldn't have sent atheists to the Moon or even let them into an astronaut program."

A number of them were, in fact, religious men. A few turned more spiritual after their lunar experience. Apollo 15's James Irwin, who walked on the Moon in August 1971, became an evangelical minister. "I felt the power of God as I'd never felt it before," Irwin later wrote. Apollo 16's Charlie Duke, one of the CapComs for Apollo 11, became active in missionary work, explaining, "I make speeches about walking *on* the Moon and walking *with* the Son."

An Internet document entitled "Onward Christian Spacemen: A Call for Christian Leadership of Manned Space Exploration" calls Christians not only to participate in manned space exploration but also to command and lead it over the likes of the "theologically naïve."

Another spiritual critic of the "godless" American space program and its "soulless" astronauts has written:

> *[The crew of Apollo 11] were not even high priests. They were altar boys: stand here, go there, do that, hold this. At best, they were vessels for others to find divine grace. We are taught nothing by [the astronauts], but we can learn from them. . . . The pilgrimage to the Moon exposed the limits of the mode of consciousness that it set out to glorify. It uncovered no new world except the one that it foolishly attempted to leave behind.*

Assertions linger that the telephone number connecting President Nixon to Armstrong and Aldrin on the lunar surface was 666-6666, a sign of the Antichrist, as well as equally ridiculous claims that the Moon landing was a conspiracy of Freemasons. (The "evidence": that Aldrin carried a Masonic flag with him in his PPK, which Buzz presented upon his return to the lodge's Sovereign Grand Commander of the Supreme Council of the World, which is true, and, second, that Neil's father was a thirty-third-degree Mason. Stephen Armstrong was a Mason, but Neil does not know his rank.)

Even more deeply entrenched is the rumor that Neil Armstrong converted to Islam.

For the past three and a half decades, stories have been repeated all around the Muslim world that when Armstrong and Aldrin walked on the Moon, they heard a voice singing in a strange language that they did not understand. Only later, after returning to Earth, did Armstrong realize that what he heard on the lunar surface was the *adhan,* the Muslim call to prayer. Neil then allegedly converted to Islam, moved to Lebanon (the country in the Middle East, not Lebanon, Ohio), and subsequently visited several Muslim holy places, including the Turkish *masjid* where Malcolm X once prayed.

The story of Armstrong's conversion grew so far and wide by the early 1980s that, not only Armstrong himself, but also an official body of the United States government, found it necessary to respond. In March 1983, the U.S. State Department sent the following message to all embassies and consulates in the Islamic world:

1. *Former astronaut Neil Armstrong, now in private life, has been the subject of press reports in Egypt, Malaysia and Indonesia (and perhaps elsewhere) alleging his conversion to Islam during his landing on the Moon in 1969. As a result of such reports, Armstrong has received communications from individuals and religious organizations, and a feeler from at least one government, about his possible participation in Islamic activities.*

2. *While stressing his strong desire not to offend anyone or show disrespect for any religion, Armstrong has advised department that reports of his conversion to Islam are inaccurate.*

3. *If post receive queries on this matter, Armstrong requests that they politely but firmly inform querying party that he has not converted to Islam and has no current plans or desire to travel overseas to participate in Islamic religious activities.*

Whatever help the State Department might have been in clarifying Armstrong's views, it wasn't enough. Requests for him to appear in Muslim countries and at Islamic events became so frequent in the mid-1980s that Neil felt compelled to act. "We were getting such a barrage of information, just inundated with questions about this, predominately from the Islamic world but also from the non-Muslim world, the latter of which was saying, 'This can't be true, can it?' Finally we decided that we needed to have something official that journalists could refer to. We again used the State Department, this time to assist in setting up a telephone press conference to Cairo, Egypt, where a substantial number of journalists from the Middle East could be there to ask me questions and get my response. That way they all heard the same thing.

"Just how much that helped is impossible to know, but it certainly didn't completely stem the questions." Some clung to the notion that the U.S. government didn't want their great American hero to be known as a Muslim, and thus was somehow forcing him publicly to deny his faith.

"Once I was visiting the Phi Delta Theta house at Purdue and a student came up that seemed to be living in the fraternity house. His father was a professor at Stanford. Apparently the young man was of Middle Eastern descent, and his father had told him about my conversion to Islam. So he asked me if it was true and I, of course, told him that it wasn't true. I could tell that he thought I was lying to him. He did not believe me. He'd been convinced that I would lie about it."

In recent years the story has even gotten embellished to include the assertion that Apollo 11 discovered that the Earth emitted radiation (which it does) and that the source of the radiation came from the Ka'ba in Mecca, proving that Mecca is "the center of the world."

Today, Vivian White tries hard to set the record straight with a form letter that states, "The reports of his conversion to Islam and of hearing the voice of the *adhan* on the Moon and elsewhere are all untrue."

Armstrong understands why such projections—phenomenal and otherwise—are made onto him. "I have found that many organizations claim me as a member, for which I am not a member, and a lot of different families—Armstrong families and others—make connections, many of which don't exist. So many people identify with the success of Apollo. The claim about my becoming a Muslim is just an extreme version of people inevitably telling me they know somebody whom I might know."

Armstrong, because he was so hard to know, turned out to be myth personified, an enigma prime to be filled with meaning.

In the late 1970s, *Chariots of the Gods?* (1969) author Erich von Däniken tried to turn Armstrong into a collaborator on his sensational (and best-selling) theory of "ancient astronauts," extraterrestrial beings who had visited Earth in the remote past and left various archaeological traces of their civilization-building activities.

In August 1976 Armstrong had accompanied a Scottish regiment, Black Watch and the Royal Highland Fusiliers, on a scientific expedition into the vast Cueva de los Tayos ("Caves of the Oil Birds") in a remote part of Ecuador first discovered by the Argentinian Juan Moricz.

At the time, Neil was unaware that in *The Gold of the Gods*, Von Däniken's 1972 follow-up to *Chariots of the Gods?*, the controversial Swiss author had described his own exploration of the Cueva de los Tayos, in which he claimed to have found considerable archaeological evidence of an extraterrestrial presence, including that certain doorways in the cave were too square to have been made naturally. "But it was the conclusion of our expedition group," relates Neil, "that they were natural formations."

Newspaper reports of the Los Tayos expedition and Armstrong's role in it made it clear that Von Däniken's claims about the caves were false. In a two-page letter written to Neil from his home in Zürich, Switzerland, on February 18, 1977, Von Däniken told the world's most famous astronaut that Armstrong's "expedition cannot possibly have been to my cave."

Von Däniken then urged Armstrong "to participate in a cave expedition which I am presently planning" whereby "relics from an extraterrestrial civilization—will be inspected."

Armstrong responded politely: "Because of my Scottish ancestry, and the fact that the U.K. side of this project was largely Scottish, I was invited to act as honorary chairman of the expedition, and I accepted. . . . I had not read your books and did not know of any connection that you might have had with the caves. I made no statements regarding any hypotheses you may have put forth. . . . I appreciate your kind invitation to join you in your forthcoming expendition, but am unable to accept."

What of "Mr. Gorsky"?

Just before reentering the LM after Apollo 11's EVA, Armstrong supposedly made the enigmatic remark, "Good luck, Mr. Gorsky." Some reporters at Mission Control attributed the remark as referencing a rival Soviet cosmonaut. However, there was no Gorsky in the Russian space program. Over the years many people questioned Armstrong as to what his statement about Mr. Gorsky meant, but Armstrong always just smiled.

The story resumes in 1995 during an address in Tampa, Florida, when Armstrong finally responded to a reporter's question about the story. Mr. Gorsky had finally died, so Neil felt he could answer the question.

When he was a kid, he was playing baseball with a friend in the backyard. His friend hit a fly ball that landed in the front of his neighbor's bedroom window. His neighbors were Mr. and Mrs. Gorsky. As he leaned down to pick up the ball, young Armstrong heard Mrs. Gorsky shouting at Mr. Gorsky, "Oral sex! You want oral sex?! You'll get oral sex when the kid next door walks on the Moon!"

As a story, "Mr. Gorsky" always gets a laugh, which was what comedian Buddy Hackett was counting on when he first delivered the joke (which Hackett apparently invented) on NBC's *Tonight Show* sometime around 1990. In spite of the ease with which the story can be debunked, and in spite of various attempts on the Internet (a search for "Armstrong" and "Gorsky" generates 4,000 hits) to expose it for the urban legend that it has become, the story is funny enough that countless people continue to read it and pass it along, no matter its origin. "There is absolutely no truth to it. I even heard Hackett tell the story at a charity golf outing."

Even during the time of Apollo 11, some believed that the Moon landings never really took place—that they were a fraud foisted upon the world for political reasons by the U.S. government. The Flat Earth Society maintained an active membership. But the idea of a Moon hoax picked up greatly in 1978 because of *Capricorn One,* a Hollywood conspiracy fantasy, not about the Moon landing, but about the first manned mission to Mars. In the tale, NASA attempted to cover for a highly defective spacecraft by forcing its astronauts before cameras in a desert film studio to act out the journey and trick the world into believing they made the trip. Though a mediocre movie, *Capricorn One*'s notion of a government conspiracy never fell out of favor with a small number of skeptics.

Inevitably, there were people who not only chose to believe in some version of the lunar conspiracy theory, but who saw a way to profit from it. In 1999, Fox TV broadcast a "documentary" entitled *Conspiracy Theory: Did We Land on the Moon?* The program was based largely on a low-budget commercial video produced by a self-proclaimed "investigative reporter" from Nashville, Tennessee. Called *A Funny Thing Happened on the Way to the Moon,* it speculated that the Moon landings were an ingenious ploy of the U.S. government to win the Cold War and stimulate the collapse of Soviet communism by forcing the Kremlin into investing massive sums of money on its own lunar program, thereby ruining the Russian economy and provoking the internal downfall of the government.

No matter that every piece of "evidence" raised by the sensationalistic program was parroting the same uninformed arguments about Apollo that had been around for over two decades—i.e., that the American flag planted by Apollo 11 appears to be waving in a place where there can be no wind; that there are no stars in any of the photographs taken on the lunar surface; that the photographs taken by the Apollo astronauts are simply "too good" to be true; that the 200-degree-plus Moon surface temperatures would have baked the camera film; that the force of the LM's descent engine should have created a crater under the module; that no one can travel safely through the "killer radiation" of the Van Allen Belts; and more. Some members of the TV viewing audience succumbed to the trickery, others to its darker legacy.

On his seventieth birthday in August 2000, Armstrong received a birthday card containing a belligerent typewritten letter from a teacher charging that the Moon landing was a hoax and inviting Neil to review the "evidence" on the Internet.

Dear Mr. Armstrong:

The least I could do was send a card for your 70th birthday, however over 30 years on from the pathetic TV broadcast when you fooled everyone by claiming to have walked upon the Moon, I would like to point out that you, and the other astronauts, are making yourselfs [sic] *a worldwide laughing stock, thanks to the Internet.*

Perhaps you are totally unaware of all the evidence circulating the globe via the Internet. Everyone now knows the whole saga was faked, and the evidence is there for all to see. We know the pictures have pasted backgrounds, who composed the pictures, and how the lunar landing and Moon walks were simulated at Langley Research Centre, in addition to why NASA faked Apollo.

Maybe you are one of those pensioners who do not surf the Internet, because you know precious little about how it works. May I suggest you visit [Web site withheld by author] *to see for yourself how ridiculous the Moon landing claim looks 30 years on.*

As a teacher of young children, I have a duty to tell them history as it truly happened, and not a pack of lies and deceit.

[Name withheld by author]

Armstrong sent the birthday card and letter on to NASA's associate administrator for policy and plans. "Has NASA ever refuted the allegations or assembled information to be used in rebuttal? I occasionally am asked questions in public forums and feel I don't do as good a job as I might with more complete information," said Neil. Subsequently, in 2002, NASA commissioned distinguished space writer and veteran UFO debunker James Oberg to write a 30,000-word monograph refuting the notion that the Apollo program was a hoax. After news of the plan for Oberg's book hit the papers, however, NASA quickly reversed course, judging that not even a judicious, well-argued refutation could successfully achieve its intended effect.

To all inquiries about the Moon hoax, Vivian White sends out the following letter:

Dear ___:

I am responding on behalf of Mr. Armstrong to your recent letter regarding the reality of the Apollo program flights.

The flights are undisputed in the scientific and technical worlds. All of the reputable scientific societies affirm the flights and their results.

The crews were observed to enter their spacecraft in Florida and observed to be recovered in the Pacific Ocean. The flights were tracked by radars in a number of countries thoughout their flight to the Moon and return. The crew sent television pictures of the voyage including flying over the lunar landscape and on the surface, pictures of lunar scenes previously unknown and now confirmed. The crews returned samples from the lunar surface including some minerals never found on Earth.

Mr. Armstrong believes that the only thing more difficult to achieve than the lunar flights would be to successfully fake them.

Mr. Armstrong accepts that individuals may believe whatever they wish. He was, however, substantially offended by the FOX program's implication that his fellow Apollo crewmen were possible accomplices in the murder of his very good friends, Grissom, White, and Chaffee, and he has indicated his displeasure to FOX.

We appreciate your inquiry and send best wishes.

Sincerely,
Vivian White
Administrative Aide

Neil understands the impulse of the conspiracy theorists, even if it is totally alien to his own rational mind. "One, people love conspiracy theories. They are very attracted to them. As I recall, after Franklin D. Roosevelt died, there were people saying that he was still alive someplace. And, of course, 'Elvis lives!' There is always going to be that fringe element on every subject, and I put this in that category. It doesn't bother me. It will all pass in time. Generally, it's almost unnoticeable except for the peaks that occur when somebody writes a book or puts out an article in a magazine or shows something on television."

Armstrong has also experienced one man's attempt to turn Armstrong's personal life into a television event of the stranger's own devising.

At the annual meeting of EDO Corporation stockholders in New York City in 2001, the man who made *A Funny Thing Happened on the Way to the Moon* showed up with a video-camera-carrying assistant. EDO president James Smith recalls the scene: "This guy shows up with a Bible and shouts out, 'Neil Armstrong, will you swear on this Bible that you went to the Moon?' Well, the audience immediately started booing the intruder very loud, but he went right on, 'Everybody else in the world knows you didn't, so why don't you just admit it?!' It quickly turned into a kind of pushy-shovy thing, so and I and a few other men got the guy out of there. Subsequent to that, we never had a meeting where we didn't hire special security."

"Had I the opportunity to run that episode over in my life," Armstrong comments, "I wouldn't have allowed my company people to usher me out of the room. I would have just talked to the crowd and said, 'This person believes that the United States government has committed fraud on all of you, and simultaneously he wants to exercise his right protected by the U.S. government to state his opinions freely to you.' "

A few months after the EDO meeting, on September 9, 2002, the same man with Bible in hand confronted Buzz Aldrin outside of a Beverly Hills hotel. A resident of the Los Angeles area, Buzz had arrived at the hotel thinking he was to be interviewed by a Japanese educational television network. At first Aldrin, his stepdaughter in tow, tried to answer the man's questions, then did his best to get away from him. But the insistent independent filmmaker dogged him out of the hotel and kept directing his assistant to keep the camera running, while shouting at Buzz, "You are a coward and a liar." Harassed to the point of complete exasperation, the seventy-two-year-old Aldrin, all 160 pounds of him, decked the thirty-seven-year-old 250-pounder with a quick left hook to the jaw. The man from Nashville filed a police report but, after watching the accuser's own tape of the incident, the L.A. County District Attorney rather forcefully declined to file charges.

As the self-proclaimed "victim" later told reporters, "If I walked on the Moon and some guy said swear on a Bible, I'd swear on a stack of Bibles."

Even before the EDO and Aldrin incidents, the same individual entered uninvited into the Armstrongs' suburban Cincinnati home. Neil's second wife Carol relates what happened: "Neil was at the office. This guy knocked at the door and there was a big dog with him, and he had a package. I opened the outside door while leaving the screen door shut, and the man said, 'Is Neil here?' I said, 'No, he's not. May I help you?' He opened the screen door and just walked in, bringing along his dog. He said, 'I want him to sign this,' and I said, 'Neil doesn't sign things anymore.' 'He'll sign this,' he uttered, and then he left.

"It sort of hit me three minutes later. All of a sudden I felt shaky."

In the following weeks, the interloper started putting letters and other things in the Armstrongs' mailbox. Some of the materials had religious overtones and most were about the Moon landing being faked. The local police department responded, "It's probably nothing, but why don't you just bring the tapes and letters and we'll take a look at them," until a call to the ABC TV station in Nashville revealed that he had never worked there, but instead was an independent filmmaker who had operated a business called ABC Video.

A few weeks later, Carol received a phone call from her neighbor: "Carol, there's this car parked out here and it's been out here for a long time." When the neighbor went out to investigate, she saw a lot of camera equipment in the backseat. The siege continued for three days, culminating in a car chase involving the Armstrongs, the intruder, and the police.

The high price of celebrity was a heavy burden that all of the early astronauts and their families had to pay, but none more dearly than the First Man—as personally unwanted as his status as a celebrity and global icon particularly was. It was an unwanted, unasked for, but inevitable, legacy that Armstrong shared with his hero, Lindbergh.

CHAPTER 35

Into the Heartland

The few puffy clouds over the ski slopes at Snowmass were a meek harbinger of the major blizzard sweeping toward Aspen's four snowcapped summits that February day in 1991. Neil rode to the top of the intermediate ski run known as Upper Hal's Hollow with Doris Solacoff, whose husband, Kotcho, was Armstrong's boyhood friend from Upper Sandusky. Neil's brother Dean, recently divorced, completed the ski quartet, who had just finished lunch. Neil had eaten a big bowl of chili with plenty of onions.

Neil remained so quiet throughout the ascent that Dorie took notice. A few hundred feet into her run, she observed Neil skiing down ever so slowly. "I don't feel too well." Noticing his face was pale and ashen, Dorie, a registered nurse, insisted on going for help. "No, just wait a second," Neil hesitated, knowing what sort of fuss would be made over him. "I feel real weak. I think I'm going to sit down and rest here for a minute."

Doris Solacoff raced to contact the ski patrol. "I have a friend that I believe is having a heart attack, and I'll tell you right where you need to come."

Down at the bottom of Upper Hal's Hollow, Kotcho and Dean had started to worry. Finally, Dorie approached, shouting, "Neil has had a heart attack, and the ski patrol is bringing him down in the rescue toboggan!"

The doctor on duty at the lodge infirmary confirmed a heart attack and administered atropine to stabilize a cardiac arrhythmia through an IV line. An ambulance transported him to Aspen Valley Hospital, where he was placed in the intensive care unit. There Armstrong experienced repeated episodes of bradycardia, or abnormal slowing down of the heart.

Armstrong's heart rate soon stabilized enough for a transfer to Denver, but the blizzard kept him in Aspen for three days. Practiced at protecting celebrities, the little resort hospital kept word of Armstrong's heart attack secret.

Kotcho, himself an Ohio physician, helped arrange for a transport by medivac from Aspen to a hospital in Cincinnati. There a team of heart specialists carried out a catheterization that linked the attack to a tiny aberrant blood vessel. The rest of his coronary arteries were clear of blockages of any kind; his heart tissue sustained only the slightest amount of permanent damage.

Released the next day with no major restrictions, Armstrong took the heart specialist at his word and flew to a business meeting. Six months later, he passed his flight physical and was put back on full flight status.

In the coming years, he would make many more visits to the Colorado ski slopes, once or twice with Kotcho, Dorie, and Dean. The trio now refers to Upper Hal's Hollow as Neil's Run.

"The day Neil had his heart attack, he was in the process of separation from Janet," explains Kotcho, "so I called his son Mark several times a day and gave him reports. The day after the attack, Janet called me and said that Gene Cernan had called her and told her about it. Gene had found out through the ski patrolman who brought Neil down, who happened to be one of Gene's friends. Gene then called Jan. She thought the news was going to make front pages all over the world and the TV and everything."

What role stress played in Armstrong's illness can never be known with certainty, but difficulties in his personal life had mounted during the previous twelve months leading up to the heart attack. His father Stephen died on February 3, 1990, in the Dorothy Love Retirement Community in Sidney, Ohio, south of Wapakoneta. His mother, Viola, passed away barely three months later. His parents, both age eighty-three, had been married for sixty years. Shortly before his mother's death, Janet had left Neil, citing years of emotional distance.

With Neil's departure from NASA in 1971, Janet Armstrong had hoped for a new beginning in suburban Cincinnati. "My husband's job was there, so that was where we went. He wanted to realize a more quiet life," having "spent all those years in the program with little time for himself."

Lebanon was a typical small town—a rural bedroom community for Cincinnati and Dayton. "I had never lived in a small town. We drove all around the area and it was the best thing outside the beltway at that time. I remember we went into the ice cream parlor and just kind of cased the place. It seemed like a safe community and a good place to raise the children. We thought we were seeing people we could identify with in the town."

The nineteenth-century farmhouse had to be gutted. "Neil did not like debt and wouldn't take out another loan, so it took seven years as we paid cash for the work to be done. It got so that the builder could answer the telephone if I wasn't there and go pick the kids up at school! He just became part of the family! It was difficult on the kids and it was difficult on me.

"It was easier for Mark than it was for Rick," but both boys were teased for being Neil Armstrong's son. According to Rick, "It was rough, but I learned to ignore it." In Rick's view, Mark had a little easier time of it: "He was much more of the social butterfly." Rick recalls farm life as "an isolation that, I think, was driven a lot by what Dad was experiencing and it had a trickle-down effect on the rest of us." Janet (and undoubtedly Neil as well) did not know that the boys were having it so rough: "It took me a couple of years before I caught on to that, because the boys wouldn't say anything to me."

Neil did some chores around the 300-plus-acre farm, if not as many as Janet would have liked. "We started by carrying between seventy and ninety head of cattle. We grew corn, soybeans, hay, and wheat." Asked whether she actually enjoyed doing the farmwork, Janet today replies, "It was something that had to be done. It was really difficult to shovel poop during the day and go out to a dinner party at night. 'Well, what do you do?' people would ask. Well, I was busy on the farm."

In 1981, a year after Neil resigned from UC, Neil and Janet became "empty-nesters" when Mark went away to Stanford University (Rick had since graduated from Wittenberg College in Ohio). "I don't think it affected Neil at all, but it certainly affected me. I felt that this was a time when we could really do things together." As it turned out, however, Neil, with all of his new corporate board responsibilities, wasn't home any more than he had been before. "The kids have gone, Neil is gone, our dog Wendy had been stolen. We had no security system. I was stuck out there in the country.

"Finally, I got tired of all this, and in 1987 I started a travel agency. In the beginning, it was cruises only. Then we added air and became a full-service travel agency. I sold that agency in 1993."

Janet's frustrations with Neil rose as her dissatisfaction with her own life increased. She tried in vain to help him get better organized. "He had so many requests for speeches and so many this and so many that—he didn't know where to start. He had to make decisions—and decision making seemed to be especially difficult for him at that time.

"The man needed help. I couldn't help him. He really didn't want me helping him. He didn't want to get angry with me, I suppose, or he didn't want me to get angry at him. That was probably smart on his part. Vivian White used to get just beside herself. She just learned to go with the flow."

Janet also tried to plan vacations for the two of them, but Neil couldn't commit—his schedule was always too busy. "I could not continue to live like that. He'd look at all sides of everything, and sometimes he'd discuss them—and I'd say, 'Just do it!' But he couldn't, or just didn't.

"In November 1987 I asked him to go skiing, but he couldn't work it into his schedule for another year." Finally in late 1988 they made it out to the slopes at Park City, Utah, where Janet persuaded him it would be fun to have a vacation home. "He had free travel, the boys could come out, and we could have a place that was so convenient, and everybody liked to ski." In early 1989, they bought a brand-new chalet-style home on the outskirts of Park City, one of the sites for the 1992 Winter Olympics. It could have been a turning point in their marriage if the couple had chosen to approach it that way, which neither did. "The fact was it took a whole year to get on his schedule to go away for a weekend! In a sense, I resented it. It really put the handwriting on the wall."

A matter of months after purchasing the Park City vacation home, Neil came home from a business trip to find a note from Janet on the kitchen table of their Lebanon farmhouse. The note said she was leaving him.

"We had family. We had grandchildren. It was a long hard decision for me. It wasn't an easy thing to do—I cried for three years before I left." Janet had prolonged her decision because "the children were still there, the nest wasn't empty, there were still things going on. I always had hoped our life together would improve with time.

"I realized the personality. I just couldn't live with the personality any-more."

Neil took it hard. "Can't you do something about it, Neil?" his friend Harry Combs asked. "No, I just can't," Neil answered. "Jan has just given up on us. She doesn't want to live that kind of life." Says Combs, "He was in the deepest depression that I've ever seen.

"It was awful. He would just sit there and glare at the table—not even move. I would ask him, 'Is there any improvement?' and he would say, 'The children are supportive, but I have no sign of ever getting her back.' There were two or three years of this stuff."

Dean confirms that Neil became very depressed: "He begged her for a long time to come back."

The separation was tragically bookended by the deaths of Neil's parents; first Stephen, then Viola. Their last few years of life had been sad and problematic ones. Stephen had suffered a series of minor strokes and thought they did not have enough money to live on. The children moved their parents into a duplex in Bisbee, Arizona, where June and her husband Jack Hoffman lived. Viola adapted well, but Stephen hated the desert. In the summer of 1989 Neil moved them to the Dorothy Love Retirement Community in Sidney, Ohio.

Stephen lived unhappily in an unassisted private apartment at the nursing home for six months and made life even more difficult for Viola. Neil was with him on February 3, 1990, when he succumbed to another series of strokes. "Dad sat straight up in bed, looked at us, and laid down and died," Neil remembers. A few days before, Stephen had motioned his wife over, whispering, "I love you."

After grieving for her husband, Viola was ready to go on living. A previous diagnosis of pancreatic cancer turned out to be a heart problem. During a visit with June in Arizona, she impulsively purchased six pairs of shoes, reveling in the indulgence. Unfortunately, her health was more fragile than anyone suspected. On Monday, May 21, 1990, back in Ohio, she died suddenly. A few days earlier, she surprised her daughter by saying, "I am not sure there really is a God. But I am very happy that I believed."

That next winter following the death of his parents and his separation from Janet, Neil suffered his heart attack. His cardiac health recouped quickly, but it would take longer to cure the heartache.

Out of ashes, if a person is lucky, a brand-new life can rise. For Neil, rejuvenation—and a type of personal redemption—began the moment he met Carol Held Knight.

Carol Knight, born to Victor Held and Rosario Cota in 1945, was a recent widow. Her husband, forty-nine-year-old Ralph Knight, had been killed in a small plane crash in Florida in 1989, on his way to see motorcycle races in Daytona. Carol was left to raise her two teenage children, Molly, fifteen, and Andrew, fourteen, and also run the family business, a small Cincinnati construction company.

The meeting between Neil and Carol in the summer of 1992 was surreptitiously arranged by mutual friends, Paul and Sally Christiansen, at a pre–golf tournament breakfast at their club in suburban Cincinnati. Out of embarrassment at sitting next to the famous astronaut, Carol said little, then left early to tend to her ill mother. Neil escorted her out to her car.

"A couple of weeks later, my son Andy and I were out in the backyard. I could hear the phone ringing. There was a very quiet voice on the other end, 'Hello.' And I said, 'Who is this?' And this quiet voice said, 'Neil.' And I said, 'Neil who?' And he said, 'Neil Armstrong.' And I said, 'Oh, what do you want?' 'What are you doing?' 'Well, actually, my son and I are trying to cut down a dead cherry tree.'

"Neil came to life and said, 'Oh, I can do that.' 'Well, you know where I live,' I answered, 'across the street from Paul and Sally.' 'Well, I'll be right over.' Thirty-five minutes later, there's a pickup truck in the driveway. Andy answered the door and Neil's standing there with a chainsaw in his hand. Andy comes back in the kitchen and he says, 'Do you know who's at the door?' I said, 'Oh, I forgot to tell you.'

Carol and Neil were married after Neil and Janet's divorce became final in 1994. There were two wedding ceremonies. Planning the family gathering, Carol said, "How does that look, Neil, June eighteenth?' He opened up his date book and said with a very serious expression, 'I have a golf tournament.' Then he looked up at me very sheepishly and said, 'But I could change it.' "

Because the State of California required a blood test for a marriage license plus a waiting period of five days, Carol and Neil first married in Ohio. The mayor of Carol's village (also a friend) presided on June 12, 1994. The Christiansens stood as their witnesses. Their California wedding took place at San Ysidro Ranch, near Calabasas Canyon in the Los Angeles area. Surrounded by mountains and on a small lawn bordered by a white rose arbor, it was, for Carol, "one of the most beautiful places I've ever seen." With them that day were only the couple's four adult children, plus Mark's wife Wendy and their two children.

The new Mr. and Mrs. Neil A. Armstrong decided to build a brand-new house on the same property where Carol's old house was standing. The one-story English-country-style home was finished in 1997. "We talked about whether we would like to live anyplace else. But all our friends were here and we had come to the stage in life where that network was really priceless."

Did Carol give much though to what it might mean to be Mrs. Neil Armstrong? "I'm sure the attention is so much less than it was thirty years ago. We have noticed most of that when we travel out of the country. But he's not recognized that much anymore."

Carol's not bothered when the media call her Janet, as appeared in photo captions in coverage of the *Columbia* memorial service in Houston in 2003. "That's fine. It's not about me.

"I definitely run interference. I will politely explain, 'Neil doesn't sign autographs anymore.' We try to give them something instead: 'How about a picture?' You have to respect their feelings, too. There have been a few times when I've been actually scared, maybe twice in the U.S. and a few times in other countries. I remember coming into an overseas airport around two in the morning. I didn't think we'd be able to get to the car, just people all over! We needed help from half a dozen policemen just to get in the car.

"Once we came back from London and we had just gotten home after the flight and just taken our suitcases in the bedroom, when the doorbell rang. I went to the door and opened it and this woman said in a British accent, 'I'm from the London *Times* and I missed you in Britain. I wanted an interview. Could I have one now?' And I just looked at her and said, 'You must be kidding.'

"Neil and I are a good balance, so we have a good partnership."

"Carol turned out to be the greatest," related Harry Combs. "A humdinger! The fellows in the Conquistadores del Cielo [an elite aerospace group founded in 1937] were just so delighted in the change we all saw in Neil. She just made a new man out of him!" Taft Broadcasting's Charlie Mechem, though he "loved Janet" and thought she was "a dynamite woman," admitted he's "nuts about Carol. I think she's done a lot to make these last eleven years of his life very happy." Gene Cernan, who has remained a good friend of Janet's from their days together at Purdue to the present, offered, "Carol is a match, a fit for Neil like a glove. As for Janet, it's a woman's right, she just got tired of being Mrs. Neil Armstrong. She wanted her own identity."

Today, Janet Shearon Armstrong (she retains the last name) still resides in Utah. She volunteers with the local homeowners association, teaches swimming, takes walks with Cassie, her golden retriever, and travels. "I'm in an investment club here, and that can take all my time. I have friends, and we do things."

Much of her time is taken traveling to visit with her two boys and her six grandchildren. After Rick graduated from Wittenberg College in 1979 with a major in biology, he trained dolphins and sea lions for a company out of Gulfport, Mississippi, then went on to Hawaii, after which he began doing dolphin shows at Ohio's Kings Island. Today, Rick, his wife, and three children live in a northern Cincinnati suburb. Mark majored in physics at

Stanford, where he also played on the golf team and helped set up the university's first student computer lab. He went to work with Symantec in Santa Monica, then he joined his former college roommate's startup, WebTV, which was eventually bought by Microsoft. Mark stayed with Microsoft in Silicon Valley until 2004, when he moved his wife and three children to the Cincinnati area. It was through Mark's interest in Apple's original Macintosh that Neil first became enthusiastic about computers, now a daily hobby.

Neither boy ever developed a strong interest in aviation. In high school, Mark did take a few flying lessons at the Lebanon airport, and soloed, but that was the end of it.

Janet wishes her ex-husband well and is still trying to understand him:

"Everyone gives Neil the greatest credit for not trying to take advantage of his fame, not like other astronauts have done."

"Yes, but look what it's done to him inside. He feels guilty that he got all the acclaim for an effort of tens of thousands of people. Someone like Jim Lovell was a different personality completely! He would just walk on and not let it bother him. Neil would let it bother him. He always was afraid of making a social mistake, and he has no reason to feel that way for he was always a well-mannered gentleman.

"He's certainly led an interesting life. But he took it too seriously to heart.

"He didn't like being singled out or to feel that people were still wanting to touch him or get his autograph. Yet he wouldn't quit signing autographs for twenty years because probably, in the bottom of his heart, he didn't think most people were trying to make money selling them."

"Are you saying that if he had gone out in the public more times over the years that the interest in him would have dwindled—that he's made himself into a type of target?"

"I agree."

Neil Armstrong today seems to be a very happy man—perhaps happier than at any other time in his life. Although he technically "retired" in the spring of 2002, he remains as busy as ever traveling around the world, giving speeches, attending events, visiting children and grandchildren, reading books, writing essays, playing golf. He attends meetings of the American Philosophical Society and frequently participates in annual sessions of the Academy of the Kingdom of Morocco, in which he has been a member since

King Hassan II established it in 1980. The only other American charter members of the Moroccan Academy (modeled after the Academie Française) were former secretary of state Henry Kissinger and Alex Haley, the author of *Roots*. At meetings in Casablanca, Neil has been presented talks on "New Knowledge of the Earth from Space Exploration" (1984), "Research Values in Contemporary Society" (1989), "The Ozone Layer Controversy" (1989; coauthored with his son Mark), and "Observations on Genetic Engineering" (1997; coauthored with his wife Carol). One of the consistent themes in Neil's presentations is "junk science," how a small amount of knowledge can be a dangerous thing, and how society should not draw a sweeping conclusion when knowledge about a subject is noticeably incomplete.

As for his personal flying, he still seizes the occasional opportunity to take control of an interesting aircraft. In 1989, when he became chairman of AIL Systems, Inc., he was invited to fly the B-1 bomber. He later flew the B-1 again for the *First Flights* television series. For that 1991 series, he also flew a number of other aircraft types, including the Harrier, helicopters, gliders, and an old Lockheed Constellation.

In the late 1990s, Armstrong sold his Cessna 310 but kept his pilot's license current for those occasions when he would be offered the chance to fly a special aircraft. In 2001, in association with his directorship of RMI Titanium Co., he flew an Airbus 320 at Airbus's headquarters in Toulouse, France. In the summer of 2004 he flew the new Eurocopter and AStar helicopters and an assortment of light aircraft. As often as he can, he still goes aloft in sailplanes, a relaxing sporting activity that he has enjoyed since the early 1960s. "He was always a natural at that," Janet recalls. "He could actually hear the thermals. It was a wonderful relief for him to be up there flying by himself."

Many people have wondered why Armstrong finally, after all these years, agreed to an authorized biography. No more explicit answer can be given than to say, "It was time." For Armstrong's foremost legacy lies in what is most genuine about his life story and what his truthful experiences can signify to today's young people—and shall signify for generations to come.

A few years back, Neil and Carol visited their good friends Dorie and Kotcho Solacoff at the home of the Solacoffs' daughter Kathy and her husband Chris Perry, a PGA Tour golfer. The youngest of the Perrys' three children, five-year-old Emily, proved to be a real firecracker. Neil took to Emily quickly, and Emily to him, and soon she had him by the hand, taking him on an expedition through her house. "I want to show you a secret, but don't tell anyone. This is a secret which no one knows about."

Up in the attic, Emily said, "Look over the mattress and look down there." There it was—a great big dead bug. "But don't tell anyone," she whispered.

Next the little girl led him into her bedroom. "This is my clock, and this is my lamp, and this is my mirror, and these are some of my books. This book is on Winnie the Pooh, and this one is about Sleeping Beauty, and this is Cinderella, and, oh, here is a book about Neil Armstrong. He was the first man on the Moon."

Then she stopped, hesitated for a moment, looked at the nice older man like Grandpa who had come to visit her in her house, and said, "Oh! Your name is Neil Armstrong, too, isn't it?"

Acknowledgments

Historians may also voyage from the Earth to the Moon. My own epic journey began three years ago, in June 2002, when Neil A. Armstrong signed a formal agreement naming me as his biographer. Actually the trip began well before that. I first wrote Mr. Armstrong about my ambition to write his life story in October 1999. A long thirty-three months later, after numerous letters and e-mails had passed back and forth between us (and a critical face-to-face private meeting—our first—in September 2001), Armstrong gave me his thumbs-up. That approval brought unprecedented access not only to Neil and his personal papers but also to his family, friends, and colleagues—many of whom, in deference to Neil, had resisted speaking openly about him before.

So, first and foremost, I wish to thank Neil Armstrong himself. Without his full and generous support, this book could never have been successfully written.

I am also indebted to Neil for the integrity with which he wanted the project carried out. He wanted the book to be an independent, scholarly biography. Although he took the opportunity to read and comment on every draft chapter, he did so only to guarantee that the book was as factual and technically correct as possible. Not once did he try to change or even influence my analysis or interpretation.

It should be clear, then, to all readers that Neil Armstrong is not in any way a coauthor of this book. In fact, I am quite sure that he does not like the book's title. He would never think to call himself the "First Man," insisting as he always has that Buzz Aldrin landed on the Moon at the very same instant he did. Also, it is not to Armstrong's liking that "First Man" sounds so biblical, so epic, so iconic; he would never express his life or legacy in those terms. But once Neil had decided to trust my effort, he was not about to interfere with my purpose. The result, I believe, is an exceptionally rare type of book: an authorized biography more candid, honest, and unvarnished than most unauthorized biographies.

Just as it took some 400,000 Americans in government, industry, and universities to carry out the Apollo program, this book could not have been produced without the help of a score of people. A complete list of people interviewed for the book appears in the bibliography; to every one of them, I express my sincere thanks. I have never—and will never—meet a finer group of individuals. Meeting them and hearing what they had to say about Neil and about their own lives and careers made me think how lucky Neil was to have had them for colleagues and friends. What I shall always remember best about my research for this book is the enchanting time I spent with all the wonderful people I interviewed. Conducting the oral history took me to eighteen states and the District of Columbia.

I owe special thanks to Neil's immediate family: to his son Rick Armstrong, his brother Dean Armstrong, and especially his sister June Armstrong Hoffman. As readers will quickly surmise, June not only provided me with many extremely informative and deeply personal insights into Neil and the history of her family, but also shared with me all of her mother's photo albums and personal papers. This "Viola material," as I came to call it, proved invaluable by significantly deepening my understanding of the family dynamics from which the young Neil emerged. For sharing her mother with me, and thus the world, I have June to thank. Jayne Hoffman, June's daughter, was also tremendously helpful in sorting out the many intricacies and riddles of the Armstrong family genealogy.

From the start I was committed to hearing firsthand from Neil's first wife, Janet Shearon Armstrong. It was impossible to tell Neil's story without telling Janet's. I was interested not only in what Janet had to say about her former husband of thirty-eight years; I was interested in Janet herself. During the Apollo years, Janet, as the wife of an astronaut and then as the wife of the first man on the Moon, became a public figure in her own right. In that context, it was critically important to examine her own experiences as a woman, wife, mother, and role model.

As hard as it was for her to do, Janet eventually agreed to a series of interviews. What she contributed, in my view, is a priceless addition to this book. If I had failed to talk with her, it would have been like missing the chance to hear from Mrs. Christopher Columbus. I only wish that arrangements could have been made to interview Janet's and Neil's youngest son, Mark Armstrong.

I also want to thank Neil's current wife, Carol Held Knight Armstrong, for the interview she granted me and for the generous and caring hospitality she showed me every time I visited the Armstrong home. Meeting Carol's charming daughter Molly Knight-VanWagenen and her two little ones was icing on the cake. I cannot say how delightful the sight was of Molly's beautiful blond daughter sitting contentedly on Grandpa Neil's lap.

A host of historians, librarians, archivists, curators, and other research professionals at various institutions helped enormously with my research. Notable among them, and deserving special thanks, were Dr. Michael Gorn, chief historian of NASA Dryden Flight Research Center in Edwards, CA, as well as Mike's staff historians Dr. Curtis Peebles and Dr. Christian Gelzer and archivist Peter Merlin; Dr. J. D. Hunley, former NASA Dryden historian; Stephen Garber and Jane Odom of the NASA Headquarters History Office; Shelly Kelly, Anna B. Peebler, and Regina Grant of the University of Houston–Clear Lake Archives and NASA Johnson Space Center History Program; Rebecca Wright of Signal/Veridian, the director of NASA Johnson Space Center's Oral History Project; Kent Carter, regional director of the National Archives and Records Administration—Southwest Region in Fort Worth, TX, and his director of archival operations Meg Hacker; Bill Hooper and Pamela T. Wilson at the Research Center of Time Inc., in New York City, as well as Time Inc.'s Richard Stolley; John Zwez, former director of the Neil A. Armstrong Museum in Wapakoneta, OH; M. Hill Goodspeed, historian at the National Museum of Naval Aviation in Pensacola, FL; Christy Haas, archives technician at the Military Personnel Records section of the National Personnel Records Center in St. Louis, MO; Garland Gouger, reference librarian at NASA Langley Research Center's Floyd L. Thompson Memorial Technical Library in Hampton, VA; Bonita Smith of Indyne, Inc., the contract historian at John H. Glenn Research Center at Lewis Field in Cleveland, OH; Jane Carlin, head of the University Libraries at the University of Cincinnati; M. Jo Derryberry, director of the Auglaize County Library in Wapakoneta; and Elizabeth Bringman, head of the Upper Sandusky (OH) Community Library.

Dr. Roger D. Launius, former NASA chief historian in Washington, DC, and current chair of the Department of Space History at the Smithsonian's National Air and Space Museum, helped me get this project started, and Dr. Tom D. Crouch of the museum's Department of Aeronautics offered guidance at various points along the way. The author of the definitive biography of the Wright brothers, my friend and fellow Ohio State graduate Tom Crouch, would himself have made a great Armstrong biographer. I also am indebted to Andrew Chaikin, author of the outstanding 1994 book

A Man on the Moon: The Voyages of the Apollo Astronauts (the basis for the HBO miniseries *From the Earth to the Moon*), for his assistance and encouragement. Dr. Douglas G. Brinkley, who in the company of the late Dr. Stephen E. Ambrose in September 2001 conducted a lengthy interview with Armstrong, provided moral support. Support from Neil Thompson, author of the 2004 biography *Light This Candle: The Life and Times of Alan Shepard,* also meant a lot to me. Dr. Stephen Waring of the University of Alabama-Hunstville history department shed significant light on Armstrong's critically important role in the Space Shuttle *Challenger* investigation.

Without the *Apollo Lunar Surface Journal* assembled over the course of many years by its editor Eric P. Jones, my understanding of what happened on the Sea of Tranquility during the Apollo 11 mission would have been much less informed and precise. I want to thank Eric for his great support of my project and particularly for his keen reading of my draft chapters relevant to the first landing. He saved me from making several major errors. Those that remain are my own.

The founder and editor of the Web site collectSPACE.com, Robert Pearlman, provided a number of important insights into space history and the popular fascination with astronauts and space memorabilia. My incessant e-mail questions to him about such details as the contents of the astronauts' PPKs could not have been answered more promptly or completely.

I also want to thank Hank Brandli, Michael Esslinger, Barbara Honegger, Neil McAleer, James McDade, Anthony Pizzitola, Herman A. Spanagel, and Roger Weiss for their letters and e-mails and for the historical materials they so generously provided me. My old friend and former editor Steve Corneliussen of Poquoson, VA, offered his usual provocative critique of the book's early chapters.

The officers and gentlemen of Fighter Squadron 51 deserve special mention for what they contributed to this book. As a group, not even the Apollo astronauts that I interviewed were more impressive to me. Special thanks go Ted Rickelton of Seattle, WA, the brother of Ensign Glenn H. "Rick" Rickelton, as well as to Rick's nephews, Glenn Rickelton of Elk Grove, CA, and Scott Rickelton of Bothell, WA, for the family's permission to quote from Ensign Rickelton's diary. I also greatly appreciate Robert Kaps's permission to quote from his Korean War journal. VF-51's Ken "K.C." Kramer supplied a ton of useful information and insights about the history of the fighter squadron. Besides sending me a huge collection of pertinent materials, Ken read and commented extensively on the draft chapters related to Neil's time in the navy. Also providing very helpful comments and criticism of those chapters were VF-51's Ernest M. Beauchamp, Hershel Gott, and Wam Mackey. William Holloway, a close friend of VF-51's James J. Ashford, also offered a penetrating review of those chapters. I wish to thank Bill Holloway also for freely sharing his manuscript account of the life of his friend Jim Ashford, one of the VF-51 aviators, like Rickelton, who was killed in Korea.

Without the support I received from my academic home, Auburn University, I could never have produced this book in a timely fashion. For the original agreement to give me the necessary time away from full-time teaching, I wish to thank former university provost Dr. John Pritchett, Vice President for Research Dr. Michael Moriarty, former deans of the college of liberal arts, Dr. John Heilman and Dr. Rebekah Pindzola, former associate dean Dr. Anthony Carey, and chair of the history department Dr. William Trimble. All of my colleagues are due my thanks for indulging my passion for my subject and my long absences from their company. In particular I wish to acknowledge the support of my fellow faculty in our Technology and Civilization program, especially Dr. Guy V. Beckwith and Dr. W. David Lewis. Auburn's eminent British history specialist Professor Daniel Szechi aided me greatly in understanding the fascinating history of the Scottish Borders.

My doctoral students never let me give up on the idea of writing the Armstrong biography. The Three Amigos—David Arnold, Amy E. Foster, and Kristen Starr—kept cheering me on even when I had given up most hope that the project would work out. David and Amy have gone on to complete excellent PhDs in space history, and Kristen is not far behind. Nor is Andrew Baird, a late addition to the coterie. I expect never to have a more able or stimulating group of graduate students. I also want to thank the countless undergraduate students I have enjoyed teaching in our freshman Technology and Civilization survey and in my courses in aerospace history.

An Auburn undergraduate student, Molly Prickett, amazingly transcribed over seventy-five of my interviews for this book. Anyone who has ever toiled to produce verbatim transcripts from tape-recorded interviews understands how tedious and time-consuming it all is. Fortunately, no one loves space history or the U.S. space program more than Molly. Auburn history graduate student David Burke also transcribed a few of the interviews. So, too, did my sister, Carol Lynn Busse. If ever a sister was more wonderful than June Armstrong, it was our family's cherished Carol.

Simon & Schuster's marvelous Denise Roy has done so many wonderful things for this book, I don't know where to begin to praise her. Denise adroitly trimmed an overly long (and frequently overwritten) manuscript into something as lean and readable as anyone could have possibly made it. Her consummate professionalism and always friendly and constructive words of encouragement inspired me to keep working for *our* book's improvement. She has spoiled me from wanting to ever work with another editor.

Prior to initiating this project, I never thought I would need, or want, a literary agent. I had no idea how to get one and could have made a bad decision. Instead, I found a kindred spirit and an angel in the intellectually radiant and spiritually magical form of Laurie Fox of the Linda Chester Agency. Every minute of my work on this book would have been worthwhile even if their only result had been becoming Laurie's friend. Laurie's husband, D. Patrick Miller, a talented and accomplished author in his own right, as Laurie herself is, also shared a number of helpful ideas. So, too, did the majestic Linda Chester herself. I also want to thank Justin Manask and Joel Gotler of Intellectual Property Group.

My immediate family "lived" this book almost as much as I did. Many times at dinner, as I sat stone silent or dazed, my mind still spinning with that day's thoughts about Armstrong's life, my wife Peggy, daughter Jennifer, and son Nathan would have to reel me in and bring me back down to Earth. But I never felt anything but their loving support for what I was doing. I am so happy that both of my children have found equivalent passions in their own lives—art history for twenty-one-year-old Jennifer and medicine for twenty-six-year-old Nathan. But I hope even more that they find partners and have children as loving, interested, and tolerant in them as three-dimensional human beings as they have been of their father.

Finally, I thank you, the reader, for investing in such a big book and, hopefully, reading it from first page to last. For you, for posterity, and for Neil, I have given it my absolute best.

—*James R. Hansen*
Auburn, AL
April 2005

Notes

GWW: Grace Walker-Wiesmann
HAG: Herbert A. Graham
HCS: Harold C. Schwan
HG: Herschel Gott
HSC: Harry S. Combs
JAH: June Armstrong Hoffman
JBB: John "Bud" Blackford
JEL: James E. Lovell
JG: John Glenn Jr.
JGM: John G. McTigue
JM: John Moore
JSA: Janet Shearon Armstrong
JZ: Jacob Zint
KCK: Ken C. Kramer
KID: Kenneth I. Danneberg
KKS: K. K. "Kotcho" Solacoff
L: *Life* magazine
LBJ: Lyndon Baines Johnson
LN: *Lima News* (Ohio)
MC: Michael Collins
MOT: Milton O. Thompson
NAA: Neil Alden Armstrong
NK: Ned Keiber
NM: Norman Mailer
NO: *The National Observer*
NPRC: National Personnel Records Center (St. Louis, MO)
NYT: *New York Times*
OFM: *Of a Fire on the Moon* (Mailer)
PFB: Paul F. Bikle
PJK: Peter J. Karnoski
RED: Richard E. Day
RFG: Richard F. Gordon Jr.
RJB: Roger J. Barnicki
RMW: Robert M. White
RTE: *Return to Earth* (Aldrin)
SA&DB: Stephen Ambrose and Douglas Brinkley (Profiles of Armstrong,
              Ambrose)
SKA: Stephen K. Armstrong
SMEL: *St. Marys Evening Leader* (Ohio)
SPB: Stanley P. Butchart
TB: *Toledo Blade*
TLA: Time-Life Archives
TS: Tom Stafford
TT: Tom Thompson
VEA: Viola Engel Armstrong
VEAP: Viola Engel Armstrong Papers
VAK: Vincent Aubrey Knudegaard

WAA: William A. Anders
WAB: William A. Bowers
WAM: William A. Mackey
WDN: *Wapakoneta Daily News* (Ohio)
WHC: *We Have Capture* (Stafford, Cassutt)
WHD: William H. Dana
WJK: William J. "Pete" Knight
WMS: Walter M. Schirra Jr.
WOL: *Wingless on Luna* (Documents, NAA)
Y&J: Chuck Yeager and Leo Janos

vii   *I: E* Joseph Campbell, *Reflections on the Art of Living.*

Prologue

1 *"missed the whole thing"* BA quoted in Andrew Chaikin, *A Man on the Moon,* p. 227.

2 "numero uno *spot"* JSA to author, Park City, UT, Sept. 11, 2004 (morning), p. 27.

3 *"anyone sneezes on the Moon"* "Borman: Why Cancel Out Nixon?" *Akron Beacon Journal,* July 13, 1969.

3 *"lunar-crazy"* Dutch comment quoted in "Europe, Too, Is Awaiting the Launch of Apollo 11," *NYT,* July 16, 1969.

3 *"the America we love"* Czech comment quoted in ibid.

3 *"12 percent of the entire Moon output is 'made in Germany' "* German comment quoted in ibid.

3 *"greatest adventure in the history of humanity"* French comment quoted in "Foreign Press Hails Apollo Mission," *TB,* July 17, 1969.

3 *"country whose people are so tired of politics"* French comment quoted in "Europe, Too, Is Awaiting," *NYT,* July 16, 1969.

3 *"three courageous men"* Pravda comment quoted in "Foreign Press Hails," *TB,* July 17, 1969.

3 *"extend imperialism into space"* Communist newspaper comment from Hong Kong quoted in ibid.

3 *"What is there in thee, moon"* John Keats quoted in John Noble Wilford, *We Reach the Moon,* p. 17.

4 *"worth all the heat and mosquitoes"* Quoted in Lacey Fosburgh, "Hundreds of Thousands Flock to Be 'There,' " *NYT,* July 16, 1969.

4 *"new era in the life of man"* Quoted in Bernard Weinraub, "Some Applaud as Rocket Lifts, But Rest Just Stare," *NYT,* July 17, 1969.

5 *"the kindling light to put men together"* Quoted in Weinraub, ibid.

5 "Incroyable!" Shriver quoted in "The VIP Guests Can Hardly Find Words," *NYT,* July 17, 1969.

5 *"the poetry of hope"* Hale Broun quoted in CBS, *10:56:20 P.M.,* p. 21.

5 *"America's inability to choose the proper priorities"* Hosea Williams quoted in
   " 'Priorities' Under Fire," *LN,* July 15, 1969.

5 *"holy ground"* Abernathy quoted in CBS, *10:56:20 P.M.*, pp. 15–16.

5 *"so much that we have yet to do"* LBJ quoted in "Johnson Hails National Effort
   Behind Apollo 11," *NYT,* July 17, 1969. A fuller citation of LBJ's remarks can
   be found in CBS, *10:56:20 P.M.*, pp. 19–20.

6 *"not a carnival atmosphere"* Sevareid quoted in CBS, *10:56:20 P.M.*, pp. 13–14.

6 *"pressure might be too great"* VEAP, "Apollo 11, 1969," Part 3:1.

6 *"never was there a prayer like this one"* Ibid.

6 *"besieged by newsmen of every category"* VEAP, "Looking Back," p. 7.

7 *"survived this only by the grace of God"* VEAP, "Apollo 11, 1969," Part 3:1.

7 *"welcomed with open arms"* Ibid., Part 3:3.

8 *"call us again before you leave?"* Ibid., Part 3:4.

8 *"feel somone squeezing your hand these days"* Ibid.

8 *"Janet, too, was full of cheerfulness"* VEAP, "Apollo 11, 1969," Part 3:4.

8 *"Stephen and I sat side by side"* Ibid., Part 3:6.

Part One: An American Genesis

11 *E* VEAP, "Our Armstrong Family," p. 4.

11 *E* NAA, "What America Means to Me," *The Reader's Digest* (Apr. 15, 1975),
    pp. 75–76.

Chapter 1: The Strong of Arm

13 *"loved every last one"* "Neil Armstrong's kinsman was hanged as a thief," *Life,*
    Mar. 24, 1972; "Neil Armstrong Spared Hanging in Scotland," *CE,* Mar. 3,
    1972.

13 *Armstrong name began illustriously* The primary source used for the early his-
    tory of the Armstrongs in Scotland is James L. Armstrong, *Chronicles of the
    Armstrongs* (Salem, MA: Higginson Book Co., 1902).

14 *emerged as a powerful force* Technically, it is inaccurate to call the Armstrongs a
    "clan," a designation reserved for Gaels from the Gaeltacht, that is, High-
    landers, with a recognized chieftain-based dynasty thought to be descended
    from the heroes of the Celtic past and with customs and traditions of gover-
    nance, law, and society all of their own.

        By contrast the "Names" of the Lowlands, like the Armstrongs, were more
    volatile associations, with few permanently recognized chieftain dynasties,
    which were organized on a feudal and personal basis rather than on the
    Gaeltacht's mix of custom and myths of common ancestry.

        Unfortunately, this has not stopped modern descendants of these families
    from calling themselves a "clan." In fact, members of the Armstrong family—
    most all of them American tourists—took advantage of the occasion of Neil
    Armstrong's Moon landing in July 1969 to establish an organization at
    Mangerton in Liddesdale, Scotland, known as the Armstrong Clan Society.
    Spinning off from this organization in the past thirty-plus years has been an

Armstrong Genealogy and History Center, Clan Armstrong Trust, and a number of dedicated Internet Web sites.

14 *"Elliots and Armstrongs never fail"* VEAP: "Our Armstrong Family," p. 1.

14 *"very ill to tame"* Quotes in this paragraph come from by far the most reliable history of the Anglo-Scottish Border reivers, Fraser, *Steel Bonnets,* p. 57.

14 *Scott identified . . ."Christie's Will"* The entirety of Sir Walter Scott's "Minstrelsy of the Scottish Border" is available online at the Web site of the Edinburgh University Library: www.walterscott.lib.ed.ac.uk/works/poetry/minstrelsy.htm

15 *Conveniently, Christie's Will* VEAP: Letter, Historical Research Associates, Co. Antrim, N. Ireland, to Mrs. Stephen Armstrong, Wapakoneta, OH, Feb. 3, 1986. This letter is part of a correspondence sequence between Historial Research Associates and Viola Armstrong.

15 *Militia muster rolls for Ulster* "Fermanagh Muster Rolls c. 1630," part of an Irish genealogy Web site called From Ireland, administered by Jane Lyons, Dublin, Ireland: www.from-ireland.net/censussubs/fermanmust1630.htm. See also "Ulster Ancestry: From the Muster Rolls of the County of Fermanagh, 1631," at www.ulsterancestry.com/muster-roll1663.html.

15 *Mary Forster* Forster (Forrester, Foster) was another one of the large Borderland reiver families. Although found more often on the English than the Scottish side, Forsters from both sides of the boundary intermarried. Sir John Forster (d. 1602) served over nearly four decades as the warden of the Middle March. The dates here are correct: he lived to be over one hundred years old. The lineage between Sir John Foster and Adam Armstrong's wife Mary Forster (born 1685) is unknown. Perhaps she was a granddaughter. If so, it would suggest a significant linkage between the Forster and Armstrong families.

16 *"first white child"* Leckey, *Tenmile Country,* pp. 538–39.

16 *"most delightful country"* Comment made by Christopher Gist, on his survey for the Ohio Company in 1750. On Gist's exploration of the Ohio Country, see Buck and Buck, *The Planting of Civilization in Western Pennsylvania,* pp. 63, 66, 71, 72, 75.

17 *ninety cents* H. G. Howland, ed., *1880 Atlas of Auglaize County* (Columbus, OH: Robert Sutton, 1880). Tax lists are also available online at www.rootsweb.com/~ohauglai/genweb/twp10.htm.

17 *Jacobus J. Van Nuys* Following the Civil War, one of the descendants of the Van Nuys family, Isaac Van Nuys, helped lay the foundation for what became the town of Van Nuys, California, north of Los Angeles. Members of today's Armstrong family believe, based on their genealogical research, that Isaac (1826–1884) may be directly related to Jacobus Van Nuys, the grandfather of Margaret Van Nuys's Stephen Armstrong.

17 *grandfather Van Nuys's legacy* VEAP: "Our Armstrong Family," pp. 8–9. In his last will and testament, dated March 28, 1834, Van Nuys ordered "the sum of one hundred dollars . . . payable to my Grandson Stephen Armstrong . . . be invested in land in the name and for the use of said Stephen Armstrong." Also in the will Jacobus bequeathed "to my grandson Stephen when he shall have arrived at the age of twenty-one years one horse, saddle and bridle and a suit of

new clothing of at least the value of one hundred dollars in all, and desire that he may stay in my family during his minority and receive an education sufficient to enable him to transact business with facility."

17 *census of 1850* "Schedule I: Free Inhabitants in Noble Township in the County of Auglaize, State of Ohio, Enumerated on the 6th Day of September 1850," available online at www.rootsweb.com/~usgenweb/oh/auglaize/census/1850/0278b.gif.

18 *Union service records* A Stephen Armstrong did fight in the Civil War, but his full identity is unknown. He served as a private in Company A of the 53rd Regiment of Ohio Infantry. This regiment was organized at Jackson, OH, from September 1861 to February 1862, when it was ordered to Paducah, KY. Under the direction of General William T. Sherman, an Ohio native, the 53rd participated in the Battle of Shiloh and the sieges of Corinth and Vicksburg.

18 *with Willis's mother Martha* The Badgley children seem to have left the River Road farm even before Stephen's Armstrong's death. In 1871 seventeen-year-old Charles Aaron Badgley went off to study dentistry—his father's own ambition—with an uncle, Aaron E. Badgley, in Winona, IL. Charles finished school, went into practice with his uncle, and eventually became a doctor of dental surgery in Greenfield, MO. Willis's half sister Hettie also moved away, marrying a man from Springfield, IL, in 1877. What happened to George and Mary Jane is unknown.

19 *vial of water from the River Jordan* VEAP: "The Willis Armstrong Family, Part 1," p. 2.

19 *half brother Ray* Ray Armstrong (b. 1895) and his first wife, whose name is not known, eventually divorced. He then married Leota Longmore Blything and lived in Pasadena, where he set up a successful electrical shop that eventually serviced the nascent motion picture industry. Upon retirement, he and Leota ("Lee") moved to Joshua Tree, CA. He died there while in his late eighties. Stephen's half sister Grace (1887–1969) married Ralph Koons in 1920, giving birth to three children: John, George, and Martha. The family stayed in the St. Marys area as farmers. Half sister Bernice (1890–1971) became a teacher in the Cleveland school district. She married a Canadian man by the name of George Wilmer. Together they had one child, Marjorie.

Chapter 2: The Strong of Spirit

20 *passage to America* "Armstrongs Urgrossvater stammt aus Ladbergen," *Münsterländishe Tageszeitung,* Sept. 12, 1969.

20 *"hurry home from the Moon"* VEAP: "With Grandpa and the Frederick W. Katter Family," p. 3; "Apple-Dumplings, Neil's Favorite Dish, Await His Return from Moon," *SMEL,* July 16, 1969.

21 *Reformed Church* "The Reformed Church in the U.S.," in *Handbook of Denominations in the United States, New Tenth Edition,* Frank S. Mead, rev. Samuel S. Hill (Nashville, TN: Abingdon Press, 2001), pp. 297–99.

21 *"Mother never preached"* Interview with JAH, Hereford, AZ, Apr. 5, 2003.

21 *"the way it is written"* VEAP, "My religion has been something very sweet."

21 *underlining and margin notations* VEAP: *The Red Letter New Testament of Our Lord and Savior Jesus Christ.*

21 *"father she never knew"* JAH: e-mail to author, Aug. 22, 2003.

21 *"loved his home and his family"* VEAP: "With Grandpa," p. 2.

21 *an "awful surgery"* Ibid., pp. 4–5.

21 *"taken one of His flock Home"* Ibid., p. 5.

21 *Katter barnyard . . . "was a cemetery"* Ibid., p. 8.

22 *"angel appeared at the foot of his bed"* Ibid., p. 12.

22 *William Ernst Korspeter* VEAP: "The Ernst Korspeter Family." Viola wrote this seven-page family history of the Korspeters in February 1977. According to a postscript, the account was given to her orally by her stepfather, William Ernst Korspeter, before he died in 1969.

22 *"sort of lonesome"* VEAP: Letter, "Dearest Friend," p. 1, in eighth-grade theme tablet.

22 *"Memory Gems"* VEAP: "Cleardale School."

22 *Jonathan Edwards* VEAP: "Sinners in the Hand of an Angry God—Jonathan Edwards," p. 3.

22 *"eyes that penetrate"* VEAP: "The House of Night—Philip Freneau," p. 3.

22 *"most charming of friends"* VEAP: Signed by Doris Fischer in "My Schoolmates" section of Blume High School yearbook, 1925.

23 *"longed to be a missionary"* VEAP: Letter to Reverend Charles Sloca PhD, Fairfield, IA, Oct. 27, 1969, p. 2.

23 *"wonderful time together"* VEAP: "The Willis Armstrong Family," p. 7.

23 *"somehow we would manage":* Ibid.

23 *"These talks with God"* VEAP: "The Willis Armstrong Family and the Stephen Armstrong Family," p. 11.

24 *"thrilled beyond words"* Ibid., p. 13.

24 *"we haven't any little Teddy yet"* VEAP: Letter to husband Stephen Armstrong, "Monday evening," Aug. 4, 1930.

24 *"I cannot save the child"* VEAP: "The Willis Armstrong Family and the Stephen Armstrong Family," p. 15.

25 *"beautiful little dear"* Ibid.

Part Two: Tranquility Base

27 *E* Interview with JAH, Wapakoneta, Aug. 14, 2002, pp. 23–24.

Chapter 3: First Child

29 *"teach the beauty of life"* VEAP: "The Willis Armstrong Family and the Stephen Armstrong Family," p. 15.

29 *"breast-feed him"* Ibid., p. 16.

29 *"hallowed place"* Ibid., p. 14.

29 *"rear him according to God's Holy Word"* Ibid., p. 16.

30 *"A little bit scared"* Ibid., p. 1.

30 *"Stand up there like a man!"* Ibid., p. 5.

30 *read street signs by age three* JAH: e-mail to author, Sept. 11, 2003.

30 *"books all around him"* SKA: Exhibit recording at Neil Armstrong Air and Space Museum, Wapakoneta, ca. June 1969.

30 *"couldn't keep him busy all the time"* "Neil Armstrong's Grade Transcript East Elementary School, St. Marys," part of feature in "Ohio Schools; Three of Neil's Teachers Here Quoted," *SMEL,* Sept. 23, 1969; "Astronaut Neil Armstrong Jumped Second Grade, East School; Teachers Remember Him As Excellent Pupil," *SMEL,* July 11, 1969.

30 *"always moving"* NAA to author, Aug. 13, 2002, p. 8. In the view of his future wife Janet Shearon (Armstrong), so much moving around from town to town as a boy did have a damaging effect on the formation of Neil's personality: "He didn't have the opportunity to develop the kind of friendships with pals like I and most children did. . . . Every place was a new place. I'm sure it had an effect on the development of his social abilities." JSA to author, Sept. 11, 2004 (afternoon), p. 28.

30 *"corner, reading a book"* JAH to author, Aug. 14, 2002, p. 13.

30 *"glue, all over everything!"* Ibid., p. 24.

30 *"Goody Two-shoes"* Ibid., p. 13.

30 *"definitely a caretaker"* Ibid., p. 16.

30 *"Jump! jump! It's okay"* Ibid., pp. 24–25.

31 *"never violated Neil's space"* DAA to author, Nov. 14, 2002, p. 11.

31 *"consumed by learning"* Ibid., p. 2.

31 *"only had two dates in high school"* Ibid., p. 8.

31 *"never competed with Neil in any way"* Ibid., p. 40.

31 *"Dean wasn't left out"* JAH to author Aug. 14, 2002, p. 19.

31 *"never experienced anything"* ALSK to author, Aug. 15, 2002, p. 30.

31 *"not made to hurt anyone"* DAA to author, Nov. 14, 2002, p. 40.

31 *" 'this game is over' "* JAH to author, Aug. 14, 2002, pp. 16–17.

31 *"a truthfulness about him"* VEA to DJH, tape 1B, p. 10.

31 *"wanted us to be good"* JAH to author, Aug. 14, 2002, p. 23.

31 *"stubborn rather than . . . opposite"* Interview with MC, Mar. 25, 2003, p. 5.

31 *"always does things on his terms"* DAA to author, Nov. 14, 2002, p. 40.

32 *"a high level of self-confidence"* JAH to author, Aug. 14, 2002, p. 20.

32 *"don't think he 'scared' that much"* DAA to author, Nov. 14, 2002, p. 40.

32 *" 'Straighten up!' "* JAH to author, Aug. 14, 2002, p. 14.

32 *"didn't think of him as being close"* NAA: e-mail to author, July 23, 2003.

32 *"never hugged"* JAH to author, Aug. 14, 2002, pp. 12–13.

32 *"Dear Mom and Family"* VEAP: NAA letter, 400 Salisbury, West Lafayette, IN, to Mrs. S. K. Armstrong, May 3, 1948.

32 *"very close and very loving"* DS to author, Wapakoneta, Aug. 15, 2002, p. 3.

32 *"one of the nicest persons"* ALSK to author, Aug. 15, 2002, p. 5.

32 *"find fault in anybody"* DS to author, Aug. 15, 2002, p. 8.

32 *"spine of the family"* AF to author, Aug. 15, 2002, p. 5.

32 *"don't remember my parents arguing"* JAH to author, Aug. 14, 2002, p. 15.

32 *"always there"* Ibid., p. 15.

32 *"the flexible one"* Ibid., p. 16.

33 *"love of the Master"* VEAP: Letter to Reverend Charles Sloca, PhD, Fairfield, IA, Oct. 27, 1969, p. 6.

33 *Taking Butchart at his word* SPB to author, Lancaster, CA, Dec. 15, 2002, p. 9.

34 *"great influence on Neil"* DS to author, Aug. 15, 2002, p. 7.

34 *"a natural for research"* Crites quoted in "Astronaut's Home Town Swept by 'Moon Craze,' " Syracuse (NY) *Post Standard,* July 4, 1969, and "Moon Was a Dream to Shy Armstrong," *Dayton Journal Herald,* July 11, 1969.

34 *"never let anyone know that he knew anything"* Crites quoted in "Neil Armstrong—All American Boy," *The Blade Sunday Magazine, TB,* Dec. 5, 1965.

34 *"did not see Neil argue"* EFK to author, Dickinson, TX, Dec. 10, 2002, p. 27.

34 *"in the crew quarters"* CDF to author, San Diego, CA, Apr. 8, 2003, p. 27.

35 *Cronkite dismissed the matter* "Face the Nation as Broadcast over the CBS Television Network and the CBS Radio Network, Sunday, August 17, 1969—11:30 A.M.–12:30 P.M.; Origination: Houston, Texas; Guests: Crew of Apollo 11; Reporters: Walter Cronkite, CBS News, David Schoumacher, CBS News, Howard Benedict, Associated Press," CBS transcript, p. 24.

35 *"just wants a good cigar"* DAA to author, Nov. 14, 2002. This comment was not recorded and thus is not part of the official transcript.

35 *"a million swords to be pierced through my heart"* VEAP: Letter to Reverend Sloca, Oct. 27, 1969, p. 5.

35 *"He seems to be inspired by God"* Ibid, p. 4.

Chapter 4: The Virtues of Smallville

36 *"out in the hinterlands"* This back-and-forth between Armstrong and MC is quoted in AC, *A Man on the Moon,* Vol. 3, p. 295.

37 *"Small-town values"* Walter M. Schirra, with Richard N. Billings, *Schirra's Space,* p. 10.

37 *"Growing up in a small town"* JG to author, Sept. 23, 2003, p. 11.

37 *"no worse and no better"* NAA to DJH, quoted in *FOM,* 112.

37 *"crawl inside the mixing vats"* NAA: e-mail to author, June 27, 2005.

37 *"save a substantial part of it for college"* NAA to author, Aug. 13, 2002, p. 10.

38 *"we had painful cramps in our legs"* Letter from KKS, Upper Sandusky, OH, to author, May 16, 2003, p. 5.

38 *"Scouts can take a lot of credit for Neil"* JBB quoted in "The Path of Scouting Leads to Outer Space," p. 4.

38 *"stars in the windows"* NAA to author, Aug. 13, 2002, pp. 11–12.

38 *"new troop"* Tape-recorded letter, JBB, Concord, NH, to author, July 25, 2003, p. 3.

38 *"a real taskmaster sort of fellow"* Ibid.

38 *"beat-up three-ring binder"* Ibid., pp. 4–5.

39 *"great acclaim under the circumstances"* JBB to author, July 25, 2003, p. 4.

39 *"less of a disciplinarian"* Ibid.

39 *"not a Scoutmaster"* NAA to author, Aug. 13, 2002, p. 12.

39 *"a wonderful combination"* JBB to author, July 25, 2003, p. 5.

39 *" 'Spit it out, it's poison!' "* Ibid., p. 5.

39 *"Neil was furious"* Ibid., pp. 5–6.

40 *"might get drafted"* NAA to author, Aug. 13, 2002, p. 12.

40 *"one song by heart"* BG to author, Wapakoneta, Aug. 15, 2002, p. 12.

40 *"music contributed to 'thought control'"* Conn Corporation, Elkhart, IN, "Conn Baritone Player: First Man on the Moon," press release, July 30, 1969.

41 *"We were so bad"* Jerre Maxson to DJH, Wapakoneta, ca. June 1969, tape IIA-2, quoted in *FOM,* p. 113.

41 *"never have been successful commercially"* NAA to author, Aug. 13, 2002, p. 13.

41 *"be sure everything was right"* BG to author, Aug. 15, 2002, p. 3.

41 *"He just had things to do"* NK to author, Aug. 15, 2002, p. 3.

41 *"never really had a steady date"* DS to author, Aug. 15, 2002, p. 6.

41 *"no romance between us"* ALSK to author, Aug. 15, 2002, p. 2.

41 *"big thing—to get the car"* DS to author, Aug. 15, 2002, pp. 3–4.

41 *"If we got in an accident"* Ibid., p. 4.

41 *"We just drove"* ALSK to author, Aug. 15, 2002, p. 16.

41 *between the little towns of New Hampshire and St. Johns* Ibid., p. 16.

42 *"hit this ditch"* DS to author, p. 4.

42 *"Stop the car here"* Ibid., p. 5.

42 *"out of the woods"* Ibid., p. 5.

42 *"He thinks, he acts"* Copy of the Blume High School yearbook for the school year 1946–47 can be reviewed at the Auglaize County Library, Wapakoneta, OH. Another copy of the yearbook is on display in Wapakoneta's Neil Armstrong Air and Space Museum.

Chapter 5: Truth in the Air

43 *"Neil's main interest"* JZ quoted in Lawrence Mosher, "Neil Armstrong: Man for the Moon: History Waits for Him," *NO,* July 7, 1969.

43 *"the possibility of life on other planets"* JZ quoted in Boothe, "Neil Dreamed of Landing on Moon Someday," *WDN,* June 27, 1969.

44 *"made of green cheese"* JZ quoted in Mosher, "Man for the Moon."

44 *picture of a smiling Zint* Dallas Boothe, "Neil Dreamed," *WDN,* June 27, 1969; "Astronomer Jakob Zint Provided Neil A. Armstrong's First Close-Up Look at the Moon," *SMEL,* June 27, 1969; Mosher, "Man for the Moon," *NO,* July 7, 1969; Al Kattman, "Astronaut Realizing Teen-Age Dream: From Auglaize Farm Home to Trip and Walk in Moon," *LN,* July 9, 1969; "Moon Was a Dream," *Dayton Journal Herald,* July 11, 1969; "Jakob Zint, Wapakoneta Astronomer, Says 'Neil's Dream Has Come True,'" *SMEL,* July 21, 1969.

44 *"Moon through Mr. Zint's lenses"* Mosher, "Man for the Moon," *NO,* July 7, 1969.

44 *"now he's up there"* JZ quoted in "Jakob Zint, Wapakoneta Astronomer," *SMEL,* July 21, 1969.

44 *"at Jake Zint's laboratory the one time"* NAA: e-mail to author, July 12, 2003.

44 *"his stories appear to be false"* Ibid.

44 *"Almost Too Logical to Be True"* Photo caption to Mosher, "Man for the Moon."

45 *"thought it was fishy"* ALSK to author, p. 31.

45 *"didn't sound right to me, either"* NK to author, p. 32.

45 *"meet the man up there"* Crites quoted in Kattman, "Astronaut Realizing Teen-Age Dream," and in Mosher, "Man for the Moon."

45 *"That's fiction"* NAA: e-mail to author, Sept. 15, 2003.

45 *"don't remember reading about the Wrights"* NAA: e-mail to author, Oct. 14, 2003.

45 *"always zooming around in the house"* SKA: exhibit recording at Neil Armstrong Air and Space Museum, Wapakoneta, OH, ca. June 1969.

45 *"I don't know what's true"* NAA to author, Cincinnati, OH, Aug. 13, 2002, p. 5.

46 *"skipped Sunday school"* SKA: exhibit recording at Neil Armstrong Air and Space Museum, Wapakoneta, ca. June 1969.

46 *"scared to death and Neil enjoyed it"* Mosher, "Man for the Moon."

46 *"never any end to the dream"* NAA to DJH, quoted in *FOM*, p. 19. See also NAA to author, Aug. 13, 2002, p. 8.

46 *"to the stars in my machine"* Tsiolkovskii quoted in A. A. Kosmodemyansky, *Konstantin Tsiolkovskii—His Life and Work* (Moscow, 1956), p. 8.

47 *"Cherry tree down"* All of the quotes from Robert Goddard appear in Esther C. Goddard, ed., *The Papers of Robert H. Goddard* (New York: McGraw-Hill, 1970), Vol. 2, pp. 623–24, 651, 840; Vol. 3, p. 1216.

47 *"can't say they were related to flying"* NAA to author, Aug. 13, 2002, p. 8.

47 *"tried it later"* NAA to DJH, not quoted in *FOM*. The phrases appear in a working draft of a chapter by DJH for *FOM*. A copy of this draft exists in the TLA.

47 *"Should I get Mama?"* JAH to author, Aug. 14, 2002, pp. 17–18.

47 *"Never to trust a dead limb"* NAA: e-mail to author, July 22, 2003.

47 *"never thought of it as being related to my character"* Ibid.

48 *"psychological backdrop to this"* NAA: e-mail to author, July 23, 2003.

48 *"obviation of failure"* Henry Petroski, *To Engineer Is Human: The Role of Failure in Successful Design,* p. 127.

48 *"focus on aviation"* NAA to author, Aug. 13, 2002, p. 5.

48 *"buy models with engines"* NAA to DJH, quoted in *FOM,* p. 114.

48 *fly ones . . . sometimes aflame* DAA to author, p. 4.

48 *"Mother would have just died"* JAH to author, pp. 18–19.

48 *"it was a rare occasion"* NAA: e-mail to author, July 23, 2003.

48 *"the model that wasn't built well"* NAA to author, Aug. 13, 2003, p. 6.

49 *"operational aspects of an airplane"* NAA to SA&DB, in *Quest,* p. 6–7.

49 *"anything I could get my hands on"* NAA to SA&DB, *Quest,* p. 7.

49 *"comic books"* Charles Brading quoted in "Moon Was a Dream."

49 *"never get off the ground"* SSK: letter to author May 16, 2003, p. 4.

49 *"fighter-type model"* AF to author, Aug. 15, 2002, p. 7.

49 *"I would win a number"* NAA to author, Aug. 13, 2002, p. 7.

49 *" 'control-line' models"* Ibid., p. 6.

49 *"absorbed a lot of new knowledge"* Ibid.

49 *"rode a bike with no fenders"* Jerre Maxson quoted in "Astronaut's Home Town Swept by 'Moon Craze,' " *Syracuse* (NY) *Post-Standard,* July 4, 1969.

49 *" 'top cylinder overhauls' "* NAA to author, Aug. 13, 2002, p. 19.

49 *"He learned to fly"* VEA to DJH, tape 1A, pp. 5–6.

49 *"around town talking, telling . . . stories"* NAA to author, Aug. 13, 2002, p. 19.

50 *"but what did I know!"* NAA to author, Aug. 13, 2002, p. 18.

50 *"didn't need a car"* SKA quoted in Mosher, "Man for the Moon."

50 *"could solo in a glider at age fourteen"* NAA to SA&DB, in *Quest,* p. 8.

50 *" 'Oh, oh, here I go!' "* NK to author, p. 11.

50 *"lone wolf"* DS quoted in John McGuire, "Neil Armstrong—All American Boy."

51 *"never expressed any fear"* JAH to author, Aug. 14, 2002, p. 21.

51 *"an exceptionally special day"* NAA to author, Aug. 13, 2002, p. 20.

51 *"didn't bounce it like I did"* NK to author, p. 11.

51 *"not like that technique at all"* NAA to author, Aug. 13, 2002, p. 19.

51 *"saw the plane go down"* DAA to author, p. 16.

52 *Lange died in Neil's arms* "Frederick C. Lange Victim of Accident," *Lima News,* July 28, 1947; "Flying Student Killed in Plane Accident Saturday," *WDN,* July 28, 1947.

52 *"pretty severe impact"* NAA to author Aug. 13, 2002, p. 21.

52 *pondering whether he should keep flying* Mrs. Stephen Armstrong as told to Lorraine Wetzel, "Neil Armstrong's Boyhood Crisis," *Guideposts* (Feb. 1970): 3–7. In *FOM,* Farmer and Hamblin wrote: "[Neil's] mother thought that he might give up flying after he saw one of his fellow students die in a plane crash. . . . Neil spent most of the next two days in his room, his mother remembered, but he did not give up flying" (p. 114). I have not been able to locate the interview in which Viola suggested this to the *Life* magazine writers, but the comments seem in character, even if it is not an accurate reflection of Neil's reaction to Carl Lange's tragic death.

52 *"never felt he was affected by it in any way"* JAH to author, Aug. 14, 2002, p. 21.

Chapter 6: Aeronautical Engineering 101

53 *"shattering the sonic wall"* These were the words of Air Force Secretary Stuart Symington when he confirmed on June 10, 1948, that the Bell X-1 had broken the sound barrier. See James Hansen, *The Bird Is on the Wing: Aerodynamics and the Progress of the American Airplane,* p. 102. For a thorough history of the X-1 program, see Richard P. Hallion, *Supersonic Flight: Breaking the Sound Barrier and Beyond,* rev. ed.

53 *"missed all the great times"* NAA: e-mail to author, Oct. 14, 2003.

56 *"very good math skills"* Doris Barr, Cincinnati, OH., to author, telephone conversation, Aug. 15, 2002. As it turned out, Armstrong probably did not need trigonometry to get into engineering school; in fact, his high school transcript did not record the course from Doris Barr.

56 *"build up the naval air reserve strength"* NAA to SB&DB, in *Quest,* p. 8.

56 *medical examination recorded* "Physical Examination for Flying," Form NAVMED AV-1 (1943), dated Mar. 7, 1947, copy in Armstrong's military records file, NPRC.

56 *"fly the airplane for seven dollars an hour"* NAA to author, Aug. 13, 2002, p. 17.

57 *"dropped the blackberries"* VEA to DJH, tape 1A, pp. 6–7.

57 *"a wonderful deal"* NAA to author, Aug. 13, 2002, p. 22. In 1947, Armstrong's

primary costs at Purdue University, all of which were covered by his navy scholarship, probably ran no higher than about $400 for the academic year. For college tuition in 1945, the GI Bill provided veterans with a maximum of $500 per academic year and out of that money the student had to pay for course fees, books, and supplies, estimated by the university at forty to fifty dollars per semester.

57 *navy appointment letter* L. C. Conwell, Commander, USN, Officer Procurement Division, to Mr. Neil Alden Armstrong, 601 West Benton, Wapakoneta, OH, May 14, 1947, copy in Armstrong's military records file, NPRC.

57 *" 'shop culture' school"* DSS: letter, King of Prussian, PA, to author, Dec. 25, 2002, p. 3.

57 *"We took all pretty much the standard stuff"* NAA to author, Aug. 13, 2002, p. 24.

57 *"Students didn't protest"* Letter: DAG to author, Nov. 30, 2002, p. 1.

57 *"tested out of freshman English"* NAA to author, Aug. 13, 2002, p. 24.

58 *"kind of a whirl"* Ibid.

58 *"sleeping in the field house"* TT: e-mail to author, Oct. 23, 2002.

58 *"Dear Mom & Family"* VEAP: NAA, 400 Salisbury, W. Lafayette, IN, to Mrs. S. K. Armstrong, 601 W. Benton, Wapakoneta, OH, May 3, 1948.

59 *"made the wrong choice"* NAA to author, Aug. 13, 2002, p. 24.

60 *"I have no idea"* NAA: e-mail to author, Oct. 26, 2003.

60 *"kids looked so young!"* NAA to SA&DB, in *Quest*, p. 14.

60 *"quiet, pleasant type"* PJK, Las Vegas: letter to author, Nov. 17, 2002, p. 3.

60 *"combination where I can do both"* NAA to author, Aug. 13, 2002, p. 45.

60 *"not rigorous enough"* Milton Clauser's views on the need to reform Purdue's aeronautical engineering curriculum are summarized in Grandt Jr. et al., *One Small Step*, p. 101.

61 *"engineering science"* For a rich historical treatment of the role of engineering science in American aeronautics, see Walter G. Vincenti, *What Engineers Know and How They Know It.* See also *From Engineering Science to Big Science: The NACA and NASA Collier Trophy Research Project Winners,* ed. Pamela E. Mack. For a specific analysis of the development of engineering science within college aeronautical engineering programs, see Amy Elizabeth Foster, "Aeronautical Science 101: The Development of Engineering Science in Aeronautical Engineering Education at the University of Minnesota," MA Thesis, University of Minnesota, Oct. 1980. Dr. Foster (PhD, Auburn University, 2005) compares the AE programs at Minnesota and Purdue.

61 *"in that Wind Tunnel class"* Dr. Leslie A. Hromas letter to author, Oct. 17, 2002, "Interactions and Thoughts About Neil."

61 *"Neil would roam"* Richard H. Petersen, La Jolla, CA: e-mail to author, Nov. 4, 2002.

61 *the days of "The Paddle"* NAA: e-mail to author, Oct. 26, 2003.

61 *"Marvin Karasek, an amazing pianist and composer"* NAA: e-mail to author, Oct. 28, 2003.

61 La Fing Stock VEAP: Copies of show programs for "Student Union Presents 'Varsity Varieties,' " Nov. 19, 1952, and Nov. 20, 1953.

62 *"trade party" cohosted by Janet's sorority* JSA to author, Sept. 10, 2004 (morning), transcript, p. 19.

62 *"damage sufficient to prevent flying it back"* NAA: e-mail to author, Dec. 3, 2002.

62 *"haul it back . . . on our grandfather's hay wagon"* DAA to author, pp. 17–18.

62 *"cease to be known as a spaceman?"* Quoted in Ira Berkow, "Cincinnati's Invisible Hero," *CD,* Jan. 17, 1976.

Part Three: Wings of Gold

65 *E* Letter, Peter J. Karnoski, Las Vegas, NV, to author, Nov. 17, 2002, p. 3.

65 *E* Quoted on the last page of James A. Michener, *The Bridges at Toko-Ri* (NY: Random House, 1953).

Chapter 7: Class 5-49

67 *Since the days of John Paul Jones* Richard C. Knott, *A Heritage of Wings: An Illustrated History of Navy Aviation,* pp. 268–69.

68 *"called us up early"* NAA to SA&DB, in *Quest,* p. 8.

69 *"NavCads"* "The NavCads were more expendable," recalled Tommy Thompson of Class 5-49. "The navy had very little invested in them as compared to having paid for two years of college for the midshipmen."

69 *"little time away from the grind"* NAA to author, Aug. 13, 2002, p. 26.

69 *"how to polish our shoes"* TT: e-mail to author, Oct. 29, 2002. Attachment: "Flight Training," p. 1.

69 *"gave everyone low grades"* NAA: e-mail to author, Nov. 11, 2003.

70 *"walked [disciplinary] 'tours' "* PJK: letter to author, Nov. 17, 2002, p. 1.

70 *only one "Delinquent Report"* "Delinquency Report, Pre-Flight, Battalion I: Aviation Training Summary," Jacket Number C-5-49-C-197, CNATRA (Chief of Naval Air Training) Files, U.S. Navy Historical Research Center, Pensacola, FL. All quotes pertaining to Armstrong's flight training come from his CNATRA file.

70 *"Neil was one of us"* PJK: letter to author, Nov. 17, 2002, pp. 1–2.

70 *"some of us just barely"* TT: e-mail to author, Oct. 29, 2002, Attachment: "Flight Training," p. 1.

71 *averaged 3.27* Grade reporting sheet, Navy Department, Bureau of Naval Personnel, Washington, DC, n.d., copy in Armstrong's military records file.

71 *"sat in the rear seat"* TT: e-mail to author, Oct. 29, 2002, Attachment: "Flight Training," p. 2. William A. Mackey ("Wam"), who instructed at Whiting Field from June 1948 to July 1949, remembers that "the instructor rode in the *back* and the student in the *front* seat." WAM, written comments to author on draft MSS, Jan. 11, 2005.

71 *"a big step up"* NAA: e-mail to author, Nov. 11, 2003.

71 *"Average to above"* Armstrong's CNATRA file.

73 *"sure of himself in that plane"* PJK: letter to author, Nov. 17, 2002, p. 2.

73 *"confident, but not cocky"* DSS: letter to author, Dec. 25, 2002, p. 3.

73 *"If it involved flying"* BJC: letter to author, Nov. 15, 2002, Attachment, p. 3.

75 *"you're indestructible!"* PJK: letter to author, Nov. 17, 2002, p. 2.
75 *"do things with perfection"* NAA to author, Aug. 13, 2002, p. 27.
75 *"every man for himself"* DSS: letter to author, Dec. 25, 2002, p. 1.
75 *"advance along his track faster"* NAA to author, Aug. 13, 2002, p. 30.
75 *"LSO had a paddle in each hand"* Ibid., p. 28.
75 *"keep both eyes open"* Ibid., pp. 28–29.
76 *"take off easily, without a catapult"* Ibid., p. 28.
76 *"very emotional achievement"* Ibid., p. 27.
76 *"highly precise kind of flying"* Ibid., p. 28.
76 *"fighter pilots always said"* NAA to SA&DB, in *Quest,* p. 9.
77 *"responsible for anybody else"* VEA to DJH, ca. June 1969, Tape 1A, p. 7.
78 *"first for bragging rights"* HAG: e-mail to author, Oct. 10, 2002.

Chapter 8: Fighter Squadron 51

79 *"given the West Coast"* NAA to author, Aug. 13, 2002, p. 31.
79 *"attached to this command in a pool status"* Officer's Fitness Report signed by Cdr. Luke H. Miller, Commanding Officer, FASRON 7, NASA San Diego, CA, Dec. 5, 1950, copy in Armstrong's military records file.
79 *"waiting for my fighter assignment"* NAA to author, Aug. 13, 2002, p. 31.
80 *"lovely flying experience"* Ibid.
80 *"single-engine pilots wanted to fly jets"* WAB: e-mail to author, Sept. 15, 2002.
80 *"mystique about flying"* KCK: e-mail to author, July 3, 2003.
80 *"a dream spot"* HAG: e-mail to author, Oct. 12, 2002.
81 *"made every plane he ever flew look good"* John Moore, *The Wrong Stuff: Flying on the Edge of Disaster,* p. 93.
81 *"can't have all four of those guys!"* WAM to author, Sept. 21, 2002, p. 3.
81 *eleven additional "nuggets"* EMB: letter to author, Nov. 12, 2002, p. 2.
81 *"fly with each of the nuggets"* EMB: letter to author, Nov. 12, 2002, p. 2.
81 *"whatever Ernie found out about me"* NAA: e-mail to author, Nov. 13, 2003.
82 *"vibration-free flow of power"* WAB: e-mail to author, Sept. 15, 2002.
82 *"high-powered race car"* HAG: e-mail to author, Oct. 20, 2002.
82 *"very short legs"* WAM to author, Sept. 21, 2002, p. 3.
82 *"one of those magic moments"* NAA to author, Aug. 13, 2002, p. 31.
82 *"quiet without being shy"* HAG: e-mail to author, Oct. 12, 2002.
83 *"very solid aviator"* WAM to author, Sept. 21, 2002, p. 13.
83 *"designated naval aviator"* EMB: letter to author, Nov. 12, 2002, p. 2.
83 *flying was . . . "a bit scarce"* NAA: e-mail to author, Nov. 14, 2002.
83 *"swept-wing MiG-15s"* HAG: e-mail to author, Oct. 20, 2002.
83 *"very young, very green"* NAA to SA&DB, in *Quest,* p. 10.
83 *"won against a MiG"* NAA to SA&DB, in *Quest,* p. 11.
84 *"didn't have particularly good handling qualities"* Ibid.
84 *"lot of fun"* WAM to author, Sept. 21, 2002, p. 5.
84 *"the best of the navy fighters"* HAG: e-mail to author, Oct. 22, 2002.
84 *"speeds tended to be higher on the jet"* NAA to author, Aug. 13, 2002, p. 32.
84 *"thought they were crazy"* NAA to SA&DB, in *Quest,* p. 10.
84 *"in proper lineal position with his contemporaries"* Chief of Naval Personnel,

Department of the Navy, Bureau of Naval Personnel, Washington, DC, to ENS Neil Alden Armstrong, USN, "Change in Date of Rank," n.d., copy in Armstrong's military records file.

85 *"great precision pilot"* KCK: e-mail to author, July 3, 2003.

85 *"skill and the nerve"* HAG: e-mail to author, Oct. 20, 2002.

85 *"graded on every landing"* KCK: e-mail to author, July 3, 2003.

85 *"first few catapult launches took faith"* HAG: e-mail to author, Oct. 20, 2002.

85 *"perilously close to the water"* NAA to author, Aug. 13, 2002, p. 38.

85 *"recommended for promotion when due"* Officer's Fitness Report signed by Capt. Austin W. Wheelock, Commanding Officer, USS *Essex,* June 30, 1951, copy in Armstrong's military records file.

86 *"a big letdown for us"* KCK: e-mail to author, July 3, 2003.

86 *"only game in town"* KCK: e-mail to EMB forwarded to author, July 3, 2003.

86 *"kick us ensigns off the ship"* Rickelton diary, July 11, 1951.

86 *"war is as good as over"* Ibid., July 25, 1951.

Chapter 9: Fate Is the Hunter

88 *"adventure of their life"* GER to William Holloway, Cincinnati, OH, Mar. 17, 1999, communicated to author in e-mail from Holloway, Dec. 3, 2003.

88 *"Same rolling, pitching"* Journal of Robert Kaps, "USS Essex (CV9), Carrier Air Group Five, 28 June 1951 to 25 March 1952," entry for Aug. 20, 1951.

88 *"broke my fist on the . . . bulkhead"* "Personal Diary of Ensign Glen Howard "Rick" Rickelton, U.S. Navy, Written During VF-51 Combat Flight Training & Korean War Service Aboard CV-9 U.S.S. Essex," entry for Aug. 20, 1951.

89 *first time navy fighters . . . ever escorted* On the Rashin raid on Aug. 25, 1951, see Richard P. Hallion, *The Naval Air War in Korea,* pp. 181–85.

89 *"The four-plane division"* NAA: e-mail to author, Nov. 25, 2003.

89 *"one of the boys"* HAG to author, June 20, 2003, p. 15.

89 *"Neil in the ready room after dinner at the blackboard"* Ibid., pp. 2–3.

89 *"Neil, where were you?"* Story told in JM, *Wrong Stuff,* pp. 120–21.

90 *"very good relationship"* KCK: e-mail to author, July 16, 2003.

90 *"delighted when I had the chance to fly with him"* NAA to SA&DB, in *Quest,* p. 13.

90 *" 'guy just doesn't care!' "* Tape-recorded letter, HCS to author, p. 5.

90 *" 'CAG, help me out' "* WAM to author, pp. 12–13.

90 *"greatest of the 'follow me, boys!' "* Quoted in Michener, "The Forgotten Heroes of Korea," *Saturday Evening Post,* May 10, 1952, p. 20.

90 *What the hell was the man thinking?* GER: letter to author, Sept. 24, 2003, p. 3.

90 *"couple of hundred more pounds of fuel"* NAA: e-mail to author, Dec. 21, 2003.

91 *"as contrary as we could"* Ibid., p. 35.

91 *"shocking incident"* Commander, Carrier Air Group Five to Commanding Officer, USS *Essex* (CV-9), "Action Report of Carrier Air Group FIVE (18 August 1951–19 September 1951," Sept. 22, 1951, p. 4, Naval Historical Center, Department of the Navy, Washington Navy Yard, Washington, DC. Accessible online at www.history.navy.mil.

91 *"heckler . . . exploded after catapult"* Kaps journal, entry for Aug. 23, 1951.

91 *"pronounced outlook on the point of survival"* Commander, Carrier Air Group Five to Commanding Officer, USS *Essex,* "Action Report of Carrier Air Group FIVE (18 August 1951–19 September 1951," Sept. 22, 1951, p. 4.

91 *"not the hero type"* Kaps journal, entry for Sept. 2, 1951.

91 *experience of Paul Gray* In *The Naval Air War in Korea,* historian Richard P. Hallion calls Commander Paul Gray of VF-54 "the Navy's own flak magnet and Wonsan harbor ditching expert" (p. 186). James A. Michener features Gray and the five times he was shot down in "The Forgotten Heroes of Korea," *The Saturday Evening Post,* May 10, 1952, pp. 19–21 and 124–28.

92 *"could have walked on it"* Rickelton diary, entry for Sept. 3, 1951.

92 *flying with John Carpenter* In some of the incorrect versions of Armstrong's flight of September 3, 1951, Neil is said to have been flying as wingman for Dick Wenzell. For example, see Thomas F. Gates, "The Screaming Eagles in Korea, 1950–1953; Part 2," *The Hook* (Winter 1996): 26.

92 "ARMSTRONG of VF-51 saved his own life" Commander, Carrier Air Group Five to Commanding Officer, USS *Essex,* "Action Report of Carrier Air Group FIVE (18 August 1951–19 September 1951," Sept. 22, 1951, p. 5.

93 "Armstrong bailed out" "One Stub Wing," *Naval Aviation News* (Dec. 1951), in section on "Korean Air War," n.p.

93 "regained control" Hallion, *The Naval Air War in Korea,* pp. 166–67.

94 *"going to snap"* NAA to author, Aug. 13, 2002, p. 36.

95 *"told me to go find out about it, so I did!"* JM, *Wrong Stuff,* p. 120. Moore's story is repeated as fact in Gates, "The Screaming Eagles," p. 24.

95 *"intended to come down in the water"* NAA to author, Aug. 13, 2002, p. 36.

95 *" 'pay the government for that helmet' "* KID to author, June 27, 2003, p. 10.

95 *"cool handling of the situation"* HAG: e-mail to author, Oct. 23, 2002.

95 *"Bailed out over Pohang"* Armstrong logbook, Sept. 3, 1951.

96 *"price to pay for a goddamn truck!"* JM, *Wrong Stuff,* p. 124.

96 *"living bejesus shot at them"* KID to author, p. 8.

96 *"lives of five pilots, one air crewman, and ten aircraft"* Commander, Carrier Air Group Five to Commanding Officer, USS *Essex,* "Action Report of Carrier Air Group FIVE (18 August 1951–19 September 1951," Sept. 22, 1951, p. 5.

96 *"Two damn fine guys lost and for what?"* Kaps journal, entry for Sept. 4, 1951.

96 *"worst part of it"* Rickelton journal, entry for Sept. 4, 1951.

96 *"it did get better"* NAA to author, Aug. 13, 2002, p. 37.

96 *"never missed an opportunity to shoot"* NAA to author, Aug. 13, 2002, p. 38.

97 *"with our hands tied"* HAG: e-mail to author, Oct. 23, 2002.

97 *"stress maybe even panic in his voice"* "Ernie Beauchamp's Account of the Banshee Crash," in "VF-51 in Korea—The Essex Cruise," by KCK and HG, undated MSS, p. 11. In November 2003, when the author received it from KCK, this manuscript was still a work in progress.

98 *"Jesus Christ, look at it burn!"* "Hersch Gott's Recollection of the Banshee Crash," in "VF-51 in Korea—The Essex Cruise," by KCK and HG, p. 16.

98 *"ducked under it as it went by"* Rickelton diary, entry made on Sept. 18, 1951, two days after the Banshee crash.

98 *"heat was horrible"* JM, *Wrong Stuff,* p. 7.

99   *"no heed of personal safety"* Commander, Carrier Air Group Five to Commanding Officer, USS *Essex,* "Action Report of Carrier Air Group FIVE (18 August 1951–19 September 1951," Sept. 22, 1951, p. 7.

99   " *'Essex hard luck' "* Kaps journal, entry for Sept. 16, 1951.

Chapter 10: The Ordeal of Eagles

101   *"unique and interesting"* NAA to author, Aug. 13, 2002, p. 41.

101   *"Never sell them short"* VEA to DJH, Wapakoneta, ca. June 1969, Tape 1B, p. 12.

102   *"get photos one day"* HG to author, June 20, 2003, p. 18.

102   *"Let's go shoot something"* GER: letter to author, Sept. 24, 2002, p. 3.

102   *"up close along the border"* NAA to author, Aug. 13, 2002, p. 40.

102   *"anxious moments but no engagements"* Kaps journal, Oct. 29, 1951.

103   *"keeps the planes from toppling over"* Kaps journal, entry for Nov. 26, 1951.

103   *"jettison armaments prior to returning"* NAA to SA&DB, in *Quest,* p. 12.

103   *"can't remember ever having come back with any ordnance"* WAM to author, p. 14.

104   *On December 14.* As Captain Austin E. Wheelock brought the *Essex* into the docks at Yokosuka after its third tour in the Sea of Japan, he ordered Operation Pinwheel, whereby, on signal from the bridge, all pilots of the ship's propeller-driven Corsairs and Skyraiders (tied down on the port side of the flight deck, propellers facing outward) were to turn their engines to full power. The resulting pinwheel effect would help the harbor tugboats pivot the carrier into its berthing position. Most of the pilots resentfully called the order "Operation Pinhead." Commander Paul N. Gray of VF-54 told his AD pilots to run the engines at no more than half power. To quell the anger of Captain Wheelock, CAG Marshall Beebe restricted VF-54 to the ship for four days while the other squadrons took liberty. Three days later, carrier division commander, Rear Admiral "Black Jack" Perry intervened on the pilots' behalf, though too late to forestall damage to pilot morale or pilot regard for the CAG. Michener would memorialize the incident in his 1953 novel *The Bridges at Toko-Ri.* See also Paul N. Gray's "The Bridges at Toko-Ri: The Real Story," in *Shipmate* (July–Aug. 1997).

104   *"sang Christmas carols"* NAA: e-mail to author, Dec. 18, 2003.

104   *"I couldn't be home"* Rickelton diary, Dec. 26, 1951.

104   *"Who's in a hurry?"* Kaps journal, Dec. 27, 1951.

105   *"HAPPY DAY!"* Ibid., Jan. 4, 1952.

105   *"good news tonight!!"* Rickelton diary, Jan. 4, 1952.

105   *"Rick shot down"* Kaps journal, Jan. 6, 1952.

105   *"our fighter pilot"* J. Glenn Rickelton: e-mail to author, Dec. 1, 2003.

105   *"come back one more time"* WAM to author, p. 19.

106   *"questioned everything"* NAA to SA&DB, in *Quest,* p. 14.

106   *"more intensity to combat"* NAA to author, Aug. 13, 2002, p. 44.

106   *"reality that you live with"* Ibid., p. 40.

106   *"stopped worrying about it"* HAG: e-mail to author, Oct. 23, 2002.

106   *"didn't cut off the supplies"* NAA to author, Aug. 13, 2002, p. 40.

107   *"cleared out of those gun emplacements"* HG to author, June 20, 2003, p. 19.

107   *"didn't ask questions much"* NAA to SA&DB, in *Quest,* p. 13.

107 *"excellent representation of the kinds of flying we were doing"* Ibid.

108 *"equally difficult places"* NAA to author, Aug. 13, 2002, p. 39.

109 *"If everybody from New Mexico was like those two boys"* WAM to author, p. 17.

109 *"Chet was a very thoughtful person"* NAA: e-mail to author, Nov. 29, 2003.

109 *"like a bunch of little kids"* Tape-recorded letter, HCS to author, p. 6.

109 *"Wam, I'm hit"* KCK: letter to author, "Comments on 'The Forgotten Heroes of Korea,' [by] James A. Michener—5/10/52 Sat[urday] Eve[ning] Post," Sept. 10, 2003, p. 4. Michener reported that Cheshire said, "Wham, I'm hit!" not understanding the reference to division leader William A. Mackey's nickname "Wam," after his initials.

109 *"get up there fast"* Ibid., p. 5.

110 *"already dead at this point"* Ibid.

110 *"clear he was going to ditch"* NAA: e-mail to author, Dec. 8, 2003.

110 *"Heaven help this world of ours"* Kaps journal, Jan. 26, 1952.

110 *"God bless you all, men"* Quoted in Michener, "The Forgotten Heroes of Korea," p. 124.

111 *"glad to have that one over"* Kaps journal, Feb. 1, 1952.

111 *"ought to go fly"* NAA to author, Aug. 13, 2002, p. 40.

111 *"trying to get out on more missions"* Tape-recorded letter, HCS to author, p. 9.

112 *"land of dreams"* Kaps journal, Mar. 11, 1952.

112 *"none will have to go through it again"* Ibid., Mar. 25, 1952.

112 *"like gold stars at Sunday school"* NAA quoted in *FOM*, p. 19.

112 "For distinguishing himself by meritorious service" Certificate awarded by the Commander of the Seventh Fleet, "The Air Medal to Ensign Neil A. Armstrong, United States Navy," June 21, 1952, copy in Armstrong's military files.

113 *"enormous respect" for the Skipper* NAA to author, Aug. 13, 2002, p. 35.

113 *"it's how you perform"* NAA to SA&DB, in *Quest*, p. 13.

113 *"we did as teams"* Ibid., 12.

113 *"click together very well"* Tape-recorded letter, HCS to author, p. 3.

114 *"fight the wrong war in the wrong place"* Michener, *Bridges at Toko-Ri.*

Part Four: The Real Right Stuff

115 *E* Captain William S. Farren, British Royal Aircraft Factory, quoted in Henry T. Tizard, "Methods of Measuring Aircraft Performances," Aeronautical Society of Great Britain, *Aeronautical Journal,* no. 82 (Apr.–June 1917), in James R. Hansen, ed., *The Wind and Beyond: A Documentary Journey into the History of Aerodynamics in America;* Vol. 1: *The Ascent of the Airplane* (Washington, DC: NASA SP-2003-4409), p. 357.

115 *E* Captain Henry T. Tizard, pilot in the Testing Squadron of the British Royal Flying Corps during World War I, and later the chair of the Royal Air Force's Committee for the Scientific Survey of Air Defense, Ibid., p. 340. Aeronautical Society of Great Britain, *Aeronautical Journal,* no. 82 (Apr.–June 1917).

Chapter 11: The Research Pilot

117 *"prophetic statement"* KCK: e-mail to author, Oct. 23, 2003, and Jan. 4, 2004.

117 *"doubt that I made the statement"* NAA: e-mail to author, Oct. 24, 2003.

117 *"extend my time in the service or swim home"* NAA to SA&DB, in *Quest,* p. 13.

118 *"presents a fine military bearing"* Officer's Fitness Report signed by Cdr. C. B. Cottingham, Air Transport Squadron 32, NAS San Diego, CA, Aug. 8, 1952, copy in Armstrong's military records file.

118 *"trick knee"* Chief of Naval Personnel, Bureau of Naval Personnel, Department of the Navy, to Commandant, Ninth Naval District, "Subj: LTJG Neil A. Armstrong, USN-R," Feb. 24, 1954, copy in Armstrong's military records file.

118 *"high degree of interest and initiative"* Report on the Fitness of Naval Reserve Officers on Inactive Duty, "Armstrong, Neil Alden," signed by LCDR Leonard R. Kozlowski, Commanding Officer, VF-724, NAS Glenview, June 5, 1954, copy in Armstrong's military records file.

118 *"outstandingly proficient Naval Aviator"* Reports on the Fitness of Naval Reserve Officers on Inactive Duty, "Armstrong, Neil Alden," signed by LCDR Kozlowski, June 30, 1955, and May 20, 1956, copies in Armstrong's military records file.

118 *"forced him to terminate his activities with this unit"* Report on the Fitness of Naval Reserve Officers on Inactive Duty, "Armstrong, Neil Alden," signed by LCDR A. A. Johnston, Commanding Officer, NRA VF-773, NAS Los Alamitos, Aug. 3, 1956, copy in Armstrong's military records file.

119 *"asked if he could come down"* NAA to author, Nov. 26, 2002, p. 1.

119 *post at Lewis laboratory* While working in Cleveland, Armstrong lived sixteen miles southeast of downtown at 424 Fair Street, Berea, Ohio.

120 *"Piloting of aircraft"* Annual Qualifications Questionnaire, Inactive Reserve, USN-R, "Armstrong, Neil Alden," June 30, 1954, copy in Armstrong's military records file.

120 *"with a view to their practical solutions"* Public Law 271, 63d Congress, approved Mar. 3, 1915. The complete text of the NACA's charter appears as Appendix A in Hansen, *Engineer in Charge,* p. 399.

120 *"Son, have you ever flown an airplane?"* Comment made by Melvin N. Gough, quoted in Laurence K. Loftin Jr., "A Research Pilot's World As Seen from the Cockpit of an NASA Engineer-Pilot," unpublished ms., July 1986, chap. 3, p. 5.

121 *"flew successfully an instrumented vehicle to greater than Mach 5"* This phrase is from the following NASA memorandum: John H. Disher, Deputy Director, Apollo Applications Program, NASA Headquarters, to Joseph E. Robbins, Administrative Officer, NASA Wallops Station, Wallops Island, VA, Aug. 1, 1969, copy provided to author by G. Merritt Preston, a former NACA Lewis engineer, copy in author's Preston file. Disher's memo informed former Wallops Island director Joseph A. Shortal's *A New Dimension: Wallops Flight Test Range, The First Fifteen Years* (Washington DC: NASA RP-1028, 1978). A shorter but more comprehensive survey is provided in Wallace, *Wallops Station and the Creation of an American Space Program* (Washington, DC: NASA SP-4311, 1997).

121 *"lot of analyzing data"* NAA to SA&DB, in *Quest,* p. 15.

121 *"it was the right one"* Ibid.

121 *"The only product of the NACA was research reports"* Ibid.

121 *"system was so precise, so demanding"* NAA to author, Nov. 26, 2002, p. 2.

122 *"like to transfer out there"* Ibid., p. 1.

122 *"San Diego to Chicago"* Tape-recorded letter, HCS to author, p. 11.
122 *"use a black marker"* KCK: e-mail to author, July 3, 2003.

Chapter 12: Above the High Desert

123 *"a superb flying place"* NAA to author, Nov. 26, 2002, p. 3.
124 *"used to get up there"* DJH interview with JSA, El Lago, TX, n.d. (ca. June 1969), p. 3. Copy in TLA.
125 *"never learned to fly a plane"* JSA essay for DJH, "People Are Always Asking Me," n.d. (ca. June 1969), p. 3.
126 *"She was all the right things"* EC to author, Feb. 10, 2003, pp. 2–3.
126 *"isn't one to rush into anything"* JSA essay for DJH, "People Are Always Asking Me," n.d. (ca. June 1969), p. 2.
126 *"Janet is as strong as horseradish"* DAA to author, p. 24.
126 *"opposites attract"* Ibid., p. 24.
126 *"see her being attracted to class"* EC to author, p. 3.
127 *"years to get to know him"* JSA to author, Sept. 10, 2004 (morning), p. 22.
127 *"six cents a mile for the trip"* JSA to DJH, quoted in *FOM,* p. 116.
127 *"It was very lovely"* VEAP: "Richley Blest," p. 2.
127 *"for one semester"* NAA to author, Nov. 26, 2002, p. 43.
128 *"a shower was a hose hung out over the tree limb"* Ibid.
128 *"loved it"* DJH interview with JSA, El Lago, TX, n.d. (ca. June 1969), p. 2. Copy in TLA.
128 *"total relaxation away from everything"* DJH interview with JSA, El Lago, TX, n.d. (ca. June 1969), p. 17. Copy in TLA.
128 *"only one stop sign away"* DJH interview with JSA, El Lago, TX, n.d. (ca. June 1969), p. 1. Copy in TLA.
128 *"wasn't very reliable"* BL to Christian Gelzer, Edwards, CA, Jan. 30, 2003, p. 7.
128 "start rolling down the hill" Milton O. Thompson, *At the Edge of Space,* p. 15.
129 *"had a '47 Dodge"* NAA to author, Nov. 26, 2002, p. 44.
129 *"would drive that way!"* BL to Gelzer, Jan. 30, 2003, p. 11.
129 *"ran the truck into a ditch"* Ibid.
130 *"kids wanted to ride with Neil"* Ibid., p. 12.
130 *"wonderful runway for those big machines"* NAA to author, Nov. 26, 2002, p. 3.
130 *"gung-ho individual"* Clyde Bailey to Michael Gorn, NASA Dryden Flight Research Center, Edwards, CA, Mar. 30, 1999. Interview transcript published in "Clyde Bailey, Richard Cox, Don Borchers, and Ralph Sparks," *The Spoken Word,* ed. Peebles, p. 25.
131 *"crappiest winter weather"* MOT, *ATEOS,* p. 4.
132 *flew a B-29 Superfortress* At Edwards, the NACA flew two B-29s. One was a P2B-1S, a navy version of the B-29A (serial number 45-21787) designated as NACA 137; the other was a JTB-29A (serial number 45-21800), with no NACA number. The P2B-1S, flown from 1951 to 1959, served primarily as the D-558-2 mother ship, and the JTB-29A, flown from 1955 to 1958, as the mother ship for the X-1 series. The NACA's B-47A (serial number 49-1900), designated as NACA 150, flew from 1953 to 1957. The NACA also flew a B-50 as a launch aircraft.
132 " *'kid is not even out of high school yet!'* " SPB to author, Dec. 15, 2002, Lan-

caster, CA, p. 8. Butchart thought so highly of Neil Armstrong that he insisted on participating in this interview even though the funeral for his wife of fifty-seven years, Miriam, had been only five days earlier.

133 *"in a learning mode"* NAA to SA&DB, in *Quest,* p. 15.

133 *(with an F-51 designation)* The precise designation of this aircraft was ETF-51D (E=Experimental, T=Test, F=Fighter, D=Model). NAA to SA&DB in *Quest,* p. 16. The NACA transferred this particular Mustang to Edwards from Langley in 1950. The P-51/F-51 was the first aircraft to employ the NACA's so-called laminar flow airfoil and could dive to around Mach 0.8. At Edwards, it was used as both a proficiency aircraft and as a chase and support plane. It was retired in 1959 after a taxiing mishap.

133 *"became more confident in my abilities"* Ibid.

133 *"flew in both positions"* NAA to author, Nov. 26, 2002, p. 5.

133 *"thought we'd hit another airplane"* SPB to author, p. 7.

134 *"good introduction to how the game went"* Ibid.

134 *"Butch, number four quit"* SPB to author, p. 12.

134 *"wasn't too concerned"* SPB to Curt Asher, Lancaster, CA, Sept. 15, 1997, p. 26. Copy in the Historical Archives, NASA Dryden Flight Research Center, Edwards, CA.

134 *"scratching my head"* SPB to author, pp. 12–13.

134 *"a windmilling propeller"* NAA to author, Nov. 26, 2002, p. 30.

135 *"get rid of the rocket plane underneath"* Ibid., p. 31.

135 *"I've got to drop you!"* Ibid., p. 13.

136 *"Neil, you got control?"* Ibid., p. 14.

136 *" 'Get your gear down!' "* Ibid.

136 *"could have turned ugly"* NAA to author, Nov. 26, 2002, p. 31.

137 *"don't think I could ever get it supersonic"* Ibid., p. 8.

137 *"if you turned, it would really slow down"* Ibid., p. 9.

137 *"a lot of landing work"* Ibid.

137 *"probable best technique?"* Ibid., p. 31.

137 *900-plus flights* This is a complete list of the aircraft that Armstrong flew during his seven-year career at Edwards. In parenthesis following the aircraft type are the numbers that the NACA/NASA assigned to the specific airplane. The first number in the designation is typically the year that the NACA received the aircraft.

Research Aircraft (jet)
Bell X-5 (50-1838)
Research Aircraft (rocket)
Bell X-1B (48-1385)
North American Aviation X-15 (56-6670)
North American Aviation X-15 (56-6672)
Research Aircraft (other)
Paraglider Research Vehicle (N9765C)
Lockheed NT-33A Shooting Star (51-4120) Cornell Laboratories
Convair NC-131B Samaritan (53-7793) Cornell Laboratories
Fighters (jet)

North American Aviation YF-86D Sabre (50-777/NACA 149)
North American Aviation F-86E Sabre (50-606/NACA 157)
North American Aviation F-100A Super Sabre (52-5778)
North American Aviation JF-100C Super Sabre (53-1709)
North American Aviation JF-100C Super Sabre (53-1712)
North American Aviation JF-100C Super Sabre (53-1717)
McDonnell YF4H-1 Phantom II (142259)
McDonnell F-101A Voodoo (53-2422) Minneapolis Honeywell
McDonnell F-101A Voodoo (53-2434)
Convair YF-102 Delta Dagger (53-1785)
Convair JF-102A Delta Dagger (54-1374)
Convair TF-102A Delta Dagger (56-2345)
Lockheed YF-104A Starfighter (55-2961)
Lockheed F-104A Starfighter (56-0734)
Lockheed JF-104A Starfighter (56-0745)
Lockheed JF-104A Starfighter (56-0749)
Lockheed F-104B Starfighter (57-1303)
Lockheed F-104D Starfighter (57-1315)
Lockheed F-104D Starfighter (57-1316)
Republic F-105 Thunderchief (54-0102)
Republic YRF-84F
Convair F-106B Delta Dart (57-2547)
Douglas F5D-1 Skylancer (139208/NACA 212)
Douglas F5D-1 Skylancer (142350/NACA 213)
Fighters (propeller driven)
North American ETF-51D Mustang (44-84958/NACA 148)
Bombers (jet)
Boeing JB-47A Stratojet (49-1900)
Bombers (propeller driven)
Boeing P2B-1S Superfortress (84029/NACA 137)
Boeing JTB-29A Superfortress (45-21800)
Trainers (jet)
Cessna T-37A (54-2737)
Cessna T-37B (56-3480)
Lockheed T-33A Shooting Star (49-0939)
Lockheed T-33A Shooting Star (51-6692)
Transports (jet)
KC-135A Stratotanker (55-3124)
Lockheed L-1329 JetStar (N9288R)
Transports (propeller driven)
Douglas R4D-5 Skytrain (17136)
Douglas JC-47D Skytrain (43-48273)
Douglas DC-3 Skytrain (N41447)
Beechcraft C-45H Expediter (51-11806/N717R)
General Aviation
Cessna L-19A Bird Dog (50-1675)
Piper PA-23 Apache (N . . . 35P)

Beechcraft (N2085D)
Rotary wing (helicopter)
Hiller H-23C Raven (56-2288)
Piasecki H-21B Workhorse (53-4380)

138 *"not do a lot of flying"* NAA to SA&DB in *Quest,* p. 18.
138 *"most intelligent of all the X-15 pilots"* MOT, *ATEOS,* pp. 2, 16.
138 *"wanting to understand everything"* BAP to author, p. 12.
138 *"set him apart from mere mortals"* WHD to author, Dec. 9, 2002, p. 7.
138 *"turned out Neil was right"* WHD to author, Ibid., pp. 6–7.
139 *"circles around many test pilots, engineering-wise"* GJM to author, p. 21.
139 *"did not have that bias"* Ibid., p. 7.
139 *"more mechanical than it is flying"* WJK to author, p. 9.
139 *"prejudiced for the fact that this guy's been a NACA"* CCK to author, p. 7.
140 *"evaluating a man from a test-pilot-performance capability"* Ibid.

Chapter 13: At the Edge of Space

144 *"first techniques for maneuvering in outer space"* This claim is made, for example, in the caption to a photograph showing Yeager in the F-104 available at http://mach1collectibles.com. The same caption also states that "NASA eventually took over the U.S. quest for space," a ridiculous assertion that the U.S. Air Force actually began the American space program.
145 *"inadvertently touched down at 170 KIAS"* NAA, Aeronautical Research Engineer and Pilot, memorandum for record, "Pilot Familiarization; X-1B #385; Flight No. 14," Aug. 15, 1957, History Archives, NASA Dryden.
145 *"didn't really fail . . . I broke it"* NAA to author, Nov. 26, 2002, p. 13.
146 *"dropped too close to Edwards Dry Lake"* NAA: e-mail to author, Jan. 22, 2004.
147 *"a complex and bothersome nuisance"* NAA to author, Nov. 26, 2002, pp. 11–12.
147 *"unique, self-adjusting system"* Ibid., p. 12.
147 *"used airplanes like the mathematician might use a computer"* Ibid., pp. 39–40.
148 *"rapidly deteriorating . . . near Mach 3"* Hallion, *On the Frontier,* p. 76.
148 *"optimum maximum energy"* Quoted in Hallion, *On the Frontier,* p. 77.
148 *"tended to blame the air force officials"* NAA: e-mail to author, Feb. 3, 2004.
148 *"often in the Simulation Lab"* NAA: e-mail to author, Feb. 3, 2004.
149 *"outputs to the instruments were improperly mechanized"* Ibid.
149 *"pilots didn't really trust simulators"* GLW to author, p. 3.
149 *"Neil believed in the simulations"* RED to author, pp. 7–8.
149 *"possible to pilot an aircraft into orbit"* NAA to author, Nov. 26, 2002, p. 34.
150 *"watch them get sick!"* RJB to author, p. 17.
150 *"persuaded ourselves at least"* NAA to author, Nov. 26, 2002, p. 34.
150 *"best simulator that had ever been built up to that time"* Ibid., p. 25.
151 *"put together a little team"* Ibid., pp. 25–26.
151 *"like a streamlined brick"* MOT, ATEOS, p. 66.
151 *"sundry combinations of speed brakes and flaps"* GJM to author, p. 5.
152 *"a 360-degree spiraling descent starting at about 40,000 feet"* Ibid.
152 *"something that the pilots, with their own experience, knew intuitively"* Ibid., p. 6.

152 " 'try theirs for a change' " Ibid., pp. 5–6.

153 " 'Here he is!' " RED to author, pp. 6–7.

153 *"flight stick should look like"* NAA to author, Nov. 26, 2002, pp. 37–38.

153 *"hinge points for one person"* Ibid., p. 37.

154 *"development of this high-speed range or 'High Range' "* Ibid., p. 10.

154 *"flying westbound against the Earth's rotation"* Ibid., p. 32.

155 *"contractor was expected to demonstrate"* Ibid., p. 26.

155 *"not party to those discussions"* Ibid., p. 27.

156 *"how a T-38 would perform"* NAA: e-mail to author, Mar. 16, 2004.

156 *"nice to have somebody along"* NAA to author, Nov. 26, 2002, p. 30.

157 *"very confined world in there"* Ibid., p. 35.

157 *"proceed with the original flight plan"* Radio "X-15-1 #670, Flight 1-18-31," Nov. 30, 1960, p. 1, History Archives, NASA Dryden.

157 *"landing would be the same"* NAA to author, Nov. 26, 2002, p. 35.

158 *"Thanks, Dad"* Radio "X-15-1 #670, Flight 1-18-31," Nov. 30, 1960, p. 4, History Archives, NASA Dryden.

158 *"Real nice flight, boy!"* Radio "X-15-1 #670, Flight 1-19-32," Dec. 9, 1960, p. 3, History Archives, NASA Dryden.

Chapter 14: The Worst Loss

161 *"just a different man"* JAH to author, Aug. 4, 2002, p. 26.

161 *"she tripped and fell"* JSA to DJH, El Lago, TX, n.d. (summer 1969), p. 4.

161 *"teaching swimming during this time"* Ibid., p. 5.

161 *"told him I was hospitalizing her"* Ibid.

162 *"never, ever complained"* Ibid.

162 *"took the radiation beautifully"* Ibid., p. 6.

162 " 'No, she'll be dead within six months' " JAH to author, Aug. 14, 2002, p. 25.

163 *"just overcame her"* JSA to DJH, n.d. (summer 1969), p. 6.

163 *"desperately wanted to do something to help"* GWW to author, p. 8.

163 *"She was a gay little thing"* Ibid., p. 9.

164 *"loved his little girl very deeply"* Ibid., p. 12.

164 Neil being very *"composed"* at the funeral JGM to author, p. 10.

165 *"always felt like that wasn't the thing to do"* GWW to author, p. 12.

165 *"a pilot thing"* Ibid., p. 6.

165 *"hurt Jan a lot"* Ibid.

165 *"Angry at God"* Ibid., p. 12.

166 *"Ricky was so happy"* Ibid., p. 11.

166 *"did things with the kids"* Ibid., p. 11.

166 *"to be alone"* Wead, *All the Presidents' Children,* p. 78.

166 *"thought his heart would break"* JAH to author, Aug. 14, 2002, p. 26.

167 *"the other men took care of the animal"* Ibid., p. 27.

167 *"time by his daughter's gravesite"* BAP to author, Dec. 19, 2002, p. 9.

167 *"quickly stepped forward and kissed her"* UPI wire story, John L. Michael, "2-Year-Old Girl Bussed by Neil," Oct. 23, 1969. A copy of this article can be found in the archives of the WDN.

167 *"never asked him . . . I couldn't"* JAH to author, Aug. 14, 2002, p. 27.

Chapter 15: Higher Resolve

168 *"hard decision for me"* NAA to DJH, n.d. (ca. spring 1969), p. 8. Copy in TLA.

168 *"bit of pie in the sky"* NAA to SA&DB, in *Quest,* p. 19.

168 *"impossible once Sputnik"* Ibid.

168 *"absolutely changed our country's view"* Ibid.

169 *"certainly aware of Mercury"* Ibid., p. 18.

169 *"didn't have that feeling at all"* NAA to author, Nov. 26, 2002, p. 60.

169 *"At the time the Mercury Program was started"* NAA to SA&DB, in *Quest,* p. 20.

169 *"I always felt that 'form follows function' "* NAA to author, Nov. 26, 2002, p. 60.

169 *"far more involved in spaceflight research than the Mercury people"* NAA quoted in *FOM,* p. 19.

170 *"risks we had in the space side of the program were probably less"* NAA to SA&DB in *Quest,* p. 17.

170 *"great dark sepulchral bridge coat"* Wolfe, *Right Stuff,* p. 17.

171 *"liked the people . . . at Edwards"* NAA to author, Nov. 26, 2002, p. 60.

171 *"our thing at Edwards"* Ibid., p. 55.

172 *"fiddled with the airplane"* Ibid.

172 *"confirmed that it could be doable"* Ibid.

173 *"pilots that were to do the development work"* Ibid., p. 58.

173 *"could have kept flying the X-15"* Ibid.

173 *"also working on the Dyna-Soar"* NAA to SA&DB, in *Quest,* p. 19.

173 *"I don't think there was a Eureka moment"* NAA to author, Nov. 26, 2002, p. 59.

174 *"accident prone"* RED to author, p. 8.

175 *"biggest bang I'd ever heard"* North American Aviation, Inc., *X-15 1960 Annual Report,* USAF Film Report, Sept. 15, 1961. Quote is from A. Scott Crossfield's onscreen appearance in this film. The NAA documentary is available on the CD-ROM that comes with Godwin, ed., *X-15: The NASA Mission Reports.*

175 *"whether there had been damage"* NAA to author, Nov. 26, 2002, p. 42.

176 *"a severe right roll occurred"* NAA, "Pilots Flight Notes," Dec. 20, 1961, p. 1, copy in NASA Dryden Historical Archives.

176 *"aspects of the MH-96"* NAA to author, Nov. 26, 2002, p. 41.

177 *"impact seemed to be somewhat harder"* NAA, "Pilot's Flight Notes," Dec. 20, 1961, p. 2.

177 *"went pretty much on plan"* NAA to author, Nov. 26, 2002, p. 47.

178 *"did not see any light"* NAA, "Rough Draft, Pilot's Comments," Apr. 6, 1962, p. 1, copy in NASA Dryden Historical Archives.

178 *"long time the second time for that engine to light up"* Ibid.

178 *"highest I'd ever gone"* NAA to author, Nov. 26, 2002, p. 48.

178 *"I thought I got the g's high enough"* Ibid.

179 *"Hard left turn, Neil!"* Transcript of radio voice communications, "X-15-2; Flight 3-4-8; April 20, 1962," p. 5, copy in NASA Dryden Historical Archives.

179 *"Of course, I'm trying to turn"* NAA to author, Nov. 26, 2002, p. 49.

179 *"no reason to suspect that ballooning would cause any trouble"* Ibid., p. 50.

179 *"sailing merrily by the field"* NAA, "Pilots Comments, Flight 3-4-8," Apr. 21, 1962, p. 2, copy in NASA Dryden Historical Archives.

179 *"whether I would be able to get back to Edwards"* NAA to SA&DB, in *Quest,* p. 17.

180 "home base in sight" Transcript of radio voice communications, "X-15-2; Flight 3-4-8; April 20, 1962," p. 5.

182 *"a hundred miles per hour, racing down that lake bed"* BAP to author, p. 7.

182 *"little old lady in Pasadena"* JGM to author, p. 6.

182 *"How far was Neil from the Joshua trees?"* Ibid., pp. 6–7.

182 *"just barely made it back to the dry lake bed"* WHD to author, p. 9.

182 *"rather funny at the time"* WJK to author, p. 4.

182 *"giggled over it a little bit"* RMW to author, p. 12.

183 *"a lax condition"* WJK to author, p. 4.

183 *"sounded like a screwup to him"* NAA to author, Nov. 26, 2002, p. 51.

183 *"there were definite limitations"* GLW to author, p. 10.

183 *"didn't realize how far up the nose had gone"* WHD to author, p. 10.

183 *"a learning thing"* NAA to author, Nov. 26, 2002, p. 52.

183 *"doing what he thought was the right thing"* WHD to author, p. 10.

184 *"guy was by the numbers"* RJB to author, p. 15.

185 *"like the back of my hand"* Y&J, *Yeager: An Autobiography,* p. 181.

185 *"think about Smith's Ranch Lake?"* Academy of Achievement, "General Chuck Yeager Interview," Cedar Ridge, CA, Feb. 1, 1991, p. 4. This interview can be accessed online at www.achievement.org/autodoc/page/yea0int-1.

185 *"damndest to talk Armstrong out of going at all"* Y&J, *Yeager,* p. 182.

186 *"touched, but we sure as hell didn't go"* Ibid.

186 *"went up there and looked it over"* NAA to author, Nov. 26, 2002, p. 22.

186 *"go back and try it again"* Ibid.

187 *"Chuck started to chuckle"* Ibid.

187 *"driver came out and he had a chain"* Ibid.

187 *"don't think anyone has ever seen the film"* Ibid., pp. 22–23.

187 *"What an air force pickup truck was doing there"* Ibid., p. 22.

187 *"Any ideas?"* Y&J, *Yeager,* p. 182.

188 *"Keep the door open and we'll jump aboard"* Academy of Achievement, "General Chuck Yeager Interview," p. 4.

188 Neil *"did not rise to the bait"* E-mail, Christian Gelzer, NASA Dryden Research Center, to author, "Re: Bill Dana," Feb. 27, 2004. This e-mail communicated responses to questions posed to WHD by Dr. Gelzer, a NASA Dryden historian, on behalf of the author.

188 *"Neil's embarrassment"* Gelzer e-mail to author, "Re: Bill WHD," Feb. 27, 2004.

188 *"when Bikle saw me he burst out laughing"* Y&J, *Yeager,* p. 182.

188 *"felt Yeager was the best"* WHD to author, Dec. 9, 2002, p. 7.

188 *"last guy at Edwards to take any advice"* Y&J, *Yeager,* p. 181.

188 *"I did take his advice!"* NAA to author, Nov. 26, 2002, p. 23.

188 *"thought I was a wild man"* Y&J, *Yeager,* pp. 108, 121.

189 *"rated them about as high as my shoelaces"* Ibid., pp. 182–83.

189 *"wasn't too good an airplane driver"* Academy of Achievement, "General Chuck Yeager Interview," p. 4.

189 *"limited understanding"* NAA to author, Nov. 26, 2002, p. 19.

189 *"just like we always did"* Ibid., p. 45.

190 *"decided to go to Nellis Air Force Base"* Ibid.

190 *"a no-radio approach"* Ibid., pp. 45–46.

190 *"a good jolt when I hit it"* Ibid., p. 46.

191 *"stretched the truth a bit"* MOT, *ATEOS,* p. 113.

191 *"Oh no, not again!"* Ibid., p. 116.

191 *"bad day all around"* NAA to author, Nov. 26, 2002, p. 46.

192 *"applied power to abort the landing and get airborne"* MOT, *ATEOS,* p. 115.

192 *"didn't diddle around"* SAB to author, p. 27.

192 *"Bikle was very pragmatic"* NAA to author, Nov. 26, 2002, p. 28.

193 *NASA formally announced* Memo, Brainerd Holmes to Webb, Dryden, and Seamans, "Subj: Selection of Additional Astronauts," Apr. 28, 1962, with enclo., "Gemini and Apollo Astronaut Selection." Also, MSC *Space News Roundup,* May 2, 1962, p. 1; *Astronautical and Aeronautical Events of 1962,* p. 56.

195 *"We wanted him in"* RED to author, Dec. 11, 2003, p. 10.

195 *"his personal affairs"* Ibid., p. 11.

195 *Yet he does credit Day* NAA: e-mail to RED, July 16, 1997, in author's Dick Day file.

196 *"He never mentioned anything to anybody"* SPB to author, Dec. 15, 2002, p. 25.

196 *"hadn't seen anything to indicate that Neil wanted to leave Edwards"* BAP to author, Dec. 19, 2002, p. 17.

196 *"Due to commitments of Mr. Neil A. Armstrong"* PFB, Director, NASA Flight Research Center, to NASA HQ, Attn: Mr. John Stack, Code RA, "Flights of United Kingdom Aircraft by Neil A. Armstrong," May 29, 1962, copy in Armstrong's personal papers.

197 *"memo was a form response"* NAA: e-mail to author, Mar. 17, 2004.

197 *"looking for qualified test pilots"* CCK to author, p. 2.

198 *"Walt Williams thought he was first rate"* Ibid.

198 *"absolutely no way"* Ibid., p. 3.

198 *"somewhat affected by the situation"* NAA to author, Nov. 26, 2002, p. 61.

Chapter 16: I've Got a Secret

202 *"around the Fourth of July"* JAH to author, Aug. 14, 2002, p. 27.

202 *"happy to get that call"* NAA to author, June 2, 2003, p. 5.

202 *"definitely on the list"* "NASA Test Pilot Named First Civilian Astronaut," *Washington Evening Star,* July 18, 1962, p. 1.

202 *"suspect that at least one civilian will be included"* Collins's letter to his father, written on Aug. 19, 1962, is quoted in MC, *CTF,* p. 29.

202 *"odds had been good he would make this cut"* Jim Lovell and Jeffrey Kluger, *Lost Moon: The Perilous Voyage of Apollo 13,* p. 187.

203 *"Nobody pressured us"* Donald K. Slayton with Michael Cassutt, *Deke!,* p. 120.

203 *"people from my own organization"* NAA to author, June 2, 2003, p. 5.

203 *"how I would grade in those categories"* Ibid.

203 *"projects of the current space program"* NAA and Euclid C. Holleman, *A Review of In-Flight Simulation Pertinent to Piloted Space Vehicles.* AGARD Report 403, 21st Flight Mechanics Panel Meeting, Paris, France, July 9–11, 1962, p. 7.

204 *"smoke was obvious"* NAA to author, Nov. 26, 2002, p. 54.

204 *"were some painful experiences"* NAA to author, June 2, 2003, p. 3.

205 *"lot of strange tests like that"* Ibid.

205 " *'Fifteen Men in a Boardinghouse Bed' "* Ibid.

206 *"guys who were stationed in Michigan"* Ibid., p. 4.

206 *"didn't find it at all difficult"* Ibid.

206 *"All thirty-two of the finalists"* Ibid., p. 5.

206 *"We did not have military pilots"* NAA: e-mail to author, Mar. 27, 2004.

206 *"difficulties . . . Mercury astronauts"* NAA to author, June 2, 2003, p. 10.

207 *"lookout for any abnormal behavior"* MC, *Carrying the Fire,* p. 29.

207 *"completely quiet"* NAA to author, June 2, 2003, p. 7.

207 *"checked in as Max"* Ibid., p. 8.

207 *"plenty of missions for all of you"* Gilruth quoted in Tom Stafford with Michael Cassutt, *We Have Capture,* p. 40.

208 *"test pilot's creed"* Slayton quoted in TS with MC, *WHC,* pp. 40–41.

208 *truly remarkable group of men* A few women did apply for astronaut selection in 1962, but as Bob Gilruth explained at the September 17, 1962, press conference, "none qualified." The other four civilian finalists for the second class of astronauts were Thomas E. Edmonds, John M. Fritz, Orville C. Johnson, and John L. Swigert. Of these, only Jack Swigert ever became an astronaut, as part of NASA's fifth class, chosen in 1966. Swigert, the first—and for many years—only unmarried astronaut ever accepted into NASA's astronaut corps, journeyed to the Moon as part of Apollo 13, replacing Thomas K. "Ken" Mattingly on the crew after he was grounded for being exposed to the German measles.

208 *"best NASA ever picked"* MC, *CTF,* p. 30.

210 *"more like junior executives"* Homer Bigart, "9 New Astronauts Named to Train for Moon Flights," *NYT,* Sept. 18, 1962, p. 1.

211 *"general challenge of the unknowns"* NAA quoted in Manned Spacecraft Center, "Trainees Comment on 'Why?,' " *NASA Roundup,* Sept. 19, 1962, p. 5.

211 *"like to be on the first team"* FB and the other members of the "New Nine" quoted in Manned Spacecraft Center, "Trainees Comment on 'Why?,' " *NASA Roundup,* Sept. 19, 1962, p. 5.

211 *"fairly unsophisticated questions"* NAA to author, June 2, 2003, p. 8.

211 *"variety of aircraft available to fly"* Ibid., p. 7.

212 *"make a 'rag wing' "* NAA to author, Nov. 26, 2002, p. 57.

212 *"Where's Milt?"* BAP to author, p. 20.

212 *"problems developing a good flight-worthy vehicle"* MOT, *ATEOS,* p. 147.

Part Five: No Man Is an Island

215 *E* MC to author.

215 *E* Eugene Cernan with Dan Davis, *Last Man on the Moon: Astronaut Gene Cernan and America's Race in Space,* p. 145.

Chapter 17: Training Days

217 *"the three grimmest days"* See McDougall, *The Heavens and the Earth,* pp. 318, 328, and Charles Murray and Catherine Bly Cox, *Apollo,* pp. 79–80.

218 *"the mantles of the single-combat warriors"* Wolfe, *Right Stuff,* pp. 101–03.

219 *"right on the brink of World War III"* NAA to SA&DB, in *Quest,* p. 23.

219 *Pete Conrad watched* Conrad's reaction described in Stafford, *We Have Capture!,* p. 41.

219 *first in a series of contractor tours* Armstrong's itinerary has been reconstructed from his Travel Request and Authorization forms, MSC, in NAA's personal papers. Signing the forms at MSC were Donald K. Slayton, the "approving official," and Paul E. Purser, the "authorizing official."

220 *"lots of food and plenty of booze"* Stafford, *We Have Capture!,* p. 42.

220 *"Every Monday morning all astronauts would get together"* Ibid., p. 43.

220 *"hardest-working bunch of guys"* George M. Low, Deputy Administrator, NASA Headquarters, to Robert Sherrod, "Further Comments on Astronaut Chapter," Oct. 8, 1974, copy in NASA History Office Archives, Washington DC, File 87–12, Box 15.

221 *"I didn't find the academic burden to be overly difficult"* NAA to author, Cincinnati, OH, June 2, 2003, p. 11.

221 *"Vomit Comet"* Flight Crew Training Report No. 27, "Period: April 22–27, 1963," in NAA's personal papers.

222 *Dilbert Dunker* Flight Crew Training Report No. 49, "Period: September 23–28, 1963," in NAA's personal papers.

222 *"at sixteen g's"* Glenn quoted in MC, *Liftoff: The Story of America's Adventure in Space,* p. 31. Glenn detailed his experiences on the Johnsville centrifuge in "The Wheel" in *We Seven,* pp. 180–87. Glenn also discusses his rides on the wheel in *John Glenn: A Memoir,* pp. 236–37 and 276–81.

222 *"get up to twenty g's"* Faget quoted in WMS, "Our Cozy Cocoon," in *We Seven,* p. 146.

222 *"dynamic runs"* Flight Crew Training Report No. 40, "Period: July 22–27, 1963," in NAA's personal papers.

222 *"That training went for"* NAA: e-mail to author, "Questions about astronaut training," Apr. 8, 2004.

223 *helicopter flight to preparations* Flight Crew Training Report No. 457, "Period: November 18–23, 1963," in NAA's personal papers.

223 *"The helicopter was not a good simulation of the lunar module control at all"* NAA to author, Cincinnati, OH, June 3, 2000 (afternoon), p. 26.

223 *"heard the news bulletin"* NAA to author, June 2, 2003 (morning), p. 18.

224 *"it was just natural that I was at the place where the simulators were"* Ibid., p. 6.

224 *"Deke just said, 'Here they are' "* Stafford, *WHC,* p. 44.

224 *"probably an easy pick for Deke"* NAA to author, June 2, 2003 (morning), p. 6.

225 *"equations of motion"* NAA to author, June 2, 2003 (morning), p. 16.

225 *"sense of being proper"* Ibid.

226 *"useful simulator"* Ibid.

226 *Lovell . . . memos* Jim Lovell, Memorandum for Astronauts, "Parasail Primer," July 26, 1963; Lovell, "Gemini Egress Development," Feb. 7, 1964; Lovell, Memorandum for Astronauts, "Ballute Test Results," Feb. 11, 1964;

Lovell, "Gemini Survival Kits," Apr. 27, 1964. Copies of all these memos and others by different astronauts were found in NAA's personal papers.

226 *"memos flying"* NAA to author, June 2, 2003 (morning), p. 12.

226 *"Some things weren't covered"* NAA to SA&DB, in *Quest,* p. 22.

226 *week in the barrel* Armstrong's "week in the barrel" is laid out in Fred Asselin, Astronaut Affairs Coordinator, Office of Public Affairs, MSC, to Neil Armstrong, Astronaut Office, MSC, June 16, 1964, in NAA's personal papers.

227 *"Quite a different responsibility"* NAA to SA&DB, in *Quest,* p. 21.

227 *"Neil presented a certain façade, a certain persona"* MC to author, Marco Island, FL, Mar. 25, 2003, p. 4.

228 *"Neil would be . . . on the thinker side"* Ibid., p. 6.

228 *"potential of being challenged"* BA to author, Albuquerque, NM, Mar. 17, 2003, p. 4.

228 *"long time coming to a solution"* RFG to author, Prescott, AZ, Apr. 12, 2003, p. 9.

228 *"Neil was patient with processes"* MC to author, Mar. 25, 2003, p. 4.

228 *"He could be stubborn"* BA to author, Mar. 17, 2003, p. 5.

228 *"Neil . . . bamboozled"* WAA to author, San Diego, CA, Sept. 8, 2003, p. 8.

228 *" meet anyone halfway"* MC to author, Mar. 25, 2003, p. 8.

228 *"Neil wasn't an expansive guy"* WAA to author, Sept. 8, 2003, p. 35.

228 *"Neil is as friendly"* JG to author, The John Glenn Institute for Public Service & Public Policy, Ohio State University, Columbus, OH, Sept. 23, 2003, p. 5.

229 *"jungle training"* Ibid., p. 4.

229 *"Neil's theory on exercise"* JG, *Glenn: A Memoir,* pp. 391–92.

229 *"That a boy, Dave!"* David Scott to author, Atlanta, GA, Feb. 1, 2003, transcript, p. 22. I interviewed Scott the afternoon of the Space Shuttle *Columbia* accident.

229 *"on his own schedule"* MC to author, Mar. 25, 2003, p. 7.

229 *"The guy was really cool under pressure"* Scott to author, Feb. 1, 2003, p. 31.

229 *"You just couldn't see through him"* BA to author, Mar. 17, 2003, p. 6.

Chapter 18: In Line for Command

230 *"I had no expectation of getting it"* NAA to author, June 2, 2003, p. 18.

230 *"actual flight assignment"* NAA to SA&DB, in *Quest,* p. 24.

231 *"how Deke assigned the crews"* NAA to author, June 2, 2003, pp. 18–19.

231 *"Some flights required more, or special, skills and experience"* Ibid., p. 18.

232 *"So he [Deke] tried to think things through ahead of time"* Ibid., p. 20.

232 *"a very loose operation"* Ibid., p. 13.

232 *"So I took a very simple approach"* Ibid., p. 21.

234 *" 'Eight days or bust was their motto' "* MC, *Liftoff,* p. 87.

234 *"backing up Gordon Cooper"* NAA to SA&DB, in *Quest,* p. 23.

235 *"Deke stood up for [Gordo]"* NAA to author, June 2, 2003, p. 30.

235 *"equal to thousands of hours in the labs"* NAA to SA&DB, in *Quest,* p. 21.

235 *"We'd get home . . . sometimes"* Ibid., p. 24.

236 *"Slayton would send astronauts out"* EFK to Roy F. Neal, Houston, TX, Mar.

19, 1998, p. 15. This interview was conducted as part of the NASA JSC Oral History Project.

236 *"We practiced the procedures"* NAA to author, June 2, 2003, p. 23.

236 *"responsibilities of the tracking station at Hawaii"* Ibid., p. 23.

236 *"We all knew the spacecraft very well"* NAA to SA&DB, in *Quest,* p. 24.

237 *"It was mostly A-to-B flying"* NAA to author, June 2, 2003, p. 2.

237 *"Morehead was a superb facility"* Ibid., p. 17.

237 *"My interests were just from a rank amateur"* Ibid.

238 *"a good visual representation"* Ibid.

238 *"we would turn the lights completely down in the cockpit"* Ibid.

238 *"We didn't get much Southern Hemisphere practice"* Dave Scott to Ken Glover, ca. 1992, sent by e-mail to author from Eric P. Jones, May 24, 2003. Under NASA sponsorship, Glover assisted Jones during the 1990s in the creation of the *Apollo Lunar Surface Journal,* available online at *www.hq.nasa.gov/alsj/.*

238 *"my sense is that the Gemini teams were more closely knit than the Apollo ones"* NAA to author, June 2, 2003, p. 27.

239 *"Ours was the first spacecraft to go into space with a fuel cell"* Gordon Cooper with Bruce Henderson, *Leap of Faith,* p. 135.

239 *"newfangled contraption"* MC, *Liftoff,* p. 87.

239 *"We actually talked to the spacecraft on VHF as it went overhead"* NAA to SA&DB, in *Quest,* p. 24.

239 *"nearly cost us our mission"* GC, *Leap of Faith,* p. 136.

239 *"we'd released a rendezvous pod"* Ibid.

240 *Tom Stafford* TS, *WHC,* p. 69.

240 *"Dave was an excellent choice"* NAA to author, June 2, 2003, p. 32.

240 *"I had some concept of what was in Deke's mind"* Ibid.

Chapter 19: Gemini VIII

243 *"super flight with great objectives"* NAA to author, June 2, 2003, p. 35.

243 *"Gemini meant the twins, Castor and Pollux"* Ibid.

243 *internal technical debate* For a detailed analysis of the debate over the selection of lunar-orbit rendezvous as the mission mode for the Moon landing, see chapter 8 of *Spaceflight Revolution* (1995), "Enchanted Rendezvous," pp. 221–68.

243 *"rendezvous and docking"* NAA: e-mail to author, May 12, 2003.

244 *troubled development* For a summary of the Agena's development problems as a rendezvous target vehicle, see chapter 13 of Barton C. Hacker and James M. Grimwood, *On the Shoulders of Titans,* "Agena on Trial," pp. 297–321.

244 *"epoxy in the catcher mechanism"* NAA to author, June 2, 2003, p. 37.

244 *"cost us the launch"* David Scott in Scott and Alexei Leonov, *Two Sides of the Moon,* p. x.

245 *"I was speechless"* VEAP, "Thinking Back," p. 4.

245 *"surprise when you really launched"* NAA to author, June 2, 2003, p. 36.

245 *reflected a "keying up"* On the X-15 aeromedical investigations, see Wendell H. Stillwell, *X-15 Research Results* (Washington, DC: NASA SP-60, 1965), pp. 89–90.

246 *"The Titan II was a pretty smooth ride"* Ibid., p. 37.

246 *"Hey, how 'bout that view!?"* Gemini VIII Voice Communications (Air-to-Ground, Ground-to-Air and On-Board Transcription), Gemini Project Files, p. 3. Copy in NARA, Southwest Repository, Ft. Worth, TX, Record Group 255, MAC Control No. C-115471.

246 *"First, all you see is blue"* NAA to author, June 2, 2003, p. 37.

247 *"worried about the engine keeping running"* Ibid., p. 38.

247 *"all those ships!"* Gemini VIII Voice Communications (Air-to-Ground, Ground-to-Air and On-Board Transcription), Gemini Project Files, p. 18. Copy in NARA, Southwest Repository, Ft. Worth, TX, Record Group 255, MAC Control No. C-115471. Armstrong's comment came at 1:29:08 elapsed time.

247 *"A fundamental requirement of rendezvous"* NAA to author, June 2, 2003, p. 40.

248 *"Then a strange thing happens"* MC, *Liftoff,* pp. 72–73.

248 *"Rendezvous simulation in Gemini"* NAA to author, June 2, 2003, p. 31.

248 *"We achieved fifty to sixty rendezvous simulations on the ground"* NAA to Barton C. Hacker, Houston, TX, Apr. 6, 1967, p. 13. Tape recording in NARA, Southwest Repository, Ft. Worth, TX, Record Group 255, Code GemOH49.

249 *"This was a teeny-tiny computer"* NAA to author, June 2, 2003, p. 38.

250 *"allowed us to arrive at the Agena"* Ibid., p. 41.

251 *"quick loose burn"* Scott quoted in *On the Shoulders of Titans,* p. 310.

251 *"one hundred thirty degrees behind the Agena"* NAA to author, June 2, 2003, p. 41.

252 *"It's hard to do at night"* Ibid., p. 42.

252 *"At that point it lit up like a Christmas tree"* Ibid.

253 *"we did what was called 'station keeping' "* Ibid.

255 *"It was very easy to fly close"* Ibid.

256 *"I was going to have him fly it, but not then"* Ibid., p. 43.

258 *"we were not in level flight like we were supposed to be"* Ibid., p. 44.

259 *"any trouble with the docking"* NAA to SA&DB, in *Quest,* p. 26.

259 *"problem or mistake, it would come from the Agena"* NAA to author, June 2, 2003, p. 34.

259 *"probably an unnecessary comment"* NAA to author, June 2, 2003, p. 44.

259 *"problem was not the Agena's"* Ibid., p. 46.

259 *"hear the thruster when it fired"* NAA to SA&DB, in *Quest,* p. 26.

260 *"tumbling gyro"* NAA to author, June 2, 2003, p. 45.

260 *"lose our ability to discriminate accurately"* Ibid.

260 *"engage the spacecraft's other control system"* Ibid., p. 46.

260 *"We found the culprit"* Ibid., p. 47.

261 *"Murphy's law says bad things always happen"* NAA to SA&DB, in *Quest,* p. 27.

262 *"I knew what the mission rules were"* NAA to author, June 2, 2003, p. 46.

263 *"I had to go back to the foundation instincts"* NAA to SA&DB, in *Quest,* p. 26.

264 *"I wanted to stay up"* NAA to Barton C. Hacker, Houston, TX, Apr. 6, 1967, p. 20.

264 *"we steered a course for Okinawa"* NAA to author, June 2, 2003, p. 49.

264 *"We appeared to be dropping at a prodigious rate"* Ibid.

265 *"coming down in Red China"* NAA to SA&DB, in *Quest,* p. 27.

265 *"We assumed it was friendly"* Ibid.

265 *"Gemini was a terrible boat"* NAA to author, June 2, 2003, p. 35.

265 *"I was very depressed"* Ibid., p. 50.

265 *"Our job was to protect Armstrong and Scott"* WMS, *Schirra's Space,* p. 173.

266 *"The wind took it right back out again!"* NAA to author, June 2, 2003, p. 51.

266 *"I'll get a gun and sink her!"* WMS, *Schirra's Space,* p. 174.

266 *"We tried to tell them everything we knew"* NAA to author, June 2, 2003, p. 52.

267 *"It was a great disappointment to us"* NAA to SA&DB, in *Quest,* p. 26.

267 *"I JUST HAD A PHONE CALL FROM NEIL ARMSTRONG"* Telegram, Hank Suydom, Houston, to Dave Snell, New York City, "RUSH PERSONAL," Mar. 29, 1966, copy in NAA personal files.

267 *run articles on Gemini VIII* In *Life,* Mar. 25, 1966, and Apr. 1, 1966.

268 *"I'll speak for both of us"* The contributions to the *Life* article entitled "A Case of 'Constructive Alarm,' " published in the Apr. 1, 1966, issue, were sent from Houston to New York by Teletype: Hank Suydam to Time, Inc., New York City, Mar. 28, 1966, copy in NAA personal files.

268 *"I know that you were not entirely satisfied with the result"* Edward K. Thompson to NAA and David Scott, Apr. 5, 1966, copy in NAA personal files.

268 *"What Went Wrong?"* United Press International, "What Went Wrong? Tapes Hold Secret," *New York World-Telegram,* Mar. 17, 1966.

268 *"We are very proud of them"* Statement issued by Pres. Lyndon B. Johnson, *Pres. Doc.,* Mar. 21, 1966, p. 400.

268 *"criticize Neil's performance"* EC, *The Last Man on the Moon,* p. 101.

269 *"turned out to be the wrong thing to do"* TS, *WHC,* p. 84.

269 *"the crew had unnecessarily activated a backup control system"* Walter Cunningham, with Mickey Herskowitz, *The All-American Boys,* pp. 91–92.

270 *"participated in that crap"* FB to author, Las Cruces, NM, Mar. 15, 2003, p. 10.

270 *"Everybody second-guessed everybody"* AB to author, Houston, TX, Feb. 7, 2003, pp. 36–37.

270 *"Neil could have done"* James McDivitt to author, Tucson, AZ, Apr. 7, 2003, p. 8.

271 *"one ring of their reentry system"* BA to author, Albuquerque, NM, Mar. 17, 2003, p. 15.

271 *"You'll never hear it from me"* JG to author, Columbus, OH, Sept. 23, 2003, p. 7.

271 *"life-threatening situation"* CCK, *Flight: My Life in Mission Control,* pp. 254, 255.

272 *"I was damn impressed with Neil"* EFK to author, Dickinson, TX, Feb. 6, 2003, p. 5.

272 *"never forget this mission's lesson"* EFK, *Failure Is Not an Option,* p. 174.

272 *"We tricked the astronauts on that one"* CKK to author, Feb. 7, 2003, p. 9.

272 *"figure out the right diagnosis"* NAA to author, June 2, 2003, p. 48.

272 *"the technicians did something that put a nick in that cable"* Ibid.

273 *"we had done everything right"* Scott, *Two Sides of the Moon,* p. 181.

273 *"remained a mystery"* NAA to author, June 2, 2003, p. 48.

273 *"They wouldn't have known what happened"* Dave Scott to author, Atlanta, GA, Feb. 1, 2003, p. 37.

273 *"a big glitch in the program"* CKK to author, Feb. 7, 2003, p. 10.

273 *"it could have been a showstopper"* Scott, *Two Sides of the Moon,* p. 180.

273 *"nothing . . . that affected their crew assignments"* MC to author, Mar. 25, 2003, p. 11.

273 *"Neil quick-thinking"* WAA to author, San Diego, CA, Sept. 8, 2003, p. 10.

273 *"even greater confidence in Neil's abilities"* CKK to author, Feb. 7, 2003, p. 12.

273 *"the crew demonstrated remarkable piloting skill"* Gilruth quoted in Manned Spacecraft Center, "Mission Evaluation Team Lauds Quick-Thinking Gemini VIII Crew," *Space News Roundup,* Apr. 1, 1966, p. 1.

274 *"parlayed a busted Gemini VIII flight into the Buck Rogers grand prize mission"* Cunningham, *The All-American Boys,* p. 92.

274 *"affect us some way in the future"* NAA to author, June 2, 2003, p. 53.

274 *"get right back into the cycle"* NAA to Barton C. Hacker, Apr. 6, 1967, p. 24.

Chapter 20: The Astronaut's Wife

275 *"space hero"* "Wapak Awaits Celebration for Hometown Spaceman," *LN,* Apr. 10, 1966.

275 *"Wapakoneta made the request"* NAA to author, June 2, 2003, pp. 53–54.

275 *"You are my people"* Carolyn Focht, " 'More Than I Deserve,' " *Columbus* (OH) *Dispatch,* Apr. 14, 1966; Al Kattman, "Proud Hometown Greets Astronaut," *Lima News,* Apr. 14, 1966.

275 *"more than I deserve"* Focht, " 'More Than I Deserve.' "

276 *"Those dear people"* VEA to DJH, Wapakoneta, OH, n.d. (ca. Mar. 1969], *Life* interview, Tape 1B, p. 18. Copy in VEAP.

276 *"Indeed, we know nothing yet"* VEAP, "Looking Back," n.d. [ca. 1976], p. 3.

277 *"Our prayers were answered"* Ibid., p. 4.

277 *"temptation . . . too great to ignore"* EC, *The Last Man on the Moon,* pp. 82–83.

277 "Life *treated the men and their families"* Letter, DJH to Perry Michael Whyte, Iowa State University, Jan. 1977, quoted in AC, *A Man on the Moon,* p. 633, n. 349.

278 *"they are really home hardly at all"* JSA to DJH, Mar. 12, 1969, p. 2.

278 *"Certainly I realize that there are risks"* Ibid., p. 1.

278 " *'I want to go see Lurton' "* Ibid., p. 6

278 *"I was furious"* JSA to author, Sept. 10, 2004 (afternoon), p. 19.

279 " *'what about the wives?' "* Ibid., p. 20.

279 *"listening but not watching"* "High Tension over the Astronauts," *Life,* Mar. 25, 1966.

279 *"But also I am a fatalist"* Ibid.

279 *"blah, blah, blah"* JSA to author, Sept. 10, 2004 (afternoon), p. 19.

279 *"Elliot was a hard worker, diligent"* NAA to author, June 2, 2003, p. 29.

280 *"qualifications as an astronaut"* Ibid.

280 " *'Charlie was a very affable fellow' "* Ibid., p. 34.

281 *"I don't have any knowledge of them having such concerns"* Ibid., p. 35.

281 *"crisscrossed with tidy streets"* AC, *A Man on the Moon,* p. 20

281 *"We were looking for property"* NAA to author, Cincinnati, OH June 2, 2002 (morning), p. 10.

282 *"We had a swimming pool"* NAA to author, June 2, 2002, p. 27.

282　*"children weren't asphyxiated"* JSA to DJH, El Lago, TX, n.d. (ca. March 1969), *Life* interview, transcript, p. 10.

282　*"He took one leap and he was over"* JSA to DJH, n.d. (ca. March 1969), p. 11.

282　*"Ed certainly had the ability"* NAA to author, June 2, 2002, p. 25.

282　*"But no . . . Neil didn't do that!"* JSA to DJH, n.d. (ca. March 1969), p. 12.

283　*"I just held my breath the whole time"* NAA to author, June 2, 2002, p. 25.

283　*"the longest journey" he ever made* JSA to DJH, n.d. (summer 1969), p. 13.

283　*"I've got an Excedrin headache"* Ibid., p. 14.

283　*"It was a terrible mess afterwards"* Ibid., p. 15.

283　*"We really made a mess of their whole place!"* Ibid., p. 16.

284　*Seabrook, Tex., April 24, 1964 (UPI)* "Home of Astronaut Burns," *NYT,* Apr. 24, 1964, p. 23.

284　*"consumed by the smoke"* JSA to DJH, n.d. (summer 1969), p. 13.

284　*"It could have been catastrophic"* NAA to author, June 2, 2003, p. 27.

284　*"I never cried"* JSA to DJH, n.d. (summer 1969), p. 14.

284　*"we had minimum furniture"* Ibid., p. 13.

285　*"I'll never forget how grateful I was to all the neighbors"* Ibid., p. 15.

285　*"a good six months"* Ibid.

285　*"His models, we saved those"* Ibid., p. 16.

285　*"It was not a 'spec' home"* NAA to author, June 2, 2003, p. 10.

285　*"just an inconvenience"* Ibid., p. 27.

286　*"I vowed I'd never build another house!"* JSA to DJH, n.d. (summer 1969), p. 17.

286　*"inspectors found the cause"* NAA to author, June 2, 2003, p. 25.

286　*"detector systems"* JSA to DJH, n.d. (summer 1969), p. 17.

287　*"married to an astronaut"* JSA tape-recording for DJH, transcribed Apr. 2, 1969, p. 5.

287　*"As his wife I do keep his clothes clean for him"* Ibid., p. 1.

287　*"It never, never shows in Neil that he's had a very distressed day"* Ibid., p. 3.

287　*"questions about his work"* JSA to DJH, Mar. 12, 1969, p. 2.

287　*"it is definitely a strain on the wife and the family"* Ibid.

288　*"miss the fun part"* Ibid., p. 3.

288　*"children are in need of something"* Ibid., p. 4.

288　*"make sure they understand what is happening"* Ibid., p. 7.

288　*"When you put your children in public"* Ibid., pp. 7–8.

288　"Something that occurred to me the other day when I was driving the car" JSA tape recording for DJH, transcribed Apr. 2, 1969, p. 1.

289　*"Living in the present is most important"* Ibid., p. 2.

289　*"it's of prime importance that you are able to understand yourself"* Ibid., pp. 1–2.

289　"maintain one's own identity" Ibid., pp. 7–8.

289　*"like a coffee"* JSA to author, Sept. 10, 2004 (afternoon), p. 28.

290　*ended in divorce or separation* On the list of those who divorced was Buzz and Joan (Archer) Aldrin, Alan and Sue (Ragsdale) Bean, Gene and Barbara (Atchley) Cernan, Pete and Jane (DuBose) Conrad, Dick and Barbara (Field) Gordon, Fred and Mary (Monroe) Haise, Edgar and Louise (Randall) Mitchell, Dave and Lurton (Ott) Scott, Tom and Faye (Shoemaker) Stafford, Alfred and Pamela (Vander Beek) Worden, John and Barbara (White) Young, and ultimately, but not until 1994, Neil and Janet (Shearon) Armstrong. Ken

Mattingly separared from his wife Elizabeth (Dailey) several years prior to her death in 1991.

290 *"my tunnel vision"* EC, *The Last Man on the Moon,* p. 68.

290 *"NASA did not have a survival handbook for our wives"* Ibid.

Chapter 21: For All America

293 *"This was my third run-through"* NAA to author, June 3, 2003, p. 1.

293 *"it wasn't going to be successful"* RFG to author, Apr. 12, 2003, p. 28.

293 *"two vehicles in formation"* NAA to author, June 3, 2003, p. 2.

294 *"We'd go out on the beach and work out trajectory procedures"* Ibid., pp. 1–2.

294 *"a very nice flight, indeed"* MC, *Liftoff,* pp. 111–12.

294 *"stable orientations while tethered"* NAA: e-mail to author, June 30, 2004.

295 *"a cool and methodical demonstration"* MC, *Liftoff,* p. 112.

295 *"Gemini was timely and synergistic"* NAA to author, June 3, 2003, p. 8.

296 *"loss of friends"* NAA: e-mail to author, July 24, 2004.

297 *"spontaneous, friendly, and extremely warm"* George Low, *Latin American Tour With Astronauts Armstrong and Gordon, October 7–31, 1966,* unpublished manuscript, Nov. 16, 1966, p. iii.

297 *"Neil and Dick were out of their cars shaking hands"* Ibid., p. 58.

298 *"whether we would get out in one piece"* Ibid., pp. 27–28.

298 *"organized campaign to embarrass us"* Ibid., p. 40.

298 *"every rooftop along the motorcade route was covered with armed soldiers"* Ibid., p. 57.

298 *"the weather in Asunción"* NAA to author, June 2, 2003, p. 55.

299 *"Fernando was Dutch"* NAA to author, June 2, 2003, p. 56.

300 *"He was not an immovable type"* Ibid., p. 54.

300 *"short little speeches"* Low, *Latin American Tour,* pp. 61–62.

300 *"official visit by a team of scientists as well as space heroes"* Ibid., p. iv.

Part Six: Apollo

301 *E* NAA to SA&DB, in *Quest,* p. 33.

Chapter 22: Out of the Ashes

305 *"non-staking-a-claim treaty"* NAA to SA&DB, in *Quest,* p. 29.

305 *a reception in the Green Room* The astronaut who best recollects the details of the White House reception for the Outer Space Treaty that took place simultaneously with the Apollo fire is Jim Lovell. See Jim Lovell and Jeffrey Kluger, *Lost Moon: The Perilous Voyage of Apollo 13,* pp. 7–12 and 21–22.

306 *"Don't leave the hotel"* Quoted in ibid., p. 23.

306 *"did not know anything"* JSA to author, Sept. 11, 2004 (morning), p. 1.

306 *"tell Pat about it before she heard it on television"* WAA to author, San Diego, CA, Apr. 8, 2003, p. 24.

307 *"unique time to share ourselves"* JSA to author, Sept. 11, 2004 (morning), p. 2.

307   *get to the Moon before the end of the decade* Quoted in Lovell and Kluger, *Lost Moon,* p. 24.

307   *"I don't blame people for anything"* NAA to author, June 3, 2003, p. 6.

307   *"it really hurt to lose them in a ground test"* NAA to SA&DB, in *Quest,* p. 28.

307   *"injuries and even deaths are easier to accept"* NAA to author, June 3, 2003, p. 6.

307   *"it was* some *bad oversight"* Ibid.

308   *"It* is *a remarkable coincidence"* Ibid., p. 7.

308   *"I was involved in doing other things"* Ibid., p. 5.

309   *"We were given the gift of time"* NAA to SA&DB, in *Quest,* p. 29.

309   *"everyone not working on fire-related matters"* MC, *Liftoff,* p. 137.

310   *"The operative word is 'may' "* NAA to author, June 3, 2003, p. 7.

Chapter 23: Wingless on Luna

314   *"lunar gravity"* NAA to author, Cincinnati, OH, June 3, 2004, p. 24.

314   *"That was a natural thing for us"* Ibid., p. 7.

314   helicopters *"could neither replicate the consequences of lunar gravity nor the handling characteristics of reaction system machines"* NAA, *Wingless on Luna,* p. 6.

315   *"wingless on Luna"* NAA used this phrase as the title of the speech he gave before the Wings Club at the Inter-Continental Hotel in New York City on May 20, 1988, "Wingless on Luna," Twenty-fifth Wings Club, General Harold R. Harris Sight Lecture. Armstrong's lecture was published as a small book later that year, with Armstrong holding the copyright.

315   *"experimental VTOL machines"* NAA to author, *WOL,* p. 6.

315   *"We were aware of that work"* NAA: e-mail to author, July 24, 2004.

316   *"Our first idea"* NAA to author, June 3, 2003, p. 24.

316   *"Campbell Soup can sitting on top of legs"* NAA to SA&DB, in *Quest,* p. 31.

317   *"You ought to go talk to them"* Gene Matranga to author, Dec. 12, 2002, p. 12.

320   *"We at the Marshall Space Flight Center"* "Concluding Remarks by Dr. Wernher von Braun About Mode Selection for the Lunar Landing Program Given to Dr. Joseph F. Shea, Acting Director (Systems) Office of Manned Space Flight," June 7, 1962, copy in Milton Ames Collection, Langley Historical Archives, NASA Langley Research Center, Hampton, VA.

321   *"Bell already had a design for the LLRV"* GJM to author, Dec. 12, 2002, p. 13.

322   *"In the lunar simulation mode"* NAA, *WOL,* p. 11.

322   *"I did go to Edwards a few times"* NAA: e-mail to author, July 24, 2004.

323   *"Neil made sure"* GJM to author, Dec. 12, 2002, p. 13.

323   *"control characteristics ideal"* NAA, *WOL,* p. 6.

323   *"an engineer's delight"* Ibid., p. 8.

323   *"It worked surprisingly well"* Ibid., p. 9.

323   *"excessively sluggish"* Ibid.

323   *"The LLRF was a clever device"* NAA to author, June 3, 2003, p. 30.

324   *"actual lunar lander would have little ground effect"* Ibid., p. 8.

324   *"Having no flying machines to simulate lunar control"* Ibid., p. 7.

324   *"prohibitively time consuming and expensive"* Ibid., p. 15.

326   *"at least I had the chance to give my input"* NAA: e-mail to author, Aug. 1, 2004.

327   *"helicopter wasn't a good simulation"* NAA to author, June 3, 2003, p. 27.

328   *"almost bad training"* WAA to author, San Diego, CA, Sept. 18, 2003, p. 22.

328   *"a hairy deal"* FB to author, Las Cruces, NM, April 15, 2003.

328   *"worry about flying it"* JEL to author, Dayton, OH, July 17, 2004.

328   *"Neil's first experiences in the LLTV"* WAA to author, Sept. 18, 2003, p. 10.

329   *"The LLTV proved to be an excellent simulator"* NAA, *WOL,* p. 15.

329   *"At that height a glitch could be fatal"* BA, *Men from Earth,* p. 187.

329   *"I wouldn't call it routine"* NAA to author, June 3, 2003, p. 27.

329   *"It's hard to compare against combat"* Ibid., p. 28.

329   *Houston sent the following priority telegram* NASA MSC, Houston, Tex., to National Aeronautics and Space Administration, Attn B. P. Helgeson and J. F. Lederer, May 6, 1968. Copy in NAA's personal files, LLRV/LLRF material.

330   *"He activated the ejection seat"* CCK, *Flight,* p. 312.

331   *"Neil was shaken up pretty badly"* BA, *Men from Earth,* p. 187.

331   *"little time to analyze alternatives"* NAA to SA&DB, in *Quest,* p. 32.

331   *"a higher wind than we normally dealt with"* GJM to author, Dec. 12, 2002, p. 15.

332   *"Neil didn't think much of that"* Ibid., p. 16.

332   *" 'An hour ago!' "* AB to author, Houston, TX, Feb. 7, 2003, pp. 23–24.

332   *"I mean, what are you going to do?"* NAA to author, June 3, 2003, p. 28.

332   *"The LLTV was . . . a high-risk vehicle"* NAA to author, June 3, 2003, pp. 28–29.

333   *"Gilruth and I were ready to eliminate it completely"* CCK, *Flight,* p. 312.

333   *"It's dangerous, damn it!"* Ibid., p. 313.

334   *"we let them keep it"* Ibid.

334   *"We are very pleased with the way it flies"* UPI, "Neil Armstrong Praises Lunar Landing Vehicle During Tests," *LN,* July 17, 1969.

334   *"absolutely required to prepare"* NAA to author, June 3, 2003, p. 29.

334   *"defend the things that you've been involved in the creation of"* Ibid.

Chapter 24: Amiable Strangers

336   *"in Mission Control"* NAA to author, Cincinnati, OH, June 3, 2003, p. 14.

337   *"that was enormously bold"* Ibid., p. 16.

337   *"I cannot imagine NASA management"* Ibid., p. 9.

338   *"but we sure had the motivation to get it done"* Ibid., p. 10.

338   *"Deke laid out his thinking about Apollo 11"* Ibid., p. 17.

338   *"it would be not right of me to pull Lovell out of line for a command"* Ibid.

339   *"I had a little difficulty in my own mind putting Aldrin above Collins"* Ibid.

339   *"Deke didn't think that Fred was quite ready for a prime crew"* Ibid., p. 18.

339   *"I was not aware of any disappointment on Fred Haise's part"* Ibid., p. 19.

340   *"I was comfortable with him"* Ibid., p. 11.

341   *"It was a remarkably trouble-free flight"* Ibid., p. 14.

342   *"We were just doing our jobs"* NAA to author, Cincinnati, OH, June 4, 2003, p. 25.

342   *"public interest all the time"* NAA to author, June 3, 2003, p. 13.

343   *"this will be the first lunar landing"* Ibid., p. 18.

343   *"Moon Team Is Named"* CPD, Jan. 10, 1969.

343   *"these are the first guys who will be concentrating the greatest extent on getting a*

landing done" Slayton comment at Apollo 11 Crew Press Conference, Manned Spacecraft Center, Jan. 10, 1969, 1A/1.

343 *"amiable strangers"* MC, *CTF,* p. 442.

344 *San Antonio . . . had "something extra going for it"* MC, quoted in *FOM,* p. 128.

344 *"A house of ill-repute was right there"* Ibid.

345 *"just a normal, active, troublesome kid"* Ibid., p. 129.

345 *"In the end I chose West Point"* Ibid.

346 *"I'd rather do something than study about it"* Ibid., p. 130.

346 *"I chose the air force"* Ibid., p. 20.

346 *"all this combination in one man"* Patricia Collins, quoted in *FOM,* p. 131.

346 *"Never . . . had [I] seen such a good lawyer's brief in six sentences"* Ibid., p. 132.

348 *"there is no Easter Bunny"* MC, quoted in *FOM,* p. 139.

348 *"I feel a bit freakish"* MC to author, Marco Island, FL, Mar. 25, 2003, p. 15.

350 *"My father must have been distressed"* BA, *RTE,* pp. 88–89.

350 *"my experience at camp"* BA, quoted in *FOM,* p. 156.

351 *"My father never gave direct instructions nor stated goals"* BA, *RTE,* p. 88.

351 *"Buzz prefers Annapolis"* BA's mother, quoted in *FOM,* p. 156.

351 *"aligned towards the army air corps"* BA to author, Albuquerque, NM, Mar. 17, 2003, p. 11.

352 *"you knew exactly where you were at all times"* BA, *RTE,* p. 111.

352 *"I fully expected my father to be disappointed"* Ibid., p. 117.

352 *"He was still lobbying for me to change to multiengine aircraft"* Ibid., p. 121.

354 *"if I didn't watch it I'd end up with a reputation as a hotshot egotist"* Ibid., p. 133.

354 *"the engineering wonders of pipes"* BA, *RTE,* pp. 93–94.

354 *"I knew I needed more formal education"* BA to author, Mar. 17, 2003, p. 10.

355 *"I was first in our class of air force officers"* BA, *RTE,* p. 146.

355 *"practical application to the air force"* Ibid.

355 *"how to please academia"* BA to author, Mar. 17, 2003, p. 12. See also, *RTE,* pp. 149–50.

355 *"They wanted me to revise"* BA to author, Mar. 17, 2003, p. 12.

356 *"If only I could join them in their exciting endeavors!"* Dedication to Aldrin's MIT doctoral thesis, copy in the MIT Library, Cambridge, MA. The author wishes to thank Dr. Debbie Douglas for securing materials related to Aldrin's doctoral thesis and his MIT education, as well as information about Aldrin Sr.'s MIT degree.

356 *"I knew darned well"* BA to author, Mar. 17, 2003, p. 10. See also *RTE,* pp. 150–51.

356 *Dr. Rendezvous* BA to author, Mar. 17, 2003, p. 13.

356 *"Buzz was very able in rendezvous matters"* NAA to author, June 3, 2003, p. 11.

357 *"I had been brash"* BA, *RTE,* pp. 160–61.

357 *"under prevailing custom I would skip two flights"* Ibid., p. 161.

357 *"Charlie felt you should been in it all along"* Ibid., p. 166.

358 *"Frank shot back that he didn't need any suggestions from me"* Ibid., p. 197.

358 *"what might be considered eccentricities"* NAA to author, June 3, 2003, p. 12.

358 *"difference between those three men"* Gunther Wendt, *Unbroken Chain,* p. 129.

359 *"Neil and I hardly knew one another"* BA to author, Mar. 17, 2003, unrecorded comment.

Chapter 25: First Out

360 *"You want to take a crack at it?"* NAA comment, Apollo 11 Crew Press Conference, Manned Spacecraft Center, Jan. 10, 1969, 1C/1.

360 *"Every step will be firmly decided prior to flight"* Ibid.

361 *"I would have preferred to go on a later lunar flight"* BA, *RTE,* p. 200.

361 *"No one had ever refused a flight"* Ibid.

361 *"I am going to land on the Moon"* Ibid., p. 201.

361 *"Aldrin to Be First Man on the Moon"* New Orleans *Times-Picayune,* Feb. 27, 1969.

362 *"Such a move, I thought, was an insult to the service"* BA, *RTE,* p. 205.

362 *"too explosive for even the subtlest maneuvering"* Ibid.

362 *"Clearly, the matter was weighing on him as well"* Ibid., p. 206.

362 *"didn't want to rule out the possibility of going first"* Ibid.

363 *"probably wouldn't have written it that way"* BA to author, Mar. 17, 2003, p. 24.

363 *"all the time struggling not to be angry with Neil"* BA, *RTE,* p. 206.

363 *"I felt that I owed it"* BA to author, Mar. 17, 2003, p. 23.

363 *"Aldrin's arguments"* EC, *Last Man on the Moon,* p. 231.

363 *"I had enough problems"* MC, *CTF,* p. 352.

364 *"everything Buzz presented"* MC to author, Mar. 25, 2003, p. 15.

364 *"I didn't really want to be first"* BA to author, Mar. 17, 2003, p. 23.

364 *"It was a little different when you were an egghead from MIT like me"* Ibid.

364 *"It would have been so inappropriate"* Ibid., p. 11. See also *RTE,* p. 206.

364 *"Whether or not I was going to be the first to step onto the Moon"* Ibid.

365 *"the subject of gossip, speculation, and awkward encounters"* Ibid., pp. 206–07.

365 *"I finally got him to promise he'd stay out of it"* Ibid., p. 206.

365 *"I went finally to George Low"* Ibid., p. 207.

365 *"weeks of speculation"* John Noble Wilford, "Armstrong Designated as First to Set Foot on Lunar Surface," *NYT,* Apr. 15, 1969.

365 *"plans called for Mr. Armstrong to be the first man out"* Aeronautics and Astronautics Chronology on Science, Technology, and Policy, 1969, p. 108.

366 *"how the matter was finally decided"* BA, *RTE,* p. 207.

366 *"Buzz's attitude took a noticeable turn"* MC, *CTF,* p. 352.

366 *"He alienated a lot of people"* Wendt, *The Unbroken Chain,* p. 129.

366 *"I always thought Aldrin would be the first"* Stephen Armstrong, quoted in "Moonman's Father Worried over Feat," *CPD,* Apr. 16, 1969.

367 *"I had no preconceived notions at that point who it would be"* NAA to author, June 4, 2003, p. 15.

367 *"The reality was that it was not something that I thought was really very important"* Ibid.

367 *"I was not aware of any of that at the time"* Ibid., p. 33.

367 *"Did Moonman Pull Rank?"* Akron Beacon Journal, June 27, 1969.

367 *"Armstrong Demands First-on-Moon Role"* Dayton Journal Herald, June 27, 1969.

368 *"Precisely why the change"* Paul Haney, quoted in "Switch Puts Armstrong First—Haney," *CPD,* June 27, 1969.

368 *"expectation . . . for Apollo"* NAA to author, June 4, 2003, p. 18.

368 *"The only firm plan ever made was the one we're going to go with"* George Low,

quoted in "Armstrong Demands First-on-Moon Role," *Dayton Journal Herald,* June 27, 1969. Before he made this statement, on June 26, Low received a call in the middle of the night from the Associated Press informing him that "they had a story that Neil Armstrong had pulled rank on Buzz Aldrin to be the first man on the surface of the moon." The AP wanted to know "whether it was true and how the decision was reached concerning who would get out of the LM first." At the office that morning, Low prepared a brief from MSC Public Affairs Officer Brian Duff that summarized his recollection of how the decision was made. Interestingly, Low concluded, "I am sure that Armstrong had made an input to this recommendation, but he, by no means, had the final say." According to Low, "the basic decision" was made by his Configuration Control Board . . . based on a recommendation by the Flight Crew Operations Directorate" at MSC. George M. Low, Manager, Apollo Spacecraft Program, to B. M. Duff, June 27, 1969, copy in the JSC archives at the University of Houston–Clear Lake.

368 *"my recommendation was never asked for or given"* NAA comment, Apollo 11 Crew Press Conference, MSC, Jan. 10, 1969, 4B/3–4.

369 *"Buzz may have felt that"* NAA to author, June 3, 2003, p. 15.

369 *"when you were pressurized in the suit"* Ibid., p. 16.

369 *"an inherent risk involved"* Ibid., p. 15.

370 *"It was a nothing thing"* AB to author, Houston, TX, Feb. 7, 2003, p. 11.

370 *"they were looking for technical reasons"* Ibid., p. 12.

370 *"Look, NASA knew both these guys"* Ibid.

371 *"the same revelation"* CCK to author, Houston, TX., Feb. 7, 2003, p. 16.

371 " *'Good God, we can't let that happen!' "* Ibid.

371 " *'He's going to be a Lindbergh' "* Ibid., p. 17.

371 *"It should be Neil Armstrong"* Ibid., p. 323.

371 *"Aldrin desperately wanted the honor"* Ibid.

372 *"Not once did we criticize his strongly held positions"* Ibid.

372 *"Collectively, we said, 'Change it' "* Ibid., p. 17.

372 *"Buzz Aldrin was crushed"* Ibid., p. 323.

372 *"That was Deke"* CCK to author, Feb. 7, 2003, p. 16.

372 *"I told him that this was a Bob Gilruth decision"* George M. Low, Memorandum for Record, "Meeting with Buzz Aldrin," Sept. 14, 1972, copy in George M. Low Papers, Box 35, RPI Archives, Rensselaer Polytechnic Institute, Troy, NY.

373 *"pretty strong evidence"* NAA to author, June 3, 2003, p. 16.

Chapter 26: Dialectics of a Moon Mission

374 *"He always rose above internecine warfare"* MC to author, Mar. 25, 2003, p. 15.

375 *"surface work"* NAA to author, June 4, 2003, p. 9.

375 *"unknowns that we couldn't simulate"* Ibid.

376 *"I was very tempted to sneak a piece of limestone up there"* Ibid., p. 11.

376 *"Jack worked diligently and endlessly"* Ibid., p. 10.

376 *"geologists in NASA"* Schmitt to author, Albuquerque, NM, Mar. 16, 2003, p. 3.

376 *"geological preparation for Apollo 11"* NAA to author, June 4, 2003, p. 9.

376 *"water for the cooling of our suits"* Ibid., p. 10.

377 *"the* best . . . *on the Moon"* Schmitt to author, Mar. 16, 2003, p. 3.

377 *"incredible machines"* MC, *Liftoff,* p. 148.

378 *"Here the fidelity broke down"* Ibid., p. 149.

378 *"On balance, the simulations were quite good"* NAA to author, June 4, 2003, p. 1.

378 *"simulators to be exactly like the real thing"* Ibid.

378 *"just tried to 'win' "* Ibid., p. 2.

378 *"some of the guys were well aware of my approach"* Ibid.

379 *"Neil suddenly appeared in his pajamas"* MC, *CTF,* p. 352.

379 *"Mike and I sat around having a drink"* BA to author, Mar. 17, 2003, p. 20.

379 *"That wouldn't have been Neil"* Ibid.

380 *"I don't recall that Buzz asked me to abort—ever"* NAA to author, June 4, 2003, p. 2.

380 *"This was a chance to test the control center"* Ibid., p. 3.

380 *"I do remember that Buzz expressed his displeasure"* Ibid.

381 *"I was a little disappointed that we didn't figure it out soon enough"* Ibid., p. 4.

382 *"Apollo 10 turned out to be very helpful there"* Ibid., p. 13.

382 *"I was very interested in additional information about the mascons"* Ibid.

382 *"we wanted to do that as accurately as we could"* Ibid.

383 *"we knew all the principal landmarks on our descent path by heart"* Ibid.

383 *"Well, Deke, it would be nice to have another month of training"* Ibid., p. 19.

384 *"Mission Rules"* CCK, *Flight,* p. 117.

386 *"more the observer than the participant"* EFK, *Failure Is Not an Option,* p. 261.

386 *"I expected him to be vocal on the mission rule strategy"* Ibid., p. 262.

387 *"I had high respect for mission rules"* NAA to author, June 4, 2003, p. 5.

387 *"Then I might have argued against it"* Ibid., p. 6.

388 *"I wondered then if he'd overrule all of us in lunar orbit"* CCK, *Flight,* p. 314.

388 *" 'No, Chris, we're ready.' "* NAA quoted in CCK, *Flight,* p. 314.

389 *"final training for a crew"* NAA, Apollo 11 Crew Press Conference, Manned Spacecraft Center, July 5, 1969, 4C/2.

389 *"amazingly relaxed"* Dr. Charles E. Berry quoted in UPI story, "Moon-Bound Trio Fit and Ready," *Dayton Journal Herald,* July 2, 1969.

389 *"potential danger from lunar contaminants"* NAA to author, June 4, 2003, p. 26.

390 *"worst word-sculptors ever assembled"* NM, *OFM,* p. 36.

390 *"razorback hogs"* Ibid., p. 24.

390 *"splash of derision"* Ibid., p. 25.

391 *"where laxatives ended and physics began"* Ibid., p. 24.

391 *"stay behind the ropes"* Brian Duff, Public Affairs Officer, Apollo 11 Crew Press Conference, Manned Spacecraft Center, July 5, 1969, 4A/1.

391 *"easy saunter of athletes"* NM, *OFM,* p. 25.

391 *"ill at ease"* Ibid., p. 26.

391 *"We're here today to talk a little bit about the forthcoming flight"* NAA, Apollo 11 Crew Press Conference, Manned Spacecraft Center, July 5, 1969, 4A/2.

392 *"We just did our work"* NAA to author, June 4, 2003, p. 18.

392 *"We thought that* Columbia *was better"* Ibid.

393 *"I had certainly read the book"* Ibid.

393 *"Mike was especially thoughtful about it"* Ibid.

393 *"settled on* Eagle" BA, *RTE,* p. 211.

393 *"historical and memorable to say"* Reporter's question, Apollo 11 Crew Press Conference, Manned Spacecraft Center, July 5, 1969, 4B/2.

394 *"what you're going to say, Neil"* Low quoted in CCK, *Flight,* p. 314.

394 *"He'd say the right thing"* CCK, *Flight,* p. 315.

394 *"The most important part of the flight"* NAA to author, Sept. 19, 2003, p. 6.

394 *"we have chosen to use some unofficial names"* NAA, Apollo 11 Crew Press Conference, Manned Spacecraft Center, July 5, 1969, 4C/2.

395 *"I wouldn't presume to question it"* Ibid., 4D/1–2.

395 *"I let other, wiser minds"* NAA to SA&DB, in *Quest,* p. 38.

396 *"that is precisely what we mean"* NAA, Apollo 11 Crew Press Conference, Manned Spacecraft Center, July 5, 1969, 4E/2.

396 *"only history can tell"* Ibid., 4B/1.

396 *"There are no alternatives"* Ibid.

397 *"I don't have the numbers"* Ibid., 4E/2.

397 *"surrendered words about as happily"* NM, *OFM,* p. 31.

397 *"characteristic mixture of modesty and technical arrogance"* Ibid., p. 32.

397 *"sly privacy of a man whose thoughts may never be read"* Ibid., p. 31.

397 *"trapped with psyche-eaters"* Ibid., p. 34.

397 *"contend in a practical way with the necessary language"* Ibid.

397 *"extraordinarily remote"* Ibid., p. 27.

397 *"a presence in the room"* Ibid., p. 33.

398 *"the man nearest to being saintly"* Ibid.

398 *"If he had been a young boy selling subscriptions"* Ibid., p. 27.

398 *"a shining knight of technology"* Ibid., p. 40.

398 *"interpret it properly, then attack it"* NAA quoted in NM, *OFM,* p. 40.

398 *"computerese"* NM, *OFM,* p. 41.

398 *"either the end of the old or the first of the new men"* Ibid., p. 40.

398 *"large reactions, large ideas"* Ibid.

399 *"It's their success more than ours"* NAA quoted in NM, *OFM,* p. 40.

399 *"he would be a hero on terms he alone would make clear"* NM, *OFM,* p. 40.

399 *"If I had a choice, I would take more fuel"* NAA quoted in NM, *OFM,* p. 40.

399 *"I think a private life is possible"* Ibid., p. 46.

399 *"spiritual neuter"* NM, *OFM,* p. 43.

399 *"just as salmon swim upstream"* NAA quoted in NM, *OFM,* pp. 43–44.

400 *"might soon prove to be prophetic"* NM, *OFM,* pp. 46–47.

400 *"a dream on which one might found a new theory of the dream"* Ibid., p. 47.

401 *"center of the suburban middle class"* Ibid.

401 *"enterprising beyond the limits of the imagination"* Ibid.

401 *"a new psychological constitution to man"* Ibid.

401 *"The century would seek to dominate nature"* Ibid., p. 48.

402 *"the metaphysical direction unknown"* Ibid., pp. 48–49

Part Seven: One Giant Leap

403 *E* Inscription cited in MC, *Liftoff,* p. 160.

403 *E* JAH in private conversation to author, Hereford, AZ, Apr. 3, 2003.

Chapter 27: Outward Bound

405   *"watching television was not high on our list"* NAA to author, June 4, 2004, p. 20.

406   *"certainly a very high-performance machine"* NAA to author, Sept. 18, 2004, p. 2.

406   *"value of the incremental approach"* Ibid.

407   *"softened the intensity"* Ibid., p. 1.

407   *"it's a key to the Moon"* Wendt, *Unbroken Chain,* p. 132.

408   *"only chance we would have had"* NAA to author, Sept. 18, 2004, p. 3.

408   *"it was fortunate that the concept never had to prove itself"* Ibid., p. 2.

408   *"It was a complete concentration on getting through each phase"* Ibid., p. 4.

409   *"Neil believes God is up there with all three of those boys"* VEA quoted in "Neil's Mother Prays for Apollo 11 Crew," *Columbus* [OH] *Dispatch,* July 18, 1969.

409   *"I told Neil to look around and not to step out if it didn't look good"* Quoted in "Moon Advice from Grandma," *Akron Beacon Journal,* July 13, 1969.

409   *"I was kind of worried at first"* Rick Armstrong quoted in "Neil Armstrong's Wife Returns to Home in Texas," *SMEL,* July 17, 1969.

409   *"This, too, shall pass"* JSA to author, Sept. 11, 2004 (morning), p. 6.

409   *"I wish they would hurry"* JSA quoted in *FOM,* p. 67.

409   *"I haven't aged a day"* JSA quoted in " 'I Don't Feel Historic,' Armstrong Wife Says," *TB,* July 17, 1969.

409   *"I don't feel historic"* Ibid.

410   *"I think you're too tired"* JSA to her son Rick, quoted in ibid.

410   *"Go" for TLI* At 00:02:26:38 mission elapsed time, CapCom Bruce McCandless told the Apollo 11 crew, "You are Go for TLI." All quotations involving communications between Mission Control and the Apollo 11 spacecraft come from *Apollo 11 Technical Air-to-Ground Transcription,* prepared during the course of the mission by MSC's Apollo Spacecraft Program Office. A copy of the transcript is available in the historical archives at the University of Houston–Clear Lake. On board Apollo 11, a voice recorder captured what the astronauts said to one another when they were not in communication with the ground. This transcript, *Apollo 11 Onboard Voice Transcription, Recorded on the Command Module Onboard Recorder Data Storage Equipment,* was produced, naturally, after *Columbia*'s return to Earth. This transcript, too, can be found in its entirety in the archives at UHCL. Regrettably, there is a major gap in the onboard voice recording. All voice data between 00:03:29:21 and 03:03:39:38—three days, ten minutes, and seventeen seconds' worth—was somehow erased during the flight, so there is no record of what the astronauts said to one another during this lengthy period of time. In the following source notes, it is noted when the quotation comes from the Onboard Recorder (OBR).

410   *"That Saturn gave us a magnificent ride"* NAA at 00:02:53:03.

410   *"the Saturn V noise was enormous"* NAA to author, Sept. 18, 2004, p. 3.

411   *"driving a wide car down a narrow alley"* MC, *Lift-off,* p. 2.

411   *"small patch of blue sky"* Ibid., p. 3.

411   *"in this holding orbit"* NAA to author, Sept. 18, 2004, p. 4.

412   *"I've lost a Hasselblad"* MC at 00:01:20:10, OBR.

412   *"How does zero g feel?"* NAA at 00:01:17:41, OBR.

413   *"Space sickness"* NAA to author, Sept. 18, 2004, p. 5.

413 *"a rule was a rule, so we sat there, helmet and gloves on"* MC, *Liftoff,* pp. 3–4.

413 *"less able, less mobile, and less facile"* NAA to author, Sept. 18, 2004, p. 8.

414 *"If the separation and docking did not work"* BA, *RTE,* p. 221.

414 *"Mike being able to pull it off"* NAA: e-mail to author, Oct. 25, 2004.

414 *"parts and pieces floating about the cabin"* BA, *RTE,* p. 221.

415 *"three albino whales inside a small tank"* MC, *Liftoff,* p. 4.

415 *"We rubbed our behinds with a special salve"* BA, *RTE,* p. 217.

415 *"entering a slow-motion domain"* MC, *Liftoff,* p. 4.

416 *"It was a commitment to excellence"* NAA to author, Sept. 18, 2004, p. 9.

416 *"I can observe the entire continent of North America"* NAA at 00:03:53:05.

416 *"The weather was good just about everywhere"* NAA at 00:04:52:19.

416 *"I didn't know what I was looking at, but I sure did like it"* MC at 00:04:53:28.

416 *"We were like a chicken on a barbecue spit"* MC, *Liftoff,* p. 4.

417 *"Great Wall of China"* NAA to SA&DB, in *Quest,* p. 38.

417 *"celestial onslaught"* Ibid.

417 *"it has an almost benign quality"* BA, *RTE,* p. 220.

418 *"If Tang was on our flight I was unaware of it"* Ibid., p. 223.

418 *"we could have shut down our altitude-control thrusters"* Ibid.

418 *"The shrimp were chosen one by one"* Ibid., p. 222.

418 *"Ah, this salmon salad!"* MC, *CTF,* p. 389.

419 *"Gee, I almost went to sleep then"* NAA at 00:02:09:38, OBR.

419 *"all the Apollo 11 crew slept well"* NAA: e-mail to author, Nov. 4, 2004.

419 *"suspended by a cobweb's light touch"* MC, *Liftoff,* p. 5.

420 *"The best thing to do is just ask 'em"* FB, *Countdown,* p. 240.

420 *"The orbit of probe Luna 15 does not intersect the trajectory of Apollo 11"* Keldysch memo quoted in FB, *Countdown,* p. 240.

421 *"high school football team beating the Miami Dolphin"* MC, *CTF,* p. 387.

421 *"I wan't thinking about Luna 15"* NAA: e-mail to author, Nov. 4, 2004.

421 *"classified briefings on the Soviet program"* Ibid., Nov. 2, 2004.

421 *"dead animals and birds"* Phrase from firsthand Soviet military eyewitness to Baikonur accident, quoted in Asif Siddiqi, *Challenge to Apollo,* pp. 691–92.

422 *"I don't remember any briefings"* NAA: e-mail to author, Nov. 2, 2004.

422 *"Vice President Spiro T. Agnew has called for putting a man on Mars by the year 2000"* CapCom (McCandless) at 00:23:14:23.

422 *"Right on, Spiro!"* MC, *CTF,* p. 387.

423 *"no recollection at all of being idle"* BA, *RTE,* p. 224.

423 *"much too busy to be bothered with selecting music"* Ibid., p. 225.

424 *"I can remember liking the theremin"* JSA: e-mail to author, Oct. 31, 2004.

424 *"whether Janet liked it or not"* NAA: e-mail to author, Nov. 4, 2004.

424 *"just a little more than a half Earth"* NAA at 01:10:01:31.

425 *"Okay, world, hold on to your hat"* MC at 01:10:07:21.

425 *"Neil's standing on his head again"* MC at 01:10:15:35.

425 *"exact words were written down"* BA, *RTE,* p. 225.

425 *"Apollo 11 signing off"* MC at 01:10:34:35.

425 *"the crew slept rather well all night"* Reported to the press by an unidentified NASA public affairs officer on the morning of July 18, 1969, at 7:00 CDT and included in the Apollo 11 Spacecraft Commentary, 16–24 July 1969, produced

concurrently with the mission by MSC. This transcript is available in the UHCL archives.

426 *"upside down"* BA, *RTE,* p. 225.

426 *"a mass of intelligent energy"* This phrase comes from an article that appeared in the July 1977 issue of *Science Digest.* The author of the article, James Mullaney, a former contributing editor to *Astronomy* magazine, wrote, "The crew of Apollo 11, during the first moon landing, reported that their capsule was paced by what appeared to be a mass of intelligent energy." For a comprehensive critique and rebuttal of this and other UFO sightings, see James Oberg, *UFOs and Outer Space Mysteries,* chap. 3.

426 *"a bright object"* In his 1976 book *UFOs: The American Scene,* author Michael Hervey asserted that in lunar orbit, while Aldrin was adjusting his camera, Buzz's "attention was suddenly drawn to a bright object resembling a snowman traveling from west to east in the sky." In fact, the only "UFO" sighted by Aldrin, Collins, and Armstrong was the Saturn LM Adapter panel, before the astronauts reached lunar orbit.

427 *"an appetite for vicarious scientific adventure and a need to externalize fear"* Walter A. McDougall, *The Heavens and the Earth,* p. 100.

428 saw the flashes *"at least two or three different times"* BA to author, Albuquerque, NM, Mar. 17, 2003, tape 2, p. 3.

428 *"fireflies" John Glenn: A Memoir,* pp. 352–53.

429 *"The food guys couldn't have cared less"* BA to author, Mar. 17, 2003, tape 2, p. 3.

429 *"Guess what? We see them with our eyes closed!"* Ibid., p. 4.

429 *"I thought I was seeing something within the cabin"* Ibid.

430 *"six people had gone outside the Van Allen Belt"* Ibid.

430 *"whatever it was, it was only a hundred miles or so away"* BA, *RTE,* p. 224.

430 *"talk about it to the ground"* BA to author, Mar. 17, 2003, tape 2, p. 3.

431 *"S-VIB is about 6,000 nautical miles"* CapCom (Charlie Duke) at 02:12:49:02.

431 *"We could see it for about forty-five seconds at a time"* BA, *RTE,* p. 224.

431 *"We did watch a slow blinking light"* NAA: e-mail to author, Oct. 25, 2004.

431 *"their velocity along the flight path"* NAA: e-mail to author, Nov. 2, 2004.

432 *"immediately after Apollo 11 we all thought it was so, 'No, no, no.'"* BA to author, Mar. 17, 2003, tape 2, p. 3.

432 *"lay their little pink bodies on the line"* MC, *Liftoff,* p. 392.

432 *"Even* Pravda *in Russia is headlining the mission and calls Neil 'The Czar of the Ship.'"* CapCom (McCandless) at 03:00:29:46.

432 *"She says that Neil is clever"* CapCom (McCandless) at 03:00:34:02.

433 *"cool, magnificent sphere"* MC, *CTF,* p. 393.

433 *"vivid contrast between the Earth and the Moon"* MC, *Liftoff,* p. 7.

433 *"It's a view worth the price of the trip"* NAA at 03:01:17:24.

434 *"If just one digit slips in our computer"* MC, *Liftoff,* p. 6.

434 *"in orbit around the Moon"* Cronkite quoted in CBS, *10:56:20 P.M.,* p. 43.

434 *"It's quiet around the world"* Ibid., p. 44.

435 *"It was like—like perfect!"* NAA at 03:04:21:56.

436 *"Ice Commander"* Gene Cernan calls Armstrong "The Ice Commander" in *The Last Man on the Moon,* so titling his chapter on Apollo 11, pp. 231–40.

437 *"Plaster of Paris gray to me"* MC at 03:03:49:32, OBR.

437 *"Well, I have to vote with the 10 crew"* BA at 03:03:58:14, OBR.

437 *"Looks tan to me"* NAA at 03:03:58:21, OBR.

437 *"There's no substitute for actually being here"* NAA at 03:04:34:34.

439 *"park a baby buggy, much less a Lunar Module"* MC, *Liftoff,* p. 7.

439 *"as the Moon sinks slowly in the west"* MC at 03:06:57:45.

439 *"If we overburned"* BA, *RTE,* p. 226.

440 *"I thought today went pretty well"* MC at 03:14:02:08, OBR.

440 *"no indication that any of the crew members are actually sleeping"* Apollo 11 Spacecraft Commentary, 16–24 July 1969, CDT 00:03, 20 July, Release 270/1. Following the sleep period prior to the day of the landing, NASA reported that Collins had slept six hours, Armstrong five and a half, and Aldrin five.

Chapter 28: The Landing

442 *Safire's statements* Bill Safire to H. R. Haldeman, "In Event of Moon Disaster," July 18, 1969; Jim Keogh, The White House, "Memorandum for Bob Haldeman, July 19, 1969. Copies in NASA History Office, Washington, DC.

443 *"Kuralt followed"* Kuralt's piece quoted in CBS, *10:56:20 P.M.,* pp. 49–50.

445 *referred to the upcoming Moon landing as "a giant step"* Ibid., p. 52.

445 *"this particular morning the system came unglued"* BA, *RTE,* p. 227.

447 *" 'why do we need that there?' "* NAA to author, Sept. 18, 2003, p. 27.

449 *"Seats were not required"* Thomas J. Kelly, *Moon Lander,* p. 63.

451 *"crosshairs were in the center"* NAA to author, Sept. 18, 2003, pp. 14–15.

451 *"couldn't land on AGS"* Ibid., p. 24.

452 *Fortunately, Stafford and Cernan* See EC, *The Last Man on the Moon,* pp. 217–18, and TS, *WHC,* pp. 130–31.

452 *" altitude limits"* NAA to author, Sept. 18, 2003, p. 17.

453 *"barnyard math"* Ibid., pp. 16–17.

453 *"all the guys in the trenches"* Ibid., p. 18.

454 *"could easily lose the signal"* NAA: e-mail to author, Nov. 24, 2004.

454 *"get the computer into the right program"* NAA to author, Sept. 18, 2003, p. 20.

455 *"take the tension"* Cronkite quoted in CBS, *10:56:20 P.M.,* p. 74.

455 *"pulled on my heart strings"* VEAP, "Apollo 11," p. 7.

455 *"strategy for the throttle profile"* NAA to author, Sept. 18, 2003, p. 21.

455 *"like a magpie"* BA, *RTE,* p. 229.

456 *"used the push-to-talk mode"* NAA to author, Sept. 18, 2003, p. 18.

456 *"did not accurately catch the ignition point"* Ibid., pp. 19–20.

457 *"Landmark visibility was good"* NAA, from the 1969 Technical Debrief, quoted in ALSJ, "The First Lunar Landing," p. 12.

457 *"wasn't going to be a welcoming committee"* NAA to author, Sept. 18, 2003, p. 20.

457 *"get landing radar into the equation"* Ibid., p. 21.

458 *"got the Earth right out our front window"* BA, 04:06:38:20 mission elapsed time.

458 *"didn't want to practice aborts"* NAA to author, Sept. 18, 2003, p. 22.

459 *"simply for readout purposes"* Cronkite quoted in CBS, *10:56:20 P.M.,* p. 76.

460 "problem had never come up in the simulators" BA, *RTE,* p. 230.

460 *"My inclination was just to keep going"* NAA to author, Sept. 18, 2003, p. 22.

461 *"go by the numbers"* Koos quoted in EFK, *Failure Is Not an Option,* p. 268.

462 *"Bales felt naked"* Ibid., p. 269.

462 *"THIS WAS NOT AN ABORT"* Koos quoted in ibid., p. 270.

463 *"same one we had in training"* Duke quoted in ibid., p. 288.

464 *"all those program alarms"* NAA to author, June 4, 2003, p. 8.

464 *"would have been helpful to have known that"* Ibid.

464 *"didn't know anything about it"* BA to author, p. 20.

465 *"intimidated"* NAA to author, June 4, 2003, p. 8.

466 *"find somebody's backyard to land in"* NAA to author, Sept. 18, 2003, p. 23.

466 *"not the place where I wanted to be landing"* Ibid.

467 *"a lot of our vision would be wiped out"* Ibid., p. 10.

467 *"pick out bumps and craters"* Ibid.

468 *"LM flew better than I expected"* Ibid., p. 24.

468 *"less traumatic"* BA quoted in *ALSJ,* "The First Lunar Landing," p. 21.

468 *"Extend it"* NAA quoted in ibid.

469 *"our gear down"* BA, from 1969 Technical Debrief, quoted in *ALSJ,* p. 24.

469 *"sheet of moving dust"* NAA to author, Sept. 18, 2003, p. 24.

470 *"translational velocity"* NAA, from 1969 Technical Debrief, quoted in *ALSJ,* p. 25.

470 *"How's the fuel?* NAA, 04:06:43:57 mission elapsed time.

470 *"never dreamed we could be flying this close to empty"* EFK, *Failure Is Not an Option,* p. 291.

470 *"no response from the crew"* Ibid.

471 *"very aware of the fuel situation"* NAA to author, Sept. 18, 2003, pp. 25–26.

471 *"liked to have a little forward motion"* Ibid., p. 27.

471 *"could hear a feather drop"* EFK, *Failure Is Not an Option,* pp. 291–92.

472 *"wasn't panic stricken about the fuel"* NAA to author, Sept. 18, 2003, p. 26.

472 *"If we had landed right on top of a rock"* Ibid, p. 25.

472 *"some merit to landing a little bit hard"* Ibid.

473 *"if there was sloshing"* Ibid.

474 *"Whew, boy! Man on the Moon!"* Cronkite quoted in CBS, *10:56:20 P.M.*, p. 77.

475 *"Okay, let's get on with it"* NAA, 04:06:46:23 mission elapsed time.

Chapter 29: One Small Step

476 *"power of millions of prayers"* VEAP, "Apollo 11," p. 7.

477 *"the same old Neil"* Stephen Armstrong, quoted in CBS, *10:56:20 P.M.*, p. 104.

477 *"opposite ends of the spectrum"* JSA to author, Sept. 11, 2004 (morning), p. 35.

477 *"I wanted to really know"* Ibid., p. 33.

478 *"didn't care whether he was Catholic"* Ibid., p. 30.

478 *"a great tense time"* Ibid., p. 33.

478 *"welcomed other people, especially the guys"* Ibid., p. 31.

479 *"daddy's going to the Moon"* Mark Armstrong quoted in *FOM,* p. 46.

479 *"asking him to talk to the boys"* JSA to author, Sept. 11, 2004 (morning), p. 33.

479 *"keep life as normal as possible"* Ibid., p. 34.

479 *"There he is! There he is!"* JSA quoted in *FOM,* p. 134.

479 *"some bird food?"* Mark Armstrong quoted in ibid.

479 *"sleep wasn't really important"* JSA to author, Sept. 11, 2004 (morning), p. 34.

480 *"in bed with Janet"* WAA to author, Sept. 18, 2003, p. 24.

480 *"he just doesn't answer"* Rick Armstrong quoted in *FOM*, p. 246.

481 *"pinpoint us more quickly than it did"* NAA to author, Sept. 18, 2003, p. 30.

481 *"You guys did a fantastic job"* MC, 04:06:58:40 mission elapsed time.

481 *"miniscule dot"* MC, *CTF*, p. 405.

482 *"can't see a darn thing but craters"* Ibid., p. 410.

482 *"get out there and get some stuff"* NAA to author, Sept. 18, 2003, p. 31.

482 *"mascons"* NAA quoted in *ALSJ*, "Post-landing activities," p. 30.

482 *"indicated that it was not safe to continue"* NAA to author, Sept. 18, 2003, p. 29.

483 *"fuel lines were not a new subject"* Ibid.

484 *"less than a serious problem"* NAA to author, Sept. 18, 2003, p. 29. For additional comments by Armstrong on the concern about tank overpressurization right after the landing, see *ALSJ*, "The First Lunar Landing," pp. 31–32.

484 *"went through all the systems checks"* NAA to author, Sept. 18, 2003, p. 29.

485 *"a degree of relaxation there"* Ibid., p. 30.

486 *"trying to just describe what we saw"* Ibid., p. 23.

486 *"too excited to sleep"* BA, *RTE*, p. 232.

486 *"outside as soon as we could"* NAA to author, Sept. 19, 2003, p. 1.

488 *"part of the Communion bread loaf"* Cronkite quoted in CBS, *10:56:20 P.M.*, p. 85.

488 *"let him do his own thing"* NAA to author, Sept. 18, 2003, p. 31.

488 *"don't remember that ever being mentioned"* Ibid.

489 *"EVA preparation checklist"* NAA, from 1969 Technical Debrief, quoted in *ALSJ*, p. 2.

489 *"lunar surface took quite a bit longer"* NAA to author, Sept. 19, 2003, p. 1.

489 *"careful of our movements"* BA, *RTE*, p. 233.

489 *"easy to bump things"* NAA to author, Sept. 19, 2003, p. 3.

490 *"never done the tests with the filters on"* Ibid., p. 4.

490 *"two hundred pounds of pressure to open that up"* Ibid.

490 *"hatch proved to be no more difficult than a lot of other maneuvers"* Ibid., p. 6.

491 *"asked Houston if they were getting a picture"* Ibid., p. 2.

491 *"not ever concerned about falling from the ladder"* Ibid., p. 6.

492 *"Armstrong is on the Moon!"* Cronkite quoted in CBS, *10:56:20 P.M.*, p. 96.

492 *"pictures were surreal"* NAA to author, Sept. 19, 2003, p. 2.

493 *"replied that he was still thinking it over"* BA, *RTE*, p. 233.

493 *"Be descriptive now, Neil"* JSA quoted in *FOM*, p. 268.

494 *"Decisions, decisions, decisions!"* Ibid., p. 258.

494 *"a very simplistic statement"* NAA to author, Sept. 19, 2003, p. 6.

494 *"can't recapture it"* Ibid., p. 7.

494 *"put it in parentheses"* Ibid., p. 8.

494 *"came across the idea for his statement"* As to what might have triggered the now immortal phrases "one small step" and "one giant leap," over the years since Apollo 11 people have expressed numerous theories, some of them tangible, a few quite fanciful. One theory, inspired by a comment Neil made in 1971 to NASA public affairs officer Robert Sherrod, suggests that the phrases derived from a children's game called Mother, May I? that Neil occasionally

played outdoors with siblings and friends during his Ohio boyhood. (NAA to Robert Sherrod, Washington DC, Sept. 23, 1971, p. 6, copy in NASA History Office Archives.) If the player takes the allotted "small steps" or "giant steps" before first saying, "Mother, May I," he or she has to return to the starting line. Today, though Neil vaguely remembers playing the game, he does not recall talking about it to Sherrod or anyone else. "I think if I said that, that it would have been more in jest than if that actually contributed" (NAA to author, Sept. 19, 2003, p. 8).

495 *"read all the [Tolkien] books"* NAA to author, Sept. 19, 2003, p. 8.

495 *"signalize [sic] the first lunar landing"* Willis Shapley to George C. Mueller, Office of Manned Space Flight, NASA Headquarters, Apr. 1969, NASA Headquarters History Office.

496 *"statements that were made"* NAA to author, Sept. 19, 2003, p. 9.

496 *"certainly wasn't conscious"* Ibid., p. 8.

496 *"almost floating as he walked"* VEAP, "Apollo 11," p. 8.

497 *"we try the clothesline technique"* NAA to author, Sept. 19, 2003, p. 5.

498 *"making our bodies into a bipod"* Ibid.

498 *"get a few quick pictures"* Ibid., p. 9.

499 *"get that camera down and hooked up"* NAA, from 1969 Technical Debrief, quoted in *ALSJ*, "One Small Step," p. 10.

499 *"stark beauty of its own"* NAA, 04:13:34:56 mission elapsed time.

501 *" 'Were you born in a barn?' "* NAA quoted in *ALSJ*, "One Small Step," p. 16.

501 *"never get the bent hatch closed again!"* BA quoted in ibid., p. 16.

501 *" one-sixth g environment"* NAA to author, Sept. 19, 2003, p. 19.

501 *"walked sideways while hooked to an assembly of cables"* Ibid.

502 *"keep a good eye out"* BA, *Men from Earth,* p. 241. See also BA, *RTE,* p. 235.

502 *"One time I came close to falling"* NAA: e-mail to author, May 20, 2005, comments on chap. 29.

502 *"first to pee in his pants"* BA, *RTE,* p. 235.

503 *"flag should just be draped down"* NAA to author, Sept. 19, 2003, p. 12.

504 *"a unique permanent wave"* BA, *RTE,* p. 237.

504 *"trouble getting it into the surface"* NAA to author, Sept. 19, 2003, p. 12.

506 *"let him do the responding"* BA, *RTE,* p. 237.

506 *"didn't say it would be the president"* NAA to author, Sept. 19, 2003, p. 13.

506 *"could sense our son was emotionally shaken"* VEAP, "Apollo 11," p. 10.

507 *"maybe it wasn't even going to happen"* NAA to author, Sept. 19, 2003, p. 13.

507 *"Neil had the camera most of the time"* BA, *RTE,* p. 236.

508 *"who took what pictures"* NAA: e-mail to author, Dec. 1, 2004.

508 *"Buzz did have the camera some of the time"* Ibid.

509 *"enormity of the situation"* BA to author, Mar. 17, 2003, p. 30.

509 *"just not the opportunity for me ever to do that"* Ibid.

509 *"Stupid me, stupid me"* MC to author, Mar. 25, 2003, p. 16. Even those who realized it at the time of Apollo have misunderstood why the omission occurred. "It's a real anomaly," Apollo 12 astronaut Dick Gordon has stated. For years Gordon believed that Buzz never had a chance to take any pictures: "Neil had the camera; Buzz didn't have the mount. The only picture Buzz took was a stereoscopic picture of the footprints" (Dick Gordon to author, Apr. 12, 2003,

p. 17). Apollo 9 commander Jim McDivitt has held the same mistaken views. *"Why are there no pictures of Neil on the surface, Jim?"* "That's easy." *"Is it?"* "Yes, the only camera they had, Neil had." *"So you are saying Buzz took no pictures?"* "Yes, I think that's right. There was only one camera, and I don't think Buzz took any pictures" (McDivitt to author, Apr. 17, 2003, p. 18). Apollo 10 and Apollo 17 astronaut Gene Cernan saw it the same way. "They took only one camera and it was on Neil's suit, and I guess Neil never handed the camera over to Buzz to take a picture. It's a tragedy" (EC to author, Feb. 10, 2003, p. 12). Same with George Franklin, the lead engineer in the Flight Crew Support Division at the Manned Spacecraft Center who was responsible for preparing the LM crew for many of their surface activities. Franklin believes that "Buzz never took a picture." *"How do you explain that?"* "Because of who had the camera." *"Was it too hard for Neil to get it off his chest bracket?"* "No, we don't know why. In the procedures, Neil was supposed to change out and he didn't. Why? I can't answer that question, why the camera was never changed over" (Franklin to author, Feb. 5, 2003, p. 7).

510   *"I find that shocking"* EFK to author, Feb. 8, 2003, p. 28.
510   *"would not accuse him of that"* CCK to author, Feb. 7, 2003, p. 20.
510   *"some nefarious plot on Buzz's part"* MC to author, Mar. 25, 2003, p. 16.
511   *"don't think it crossed his mind"* CCK to author, Feb. 7, 2003, p. 20.
511   *"practiced their photography"* AB to author, Feb. 7, 2003, pp. 5–6.
511   *"That's a possibility"* Ibid.
512   *"What I can imagine Neil thinking"* EC to author, Feb. 10, 2003, p. 12.
512   *"got out the sample bags"* NAA to author, Sept. 19, 2003, p. 17.
513   *"never been disappointed about the rocks"* NAA: e-mail to author, Dec. 23, 2004.
513   *" 'documented samples' "* Ibid.
513   *"still actively studying the Moon rocks"* Ibid.
515   *"the bubble just kept circling"* NAA to author, Sept. 19, 2003, p. 18.
516   *"amazed watching that thing bloom like a flower"* Ibid.
516   *"knew it forwards, backwards, and blindfolded"* Ibid., p. 15.
516   *"snap a picture of the crater"* Ibid., p. 20.
517   *"Not spectacular outcroppings"* Ibid.
517   *"too many interesting things to do"* NAA, from postmission press conference, quoted in *ALSJ,* "EASEP Deployment and Close-out," p. 15.
518   *"didn't mind breaking the rules"* NAA to author, Sept. 19, 2003, p. 15.
518   *"dust in an oxygen environment can be flammable"* Ibid., p. 22.
519   *"inordinate amount of force"* NAA, from 1969 Technical Debrief, quoted in *ALSJ,* "EASEP Deployment and Close-out," p. 19.
519   *"pulled the packet out and tossed it onto the surface"* BA, *RTE,* p. 238.
520   *"sort of guarded"* BA quoted in *ALSJ,* "EASEP Deployment and Close-out," p. 22.
520   *"how I got up to the third step"* NAA to author, Sept. 19, 2003, p. 23.
520   *"jump pretty high"* Ibid.
522   *"Like colts almost"* Cronkite to Sevareid, quoted in CBS, *10:56:20 P.M.*, p. 103.
523   *"their own personal items"* Anonymous NASA MSC official quoted in Nicholas C. Chriss, "Astros Take Secrets, But They're Personal," *New York Post,* May 22,

1969. See also Donald K. Slayton, Director of Flight Crew Operations to NASA Headquarters, Attn: Mr. Julian Scheer, "Astronaut PPKs," Oct. 22, 1968, NARA Fort Worth, RG 255.

523   *"had to make a list"* AB quoted in *Air & Space Smithsonian* (Dec. 1994–Jan. 1995).

523   *"something memorable for her"* Cronkite quoted in CBS, *10:56:20 P.M.*, p. 85.

524   *"not even worthy of being typed up"* BA, *RTE*, p. 214.

525   *"1974 memorandum for the NASA Associate Administrator Rocco Petrone* Robert Pearlman: e-mail to author, Dec. 29, 2004.

525   *"total weight of this kit shall not exceed"* See "Astronaut Preference Kit Policy," n.d., at www.collectspace.com/resources/flown_apollo_apk.html.

526   *"small flags are to be carried in a plastic vacuum"* NASA Press Release 69–83E, July 3, 1969. I wish to thank Robert Pearlman for providing a copy of this memorandum.

527   *"In my PPK"* NAA: e-mail to author, Dec. 22, 2004.

527   *"didn't bring anything else for myself"* NAA to author, Sept. 19, 2003, p. 23.

527   *"if I wanted to send anything"* JSA to author, Sept. 11, 2004 (morning), p. 39.

Chapter 30: Return to Earth

529   *"unknowns were rampant"* NAA quoted in *Quest*, p. 38.

529   *"on that scale was probably a thirteen"* Ibid.

529   *"truckload of equipment inside that cockpit"* NAA, from the 1969 Technical Debrief, quoted in *ALSJ*, "Trying to Rest," pp. 3–4.

531   *"Each PLSS bounced on the porch"* BA, quoted in ibid., p. 13.

531   *"giving the packages the heave-ho"* Ibid.

531   *"last item jettisoned"* NAA, quoted in ibid., p. 13.

532   *"scent of wet ashes"* Ibid., p. 16.

532   *"like it was going to catch fire"* BA, quoted in ibid.

532   *"postpone our answer to that one"* NAA, 04:18:44:01 mission elapsed time.

532   *"couldn't tell if I was tired"* NAA to author, Sept. 19, 2003, p. 25.

532   *"couple hundred pages of checklist items"* Ibid., p. 24.

532   *"engine cover"* Ibid. See also *ALSJ*, "Trying to Rest," pp. 22–26.

533   *"temperature got quite brisk"* Ibid., p. 24.

533   *"had never heard this thing run"* Ibid., p. 25.

533   *"quality of sleep was poor"* NAA quoted in *ALSJ*, "Trying to Rest," p. 23.

533   *"had the better sleeping place"* BA, from the 1969 Technical Debrief, quoted in *ALSJ*, "Trying to Rest," p. 25.

533   *"get by with a low amount of sleep"* NAA to author, Sept. 19, 2003, p. 25.

534   *"overflow of program alarms"* Ron Evans, 05:01:41:14 mission elapsed time.

534   *"wasn't hard to recreate what I'd just seen"* NAA to author, Sept. 19, 2003, p. 26.

534   *"smooth crater field"* NAA, 05:03:10:32 mission elapsed time.

535   *"ascent was a very simple trajectory"* NAA to author, Sept. 19, 2003, p. 26.

536   *"we've been this nervous"* Cronkite to Schirra, quoted in CBS, *10:56:20 P.M.*, p. 123.

536   *"in deep concentration with our Lord"* VEAP, "Apollo 11," p. 10.

537 *"see the American flag fall over"* BA, *RTE,* p. 239.

538 *"Oh, boy! Their words 'beautiful'"* Cronkite quoted in CBS, *10:56:20 P.M.,* p. 124.

538 "Columbia *has no landing gear"* MC, *Liftoff,* p. 10.

538 *"eight hundred and fifty chances for me to screw it up"* MC, *CTM,* p. 417.

538 *"One little hiccup and they are dead men"* Ibid., p. 418.

539 *"we felt comfortable in the situation"* NAA to author, Sept. 19, 2003, p. 27.

539 *"like a rocking chair going up and down"* Ibid., p. 28.

539 *"going right down U.S. 1"* NAA, 05:04:25:35 mission elapsed time.

539 *"pretty spectacular ride"* NAA, 05:24:27:17 mission elapsed time.

539 *"Three hours may seem like a long time"* BA, *RTE,* p. 340.

540 *"black-magical manipulations"* MC, *CTM,* p. 419.

540 *"make their move, thrusting toward me"* Ibid., pp. 420–21.

541 *"stay exactly on their prescribed approach path"* Ibid., p. 421.

542 *"feel that it is going to happen"* Ibid., pp. 421–22.

544 *"flew it right into gimbal lock"* NAA to author, Sept. 19, 2003, p. 29.

544 *"the surprise of my life"* MC, *CTM,* p. 423.

544 *"if this retraction fails"* Ibid.

544 *"busy there for a couple seconds"* MC, mission elapsed time.

545 *"cavort about a little bit"* MC, *CTM,* p. 423.

545 *"Our boys were together"* VEAP, "Apollo 11," p. 11.

545 "Man has finally visited the Moon" Cronkite quoted in CBS, *10:56:20 P.M.,* p. 131.

546 *"dusting each other by hand"* BA, *RTE,* p. 240.

546 *"a fond farewell"* NAA to author, Sept. 19, 2003, p. 30.

547 *"something I have wondered about myself"* Ibid.

547 *started throwing question after question at his mates* See also MC, *CTF,* p. 424.

547 *"don't want to be a permanent Moon satellite"* MC, *Liftoff,* p. 10.

547 *"been in for a long lonely ride"* NAA to author, Sept. 19, 2003, p. 33.

548 *"possible to get that attitude wrong?"* Ibid.

549 *"tiny Earth growing"* MC, *Liftoff,* p. 11.

549 *"TV broadcasts served a useful purpose"* NAA to author, Sept. 19, 2003, p. 34.

552 *"vote of appreciation"* Cronkite quoted in CBS, *10:56:20 P.M.,* pp. 144–45.

553 *"slightly altered skp maneuver for reentry"* NAA to author, Sept. 19, 2003, p. 33.

554 *"orange-and-white blossoms"* MC, *Liftoff,* p. 13. See also MC, *CTF,* p. 448

554 *"seas weren't supposed to be too bad"* NAA to author, Sept. 19, 2003, p. 34.

554 *"hanging from the straps"* Ibid., p. 35.

554 *"in front of television cameras tossing our cookies"* BA, *RTE,* p. 4.

555 *"Don't take off your BIGs"* Carpentier quoted in *FOM,* p. 362.

556 *"we all felt pretty good"* NAA to author, Sept. 19, 2003, p. 35.

556 *"get it behind us so that we could celebrate"* Ibid., p. 36.

557 *"tend to be a little exaggerative"* Ibid.

557 *"can only say it was out of this world"* JSA quoted in "Apollo Crew's Families Also in World Spotlight," *TB,* July 25, 1969.

557 *"Stephen came to my rescue and kissed me"* VEAP, "Apollo 11," p. 13.

558 *"confirmation that all . . . was okay"* NAA to author, Sept. 19, 2003, p. 36.

558 *"taking our leisure until we were totally off schedule"* BA, *RTE,* p. 11.

558 *"And now it begins"* Quoted in ibid., p. 12.

559 *"position to see all that stuff"* NAA to author, Sept. 19, 2003, p. 36.

559 *"You lucky sons of bitches"* Admiral John S. McCain, quoted in BA, *RTE,* p. 12.

559 *"Somebody somewhere had made that decision"* Ibid., p. 13.

559 *"We had cocktail hour"* NAA to author, Sept. 19, 2003, p. 36.

559 *"bumped and swayed down onto the truck bed"* BA, *RTE,* p. 14.

559 *"can't get men off the airplane"* Carpentier quoted in ibid.

559 *"Everyone was assembled to greet us"* NAA to author, Sept. 19, 2003, p. 37.

560 *"Had she expected to be contaminated in advance?"* BA, *RTE,* p. 16.

560 *" 'Hello, Mom, this is Neil.' "* VEAP, "Apollo 11," p. 14.

561 *"that time was very valuable to us personally"* NAA to author, Sept. 19, 2003, p. 37.

561 *"photos helped them ask their questions"* Ibid., p. 38.

562 *"rivalries or arguments"* BA, *RTE,* p. 22.

562 *"most difficult part of your mission"* Lovell, 08:01:02:32 mission elapsed time.

562 *"We were not naïve"* NAA to author, Sept. 19, 2003, p. 35.

Chapter 31: For All Mankind

564 *"a sort of new enlightenment"* NAA quoted in *FOM,* pp. 337–38.

565 *"never comfortable speaking"* JSA to author, Sept. 11, 2004 (morning), p. 50.

566 *"problems of a five-year-old boy in a candy store"* NAA, from Aug. 12, 1969, press conference in Houston, quoted in "Problems of a 5-Year-Old Boy in a Candy Store," *The National Observer* [Silver Springs, MD], Aug. 18, 1969.

566 *"last thing we're prepared for"* NAA quoted in "Millions See Two Parades," *LN,* Aug. 13, 1969.

566 *"advised not to reach out and shake hands"* BA, *RTE,* p. 30.

566 *"never seen so many people"* JSA to author, Sept. 11, 2004 (morning), p. 44.

566 *"threw out IBM punch-cards"* NAA to author, Sept. 19, 2003, p. 35.

567 *"jaws ached from smiling"* BA, *RTE,* p. 33.

567 *"exciting to be in those cities"* JSA to author, Sept. 11, 2004 (morning), p. 44.

567 *"aggregations of people"* NAA to author, Sept. 19, 2003, p. 38.

568 *"important adventure"* Agnew quoted in John C. Waugh, "A Grateful Nation Acclaims Its Space Heroes," *Christian Science Monitor,* Aug. 15, 1969.

568 *"Armstrong choked back tears"* "49-Day World Trip Awaits Astronauts," UPI story in *LN,* Aug. 14, 1969.

569 *"more eloquent because they were unstudied"* "Homage to the Men from the Moon," *Time,* Aug. 22, 1969.

569 *"impressive occasion for everyone"* NAA to author, Sept. 19, 2003, p. 39.

569 ultimate *"Texas barbecue"* Bernard Weinraub, "Houston Parade Honors Apollo 11 Crew in Finale of U.S. Fetes," *NYT,* Aug. 17, 1969.

569 *"no idea what the future is going to hold":* NAA, official CBS transcript of *Face the Nation,* Aug. 17, 1979.

571 *"looking for a place to get away"* NAA to author, Sept. 22, 2003, p. 32.

571 *"yesterday's when I'd like to have him!"* HSC to author, Oct. 7, 2003, p. 2.

573 *"sitting in ninety degree heat"* NK to author, Aug. 15, 2002, pp. 22–23.

573 *"One of Hope's jokes"* AF: e-mail to author, Aug. 25, 2002.

573   *"spout these great words of wisdom"* ALSK to author, Aug. 15, 2002, p. 14.

573   *"a Buckeye on the Moon"* NAA quoted in Al Kattman, "Neil Armstrong Returns Home for Hero's Welcome," *LN,* Sept. 7, 1969.

574   *"Mr. Speaker, Mr. President"* NAA before joint session of Congress, quoted in "Armstrong Addresses Congress," *LN,* Sept. 21, 1969.

576   *"We zipped up, lined up"* BA, *RTE,* p. 49.

576   *"We raised hell"* Ibid., p. 51.

576   *"take care of Americans in America"* Ibid., p. 55.

577   *tape-record a travelogue:* Transcript of Neil's travelogue in NAA's personal papers, "Giant Step" file.

577   *"situation in Belgium"* JSA to author, Sept. 11, 2004 (morning), p. 46.

577   *"broke my goddamn ankle!"* MC quoted in *RTE,* p. 65.

577   *"irresponsible to ask us to be on television"* NAA to author, Sept. 19, 2003, p. 43.

577   Carpentier *"conned into going on television"* BA, *RTE,* p. 70.

578   *"dancers all moved back to watch"* Ibid., p. 76.

578   *"right thing to be doing"* NAA to author, Sept. 19, 2003, p. 35.

578   *"liquor everywhere"* BA, *RTE,* p. 74.

578   *"some disturbing symptoms in Buzz"* MC, *CTF,* p. 465.

578   *"Had I been more observant"* NAA to author, Sept. 19, 2003, p. 44.

579   *"must confess, my feelings were hurt"* BA, *RTE,* p. 47.

579   *"Buzz used notes"* JSA to author, Sept. 11, 2004 (morning), p. 50.

579   *"president was quite nice"* NAA to author, Sept. 19, 2003, p. 45.

580   *"More can be gained from friendship"* NAA, commencement speech, Wittenberg College, Nov. 1969, copy in NAA personal papers. See also "Wittenberg Honors Armstrong," *Akron Beacon Journal,* Nov. 24, 1969.

581   *"soldiers rushed the stage to talk with Neil"* Bob Hope, *The Last Christmas Show* (Garden City, NY: Doubleday & Co., 1974), p. 283.

581   *"that's a great question"* NAA quoted in ibid. A four-page typescript copy of the section in Bob Hope's *The Last Christmas Show* was found in VEAP.

581   *"anything to cheer them up"* NAA to author, Sept. 22, 2003, p. 2.

581   *"fairly close to combat zones"* Ibid.

582   *"probably best way to handle the whole situation"* JSA: e-mail to author, Oct. 31, 2004.

582   *"Committee on Space Research"* NAA to author, Sept. 22, 2003, pp. 6–7.

582   *"tumultuous welcome from a predominantly Russian audience"* "Wild Applause Welcomes Armstrong in Leningrad," *CPD,* May 26, 1970.

583   *"Kosygin shook his finger"* NAA to author, Sept. 22, 2003, p. 2. See also "Kosygin 'Sees' Moon with Armstrong's Aid," *CPD,* June 3, 1970.

Part Eight: Dark Side of the Moon

585   *E* NAA to author, Cincinnati, OH, June 2, 2004, p. 10.

585   *E* NAA to SA&DB, Houston, TX, Sept. 19, 2001, interview transcript, p. 88.

Chapter 32: Standing Ground

587 *"Washington jobs"* NAA to author, Sept. 22, 2003, p. 5.

587 *"something I could do"* Ibid.

587 *"not a desk job person"* JSA to author, Sept. 11, 2004 (afternoon), p. 3.

587 *"Why analog technology?"* Gorn, *Expanding the Envelope*, pp. 322–23.

588 *"didn't have a choice"* NAA to author, Sept. 22, 2003, p. 1.

588 *"meet a lot of Washington people"* JSA to author, Sept. 11, 2004 (afternoon), p. 3.

588 *"maintain my flight currency"* NAA to author, Sept. 22, 2003, p. 6.

589 *"my answer wasn't to his liking"* Ibid.

589 *"just wanted to be a professor"* Ibid., p. 13.

590 *"accept Neil Armstrong's resignation"* James C. Fletcher quoted in "Neil Armstrong to Leave NASA," NASA Flight Research Center *Express* 14 (Aug. 28, 1971): 2. See also "Armstrong Quitting NASA to Be Cincy U Professor," *Akron Beacon Journal,* Aug. 26, 1971.

590 *"Christopher Columbus as a professor of navigation"* Editorial, "Professor Armstrong," *CE,* Aug. 28, 1971.

590 *"pimp for UC"* See "NR Apologizes," in *Cincinnati News Record,* Apr. 11, 1975. In an April 8, 1975, story about UC's lobbying for a $15.5 million state subsidy increase, the newspaper said UC officials "hoped" Armstrong "will pimp for UC." The paper apologized to Armstrong and assured him that "we did not seek to maliciously malign his reputation as an academician or an historical figure."

590 *"Returning to Ohio wasn't a consideration"* NAA to author, Sept. 22, 2003, p. 15.

590 *"Cincinnati's was a pretty good department"* Ibid., p. 14.

591 *"been on the Moon"* Anonymous University of Cincinnati spokesman quoted in "People" sections of *Time* and *Newsweek,* Sept. 6, 1971.

591 *"felt comfortable with all of them"* Ibid., p. 14.

591 *"taught three quarters a year"* Ibid., p. 16.

592 *"last student out the door"* Dave Burrus: e-mail to author, Mar. 15, 2003.

592 *"Give him a break"* Burrus quoted in "Armstrong Holds 1st UC Class; Former Astronaut Shuns Press," *Akron Beacon Journal,* Jan. 4, 1972.

592 *"journalists aren't always very thoughtful"* NAA to author, Sept. 22, 2003, p. 16.

592 *"disappointed in her not being truthful"* Ibid., p. 17.

592 *"courses most important to me personally"* Ibid., p. 15.

592 *"make the tests challenging"* Ibid., p. 19.

593 *"couldn't work the system"* Ibid., p. 18.

593 *"burdened with lots of new rules"* Ibid., p. 21.

593 *"legally circumvent this envelope of instructions"* Ibid., p. 22.

594 *"couldn't remain in that kind of job"* Ibid., p. 23.

594 *"just irritating"* Ibid., p. 24.

594 *"personal career pursuits lead him into other activities"* UC president Henry R. Winkler quoted in UPI story, *CE,* Jan. 18, 1980.

594 *"why he was leaving"* Ron Houston quoted in Kathleen Haddad, "Neil Armstrong Resigns; Plans Unknown," *Cincinnati News Record,* Jan. 23, 1980.

594 *"economic status of his family"* Winkler quoted in ibid.

594 *"get tired of it after a while"* Ken Service quoted in ibid.

595 *"hadn't done anything like it before"* NAA to author, Sept. 22, 2003, p. 30.

596 *"inroads with people we'd like to see"* Richard Teichgraber quoted in Dan Bearth, "Moon Walker Joins Oil Rig Firm," *Wichita Eagle and Beacon,* Mar. 15, 1980. See also "Armstrongs Launch Own Firm," *Anderson* [IN] *Herald,* Jan. 26, 1980; "Oil Drilling Rig Firm Hires Armstrong to Promote Sales," *CPD,* Mar. 16, 1980; and "Armstrong Takes Oil Job," *Virginian-Pilot,* Mar. 17, 1980.

596 *"turned down a lot more than I accepted"* NAA to author, Sept. 22, 2003, p. 31.

596 *"company wanted more technical competence"* Ibid., p. 33.

596 *"one of the seven or eight"* Ibid., p. 31.

597 *"wasn't that way with Neil"* CSM to author, June 25, 2003, p. 1.

597 *"Neil fit in perfectly"* Ibid., p. 3.

597 *"wonderfully compatible"* Ibid., p. 4.

597 *"would you take one small step forward?"* Ibid., p. 5.

597 *" 'Is this the man who went to the Moon?' "* Ibid., p. 9.

598 *"recovering from the* Challenger *accident"* James R. Wilson to author, June 23, 2003, p. 4.

599 *"gave us instant credibility"* Devere Burt to author, June 3, 2003, p. 6.

600 *"bang the big Boilermaker drum"* Stephen Beering, May 30, 2003, p. 11.

600 *"not in any way drawn to the political world"* NAA to author, June 2, 2004, p. 4.

600 *"Armstrong Possible Chief of Nixon's Ohio Race"* Joe Rice, "Political Parade," *Akron Beacon Journal,* Apr. 16, 1972.

600 *"approached to run for various positions"* NAA to author, June 2, 2004, p. 4.

600 *"not politic to express those views"* Ibid., p. 5.

601 *"for people more thoughtful and experienced in international relations"* Ibid., p. 6.

Chapter 33: To Engineer Is Human

602 *"pocket-protector nerdy engineer"* NAA address to National Press Club, Feb. 22, 2000, Washington DC, quoted in Paul Hoversten, "Neil Armstrong: Basically a 'Nerdy Engineer,' " accessed at space.com. See also Reuters story, "One Small Step, One Small Click," from Wired News, accessed at *http://www.wired.com/news/print/0,1294,34491,00.html.*

603 *"unusual combination of mistakes"* See Conclusions of NASA's *Report of Apollo 13 Review Board,* June 15, 1970, copy in Record Group 255, Box 10, NARA Fort Worth.

603 *"stupid and preventable accident"* CCK, *Flight,* p. 339.

603 *"Cortright wouldn't budge"* Ibid.

603 *"Apollo 13 investigation"* NAA: e-mail to author, Jan. 19, 2005.

603 *"leaves an impression not easily forgotten"* NAA quoted in "Armstrong: Don't Neglect Space Effort," *NYT,* June 12, 1971.

604 *"a new world ecology"* NAA quoted in "Armstrong Warns of Man's Extinction," *CPD,* June 12, 1971.

604 *"purpose of all those Moon walks"* NAA quoted in "Armstrong Envisions Great Space Benefits for Earth," *CE,* Feb. 9, 1972.

604 *"satellites will provide complete libraries"* Ibid.

604 *"future is not something I know"* NAA quoted in "Neil Armstrong Proves to Be Very Much an Earthling," *Chicago Daily News,* Aug. 11, 1977.

604 *"need to build a new world"* NAA quoted in "Armstrong Says New Settlers Will Live on Moon in Future," *Kentucky Newsclip,* June 18, 1974.

604 " *'preservation of its principles?'* " NAA quoted in Arthur J. Snider, "Some Advice to Earthmen from the First Man on the Moon," *Chicago Daily News,* n.d. [Aug. 1977].

605 *"Armstrong Has No Comment for Last Shot"* Bill Sloat article in *Florida Today,* Dec. 7, 1972.

605 *"closed-mouth son of a bitch"* Anonymous University of Cincinnati professor quoted in ibid.

605 *"not very easy to find"* UC press officer Al Kuttner quoted in ibid.

605 *"does not give out interviews"* Ruta Bankovikis quoted in Bill Sloat, "Armstrong Has No Comment for Last Shot," *Florida Today,* Dec. 7, 1972.

605 *"Invisiblest"* "Cincinnati Superlatives: The Invisiblest," in *Cincinnati Enquirer Sunday Magazine,* Dec. 6, 1974.

605 *"Armstrong Out of Seclusion"* Nicholas C. Chriss article (L.A. Times News Service), *Florida Today,* Mar. 8, 1974.

605 *"Armstrong Stays Alone in His Private Orbit"* Ira Berkow article [Newspaper Enterprise Association] as printed in *Rocky Mount* [NC] *Telegram,* Dec. 1, 1975.

605 *"Neil Armstrong, Where Are You?"* Article in *Birmingham Magazine,* Oct. 1976.

605 *"Cincinnati's Invisible Hero"* Berkow article as printed in *CE,* n.d. [1976].

605 *"The Hermit of Cincinnati"* Berkow article as printed in *Vancouver* [WA] *Columbian,* Feb. 19, 1976.

605 *"In Search of Neil Armstrong"* Sandra Earley article in *Atlanta Journal and Constitution Magazine,* May 20, 1979.

605 *"Will Neil Armstrong ever return to public life?"* Robin Adams Sloan, "Gossip Column," *Cincinnati Post,* Sept. 6, 1974.

605 *"quit NASA and became a recluse"* Gordon Cooper, *Leap of Faith,* p. 202.

606 *"chastise Neil for being too Lindbergh-like"* JEL to author, July 17, 2004, p. 20.

606 *"given a large number of press conferences"* NAA to author, Sept. 22, 2003, p. 29.

608 *"First Moon Man Hurt on Barn Door"* *Sacramento Bee,* Nov. 12, 1978.

608 *"Louisville Surgery Team Rejoins Armstrong's Finger"* *Cincinnati Post,* Nov. 13, 1978.

608 *"From Moon Walk to Microsurgery"* Michael Marriott article in *Louisville Courier-Journal,* Nov. 17, 1978.

608 *"Armstrong Blasts Off After Touchy Operation"* Jon Clemens article in *Louisville Courier-Journal,* Nov. 15, 1978.

608 *"One Small Tip: Moon Walker Leaves City with a Restored Finger"* Ibid.

608 *"incur routine injuries"* NAA quoted in "Armstrong Heads Home, May Leave Ring," *CPD,* Nov. 17, 1978.

609 *"Speak to Us, Neil"* CE, May 26, 1979.

609 *"A giant leap for the press"* *Philadelphia Inquirer,* May 26, 1979.

609 *"First Person on Moon Will Step Out of Anonymity"* *Milwaukee Journal,* Feb. 7, 1979.

609 *"Armstrong Reticent Talking of Moon Walk 10 Years Later"* *Cincinnati Post,* Apr. 1, 1979.

609 *"The Search Goes On"* "People Today" section, *CE,* Mar. 4, 1979.

609 *"trip to the North Pole"* NAA to author, June 2, 2004, pp. 21–22. NAA's personal files contain correspondence and notes pertinent to the polar expedition, including a signed certificate from the Polar Bear Chapter of the Order of Arctic Adventurers, substantiating that Armstrong crossed the Arctic Circle and reached 90 degrees North.

609 *"aggressive civilian space agenda"* See *Pioneering the Space Frontier: The Report of the National Commission on Space* (Toronto and New York: Bantam Books, 1986).

609 *"long-range plan"* NAA to author, June 2, 2004 (after-noon), p. 1.

609 *"fewer number of recommendations a commission makes"* Ibid., p. 2.

610 *"not today sitting on everyone's desk"* Ibid.

610 *"put on the line with Mr. Reagan"* Ibid., p. 1.

610 *"Rogers seemed to be very interested in doing this job"* Ibid.

611 *"Bill Rogers was Mr. Outside"* Ibid., p. 2.

611 *"gave me the job of running the operational side of the committee"* Ibid.

611 *"Neil was Mr. Inside"* Donald Kutyna to author, Mar. 20, 2004, p. 3.

611 *"investigation's timetable"* NAA to author, June 2, 2004 (morning), p. 3.

611 *"be aware of how public opinion was being expressed through the media"* Ibid.

611 *"ought to be one investigation"* Ibid., p. 4.

612 *"opportunity for some people to play to the cameras"* Ibid.

612 *"spent the most time on the accident itself"* Ibid., p. 15.

613 *"no such prohibitions from our chairman"* Ibid., p. 9.

613 *" 'Mrs. Mitchell, this commission is not about interesting.' "* Ibid.

613 *"in the back of this elevator"* Kutyna to author, Mar. 20, 2004, p. 7.

613 *"the same conclusions"* NAA to author, June 2, 2004 (morning), p. 9.

614 *Transcripts of the public hearings into* Challenger The transcripts of the Rogers Commission hearings can be accessed through *http://history.nasa.gov.* See also *Report to the President by the Presidential Commission on the Space Shuttle Challenger Accident,* 5 vols., June 6, 1986. Volumes 4 and 5 contain the hearings transcripts.

614 *"in answer to Mr. Armstrong's questions"* Hearings of the Presidential Commission on the Space Shuttle Challenger accident, May 2, 1986, Session, Excerpt No. 2866.

615 *"opinions or hypotheses"* NAA to author, June 2, 2004 (morning), p. 10.

615 *"unanimous in the commission"* Ibid.

615 *"don't tell NASA to do something it can't do"* Ibid., p. 11.

615 *"everyone felt fully invested in it"* Ibid.

616 *"for nature cannot be fooled"* For Feynman's discussion of his minority report, see Feynman as told to Ralph Leighton, *What Do You Care What Other People Think? Further Adventures of a Curious Character* (New York: Norton, 1988).

617 *"first impression is usually wrong"* NAA quoted in Sharon Turco, "Armstrong: Don't Jump to Conclusions," *CE,* Feb. 3, 2003.

617 *"immortal as a species"* NAA to author, June 2, 2004 (afternoon), p. 14.

617 *"Moon remains our first objective"* Ibid., pp. 16–17.

618 *"suspicious of space tourism"* Ibid., p. 17.

618 *"know that we can go to Mars"* Ibid., p. 16.

618 *"back to the Moon makes sense"* Ibid.

618 *"Our president has introduced a new initiative"* NAA acceptance speech for Rotary National Award for Space Achievement, Houston, TX, Mar. 11, 2004, quoted in Mark Carreau, "Armstrong Endorses Bush's Mars, Moon Plan," *Houston Chronicle,* Mar. 12, 2004.

619 *"Mars enthusiast"* NAA to author, June 2, 2004 (afternoon), p. 17.3.

619 *"party to an international treaty on uses of the Moon"* Ibid., p. 15.

619 *"evidence of the Chinese"* Ibid., p. 18.

619 *"My exploration came totally as a by-product of that"* Ibid., p. 23.

Chapter 34: The Astronaut as Icon

620 *"touring him around"* NAA to author, June 4, 2003, p. 32.

620 *"Anne Morrow"* JSA to author, Sept. 11, 2004 (morning), p. 2.

620 *"never experienced such a sense of power"* Charles A. Lindbergh quoted in A. Scott Berg, *Lindbergh,* p. 537.

620 *"accepted an invitation from Neil A. Armstrong"* Ibid.

620 *"I might have"* NAA to author, June 4, 2003, p. 32.

620 *"beautifully executed mission"* Lindbergh quoted in Berg, *Lindbergh,* p. 537.

621 *"seated next to each other at the banquet"* NAA to author, June 4, 2003, p. 33.

621 *"more chance to look around"* Lindbergh quoted in Berg, *Lindbergh,* p. 537.

621 *"certain similarities in the two events"* NAA quoted in Mark Bowden, "Unlike Lindbergh, Adoration of Public Eluded Neil Armstrong, First Man on Moon," newspaper clipping, n.d. [May 1977], source unknown, in VEAP.

621 *"more unlike than alike"* NAA quoted in ibid.

621 *"understand his predicament"* Ibid.

621 *"told me never to sign autographs"* NAA to author, June 4, p. 33.

622 *"most people don't know our home address"* NAA to author, Sept. 22, 2003, p. 27.

622 *"my accountant put an ad in the paper"* Ibid., p. 28.

622 *"I don't ask!"* Vivian White to author, May 29, 2003, p. 2.

622 *"sat down at a folding card table"* Ibid., p. 1.

622 *"he just quit signing"* Ibid., p. 6.

623 *"I sign it"* Ibid., p. 5.

623 *"never answer personal questions"* Ibid., p. 3.

623 *"hello to all my fellow Scouts"* NAA, 02:08:42:31 mission elapsed time. See also "Armstrong Likens Eagle Scout to Astronaut," *CPD,* Feb. 7, 1972.

623 *"Scouts don't do right"* NAA to author, Sept. 22, 2003, p. 28.

623 *"no way he could do it"* Vivian White to author, May 29, 2003, p. 5.

623 *"no official association with them"* NAA to author, Sept. 22, 2003, p. 29.

624 *founder of collectSPACE* Pearlman: e-mail to author, Jan. 21, 2005.

625 *"never, ever quoted myself"* NAA to author, June 2, 2004 (afternoon), p. 12.

626 *"Daddy will be so pleased"* Patricia Nixon quoted in "Armstrong Opens Space Museum," *Washington Post,* July 21, 1972.

626 *"just here to see the museum"* NAA quoted in ibid.

626 *"I should have been asked"* NAA to author, Sept. 22, 2003, p. 37.

627 *"Hallmark case was simple"* NAA to author, June 2, 2004 (afternoon), p. 12.

628 *"NASA hadn't been very careful"* Ibid.

629 *"bring the Truth to His Creation"* Wernher von Braun quoted in George W. Cornell, "Space Expert Sees New Awareness of God," *CPD,* July 19, 1969.

629 *"ecstasy of this prophetic day"* Pope Paul VI quoted in *Baltimore Sun,* July 21, 1969, A4. See also "Pope Praises Plans for Moon Landing," *NYT,* July 14, 1969.

629 *"this righteous Lunar flight"* Reverend Herman Weber quoted in "St. Paul United Church of Christ Pastor Offers Prayer," *Wapakoneta Daily News,* July 16, 1969.

629 *"base for all tranquility, for all peace?"* Sermon by Reverend Charles Sloca, Fairfield, IA, "Vision Via Television," copy in VEAP.

629 *"most important keystone in his ego-structure"* Dan L. Thrapp [Los Angeles Times/Washington Post Service], "Moon Walk to Shift Man-God Views," *Dayton Journal Herald,* July 19, 1969.

629 *"astronauts were religious men"* Ming Zhen Shakya, "A Nobel Prize, Lunar Communion, the Beatitudes, and a Song of David's," n.d., accessed at www.hsuyun.org/Dharma/zbohy/Literature/essay/mzs/beatitudes.html. Ms. Ming Shen identified herself as belonging to the Zen Buddhist Order of Hsu Yun.

630 *"felt the power of God as I'd never felt it before"* James Irwin quoted in Charles W. Colson, "Astronauts Who Found God: A Spiritual View of Space," Nov. 5, 1998, accessed at www.fuw.edu.pl/~pniez/breakpoint.html.

630 *"walking* with *the Son"* Charles Duke quoted in ibid.

630 *"Onward Christian Spacemen"* Anonymous essay, n.d., accessed at www.graceunknown.com/Scholastica/OnwardChristianSpacemen.html.

630 "were not even high priests" Gillies Macbain, "Pilgrimage to the Moon," n.d., accessed at www.aislingmagazine.com/Anu/articles/TAM17/Moon.html. Macbain identified himself as "a writer, philosopher, and organic farmer" living in County Tipperary, Ireland.

631 *U.S. State Department sent the following message* Secretary of State, U.S. Department of State, Washington, DC, to Middle Eastern and Pacific Diplomatic Posts, "Subject: Alleged Conversion of Neil Armstrong," Mar. 2, 1983, copy in NAA's personal files. In NAA's personal papers, there is a very large file pertaining to this subject as well as to Neil's attempts to dispel the rumor. Some of the contents involve messages circulated worldwide within the United States Information Agency (USIA). The following is a sampling of headlines from articles published in the Islamic world about Armstrong's alleged conversion: "American Astronaut Embraces Islam," *Radiance Delhi,* Mar. 20, 1983; "Did Armstrong Hear Azan on the Moon?" *Gulf News,* Apr. 2, 1983; and "Neil Armstrong Embraces Islam," *Yaqeen International,* Apr. 22, 1983. Among the many letters written to Armstrong from people around the world about his alleged conversion, as many came from Christians hoping that the rumors were not true as from Muslims hoping that they were.

631 *"certainly didn't completely stem the questions"* NAA to author, June 2, 2004 (afternoon), p. 9. Neil's teleconference took place on May 23, 1983. See USIA, Satellite Speakers Staff, "Subject: TelePress Conference: Neil Armstrong/Cairo; Topic: Disinformation in Egypt on Armstrong's Supposed Conversion to Islam," May 20, 1983, copy in NAA's personal files.

632 *"convinced that I would lie"* NAA to author, June 2, 2004 (afternoon), p. 10.

632 *Mecca is "the center of the world"* "Islamic Science: Neil Armstrong Proved Mecca is the Center of the World" (Interview with Dr. Abd Al-Baset of the Egyptian National Research Center), Clip No. 545, Jan. 16, 2005, accessed at www.memrity.org/Transcript.asp?P1=545.

632 *"many organizations claim"* NAA to author, June 2, 2004 (afternoon), p. 9.

633 *"expedition cannot possibly have been to my cave"* Erich von Däniken, Bonstetten (Zürich), Switzerland, to NAA, Feb. 18, 1977, in NAA's personal files.

633 *"no statements regarding any hypotheses"* NAA to Erich von Däniken, Feb. 24, 1977, in NAA's personal files.

634 *"absolutely no truth to it"* Private conversation, NAA to author, June 2, 2004.

635 *"Has NASA ever refuted the allegations"* NAA to Lori Garver, Associate Administrator for Policy & Plans, Code Z, NASA Headquarters, Washington, DC, Aug. 10, 2000, copy in NAA's personal files.

636 *"people love conspiracy theories"* NAA to author, June 2, 2004, p. 7.

637 *"hire special security"* James Smith to author, July 17, 2003, p. 14.

637 *"opportunity to run that episode"* NAA to author, June 2, 2004 (afternoon), p. 8.

637 *confronted Buzz Aldrin* See Sheila Burke, "Nashville Filmmaker Confronts Former Astronaut Buzz Aldrin" Feb. 9, 2002, accessed at Tennessean.com.

637 *"All of a sudden, I felt shaky"* CKA to author, June 3, 2004, p. 12.

Chapter 35: Into the Heartland

640 *"Neil had his heart attack"* KKS in letter to author, May 16, 2003.

640 *"My husband's job was there"* JSA to author, Sept. 11, 2004 (afternoon), p. 6.

640 *"never lived in a small town"* Ibid., p. 9.

641 *"easier for Mark than it was for Rick"* Ibid., p. 7.

641 *"learned to ignore it"* Rick Armstrong to author, Sept. 22, 2003, p. 18.

641 *"boys wouldn't say anything to me"* JSA to author, Sept. 11, 2004 (afternoon), p. 8.

641 *"something that had to be done"* Ibid., p. 13.

641 *"shovel poop during the day"* Ibid.

641 *"stuck out there in the country"* Ibid., p. 20.

641 *"got tired of all this"* Ibid., p. 19.

641 *"The man needed help"* Ibid., p. 23.

642 *"could not continue to live like that"* Ibid., p. 24.

642 *"took a whole year to get on his schedule"* Ibid., p. 25.

642 *"cried for three years before I left"* Ibid.

642 *"couldn't live with the personality anymore"* Ibid.

642 *"the deepest depression"* HSC to author, Oct. 7, 2003, p. 8.

642 *"begged her for a long time to come back"* DAA to author, Nov. 14, 2002, p. 31.

643 *"Dad sat straight up in bed"* JHA to author, Apr. 5, 2003, author's notes, p. 1.

643 *"very happy that I believed"* Ibid., p. 2.

644 *" 'Neil who?' "* CKA to author, June 3, 2004, p. 3.

644 *"all our friends were here"* Ibid., p. 6.

645 *"It's not about me"* Ibid.

645 *"definitely run interference"* Ibid.

645 *"You must be kidding"* Ibid., p. 13.

645 *"A humdinger!"* HSC to author, Oct. 7, 2003, p. 11.

645 *"nuts about Carol"* CSM to author, June 25, 2003, p. 16.

645 *"got tired of being Mrs. Neil Armstrong"* EC to author, Feb. 10, 2003, p. 22.

645 *"have friends, and we do things"* JSA to author, Sept. 11, 2004 (afternoon), p. 25.

646 *"look what it's done to him inside"* Ibid., p. 28.

646 *"too seriously to heart"* Ibid., p. 34.

647 *"could actually hear the thermals"* Ibid., p. 36.

648 *"show you a secret"* KKS in letter to author, May 16, 2003.

Bibliography

Primary Sources

NONARCHIVED PRIVATE PAPERS

Papers of Neil A. Armstrong. Lebanon and Cincinnati, OH.
Papers of Viola Engel Armstrong and Armstrong Family. Hereford, AZ (Property of June Armstrong Hoffman).
Personal Diary of Ensign Glen Howard "Rick" Rickelton, U.S. Navy, Written During V-51 Combat Flight Training & Korean War Service Aboard CV-9 USS *Essex*, Rickelton Family Papers, Elk Grove, CA, and Seattle, WA.
Personal Diary of Robert Kaps, USS *Essex* (CV-9), Carrier Air Group Five, 28 June 1951 to 25 March 1952.

ARCHIVAL COLLECTIONS

Archives of Aerospace Exploration. University Libraries, Virginia Polytechnic Institute and State University. Blacksburg, VA.
Auglaize County Public Library. Wapakoneta, OH. Neil A. Armstrong Newspaper Files.
Emil Buehler Naval Aviation Library. National Museum of Naval Aviation. Pensacola, FL.
John Glenn Archives. The Ohio State University Archives. Columbus, OH.
NASA Dryden Flight Research Center. Historical Archives. Edwards, CA.
NASA Headquarters History Office. Washington, DC.
National Personnel Records Center. Military Personnel Records. St. Louis, MO.
Naval Historical Center. Department of the Navy, Washington Navy Yard. Washington, DC.
Neil A. Armstrong Museum. Newspaper files. Wapakoneta, OH.
Nixon Presidential Materials. National Archives at College Park. College Park, MD.
Ohio Historical Society. Columbus, OH.
Purdue University Library and Archives. West Lafayette, IN.
Records of NASA Dryden Flight Research Center. National Archives and Records Administration—Pacific Region. Laguna Nigel, CA.
Records of NASA Glenn Research Center. National Archives and Records Administration—Midwest Region. Chicago, IL.

Records of NASA Headquarters. National Archives and Records Administration—East Region. College Park, MD. Record Group 255.

Records of NASA Johnson Space Center. National Archives and Records Administration—Southwest Region. Fort Worth, TX. Record Group 255.

Records of NASA Johnson Space Center. Library and Archives of the University of Houston–Clear Lake. Clear Lake, TX.

Records of NASA Kennedy Space Center. National Archives and Records Administration—Southeast Region. Atlanta, GA. Record Group 255.

Records of NASA Langley Research Center. National Archives and Records Administration—Atlantic Region. Philadelphia, PA. Record Group 255.

Renssalaer Polytechnic Institute University Archives, Troy, NY. George M. Low Papers.

Time-Life Archives. Time-Life Building. New York City.

University of Cincinnati Archives. Cincinnati, OH.

Wyandot County Public Library. Newspaper files. Upper Sandusky, OH.

DOCUMENTS

Works of Neil A. Armstrong, Published and Unpublished

"Future Range and Flight Test Area Needs for Hypersonic and Orbital Vehicles," *Proceedings of Professional Pilots Symposium on Air Space Safety,* 1958. Also appeared in *Society of Experimental Test Pilots* 3 (Winter 1959).

"Flight and Analog Studies of Landing Techniques Pertinent to the X-15 Airplane," *Research-Airplane-Committee Report on Conference on the Progress of the X-15 Project,* NACA-CONF-30-Jul-58, July 30, 1958. Coauthors: Thomas W. Finch, Gene J. Matranga, Joseph A. Walker.

"Test Pilot Views on Space Ventures," *Proceedings of ASME Aviation Conference,* Mar. 1959.

"Approach and Landing Investigation at Lift-Drag Ratios of 2 to 4 Utilizing a Straight-Wing Fighter Airplane," *NASA TM X-31,* Aug. 1959. Coauthor, Gene J. Matranga.

"Utilization of the Pilot in the Launch and Injection of a Multistage Orbital Vehicle," *IAS Paper 60-16,* 1960. Coauthors: E. C. Holleman and W. H. Andrew.

"X-15 Operations: Electronics and the Pilot," *Astronautics* 5 (May 1960): 42–3, 76–8.

"Development of X-15 Self-Adaptive Flight Control System," *Research-Airplane-Committee Report on Conference on the Progress of the X-15 Project,* 1961. Coauthors: R. P. Johannes and T. C. Hays.

"Flight-Simulated Off-the-Pad Escape and Landing Maneuvers for a Vertically Launched Hypersonic Glider," *NASA TM X-637,* March 1962. Coauthors: G. J. Matranga and William H. Dana.

"The X-15 Flight Program," *Proceedings of the Second National Conference on the Peaceful Uses of Space,* Seattle, WA, May 8–10, 1962. Coauthors: Joseph A. Walker, Forrest S. Petersen, Robert M. White.

"A Review of In-Flight Simulation Pertinent to Piloted Space Vehicles," *AGARD Report 403,* 21st Flight Mechanics Panel Meeting, Paris, France, July 9–11, 1962. Coauthor, Euclid C. Holleman.

"Pilot Utilization During Boost," Inter-Center Technical Conference on Control Guidance and Navigation Research for Manned Lunar Missions, Ames Research Center, Moffett Field, CA, July 24–25, 1962. Coauthor, Euclid C. Holleman.

"X-15 Hydraulic Systems Performance," *Hydraulics and Pneumatics,* Dec. 1962.

"Gemini Manned Flight Programs," *Proceedings of the Society of Experimental Test Pilots,* 8th Symposium, 1964.

"Controlled Reentry," *Gemini Summary Conference,* Houston, Texas, Feb. 1967. Multiple coauthors.

"Safety in Manned Spaceflight Preparation: A Crewman's Viewpoint," *AIAA,* 4th Annual Meeting, Oct. 1967.

"Apollo Flight Crew Training in Lunar Landing Simulators," *AIAA Paper 68-254,* 1968. Coauthor, S. H. Nassiff.

"Lunar Landing Strategy," *Proceedings of the Society of Experimental Test Pilots,* 13th Symposium, 1969.

"The Blue Planet," World Wildlife Fund, London, England, Nov. 1970.

"Lunar Surface Exploration," COSPAR, Leningrad, USSR, 1970, and Akademie-Verlag, Berlin, 1971.

"Change in the Space Age," The Mountbatten Lecture, University of Edinburgh, Mar. 1971.

"Out of This World," *Saturday Review/World,* Aug. 24, 1974.

"Apollo Double Diaphragm Pump for Use in Artificial Heart-Lung Systems," *AAMI National* Meeting, Mar. 1975. Coauthors: H. J. Heimlich, E. A. Patrick, G. R. Rieveschl.

"Intra-Lung Oxygenation for Chronic Lung Disease," Benedum Foundation, 1976. Coauthors: H. J. Heimlich, E. A. Patrick, G. R. Rieveschl.

"What America Means to Me," *The Reader's Digest,* June 1976, pp. 75–76.

"A Citizen Looks at National Defense," *National Defense,* Sept.–Oct. 1978.

"The Learjet Longhorn, First Jet with Winglets," *Proceedings of the Society of Experimental Test Pilots,* 22nd Symposium, 1978. Coauthor, P. J. Reynolds.

Commencement Address, University of Cincinnati June 13, 1982.

"New Knowledge of the Earth from Space Exploration," Academy of the Kingdom of Morocco, Casablanca, 1984. Coauthor, P. J. Lowman.

Wingless on Luna. 25th Wings Club General Harold R. Harris "Sight" Lecture, Presented at Inter-Continental Hotel, New York City, May 20, 1988. New York: Wings Club, 1988.

"Research Values in Contemporary Society," Academy of the Kingdom of Morocco, Casablanca, 1989.

"Reflections by Neil Armstrong: We Joined Hands to Meet Challenge of Apollo Mission," *Cincinnati Enquirer,* July 20, 1989.

"The Ozone Layer Controversy," Academy of the Kingdom of Morocco, Casablanca, 1993. Coauthor, Mark S. Armstrong.

"Engineering Aspects of a Lunar Landing," The Lester D. Gardner Lecture, Massachusetts Institute of Technology, May 3, 1994. Coauthor, Robert C. Seamans.

"Pressure Vessel Considerations in Aerospace Operations," National Board of Boiler and Pressure Vessel Inspectors, Anchorage, AL, 1995.

"Observations on Genetic Engineering," Academy of the Kingdom of Morocco, Rabat, 1997. Coauthor, Carol Knight Armstrong.

OTHER PRIMARY DOCUMENTS

Bennett, Floyd V. *Mission Planning for Lunar Module Descent and Ascent.* Washington, DC: NASA Technical Note MSC-04919, Oct. 1971.

CBS Television Network, *10:56:20 P.M., 7/20/69.* New York: Columbia Broadcasting System, 1970.

Godwin, Robert, ed. *X-15: The NASA Mission Reports.* Burlington, Ontario: Apogee Books, 2000.

————. *Dyna-Soar: Hypersonic Strategic Weapons System.* Burlington, Ontario: Apogee Books, 2003.

————. *Apollo 11: The NASA Mission Reports.* 3 vols. Burlington, Ontario: Apogee Books, 1999–2002.

Jones, Eric P., *Apollo Lunar Surface Journal.*

Low, George M. *Latin American Tour with Astronauts Armstrong and Gordon, 7–31 Oct. 1966.* NASA Manned Spacecraft Center: Unpublished mss., Nov. 16, 1966.

NASA Lyndon B. Johnson Space Center. *Biomedical Results of Apollo.* Washington, DC: NASA SP-368, 1975.

NASA Manned Spacecraft Center. *Apollo 11 Onboard Voice Transcription, Recorded on the Command Module Onboard Recorder Data Storage Equipment.* Houston: Manned Spacecraft Center, Aug. 1969.

NASA Manned Spacecraft Center. *Apollo 11 Preliminary Science Report.* Washington, DC: NASA SP-214, 1969.

NASA Manned Spacecraft Center. *Apollo 11 Spacecraft Commentary, July 16–24, 1969.*

NASA Manned Spacecraft Center. *Apollo 11 Technical Air-to-Ground Voice Transcription.* Prepared for Data Logistics Office Test Division, Apollo Spacecraft Program Office, July 1969.

National Commission on Space. *Pioneering the Space Frontier: The Report of the National Commission on Space.* Toronto and New York: Bantam Books, May 1986.

"Neil Armstrong's Comments on Behalf of the Apollo 11 Crew," Langley Medal Awards Ceremony, July 20, 1999, National Air and Space Museum, Washington, DC.

"Remarks by Neil A. Armstrong upon Receipt of National Space Trophy," 2004 Rotary National Award for Space Achievement, Houston, TX.

"Statement by Neil Armstrong at the White House," NASA Release, July 20, 1994.

U.S. News and World Report. *U.S. on the Moon: What It Means To Us.* Washington, DC: U.S. News and World Report, 1969.

NEWSPAPERS AND PERIODICALS

Akron Beacon Journal
Baltimore Evening Sun

Boston Globe
Chicago Tribune
Christian Science Monitor
Cincinnati Enquirer
Cincinnati Post
Cleveland Plain Dealer
Cleveland Press
Columbus (Ohio) *Citizen-Journal*
Columbus (Ohio) *Dispatch*
Dayton Daily News
Florida Today
Houston Chronicle
Lebanon (Ohio) *Western Star*
Life
Lima (Ohio) *Citizen*
Lima (Ohio) *News*
Los Angeles Times
NASA X-Press (NASA Dryden)
National Observer
Newsweek
New York *Daily News*
New York Times
Seattle Daily Times
Space News Roundup (NASA Manned Spacecraft Center/JSC)
St. Marys (Ohio) *Evening Leader*
Time
Toledo Blade
Wall Street Journal
Wapakoneta Daily News
Washington Post

Interviews

CONDUCTED BY AUTHOR

Aicholtz, John, June 5, 2003, Cincinnati.
Aldrin, Buzz, Mar. 17, 2003, Albuquerque, NM.
Anders, Valerie, Apr. 8, 2003, San Diego; July 17, 2004, Dayton.
Anders, William A., Apr. 8, 2003, San Diego.
Armstrong, Carol Knight, June 2004, Cincinnati.
Armstrong, Dean, Nov. 14, 2002, Bonita Springs, FL.
Armstrong, Janet Shearon, Sept. 10–11, 2004, Park City, UT.
Armstrong, Neil A., Cincinnati.
- Aug. 13, 2002.
- Nov. 26, 2002.
- June 2–4, 2003.
- Sept. 18–19 and 22, 2003.
- June 2–3, 2004.

Armstrong, Rick, Sept. 22, 2003, Cincinnati.

Armstrong Hoffman, June,
- Aug. 14, 2002, Wapakoneta, OH.
- Apr. 4–5, 2003, Hereford, AZ.
- June 7, 2003, Wapakoneta.

Baker, Steve, June 5, 2003, Cincinnati.

Barnicki, Roger J., Dec. 11, 2002, Lancaster, CA.

Barr, Doris, Aug. 15, 2002, Cincinnati (telephone).

Bean, Alan, Feb. 7, 2003, Houston.

Beering, Stephen, May 30, 2003, Carmel, IN.

Bennett, Floyd V., Feb. 8, 2003, Houston.

Blackford, John "Bud," July 25, 2003, Concord, NH.

Borman, Frank, Apr. 15, 2003, Las Cruces, NM.

Borman, Susan, Apr. 15, 2003, Las Cruces, NM (telephone).

Brading, Charles, Jr., Aug. 17, 2003, Wapakoneta, OH.

Burrus, David, June 5, 2003, Cincinnati.

Burt, Devere, June 3, 2003, Cincinnati.

Butchart, Stanley P., Dec. 15, 2002, Lancaster, CA.

Cargnino, Larry, Nov. 29, 2002, West Lafayette, IN.

Carpentier, Dr. William, Feb. 8, 2003, Seabrook, TX.

Cernan, Eugene A., Feb. 10, 2003, Houston.

Collins, Michael, Mar. 25, 2003, Marco Island, FL.

Combs, Harry, Oct. 7, 2003, Orlando, FL.

Crossfield, A. Scott, July 17, 2004, Dayton, OH.

Dana, William H., Dec. 9, 2003, Edwards, CA.

Danneberg, Kenneth I., June 27, 2002, Denver.

Day, Richard E., Dec. 11, 2003, Palmdale, CA.

Frame, Arthur, Aug. 15 and 17, 2002, Wapakoneta.

Franklin, George C., Feb. 5, 2003, Houston.

Friedlander, Charles D., Apr. 8–9, 2003, San Diego.

Glenn, John H., Sept. 23, 2003, Columbus, OH.

Gordon, Linda, Apr. 12, 2003, Prescott, AZ.

Gordon, Richard F., Jr., Apr. 12, 2003, Prescott, AZ.

Gott, Herschel, June 20, 2003, Los Altos, CA.

Gustafson, Bob, Aug. 15, 2002, Wapakoneta.

Heimlich, Dr. Henry, June 5, 2003, Cincinnati.

Hollemon, Charles, Nov. 21, 2002, West Lafayette.

Keating, William, June 5, 2003, Cincinnati.

Keiber, Ned, Aug. 15, 2002, Wapakoneta, OH.

Kinne, Tim, June 5, 2003, Cincinnati.

Kleinknecht, Kenneth S., June 27, 2003, Littleton, CO.

Knight, William "Pete," Dec. 15, 2002, Palmdale, CA.

Knudegaard, Vincent Aubrey, Sept. 11, 2002, Auburn, AL.

Kraft, Chris, Feb. 7, 2003, Houston.

Kranz, Eugene, Feb. 8, 2003, Friendswood, TX.

Kutyna, Donald J., Mar. 20, 2004, Colorado Springs.

Love, Betty, Jan. 30, 2003, Edwards, CA (Conducted by Christian Gelzer).

Lovell, James A., July 17, 2004, Dayton.

Lovell, Marilyn, July 17, 2004, Dayton.

Lunney, Glynn, Feb. 6, 2003, Houston.

Mackey, William A., Sept. 21, 2002, Tuscaloosa, AL.

Mallick, Donald L., Dec. 12, 2002, Lancaster, CA.

Matranga, Gene J., Dec. 12, 2002, Lancaster, CA.

McDivitt, James A., Apr. 7, 2003, Tucson, AZ.

McTigue, John G., Dec. 9, 2002, Lancaster, CA.

Mechem, Charles S., Jr., June 25, 2003, Jackson Hole, WY.

Meyer, Russ, Oct. 7, 2003, Orlando, FL.

North, Warren J., Apr. 11, 2003, Phoenix.

Palmer, George, Nov. 21, 2002, West Lafayette.

Peterson, Bruce A., Dec. 9, 2002, Lancaster, CA.

Preston, G. Merritt, Mar. 27, 2003, Melbourne, FL.

Rogers, James, June 5, 2003, Cincinnati.

Schiesser, Emil, Feb. 4, 2003, Seabrook, TX.

Schirra, Walter M. Jr., Apr. 8, 2003, San Diego.

Schmitt, Harrison H. "Jack," Mar. 16, 2003, Albuquerque.

Schuler, Dudley, Aug. 15, 2002, Wapakoneta, OH.

Schwan, Harold C., Oct. 17, 2002, Chesterfield, MO.

Scott, David R., Feb. 1, 2003, Atlanta.

Shaw-Kuffner, Alma Lou, Aug. 15, 2002, Wapakoneta.

Smith, James M., July 17, 2003, New York City.

Solacoff, Doris, June 1, 2003, Upper Sandusky, OH.

Solacoff, K. K. "Kotcho," June 1, 2003, Upper Sandusky, OH.

Spitzen, Ralph, June 5, 2003, Cincinnati.

Stear, Mark, June 5, 2003, Cincinnati.

Townley, Diana, June 5, 2003, Cincinnati.

Townley, Gary, June 5, 2003, Cincinnati.

Walker-Wiesmann, Grace, Dec. 14, 2002, Reedley, CA.

Waltman, Gene L., Dec. 19, 2002, Edwards, CA.

White, Robert M., Nov. 12, 2002, Sun City Center, FL.

White, Vivian, May 29, 2003, Lebanon, OH.

Wilson, James R., June 23, 2003, Park City, UT.

Windler, Milton L., Feb. 4, 2003, Friendswood, TX.

Zwez, John, Aug. 14, 2002, Wapakoneta, OH.

CONDUCTED BY OTHER RESEARCHERS

Albrecht, William P., Feb. 16, 2001, Edwards, CA (Curtis Peebles).

Aldrin, Edwin E., July 7, 1970, Houston, TX (Robert B. Merrifield).

Algranti, Joseph S., Mar. 15, 1968, Houston, TX (Robert B. Merrifield); Aug. 10, 1998, Chapel Hill, NC (Erik Carlson).

Anders, William A., Oct. 8, 1997, Houston (Paul Rollins).

Arabian, Donald D., Feb. 3, 2000, Cape Canaveral (Kevin M. Rusnak).

Armitage, Peter J., Aug. 20, 2001, Houston (Kevin M. Rusnak).

Armstrong, Janet Shearon, Mar. 12, 1969, Houston *(Life)*.

Armstrong, Neil A.,
- Sept. 1, 1964, Houston *(Life)*.
- Summer 1965, Houston *(Life)*.
- Apr. 6, 1967, Houston (Barton C. Hacker).
- Feb. 23, 1969, Houston *(Life)*.
- Mar. 2, 1969, Houston *(Life)*.
- Mar. 12, 1969, Houston *(Life)*.
- Aug. 7, 1969, Houston *(Life)*.
- Sept. 23, 1971, Washington, DC (Robert Sherrod).
- Oct. 11, 1988, Cincinnati (Andrew Chaikin).
- Mar. 6, 1989 (Neil McAleer: phone interview).
- Sept. 19, 2001, Houston (Stephen E. Ambrose and Douglas Brinkley).

Armstrong, Viola, May 9, 1969, Wapakoneta, OH (Dora Jane Hamblin).

Bean, Allan, Apr. 10, 1984, Houston (W. David Compton).

Bond, Aleck C., Sept. 3, 1998, Houston (Summer Chick Bergen).

Borman, Frank, Apr. 13, 1999, Las Cruces, NM (Catherine Harwood).

Bostick, Jerry C., Feb. 23, 2000, Marble Falls, TX (Carol Butler).

Butchart, Stanley P., Sept. 15, 1997, Lancaster, CA (Curt Asher).

Carlton, Robert L., Mar. 29, Apr. 10, and Apr. 19, 2001, Houston (Kevin M. Rusnak).

Carpenter, M. Scott, Mar. 30, 1998, Houston (Michelle Kelly).

Catterson, A. Duane, Feb. 17, 2000, Houston (Carol Butler).

Cernan, Eugene A., Apr. 6, 1984, Houston (W. David Compton).

Charlesworth, Clifford E., Dec. 13, 1966, Houston (Vorzimmer).

Chilton, Robert G., Mar. 30, 1970, Houston (Loyd Swenson).

Collins, Michael, Oct. 8, 1997, Houston (Michelle Kelly).

Crossfield, A. Scott, Feb. 3, 1998, Lancaster, CA (Peter Merlin).

Dana, William H., Nov. 14, 1997, Edwards, CA (Peter Merlin); Mar. 9, 1999, Edwards, CA (Michael Gorn).

Day, Richard E., May 1, 1997, Edwards, CA (J. D. Hunley).

Donlan, Charles J., Apr. 27, 1998, Washington, DC (Jim Slade).

Drake, Hubert M., Nov. 15, 1966, Edwards, CA (Jim Krier and J. D. Hunley); Apr. 16, 1997, Edwards, CA (J. D. Hunley).

Duke, Charles M., Mar. 12, 1999, Houston (Doug Ward).

Fendell, Edward I., Oct. 19, 2000, Houston (Kevin M. Rusnak).

Franklin, George C., Oct. 3, 2001, Houston (Kevin M. Rusnak).

Fulton, Fitzhugh L., Jr., Aug. 7, 1997, Edwards, CA (J. D. Hunley).

Gordon, Richard F., Jr., Oct. 17, 1997, Houston (Michelle Kelly).

Griffin, Gerald D., Mar. 12, 1999, Houston (Doug Ward).

Grimm, Dean F., Aug. 17, 2000, Parker, CO (Carol Butler).

Haines, Charles R., Nov. 7, 2000, Houston (Kevin M. Rusnak).

Haise, Fred, Jr., Mar. 23, 1999, Houston (Doug Ward).

Hodge, John D., Apr. 18, 1999, Great Falls, VA (Rebecca Wright).

Honeycutt, Jay F., Mar. 22, 2000, Houston (Rebecca Wright).

Hutchinson, Neil B., June 5, 2000, Houston (Kevin M. Rusnak).

Kelly, Thomas J., Sept. 19, 2000, Cutchogue, NY (Kevin M. Rusnak).

Kleinknecht, Kenneth S., Sept. 10, 1998, Littleton, CO (Carol Butler) July 25, 2000, Houston (Carol Butler).

Kranz, Eugene F., Jan. 8, 1999, Houston (Rebecca Wright); Apr. 28, 1999, Houston (Roy Neal).

Love, Betty, Apr. 10, 1997, Edwards, CA (Michael Gorn); May 6, 2002, Palmdale, CA (Rebecca Wright).

Lovell, James A., Jr., May 25, 1999, Houston (Ron Stone).

Low, George M., Jan. 9, 1969, Houston (Robert B. Merrifield).

Lunney, Glynn S., Jan. 28, Feb. 8, and Apr. 26, 1999, Houston (Carol Butler).

Mattingly, Thomas K., II, Nov. 6, 2001, Costa Mesa, CA (Rebecca Wright).

McDivitt, James A., June 29, 1999, Elk Lake, MI (Doug Ward).

Maxson, Jerre, May 9, 1969, Wapakoneta, OH (Dora Jane Hamblin).

Mitchell, Edgar D., Sept. 3, 1997, Houston (Sheree Scarborough).

North, Warren J., Mar. 14, 1968, Houston (Robert B. Merrifield); Sept. 30, 1998, Houston (Summer Chick Bergen).

O'Hara, Delores B. "Dee," Apr. 23, 2002, Mountain View, CA (Rebecca Wright).

Preston, G. Merritt, Feb. 1, 2000, Indian Harbor Beach, FL (Carol Butler).

Saltzman, Edwin J., Dec. 3, 1997, Edwards, CA (J. D. Hunley).

Schirra, Walter M., Jr., Dec. 1, 1998, San Diego (Roy Neal).

Schmitt, Harrison H. "Jack," May 30, 1984, Houston (W. D. Compton); July 14, 1999, Houston (Carol Butler).

Schweickart, Russell L., Oct. 19, 1999, Houston (Rebecca Wright).

Seamans, Robert C., Nov. 20, 1998, Beverly, MA (Michelle Kelly) June 22, 1999, Cambridge, MA (Carol Butler).

Shea, Joseph F., May 16, 1971, Weston, MA (Robert Sherrod).

Sherman, Howard, Feb. 11, 1970, Bethpage, NY (Ivan Ertel).

Slayton, Donald K., Oct. 17, 1967, Houston (Robert B. Merrifield); Oct. 15, 1984, Houston (W. D. Compton).

Stafford, Thomas, Oct. 15, 1997, Houston (William Vantine).

Thompson, Milton O., Sept. 22, 1983, Edwards, CA (Larry Evans).

E-MAIL AND LETTER CORRESPONDENCE WITH AUTHOR

Aldrin, Buzz, Los Angeles, CA.

Armstrong, Janet Shearon, Park City, UT.

Armstrong, Neil A., Cincinnati.

Armstrong-Hoffmann, June, Hereford, AZ.

Baker, Steve, Cincinnati.

Beauchamp, Ernest M., Corona Del Mar, CA.

Bowers, William "Bill."

Brandli, Hank, Melbourne, FL.

Burke, Mel, Edwards, CA.

Burrus, David, Cincinnati.

Campbell, Nick, Denver, CO.

Clingan, Bruce, Troy, OH.

Danneberg, Kenneth I., Denver, CO.

Day, Richard E., Palmdale, CA.

Esslinger, Michael, Monterey, CA.

Friedlander, Charles D., San Diego.

Gardner, Donald A., Clinton, IN.
Gates, Charles, Denver.
Gott, Herschel, Los Altos, CA.
Graham, Herb A.
Hamed, Awatef, Cincinnati.
Hayward, Tom.
Hoffman, Jayne, River Falls, WI.
Honneger, Barbara, Monterey, CA.
Hromas, Leslie A., Rolling Hills, CA.
Huston, Ronald, Cincinnati.
Jones, Eric P., Australia.
Karnoski, Peter, Las Vegas, NV.
Kinne, Tim, Cincinnati.
Klingan, Bruce E., Bellevue, WA.
Koppa, Rodger J., College Station, TX.
Kraft, Chris, Houston.
Kramer, Ken, Houston and San Diego.
Kranz, Eugene F., Houston.
Kutyna, Donald J., Colorado Springs.
Mackey, William A., Tuscaloosa, AL.
Mechem, Charles S. Jr., Loveland, OH.
Pearlman, Robert, Houston.
Perich, Pete, Warren, OH.
Petersen, Richard H., La Jolla, CA.
Petrone, Rocco, Palos Verdes Peninsula, CA.
Rickelton, Glen, Elk Grove, CA.
Rickelton, Ted, Seattle, WA.
Russell, George E. "Ernie," Cashion, OK.
Schwan, Harold C., Chesterfield, MO.
Scott, David R., London, England.
Slater, Gary L., Cincinnati.
Spanagel, Herman A., Satellite Beach, FL.
Spitzen, Ralph E., Columbus, OH.
Stear, Mark, Cincinnati.
Stephenson, David S., King of Prussia, PA.
Thompson, Tom, Rancho Palos Verde, CA.
Walker-Wiesmann, Grace, Reeedley, CA.
White, Vivian, Lebanon, OH.

Secondary Sources

BOOKS

Aldrin, Buzz, and Malcolm McConnell. *Men from Earth.* 2nd ed. New York: Bantam Falcon Books, 1991.
Aldrin, Edwin E. Jr. with Wayne Warga. *Return to Earth.* New York: Random House, 1973.

Allday, Jonathan. *Apollo in Perspective: Spaceflight Then and Now.* Bristol and Philadelphia: Institute of Physics Publishing, 2000.

Armstrong, Robert Bruce. *The History of Liddesdale.* Vol. I. Edinburgh, 1883.

Arnold, H. J. P., ed. *Man in Space: An Illustrated History of Spaceflight.* New York: Smithmark, 1993.

Baker, David. *The History of Manned Spaceflight.* New Cavendish Books, 1981. Reprint. New York: Crown Publishers, 1982.

Ball, John. *Edwards: Flight Test Center of the USAF.* New York: Duell, Sloan, and Pearce, 1962.

Barbour, John. *Footprints on the Moon.* New York: Associated Press, 1969.

Bean, Alan. *Apollo: An Eyewitness Account by Astronaut/Explorer Artist/Moonwalker Alan Bean.* Shelton, CT: Greenwich Workshop, Inc., 1998.

Berg, A. Scott. *Lindbergh.* New York: G. P. Putnam's Sons, 1998.

Bilstein, Roger. *Stages to Saturn: A Technological History of the Apollo/Saturn Launch Vehicles.* Washington, DC: NASA SP-4206, 1980.

———. *Orders of Magnitude: A History of the NACA and NASA, 1915–1990.* Washington, DC: NASA SP-4406, 1989.

Borman, Frank, with Robert J. Serling. *Countdown.* New York: Morrow, 1988.

Bowman, Martin W. *Lockheed F-104 Starfighter.* London: Crowood Press, 2001.

Boyne, Walter J., and Lopez, Donald S. *The Jet Age: Forty Years of Jet Aviation.* Washington, DC: Smithsonian Institution Press, 1979.

Brooks, Courtney G., James M. Grimwood, and Loyd S. Swenson Jr. *Chariots for Apollo: A History of Manned Lunar Spacecraft.* Washington, DC: NASA SP-4205, 1979.

Burrows, William E. *This New Ocean: The Story of the First Space Age.* New York: Modern Library, 1999.

Carpenter, M. Scott, Gordon L. Cooper Jr., John H. Glenn Jr., Virgil I. Grissom, Walter M. Schirra Jr., Alan B. Shepard, and Donald K. Slayton. *We Seven.* New York: Simon & Schuster, 1962.

Cayton, Andrew R. L. *Ohio: The History of a People.* Columbus: Ohio State University Press, 2002.

Cernan, Eugene, with Don Davis. *The Last Man on the Moon: Astronaut Gene Cernan and America's Race in Space.* New York: St. Martin's Griffin, 1999.

Chaikin, Andrew. *A Man on the Moon.* New York and London: Penguin Group, 1994.

———. *A Man on the Moon.* 3 vols. (I: *One Giant Leap;* II: *The Odyssey Continues;* III: *Lunar Explorers*). Alexandria, VA: Time-Life Books, 1999.

Collins, Michael. *Carrying the Fire: An Astronaut's Journeys.* New York: Farrar, Straus and Giroux, 1974.

———. *Liftoff: The Story of America's Adventure in Space.* New York: Grove Press, 1988.

Compton, W. David. *Where No Man Has Gone Before: A History of the Apollo Lunar Exploration Missions.* Washington, DC: NASA SP-4214, 1989.

Cooper, Gordon, with Bruce Henderson. *Leap of Faith: An Astronaut's Journey into the Unknown.* New York: HarperTorch, 2000.

Cooper, Henry S. F. Jr. *Apollo on the Moon.* New York: Dial, 1973.

———. *Moon Rocks.* New York: Dial, 1970.

Corn, Joseph J. *The Winged Gospel: America's Romance with Aviation, 1900–1950.* New York and Oxford: Oxford University Press, 1983.

Cortright, Edgar M., ed., *Apollo Expeditions to the Moon.* Washington, DC: NASA SP-350, 1975.

Cunningham, Walter, with Mickey Herskowitz. *The All-American Boys.* New York: Macmillan, 1977.

Dawson, Virginia P. *Engines and Innovation: Lewis Laboratory and American Propulsion Technology.* Washington, DC: NASA SP-4306, 1991.

Dethloff, Henry C. *Suddenly, Tomorrow Came . . . : A History of the Johnson Space Center.* Washington, DC: NASA SP-4307, 1993.

Duke, Charlie and Dotty. *Moonwalker.* Nashville: Oliver-Nelson Books, 1990.

Emme, Eugene M. *Two Hundred Years of Flight in America: A Bicentennial Survey.* San Diego: American Astronautical Society, 1977.

Engen, Donald. *Wings and Warriors: Life as a Naval Aviator.* Washington and London: Smithsonian Institution Press, 1997.

Farmer, Gene, and Dora Jane Hamblin. *First on the Moon.* New York: Little, Brown, and Co., 1969.

Fraser, George MacDonald. *The Steel Bonnets: The Story of the Anglo-Saxon Border Reivers.* London: Collins Harvill, 1989.

Fries, Sylvia Doughty. *NASA Engineers and the Age of Apollo.* Washington, DC: NASA SP-4104, 1992.

Gainor, Chris. *Arrows to the Moon: Avro's Engineers and the Space Race.* Burlington, Ontario: Apogee Books, 2001.

Garber, Stephen J., ed. *Looking Backward, Looking Forward: Forty Years of U.S. Human Spaceflight Symposium, 8 May 2001.* Washington, DC: NASA SP-2002-4107, 2002.

Glenn, John, with Nick Taylor. *John Glenn: A Memoir.* New York and Toronto: Bantam Books, 1999.

Goldstein, Laurence. *The Flying Machine and Modern Literature.* Bloomington: Indiana University Press, 1986.

Gorn, Michael H. *Expanding the Envelope: Flight Research at NACA and NASA.* Lexington: University Press of Kentucky, 2001.

Grandt, A. F. Jr., W. A. Gustafson, and L. T. Cargnino. *One Small Step: The History of Aerospace Engineering at Purdue University.* West Lafayette: School of Aeronautics and Astronautics, Purdue University, 1996.

Gray, George W. *Frontiers of Flight: The Story of NACA Research.* New York: Knopf, 1948.

Gray, Mike. *Angle of Attack: Harrison Storms and the Race to the Moon.* New York: W. W. Norton & Co., 1992.

Gunston, Bill. *Attack Aircraft of the West.* London: Ian Allan, 1974.

Hacker, Barton C., and James M. Grimwood. *On the Shoulders of Titans: A History of Project Gemini.* Washington, DC: NASA SP-4203, 1977.

Hallion, Richard P. *On the Frontier: Flight Research at Dryden, 1946–1981.* Washington, D.C.: NASA SP-4303, 1988.

———. *Supersonic Flight: Breaking the Sound Barrier and Beyond,* rev. ed. Washington, DC: Brassey's, 1997.

———. *Test Pilots: The Frontiersmen of Flight,* rev. ed. Washington and London: Smithsonian Institution Press, 1988.

———. *The Naval Air War in Korea.* New York: The Nautical & Aviation Publishing Co. of America, 1986.

Hansen, James R. *The Bird Is on the Wing: Aerodynamics and the Progress of the American Airplane.* College Station: Texas A&M University Press, 2003.

———. *Engineer in Charge: A History of the Langley Aeronautical Laboratory, 1917–1958.* Washington, DC: NASA SP-4305, 1987.

———. *Spaceflight Revolution: NASA Langley From Sputnik to Apollo.* Washington, DC: NASA SP-4308, 1995.

Harland, David M. *How NASA Learned to Fly in Space: An Exciting Account of the Gemini Missions.* Burlington, Ontario: Apogee Books, 2004.

Henes, Donna. *The Moon Watcher's Companion.* New York: Marlowe & Company, 2002.

Heppenheimer, T.A. *Countdown: A History of Space Flight.* New York: John Wiley & Sons, 1997.

Hurt, Douglas R. *The Ohio Frontier: Crucible of the Old Northwest, 1720–1830.* Bloomington: Indiana University Press, 1996.

Illiff, Kenneth W., and Curtiss L. Peebles. *From Runway to Orbit: Reflections of a NASA Engineer.* Washington, DC: NASA SP-2004-4109, 2004.

Irwin, James B., with William A. Emerson Jr. *To Rule the Night.* Philadelphia: Holman (Lippincott), 1973.

Irwin, Mary, with Madelene Harris. *The Moon Is Not Enough.* Grand Rapids: Zondervan Corporation, 1978.

Jenkins, Dennis. *Hypersonics Before the Shuttle: A Concise History of the X-15 Research Airplane.* Monographs in Aerospace History No. 18. Washington, DC: NASA SP-2000-4518, June 2000.

Jones, Robert Leslie Jones. *The History of Agriculture in Ohio to 1880.* Kent, OH: Kent State University Press, 1983.

Kelly, Thomas J. *Moon Lander: How We Developed the Apollo Lunar Module.* Washington and London: Smithsonian Institution Press, 2001.

King, Elbert A. *Moon Trip: A Personal Account of the Apollo Program and Its Science.* Houston: University of Houston Press, 1989.

Knepper, George. *Ohio and Its People.* Kent, OH, and London, England: Kent State University Press, 1989.

Knott, Richard C. *A Heritage of Wings: An Illustrated History of Naval Aviation.* Annapolis: Naval Institute Press, 1997.

Kraft, Chris. *Flight: My Life in Mission Control.* New York and London: Plume Books, 2001.

Kranz, Gene. *Failure Is Not an Option: Mission Control from Mercury to Apollo 13 and Beyond.* New York and London: Simon & Schuster, 2000.

Lambright, W. Henry. *Powering Apollo: James E. Webb of NASA.* Baltimore and London: Johns Hopkins University Press, 1995.

Launius, Roger D. *Apollo: A Retrospective Analysis.* Monographs in Aerospace History No. 3. Washington, DC: Government Printing Office, July 1994.

Lay, Beirne Jr. *Earthbound Astronauts: The Builders of Apollo-Saturn.* Englewood Cliffs, NJ: Prentice-Hall, 1971.

Leckey, Howard L. *The Tenmile Country and Its Pioneer Families: A Genealogical History of the Upper Monogahela Valley.* Salem, MA: Higginson Book Co., 1950.

Levine, Arnold S. *Managing NASA in the Apollo Era.* Washington, DC: NASA SP-4102, 1982.

Lewis, Richard S. *Appointment on the Moon.* New York: Ballantine, 1969.

———. *The Voyages of Apollo: The Exploration of the Moon.* New York: Times Book Company, 1974.

Life, Special Issue, "Man in Space: An Illustrated History from Sputnik to Columbia," March 17, 2003.

Loftin, Laurence K. Jr. *Quest for Performance: The Evolution of Modern Aircraft.* Washington, DC: NASA SP-468, 1985.

Lovell, Jim, and Jeffrey Kluger. *Lost Moon: The Perilous Voyage of Apollo 13.* Boston and New York: Houghton Mifflin, 1994.

Mack, Pamela E., ed. *From Engineering Science to Big Science: The NACA and NASA Collier Trophy Research Project Winners.* Washington, DC: NASA SP-4219, 1998.

MacKinnon, Douglas, and Joseph Baldanza. *Footprints.* Illustrated by Alan Bean. Washington, DC: Acropolis Books, 1989.

Mailer, Norman. *Of a Fire on the Moon.* New York: Little, Brown and Co., 1969.

Masursky, Harold, G. William Colton, and Farouk El-Baz, eds. *Apollo Over the Moon: A View from Orbit.* Washington, DC: NASA SP-362, 1978.

McCurdy, Howard E. *Space and the American Imagination.* Washington and London: Smithsonian Institution Press, 1997.

McDougall, Walter A. *The Heavens and the Earth: A Political History of the Space Age.* New York: Basic Books, 1985.

Michener, James A. *The Bridges at Toko-Ri.* New York: Random House, 1953.

Miller, Ronald, and David Sawers. *The Technical Development of Modern Aviation.* New York: Praeger, 1970.

Moore, John. *The Wrong Stuff: Flying on the Edge of Disaster.* North Branch, MN: Specialty Press, 1997.

Murray, Charles, and Catherine Bly Cox. *Apollo: The Race to the Moon.* New York: Simon & Schuster, 1989.

Mutch, Thomas A. *A Geology of the Moon: A Stratigraphic View.* Princeton: Princeton University Press, 1970.

NASA. *Managing the Moon Program: Lessons Learned from Project Apollo.* Monographs in Aerospace History No. 14. Washington, DC: Government Printing Office, July 1999.

NASA. *Proceedings of the X-15 First Flight 30th Anniversary Celebration.* Washington, DC: NASA Conference Publication 3105, 1991.

Newell, Homer E. *Beyond the Atmosphere: Early Years of Space Science.* Washington, DC: NASA SP-4211, 1980.

Newton, Wesley P., and Robert R. Rea. *Wings of Gold: An Account of Naval Aviation Training in World War II.* Tuscaloosa: University of Alabama Press, 1987.

Oberg, James E. *Red Star in Orbit.* New York: Random House, 1981.

Peebles, Curtis. *The Spoken Word: Recollections of Dryden History, the Early Years.* Washington, DC: NASA SP-2003-4530, 2003.

Pellegrino, Charles R., and Joshua Stoff. *Chariots for Apollo: The Making of the Lunar Module.* New York: Atheneum, 1985.

Petroski, Henry. *To Engineer Is Human: The Role of Failure in Successful Design.* New York: Vintage Books, 1992.

Reeder, Charles Wells. *The Interurbans of Ohio.* Columbus: Ohio State University Press, 1906.

Reid, Robert L. *Always a River: The Ohio River and the American Experience.* Bloomington: Indiana University Press, 1991.

Reynolds, David. *Apollo: The Epic Journey to the Moon.* New York and San Diego: Harcourt, 2002.

Roland, Alex. *Model Research: The National Advisory Committee for Aeronautics.* 2 vols. Washington, DC: NASA SP-4103, 1985.

Rosof, Barbara D. *The Worst Loss: How Families Heal from the Death of a Child.* New York: Henry Holt and Company, 1994.

Saltzman, Edwin J., and Theodore G. Ayers. *Selected Examples of NACA/NASA Supersonic Research.* Dryden Flight Research Center, Edwards AFB, CA: NASA SP-513, 1995.

Schirra, Walter M. Jr., with Richard N. Billings, *Schirra's Space.* Boston: Quinlan Press, 1988.

Scott, David, and Alexei Leonov. *Two Sides of the Moon.* New York: Thomas Dunne Books [St. Martin's Press], 2004.

Scott, Walter. *Minstrelsy of the Scottish Border.* 3 vols. London, 1869; Singing Tree, 1967.

Seamans, Robert C. Jr. *Aiming at Targets: The Autobiography of Robert C. Seamans, Jr.* Washington, DC: NASA SP-4106, 1996.

Siddiqi, Asif A. *Challenge to Apollo: The Soviet Union and the Space Race, 1945–1974.* Washington, DC: NASA SP-2000-4408, 2000.

Slayton, Donald K., with Michael Cassutt. *Deke! U.S. Manned Space: From Mercury to Shuttle.* New York: Forge, 1994.

Spudis, Paul D. *The Once and Future Moon.* Washington and London: Smithsonian Institution Press, 1996.

Stafford, Tom, with Michael Cassutt. *We Have Capture.* Washington and London: Smithsonian Institution Press, 2002.

Sullivan, Scott P. *Virtual Apollo: A Pictorial Essay of the Engineering and Construction of the Apollo Command and Service Modules.* Burlington, Ontario: Apogee Books, 2003.

———. *Virtual LM: A Pictorial Essay of the Engineering and Construction of the Apollo Lunar Module.* Burlington, Ontario: Apogee Books, 2004.

Taylor, Stuart Ross. *Lunar Science: A Post-Apollo View.* New York: Pergamon, 1975.

Thompson, Milton O. *At the Edge of Space: The X-15 Flight Program.* Washington and London: Smithsonian Institution Press, 1992.

Thompson, Neal. *Light This Candle: The Life and Times of Alan Shepard, America's First Spaceman.* New York: Crown Publishers, 2004.

Thruelson, Richard. *The Grumman Story.* New York: Praeger, 1976.

Trento, Joseph J. *Prescription for Disaster: From the Glory of Apollo to the Betrayal of the Shuttle.* New York: Crown Publishers, 1987.

Upton, Jim. *Lockheed F-104 Starfighter.* Minneapolis: Specialty Press, 2003.

Vaughn, Diane. *The Challenger Launch Decision: Risky Technology, Culture, and Deviance at NASA.* Chicago: University of Chicago Press, 1997.

Vincenti, Walter G. *What Engineers Know and How They Know It: Analytical Studies from Aeronautical History.* Baltimore and London: The Johns Hopkins University Press, 1990.

Wachhorst, Wyn. *The Dream of Spaceflight: Essays on the Near Edge of Infinity.* New York: Basic Books, 2000.

Wallace, Harold D. *Wallops Station and the Creation of an American Space Program.* Washington, DC: NASA SP-4311, 1997.

Wallace, Lane. *Flights of Discovery: 50 Years at the NASA Dryden Flight Research Center.* Washington, DC: NASA SP-4309, 1996.

Waltman, Gene L. *Black Magic and Gremlins: Analog Flight Simulations at NASA's Flight Research Center.* Monographs in Aerospace History No. 20. Washington, DC: NASA SP-2000-4250, 2000.

Wead, Doug. *All the Presidents' Children.* New York and London: Atria Books, 2003.

Wendt, Guenter, and Russell Still. *The Unbroken Chain.* Burlington, Ontario: Apogee Books, 2001.

Wiley, Samuel T., ed. *Biographical and Historical Cyclopedia of Indiana and Armstrong Counties, Pennsylvania.* Philadelphia: Gresham & Co., 1891.

Wilford, John Noble. *We Reach the Moon.* New York: Bantam Books, 1969.

Wilhelms, Don E. *The Geologic History of the Moon.* Washington, DC: U.S. Geological Survey Professional Paper 1348, 1987.

————. *To a Rocky Moon: A Geologist's History of Lunar Exploration.* Tucson and London: University of Arizona Press, 1993.

Wolfe, Tom. *The Right Stuff.* New York: Farrar, Straus and Giroux, 1979.

Yeager, Chuck, and Leo Janos. *Yeager: An Autobiography.* Toronto and New York: Bantam Books, 1985.

Young, James O. *Meeting the Challenge of Supersonic Flight.* Edwards AFB, CA: U.S. Air Force Flight Test Center History Office, 1997.

ARTICLES

Asher, Gerald. "Of Jets and Straight Decks: USS Essex and Her Air Wings, 1951–1953," *Airpower* 32 (Nov. 2002): 26–40.

Brinkley, Douglas. "The Man and the Moon," *American History* 39: 26–37, 78–79.

Gates, Thomas F. "The Screaming Eagles in Korea, 1950–1953: Fighting 51, Part II," *The Hook* 24 (Winter 1996): 19–31.

Gray, Paul N. "The Bridges at Toko-Ri: The Real Story," *Shipmate* (July–Aug. 1997).

Home-Douglas, Pierre. "An Engineer First," *Prism* 13: 42–45.

Honegger, Barbara, and USAF Lt. Col. (Ret.) Hank Brandli. "Saving Apollo 11," *Aviation Week and Space Technology* (Dec. 13, 2004): 78–80.

Kaufman, Richard F. "Behind the Bridges at Toko-Ri," *Naval Aviation News* 84 (Mar.–Apr. 2002): 18–23.

Michener, James A. "The Forgotten Heroes of Korea," *The Saturday Evening Post,* May 10, 1952, 19–21 and 124–28.

Reilly, John. "The Carriers Hold the Line," *Naval Aviation News* 84 (May–June 2002): 18–23.

Thompson, Warren E. "The Reality Behind Toko-Ri," *Military Officer* 1 (June 2003): 54–59.

PROFILES OF ARMSTRONG

Abramson, Rudy. "A Year Later: Armstrong Still Uneasy in Hero Role," *Los Angeles Times,* July 19, 1970.

Ambrose, Stephen E., and Douglas Brinkley. "NASA Johnson Space Center Oral History Project Oral History Transcript: Neil A. Armstrong," *Quest: The History of Spaceflight Quarterly* 10 (2003). It is also available online at www.jsc.nasa.gov/oral_histories.

Andry, Al. "America's Enigmatic Pioneer," *Cincinnati Post,* July 20, 1989.

"Armstrong Aimed at Moon Walk," *Dayton Journal Herald,* July 10, 1969.

"Armstrong Still the Same Old Neil," *Lincoln* [NE] *Journal,* July 20, 1978.

Babcock, Charles. "Moon Was Dream to Shy Armstrong," *Dayton Journal Herald,* July 11, 1969.

Bebbington, Jim. "Armstrong Remembers Landing, Delights Auglaize Show Crowd," *Dayton Daily News,* July 18, 1994.

Benedict, Howard. "Ten Men on the Moon," *Florida Today,* Dec. 3, 1972.

Berkow, Ira. "Neil Armstrong Stays Alone in His Private Orbit," *Rocky Mount* [NC] *Telegram,* Dec. 15, 1975.

———. "Cincinnati's Invisible Hero," *Cincinnati Post,* Jan. 17, 1976.

Brinkley, Douglas. "The Man on the Moon," *American History* 39 (Aug. 2004): 26–37, 78.

Chriss, Nicholas C. "After Tranquility, Astronauts Lives Were Anything but Tranquil," *Houston Chronicle,* July 16, 1989.

Cohen, Douglas. "Private Man in Public Eye," *Florida Today,* July 20, 1989.

Conte, Andrew. "The Silent Spaceman: 30 Years After Moon Landing, Armstrong Still Shuns Spotlight," *Cincinnati Post,* July 17, 1999.

Cromie, William. "Armstrong Plays Down His Mark on History," *Washington Sunday Star,* July 13, 1969.

Dillon, Marilyn. "Moon Walk Remains a Thrill," *Cincinnati Enquirer,* June 12, 1979.

Domeier, Douglas. "From Wapakoneta to the Moon," *Dallas Morning News,* June 21, 1969.

Dunn, Marcia. "Neil Armstrong, 30 Years Later: Still Reticent After All These Years," Associated Press story, July 20, 1999, accessed at ABCNEWS.com.

Earley, Sandra. "In Search of Neil Armstrong," *Atlanta Journal and Constitution Magazine,* May 20, 1979.

Furlong, William (World Book Science Service). "Bluntly, He Places Ideas Above People," *Lima News,* June 13, 1969.

Galewitz, Phil. "Astronaut's Museum Speaks for Him," *Palm Beach Post,* Feb. 16, 2003.

Graham, Tim. "A Rare Talk with the Man from the Moon," *Cincinnati Post,* Mar. 3, 1979.

Greene, Bob. "Neil Armstrong Down to Earth," *St. Louis Post-Dispatch,* May 10, 1979.

———. "A Small Town and a Big Dream," *Cincinnati Post,* Oct. 24, 1992.

Harvey, Paul. "Neil Called Semi-Recluse," *Cincinnati Enquirer,* May 13, 1981.

Hatton, Jim. "Neil Says Feet Firmly on Terra Firma," *Cincinnati Enquirer,* Dec. 2, 1974.

Home-Douglas, Pierre. "An Engineer First," *Prism* 13 (summer 2004): 42–45.

Johnston, John, Saundra Amrhein, and Richelle Thompson. "Neil Armstrong, Reluctant Hero," *Cincinnati Enquirer,* July 18, 1999.

Kent, Fraser. " 'Good, Gray Men' Fly to Moon," Cleveland *Plain Dealer,* July 15, 1969.

Knight News Service. "Armstrong the Star Sailor Born to High Flight," *Cincinnati Enquirer,* July 20, 1979.

Lawson, Fred. "Hero Seeks Privacy After Moon Walk," *Dayton Daily News,* July 15, 1984.

Lyon, David. "Moon's Armstrong Just Guy Next Door to Neighbors," *Dayton Daily News,* Dec. 7, 1972.

Martin, Chuck. "Lebanon's Code of Silence Shields Armstrong," *Cincinnati Enquirer,* July 18, 1999.

Mason, Howard. "After the Moon: What Does an Astronaut Do?" *New York Times Magazine,* Dec. 3, 1972.

Mosher, Lawrence. "Neil Armstrong: From the Start He Aimed for the Moon," *National Observer,* July 7, 1969.

"Neil Armstrong, Man for the Moon," *The National Observer,* July 7, 1969.

Purdy, Matthew. "In Rural Ohio, Armstrong Quietly Lives on His Own Dark Side of the Moon," *New York Times,* July 20, 1994.

Reardon, Patrick. "A Quiet Hero Speaks: Neil Armstrong Finally Opens Up," *Chicago Tribune,* Sept. 27, 2002.

Recer, Paul. "U.S. Moonmen Returned to Earth Changed Men," *Cincinnati Enquirer,* July 30, 1972.

Ronberg, Gary. "A Private Lifetime on Earth," *Philadelphia Enquirer,* July 18, 1979.

Rosensweig, Brahm. "Whatever Happened to Neil Armstrong?" Discovery Channel, accessed at www.exn.com, July 6, 1999.

Salvato, Al. "In Search of the Man on the Moon," *Cincinnati Post,* July 16, 1994.

Sator, Darwin. "Astronaut Armstrong Firmly Planted on Earth," *Dayton Daily News,* May 8, 1975.

Sawyer, Kathy. "Neil Armstrong's Hard Bargain with Fame," *Washington Post Magazine,* July 11, 1999.

Sell, Mark. "Armstrong: 'It's Over; and I'd Like to Forget It,' " *Florida Today,* Oct. 1, 1978.

Shepherd, Shirley. "On Wapakoneta, Astronaut Neil Armstrong and a Reporter's Woes," *Muncie* [IN] *Star,* July 1, 1969.

Snider, Arthur J. "Neil Armstrong Proves to Be Very Much an Earthling," *Chicago Daily News,* Aug. 11, 1977.

Stanford, Neal. "Pride in Achievement: NASA Hails Apollo Program as 'Triumph of the Squares,' " *Christian Science Monitor,* July 16, 1969.

Stevens, William K. "The Crew: What Kind of Men Are They?" *New York Times,* July 17, 1969.

Van Sant, Rick. "Nine Years Later, Moon-Walker Still Not Star-Struck," *Cincinnati Post,* July 20, 1978.

Wheeler, Lonnie. "The Search Goes On," *Cincinnati Enquirer,* Mar. 4, 1979.

Wilford, John Noble. "Three Voyages to the Moon: Life After Making History on TV," *New York Times,* July 17, 1994.

Wolfe, Christine. "Just Professor, Not Spaceman," *Cincinnati Enquirer,* June 19, 1988.

Wright, Lawrence. "Ten Years Later: The Moonwalkers," *Look* (July 1979): 19–32.

REFERENCE SOURCES

Angelo, Joseph A. Jr. *The Dictionary of Space Technology.* New York: Facts on File, Inc., 1982.

Cassutt, Michael. *Who's Who in Space: The First 25 Years.* Boston: G. K. Hall & Co., 1987.

Hawthorne, Douglas B. *Men and Women of Space.* San Diego: Univelt, Inc., 1992.

Heiken, Grant, David Vaniman, and Bevan M. French. *Lunar Sourcebook: A User's Guide to the Moon.* New York: Cambridge University Press, 1991.

Jenkins, Dennis, Tony Landis, and Jay Miller. *American X-Vehicles: An Inventory: X-1 to X-50.* Monographs in Aerospace History No. 31. Washington, DC: NASA SP-2003-4531, June 2003.

Launius, Roger D., and J. D. Hunley. *An Annotated Bibliography of the Apollo Program.* Monographs in Aerospace History No. 2. Washington, DC: Government Printing Office, July 1994.

Orloff, Richard W. *Apollo by the Numbers: A Statistical Reference.* Washington, DC: NASA SP-2000-4029, 2000.

Portree, David S. F., and Robert C. Trevino. *Walking to Olympus: An EVA Chronology.* Washington, DC: NASA Monographs in Aerospace History Series No. 7, Oct. 1997.

Stillwell, Wendell H. *X-15 Research Results.* Washington, DC: NASA SP-60, 1965.

Surveyor Program [Office]. *Surveyor Program Results.* Washington, DC: NASA SP-184, 1969.

The Apollo Spacecraft: A Chronology. Four vols: Vol. I: "Through November 7, 1962," Ivan D. Irtel and Mary Louise Morse, eds.; Vol. II: "November 8, 1962–September 30, 1964," Mary Louise Morse and Jean Kernahan Bays, eds.; Vol. III: "October 1, 1964–January 20, 1966," Courtney G. Brooks and Ivan D. Ertel, eds.; Vol. IV: "January 21, 1966–July 13, 1974," Ivan D. Ertel and Roland W. Newkirk with Courtney G. Brooks, eds. Washington, DC: NASA SP-4009. 1969, 1973, 1976, 1978.

Wells, Helen T., Susan H. Whitely, and Carrie E. Karegeannes. *Origins of NASA Names.* Washington, DC: NASA SP-4402, 1976.

JUVENILE LITERATURE

Brown, Don. *One Giant Leap: The Story of Neil Armstrong.* Boston: Houghton Mifflin Company, 1998.

Connolly, Sean. *Neil Armstrong: An Unauthorized Biography.* Hong Kong: Heinemann Library, 1999.

Dunham, Montrew. *Neil Armstrong, Young Flyer.* New York: Aladdin Paperbacks (Simon & Schuster), 1996.

Kramer, Barbara. *Neil Armstrong, the First Man on the Moon.* Berkeley Heights, NJ: Enslow Publishers, Inc., 1997.

Rau, Dana Meachen, *Neil Armstrong.* Children's Press [Rookie Biographies], 2003.

Westman, Paul. *Neil Armstrong, Space Pioneer.* Minneapolis: Lerner Publications Company, 1980.

Zemlicka, Shannon. *Neil Armstrong.* Minneapolis: Lerner Publications Company, 2002.

Index

Photo Credits

Grateful acknowledgment is made to the following for permission to reproduce photographs:

June Armstrong Hoffmann: 1–10, 12–15, 24–26, 32, 40, 45, 70–71

K. K. Solacoff: 11

William A. Mackey: 16–19

National Aeronautics and Space Administration: 20–23, 27–31, 33, 35–39, 41–44, 47, 48, 50–58, 60–69, 72, 73

Michael Esslinger: 34

Edmund Osinski: 46

Time-Life, Inc.: 49

U.S. Geological Survey: 59

Neil A. Armstrong: 74

Back Cover Photo Credits and Captions (clockwise from top left)

1. Fourteen-year-old Neil with one of his model airplanes in 1944. (June Armstrong Hoffman)
2. Neil on board the USS *Cabot* following his first landings on an aircraft carrier, March 2, 1950. (Neil A. Armstrong)
3. Sixty-one-year-old Armstrong at the controls of the SR-71 Blackbird during a visit to NASA Dryden Flight Research Center in 1991. (NASA)
4. Armstrong performs rendezvous and docking simulations as backup commander of Gemini XI in 1966. (NASA)
5. Test pilot Armstrong stands in front of the rocket-powered X-15 number one after his flight in the plane on November 30, 1960. (NASA)
6. Armstrong in his "Snoopy" cap prior to boarding the flight of Apollo 11. (NASA)
7. Center: Neil as the commander leads the way into a transport van as the crew of Apollo 11 depart Kennedy Space Center's Manned Spacecraft Operations Building for Launch Complex 39A. (NASA)